TAKING SIDES

Clashing Views in

Drugs and Society

SEVENTH EDITION

Selected, Edited, and with Introductions by

Raymond Goldberg
State University of New York College at Cortland

Mc
Graw
Hill
**Contemporary
Learning Series**
A Division of The McGraw-Hill Companies

To Norma, Tara, and Greta

Cover image: Photos.com

Cover Acknowledgment
Maggie Lytle

Manufactured in the United States of America

Seventh Edition

123456789DOCDOC98765

Library of Congress Cataloging-in-Publication Data
Main entry under title:
Taking sides: clashing views on controversial issues in drugs and society/selected, edited, and with introductions by Raymond Goldberg.—7th ed.
includes bibliographical references and index.
1. Drug abuse—Social aspects. I. Goldberg, Raymond, *comp.*
362.29

0-07-319498-0
ISSN: 1094-7566

Printed on Recycled Paper

Preface

One of the hallmarks of a democratic society is the freedom of its citizens to disagree. This is no more evident than on the topic of drugs. The purpose of this seventh edition *of Taking Sides: Clashing Views in Drugs and Society* is to introduce drug-related issues that (1) are pertinent to the reader and (2) have no clear resolution. In the area of drug abuse, there is much difference of opinion regarding drug prevention, causation, and treatment. For example, should drug abuse be prevented by increasing enforcement of drug laws or by making young people more aware of the potential dangers of drugs? Is drug abuse caused by heredity, personality characteristics, or environment? Is drug abuse a medical, legal, or social problem? Should places such as RAVE parties be closed down because of possible drug use? Should schools administer drug tests on their students?

The answers to the preceding questions have many implications. If addiction to drugs is viewed as hereditary rather than as the result of flaws in one's character or personality, then a biological rather than a psychosocial approach to treatment may be pursued. If the consensus is that the prevention of drug abuse can be achieved by eliminating the availability of drugs, then more money and effort will be allocated for interdiction and law enforcement than education. If drug abuse is viewed as a legal problem, then prosecution and incarceration will be the goal. If drug abuse is identified as a medical problem, then abusers will be given treatment. However, if drug abuse is deemed a social problem, then energy will be directed at underlying social factors, such as poverty, unemployment, health care, and education. Not all of the issues have clear answers. One may favor increasing penalties for drug violations *and* improving treatment services. And it is possible to view drug abuse as a medical *and* social *and* legal problem.

The issues debated in this volume deal with both legal and illegal drugs. Although society seems most interested in illegal drugs, it is quite pertinent to address issues related to legal drugs because they cause more deaths and disabilities. No one is untouched by drugs, and everybody is affected by drug use and abuse. Billions of tax dollars are channeled into the war on drugs. Thousands of people are treated for drug abuse, often at public expense. The drug trade spawns crime and violence. Medical treatment for illnesses and injuries resulting from drug use and abuse creates additional burdens to an already extended health care system. Babies born to mothers who used drugs while pregnant are entering schools, and teachers are expected to meet the educational needs of these children. Ritalin is prescribed to several million students to deal with their lack of attention in the classroom. Drunk drivers represent a serious threat to our health and safety while raising the cost of everyone's automobile insurance. The issues debated here are not whether drug abuse is a problem, but what should be done to rectify this problem.

Many of these issues have an immediate impact on the reader. For example, Issue 3, *Will a Lower Blood Alcohol Level for Drunk Driving Reduce Automobile*

Accidents? will likely affect the amount of alcohol that people consume before driving. Issue 14, *Does Secondhand Smoke Endanger the Health of Nonsmokers?* is relevant to smokers and nonsmokers because restrictions on smoking are discussed. Issue 10, *Are Psychotherapeutic Drugs Effective for Treating Mental Illness?* is important because millions of people have been diagnosed with depression or some other type of mental illness. And the question *Should Laws Prohibiting Marijuana Use Be Relaxed?* (Issue 9) may be relevant because the federal government spends billions of dollars to prevent marijuana use.

Plan of the Book   In this seventh edition of *Taking Sides: Clashing Views in Drugs and Society*, there are 38 selections dealing with 19 issues. Each issue is preceded by an *Introduction* and followed by a *Postscript*. The purpose of the Introduction is to provide some background information and to set the stage for the debate as it is argued in the "yes" and "no" selections. The Postscript summarizes the debate and challenges some of the ideas brought out in the two selections, enabling the reader to see the issue in other ways. Included in the Postscripts are additional suggested readings on the issue. The Issues, Introductions, and Postscripts are designed to stimulate readers to think about and achieve an informed view of some of the critical issues facing society today. Internet site addresses (URLs) provided at the beginning of each Part should prove useful as starting points for further research. At the back of the book is a list of all the *Contributors to this Volume*. This section gives information on the physicians, professors, authors, and policymakers whose views are debated here.

   Taking Sides: Clashing Views in Drugs and Society is a tool to encourage critical thinking. In reading an issue and forming your own opinion, you should not feel confined to adopt one or the other of the positions presented. Some readers may see important points on both sides of an issue and may construct for themselves a new and creative approach. Such an approach might incorporate the best of both sides, or it might provide an entirely new vantage point for understanding.

Changes to this Edition   This sixth edition represents a significant revision. Five of the 19 issues are completely new: *Are Laws Against Drug Legalization Effective?* (Issue 1); *Should Drug Addition Be Considered a Disease?* (Issue 6); *Do Steroids Pose a Large Risk to Athletes and Others Who Use Them?* (Issue 7); *Should Laws Prohibiting Marijuana Use Be Related?* (Issue 9); *Are Psychotherapeutic Drugs Effective for Treating Mental Illness?* (Issue 10); *Is Ritalin an Effective Drug for Treating Attention Deficit/Hyperactivity Disorder?* (Issue 12); *Does Secondhand Smoke Enhanger the Health of Nonsmokers?* (Issue 14); *Is Alcoholism Hereditary?* (Issue 15); *Should Moderate Alcohol Consumption Be Encouraged?* (Issue 16); *Should Schools Drug-Test Students?* (Issue 17); and, *Do Tobaccco Advertisements Influence People to Smoke?* (Issue 19). For each of the remaining eight issues from the previous edition, one or both selections are replaced to reflect more current points of view.

A Word to the Instructor   An *Instructor's Manual With Test Questions* (multiple-choice and essay) and a general guidebook called *Using Taking Sides in* *the Classroom*, which discusses methods and techniques for implementing the pro-con approach into any classroom setting, can be obtained from the publisher. An online version of *Using Taking Sides in the Classroom* and a correspondence service for *Taking Sides* adopters can be found at http://www.mhcls.com/usingts/.

   Taking Sides: Clashing Views in Drugs and Society is only one title in the *Taking Sides* series. If you are interested in seeing the table of contents for any of the other titles, please visit the Taking Sides Web site at http://www.mhcls.com/takingsides/.

Acknowledgments   A number of people have been most helpful in putting together this Seventh edition. I would like to thank those professors who adopted the Sixth edition of this book and took the time to make suggestions for this subsequent edition:

Donald Brodeur
Sacred Heart University

Owen Cater
California State University, Sacramento

Mark Kaelin
Montclair State University

I am also grateful to my students and colleagues, who did not hesitate to share their perceptions and to let me know what they liked and disliked about the sixth edition. Without the editorial staff at McGraw-Hill Contemporary Learning Series, this book would not exist. The insight and professional contributions have been most valuable. Their thoughtful perceptions and encouragement were most appreciated. In no small way can my family be thanked. I am grateful for their patience and support.

                                    Raymond Goldberg
                          State University of New York at Cortland

Contents In Brief

Contents

PART 1   DRUGS AND PUBLIC POLICY   1

Issue 1.   Are Laws Against Drug Legalization Effective?   2

Asa Hutchinson, a former administrator with the Drug Enforcement Agency and a current administrator with Homeland Security, maintains that better enforcement of drug laws has resulted in a decrease in drug use and reduced the availability of illegal drugs. Hutchinson contends that drug legalization would not eliminate drug-related violence and harms caused by drugs. Author Sanho Tree states that one-fourth of all prisoners are incarcerated for nonviolent drug offenses. Stricter law enforcement may reduce the availability of drugs, states Sanho, but the stricter enforcement exacerbates the problem by increasing the cost of drugs and, subsequently, the need to commit more crimes. Focusing only on drug use overlooks the reasons that resulted in a prisoner's drug use in the first place.

Issue 2.   Should the United States Put More Emphasis on Stopping the Importation of Drugs?   18

The Office of National Drug Control Policy (ONDCP) argues that the importation of drugs must be stopped to reduce drug use and abuse. If the supply of drugs being trafficked across American borders is reduced, then there would be fewer drug-related problems. The ONDCP maintains that a coordinated international effort is needed to combat the increased production of heroin, cocaine, and marijuana. Cathy Inouye, a human rights volunteer for NGO SEDEM (Seguridad en Democracia), feels that the corroboration of numerous U.S. leaders with leaders in foreign governments has resulted in continued human rights abuses and has enriched those leaders in countries where the drug trade is prominent. Inouye notes that the federal government should re-examine its role of cooperation with other governments, especially those involved in the drug trade.

Thomas S. Dee, an economics professor at Swarthmore College, supports a .08 blood alcohol concentration (BAC). Dee maintains that alcohol-related fatalities are lower in those states that adopted the .08 BAC. Dee concludes that an estimated 1200 fewer deaths would result from the adoption of such a limit. The General Accounting Office (GAO) states that the evidence supporting the beneficial effects of establishing a lower blood alcohol level for drunk driving is inconclusive. The GAO maintains that the government's methods for determining the effectiveness of instituting a lower blood alcohol level are faulty and that rates for drunk driving have declined regardless of changes in BAC legal limits.

The Office of National Drug Control Policy (ONDCP) states that the nature of rave parties may encourage the use of club drug because party-goers dance and remain active for long periods of time. Drugs such as Rohypnol and GHB, which are colorless and tasteless, are used to sedate unsuspecting victims who are then sexually assaulted. Other club drugs discussed are ketamine (Special K) and Ecstasy. Jacob Sullum, a senior editor at *Reason* magazine, contends that the effects of drugs such as Ecstasy are exaggerated, particularly with regard to sexual behavior. Sullum refers to the history of marijuana and how it was deemed a drug that would make people engage in behaviors in which they would not typically engage. Sullum maintains that the public's reaction to club drugs is unjustified.

Paul A. Logli, an Illinois prosecuting attorney, argues that it is the government's duty to enforce every child's right to begin life with a healthy, drug-free mind and body. Logli maintains that pregnant women who use drugs should be prosecuted because they harm the life of their unborn children. He feels that it is the state's responsibility to ensure that every baby is born as healthy as possible. Carolyn Carter, a social work professor at Howard University, argues that the stigma of drug use during pregnancy has resulted in the avoidance of treatment. Carter asserts that the prosecution of pregnant drug users is unfair because poor women are more likely to be the targets of such

Robert A. Levy, a senior fellow at the Cato Institute, and Rosalind B. Marimont, a mathematician and scientist who retired from the National Institute of Standards and Technology, claim that the government distorts and exaggerates the dangers associated with cigarette smoking. Levy and Marimont state that factors such as poor nutrition and obesity are overlooked as causes of death among smokers. They note that cigarette smoking is harmful, but the misapplication of statistics should be regarded as "junk science." The 2004 Surgeon General's report on smoking states that the evidence pointing to the dangers of smoking is overwhelming. The report clearly links cigarette smoking to various forms of cancer, cardiovascular diseases, respiratory diseases, reproductive problems and a host of other medical conditions.

Ethan Nadelmann, founder and executive director of the Drug Policy Foundation, argues that law enforcement officials are overzealous in prosecuting individuals for marijuana possession. Eighty-seven percent of marijuana arrests are for possession of small amounts of the drug. The cost of marijuana enforcement to U.S. taxpayers ranges from $10 to $15 billion. In addition, punishments are unjust because they vary greatly. The Office of National Drug Control Policy (ONDCP) contends that marijuana is not a harmless drug. Besides causing physical problems, marijuana affects academic performance and emotional adjustment. Moreover, dealers who grow and sell marijuana may become violent to protect their commodity.

Medical doctor Bruce M. Cohen maintains that psychiatric medicines are very beneficial in enabling individuals with a variety of illnesses to return to normal aspects of consciousness. Cohen points out that people with conditions such as anxiety, depression, and psychosis respond very well to medications. These types of drugs have been utilized successfully for hundreds of years. Medical doctor Charles Whitfield questions the effectiveness of psychiatric drugs, especially antidepressant drugs. Whitfield maintains that the increase in the use of psychotherapeutic drugs results from their promotion by the pharmaceutical industry. The Food and Drug Administration (FDA), the government agency charged with protecting the public from harmful drugs, has an advisory committee consisting of members wo are paid by drug companies.

The writers from *Men's Health* describe caffeine as an addictive substance whose use results in withdrawal symptoms. The stimulating effects of caffeine are muted by tolerance that develops to the drug. In large amounts, caffeine consumption can cause anxiety and panic. The writers from the *Harvard Women's Health Watch* discuss the benefits of coffee. Although caffeine may have addictive qualities, its dangers are overstated. Caffeine's effects on the cardiovascular system are modest. Benefits of caffeine include reducing the risk of type 2 diabetes and developing gallstones, liver disease, and Parkinson's disease. In addition, caffeine improves cognitive functioning and physical performance.

Writer Michael Fumento disputes the idea that Ritalin is overprescribed. He notes that there are many myths associated with Ritalin. Its use does not lead to abuse and addiction. Fumento argues that Ritalin is an excellent medication for ADHD. It is possible that the drug is underutilized. Writers Farhang Khosh and Deena Beneda contend that Ritalin addresses the symptoms, but not the causes, of ADHD. Moreover, Ritalin has short- and long-term side effects such as appetite suppression, weight loss, and stunted growth. Khosh and Beneda state that Ritalin may cause paranoid symptoms in individucals who take large amounts chronically. In addition, they say that Ritalin inhibits emotions. They recommend exploring alternative treatments like nutritional therapies, herbs, and homeopathy.

Merrill Matthews, Jr., a health policy advisor with the American Legislative Exchange Council, feels that the advertising of prescription drugs directly to consumers will result in better-informed consumers. Concerns that the cost of prescription drugs will rise due to the cost of advertising drugs are unfounded. Instead, advertising drugs creates competition among manufacturers, resulting in lower costs. Additionally, communication between doctors and patients may improve because patients are more knowledgeable about drugs. Writer Katharine Greider notes that drug advertising has increased the number of visits by patients to their physicians as well as the number of prescriptions written at the request of consumers. Also, many consumers may not have the clinical or pharmacological background to comprehend information in drug advertisements.

Author Georgina Lovell argues that secondhand smoke is the third-leading cause of preventable disease, disability, and death in the United States. Secondhand smoke, according to Lovell, is never totally removed from any indoor room. Moreover, secondhand smoke has greater levels of poisons than the smoke inhaled by smokers through a filtered tip of a cigarette. Statisticians J. B. Copas and J. Q. Shi argue that research demonstrating that secondhand smoke is harmful is biased. They contend that many journals are more likely to publish articles if secondhand smoke is shown to be deleterious and that the findings of many studies exaggerate the adverse effects of secondhand smoke.

The National Institute on Alcohol Abuse and Alcoholism (NIAAA) contends that heredity plays a large role in the development of alcoholism. Family environment may play a role in whether one becomes an alcoholic, but individuals inherit characteristics that increase the possibility of developing alcoholism. The NIAAA notes that identical twins are twice as likely to become alcoholic as fraternal twins. Grazyna Zajdow, a lecturer in sociology at Deakin University, maintains that the concept of alcoholism results from a social construct of what it means to be alcoholic. Because alcoholism is a social stigma, it is viewed as a disease rather than as a condition caused by personal and existential pain. Environmental conditions, especially consumerism, says Zajdow, are the root cause of alcoholism.

Kenneth J. Mukamal, a physician at the Beth Israel Deaconess Medical Center in Boston, and associates report that men who consume alcohol at least three to four times a week have less risk of coronary heart disease, regardless of the type of alcohol consumed. Binge drinking, not moderate use, increases the risk of coronary heart disease. The report from the National Institute on Alcohol Abuse and Alcoholism (NIAAA) cautions against the moderate use of alcohol because individuals vary in their response to alcohol. In addition, the benefits of moderate alcohol consumption may be overstated because people who drink alcohol moderately may engage in healthier practices such as eating more nutritiously and exercising more regularly.

The Office of National Drug Control Policy (ONDCP), an agency of the federal government, maintains that it is important to test students for illicit drugs because academic achievement is impaired by drug use. Use of drugs such as marijuana impedes memory and learning, and Ecstasy use may result in long-term brain damage. Fatema Gunja and associates maintain that drug testing is ineffective and that the threat of drug testing may dissuade students from participating in extracurricular activities. In addition, drug testing is costly, it may make schools susceptible to litigation, and it undermines relationships of trust between students and teachers. Drug testing, according to Gunja and others, does not effectively identify students who may have serious drug problems.

The Office of Applied Studies, a research branch of the U.S. Department of Health and Human Services, contends that individuals in drug treatment are less likely to use drugs following treatment and are less likely to engage in criminal behavior. Moreover, the longer a person stays in treatment, the more effective it is. The report from the United Nations Office on Drugs and Crime argues that drug abuse treatment does not cure drug abuse. Most people who go through drug treatment relapse. Drug abuse treatment does not get at the root causes of drug abuse: crime, family disruption, loss of economic productivity, and social decay. At best, treatment may minimize drug abuse.

Author Georgina Lovell maintains that the tobacco industry purposely targets women and children with advertisements. Cigarette advertisements appeal to women by emphasizing the independence that comes from smoking and by showing that smoking helps to keep one slim. To illustrate the effectiveness of cigarette advertisements, smoking by high school girls increased dramatically throughout the 1990s. One of the most successful advertising campaigns was the use of Joe Camel to get adolescents to smoke. Alyse R. Lancaster and Kent M. Lancaster, communication professors at the Universities of Florida and Michigan, respectively, argue that the vast majority of teens are exposed to cigarette advertisements yet only a small percentage actually take up smoking.

Introduction

Drugs: Divergent Views

An Overview of the Problem

The topic of drugs remains a controversial topic in today's society—very few topics generate as much debate and concern. Drug use, either directly or indirectly, affects everyone. Drugs and issues related to drugs are evident in every aspect of life. There is much dismay that drug use and abuse cause many of the problems that plague society. Individuals, families, and communities are adversely affected by drug abuse, and many people wonder if the very fabric of society will continue to experience decay because of the abuse of drugs. The news media are replete with horrific stories about people under the influence of drugs who commit crimes or perpetrate violence against others; of people who die senselessly; of men, women, and children who compromise themselves for drugs; and of women who deliver babies that are addicted or impaired by drugs. In some countries, drug cartels have a major impact on government. Clearly, one does not need to be a drug user to experience its deleterious effects.

From conception until death, almost everyone is touched by drug use. For example, stimulants such as Ritalin are prescribed for children so that they can learn or behave better in school. Some college students take stimulants so that they can stay up late to write a term paper or lose a few pounds. Many teenagers take drugs because they want to be accepted by their friends or use drugs to cope with daily stresses and increasing responsibilities. For many people, young and old, the elixir for relaxation may be sipped, swallowed, smoked, or sniffed. Some people who live in poverty-stricken conditions anesthetize themselves with drugs as a way to "escape" from their unpleasant environment. On the other hand, some individuals who seem to have everything immerse themselves in drugs, possibly out of boredom. To contend with the ailments that accompany getting older, the elderly often rely on drugs. Many people use drugs to confront their pains, problems, frustrations, and disappointments. Others take drugs because they like their effects or one simply curious. Some people just want to experience more happiness in their lives. Whether medicinal drugs should be prescribed to alter one's consciousness and to make oneself happy is debated in Issue 10.

Background on Drugs

Drugs are an integral part of society. The popularity of various drugs rises and falls with the times. For example, according to annual surveys of 8th-, 10th-, and 12th-grade students in the United States, the use of LSD and marijuana has increased in this age group throughout the 1990s despite a decline in use throughout the 1980s (Johnston, O'Malley, and Bachman, 2002). Especially alarming is the fact that the largest increase in drug use in the 1990s occurred among 8th-grade students. Use of one particular drug, Ecstasy, increased significantly in the late 1990s. However, in 2002, use of many types of drugs has declined. Nevertheless, Ecstasy and other club drugs remain popular with many young people. Issue 4 examines whether we should be concerned about the use of club drugs.

Understanding the history and role of drugs in society is critical to our ability to address drug-related problems. Drugs have been used throughout human history. Alcohol played a significant role in the early history of the United States. According to Lee (1963), for example, the Pilgrims landed at Plymouth Rock because they ran out of beer. Marijuana use dates back nearly 5,000 years, when the Chinese Emperor Shen Nung prescribed it for medical ailments like malaria, gout, rheumatism, and gas pains. Ironically, 5,000 years after marijuana was first used medicinally, its medicinal value remains a matter of contention. Some issues simply refuse to go away. Hallucinogens have existed since the beginning of humankind and have been used for a variety of reasons. For example, hallucinogens were used to enhance beauty or to cast spells on enemies. About 150 of the estimated 500,000 different plant species have been used for hallucinogenic purposes (Schultes and Hofmann, 1979).

Opium, from which narcotics are derived, was written about extensively by the ancient Greeks and Romans; opium is referred to in Homer's *Odyssey* (circa 1000 B.C.). In the Arab world, opium and hashish were widely used (primarily because alcohol was forbidden). The Arabs were introduced to opium through their trading in India and China. Arab physician Avicenna (A.D. 1000) wrote an extensive medical textbook in which he describes the benefits of opium. Ironically, Avicenna died from an overdose of opium and wine. Eventually, opium played a central role in a war between China and the British government.

The most commonly consumed drug throughout the world is caffeine. More than 9 out of every 10 Americans drink beverages that include caffeine. Coffee dates back to A.D. 900, when, to stay awake during lengthy religious vigils, Muslims in Arabia consumed coffee. However, coffee was later condemned because the Koran, the holy book of Islam, described coffee as an intoxicant (Brecher, 1972). Drinking coffee became a popular activity in Europe, although it was banned for a short time. In the mid-1600s, coffeehouses were prime locations for men to converse, relax, and do business. Medical benefits were associated with coffee, although England's King Charles II and English physicians tried to prohibit its use. Many claims have been made regarding the safety of caffeine. Issue 11 discusses whether the consequences of caffeine consumption outweigh its benefits.

Coffeehouses served as places of learning. For a one-cent cup of coffee, one could listen to well-known literary and political leaders (Meyer, 1954). Lloyd's of London, the famous insurance company, started around 1700 from Edward Lloyd's coffeehouse. However, not everyone was pleased with these "penny universities," as they were called. In 1674, in response to the countless hours men spent at the coffeehouses, a group of women published a pamphlet entitled *The Women's Petition Against Coffee*, which criticized coffee use. Despite the protestations against coffee, its use proliferated. Today, more than 325 years later, coffeehouses are still flourishing as centers for relaxation and conversation.

Coca leaves, from which cocaine is derived, have been chewed since before recorded history. Drawings found on South American pottery illustrate that coca chewing was practiced before the rise of the Incan Empire. The coca plant was held in high regard—considered a present from the gods, it was used in religious rituals and burial ceremonies. When the Spaniards arrived in South America, they tried to regulate the natives' coca chewing but were unsuccessful. Cocaine was later included in the popular soft drink Coca-Cola. Another stimulant, amphetamine, was developed in the 1920s and was originally used to treat narcolepsy. It was later prescribed for treating asthma and for weight loss. Today the stimulant Ritalin is given to approximately 6 million school-age children annually to address attention deficit disorders. Some people claim that too many children are receiving Ritalin while others feel that not enough students are receiving the drug. This raises the question of whether or not Ritalin is being overprescribed (Issue 12).

Minor tranquilizers, also called "antianxiety drugs," were first marketed in the early 1950s. The sales of these drugs were astronomical. Drugs to reduce anxiety were in high demand. Another group of antianxiety drugs are benzodiazepines. Two well-known benzodiazepines are Librium and Valium; the latter ranks as the most widely prescribed drug in the history of American medicine. Xanax, which has replaced Valium as the minor tranquilizer of choice, is one of the five most prescribed drugs in the United States today. Minor tranquilizers are noteworthy because they are prescribed legally to alter one's consciousness. Mind-altering drugs existed prior to minor tranquilizers, but they were not prescribed for that purpose. In many instances, consumers request prescribed drugs from their physicians after seeing them advertised in the media. Is it a good practice for patients to encourage their physicians to prescribe drugs based on seeing an advertisement? Issue 13 examines whether there should be more regulation on advertising prescription drugs directly to consumers.

Combating Drug Problems

The debates in *Taking Sides: Clashing Views in Drugs and Society* confront many important drug-related issues. For example, what is the most effective way to reduce drug abuse? Should laws preventing drug use and abuse be more strongly enforced, or should drug laws be less punitive? How can the needs of individuals be met while serving the greater good of society? Should drug abuse be seen as a public health problem or a legal problem? Are drugs an American problem or an international problem? The debate whether the drug problem should be fought nationally or internationally is addressed in Issue 2. One could argue that America would benefit most by focusing its attention on stopping the proliferation of drugs in other countries. Others feel that reducing the demand for drugs should be the primary focus. If federal funding is limited, should those funds focus on reducing the demand for drugs or on stopping their importation?

One of the oldest debates concerns whether drug use should be decriminalized. In recent years, this debate has become more intense because well-known individuals such as political analyst William F. Buckley, Jr., and economist Milton Friedman have come out in support of changing drug laws. For many people, the issue is not whether drug use is good or bad, but whether people should be punished for taking drugs. Is it worth the time and expense for law enforcement officials to arrest nonviolent drug offenders? One question that is basic to this debate is whether drug decriminalization causes more or less damage than keeping drugs illegal. Issue 1 addresses the question of whether drugs should be decriminalized.

A major emphasis in society today is on competition, especially athletic competition. With a win-at-all-cost mentality, many athletes try to get the upper edge. One way to achieve this is through the use of performance-enhancing drugs. Issue 7 discusses whether athletes who use anabolic steroids are engaging in high-risk behavior.

In a related matter, should potentially harmful drugs be restricted even if they may be of medical benefit? Some people are concerned that drugs used for medical reasons may be illegally diverted. Yet, most people agree that patients should have access to the best medicine available. In referenda in numerous states, voters have approved the medical use of marijuana. Is the federal government consistent in allowing potentially harmful drugs to be used for medical purposes? For example, narcotics are often prescribed for pain relief. Is there a chance that patients who are given narcotics will become addicted? Issue 9 debates whether or not marijuana has a legitimate medical use. Issue 6 looks at the issue of drug addiction and whether addiction is based on heredity or if it is a choice that people make.

Many of the issues discussed in this book deal with drug prevention. As with most controversial issues, there is a lack of consensus on how to prevent drug-related problems. For example, Issue 5 debates whether or not prosecuting women who use drugs during pregnancy will affect drug use by other women who become pregnant. Will pregnant women avoid prenatal care because they fear prosecution? Will newborns be better served if pregnant women who use drugs are charged with child abuse? Are these laws discriminatory, since most cases that are prosecuted involve poor women?

Some contend that drug laws discriminate not only according to social class, but also according to age and ethnicity. Many drug laws in the United States were initiated because of their association with different ethnic groups: Opium smoking was made illegal after it was associated with Chinese immigrants (Musto, 1991); cocaine became illegal after it was linked with blacks; and marijuana was outlawed after it was linked with Hispanics.

Drug-related issues are not limited to illegal drugs. Tobacco and alcohol are two pervasive legal drugs that generate much debate. For example, are the adverse effects of smoking exaggerated (Issue 8)? Should nonsmokers be concerned about the effects of secondhand smoke (Issue 14)? With regard to alcoholism, should alcoholics totally abstain from alcohol or can learn to drink moderately (Issue 16)? Other issues relating to legal drugs deal with whether or not the legal blood alcohol concentration limit for driving while intoxicated should be lowered (Issue 3).

Gateway Drugs

Drugs like inhalants, tobacco, and alcohol are considered "gateway" drugs. These are drugs that are often used as a prelude to other, usually illegal, drugs. Inhalants are composed of numerous products, ranging from paints and solvents to glues, aerosol sprays, petroleum products, cleaning supplies, and nitrous oxide (laughing gas). Inhalant abuse in the United States is a relatively new phenomenon. It seems that until the media starting reporting on the dangers of inhalant abuse, its use was not particularly common (Brecher, 1972). This raises a question regarding the impact of the media on drug use. Issue 19 explores whether tobacco advertisements increase tobacco use by young people.

Advertisements are an integral part of the media, and their influence can be seen in the growing popularity of cigarette smoking among adolescents. In the 1880s, cigarette smoking escalated in the United States. One of the most important factors contributing to cigarettes' popularity at that time was the development of the cigarette-rolling machine (previously, cigarettes could be rolled at a rate of only four per minute). Also, cigarette smoking, which was considered an activity reserved for men, began to be seen as an option for women. As cigarettes began to be marketed toward women, cigarette smoking became more widespread.

As one can see from this introduction, numerous factors affect drug use. One argument is that if young people were better educated about the hazards of drugs and were taught how to understand the role of the media, limits on advertising would not be necessary.

Drug Prevention and Treatment

Some people maintain that educating young people about drugs is one way to prevent drug use and abuse. Studies show that by delaying the onset of drug use, the likelihood of drug abuse is reduced. In the past, however, drug education had little impact on drug-taking behavior (Goldberg, 2006). Similarly, what effect do advertising campaigns have on drug use? Whether young people are influenced by the media to use drugs, especially tobacco, is debated in Issue 19.

Another way to reduce drug abuse that has been heavily promoted is drug abuse treatment. However, is drug abuse treatment effective? Does it prevent recurring drug abuse, reduce criminal activity and violence, and halt the spread of drug-related disease? Issue 18 examines whether drug abuse treatment affects these outcomes. A study by Glass (1995) showed that methadone maintenance, a treatment for heroin addiction, may have some benefits. But do those benefits outweigh the costs of the treatment? If society feels that treatment is a better alternative to incarceration, it is imperative to know if treatment works.

Distinguishing Between Drug Use, Misuse, and Abuse

Although the terms *drug, drug misuse,* and *drug abuse* are commonly used, they have different meanings to different people. Defining these terms may seem simple at first, but many factors affect how they are defined. Should a definition for a drug be based on its behavioral effects, its effects on society, its pharmacological properties, or its chemical composition? One simple, concise definition of a drug is "any substance that produces an effect on the mind, body, or both." One could also define a drug by how it is used. For example, if watching television and listening to music are forms of escape from daily problems, should they also be considered drugs?

Legal drugs cause far more death and disability than do illegal drugs, but society appears to be most concerned with the use of illegal drugs. The potential harms of legal drugs tend to be minimized. By viewing drugs as illicit substances only, people can fail to recognize that commonly used substances such as caffeine, tobacco, alcohol, and over-the-counter preparations are drugs. If these substances are not perceived as drugs, people might not acknowledge that they can be misused or abused.

Definitions for misuse and abuse are not affected by a drug's legal status. Drug misuse refers to the inappropriate or unintentional use of drugs. Someone who smokes marijuana to improve his or her study skills is misusing marijuana because the drug impairs short-term memory. Drug abuse alludes to physical, emotional, financial, intellectual, or social consequences arising from chronic drug use. Under this definition, can a person abuse food, aspirin, soft drinks, or chocolate? Also, should a person be free to make potentially unhealthy choices?

The Cost of the War on Drugs

The United States government spends billions of dollars each year to curb the rise in drug use. A major portion of that money goes toward law enforcement. The military uses vast sums of money to intercept drug shipments, while foreign governments are given money to help them with their own wars on drugs. A smaller portion of the funds is used for treating and preventing drug abuse. One strategy to eliminate drug use is drug testing. Currently, men and women in the military, athletes, industrial employees, and others are subject to random drug testing.

The expense of drug abuse to industries is staggering: Experts estimate that about 14 percent of full-time construction workers in the United States between the ages of 18 and 49 use illicit drugs while at work (Gerber and Yacoubian, 2002). The cost of drug abuse to employers is approximately $171 billion each year (Kesselring and Pittman, 2002). Compared to nonaddicted employees, drug-dependent employees are absent from their jobs more often, and drug users are less likely to maintain stable job histories than nonusers. In its report *America's Habit: Drug Abuse, Drug Trafficking and Organized Crime*, the President's Commission on Organized Crime supported testing all federal workers for drugs.

It further recommended that federal contracts be withheld from private employers who do not implement drug-testing procedures (Brinkley, 1986).

One trend that has developed in recent years is the drug testing of students, especially student/athletes. Nearly one in five schools in the United States drug-tests athletes (Yamaguchi, Johnston, and O'Malley, 2003). Whether drug testing violates the privacy of high school and college athletes has not been totally resolved because court rulings on this matter have been inconsistent. The Supreme Court's most recent ruling indicated that a school district has the right to drug test **all** students who are involved with extracurricular activities. Whether or not drug-testing students reduces the likelihood of drug use is unclear. Two concerns related to this issue are cost and consequences. In times when school budgets are tight, is drug testing worth the expense? Also, what are the consequecnes if students test positive for drug use? Issue 17 examines the issue of whether or not schools should drug-test students.

How serious is the drug problem? Is it real, or is there simply an unreasonable hysteria regarding drugs? In the United States there has been a growing intolerance toward drug use during the last 20 years (Musto, 1991). Drugs are a problem for many people—they can affect one's physical, social, intellectual, and emotional health. Ironically, some people take drugs because they produce these effects. Individuals who take drugs receive some kind of reward from the drug; the reward may come from being associated with others who use drugs or from the feelings derived from the drug. If these rewards were not present, people would likely cease using drugs.

The disadvantages of drugs are numerous: They interfere with career aspirations and individual maturation. They have also been associated with violent behavior; addiction; discord among siblings, children, parents, spouses, and friends; work-related problems; financial troubles; problems in school; legal predicaments; accidents; injuries; and death. Yet, are drugs the cause or the symptom of the problems that people have? Perhaps drugs are one aspect of a larger scenario in which society is experiencing much change and in which drug use is merely another thread in the social fabric.

References

E. M. Brecher, *Licit and Illicit Drugs* (Little, Brown, 1972).

J. Brinkley, "Drug Use Held Mostly Stable or Better," *The New York Times* (October 10, 1986).

J. K. Gerber and G. S. Yacoubian, "An Assessment of Drug Testing Within the Construction Industry," *Journal of Drug Education* (vol. 32, no. 1, 2002) pp. 53–68.

R. M. Glass, "Methadone Maintenace: New Research on a Controversial Treatment," *Journal of the American Medical Association* (vol. 269, no. 15, 1995), pp. 1995–1996.

R. Goldberg, *Drugs Across the Spectrum* (Wadsworth Publishing, 2006).

L. D. Johnston, P.M. O'Malley, and J. G. Bachman, *Monitoring the Future* (National Institute on Drug Abuse, 2002).

R. G. Kesselring and J. P. Pittman, "Drug Testing Laws and Employment Injuries," *Journal of Labor Research* (vol. 32, no. 2, 2002), pp. 293–302.

H. Lee, *How Dry We Were: Prohibition Revisited* (Prentice Hall, 1963).

H. Meyer, *Old English Coffee Houses* (Rodale Press, 1954).

D. F. Musto, "Opium, Cocaine and Marijuana in American History," *Scientific American* (July 1991), pp. 40–47.

R. E. Schultes and A. Hofmann, *Plants of the Gods: Origins of Hallucinogenic Use* (McGraw-Hill, 1979).

R. Yamaguchi, L. D. Johnston, and P. M. O'Malley, "Relationship Between Student Illicit Drug Use and School Drug-testing Policies," *Journal of School Health* (April 2003), pp. 159–165.

Drug Policy Alliance

Formerly the Drug Policy Foundation, this site is an excellent source of information dealing with legal issues as they relate to drugs

http://www.drugpolicy.org

Office of National Drug Control Policy (ONDCP)

This site provides information regarding the government's position on many drug-related topics. Funding allocations by the federal government to deal with drug problems is included also.

http://www.whitehousedrugpolicy.gov

National Institute on Drug Abuse—Club Drugs

Current information regarding club drugs such as Ecstasy, Rohypnol, ketamine, methamphetamines, and LSD can be accessed through this site.

http://www.clubdrugs.org\

DanceSafe

This organization attempts to reduce the harm of the drug Ecstasy by testing pills to determine whether the contents are Ecstasy or some type of adulterant.

http://www.dancesafe.org

National Institute on Drug Abuse (NIDA)

Health risks associated with anabolic steroids and strategies for preventing steroid abuse can be obtained at this location.

http://www.steroidabuse.org

CASA—The National Center on Addiction and Substance Abuse at Columbia University

This organization's website contains highlights of various studies it conducts on drug-related topics.

http://www.casacolumbia.org

Drugs and Public Policy

*D*rug abuse causes a myriad of problems for society: The psychological and physical effects of drug abuse can be devastating; many drugs are addictive; drug abuse can wreak havoc on families; disability and death result from drug overdoses; and drugs frequently are implicated in crimes, especially violent crimes. Identifying drug-related problems is not difficult. What is unclear is the best course of action to take when dealing with these problems.

Three scenarios exist for dealing with drugs: Policies can be made more restrictive, they can be made less restrictive, or they can remain the same. The position one takes depends on whether drug use and abuse are seen as legal, social, or medical problems. Perhaps the issue is not whether drugs are good or bad, but how to minimize the harm of drugs. The debates in this section explore these issues.

- Are Laws Against Drug Legalization Effective?

- Should the United States Put More Emphasis on Stopping the Importation of Drugs?

- Will a Lower Blood Alcohol Level for Drunk Driving Reduce Automobile Accidents?

- Should We Be Concerned About "Club Drugs"?

- Should Pregnant Drug Users Be Prosecuted?

- Should Drug Addiction Be Considered a Disease?

- Do Steroids Pose a Large Risk to Athletes and Others Who Use Them?

ISSUE 1

Are Laws Against Drug Legalization Effective?

YES: Asa Hutchinson, from "An Effective Drug Policy to Protect America's Youth and Communities," *Fordham Urban Law Journal* (January 2003)

NO: Sanho Tree, from "The War at Home: Our Jails Overflow with Nonviolent Drug Offenders. Have We Reached the Point Where the Drug War Causes More Harm Than the Drugs Themselves?" *Sojourners* (May–June 2003)

ISSUE SUMMARY

YES: Asa Hutchinson, a former administrator with the Drug Enforcement Agency and a current administrator with Homeland Security, maintains that better enforcement of drug laws has resulted in a decrease in drug use and reduced the availability of illegal drugs. Hutchinson contends that drug legalization would not eliminate drug-related violence and harms caused by drugs.

NO: Author Sanho Tree states that one-fourth of all prisoners are incarcerated for nonviolent drug offenses. Stricter law enforcement may reduce the availability of drugs, states Sanho, but the stricter enforcement exacerbates the problem by increasing the cost of drugs and, subsequently, the need to commit more crimes. Focusing only on drug use overlooks the reasons that resulted in a prisoner's drug use in the first place.

In 2004 the federal government allocated nearly $19 billion to control drug use and to enforce laws that are designed to protect society from the perils created by drug use. Some people believe that the government's war on drugs could be more effective but that governmental agencies and communities are not fighting hard enough to stop drug use. They also hold that laws to halt drug use are too few and too lenient. Others contend that the war against drugs is unnecessary—that, in fact, society has already lost the war on drugs. These individuals feel that the best way to remedy drug problems is to end the fight altogether by ending the criminalization of drug use.

There are conflicting views among both liberals and conservatives on whether legislation has had the intended result of curtailing the problems of drug use. Many argue that legislation and the criminalization of drugs have been counterproductive in controlling drug problems. Some suggest that the criminalization of drugs has actually contributed to and worsened the social ills associated with drugs. Proponents of drug legalization maintain that the war on drugs, not drugs themselves, is damaging to American society. They do not advocate drug use; they argue only that laws against drugs exacerbate problems related to drugs.

Proponents of drug decriminalization argue that the strict enforcement of drug laws damages American society because it drives people to violence and crime. These people overburden the court system, thus rendering it ineffective. Moreover, proponents contend that the criminalization of drugs fuels organized crime, allows children to be pulled into the drug business, and makes illegal drugs themselves more dangerous because they are manufactured without government standards or regulations. Hence, drugs may be adulterated or of unidentified potency. Decriminalization advocates also argue that decriminalization would take the profits out of drug sales, thereby decreasing the value of and demand for drugs. In addition, the costs resulting from law enforcement are far greater to society than the benefits of criminalization.

Some decriminalization advocates argue that the federal government's prohibition stance on drugs is an immoral and impossible objective. To achieve a "drug-free society" is self-defeating and a misnomer because drugs have always been a part of human culture. Furthermore, prohibition efforts indicate a disregard for the private freedom of individuals because they assume that individuals are incapable of making their own choices. Drug proponents assert that their personal sovereignty should be respected over any government agenda, including the war on drugs.

People who favor decriminalizing drugs feel that decriminalization would give the government more control over the purity and potency of drugs and that the international drug trade would be regulated more effectively. Decriminalization, they argue, would take the emphasis off of law enforcement policies and allow more effort to be put toward education, prevention, and treatment. Decriminalization advocates assert that most of the negative implications of drug prohibition would disappear.

Opponents of this view maintain that decriminalization is not the solution to drug problems and that it is a very dangerous idea. Decriminalization, they assert, will drastically increase drug use because if drugs are more accessible, more people will turn to drugs. This upsurge in drug use will come at an incredibly high price: American society will be overrun with drug-related accidents, loss in worker productivity, and hospital emergency rooms filled with drug-related emergencies. Drug treatment efforts would be futile because users would have no legal incentive to stop taking drugs. Also, users may prefer drugs rather than rehabilitation, and education programs may be ineffective in dissuading children from using drugs.

In the following selections, Asa Hutchinson explains why he feels drugs should remain illegal, while Sanho Tree describes the detrimental effects that he believes occur as a result of drug criminalization.

Asa Hutchinson
 **YES**

An Effective Drug Policy to Protect America's Youth and Communities

Introduction

Drug abuse and addiction, and the government's response to these problems, are frequently and appropriately a topic of public debate. Some argue that because we have not completely eradicated all illegal drug abuse, we should legalize the manufacture and distribution of all drugs, including cocaine, "crack" cocaine, Ecstasy, heroin, and other drugs that are highly addictive and dangerous. Some people agree that certain illegal drugs should remain illegal, but that other drugs, marijuana, for example, should be legalized, or, at least, decriminalized. Some of these proposals stem from frustrations that the problem of drug abuse has not been completely solved, and that this problem would be better dealt with as a medical or health issue. In addition, proponents of legalization and decriminalization claim that the federal government focuses entirely on criminal enforcement, and not on prevention and treatment. Proponents of marijuana legalization or decriminalization claim that smoking marijuana is safe, it has a proven medical use, and the criminal laws are being used to impose harsh prison sentences on people that used or possessed small amounts of marijuana. These claims have no factual or scientific basis. Before drawing any conclusions about the effectiveness of federal drug policy, it would be helpful to review the federal government's successes to date, review the scientific studies concerning marijuana use, and apply what has been learned from the past to our present circumstances and future drug strategy.

Drug Use in America

Proponents of legalization frequently cite the large number of illegal drug abusers in America as a basis to legalize some or all drugs. These are the facts. 7.1 percent of the U.S. population aged twelve or older uses illegal drugs. Recent statistics indicate that drug use by persons aged twelve and older went from 6.3 percent in 2000 to 7.1 percent in 2001. Over the longer term, however,

From *Fordham Urban Law Journal*, vol. 30, issue 2, January 2003, pp. 441–464. Copyright © 2003 by Fordham Urban Law Journal. Reprinted by permission. This article was originally published in the *Fordham Urban Law Journal* as *An Effective Drug Policy to Protect America's Youth and Communities*, 30 Fordham Urb. L.J. 441 (2003). References omitted.

per capita drug use in America is down by one-half since the late 1970s. Since the age groups that report the highest percentage of drug use are ages fourteen through twenty-five, it is clear that when we reduce illegal drug use, we are reducing the number of young people harmed by the health and other consequences of illegal drugs. In addition, per capita cocaine use is down by seventy-three percent during the same period. In a recent survey conducted by the National Center on Addiction and Substance Abuse at Columbia University, almost two-thirds of teenagers said that their school is drug free. For the first time in the seven-year history of the survey, a majority of public school students reported drug-free schools. According to the survey, "[t]eens who attend drug-free schools are at roughly half the risk of substance abuse of teens who attend schools where drugs are used, kept or sold."

Law Enforcement Is Preventing a Significant Amount of Illegal Drugs from Reaching our Communities

In addition to an overall reduction in the number of persons abusing illegal drugs, law enforcement has made significant inroads in the fight against traffickers. The strategy against traffickers is proactive, targeting growers, the chemicals needed to manufacture or process illegal drugs, and the flow of illegal drugs into the United States. The DEA's priority mission is the long-term immobilization of major drug trafficking organizations through removal of their leaders, termination of their trafficking networks, seizure of their assets, and dismantling their organizational structure. For example, DEA's Operation Purple is working in twenty-eight countries to prevent the diversion of potassium permanganate, a chemical needed to manufacture cocaine, to cocaine producers. Operations Crossroads II and Caribe I involved year-long investigations that targeted an international organization based in Puerto Rico that trafficked in multi-hundred kilogram quantities of cocaine and multi-kilogram quantities of heroin and laundered millions of United States dollars in drug proceeds. Operation Landslide targeted a Mexican organization that brought significant quantities of black-tar heroin, often accompanied by cocaine and methamphetamine, into California for distribution to thirty-one cities in eleven states. The third phase of Operation Mountain Express has, to date, arrested one hundred people involved in diverting precursor chemicals needed to manufacture methamphetamine. Operation Perfect Storm was a seventeen month investigation that targeted a heroin and cocaine trafficking organization operating in New York, New Jersey, and Florida, resulting in the seizure of 2,700 kilograms of cocaine, seventeen kilograms of heroin, and the arrest of one hundred and forty-four defendants. The DEA's accomplishments in investigating international and domestic drug trafficking organizations are both significant and measurable.

Federal agencies involved in drug interdiction regularly seize large quantities of illegal drugs before they enter the United States. In addition to international efforts, the DEA and other law enforcement agencies seize large quantities of illegal drugs manufactured or grown domestically. These domestic traffickers, like their international counterparts, target America's youth.

DEA investigations also target domestic and international money laundering. Although arrests of individuals have a significant impact upon drug organizations, labor can often be replaced. Money laundering investigations, however, deprive drug trafficking organizations of the money they need to operate and survive. Successful money laundering investigations lead to the arrest of upper-level principals, and the permanent dismantling of drug organizations.

In addition to enforcement programs directed at international and domestic trafficking, the DEA collects, collates, and disseminates drug intelligence to local, state, federal, and foreign law enforcement agencies. This sharing of intelligence effectively channels law enforcement resources throughout America and the world to target drug organizations. . . .

Federal Law Enforcement Agencies Focus on Drug Traffickers

Federal law enforcement authorities investigate and prosecute the growers, manufacturers, shippers, and distributors of dangerous and addictive illegal drugs. The overwhelming majority of federal resources focus on the supply side of the illegal drug stream and target mid- and upper-level traffickers. These figures are borne out by federal sentencing statistics. In fiscal year ("FY") 2001, a total of 24,504 defendants were convicted of federal drug trafficking and drug communication offenses. During the same period, a total of 586 defendants were convicted for possession of a controlled substance. Within the geographical jurisdiction of the United States Court of Appeals for the Third Circuit, an area comprising Pennsylvania, New Jersey, Delaware, and the Virgin Islands, a total of seventeen people were convicted of drug possession in federal court. Nationwide, a total of 255 defendants were sentenced to federal prison for drug possession offenses, another 262 received probationary sentences, and a total of thirty received split sentences involving confinement and probation. In the Third Circuit, a total of three defendants were sentenced to prison for drug possession, twelve were sentenced to probation, and two were sentenced to a combination of confinement and probation. Contrary to claims by drug legalization advocates, offenders in this group were not overwhelmingly first-time offenders. Rather, offenders convicted of heroin and crack cocaine possession offenses had a median criminal history category of three. Offenders convicted of marijuana possession offenses possessed a median of thirty-seven grams of marijuana, far more than the single joint often claimed by advocates of legalization.

In addition to supporting local and state drug courts, the federal statutory framework is set up to handle first time offenders convicted of non-violent drug trafficking crimes by making them eligible for the "safety-valve" provision of Title 18 of the United States Code and the Federal Sentencing Guidelines, and receive a punishment below the statutory mandatory-minimum sentences and applicable guideline sentencing range. All federal drug offenders that provide substantial assistance to the government in the investigation or prosecution of their co-conspirators or bosses can also receive a reduced sentence. These facts establish that the federal drug sentencing laws are not being used to impose draconian sentences on first-time, non-violent, lower-level drug offenders.

Local and state law enforcement authorities similarly focus on drug dealers, and not on drug users. State criminal laws concerning drug possession focus on rehabilitative and restorative programs, rather than automatic incarceration for drug users. In Michigan, as in many other states, minor drug offenders can obtain drug treatment without any judgment of conviction being entered. First-time drug offenders charged with possession, and first- and second-time offenders charged with use, can be placed on probation and required to participate in drug treatment. Upon successful completion of the program, defendants' records are expunged. Some claim that prisons are full of first-time offenders serving lengthy sentences for possession of small amounts of marijuana. This claim is not supported by the facts. In Michigan, for example, the penalty for the use of small amounts of marijuana is a maximum of up to ninety days in prison, or a fine of up to one-hundred dollars. In more serious cases, Michigan judges can impose sentences below the guidelines, where the judge determines that it is appropriate. A recent study conducted by the Michigan Department of Corrections determined that out of a state prison population of more than 47,000, only five hundred people were in prison for drug possession. Of that five hundred, 485 had actually been convicted of multiple offenses, or had been sentenced to prison after negotiating a guilty plea to the lesser crime of drug possession. A total of fifteen people out of population of 47,000 were in prison on first-time drug possession charges.

The Perils of Legalization

A. Legalization of Marijuana or Any Other Drug Would Not Eliminate the Black Market

Marijuana is viewed by some as a harmless and safe drug. Proponents argue that it should be legalized to eliminate the black market sale of marijuana, and associated criminal activity. Even proponents of the legalization of marijuana would prohibit the sale or distribution to minors. Even after establishing the bureaucracy necessary to license and monitor the marijuana growers, distributors and sellers, a black market would still exist to supply marijuana to minors and to others that do not want to pay for the regulated, more expensive, legal marijuana. Because a large portion of illegal drugs are used by people under the age of twenty-one, the black market would continue to flourish as a source of illegal drugs for minors that would not be able to legally obtain them. Sellers seeking to avoid the license or inspection fees associated with legal marijuana sales would simply sell their product on the black market. The government would be forced to spend substantial sums to ensure compliance with license and inspection protocols established to monitor the safety and purity of the marijuana.

Similar restrictions would necessarily apply to efforts to legalize all illegal drugs, including cocaine, heroin, methamphetamine, lysergic acid diethylamide ("LSD"), Ecstasy, and phencyclidine ("PCP"). Significant expenditures on drug-related law enforcement and regulation would continue. These expenditures would continue, in part, because it is unlikely that pure drugs would be allowed. In addition, absent a program of unlimited free drugs to anyone that asked for them, law enforcement would still be required to enforce restrictions on sales to minors, and to prohibit the manufacture, sale, or possession of drugs that are impure or too potent.

Considerable expenditures would also be needed to prevent unlicensed and untaxed drugs from reaching the United States to be sold on the black market. Rather than quietly going away, international and domestic criminal organizations would simply recast themselves to meet and create new drug markets. New markets might involve unregulated and untaxed, and therefore, lower priced drugs, or minors that cannot obtain drugs under the government's plan. Another new market might involve sales to drug abusers that have already consumed their "legal" allotment. It is preposterous to conclude that criminal organizations operating outside the United States would willingly forego their profits because of a plan that distributes some amount of drugs to certain authorized "consumers" of it. Similarly, domestic drug gangs terrorizing communities will shift marketing strategies to meet new demands. Drug cartels would continue to employ violence and corruption to protect their product, profit margins, and markets; law enforcement costs would continue to rise, and not become available for education or treatment.

While the violence inflicted by international cartels and domestic traffickers is significant, violence suffered by America's youth in our cities and towns would continue to devastate society. The truth is that unless all illegal drugs are decriminalized, made available upon demand, with a high degree of purity, to all people, regardless of age, and free of charge, the black market for drugs will continue to exist.

B. Legalization of Some or All Illegal Drugs Will Not Eliminate Drug-Related Violence and Other Drug-Related Harms

Contrary to the claims of advocates, legalization of some or all illegal drugs will not eliminate the violence associated with drug abuse. Drug use affects one's mind, and it changes behavior. Drugs are illegal because they harm people. In 1999, there were 19,102 deaths from drug-induced causes. In 2000, there were a total of 601,776 drug-related emergency room episodes. More than half of those arrested in 1999 tested positive for illegal drugs at the times of their arrest. Six times as many murders are committed by people under the influence of drugs, as those committed by people who are looking to buy drugs. Twenty-four percent of the people that assault police officers are under the influence of illegal drugs. It was determined in the same study that seventy-two percent of police assailants had a history of drug law violations. Other negative effects of illegal drug use are well established. For example, a

United States Postal Service study that examined twenty-nine acts of violence involving postal workers that resulted in thirty-four murders determined that twenty of the perpetrators involved had a history of substance abuse, or were under the influence of illegal drugs or alcohol at the time of the crime. People suffering from the effects of illegal drug use will continue to pose a danger to themselves and others. They will continue to commit crimes in order to get money to buy their drugs from legal or black market suppliers, or they will commit crimes to rob lawful possessors of their drugs. In any case, violent crime will continue to occur, most likely at a greater scale. . . .

Our Efforts to Solve the Problem of Illegal Drugs Involves New Ideas

Local, state, and federal governments are employing new ideas in solving illegal drug use. While law enforcement is taking advantage of the latest technology to acquire and share information, all levels of government are implementing new ideas to address drug use and addiction. Since such a large portion of all defendants have been involved in some form of drug use, criminal justice agencies are incorporating effective drug treatment programs into their programs, and judges are fashioning sentences that include an opportunity to treat drug addiction. Defendants facing minor drug or other non-violent criminal charges are given a rehabilitation option to work toward a better, drug-free life. These defendants are given opportunities to learn job skills, perform community service, undergo drug treatment with accountability, and, if successfully completed, have their record expunged. The National Drug Control Strategy, as explained above, includes more funds than ever to provide drug use prevention education and treatment. These efforts at prevention are multifaceted, offering programs to people in many different circumstances. The Strategy funds treatment for pregnant mothers, to offer a healthy, drug-free life to mother and child. It provides money to get the anti-drug message out to a large segment of our population through a targeted media campaign, and also provides funding for treatment to prisoners. Importantly, the Strategy does not exclude anyone from treatment and encourages a return to a productive, rewarding life.

New ideas are not limited to big, far-reaching programs with large budgets. DEA's Integrated Drug Enforcement Assistance program puts a face on government by placing trained and experienced DEA Special Agents in communities. These Special Agents partner with civic, business, government, and religious leaders to solve drug problems and the underlying circumstances that breed drug abuse.

We should not forget that those most at risk are our young people. The National Household Survey on Drug Abuse found that out of the 15.9 million illegal drug users twelve or older, young people ages fourteen to twenty-five are the largest percentage users of illegal drugs, and that there is a significant drop in the reported use of illegal drugs after the age of twenty-five. For example, 10.9 percent of children fourteen-or fifteen-years old report illegal drug use in the past month. Among young people ages sixteen or seventeen, 17.8 percent report illegal drug use in the period. Among youth age eighteen to twenty,

22.4 percent reported illegal drug use, and 16.3 percent of young people age twenty-one to twenty-five report illegal drug use. Everyone agrees that individuals who grow, manufacture, distribute, or sell illegal drugs that find their way to these young people should face severe criminal penalties.

Common sense dictates that once the criminal penalties are removed for drug trafficking offenses, the flow of drugs to young people will increase substantially, with dire consequences. Children and young people going through the formative years of their lives will be surrounded with mind- and personality-altering drugs. While the percentage of overall illegal drug users at present is relatively low, the potential harms caused by illegal drugs is high. A single airplane pilot, train engineer, or eighteen-wheel truck driver doing her job while impaired by a mind- or personality-altering drug poses a much greater danger to public safety, than one who is drug free.

Conclusion

People who know the facts and understand the problem realize that a small percentage of the population uses drugs. The solution to drug abuse is vigilance coupled with thoughtful planning and action; we should not surrender to the problem. It is always interesting to look at issues from a theoretical standpoint. The reality is that drugs are illegal because they are dangerous. They cause pain and suffering to individuals and families, as well as neighborhoods and communities, and cost our society substantial sums of money. There is no reason to think that allowing the free flow of any mind altering illegal drug in America would reduce the number of users or addicts, or reduce the overall cost of protecting our citizens from its harms.

Common sense tells us that we must work to reduce the number of people using illegal drugs. Legalization would substantially increase the number of people in school or college, at work, or in business, who would suffer the residual effects of a drug that has no useful purpose. At a time when we are working to improve public health by reducing alcohol and tobacco use by teens, when we check identification before we sell cigarettes or alcohol to someone, it seems counterintuitive that a small but vocal minority is working to create a society in which there is free access to the chemicals that we know are dangerous to individuals and society.

The facts on this issue make a strong case for a national policy geared toward effective drug abuse education and prevention, and treatment for people dependent on illegal drugs. Our nation should also continue to conduct research to determine the most effective means of educating children and youth about the dangers of illegal drugs and the best ways to rehabilitate illegal drug users. On the supply side, the criminal justice system should continue to impose sanctions on people and organizations that are in the business of growing, manufacturing, transporting, and distributing illegal drugs. . . .

NO ↩

The War at Home: Our Jails Overflow with Nonviolent Drug Offenders. Have We Reached the Point Where the Drug War Causes More Harm Than the Drugs Themselves?

In 1965, Sen. Robert F. Kennedy tried to promote an enlightened drug policy before our country declared war on its own citizens. He told Congress, "Now, more than at any other time in our history, the addict is a product of a society which has moved faster and further than it has allowed him to go, a society which in its complexity and its increasing material comfort has left him behind. In taking up the use of drugs the addict is merely exhibiting the outer-most aspects of a deep-seated alienation from this society, of a combination of personal problems having both psychological and sociological aspects."

Kennedy continued, "The fact that addiction is bound up with the hard core of the worst problems confronting us socially makes it discouraging at the outset to talk about 'solving' it. 'Solving' it really means solving poverty and broken homes, racial discrimination and inadequate education, slums and unemployment. . . ." Thirty-eight years later, the preconditions contributing to drug addiction have changed little, but our response to the problem has become overwhelmingly punitive.

When confronted with illegal behavior, legislators have traditionally responded by escalating law enforcement. Yet countries such as Iran and China that routinely use the death penalty for drug offenses still have serious drug problems. Clearly there are limits to what can be achieved through coercion. By treating this as a criminal justice problem, our range of solutions has been sharply limited: How much coercion do we need to make this problem go away? No country has yet found that level of repression, and it is unlikely many Americans would want to live in a society that did.

From *Sojourners*, vol. 32, issue 3, May/June 2003, pp. 20–27. Copyright © 2003 by Sojourners. Reprinted by permission from Sojourners. 1-800-714-7474. www.sojo.net.

As the drug war escalated in the 1980s, mandatory minimum sentencing and other Draconian penalties boosted our prison population to unprecedented levels. With more than 2 million people behind bars (there are only 8 million prisoners in the entire world), the United States—with one-twenty-second of the world's population—has one-quarter of the planet's prisoners. We operate the largest penal system in the world, and approximately one quarter of all our prisoners (nearly half a million people) are there for nonviolent drug offenses—that's more drug prisoners than the entire European Union incarcerates for all offenses combined, and the EU has over 90 million more citizens than the United States. Put another way, the United States now has more nonviolent drug prisoners alone than we had in our entire prison population in 1980.

If the drug war were evaluated like most other government programs, we would have tried different strategies long ago. But our current policy seems to follow its own unique budgetary logic. A slight decline in drug use is used as evidence that our drug war is finally starting to work and therefore we should ramp up the funding. But a rise in drug use becomes proof that we are not doing enough to fight drugs and must therefore redouble our efforts and really ramp up the funding. Under this unsustainable dynamic, funding and incarceration rates can only ratchet upward. When Nixon won reelection in 1972, the annual federal drug war budget was approximately $100 million. Now it is approaching $20 billion. Our legislators have been paralyzed by the doctrine of "if at first you don't succeed, escalate."

Internationally, our drug war has done little more than push drug cultivation from one region to the next while drugs on our streets have become cheaper, purer, and more plentiful than ever. Meanwhile, the so-called collateral damage from our international drug war has caused incalculable suffering to peasant farmers caught between the crossfire of our eradication policies and the absolute lack of economic alternatives that force them to grow illicit drug crops to feed their families. Unable to control our own domestic demand, our politicians have lashed out at other peoples for daring to feed our seemingly insatiable craving for these substances. We have exported our failures and scapegoated others.

'It's the Economy, Stupid'

Many legislators approve increased drug war funding because they are true believers that cracking down is the only way to deal with unlawful conduct. Others support it out of ignorance that alternative paradigms exist. But perhaps most go along with the drug war for fear of being depicted as "soft on drugs" in negative campaign ads at election time.

In recent years, there has been an increasingly lively debate on whether nonviolent drug offenders should receive treatment or incarceration. As legislators gradually drift toward funding more badly needed treatment slots, an important dynamic of the drug economy is still left out of the national debate: the economics of prohibition. Elected officials and much of the media have been loath to discuss this phenomenon at the risk of being discredited as a "legalizer," but until a solution is found concerning this central issue, many of the societal problems concerning illicit drugs will continue to plague us. Trying to find a sustainable solution to manage the drug problem without discussing the consequences of prohibition is like taking one's car to the mechanic for repair but not allowing the hood to be opened. The time has come to take a look under the hood of our unwinnable drug war.

Under a prohibition economy where there is high demand, escalating law enforcement often produces the opposite of the intended result. By attempting to constrict supply while demand remains high, our policies have made these relatively worthless commodities into substances of tremendous value. The alchemists of the Middle Ages tried in vain for centuries to find a formula to turn lead into gold, but it took our drug warriors to perfect the new alchemy of turning worthless weeds into virtual gold. Some varieties of the most widely used illicit drug, marijuana, are now worth their weight in solid gold (around $350 per ounce). Cocaine and heroin are worth many, many times their equivalent weight in gold. In a world filled with tremendous poverty, greed, and desire, we cannot make these substances disappear by making them more valuable.

Another factor we have failed to take into account is the virtually inexhaustible reservoir of impoverished peasants who will risk growing these crops in the vast regions of the world where these plants can flourish. According to the U.N. Development Program and the World Bank, there are 1.2 billion people in the world who live on less than $1 a day. Imagine paying for housing, food, clothing, education, transportation, fertilizer, and medicine on less than $1 a day. Now imagine the temptation of putting a worthless seed into the soil and coming up with an illicit crop that can mean the difference between simple poverty or slow starvation for you and your family. We cannot escalate the value of such commodities through prohibition and not expect desperately poor farmers to plant any crop necessary to ensure their survival.

A "Harm Reduction" Approach

Of all the laws that Congress can pass or repeal, the law of supply and demand is not one of them. Neither is the law of evolution nor the law of unintended consequences. The drug trade evolves under Darwinian principles—survival of the fittest. Our response of increasing law enforcement ensures that the clumsy and inefficient traffickers are weeded out while the smarter and more adaptable ones tend to escape. We cannot hope to win a war on drugs when our policies see to it that only the most efficient drug operations survive. Indeed, these survivors are richly rewarded because we have constricted just enough supply to increase prices and profits while "thinning out the herd" by eliminating their competition for them. Through this process of artificial selection, we have been unintentionally breeding "super traffickers" for decades. Our policy of attacking the weakest links has caused tremendous human suffering, wasted countless lives and resources, and produced highly evolved criminal operations.

Our policy of applying a "war" paradigm to fight drug abuse and addiction betrays a gross ignorance of the dimensions of this medical problem and its far-reaching social and economic consequences. Wars employ brute force to extract political concessions from rational state actors. Drugs are articles of commerce that do not respond to fear, pain, or congressional dictates. However, around these crops revolve hundreds of thousands, indeed millions, of individuals responding to the artificially inflated value of these essentially worthless agricultural products. For every trafficker that our "war" manages to stop, a dozen others take his or her place because individuals—whether acting out of poverty, greed, or addiction—enter the drug economy on the assumption they won't get caught, and most never are. No "war" can elicit a unified political capitulation from actors in such diverse places as Southeast Asia, the Andes, suburbia, and the local street corner. Such a war can never be won, but a "harm reduction" approach offers ways to contain and manage the problem.

Guns and helicopters cannot solve the problems of poverty in the Andes or addiction in the United States. Moreover, our policies of employing more police, prosecutors, and prisons to deal with the drug problem is like digging more graves to solve the global AIDS pandemic—it solves nothing. As sociologist Craig Reinarman notes, our policies attack the symptoms but do little to address the underlying problems. "Drugs are richly functional scapegoats," Reinarman writes. "They provide elites with fig leafs to place over the unsightly social ills that are endemic to the social system over which they preside. They provide the public with a restricted aperture of attribution in which only the chemical bogey man or lone deviant come into view and the social causes of a cornucopia of complex problems are out of the picture."

Until we provide adequate resources for drug treatment, rehabilitation, and prevention, the United States will continue to consume billions of dollars worth of drugs and impoverished peasants around the world will continue to grow them. The enemy is not an illicit agricultural product that can be grown all over the world; rather, our policies should be directed against poverty, despair, and alienation. At home and abroad, these factors drive the demand for illicit drugs which is satisfied by an inexhaustible reservoir of impoverished peasant farmers who have few other economic options with which to sustain themselves and their families.

Some day, there will be a just peace in Colombia and a humane drug control policy in the United States. Until then, we are mortgaging the future, and the most powerless among us must pay most of the interest. That interest can be seen in the faces of the campesinos and indigenous peoples caught in the crossfire of our Andean drug war; it can be seen in the millions of addicts in the United States who cannot get treatment they need; it can be seen in the prisons filled with nonviolent drug offenders; and it can be seen in the poverty, despair, and alienation around the world because we choose to squander our resources on harmful programs while ignoring the real needs of the dispossessed.

Because we have witnessed the damage illicit drugs can cause, we have allowed ourselves to fall prey to one of the great myths of the drug warriors: Keeping drugs illegal will protect us. But drug prohibition doesn't mean we control drugs, it means we give up the right to control them. Under prohibition, the people who control drugs are by definition criminals—and, very often, organized crime. We have made a deliberate choice not to regulate these drugs and have been paying the price for the anarchy that followed. These are lessons we failed to learn from our disastrous attempt at alcohol prohibition in the 1920s.

On the other hand, the philosophy of "harm reduction" offers us a way to manage the problem. Briefly put, this means we accept the premise that mind altering substances have always been part of human society and will not disappear, but we must find ways to minimize the harm caused by these substances while simultaneously minimizing the harm caused by the drug war itself. We have reached the point where the drug war causes more harm than the drugs themselves—which is the definition of a bankrupt policy. Drug abuse and addiction are medical problems, not criminal justice problems, and we should act accordingly.

Some examples of harm reduction include comprehensive and holistic drug treatment for addicts who ask for it, overdose prevention education, clean needle exchange to reduce the spread of HIV and hepatitis, methadone maintenance for heroin addicts, and honest prevention and education programs instead of the ineffective DARE program.

We already know what doesn't work—the current system doesn't work—but we are not allowed to discover what eventually will work. Our current policy of doing more of the same is doomed to failure because escalating a failed paradigm will not produce a different result. However, by approaching the problem as managers rather than moralizers, we can learn from our mistakes and make real progress. It is our current system of the drug war that is the obstacle to finding an eventual workable system of drug control.

POSTSCRIPT

Are Laws Against Drug Legalization Effective?

Hutchinson asserts that utilizing the criminal justice system to maintain the illegal nature of drugs is necessary to keep society free of the detrimental effects of drugs. Decriminalizing the use of drugs is unwise and dangerous. He argues that international control efforts, interdiction, and domestic law enforcement are effective and that many problems associated with drug use are mitigated by drug regulation policies. He maintains that drug criminalization is a feasible and desirable means of dealing with the drug crisis.

Tree charges that the advantages of maintaining illegality are far more destructive than any conceivable benefits of legalization. He professes that if drug laws remain stringent, the result would be more drug users in prison and that drug abusers and addicts would engage in more criminal activity. Also, there is the possibility that more drug-related social problems would occur. Tree concludes that society cannot afford to retain its intransigent position on drug legalization. The potential risks of the current federal policies on drug criminalization outweigh any potential benefits.

Decriminalization proponents argue that drug laws have not worked and that the drug battle has been lost. They believe that drug-related problems would disappear if decriminalization were implemented. Citing the legal drugs alcohol and tobacco as examples, legalization opponents argue that decriminalizing drugs would not decrease profits from the sale of drugs (the profits from cigarettes and alcohol are incredibly high). Moreover, opponents argue, decriminalizing a drug does not make its problems disappear (alcohol and tobacco have extremely high addiction rates as well as a myriad of other problems associated with their use).

Many European countries, such as the Netherlands and Switzerland, have a system of legalized drugs, and most have far fewer addiction rates and lower incidences of drug-related violence and crime than the United States. These countries make a distinction between soft drugs (those identified as less harmful) and hard drugs (those with serious consequences). However, would the outcomes of decriminalization in the United States be the same as in Europe? Decriminalization in the United States could still be a tremendous risk because its drug problems could escalate and recriminalizing drugs would be difficult. This was the case with Prohibition in the 1920s, which, in changing the status of alcohol from legal to illegal, produced numerous crime- and alcohol-related problems.

Many good articles debate the pros and cons of this issue. These include "No Surrender: The Drug War Saves Lives" by John Walters (*National Review*, September 27, 2004), the current director of the Office of National Drug Control

Policy; "The Economics of Drug Prohibition and Drug Legalization" by Jeffrey A. Miron (*Social Research*, Fall 2001); "Marijuana, Heroin, and Cocaine: The War on Drugs May be a Disaster, But Do We Really Want a Legalized Peace?" by Robert Maccoun and Peter Reuter (*The American Prospect*, June 3, 2002); and "A Quagmire for Our Time: The War on Drugs," by Peter Schag (*The American Prospect*, August 13, 2001).

ISSUE 2

Should the United States Put More Emphasis on Stopping the Importation of Drugs?

YES: Office of National Drug Control Policy, from *The National Drug Control Strategy* (February 2005)

NO: Cathy Inouye, from "The DEA, CIA, DoD, & Narcotrafficking," *Z Magazine* (July/August 2004)

ISSUE SUMMARY

YES: The Office of National Drug Control Policy (ONDCP) argues that the importation of drugs must be stopped to reduce drug use and abuse. If the supply of drugs being trafficked across American borders is reduced, then there would be fewer drug-related problems. The ONDCP maintains that a coordinated international effort is needed to combat the increased production of heroin, cocaine, and marijuana.

NO: Cathy Inouye, a human rights volunteer for NGO SEDEM (Seguridad en Democracia), feels that the corroboration of numerous U.S. leaders with leaders in foreign governments has resulted in continued human rights abuses and has enriched those leaders in countries where the drug trade is prominent. Inouye notes that the federal government should re-examine its role of cooperation with other governments, especially those involved in the drug trade.

$\mathbf{S}$ince the beginning of the 1990s, overall drug use in the United States has increased. Up to now, interdiction has not proven to be successful in slowing the flow of drugs into the United States. Drugs continue to cross U.S. borders at record levels. This point may signal a need for stepped-up international efforts to stop the production and trafficking of drugs. Conversely, it may illustrate the inadequacy of the current strategy. Should the position of the U.S. government be to improve and strengthen current measures or to try an entirely new approach?

Some people contend that rather than attempting to limit illegal drugs from coming into the United States, more effort should be directed at reducing the demand for drugs and improving treatment for drug abusers. Foreign countries would not produce and transport drugs like heroin and cocaine into the United States if there were no market for them. Drug policies, some people maintain, should be aimed at the social and economic conditions underlying domestic drug problems, not at interfering with foreign governments.

Many U.S. government officials believe that other countries should assist in stopping the flow of drugs across their borders. Diminishing the supply of drugs by intercepting them before they reach the user is another way to eliminate or curtail drug use. Critical elements in the lucrative drug trade are multinational crime syndicates. One premise is that if the drug production, transportation, distribution, and processing functions as well as the money laundering operations of these criminal organizations can be interrupted and eventually crippled, then the drug problem would abate.

In South American countries such as Peru, Colombia, and Bolivia, where coca—from which cocaine is processed—is cultivated, economic aid has been made available to help the governments of these countries fight the cocaine kingpins. An alleged problem is that a number of government officials in these countries are corrupt or fearful of the cocaine cartel leaders. One proposed solution is to go directly to the farmers and offer them money to plant crops other than coca. This tactic, however, failed in the mid-1970s, when the U.S. government gave money to farmers in Turkey to stop growing opium poppy crops. After one year the program was discontinued due to the enormous expense, and opium poppy crops were once again planted.

Drug problems are not limited to the Americas. Since the breakup of the Soviet Union, for example, there has been a tremendous increase in opium production in many of the former republics. These republics are in dire need of money, and one source of income is opium production. Moreover, there is lax enforcement by police officials in these republics.

There are many reasons why people are dissatisfied with the current state of the war on drugs. For example, the casual user is generally the primary focus of drug use deterrence. This is viewed by many people as a form of discrimination because the vast majority of drug users and sellers who are arrested and prosecuted are poor, members of minorities, homeless, unemployed, and/or disenfranchised. Also, international drug dealers who are arrested are usually not the drug bosses but lower-level people working for them. Finally, some argue that the war on drugs should be redirected away from interdiction and enforcement because they feel that the worst drug problems in society today are caused by legal drugs, primarily alcohol and tobacco.

The following selections address the issue of whether or not the war on drugs should be fought on an international level. The Office of National Drug Control Policy takes the view that international cooperation is absolutely necessary if we are to stem the flow of drugs and reduce drug-related problems in the United States. Cathy Inouye argues that an international approach to dealing with drugs has been ineffective because many of the foreign countries receiving U.S. financial aid profit from the drug trade and that many of these countries engage in numerous human rights violations.

Disrupting the Market:
Attacking the Economic
Basis of the Drug Trade

The strategy of the U.S. Government is to disrupt the market for illegal drugs—and to do so in a way that both reduces the profitability of the drug trade and increases the costs of drugs to consumers. In other words, we seek to inflict on this business what every legal business fears—escalating costs, diminishing profits, and unreliable suppliers.

But how do we disrupt a market whose profits seem limitless?

First, it is important to understand that the drug trade is not in fact limitlessly profitable. Like every other business, the supply of and demand for illegal drugs exist in equilibrium; there is a price beyond which customers, particularly young people, will not pay for drugs. It follows that, when supplies are disrupted, prices go up, or drug supplies become erratic. Prices rising too much can precipitate a crisis for the individual user, encouraging an attempt at drug treatment. Use, in turn, goes down.

But that begs the question of how to disrupt.

Many drug trafficking organizations are complex, far-flung international businesses, often compared to multinational corporations. Yet others have more in common with the vast numbers of small networked businesses that exploit the communications revolution to get the best deal and price on goods and services almost anywhere on the globe. These organizations function as networks, with business functions accomplished by loosely aligned associations of independent producers, shippers, distributors, processors, marketers, financiers, and wholesalers. Such networked organizations pose special challenges to law enforcement and interdiction forces, because the very nature of a network is to be resistant to the disruption or dismantling of individual business entities. As this Strategy demonstrates, networked organizations are not immune from being attacked, disrupted, and dismantled.

One way to severely disrupt a networked organization is to damage or destroy most of the elements in one horizontal layer of the network—especially a layer requiring critical contacts or skills—faster than the organization can replace them.

From "The President's National Drug Control Strategy," Office of National Drug Control Policy, February 2005.

For instance, typically, a Colombian trafficking organization may sell partially refined cocaine to a second organization, which routes it through final processing and then sells it to a broker. The broker may then sell to a second trafficking organization, which hires a transporter in conjunction with other traffickers to spread risk. The transporter typically moves the finished cocaine to Mexico in exchange for a portion of the profits. Once in Mexico, the cocaine is handled by entirely different sets of transporters and wholesalers. A Colombian transporter who can choose from among a dozen wholesalers cannot be disrupted simply by targeting a single wholesaler group. The transporter can, however, be significantly disrupted if, for example, eight of twelve wholesalers have been disrupted or taken out of operation.

This Strategy describes how the U.S. Government, in concert with international allies, is seeking to target networks by attacking entire business sectors, such as the transporter sector. The Strategy lays out several examples, including destroying the economic basis of the cocaine production business in South America by fumigating the coca crop, seizing enormous and unsustainable amounts of cocaine from transporters, and selectively targeting major organization heads for law enforcement action and, ultimately, extradition and prosecution in the United States. Rather than provide an encyclopedic discussion of all supply reduction programs, the Strategy articulates examples of the creative ways in which the U.S. Government is hurting the drug trade.

Attacking the Means of Production

After years of steady increases, cocaine production in the Andes is, for the third straight year, decreasing. An aggressive program of eradication, begun in earnest with the election in mid-2002 of Colombian President Alvaro Uribe, has cut Colombia's potential cocaine production by one-third compared with the year before he took office. And, although final production estimates for last year are not yet available, 2004 was the third consecutive record year for eradication, with 120,713 hectares sprayed by the eradication forces of the Colombian National Police against coca plantations, which had totaled 113,850 hectares at the end of 2003. In other words, Colombian forces sprayed enough herbicide to cover more than the entire coca crop as it stood at the beginning of 2004, leaving many growers in the unenviable position of replanting at a furious pace to maintain production, relocating to other areas, or getting out of the business altogether.

Crucially, progress in Colombia has not been offset by increases in Peru or Bolivia. There was a net decrease in the total area cultivated in those countries in 2003, including a remarkable 15 percent drop in Peru. Only trace amounts of coca are cultivated in neighboring Venezuela, Ecuador, Panama, and Brazil.

Coca eradication remains a major and unavoidable problem for traffickers because of the crop's inherent vulnerability. We can locate the coca fields and destroy them before the raw material is harvested and processed and becomes invisible in the illicit smuggling world. Large-scale eradication is an effective means of targeting trafficker networks because most growers are affected, reducing the production available to all traffickers. With Colombia producing one-third less cocaine than it was just two years earlier, there simply is less to go around.

Eradication has dramatically reduced cocaine production capacity. It is also denying the narcoterrorists crucial revenues—reducing the amount of money flowing into the coffers of the Revolutionary Armed Forces of Colombia (FARC) at a time when the guerrilla movement is under sustained attack by the Colombian military.

The Government of Colombia continues its relentless attack on poppy cultivation and heroin production. Eradication programs supported by the U.S. Department of State sprayed or manually eradicated 4,152 hectares during 2004—an amount almost equal to the entire poppy crop at the end of 2003, the most recent year for which cultivation data is available. To put further pressure on heroin traffickers, President Uribe has advanced an initiative to seize farms involved in the cultivation of illicit crops, especially poppy.

Bigger Seizures through Better Intelligence: Disrupting the Market by Targeting Transporters

Coca eradication in Colombia represents a strategic opportunity to target the drug crop at a vulnerable point—when it is growing in the field and exposed to attack. Another key trafficker vulnerability occurs with the shipment by go-fast boats and fishing vessels of hundreds of tons of cocaine annually, typically from Colombia to Mexico en route to the United States.

The extent of this vulnerability can be summed up in a single fact: Since 2000, we have consistently increased the amount of U.S.-bound cocaine seized each year in the transit zone—even as potential production has dropped by roughly 100 metric tons a year of export-quality cocaine.

In 2003, the United States and our allies seized or forced the jettisoning of 210 metric tons of cocaine headed through the transit zone before it could reach U.S. consumers. Adding in seizures in South America, Mexico, and elsewhere, the United States and our allies removed 401 metric tons of cocaine— about half of the world's potential production—from distribution channels.

In 2004, those figures rose to 248 and 430 metric tons, respectively— against a backdrop of declining production in Latin America.

That this occurred despite periodic redeployments of interdiction forces to cover homeland security missions is strong testament to the crucial role of intelligence. Simply put, better intelligence has produced more seizures and a more efficient interdiction system.

Much of that intelligence has been the result of an unusually productive military-law enforcement collaboration. But even the best intelligence is not worth having if the interdiction assets are not there to act on it. Supportive interdiction agency leadership from the Departments of Homeland Security and Defense have managed to maintain interdiction force structure commitments despite the demands of other homeland security missions and the war on terror.

Complementing the exceptional success of operations targeting transit zone cocaine movement, the Colombian Navy, Marines, and the Colombian National Police have developed their own joint capability to disrupt cocaine export at Colombian north and west coast staging areas, where cocaine is positioned before being loaded onto fishing vessels and go-fast boats. These and other Colombian operations seized about 74 metric tons of cocaine in 2004 and are poised to expand in 2005.

Dismantling Transporter Networks: A Law Enforcement Case Study

As we have seen, attacks on networks can involve focused enforcement by interdiction forces, as with the remarkably successful efforts against trafficker movements departing Colombia. They can involve strategic efforts against a market segment, as is the case with coca eradication programs in the Andes. But they can also be a product of law enforcement operations, which have the capacity to eradicate major organizations root and branch.

One such operation, which came to fruition in 2004, coincided with a significant reduction in the flow of cocaine to the United States through the Caribbean—a reduction that continues to this day.

For years, about one-third of the cocaine heading toward the United States was moved through the Greater Antilles toward Florida. Approximately 10 percent of the total U.S. supply was handled by two organizations, one run by Colombian CPOT Elias Cobos-Muñoz and the second headed by Melvin Maycock and Pedro Smith.

.TWO ORGANIZATIONS—ONE REINVENTED INTERDICTION SYSTEM

To a great degree, the effectiveness of the U.S. Government's interdiction effort is the result of creative collaboration between different types of organizations: those in the military and interdiction fields and those in Federal law enforcement.

- Operation Panama Express, an Organized Crime Drug Enforcement Task Force (OCDETF) initiative managed jointly by DEA, FBI, and the Bureau of Immigration and Customs Enforcement, has greatly expanded interdiction-related intelligence collection and dissemination and ensured that follow-on investigations and prosecutions continue to develop intelligence leads and sources.
- Joint Interagency Task Force South is a primary consumer of the intelligence created by Panama Express. Known as JIATF-South, the task force provides one of the most sophisticated command, control, communications, and intelligence centers in the world, capable of fusing all-source intelligence and using it to drive ongoing interdiction operations.
- Interdiction-related intelligence for JIATF-South and Operation Panama Express is provided by the El Paso Intelligence Center, through its participation in a multiagency program that analyzes drug trafficking organizations traveling through the eastern Pacific Ocean and the Caribbean Sea.

SEVEN DAYS IN SEPTEMBER: INTERDICTION AGENCIES AND THE POWER OF TEAMWORK

In the span of seven days this past September, two fishing vessels yielded the largest and the second-largest maritime cocaine seizures in history—some 26 metric tons, or more than a month's supply for U.S. cocaine markets.

For the crew of the *Lina Maria*, the first indication that something had gone wrong was the appearance overhead of a propeller-driven aircraft belonging to the Bureau of Immigration and Customs Enforcement (ICE). The Cambodian-flagged vessel was identified some 300 miles southwest of the Galapagos Islands and tracked until a Coast Guard boarding team embarked on a U.S. Navy frigate could complete preparations for the boarding. The Coast Guard team boarded the vessel and within minutes had taken control of the bridge and the engine room, locating some 13.9 metric tons of cocaine in short order.

Intelligence collected during that seizure was then turned against another target. The *San Jose* was located by a maritime patrol aircraft of the Coast Guard, after an arduous search within an area roughly the size of the United States. Once again, a special Coast Guard detachment effected the boarding, this time seizing 12.1 metric tons of cocaine. Two additional seizures within the next month brought the total to 39 metric tons.

The chain of events that ended with the takedown of the *Lina Maria* and the *San Jose* began where such events typically start—with actionable intelligence. In this case, agents of the DEA, FBI and Department of Homeland Security had spent years developing enough intelligence on the movement of vessels like the *Lina Maria* to permit an educated guess as to the vessel's course and whereabouts. The takedowns were also made possible by Joint Interagency Task Force South, which coordinated a search by Navy ships as well as ICE, Navy, and Coast Guard maritime patrol aircraft.

A 29-month DEA-led investigation led to the arrest of all three CPOT targets, as well as more than 50 of their colleagues in Colombia, Panama, Jamaica, The Bahamas, the United States, and Canada.

More important, it disrupted organizations supplying an estimated 10 percent of the cocaine imported into the United States—roughly 30 metric tons per year. In seeming confirmation of this disruption, which was amplified by the deployment of international forces following the ouster of President Jean Bertrand Aristide in Haiti, intelligence estimates assess that there has been a significant reduction in the amount of cocaine flowing through the central and eastern Caribbean to the United States—from roughly one-third of total flow to perhaps 10 percent.

Cases like those pursued under the Caribbean Initiative will cause an even greater impact on the flow of drugs entering the United States as law enforcement pays renewed attention to the enduring problem of financial support services. This is a key effort in that major traffickers, whether international or domestic, typically insulate themselves from their drug distribution networks, but almost all remain closely linked to the proceeds of their trade. Efforts in this area are already bearing fruit. DEA's asset seizures are up from $383 million during fiscal year 2003 to $523 million in 2004, and the number of seizures valued more than $1 million rose by more than half.

In order to continue the illicit production of cocaine, sources of supply must move their proceeds out of the United States to a place where these funds can be used to finance future drug supplies. Strategically targeting these monies for seizure and denying revenue to international sources of drug supply will cause the significant disruption to the supply of illegal drugs entering the United States and is a major focus of the Department of Homeland Security, through the Bureau of Immigration and Customs Enforcement, and the Department of Justice, through the OCDETF program.

Such efforts include the bulk currency initiative, in which DEA, ICE, and the Internal Revenue Service are collaborating to ensure the coordination of all U.S. highway interdiction money seizures and related intelligence; the black market peso exchange initiative, targeting the largest known money laundering system in the Western Hemisphere, responsible for moving an estimated $4 billion worth of drug proceeds annually from the United States to Colombia; and the wire remitter initiative, which tracks drug proceeds that are sent from the United States to Latin America as well as other countries where drug production and drug-related money laundering are prevalent. . . .

Cathy Inouye  **NO**

The DEA, CIA, DoD, & Narcotrafficking

The U.S. Military and the Drug Enforcement Administration (DEA) are at it again, this time in Guatemala. The State Department's recently released 2003 International Narcotics Control Strategy Report states that Guatemala has become "the preferred Central American staging point for cocaine shipments northwards to Mexico and the United States." That Guatemala is a major transport route for illegal drugs is nothing new and neither is the DEA's presence here. However, what is new and troubling is the U.S. government's recent overtures of military aid towards Guatemala and the reimplementation of Plan Mayan Jaguar, a joint DEA-Department of Defense project that sets no limit on the number of U.S. military and DEA personnel that could be deployed in Guatemala on joint anti-narcotrafficking operations. Add to this the familiar irony that many of the drug kingpins in the country benefited from previous trainings by either the DEA or the CIA and all the pieces are in place for more chaos and disaster in this latest chapter in the war on drugs.

Less than two years ago, Plan Mayan Jaguar was put on ice due to what the State Department termed "corruption in Guatemala's special counternarcotics force, within the National Civil Police and . . . threats against human rights workers." A month later, Otto Reich, assistant secretary of state for Latin American Affairs, further lambasted the government of Guatemala, pointedly stating, "Retired military officials, linked to violent organized crime, have significant influence within the armed forces, the police, the Executive powers, and the Judiciary." These criticisms are all the more pointed, given that Otto Reich, who directed the State Departments Office for Public Diplomacy during the height of the Iran-contra scandal, is no liberal-leaning diplomat. Reich also cited a report by Minugua, the United Nations presence in Guatemala, that referred to "growing indications" of links between the police, the Public Ministry, military intelligence, and clandestine groups that "operate with impunity" in the country.

Guatemalan human rights organizations and international analysts believe that these clandestine groups work at the behest of a hidden power structure, made up of former military, business leaders, drug tycoons, and politicians. According to a report by the Washington Office on Latin Affairs,

From *Z Magazine*, July/August 2004, pp. 49–53. Copyright © 2004 by Institute for Social & Cultural Communication. Reprinted by permission.

this power structure uses the appearance of democracy within Guatemala as a façade behind which to order the intimidation and occasional execution of journalists, activists, and other members of civil society. Amnesty International put it best when they referred to Guatemala as a Corporate Mafia State. Terrorizing activists and buying the judiciary accomplishes their goal of total impunity and allows this group of people to make a fortune while, according to the United Nations, over 80 percent of the population lives in poverty.

What role does the DEA and the U.S. military have to play in this debacle? During the 1980s, the U.S. military and the CIA played an active support role in Guatemala's transition from military to civilian rule. This transition was orchestrated by the Guatemalan military seeking to maintain power behind the scenes while creating a sense of legitimacy for the Guatemalan government through the appearance of democracy. The Guatemalan military was aided in this project by U.S. agencies whose main objective was not to do anything about the Guatemalan military's continuing human rights abuses, but rather to "professionalize" the force. This idea of creating an efficient, though not necessarily just, military apparatus and later police force, was taken up by the DEA in its attempts to control the flow of drugs through the country. This desire for efficiency led the DEA, the CIA, and the DoD to collaborate with the country's military intelligence, a move that proved to be the equivalent of striking a deal with the devil. The criminal element in the country's military intelligence—a Guatemalan institution that has excelled in the art of forced disappearance, torture, and assassination—used the support of these U.S. agencies to their own benefit, becoming heads of narcotrafficking cartels and key players in the hidden network that is the real power in Guatemala.

This power dynamic had become so entrenched and the government's relationship with narcotrafficking so obvious that at the beginning of 2003, the U.S. government decertified Guatemala as a country active in the fight against drug trafficking. Plan Mayan Jaguar appeared to be suspended indefinitely and even the continuation of a type of military aid known as Expanded IMET seemed to be in jeopardy. Guatemalan human rights activists cheered the move as a condemnation of the country's rampant corruption and deteriorating human rights situation. But the decertification lasted less than a year. By September 2003, Plan Mayan Jaguar was back on track. By February 2004, the Guatemalan Congress broadened the mandate of Plan Mayan Jaguar to allow more U.S. troops in Guatemala to conduct joint counternarcotraffic patrols with Guatemalan officials, a move that was opposed by some Guatemalan politicians who see the plan as a threat to Guatemalan sovereignty.

So what changed in Guatemala to drastically alter the U.S. government's official stance? Not much. Sure, there was an election that replaced pro-military President Portillo with pro-business President Berger. But this change is in many ways cosmetic, as the behind-the-scenes power structure in Guatemala remains in place. Also, Guatemala's re-certification and the re-implementation of Plan Mayan Jaguar happened before the Portillo regime left office. The explanation lies in Guatemala's strategic position in the larger war on drugs.

Plan Mayan Jaguar fits in the strategy of Operation Central Skies. Coupled with Plan Colombia, a billion dollar program designed to stop drug production "at the source" (i.e., in the South American Andes region), Operation Central Skies, with a smaller, though still significant, operating budget, is an attempt to stop the inflow of these same South American drugs through Central America, Mexico, and on into the United States. Operation Central Skies, administered by the U.S. Department of Defense, began in 1998 as a means to provide military aid, primarily in the form of helicopters and personnel, to various Central American governments for use in anti-narcotrafficking operations. Guatemala has participated in Operation Central Skies "deployments," as have security forces from Costa Rica, Belize, El Salvador, and Honduras. Several officers have been trained under the auspices of Operation Central Skies, many in the School of the Americas.

Guatemalan security forces have been denied full admission to the School of the Americas due to their atrocious human rights records and indices of corruption. This is highly ironic, as, during the Cold War, administrators of the School of the Americas trained the Guatemalan military intelligence in the polarizing "us-against-them" mind-set that served as a justification for Guatemala's notorious record of human rights abuse. However, Guatemalans can still attend partial U.S. military training through a program called Expanded International Military Education and Training program (E-IMET). Officials at the U.S. Department of Defense justifiy their actions by saying that these training courses will create a more professional military, thus strengthening Guatemala's democracy. This claim is doubtful.

The CIA was involved in attempts in the late 1980s and early 1990s to "professionalize" the military intelligence apparatus, which is believed to be responsible for the majority of human rights abuses throughout the civil war and up to the present day. CIA support enabled Guatemala to construct a new military intelligence academy in the capital and provide intelligence gathering technology to intelligence services. The goal of these attempts at professionalization was not to confront the atrocious human rights abuses and criminal mentality possessed by the military intelligence services, but to increase their efficiency. This was a dangerous policy, as, even at that time, Guatemalan Minister of Defense Gramajo acknowledged that the intelligence services were "out of control," operating with their own mandate often against the wishes of the military hierarchy or the civilian government.

Since that time, the situation has only grown worse, as key players in the intelligence services have allegedly become the heads of organized crime. One example is retired General Luis Francisco Ortega Menaldo, who has been described as "the most powerful man in Guatemala." Ortega Menaldo had an illustrious history in military intelligence during the Lucas regime in Guatemala (1978–1982). Working in a military intelligence office within the Ministry of Public Finance, Ortega Menaldo was responsible for detecting suspicious shipments likely meant for the left-wing guerrillas. In this capacity he allegedly held shipment containers hostage at the borders, forcing the owners to pay an informal "tax" to release their goods. By the time he was appointed as head of the elite military intelligence unit in the country, the

Estado Mayor Presidencial (EMP) in 1991, he was already involved in narcotics trafficking and was in the center of a highly evolved criminal network. At this point in his career, he came into contact with the DEA, which was working closely with military intelligence officials to coordinate anti-narcotrafficking operations. According to Jose Reubén Zamora, a Guatemalan journalist, Ortega Menaldo and his associates were able to use this contact to their own benefit, expanding their criminal network with impunity.

Ortega Menaldo retired in 1996, when a close colleague of his, Alfredo Moreno Molina, long suspected of being involved in drug trafficking, was arrested for tax fraud, falsification of documents, and illicit enrichment. Ortega Menaldo was himself investigated for possible links to organized crime two weeks after the United States government suspended his visa in 2002 on the grounds of his suspected links to narcotics trafficking. Also under investigation for involvement in narcotics trafficking was retired Colonel Jacobo Esdras Salán Sanchez, another member of Guatemala's military intelligence and a graduate of the School of the Americas. Salán Sanchez also worked closely with the DEA, a relationship that ended badly when the DEA accused him of stealing confiscated drugs. Despite their now rocky relationship with the U.S. government, Ortega Menaldo and Salán Sanchez apparently continue to profit from their one-time patrons, the CIA and DEA. Guatemalan media reports speculate that much of the fancy gadgetry the CIA provided the Guatemalan military intelligence in the early 1990s has been used by Ortega Menaldo and his colleagues to spy on rival cartels and intimidate the judges and prosecutors who were charged with bringing them to justice.

Given the corrupt nature of the Guatemalan judiciary system, Moreno Molino, Salán Sanchez, and Ortega Menaldo have been cleared of any wrong doing. Moreno Molino was absolved by Judge Ruiz Wong of the Tenth Court of Appeals, who had himself been implicated in Moreno Molino's criminal network. The investigation of Ortega Menaldo was called a "clown show" by Iduvina Hernandez of the Guatemalan NGO SEDEM. She stated, "This trial seems like a show that will only put at risk whatever judge seeks to follow through on the case." After a year of haphazard investigation, during which the chief prosecutor was shot at by unknown assailants, Ortega Menaldo was also cleared of any links to organized crime. By the mid-1990s, the DEA must have realized that using Guatemala's military intelligence services to uphold the law was impossible. The DEA shifted its focus to developing an anti-narcotics squad within the National Civil Police. In a fact sheet prepared by the U.S. Embassy in Guatemala, the DEA is said to be training and financing Guatemala's anti-narcotics programs. The DEA "provided the impetus for the establishment of the elite counternarcotics force, the Department of Antinarcotics Operations (DOAN). Today (1996), the DOAN has various specialized counternarcotics units that are equipped and trained" by the DEA. Unfortunately, though not surprisingly, the DOAN had to be completely disbanded in 2002 due to rampant corruption and cooperation with the drug cartels they were supposed to be investigating.

Part of the blame for the continued miscalculation of the DEA, in concert with the DoD and the CIA, is a flawed oversight system and the overt optimistic, often misleading reports that these organizations make to themselves. In the 1999 International Narcotics Control Strategy Report, the State Department commends the government of Guatemala for "working, with USG (United States Government) assistance to develop effective integrated law enforcement and counternarcotics training programs to improve the quality of this small elite force (the DOAN)." The 2003 report skips over the complete failure of the DOAN and credits the formation of the Antinarcotics Information and Analysis Service (SAIS) as one of the greatest advances in the Guatemalan war on drugs. The report overlooks the fact that the SAIS is beset by the exact same corruption and abuse of authority problems as its predecessor. One of Guatemala's national newspapers, *Prensa Libre*, reports that in its one year of existence, the SAIA has been accused of torture, illegal detentions, robbery of drugs, and assassination.

The State Department isn't the only federal department analyzing Central America through rose-tinted glasses. In his 2000 testimony before the House Appropriations Committee, James Bodner, principal deputy undersecretary of defense for policy, makes the extraordinary claim that full IMET funding should be extended to Guatemala because of the "Guatemalan military's vigorous efforts to comply with the Peace Accords" and the "strong support" President Portillo had demonstrated for "respecting human rights." There aren't enough words in the English language to convey the utter falseness of these two claims. The Peace Accords were signed in 1996 between representatives of the Guatemalan government and leftist guerrilla groups. They were a comprehensive agreement outlining plans for everything from civilian control of the military to land reform to indigenous language rights. The Peace Accords remain unimplemented and human rights activists, international observers, and even representatives of the State Department lay the blame with certain members of the Guatemalan military. As for Bodner's analysis of the Portillo regime, perhaps he can be forgiven, since at the time of his testimony Portillo's government had not yet proven itself to be the most corrupt in the modern history of Guatemala, sponsoring a wave of political violence that would rip through the country in 2002 and 2003.

Despite these destructively optimistic reviews of the political reality in Guatemala, the United States does possess the correct intelligence on the area. In an interview with the Guatemalan press in 2002, Stephen MacFarland, business attaché to the U.S. Embassy in Guatemala, stated, "We (the United States) are preoccupied by the existence of parallel powers in this country and their links with narcotrafficking . . . we are preoccupied by the influence they can have in this country, especially over certain aspects of the armed forces." But it looks like the State Department analysis has once again fallen on deaf ears, as the Guatemalan government now courts the Bush Jr. administration for an end to the 1977 congressional embargo against military aid. The DEA, CIA, and DoD have been able to side step this prohibition through an accounting loophole, however, the Bush Jr. administration is contemplating renewing official military aid in June of this year. "During his visit to Washington, George W. Bush offered Guatemalan President Óscar Berger helicopters, planes, and communication equipment to modernize Guatemala's army," stated *Prensa Libre*. Berger told the press that "a team of experts will be coming here (at the end of May) to analyze what help the United States can give to modernize the Army."

Presumably, the current administration hopes that this latest round of "modernization" of arguably the most corrupt and brutal armed forces in Latin America will lead to a victory in the Central American front of the "war on drugs." Likely the team of experts they are sending to Guatemala will gloss over the dense politics of this Central American country, equating a "professional" army with one that follows the rule of law and has an understanding of human rights. This is a dangerous assumption, given that past and continuing actions of the CIA, DEA, and DoD have only succeeded in the creation of an efficient criminal apparatus that masquerades as the forces of law and order. So it looks like we're in for another round of lunacy in the war on drugs. Operation Mayan Jaguar will be in effect for at least the next two years—during which time the DEA can expect to play a part in strengthening the drug network in Guatemala. Seminars on professionalism and a couple of CH-47 Chinook helicopters won't be able to change the economic and political realities that give rise to rampant corruption in Guatemala. Initiatives by U.S. agencies won't be able to tackle the legions of corrupt and underpaid police officers, the manipulative intelligence service that honed its criminal capacities with equipment and training by the CIA or the 80 percent of the population that lives in poverty and could use a few extra dollars by transporting drugs from one end of their country to the other. Even if Operation Central Skies does somehow manage to limit the flow of drugs through Central America, the victory would be questionable. The drugs aren't going to stay in South America. Another "preferred staging point" will be found, possibly a return to transporting cocaine through the Caribbean, as was the case in the 1980s.

Trying to decipher the purposes of all these code named antinarcotrafficking joint operations has become impossible, especially from the perspective of the host country. But there is something telling about the attitudes of the DoD and the DEA blithely writing their optimistic annual country reports, asking for more money.

The war on drugs is not about drugs, but about self-justification. The more corrupt the security forces are in Guatemala, the more apparent the need to have some U.S. personnel down there, keeping an eye on things. The continuing failures to get the Guatemalan police to stop stealing cocaine from drug busts works fine for the DEA, as long as they get more funding to professionalize the force. Meanwhile, the U.S. military can maintain a presence, protecting any U.S. interests that need protecting. Daniel Lazare's analysis in the *NACLA Report on the Americas* is astute: "The goal (of the drug war) has not been to stamp out drugs per se, but to create a war-time atmosphere of hysteria in which the government would feel justified in using extraordinary measures to counter an extraordinary threat. Rather than eradication, the purpose of the drug war is . . . war itself." Using this analysis, Operation Central Skies makes perfect sense and the people in the DEA and the DoD are doing a fine job.

References

1. U.S. Department of State. *International Narcotics Control Strategy Report, 2003.* Released By the Bureau for International Narcotics and Law Enforcement Affairs. Washington DC. March 2004.

2. Pérez, Sonia D. (2002) Maya Jaguar sin apoyo de EEUU. *Prensa Libre.* September 12, 2002: 5.

3. Alvarado, H. and Jiménez, J. (2002) EE.UU. vincula al Gobierno con crimen organizado. *Siglo Veintiuno.* October 11, 2002: 4–5.

4. Peacock, Susan C. and Beltrán, A. (2003) *Hidden Powers in Post-Conflict Guatemala.* WOLA: Washington.

5. Schirmer, Jennifer. (1999) *Las Intimidades Del Proyecto Político de los Militares en Guatemala.* FLACSO: Guatemala. (Spanish Translation of *A Violence Called Democracy*)

6. Zamora, Jose Ruben. (2002) El Crimen Organizade, el Ejército, y el Futuro de los Guatemaltecos. *El Periodico.* November 12, 2002: 2–4.

7. ibid.

8. Pérez, Sonia D. (2002) Investigarán a Cinco Militares. *Prensa Libre.* October 24 2002: 3.

9. Narcotics Affairs Section—United States Embassy n Guatemala. *Fact Sheet: Counter-Narcotics Programs in Guatemala.* March 27, 1996.

10. U.S. Department of State. *International Narcotics Control Strategy Report, 1999.* Released By the Bureau for International Narcotics and Law Enforcement Affairs. Washington DC. March 2000.

11. U.S. Department of State. *International Narcotics Control Strategy Report, 2003.*

12. Presa Libre Staff. (2003) Saia repite los errores del Doan. *Prensa Libre.* October 24, 2003. p 12.

13. Mr. James Bodner, Principal Deputy Undersecretary of Defense for Policy. Testimony Before the Houe Appropriations Committee, Foreign Operations Subcommittee. April 6, 2000.

14. Paredes Diaz, Jennyffer. (2002) Fisk pide actuar contra corrupción y narcotráfico. *Prensa Libre.* November 13, 2002: 3.

15. Gonzaléz, Francisco. (2004) EE.UU. Analizará Dar Equipo al Ejecito. *Prensa Libre.* May 5, 2004.

16. Lazare, Daniel. (2001) A Battle Against Reason, Democracy and Drugs: The Drug War Deciphered. *NACLA Report on the Americas 35* (1): 13–17.

POSTSCRIPT

Should the United States Put More Emphasis on Stopping the Importation of Drugs?

The drug trade spawns violence; people die from using drugs; families are ruined by the effects of drugs; prisons are filled with people involved with illegal drugs; and drugs can devastate aspirations and careers.

Two paths that are traditionally followed involve reducing either the supply of drugs or the demand for drugs. Four major agencies involved in the fight against drugs in the United States—the Drug Enforcement Administration (DEA), the Federal Bureau of Investigation (FBI), the U.S. Customs Service, and the U.S. Coast Guard—have seized thousands of pounds of marijuana, cocaine, and heroin during the past few years. Drug interdiction appears to be reducing the availability of drugs. But what effect does drug availability have on use? If a particular drug is not available, would other drugs be used in its place? Would the cost of drugs increase if there were a shortage of drugs? If costs increase, would violence due to drugs go up as well?

Annual surveys of 8th-, 10th-, and 12th-grade students indicate that availability is not a major factor in drug use. Throughout the 1980s, drug use declined dramatically even though marijuana and cocaine could be obtained easily. According to the surveys, the perceived harm of these drugs, not their availability, is what affects students' drug use.

Efforts to prevent drug use may prove fruitless if people have a natural desire to alter their consciousness. In his 1989 book *Intoxication: Life in the Pursuit of Artificial Paradise* (E. P. Dutton), Ronald Siegel contends that the urge to alter consciousness is as universal as the craving for food and sex.

Articles that examine international efforts to deal with the issue of drugs include "The New Opium War," by Matthew Quirk" (*The Atlantic Monthly*, March 2005), "The Price of Powder," (*The Economist*, November 27, 2004), "U.S. Versus Them: Challenging America's War on Drugs—U.S. Policy," by Susan Taylor Martin (*St. Petersburg Times*, July 29, 2001); "Narcoterrorism as a Threat to International Security," by Stephen Blank (*World and I*, December 2001); and "Addicted to the Drug War," by Kenneth Sharp (*The Chronicle of Higher Education*, October 6, 2000).

ISSUE 3

Will a Lower Blood Alcohol Level for Drunk Driving Reduce Automobile Accidents?

YES: Thomas S. Dee, from "Does Setting Limits Save Lives? The Case of 0.08 BAC Laws," *Journal of Policy Analysis and Management* (vol. 20, no. 1, 2001)

NO: General Accounting Office, from "How Effective Are '.08' Drunk-Driving Laws?" *Consumers' Research Magazine* (August 1999)

ISSUE SUMMARY

YES: Thomas S. Dee, an economics professor at Swarthmore College, supports a .08 blood alcohol concentration (BAC). Dee maintains that alcohol-related fatalities are lower in those states that adopted the .08 BAC. Dee concludes that an estimated 1200 fewer deaths would result from the adoption of such a limit.

NO: The General Accounting Office (GAO) states that the evidence supporting the beneficial effects of establishing a lower blood alcohol level for drunk driving is inconclusive. The GAO maintains that the government's methods for determining the effectiveness of instituting a lower blood alcohol level are faulty and that rates for drunk driving have declined regardless of changes in BAC legal limits.

When discussions of drinking and driving arise, many people justifiably express concern. Too many people die needlessly because of others' poor judgment regarding whether they can safely operate a motor vehicle after drinking. However, the news is not all bad. In the last 20 years, the number of alcohol-related driving fatalities in the United States has decreased significantly. In the early 1980s, about 26,000 people died each year because of drivers under the influence of alcohol. In 1998, the number of people killed in automobile accidents on American highways because of drunk drivers was around 17,000. This represents a 30 percent decline. That number has crept up in recent years. Despite this significant reduction, few would argue against further improvement.

The figure of 17,000 alcohol-related automobile fatalities represents the number of people who were killed by a driver who was legally intoxicated at the time of the accident. Missing from this figure is the number of people who were killed by drivers who may have been drinking but who were not legally drunk. However, one does not need to be drunk to be impaired. A number of studies have demonstrated that driving ability is impaired with a blood alcohol concentration (BAC) level as low as .04.

The blood alcohol concentration (BAC), sometimes referred to as blood alcohol level (BAL), is the amount of alcohol that is in a person's body as measured by the weight of the alcohol in a certain volume of blood. A person's BAC can be measured by testing the blood, breath, urine, or saliva. The United States Senate approved a national blood alcohol level standard of .08 in March 1998. States refusing to adopt this new standard will be in jeopardy of losing federal funding for highways. One aspect of the debate focused on whether the federal government should interfere in what many senators see as a state's option. Research indicates that lowering the BAC limit from .10 or higher to .08 reduces the number of people who get behind the wheel of a car after drinking. However, the senators are not debating whether a lower standard like .08 is desirable, but what the role of the federal government should be in this matter.

The precedent for penalizing states who refuse to adopt the .08 blood alcohol level standard was set in the early 1980s when President Ronald Reagan threatened to withdraw highway funds from states that did not raise the drinking age to 21. That situation, like the current issue, raises a fundamental question: Should the federal government have the right to dictate to individual states what is an acceptable BAC standard? Is the role of government to conduct research in order to allow states to make informed decisions? If, as Senator Jack Reed (D-Rhode Island) has indicated, a .08 BAC saves between 500 and 600 lives a year, shouldn't the federal government take a more strident stand? Yet, is the research cited by these senators accurate? Should government impose laws where the research is suspect?

In the following selections, Thomas S. Dee argues that the need to lower the acceptable blood alcohol level for drunk driving is clear. The federal government should support a national blood alcohol concentration standard of .08 for driving while intoxicated to save lives and to prevent serious injuries. The General Accounting Office does not dispute the fact that automobile accidents have declined over the past two decades, but it questions the validity of these studies. The GAO asserts that the decline in automobile accidents may have occurred despite changes in the law.

Thomas S. Dee

 **YES**

Does Setting Limits Save Lives?
The Case of 0.08 BAC Laws

Abstract

Nineteen states have established laws that make it illegal per se to drive with a blood alcohol concentration (BAC) of 0.08. The controversy over extending this stricter definition throughout the nation has focused largely on whether the state laws have been effective at saving lives. Prior evidence on this question has been mixed as well as criticized on several methodological grounds. This study presents novel, panel-based evaluations of 0.08 BAC laws, which address the potential methodological limitations of previous studies. The results of this study indicate that 0.08 BAC laws have been effective in reducing the number of traffic fatalities, particularly among younger adults. These estimates suggest that the nationwide adoption of 0.08 BAC laws would generate substantial gains, reducing the annual count of traffic fatalities by at least 1200.

Introduction

Over the last 25 years, almost every state has adopted a law that makes it illegal per se to drive with certain blood alcohol concentrations (BAC).[1] Most states initially established this limit at a BAC of 0.10 or higher. However, by the end of 1998, 14 states had established an illegal per se limit at a BAC of 0.08 (Table 1).[2] The continued expansion of this stricter standard has been strongly advocated by law enforcement groups, insurance industry advocates, and traffic safety organizations like Mothers Against Drunk Driving (MADD) who claim that these regulations can save lives by reducing the prevalence of drunk driving. However, these claims have also been contested aggressively by the alcohol and restaurant industries, which argue that this regulation merely punishes responsible social drinkers who pose no threat to others. Over the last several years, much of this debate has focused on possible actions by the federal government to compel all states to adopt this stricter BAC standard. In particular, in March of 1998, the Senate approved by a vote of 62 to 32 a transportation appropriations bill that would withhold federal highway funds from states that do not adopt an illegal per se limit of 0.08.

From Thomas S. Dee, "Does Setting Limits Save Lives? The Case of 0.08 BAC Laws," *Journal of Policy Analysis and Management*, vol. 20, no. 1 (2001). Copyright © 2001 by The Association for Public Policy Analysis and Management. Reprinted by permission.

Table 1

Effective Dates of 0.08 BAC Laws and Administrative License Revocations, 1982 1998

State	Effective Dates	
	Illegal Per Se at 0.08 BAC	Administrative License Revocation
Alabama	August 1995	August 1996
California	January 1990	July 1990
Florida	January 1994	October 1990
Idaho	July 1997	July 1994
Illinois	July 1997	January 1986
Kansas	July 1993	July 1988
Maine	August 1988	January 1986
New Hampshire	January 1994	July 1992
New Mexico	January 1994	July 1984
North Carolina	October 1993	October 1983
Oregon	October 1983	July 1984
Utah	August 1983	August 1983
Vermont	July 1991	December 1989
Virginia	July 1994	January 1995

Note: Hawaii, Washington, Texas, Kentucky, and Rhode Island also adopted 0.08 BAC laws in 1995, 1999, 1999, 2000, and 2000, respectively.

The Clinton administration also endorsed this legislation. However, there was less support for this measure among Republican leaders in the House. After a period of intense lobbying, the Senate's initial decision was reversed: the final legislation did not withhold highway funds from states without a 0.08 BAC standard. And there was no threat of a presidential veto in response to this change (Pianin, 1998).[3] Commentators attributed the demise of this drunk-driving legislation in part to aggressive lobbying by the alcohol and restaurant industries as well as to a propensity among many legislators to allow states to make these decisions for themselves (Weisman, 1998). However, unclear statistical evidence on the effects of previous state-level 0.08 BAC laws was also cited as an important part of the public debate. The final legislation acknowledged this concern by directing the General Accounting Office (GAO) to evaluate the existing studies of the efficacy of state 0.08 BAC laws. In their subsequent report, the GAO (1999) cited several methodological concerns with this research in concluding that available evidence had not clearly established that the state-level 0.08 BAC laws actually reduced alcohol-related traffic fatalities.[4]

These concerns about the uncertain effects of state-level experiences with 0.08 BAC laws are likely to surface again: in its most recent transportation appropriations bill, the Senate has again approved the withholding of highway funds from states that do not have a 0.08 BAC standard. This study addresses these issues by presenting new empirical evidence on how state-level 0.08 BAC laws influenced traffic fatalities. These evaluations are based on data and empirical specifications that address the potential methodological limitations of the prior research reviewed in GAO (1999). For example, these evaluations are based on a relatively long (1982–1998) panel of annual state-level data on traffic fatality rates, instead of data on alcohol involvement in fatal crashes.[5] Furthermore, the specifications adopted here improve upon much of the previous literature partly by introducing a broader set of controls for potentially confounding and omitted determinants of traffic safety. These include explicit regressors that control for several of the key traffic-related policies that were also being introduced within states over this period (for example, other drunk-driving policies, seat-belt laws, speed limits). New state regulations that allow licensing authorities to revoke the driver's license of allegedly drunk drivers before any court action (administrative license revocations) are of particular concern in this context. More specifically, several of the states that introduced 0.08 BAC laws introduced administrative license revocations almost simultaneously (Table 1). Some studies have been criticized for failing to control for the possibly confounding influence of this contemporaneous drunk-driving policy (GAO, 1999).

Furthermore, several traffic safety studies have recognized that other important and unobserved determinants of traffic safety may vary substantially from one geographic area to another as well as over time periods (for example, state-specific or year-specific cultural sentiment toward drunk driving). As in these studies (for example, Benson, Rasmussen, and Mast, 1999; Cook and Tauchen, 1984; Dee, 1999; Evans and Graham, 1988; Evans, Neville, and Graham, 1991; Mast, Benson, and Rasmussen, 1999; Ruhm, 1996; Young and Likens, 2000), the results presented here control for the influence of these unobserved and potentially confounding omitted variables through the use of state and year fixed effects. This study also presents some counterfactual evaluations that validate this study's key inferences by exploiting the patterns in the timing of alcohol involvement in fatal traffic accidents. It is well known that traffic fatalities that occur on weekends and at night are substantially more likely to involve drunk driving than those that occur during the day or on weekdays. This pattern presents a compelling opportunity to evaluate the reliability of the inferences presented here. More specifically, if the fixed effects specifications were generating reliable inferences, life-saving benefits of introducing drunk-driving policies like 0.08 BAC laws would be expected to be relatively concentrated in observed reductions of weekend and nighttime traffic fatalities. If, in contrast, these models suggest that such policies are more effective in reducing daytime and weekday traffic fatalities, it would point to the possible existence of confounding specification errors.

The results of these evaluations clearly indicate that the adoption of state-level 0.08 BAC laws generated large and statistically significant reductions in the prevalence of traffic fatalities. Furthermore, these results suggest that the law-driven reductions in traffic fatalities were particularly large among teenagers and young adults. However, it is important to note that 0.08 BAC laws were almost never in effect without administrative license revocations (Table 1). This implies that the "direct" effects of 0.08 standards cannot be effectively distinguished from its potentially interactive effects with administrative license revocations. However, from a policy perspective, this caveat is not particularly constraining given that most states already have administrative license revocations in place. In particular, even under the conservative assumption that 0.08 BAC laws would only save lives when combined with administrative license revocations already in effect, the results presented here suggest that the nationwide adoption of this policy would reduce traffic fatalities by roughly 1200 annually.

Evaluating 0.08 BAC Laws

According to the National Highway Traffic Safety Administration (NHTSA), an average 170-pound man would reach a BAC of 0.08 by consuming his fifth 12-ounce beer (4.5 percent alcohol by volume) within a two-hour period (GAO, 1999). An average 120-pound woman would have a BAC of 0.08 after consuming three beers over the same period.[6] Varied evidence suggests that driving at such levels of intoxication is associated with increased traffic fatality risk (Levitt and Porter, 1999; Zador, 1991; Zador, Krawchuk, and Voas, 2000). For example, Zador, Krawchuk, and Voas (2000) found that the fatality risk for drivers with blood alcohol concentrations between 0.08 and 0.10 was at least six times higher than for sober drivers and that the increased risk was particularly high among young males. Similarly, NHTSA claims that impairment of visual function, reaction time, steering, and emergency responsiveness is substantial among drivers with a 0.08 BAC (GAO, 1999). However, alcohol industry associations have disputed this evidence and suggested that a nationwide 0.08 BAC law would only punish "responsible social drinking."[7]

More direct evidence on the potential efficacy of 0.08 BAC laws has been based on reduced-form evaluations of the available state-level experiences with such regulations. More specifically, seven studies have evaluated how the adoption of 0.08 BAC laws may have influenced the proportion of alcohol involvement in fatal crashes and the number of alcohol-related fatalities (GAO, 1999). Two studies focused on the effects of California's 0.08 BAC law, which was adopted at the beginning of 1990 (NHTSA, 1991; OTS, 1995). The first of these studies reported a 12 percent decline in alcohol-related fatalities after the adoption of the 0.08 BAC law. However, the GAO criticized this study in part because the post-law period was so short and because just six months into this post-law period, California introduced administrative license revocations for drunk drivers (Table 1). The second California study, which was based on four years of data, reported mixed results regarding the 0.08 BAC law. NHTSA (1994) examined data from five states that adopted 0.08 BAC laws (California, Maine, Oregon, Utah, and Vermont). This study considered how six measures of alcohol involvement (driver involvement in fatal crashes by certain BAC levels, nighttime involvement) changed after the adoption of 0.08 BAC laws in these five states. They reported significant decreases in nine of the 30 measures. Hingson, Heeren, and Winter (1996) also evaluated the changed rates of alcohol involvement in fatal crashes for these five states. However, this study compared the changes in these states with those in nearby comparison states to provide potential controls for the shared but unobserved time-series determinants of alcohol involvement.[8] Nonetheless, both of these studies have been reasonably criticized for failing to control for other important time-varying determinants. In particular, as Hingson, Heeren, and Winter (1996) recognized, three of the five states in these studies also adopted administrative license revocations within only 10 months of their 0.08 BAC law (Table 1). The study by Hingson, Heeren, and Winter (1996) has also been criticized for the potentially problematic nature of the comparison states.[9]

NHTSA released three other studies on 0.08 BAC laws in April of 1999. One of these studies (Foss, Stewart, and Reinfurt, 1998) focused on North Carolina and concluded that the 0.08 BAC law had no clear effect and that reductions in alcohol-related traffic fatalities appeared to be part of a long-term trend that began before the adoption of a 0.08 BAC law. Apsler et al. (1999) presented time-series evaluations for the 11 states that had a 0.08 BAC law by the end of 1994. They found that 0.08 BAC laws significantly reduced alcohol involvement in only two to five of these 11 states. Voas, Tippetts, and Fell (2000) conducted an evaluation of 0.08 BAC laws by estimating regression models based on quarterly data from all 50 states and the District of Columbia from 1982 through 1997. These regression models included controls for other determinants of alcohol involvement such as administrative license revocations, vehicle miles traveled, urbanicity, shared trends, and fixed state-level variables for whether each state had adopted certain traffic safety policies at any time over this period.[10] They found that 0.08 BAC laws reduced the involvement of drinking drivers relative to sober drivers. GAO (1999) criticizes this study in part for excluding young drivers, noting that many young drivers have been prosecuted under the 0.08 BAC law in California.

In reviewing the mixed evidence from these seven state-level studies, GAO (1999) concluded that they fell short of clearly establishing the efficacy of 0.08 BAC laws. This study presents novel evaluations of the effect of 0.08 BAC laws, which address the potential methodological limitations of these previous studies. One class of innovations in this study simply involves the nature of the data being analyzed. The evaluations presented here are based on annual state-level panel data on traffic fatality rates from 1982 to 1998. These data are sufficiently recent to provide observations well after most states enacted 0.08 BAC laws (Table 1). Furthermore, these data reflect total fatalities including those among young adults who were excluded from some prior studies (for example, NHTSA, 1994; Voas, Tippetts, and Fell, 2000).[11] And some of the evaluations presented here focus specifically on traffic fatality rates among younger adults. However, another potentially important distinction in the data set under study here is simply that the key outcomes are traffic fatality rates. Most studies have instead examined how 0.08 BAC laws influenced rates of alcohol involvement in fatal crashes. The rate of alcohol involvement in crashes is undoubtedly a policy-relevant outcome as it is strongly associated with fatality risk. However, tests for alcohol involvement are not actually conducted and recorded for all fatal crashes. Therefore, NHTSA has simply imputed much of the available data on alcohol involvement. In contrast, the actual number of traffic fatalities, which are ultimately the outcome of interest, is essentially observed without error in each state and year.[12] Similarly, other key attributes of fatal crashes known to be associated with alcohol use (time of accident, age of victims) are also recorded for nearly all accidents and allow construction of alcohol-sensitive measures of traffic fatalities.

A second class of innovations in this study involves the research design employed to identify the effects of 0.08 BAC laws. The most recent studies on 0.08 BAC laws have employed multiple regression techniques to purge the potentially confounding influence of other observed and unobserved determinants of traffic safety (Apsler et al., 1999; Voas, Tippetts, and Fell, 2000). However, the number of controls included in previous studies may be too limited. The period over which 0.08 BAC laws were adopted was characterized by considerable within-state variation in other important policies related to traffic safety (other drunk-driving measures, seat-belt laws, speed limits, etc.). Furthermore, other less tangible attributes that influence traffic safety may also vary substantially from one geographic area to another and over periods of time (for example, state-specific or period-specific cultural sentiment toward drunk driving). By definition, such unobserved determinants are inherently difficult to measure. However, omitting controls for these determinants could easily bias statistical inferences regarding traffic safety measures as well as attenuate the precision of those inferences. Several empirical studies of traffic safety have controlled for such omitted variable biases by introducing state and year fixed effects, which unambiguously purge the influence of unobserved state-specific determinants as well as shared, year-specific determinants.[13] This study presents multiple regression results based on such two-way fixed effects models. As noted earlier, the method adopted by Hingson, Heeren, and Winter (1996) is conceptually consistent with this approach because it relies on comparing the within-state changes in 0.08 BAC states with the contemporaneous changes in states that did not adopt 0.08 BAC laws. However, the two-way fixed effects models presented here generalize this approach in at least two important ways. One is that the effective "comparison" states are less selective because they are drawn from the entire nation. The second is that it allows for other important robustness checks because other variables reflecting important state policy changes over this period can easily be included as controls.

Nonetheless, even the use of fixed effects and an expanded set of control variables does not obviate all reasonable concerns about the possibly confounding influence of omitted variables or other specification errors. As an additional check on these results, this study presents evidence from counterfactual estimations that attempt to exploit the patterns in the timing of alcohol-related accidents. It is well established that the rates of alcohol involvement in fatal crashes are substantially larger during weekends and at nighttime.[14] For example, NHTSA (1999) reports that, in 1988, 49 percent of the drivers killed during weekends were in accidents involving someone who was intoxicated (that is, a BAC of at least 0.10). In contrast, only 29 percent of the drivers killed during weekdays in 1988 were in accidents involving someone who was intoxicated. Similarly, the rate of alcohol involvement for driver fatalities in 1988 was 56 percent at night and 16 percent during the day.[15] Because of these patterns, several empirical studies of alcohol policies (including this one) have focused on these alcohol-sensitive weekend or nighttime outcomes. However, the much lower rates of alcohol involvement in weekday and daytime fatalities also present a compelling opportunity. More specifically, if the conventional regression models were generating reliable inferences about the effects of 0.08 BAC laws, one would reasonably expect these effects to be smaller in similarly specified models of weekday or daytime traffic fatalities. However, if 0.08 BAC laws appeared to have relatively large and statistically significant effects in such models, it would suggest a confounding specification error. This study presents such counterfactual evidence by comparing the results from similarly specified models of weekend, weekday, nighttime, and daytime traffic fatality rates. These ad hoc comparisons are particularly useful in this context because they provide a compelling way of validating the inferences from these models without simply introducing additional controls that exhaust the already limited sample variation in 0.08 BAC laws and traffic fatalities. However, the power of these simple comparisons as a specification test should not be overstated. Comparisons of evaluation results for models of daytime, nighttime, weekend, and weekday traffic fatalities may yield a plausible heterogeneity even in the presence of some specification error. Furthermore, drunk-driving measures such as 0.08 BAC laws may actually have no detectable effects on daytime and weekday traffic fatalities if efforts at enforcement are substantially lower during these periods. Alternatively, 0.08 BAC standards may have larger effects on weekday and daytime fatalities if those at risk for driving drunk during these periods are more responsive to illegal per se laws. Nonetheless, the patterns of response heterogeneity across these types of traffic fatalities can provide a useful additional commentary on this study's main results. . . .

Conclusions

Over the last 20 years, an extensive array of legislative initiatives has attempted to reduce the prevalence of drunk driving. Although, by most accounts, these efforts have been successful, drunk driving continues to exact a heavy toll. In 1998, 38 percent of the 41,471 traffic fatalities in the United States were classified as alcohol-involved (NHTSA, 1999). Such disturbing facts motivate the continued legislative efforts to discourage risky drunk driving. The focus of the most recent activity has largely been on state laws that establish an explicit blood alcohol concentration (BAC) at which it is illegal per se to drive. In most states, this standard has been set at a BAC of 0.10. However, to date, 19 states have adopted a stricter BAC standard of 0.08. Further expansion of this stricter drunk-driving standard has been under consideration in most states as well as at the federal level. The nationwide adoption of 0.08 BAC laws has been strongly supported by traffic safety advocates who argue that these regulations save lives by reducing driving at unsafe BAC levels. However, these claims have also been aggressively contested by the alcohol and restaurant industries, which argue that these regulations merely punish responsible social drinking. In 1998, a federal proposal sought to withhold highway funds from states that do not adopt a 0.08 BAC standard. Congressional negotiators ultimately rejected that proposal after a period of intense lobbying that one official characterized as "deep emotions versus deep pockets" (Dao, 1998).

However, much of the controversy over extending the 0.08 BAC standard has also focused on arguably legitimate concerns about the mixed empirical evidence on the efficacy of the earliest state laws. In particular, evaluations of 0.08 BAC laws have been explicitly criticized on a variety of methodological grounds (GAO, 1999). This study presents novel evaluations of state-level 0.08 BAC laws that address the criticisms raised in the GAO report as well as several specification issues that are not. The regression models presented here examine these potential shortcomings through the analysis of a relatively long and recent panel data set on traffic fatalities and through the inclusion of additional controls for other contemporaneous and potentially confounding determinants of traffic safety. The results suggest that methodological criticisms, like those raised in GAO (1999), are indeed valid. In particular, these evaluations indicated that the failure to control for the influence of other traffic safety policies could lead to highly inflated estimates of the life-saving benefits of 0.08 BAC laws.

Nonetheless, the results of these evaluations also demonstrated that state-level 0.08 BAC laws have generated statistically significant reductions in traffic fatality rates. The preferred specification indicate that this stricter BAC standard reduced fatality rates by 7.2 percent. This evidence appears to be quite robust and was validated, in part, by the results of counterfactual estimations that exploited the timing of alcohol involvement in fatal traffic accidents. Interestingly, these results also indicate that these policy-induced reductions in traffic fatalities were particularly large among younger drivers. One relevant caveat to these results is that the direct effects of 0.08 BAC laws cannot be clearly distinguished from their potentially interactive effects with administrative license revocations because states that adopted the 0.08 BAC standard almost always had administrative license revocations in effect (Table 1). However, this qualification is not particularly constraining with respect to the policy relevance of these results in light of the fact that most states have already adopted administrative license revocations. For example, the U.S. Congress is currently reconsidering withholding highway funds from any state without a 0.08 BAC standard. This study's results suggest that federal actions that led to the nationwide expansion of 0.08 BAC laws would generate a considerable reduction in the number of annual traffic fatalities. More specifically, this study's results can be used to estimate the number of lives that would be saved annually by expanding the 0.08 BAC standard under the conservative assumption that this policy would only be effective in states that already have administrative license revocations. Twenty-three states (excluding Alaska) currently have administrative license revocations but have not yet adopted 0.08 BAC laws. In these states, during 1998, there were roughly 90.1 million people and the total traffic fatality rate averaged 18.7 per 100,000 in the population. A 7.2 percent reduction in traffic fatality rates in these states would imply roughly 1200 lives saved annually. . . . [T]hese saved lives would be disproportionately young. In considering the policy implications of such simulations and the future of BAC standards in the United States, it should also be noted that other types of evidence point to the likely efficacy of 0.08 BAC laws. Medical evidence suggests that driver ability is significantly impaired at this BAC level. Studies based on actual crash data (Levitt and Porter 1999; Zador, Krawchuk, and Voas, 2000) also demonstrate a sharply increased risk associated with driving at relatively modest BAC levels, which may not be conventionally associated with drunk driving.

Notes

1. Only Massachusetts and South Carolina have no established BAC at which it is illegal per se to drive. BAC is measured as the weight of alcohol in a certain volume of blood and can be determined through the analysis of blood, urine, breath and saliva.

2. Since then, five other states (Hawaii, Washington, Texas, Kentucky, and Rhode Island) have also adopted 0.08 BAC laws. Several other industrialized nations also define drunk-driving at a BAC of 0.08 or lower.

3. However, as part of the compromise, the legislation allocated $500 million for incentive grants to states that adopted the 0.08 BAC standard.

4. However, GAO (1999) noted that there were "strong indications" that the interaction of these laws with other drunk-driving measures may be effective. The GAO study also suggested that direct medical evidence of driver impairment at such BAC levels should be considered.

5. One criticism of some previous studies has been that they have had too little data after the adoption of 0.08 BAC laws. Another potential shortcoming in prior studies of 0.08 BAC laws has been the focus on rates of alcohol involvement in fatal crashes. Since alcohol involvement in fatal crashes is not always determined, much of the available data are actually imputed. In contrast, the prevalence of traffic fatalities, which are arguably the true outcome of interest, is essentially observed in every state and year without error.

6. Such calculations vary because the absorption of alcohol into the bloodstream depends on a number of individual characteristics, such as age.

7. Public rhetoric on how many drinks it actually takes to reach a 0.08 BAC (and, by implication, what may constitute responsible social drinking) has often been based on misleadingly varied choices of weight, gender, and drink type for a representative person (Gawande, 1998).

8. This approach is analogous to a basic "difference-in-differences" estimator, since it compares changes in the "treatment" state to contemporaneous changes in the "control" states. The preferred regression specifications adopted here, which include state and year fixed effects, provide a more general and flexible variation on this basic identification strategy.

9. For example, California was paired with Texas. GAO (1999) suggests that, in this context, it is better to compare "treatment" states to several states or the rest of the nation. The two-way fixed effects specifications employed here effectively adopt this approach and allow the introduction of other potentially relevant controls that vary within states over time.

10. However, these specifications included trend variables instead of year fixed effects. They also omitted unrestrictive state fixed effects, including instead time-invariant dummy variables for states that had certain traffic safety policies

any time over the study period. Their specifications also excluded variables representing other potentially important policies that varied within states over this period (speed limits and other drunk-driving policies).

11. GAO (1999) noted that in 1997, more under-21 California drivers were convicted under the state's 0.08 BAC law than under the "zero tolerance" law.

12. Since 1975, NHTSA has obtained data on all traffic-related fatalities through its Fatal Accident Reporting System (FARS). The economic literature on traffic safety has focused almost exclusively on fatalities as the key dependent variable (for example, Chaloupka, Saffer, and Grossman, 1993; Cook and Tauchen, 1984; Dee, 1999; Evans and Graham, 1988; Evans, Neville, and Graham, 1991; Mast, Benson, and Rasmussen, 1999; Ruhm, 1996; Young and Likens, 2000).

13. Ruhm (1996) addressed this issue directly and finds that the omission of such controls can lead to confounded inferences about alcohol-related traffic safety policies.

14. NHTSA (1999) defines the weekend as the period from 6:00 PM on Friday to 5:59 AM on Monday and defines nighttime as the period from 6:00 PM to 5:59 AM. These definitions are also adopted here.

15. These patterns of alcohol involvement are typical even though they are partly based on imputed data and are only for 1988 drivers. According to the author's calculations with the 1982–1998 FARS data on all traffic fatalities, the patterns of police-reported rates of alcohol involvement are quite similar.

References

Apsler, R., Char, A.R., Harding, W.M., & Klein, T.M. (1999). The effects of 0.08 BAC laws. Washington, DC: National Highway Traffic Safety Administration.

Benson, B.L., Rasmussen, D.W, & Mast, B.D. (1999). Deterring drunk driving fatalities: An economics of crime perspective. International Review of Law and Economics, 19(2), 205–225.

Chaloupka, F.J., Saffer, H., & Grossman, M. (1993). Alcohol-control policies and motor-vehicle fatalities. Journal of Legal Studies, 22(1), 161–186.

Cook, P.J. & Tauchen, G. (1984). The effect of minimum drinking age legislation on youthful auto fatalities, 1970–1977. Journal of Legal Studies, 13, 169–190.

Dao, J. (1998). Highway bill accord rejects tougher standard on alcohol. The New York Times, A1.

Dee, T.S. (1999). State alcohol policies, teen drinking and traffic fatalities. Journal of Public Economics, 72(2), 289–315.

Evans, W.N. & Graham, J.D. (1988). Traffic safety and the business cycle. Alcohol, Drugs and Driving, 4(1), 31–38.

Evans, W.N., Neville, D., & Graham, J.D. (1991). General deterrence of drunk driving: Evaluation of recent American policies. Risk Analysis, 11(2), 279–289.

Foss, R.D., Stewart, J.R., & Reinfurt, D.W. (1998). Evaluation of the effects of North Carolina's 0.08% BAC law. Washington, DC: National Highway Traffic Safety Administration.

GAO [U.S. General Accounting Office] (1999). Highway Safety: Effectiveness of State .08 Blood Alcohol laws. Washington, DC: GAO.

Gawande, A. (1998). One for my baby, but 0.08 for the road. Slate Magazine. (http://slate.msn.com/MedicalExaminer/98-02-26/MedicalExaminer.asp).

Hingson, R., Heeren, T., & Winter, M. (1996). Lowering state legal blood alcohol limits to 0.08%: The effect on fatal motor vehicle crashes. American Journal of Public Health, 86(9), 1297–1299.

Levitt, S.D. & Porter, J. (1999). Estimating the effect of alcohol on driver risk using only fatal accident statistics. Working Paper 6944. Cambridge, MA: National Bureau of Economic Research.

Mast, B.D., Benson, B.L., & Rasmussen, D.W. (1999). Beer taxation and alcohol-related traffic fatalities. Southern Economic Journal, 66(2), 214–249.

NHTSA [National Highway Traffic Safety Administration]. (1991). The effects following the implementation of .08 BAC limit and an administrative per se Law in California. Washington, DC: NHTSA.

NHTSA [National Highway Traffic Safety Administration]. (1994). A preliminary assessment of the impact of lowering the illegal BAC per se limit to 0.08 in five states. Washington, DC: NHTSA.

NHTSA [National Highway Traffic Safety Administration]. (1999). Traffic safety facts 1998—alcohol. Washington, DC: U.S. Department of Transportation.

OTS [Office of Traffic Safety]. (1995). The general deterrent impact of California's .08% blood alcohol concentration limit and administrative per se license suspension laws. Office of Traffic Safety, State of California.

Pianin, E. (1998). How pressure politics bottled up a tougher drunk-driving rule. The Washington Post. Washington, DC: A20.

Ruhm, C.J. (1996). Alcohol policies and highway vehicle fatalities. Journal of Health Economics, 14(5), 583–603.

Voas, R.B., Tippetts, A.S., & Fell, J. (2000). The relationship of alcohol safety laws to drinking drivers in fatal crashes. Accident Analysis and Prevention, 32, 483–492.

Weisman, J. (1998). Industry may kill alcohol measure. The Baltimore Sun. Baltimore, MD: 1A.

Young, D. & Likens, T. (2000). Alcohol regulation and auto fatalities. International Review of Law and Economics, 20(1), 107–126.

Zador P.L. (1991). Alcohol-related relative risk of fatal driver injuries in relation to driver age and sex. Journal of Studies on Alcohol, 52(4), 302–310.

Zador, P.L., Krawchuk, S.A., & Voas, R.B. (2000). Alcohol-related relative risk of driver fatalities and driver involvement in fatal crashes in relation to driver age and sex: An update using 1996 data. Journal of Studies on Alcohol, 61(3), 387–395.

NO  General Accounting Office

How Effective Are ".08" Drunk-Driving Laws?

Inconclusive Results

State efforts to combat drunk driving have, by all accounts, worked to good effect. Alcohol-related fatalities have declined sharply over the past 15 years. Currently, it is illegal in every state to drive while under the influence of alcohol. In addition, all but two have blood alcohol "per se" laws—laws that make it unlawful for a person to drive with a specific amount of alcohol in his blood. How low this amount should be has drawn controversy. Thirty-two states have set this limit at .10 BAC (blood alcohol content). In 16 states, however, the per se limit is 20% lower, or .08 BAC, and the Clinton Administration has pushed to extend this limit to other states, raising concerns that drivers who pose little threat on the highways will be unfairly penalized. As the following excerpts from a recent General Accounting Office report reveal, the effectiveness of these '.08' limits has not been sufficiently supported by the safety data, despite official assertions to the contrary.—Ed.

Since 1970, the National Highway Traffic Safety Administration (NHTSA) has espoused a "systems approach" to reducing drunk driving, including enforcement, judicial, legislative, licensing, and public information components. In 1997, NHTSA published an action plan developed with other participants to reduce alcohol-related driving fatalities to 11,000 by the year 2005. This plan recommended that all states pass a wide range of laws, including ones establishing .08 BAC limits, license revocation laws— under which a person deemed to be driving under the influence has his or her driving privileges suspended or revoked—comprehensive screening and treatment programs for alcohol offenders, vehicle impoundment, "zero tolerance" BAC and other laws for youth, and primary enforcement laws for safety belts. The plan also called for increased public awareness campaigns, with an emphasis on target populations such as young people and repeat offenders.

From General Accounting Office, "How Effective Are '.08' Drunk-Driving Laws?" *Consumers' Research Magazine,* vol. 82, no. 8 (August 1999). Copyright © 1999 by Consumers' Research, Inc. This article was excerpted from *Highway Safety: Effectiveness of State .08 Blood Alcohol Laws,* General Accounting Office (June 23, 1999). Washington, D.C.: U.S. Government Printing Office, 1999. Reprinted by permission of *Consumers' Research Magazine.*

The value of public education and enforcement has been demonstrated in a number of studies. A recent NHTSA evaluation of a sobriety checkpoint program in Tennessee, a state with a .10 BAC limit, concluded that the program and its attendant publicity reduced alcohol-related fatal accidents in that state by 20.4%.

━◦◉◦━

One of NHTSA's principal arguments for nationwide adoption of .08 BAC laws is that the medical evidence of drivers' impairment at that level is substantial and conclusive. According to NHTSA, reaction time, tracking and steering, and emergency responses are impaired at even low levels, and substantially impaired at .08 BAC. As a result, the risk of being in a motor vehicle crash increases when alcohol is involved, and increases dramatically at .08 BAC and higher levels. In contrast to NHTSA's position, industry associations critical of .08 BAC laws contend that .08 BAC is an acceptable level of impairment for driving a motor vehicle and that these laws penalize "responsible social drinking."

These associations also believe that .08 BAC laws do not address the problem of drunk driving because many more drivers using alcohol are reported at the "high" BAC levels (above .10 BAC) than at the lower BAC levels. Because we were directed to review the impact of .08 BAC laws on the number and severity of crashes involving alcohol, we did not review the medical evidence on impairment or other arguments in favor of or in opposition to .08 BAC laws.

NHTSA also believes that lowering the BAC limit to .08 is a proven effective measure that will reduce the number of crashes and save lives. For example, in a December 1997 publication, NHTSA stated that "recent research . . . has been quite conclusive in showing the impaired driving reductions already attributable to .08, as well as the potential for saving additional lives if all states adopted .08 BAC laws." In May 1998, the NHTSA Administrator stated, "The traffic safety administration is aware of four published studies, . . . [and] each study has shown that lowering the illegal blood alcohol limit to .08 is associated with significant reductions in alcohol-related fatal crashes." In a fact sheet distributed to state legislatures considering these laws, NHTSA stated that the agency's "analysis of five states that lowered the BAC limit to .08 showed that significant decreases in alcohol-related fatal crashes occurred in four out of the five states as a result of the legislation." NHTSA used these study results to encourage states to enact .08 BAC laws, testifying in one instance before a state legislature: "We conservatively project a 10% reduction in alcohol-related crashes, deaths, and injuries" in the state.

Seven studies have been published assessing the effect of .08 BAC laws on motor vehicle crashes and fatalities in the United States. Four studies published between 1991 and 1996 assessed the effectiveness of .08 BAC laws in the five states that enacted them between 1983 and 1991. On April 28, 1999, NHTSA released three additional studies.

Early studies had limitations and raised methodological concerns
Although NHTSA characterized the first four studies on the effectiveness of .08
BAC laws as conclusively establishing that .08 BAC laws resulted in substantial
reductions in fatalities involving alcohol, we found that three of the four studies
had limitations and raised methodological concerns that called their conclusions into question. For example, while a NHTSA-endorsed Boston University
study concluded that 500 to 600 fewer fatal crashes would occur each year if
all states adopted .08 BAC laws, this study has been criticized for, among other
reasons, its method of comparing states; and a recent NHTSA study characterized the earlier study's conclusion as "unwarranted." The fourth study reported
mixed results. Therefore, these studies did not provide conclusive evidence that
.08 BAC laws by themselves have resulted in reductions in drunk driving crashes
and fatalities. A task force of the New Jersey State Senate examined this evidence
and, in a report issued in December 1998, reached a similar conclusion.

***

Recent studies are more comprehensive, but results are mixed   On April 28,
1999, NHTSA released three studies that it sponsored. These studies are
more comprehensive than the earlier studies and show many positive
results but fall short of conclusively establishing that .08 BAC laws by
themselves have resulted in reductions in alcohol-related fatalities. For
example, during the early 1990s, when the involvement of alcohol in traffic fatalities declined from around 50% to nearly 40%—a trend in states
with both .08 BAC and .10 BAC laws—eight states' .08 BAC laws became
effective, and the recent studies disagree on the degree to which .08 BAC
laws played a role. Two of the studies reached different conclusions about
the effect of one state's .08 BAC law; one concluded that the law brought
about reductions in drunk driving deaths in North Carolina, while
another concluded that the state's reductions occurred as the result of a
long-term trend that began before the law was enacted.

    In a statement releasing the three studies, NHTSA credited the nation's
progress in reducing drunk driving to a combination of strict state laws and
tougher enforcement, and stated that "these three studies provide additional
support for the premise that .08 BAC laws help to reduce alcohol-related
fatalities, particularly when they are implemented in conjunction with other
impaired driving laws and programs."

Eleven-state study   An April 1999 NHTSA study of 11 states with .08 BAC
laws assessed whether the states experienced statistically significant reductions in three measures of alcohol involvement in crashes after the law took
effect: (1) the number of fatalities in crashes in which any alcohol was
involved, (2) the number of fatalities in crashes where drivers had a BAC of
.10 or greater ("high BAC"), and (3) the proportion of fatalities involving
"high BAC" drivers to fatalities involving sober drivers. The study performed
a similar analysis for license revocation laws and also modeled and controlled
for any pre-existing long-term declining trends these states may have been

experiencing when their .08 BAC laws went into effect. The study found that five of the 11 states had reductions in at least one measure and that two of the 11 states had reductions in all three measures.

❧

The study was careful not to draw a causal relationship between the reductions it found and the passage of .08 BAC laws by themselves. Rather, it concluded that .08 BAC laws added to the impact that enforcement, public information, and legislative activities, particularly license revocation laws, were having. In addition to the two states where .08 BAC and license revocation laws were found to be effective in combination, the study noted that the five states with .08 BAC laws that showed reductions already had license revocation laws in place. One of the authors told us that this suggested the .08 BAC laws had the effect of expanding the scope of the license revocation laws to a new portion of the driving public.

University of North Carolina study   A NHTSA-sponsored study by the University of North Carolina concluded, in contrast to the 11-state study, that the .08 BAC law in North Carolina had little clear effect. The study examined alcohol-related crashes and crashes involving drivers with BACs greater than .10 from 1991 through 1995; compared fatalities among drivers with BACs greater than .10 in North Carolina with such fatalities in 11 other states; and compared six measures of alcohol involvement in North Carolina and 37 states that did not have .08 BAC laws at that time. The study controlled for and commented on external factors that could confound the results, such as the state's sobriety checkpoints, enforcement, and media coverage. The study found the following:

- No statistically significant decrease in alcohol-related crashes after passage of North Carolina's .08 BAC law in three direct and two "proxy" measures.
- A continual decline in the proportion of fatally injured drivers with BACs equal to or greater than .10 but no abrupt change in fatalities that could be attributed to the .08 BAC law.
- Decreases in alcohol-related crashes in North Carolina and in the 11 other states studied. While North Carolina's decreases were greater, the study concluded that no specific effects could be attributed to the .08 BAC law.
- No statistically significant difference between North Carolina and 37 states without .08 BAC laws in four of the six measures. While reductions in police-reported and estimated instances of alcohol involvement were found to be statistically significant, these reductions happened 18 months before North Carolina lowered its BAC limit. The authors attributed these decreases, in part, to increased enforcement.

The study concluded that the .08 BAC law had little clear effect on alcohol-related fatalities in North Carolina, that a downward trend was already occurring before North Carolina enacted its .08 BAC law, and that this trend was not affected by the law. The authors offered several possible explanations, including (1) the effects of the .08 BAC laws were obscured by a broader change in drinking-driving behavior that was already occurring; (2) North Carolina had made substantial progress combating drunk driving and that the remaining drinking and driving population in North Carolina was simply not responsive to the lower BAC law; and (3) .08 BAC laws are not effective in measurably affecting the behavior of drinking drivers.

50-state study   The third April 1999 NHTSA study evaluated .08 BAC laws by comparing two groups—states with .08 BAC laws with states with .10 BAC laws, before and after the laws were passed. This study concluded that states that enacted .08 BAC laws experienced an 8% reduction in the involvement of drivers with both high and low BACs when compared with the involvement of sober drivers. The study estimated that 274 lives have been saved in the states that enacted .08 BAC laws and that 590 lives could be saved annually if all states enacted .08 BAC laws.

While more comprehensive than other studies, the study used a method to calculate the 8% reduction that is different from, and thus not directly comparable, to those for fatality estimates reported in other studies and publications. In particular, this method can produce a numerical effect that is larger than other methods.

❦

Another reason why this study's results cannot be directly compared to other studies' is because it did not include data for drivers under 21. In 1997, drivers under 21 accounted for around 14% of the drivers in fatal crashes and about 12% of the drivers in fatal crashes involving alcohol.

Including persons under 21 years old would have changed these study results. In particular, the study would have found no statistically significant reductions associated with .08 BAC laws for drivers at low BAC levels. The findings regarding drivers at high BAC levels—a group that contains over three times as many drivers—would have remained substantially unchanged.

The study warns that "it is important to interpret estimates of lives saved due to any single law with considerable caution." In particular, as the study notes, factors such as public education, enforcement, and changes in societal norms and attitudes toward alcohol have produced long-term reductions in drunk driving deaths over many years. This study did more to control for extraneous factors than any of the other multi-state studies, but this is inherently difficult to do, and in this case the authors estimate that 50% to 60% of the reductions in alcohol-related fatalities are explained by the laws it reviewed and the other factors it considered, a moderate level for statistical analyses of this type. Because of the uncertainties, the study's estimate of lives saved is also expressed as a range—and the number of lives saved in states with .08 BAC laws could have been as few as 88 or as many as 472.

While the study reported results for the three laws it reviewed, including .08 BAC laws, the study also concluded that "the attribution of savings to any single law should be made with caution since each new law builds to some extent on existing legislation and on other ongoing trends and activities."

◦◉◦

While indications are that .08 BAC laws in combination with other drunk-driving laws, as well as sustained public education and information efforts and strong enforcement, can be effective, the evidence does not conclusively establish that .08 BAC laws by themselves result in reductions in the number and severity of crashes involving alcohol. Until recently, limited published evidence existed on the effectiveness of .08 BAC laws, and NHTSA's position— that this evidence was conclusive—was overstated. In 1999, more comprehensive studies have been published that show many positive results, and NHTSA's characterization of the results has been more balanced. Nevertheless, these studies fall short of providing conclusive evidence that .08 BAC laws by themselves have been responsible for reductions in fatal crashes.

Because a state enacting a .08 BAC law may or may not see a decline in alcohol-related fatalities, it is difficult to predict accurately how many lives would be saved if all states passed .08 BAC laws. The effect of a .08 BAC law depends on a number of factors, including the degree to which the law is publicized; how well it is enforced; other drunk driving laws in effect; and the unique culture of each state, particularly public attitudes concerning alcohol.

As drunk driving continues to claim the lives of thousands of Americans each year, governments at all levels seek solutions. Many states are considering enacting .08 BAC laws, and the Congress is considering requiring all states to enact these laws. Although a strong causal link between .08 BAC laws by themselves and reductions in traffic fatalities is absent, other evidence, including medical evidence on impairment, should be considered when evaluating the effectiveness of .08 BAC laws. A .08 BAC law can be an important component of a state's overall highway safety program, but a .08 BAC law alone is not a "silver bullet." Highway safety research shows that the best countermeasure against drunk driving is a combination of laws, sustained public education, and vigorous enforcement.

Five Bottles of Beer

On average, according to NHTSA, a 170-pound man reaches .08 BAC after consuming five 12-ounce beers (4.5% alcohol by volume) over a two-hour period. A 120-pound woman reaches the same level after consuming three beers over the same period. NHTSA publishes a BAC estimator that computes the level of alcohol in a person's blood on the basis of the person's weight and gender and the amount of alcohol consumed over a specified period of time.

This estimator assumes average physical attributes in the population; in reality, alcohol affects individuals differently, and this guide cannot precisely predict its effect on everyone. For example, younger people have higher concentrations of body water than older people; therefore, after consuming the same amount of alcohol, a 170-pound 20-year-old man attains a lower BAC level on average than a 170-pound 50-year-old man.

NHTSA's estimator shows that the difference between the .08 BAC and .10 BAC levels for a 170-pound man is one beer over two hours. The difference between the .08 BAC and .10 BAC levels for a 120-pound woman is one-half a beer over the same time period.

Alcohol use is a significant factor in fatal motor vehicle crashes. In 1997, the most recent year for which data are available, there were 16,189 alcohol-related fatalities, representing 38.6% of the nearly 42,000 people killed in fatal crashes that year. In the states with .08 BAC laws, alcohol was involved in 36% of all traffic fatalities, lower than the national average and the 39.5% rate of alcohol involvement in the rest of the states. Utah had the lowest level at 20.6%; the District of Columbia had the highest at 58.5%. Among the 10 states with the lowest levels of alcohol-related fatalities, three were states with .08 BAC laws and seven were states with .10 BAC laws. Among the 10 states with the highest levels of alcohol-related fatalities, two were states with .08 BAC laws, seven were states with .10 BAC laws, and one had no BAC per se law.

Although alcohol use remains a significant factor in fatal crashes, fatalities involving alcohol have declined sharply over the past 15 years. In 1982, 25,165 people died in crashes involving alcohol, 57.3% of the nearly 44,000 traffic fatalities that year. The proportion of fatal crashes that involved alcohol declined during the 1980s, falling below 50% for the first time in 1989. The involvement of alcohol in fatal crashes declined markedly in the early 1990s, from about 50% of the fatal crashes in 1990 to nearly 40% in 1994. During this time, the number of people killed in crashes involving alcohol declined by around 25%. The proportion of fatalities involving alcohol rose slightly in the next two years before falling, in 1997, to its lowest level since 1982.

POSTSCRIPT

Will a Lower Blood Alcohol Level for Drunk Driving Reduce Automobile Accidents?

An important follow-up question to the discussion of whether a national BAC standard of .08 for driving while intoxicated would reduce the number of alcohol-related accidents, would be is the federal government unreasonably imposing laws when the evidence for those laws can be seen as questionable? Is the federal government being presumptuous in trying to implement a policy that it feels is best for its citizens? On the other hand, if it has been shown that a .08 blood alcohol limit lowers the rate of alcohol-related accidents, doesn't the federal government have a moral and ethical obligation to prevent these accidents?

Alcohol abuse is a serious problem. Although restricting a person from drinking and driving may not reduce the incidence of alcohol abuse, it may reduce other problems. Driving a motor vehicle after drinking alcohol is clearly dangerous. Not only are the drinker and the drinker's passengers endangered, but anyone else who may be driving a car in the vicinity of the drunk driver is at risk. Thousands of people, including pedestrians, are killed or maimed each year by drunk drivers. Boating while intoxicated, although not particularly a focus of this issue, has also become a problem. Lowering the blood alcohol limit to .08 may not reduce alcohol abuse for boaters and drivers, but it may reduce the risks faced by others.

Balancing the rights of individuals against the need of the federal government to implement a policy that it believes is right is a recurring issue. There is a lack of consistency in the matter of federal and state laws. During the oil crisis of the 1970s, for example, the federal government required states to have speed limits no higher than 55 miles per hour. Yet, each state has its own laws regarding the sale of alcohol. There is little debate that reducing the number of alcohol-related accidents is a high priority. However, how far should the federal government go to ensure that this occurs? Should the federal government dictate how we should act, or should it recommend how we should not act? In addition, is it clear that a lower blood alcohol level would result in fewer automobile accidents?

Several excellent articles and reports examine the issue of drinking and driving. A report from the National Institute on Alcohol Abuse and Alcoholism by Ralph Hingson and Michael Winter, entitled *Epidemiology and Consequences of Drinking and Driving*, examines the role of alcohol in traffic crashes. The National Safety Council and the National Highway Traffic Safety Administration's publication, *Setting Limits, Saving Lives* (2000), specifically addresses the effects of a .08 blood alcohol level on automobile accidents. Another publication is *Drinking and Driving: Factors Influencing Accident Risk,* by the National Institute on Alcohol Abuse and Alcoholism. The impact of drinking and driving on the fatality rate of children is discussed by R.A. Shults in "Child Passenger Deaths Involving Drinking Drivers—United States, 1997–2001 (*Morbidity and Mortality Weekly* Report, February 6, 2004).

ISSUE 4

Should We Be Concerned About "Club Drugs"?

YES: Office of National Drug Control Policy, from *Club Drugs* (Office of National Drug Control Policy, January 12, 2005)

NO: Jacob Sullum, from "Sex, Drugs and Techno Music," *Reason* (January 2002)

ISSUE SUMMARY

YES: The Office of National Drug Control Policy (ONDCP) states that the nature of rave parties may encourage the use of club drugs because party-goers dance and remain active for long periods of time. Drugs such as Rohypnol and GHB, which are colorless and tasteless, are used to sedate unsuspecting victims who are then sexually assaulted. Other club drugs discussed are ketamine (Special K) and Ecstasy.

NO: Jacob Sullum, a senior editor at *Reason* magazine, contends that the effects of drugs such as Ecstasy are exaggerated, particularly with regard to sexual behavior. Sullum refers to the history of marijuana and how it was deemed a drug that would make people engage in behaviors in which they would not typically engage. Sullum maintains that the public's reaction to club drugs is unjustified.

$\mathbf{A}$ccording to national surveys of secondary students in the United States, the use of club drugs, especially Ecstasy (MDMA), has risen significantly over the past decade. In the most recent survey, nearly eight percent of high school seniors have used Ecstasy. Not surprisingly, the number of people admitted to emergency rooms due to adverse reactions to Ecstasy and other club drugs has also increased. In 2002, more than 3,300 people were admitted to emergency rooms due to GHB, over 4,000 emergency room visits were attributed to Ecstasy, and 260 people were admitted to emergency rooms due to Ketamine (Special K). The number of emergency room visits due to Ecstasy and GHB jumped significantly from the mid-1990s to the present.

The use of GHB, Ecstasy, Rohypnol, and Ketamine is not limited to those who attend rave parties. A *Time* magazine article indicates that these drugs are showing up in hip-hop parties, on Bourbon Street in New Orleans, and in many other places. However, their use at rave parties is not unusual. Making rave parties illegal will not stop the use of these drugs, but it would remove one venue where their use occurs. Also, according to some drug experts, drug use at rave parties is deeply embedded in the culture of these parties. Is making rave parties illegal an effective strategy for reducing the use of club drugs? Further, would people who attend rave parties but who do not use drugs be unfairly penalized if such parties were outlawed?

Attempts to make rave parties and similar activities illegal are occurring on the national level as well as on the local level. A bipartisan bill was introduced into the Senate "to prohibit an individual from knowingly opening, maintaining, managing, controlling, renting, leasing, making available for use, or profiting from any place for the purpose of manufacturing, distributing, or using any controlled substance, and for other purposes." This act is referred to as the "Reducing Americans' Vulnerability to Ecstasy Act of 2002" or the "RAVE Act." Penalties could include 20 years in prison or a fine of $250,000 or twice the gross receipts derived from each violation, whichever is more.

One reason for the RAVE Act is that raves have become a way to exploit American youth. They are manipulating young people as a means of making money. One potential problem with the bill is that its language is broad enough to close down any business or establishment where any drug use or transaction occurs. There is concern that drug use at these parties will lead to adverse physical reactions as well as reckless behavior. One consequence of Ecstasy use is dehydration. To capitalize on this effect, some club owners charge excessive amounts of money for water. Others have "chilling rooms" where one can go, for a price. Those individuals objecting to rave parties point to these examples as proof that club owners are engaging in exploitation. One potential problem with the bill is that its language is broad enough to close down any business or establishment where any drug use or transaction occurs. In Chicago, the city council passed an ordinance to put building owners or managers in jail if they allow raves to be held on their property.

One of the problems associated with buying illegal drugs is that they are not always what they are purported to be—one cannot be sure of the authenticity of the drug being purchased. Moreover, if people are sold a bogus drug, then have no legal recourse. DanceSafe, a group that attends a number of rave parties, tests pills for purity. Anyone who purchases an Ecstasy pill can have this group test it to determine whether it is indeed Ecstasy. DanceSafe attempts to reduce the harm associated with misidentified drugs. One could argue that the presence of DanceSafe gives the impression that rave patrons can safely use Ecstasy.

The following selections debate whether we should be concerned about club drugs. The effects of club drugs represent a serious threat to the physical and emotional well-being of young people, according to Office of National Drug Control Policy (ONDCP). Because of the drugs' presence at rave parties, the ONDCP contends that these parties should be illegal. Jacob Sullum acknowledges that drugs like Ecstasy have the potential to cause harm. In addition, Sullum notes that many drugs sold as Ecstasy are something else entirely. However, he feels that warnings associated with drugs are blown out of proportion. Sullum also does not support closing down rave parties.

 **YES**

Club Drugs: MDMA/Ecstasy, Rohypnol, GHB, Ketamine

Overview

In recent years, certain drugs have emerged and become popular among teens and young adults at dance clubs and "raves." These drugs, collectively termed "club drugs," include MDMA/Ecstasy (methylenedioxymethamphetamine), Rohypnol (flunitrazepam), GHB (gamma hydroxybutyrate), and ketamine (ketamine hydrochloride).

Producing both stimulant and psychedelic effects, MDMA is often used at parties because it enables party-goers to dance and remain active for long periods of time. This substance is usually ingested in tablet form, but can also be crushed and snorted, injected, or used in suppository form.

The tasteless and odorless depressants Rohypnol and GHB are often used in the commission of sexual assaults due to their ability to sedate and intoxicate unsuspecting victims. Rohypnol, a sedative/tranquilizer, is legally available for prescription in over 50 countries outside of the U.S. and is widely available in Mexico, Colombia, and Europe. Although usually taken orally in pill form, reports have shown that some users grind Rohypnol into a powder and snort the drug.

GHB, available in an odorless, colorless liquid form or as a white powder material, is taken orally, and is frequently combined with alcohol. In addition to being used to incapacitate individuals for the commission of sexual assault/rape, GHB is also sometimes used by body builders for its alleged anabolic effects.

The abuse of ketamine, a tranquilizer most often used on animals, became popular in the 1980s, when it was realized that large doses cause reactions similar to those associated with the use of PCP, such as dream-like states and hallucinations. The liquid form of ketamine can be injected, consumed in drinks, or added to smokable materials. The powder form can also be added to drinks, smoked, or dissolved and then injected. In some cases, ketamine is being injected intramuscularly.

From "Club Drugs," Office of National Drug Control Policy, January 12, 2005. Notes omitted.

Extent of Use

According to the 2003 National Survey on Drug Use and Health, an estimated 10.9 million Americans aged 12 or older tried MDMA at least once in their lifetimes, representing 4.6% of the U.S. population in that age group. The number of past year MDMA users in 2003 was 2.1 million (0.9% of the population aged 12 and older) and the number of past month MDMA users was 470,000 (0.2%). The past year and past month figures are down from 2002 when approximately 3.2 million (1.3% of the population aged 12 and older) reported past year MDMA use and 676,000 (0.3%) reported past month MDMA use.

Among 12–17 year olds surveyed in 2003, 2.4% reported lifetime MDMA use, 1.3% reported past year MDMA use, and 0.4% reported past month MDMA use. Among 18–25 year olds surveyed in 2003, 14.8% reported lifetime MDMA use, 3.7% reported past year MDMA use, and 0.7% reported past month MDMA use.

The Youth Risk Behavior Surveillance System (YRBSS) study by the Centers for Disease Control and Prevention (CDC) surveys high school students on several risk factors including drug and alcohol use. For the first time in 2003, the YRBSS collected data on lifetime use of MDMA. Results of the 2003 survey indicate that 11.1% of high school students reported using MDMA at some point in their lifetimes (11.6% of male students and 10.4% of female students). The 2003 lifetime MDMA figures broken down by grade are as follows: 10.9% for 9th graders, 9.0% for 10th graders, 11.4% for 11th graders, and 12.8% for 12th graders.

According to students surveyed as part of the 2004 Monitoring the Future study, 2.8% of eighth graders, 4.3% of tenth graders, and 7.5% of twelfth graders reported using MDMA at least once during their lifetimes.

Percent of Students Reporting MDMA Use, 2003 2004

	8th Grade		10th Grade		12th Grade	
	2003	2004	2003	2004	2003	2004
Past month	0.7%	0.8%	1.1%	0.8%	1.3%	1.2%
Past year	2.1	1.7	3.0	2.4	4.5	4.0
Lifetime	3.2	2.8	5.4	4.3	8.3	7.5

Approximately 42.5% of eighth graders, 52% of tenth graders, and 57.7% of twelfth graders surveyed in 2004 reported that using MDMA once or twice was a "great risk."

Percent of Students Reporting Risk of Using MDMA, 2003–2004

Percent Saying "Great Risk"	8th Grade		10th Grade		12th Grade	
	2003	2004	2003	2004	2003	2004
Try MDMA once/twice	41.9%	42.5%	49.7%	52.0%	56.3%	57.7%
Use MDMA occasionally	65.8	65.1	71.7	74.6	n/a	n/a

One percent of eighth graders and 1.2% of tenth graders surveyed in 2004 reported using Rohypnol at least once during their lifetimes (twelfth grade data are not available for Rohypnol).

Percent of Students Reporting Rohypnol Use, 2003–2004

	8th Grade		10th Grade		12th Grade	
	2003	2004	2003	2004	2003	2004
Past month	0.1%	0.2%	0.2%	0.3%	n/a	n/a
Past year	0.2	0.6	0.6	0.7	1.3	1.6
Lifetime	1.0	1.0	1.0	1.2	n/a	n/a

Additional Monitoring the Future results for 2004 indicate that 0.7% of eighth graders, 0.8% of tenth graders, and 2.0% of twelfth graders reported past year use of GHB. Data showing lifetime and past month use of GHB and ketamine were not captured in the survey.

Percent of Students Reporting Past Year GHB & Ketamine Use, 2003–2004

	8th Grade		10th Grade		12th Grade	
	2003	2004	2003	2004	2003	2004
GHB	0.9%	0.7%	1.4%	0.8%	1.4%	2.0%
Ketamine	1.1	0.9	1.9	1.3	2.1	1.9

During 2003, 12.9% of college students and 15.3% of young adults (ages 19–28) reported using MDMA at least once during their lifetimes.

Percent of College Students & Young Adults Using MDMA, 2003

Past Use of MDMA	College Students	Young Adults
Past month	1.0%	0.8%
Past year	4.4	4.5
Lifetime	12.9	15.3

Health Effects

Using MDMA can cause serious psychological and physical damage. The possible psychological effects include confusion, depression, anxiety, and paranoia and may last weeks after ingesting the substance. Physically, a user may experience nausea, faintness, and significant increases in heart rate and blood pressure. MDMA use can cause hyperthermia, muscle breakdown, seizures, stroke, kidney and cardiovascular system failure, and may lead to death. Also, chronic use of MDMA has been found to produce long-lasting, possibly permanent, damage to the sections of the brain critical to thought and memory.

Rohypnol, GHB, and ketamine are all central nervous system depressants. Lower doses of Rohypnol can cause muscle relaxation and can produce general sedative and hypnotic effects. In higher doses, Rohypnol causes a loss of muscle control, loss of consciousness, and partial amnesia. When combined with alcohol, the toxic effects of Rohypnol can be aggravated. The sedative effects of Rohypnol begin to appear approximately 15–20 minutes after the drug is ingested. The effects typically last from 4–6 hours after administration of the drug, but some cases have been reported in which the effects were experienced 12 or more hours after administration.

GHB has been shown to produce drowsiness, nausea, unconsciousness, seizures, severe respiratory depression, and coma. Additionally, GHB has increasingly become involved in poisonings, overdoses, date rapes, and fatalities.

The use of ketamine produces effects similar to PCP and LSD, causing distorted perceptions of sight and sound and making the user feel disconnected and out of control. The overt hallucinatory effects of ketamine are relatively short-acting, lasting approximately one hour or less. However, the user's senses, judgement, and coordination may be affected for up to 24 hours after the initial use of the drug. Use of this drug can also bring about respiratory depression, heart rate abnormalities, and a withdrawal syndrome.

The number of emergency department (ED) MDMA mentions reported to the Drug Abuse Warning Network (DAWN) has increased from 421 in 1995 to 4,026 in 2002. During this same time period, the number of GHB mentions increased from 145 to 3,330. The number of ketamine ED mentions has increased from 81 in 1996 to 260 in 2002.

Arrests & Sentencing

The number of arrests by the Drug Enforcement Administration (DEA) for MDMA-related offenses has declined from 1,930 in 2001 to 1,346 in 2002. The proportion of MDMA-related arrests to all DEA arrests for any major drug decreased from 5.7 percent in 2001 to 4.7 percent in 2002.

The Department of Justice reports that MDMA was involved in 153 Organized Crime Drug Enforcement Task Force (OCDETF) investigations during FY 2002, a decrease from 188 in FY2001, but still higher than 107 such investigations in FY 2000. The number of OCDETF indictments filed in which an MDMA trafficking offense was reported in the indictment has decreased from 212 in 2001 to 191 in 2002.

According to DEA, the number of arrests for GHB-related offenses increased from 0 in 2002 to 9 in 2003. The number of GHB-related investigations by DEA also increased from 8 in 2002 to 19 in 2003. However, from FY 2002 to FY 2003, the number of OCDETF GHB- and GBL-related investigations and indictments decreased. The number of GHB- and GBL-related OCDETF investigations decreased from 18 in FY 2002 to 11 in FY 2003; the number of indictments decreased from 9 in FY 2002 to 2 in FY 2003.

In response to the Ecstasy Anti-Proliferation Act of 2000, the U.S. Sentencing Commission increased the guideline sentence for trafficking MDMA. The new amendment, enacted on November 1, 2001, increases the sentence for trafficking 800 MDMA pills by 300%, from 15 months to 5 years. It also increases the penalty for trafficking 8,000 pills by nearly 200%, from 41 months to 10 years.

Production & Trafficking

MDMA is primarily manufactured in clandestine laboratories located in Europe, particularly the Netherlands and Belgium. From these labs, MDMA is transported to the U.S. and other countries using a variety of means, including commercial airlines, express mail services, and sea cargo. Currently, Los Angeles, Miami, and New York are the major gateway cities for the influx of MDMA from abroad.

From 2001 to 2002, the amount of MDMA seized by Federal agencies decreased from 4,639,540 dosage units in 2001 to 3,495,960 dosage units in 2002. According to seizure data collected by the DEA's El Paso Intelligence Center (EPIC), the number of MDMA dosage units seized at U.S. points-of-entry (POEs) arriving from foreign source or transit countries decreased from 8,071,127 in 2000, to 6,699,882 in 2001, to 3,395,036 in 2002. EPIC reports that of the 3,395,036 MDMA tablets seized at POEs in 2002, approximately 3,229,311 were transported via commercial air carriers, 103,925 via private and commercial vehicles, and 61,800 via commercial maritime vessels.

GHB, GHB kits, and recipes for making GHB can be found on the Internet. DEA El Paso Intelligence Center (EPIC) National Clandestine Laboratory Seizure System (NCLSS) data show that the number of reported GHB laboratory seizures is low and decreased from 13 in 2001 to 7 in 2002 to 2 in 2003.

Rohypnol, legally produced and sold in Latin America and Europe, is typically smuggled into the U.S. using mail or delivery services. States along the U.S. border with Mexico have the most significant activity related to Rohypnol being mailed or brought into the U.S. via couriers from Mexico. Since the mid-1990s, the number of Rohypnol seizures in the U.S. have decreased. In 1995, a high of 164,534 dosage units of Rohypnol were seized, while in 2000, less than 5,000 dosage units were seized.

Legitimately used by veterinarians, ketamine is sometimes stolen from animal hospitals and veterinary clinics. DEA reporting also indicates that some of the ketamine available in the U.S. has been diverted from pharmacies in Mexico. Since first recorded in 1999, the number of ketamine seizures reported by the DEA has increased each year. Seizures of this drug have increased from 4,551 dosage units in 1999 to 1,154,463 in 2000. DEA data also indicate that 581,677 dosage units were seized from January to June 2001.

Legislation

MDMA, GHB, Rohypnol, and ketamine have all been scheduled under the Controlled Substance Act (CSA), Title II of the Comprehensive Drug Abuse Prevention and Control Act of 1970. The Schedules of the club drugs are as follows:

- MDMA—Schedule I as of 1998
- GHB—Schedule I as of 2000

- Rohypnol—Schedule IV as of 1984
- Ketamine—Schedule III as of 1999

Street Terms

GHB	Ketamine	MDMA	Rohypnol
Goop	Cat valium	Disco biscuit	Forget me drug
Grievous bodily harm	K	Hug drug	Mexican valium
Max	Jet	Go	Roaches
Soap	Super acid	XTC	Roofies

Sex, Drugs, and Techno Music

[In 2001], the Chicago City Council decided "to crack down on wild rave parties that lure youngsters into environments loaded with dangerous club drugs, underage drinking and sometimes predatory sexual behavior," as the *Chicago Tribune* put it. The newspaper described raves as "one-night-only parties . . . often held in warehouses or secret locations where people pay to dance, do drugs, play loud music, and engage in random sex acts." Taking a dim view of such goings-on, the city council passed an ordinance threatening to jail building owners or managers who allowed raves to be held on their property. Mayor Richard Daley took the occasion to "lash out at the people who produce the huge rogue dance parties where Ecstasy and other designer drugs are widely used." In Daley's view, rave promoters were deliberately seducing the innocent. "They are after all of our children," he warned. "Parents should be outraged by this."

The reaction against raves reflects familiar anxieties about what the kids are up to, especially when it comes to sex. As the chemical symbol of raves, MDMA—a.k.a. Ecstasy—has come to represent sexual abandon and, partly through association with other "club drugs," sexual assault. These are not the only fears raised by MDMA. The drug, whose full name is methylenedioxymethamphetamine, has also been accused of causing brain damage and of leading people astray with ersatz feelings of empathy and euphoria (concerns discussed later in this article). But the sexual angle is interesting because it has little to do with the drug's actual properties, a situation for which there is considerable precedent in the history of reputed aphrodisiacs.

A relative of both amphetamine and mescaline, MDMA is often described as a stimulant with psychedelic qualities. But its effects are primarily emotional, without the perceptual changes caused by LSD. Although MDMA was first synthesized by the German drug company Merck in 1912, it did not gain a following until the 1970s, when the psychonautical chemist Alexander Shulgin, a Dow researcher turned independent consultant, tried some at the suggestion of a graduate student he was helping a friend supervise. "It was not a psychedelic in the visual or interpretive sense," he later wrote, "but the lightness and warmth of the psychedelic was present and quite remarkable." MDMA created a "window," he decided. "It enabled me to see out, and to see my own insides, without distortions or reservations."

From Jacob Sullum, "Sex, Drugs and Techno Music," *Reason*, vol. 33, no. 8 (January 2002). Copyright © 2002 by The Reason Foundation, 3415 S. Sepulveda Blvd., Suite 400, Los Angeles, CA 90034. http://www.reason.com. Reprinted by permission.

After observing some striking examples of people who claimed to have overcome serious personal problems (including a severe stutter and oppressive guilt) with the help of MDMA, Shulgin introduced the drug to a psychologist he knew who had already used psychedelics as an aid to therapy. "Adam," the pseudonym that Shulgin gave him (also a nickname for the drug), was on the verge of retiring, but was so impressed by MDMA's effects that he decided to continue working. He shared his techniques with other psychologists and psychiatrists, and under his influence thousands of people reportedly used the drug to enhance communication and self-insight. "It seemed to dissolve fear for a few hours," says a psychiatrist who tried MDMA in the early '80s. "I thought it would have been very useful for working with people with trauma disorders." Shulgin concedes that there was "a hint of snake-oil" in MDMA's reputed versatility, but he himself considered it "an incredible tool." He quotes one psychiatrist as saying, "MDMA is penicillin for the soul, and you don't give up penicillin, once you've seen what it can do."

Shulgin did not see MDMA exclusively as a psychotherapeutic tool. He also referred to it as "my low-calorie martini," a way of loosening up and relating more easily to others at social gatherings. This aspect of the drug came to the fore in the '80s, when MDMA became popular among nightclubbers in Texas, where it was marketed as a party drug under the name *Ecstasy*. The open recreational use of Ecstasy at clubs in Dallas and Austin brought down the wrath of the Drug Enforcement Administration [DEA], which decided to put MDMA in the same legal category as heroin. Researchers who emphasized the drug's psychotherapeutic potential opposed the ban. "We had no idea psychiatrists were using it," a DEA pharmacologist told *Newsweek* in 1985. Nor did they care: Despite an administrative law judge's recommendation that doctors be allowed to prescribe the drug, the ban on MDMA took effect the following year.

Thus MDMA followed the same pattern as LSD, moving from discreet psychotherapeutic use to the sort of conspicuous consumption that was bound to provoke a government reaction. Like LSD, it became illegal because too many people started to enjoy it. Although the DEA probably would have sought to ban any newly popular intoxicant, the name change certainly didn't help. In *Ecstasy: The MDMA Story*, Bruce Eisner quotes a distributor who claimed to have originated the name *Ecstasy*. He said he picked it "because it would sell better than calling it 'Empathy.' 'Empathy' would be more appropriate, but how many people know what it means?" In its traditional sense, *ecstasy* has a spiritual connotation, but in common usage it simply means intense pleasure—often the kind associated with sex. As David Smith, director of the Haight-Ashbury Free Clinic, observed, the name "suggested that it made sex better." Some marketers have been more explicit: A 1999 article in the *Journal of Toxicology* (headlined "SEX on the Streets of Cincinnati") reported an analysis of "unknown tablets imprinted with 'SEX'" that turned out to contain MDMA.

Hyperbolic comments by some users have reinforced Ecstasy's sexual connotations. "One enthusiast described the feeling as a six-hour orgasm!" exclaimed the author of a 2000 op-ed piece in Malaysia's *New Straits Times*, picking up a phrase quoted in *Time* a couple of months before. A column in *The Toronto Sun*, meanwhile, stated matter-of-factly that MDMA "can even make you feel like a six-hour orgasm." If simply taking MDMA makes you feel that way, readers might reasonably conclude, MDMA-enhanced sex must be indescribably good.

Another reason MDMA came to be associated with sex is its reputation as a "hug drug" that breaks down emotional barriers and brings out feelings of affection. The warmth and candor of people who've taken MDMA may be interpreted as flirtatiousness. More generally, MDMA is said to remove fear, which is one reason psychotherapists have found it so useful. The same effect could also be described as a loss of inhibitions, often a precursor to sexual liaisons. Finally, users report enhanced pleasure from physical sensations, especially the sense of touch. They often trade hugs, caresses, and back rubs.

Yet the consensus among users seems to be that MDMA's effects are more sensual than sexual. According to a therapist quoted by Jerome Beck and Marsha Rosenbaum in their book *Pursuit of Ecstasy*, "MDMA and sex do not go very well together. For most people, MDMA turns off the ability to function as a lover, to put it indelicately. It's called the love drug because it opens up the capacity to feel loving and affectionate and trusting." At the same time, however, it makes the "focusing of the body and the psychic energy necessary to achieve orgasm . . . very difficult. And most men find it impossible. . . . So it is a love drug but not a sex drug for most people."

Although this distinction is widely reported by users, press coverage has tended to perpetuate the connection between MDMA and sex. In 1985 *Newsweek* said the drug "is considered an aphrodisiac," while *Maclean's* played up one user's claim of "very good sexual possibilities." *Life* also cited "the drug's reputation for good sex," even while noting that it "blocks male ejaculation." More recently, a 2000 story about MDMA in *Time* began by describing "a classic Southeast Asian den of iniquity" where prostitutes used Ecstasy so they could be "friendly and outgoing." It warned that "because users feel empathetic, ecstasy can lower sexual inhibitions. Men generally cannot get erections when high on e, but they are often ferociously randy when its effects begin to fade." The story cited a correlation between MDMA use and "unprotected sex." A cautionary article in *Cosmopolitan* began with the account of "a 28-year-old lawyer from Los Angeles" who brought home a man with whom she felt "deeply connected" under the influence of MDMA. "We would have had sex, but he couldn't get an erection," she reported. "The next day, I was horrified that I had let a guy I couldn't even stand into my bed!"

Rape Drugs

MDMA has been linked not just to regrettable sexual encounters but to rapes in which drugs are used as weapons. The connection is usually made indirectly, by way of other drugs whose effects are quite different but which are also popular at raves and dance clubs. In particular, the depressants GHB and Rohypnol have acquired reputations as "date rape drugs," used to incapacitate victims to whom they are given surreptitiously. Needless to say, this is not the main use for these substances, which people generally take on purpose because they like their effects. It's not clear exactly how often rapists use GHB or Rohypnol, but such cases are surely much rarer than the hysterical reaction from the press and Congress (which passed a Date Rape Drug Prohibition Act [in 2001]) would lead one to believe. The public has nonetheless come to view these intoxicants primarily as instruments of assault, an impression that has affected the image of other "club drugs," especially MDMA.

Grouping MDMA with GHB and Rohypnol, a 2000 Knight Ridder story warned that the dangers of "club drugs" include "vulnerability to sexual assault." Similarly, the *Chicago Tribune* cited Ecstasy as the most popular "club drug" before referring to "women who suspect they were raped after they used or were slipped a club drug." In a *Columbus Dispatch* op-ed piece, pediatrician Peter D. Rogers further obscured the distinction between MDMA and the so-called rape drugs by saying that "Ecstasy . . . comes in three forms," including "GHB, also called liquid Ecstasy," and "Herbal Ecstasy, also known as ma huang or ephedra" (a legal stimulant), as well as "MDMA, or chemical Ecstasy." He asserted, without citing a source, that "so-called Ecstasy"—it's not clear which one he meant—"has been implicated nationally in the sexual assaults of approximately 5,000 teen-age and young adult women." Rogers described a 16-year-old patient who "took Ecstasy and was raped twice. She told me that she remembers the rapes but, high on the drug, was powerless to stop them. She couldn't even scream, let alone fight back." If Rogers, identified as a member of the American Academy of Pediatrics' Committee on Substance Abuse, had trouble keeping the "club drugs" straight, it's not surprising that the general public saw little difference between giving a date MDMA and slipping her a mickey.

As the alleged connections between MDMA and sex illustrate, the concept of an aphrodisiac is complex and ambiguous. A drug could be considered an aphrodisiac because it reduces resistance, because it increases interest, because it improves ability, or because it enhances enjoyment. A particular drug could be effective for one or two of these purposes but useless (or worse) for the others. Shakespeare observed that alcohol "provokes the desire, but it takes away the performance." Something similar seems to be true of MDMA, except that the desire is more emotional than sexual, a sense of closeness that may find expression in sex that is apt to be aborted because of difficulty in getting an erection or reaching orgasm. Also like alcohol, MDMA is blamed for causing people to act against their considered judgment. The concern is not just that people might have casual sex but that they might regret it afterward.

Surely this concern is not entirely misplaced. As the old saw has it, "Candy is dandy, but liquor is quicker." When drinking precedes sex, there may be a fine line between seducing someone and taking advantage, between lowering inhibitions and impairing judgment. But the possibility of crossing that line does not mean that alcohol is nothing but a trick employed by cads. Nor does the possibility of using alcohol to render someone incapable of resistance condemn it as a tool of rapists.

The closest thing we have to a genuine aphrodisiac—increasing interest, ability, and enjoyment—is Viagra, the avowed purpose of which is to enable people to have more and better sex. Instead of being deplored as an aid to hedonism, it is widely praised for increasing the net sum of human happiness. Instead of being sold on the sly in dark nightclubs, it's pitched on television by a former Senate majority leader. The difference seems to be that Viagra is viewed as a legitimate medicine, approved by the government and prescribed by doctors.

But as Joann Ellison Rodgers, author of *Drugs and Sexual Behavior*, observes, "there is great unease with the idea of encouraging sexual prowess. . . . At the very least, drugs in the service of sex do seem to subvert or at least trivialize important aspects of sexual experiences, such as love, romance, commitment, trust and health." If we've managed to accept Viagra and (to a lesser extent) alcohol as aphrodisiacs, it may be only because we've projected their darker possibilities onto other substances, of which the "club drugs" are just the latest examples.

Signal of Misunderstanding

The current worries about raves in some ways resemble the fears once symbolized by the opium den. The country's first anti-opium laws, passed by Western states in the late 19th century, were motivated largely by hostility toward the low-cost Chinese laborers who competed for work with native whites. Supporters of such legislation, together with a sensationalist press, popularized the image of the sinister Chinaman who lured white women into his opium den, turning them into concubines, prostitutes, or sex slaves. Although users generally find that opiates dampen their sex drive, "it was commonly reported that opium smoking aroused sexual desire," writes historian David Courtwright, "and that some shameless smokers persuaded 'innocent girls to smoke in order to excite their passions and effect their ruin.'" San Francisco authorities lamented that the police "have found white women and Chinamen side by side under the effects of this drug—a humiliating sight to anyone who has anything left of manhood." In 1910 Hamilton Wright, a U.S. diplomat who was a key player in the passage of federal anti-drug legislation, told Congress that "one of the most unfortunate phases of the habit of smoking opium in this country" was "the large number of women who [had] become involved and were living as common-law wives or cohabiting with Chinese in the Chinatowns of our various cities."

Fears of miscegenation also played a role in popular outrage about cocaine, which was said to make blacks uppity and prone to violence against whites, especially sexual assault. In 1910 Christopher Koch, a member of the Pennsylvania Pharmacy Board who pushed for a federal ban on cocaine, informed Congress that "the colored people seem to have a weakness for it. . . . They would just as leave rape a woman as anything else, and a great many of the southern rape cases have been traced to cocaine." Describing cocaine's effect on "hitherto inoffensive, law abiding negroes" in the *Medical Record*, Edward Huntington Williams warned that "sexual desires are increased and perverted."

Marijuana, another drug that was believed to cause violence, was also linked to sex crimes and, like opium, seduction. Under marijuana's influence, according to a widely cited 1932 report in *The Journal of Criminal Law and Criminology*, "sexual desires are stimulated and may lead to unnatural acts, such as indecent exposure and rape." The authors quoted an informant who "reported several instances of which he claimed to have positive knowledge, where boys had induced girls to use the weed for the purpose of seducing them." The federal Bureau of Narcotics, which collected anecdotes about marijuana's baneful effects to support a national ban on the drug, cited "colored students at the Univ. of Minn. partying with female students (white) smoking [marijuana] and getting their sympathy with stories of racial persecution. Result pregnancy." The bureau also described a case in which "two Negroes took a girl fourteen years old and kept her for two days in a hut under the influence of marijuana. Upon recovery she was found to be suffering from syphilis."

Drug-related horror stories nowadays are rarely so explicitly racist. A notable and surprising exception appears in the 2000 film *Traffic*, which is critical of the war on drugs but nevertheless represents the utter degradation of an upper-middle-class white teenager who gets hooked on crack by showing her having sex with a black man. Whether related to race or not, parental anxieties about sexual activity among teenagers have not gone away, and drugs are a convenient scapegoat when kids seem to be growing up too fast.

The link between drugs and sex was reinforced by the free-love ethos of the '60s counterculture that embraced marijuana and LSD. In the public mind, pot smoking, acid dropping, and promiscuous sex were all part of the same lifestyle; a chaste hippie chick was a contradiction in terms. When Timothy Leary extolled LSD's sex-enhancing qualities in a 1966 interview with *Playboy*, he fueled the fears of parents who worried that their daughters would be seduced into a decadent world of sex, drugs, and rock 'n' roll. The Charles Manson case added a sinister twist to this scenario, raising the possibility of losing one's daughter to an evil cult leader who uses LSD to brainwash his followers, in much the same way as Chinese men were once imagined to enthrall formerly respectable white girls with opium.

The alarm about the sexual repercussions of "club drugs," then, has to be understood in the context of warnings about other alleged aphrodisiacs, often identified with particular groups perceived as inferior, threatening, or both. The fear of uncontrolled sexual impulses, of the chaos that would result if we let our basic instincts run wild, is projected onto these groups and, by extension, their intoxicants. In the case of "club drugs," adolescents are both victims and perpetrators. Parents fear for their children, but they also fear them. When Mayor Daley warned that "they are after all of our children," he may have been imagining predators in the mold of Fu Manchu or Charles Manson. But the reality is that raves—which grew out of the British "acid house" movement, itself reminiscent of the psychedelic dance scene that emerged in San Francisco during the late '60s—are overwhelmingly a youth phenomenon.

The experience of moving all night to a throbbing beat amid flickering light has been likened to tribal dancing around a fire. But for most people over 30, the appeal of dancing for hours on end to the fast, repetitive rhythm of techno music is hard to fathom. "The sensationalist reaction that greets every mention of the word *Ecstasy* in this country is part of a wider, almost unconscious fear of young people," writes Jonathan Keane in the British *New Statesman*, and the observation applies equally to the United States. For "middle-aged and middle-class opinion leaders . . . E is a symbol of a youth culture they don't understand."

This is not to say that no one ever felt horny after taking MDMA. Individual reactions to drugs are highly variable, and one could probably find anecdotes suggesting aphrodisiac properties for almost any psychoactive substance. And it is no doubt true that some MDMA users, like the woman quoted in *Cosmo*, have paired up with sexual partners they found less attractive the morning after. But once MDMA is stripped of its symbolism, these issues are no different from those raised by alcohol. In fact, since MDMA users tend to be more lucid than drinkers, the chances that they will do something regrettable are probably lower.

I Love You Guys

Another alcohol-related hazard, one that seems to be more characteristic of MDMA than the risk of casual sex or rape, is the possibility of inappropriate emotional intimacy. The maudlin drunk who proclaims his affection for everyone and reveals secrets he might later wish he had kept is a widely recognized character, either comical or pathetic depending upon one's point of view. Given MDMA's reputation as a "love drug," it's natural to wonder whether it fosters the same sort of embarrassing behavior.

Tom Cowan, a systems analyst in his 30s, has used MDMA a few times, and he doesn't think it revealed any deep emotional truths. (All names of drug users in this story are pseudonyms.) "For me," he says, "it was almost too much of a fake. . . . It was too artificial for me. . . . I felt warm. I felt loved. All of those sensations came upon me. . . . I had all these feelings, but I knew that deep down I didn't feel that, so at the same time there was that inner struggle as far as just letting loose and just being. . . . That was difficult because of the fakeness about it for me." More typically, MDMA users perceive the warm feelings as real, both at the time and in retrospect. Some emphasize an enhanced connection to friends, while others report a feeling of benevolence toward people in general.

"I was very alert but very relaxed at the same time," says Alison Witt, a software engineer in her 20s. "I didn't love everybody. . . . It's a very social drug, and you do feel connected to other people, but I think it's more because it creates a sense of relaxation and pleasure with people you're familiar with." Walter Stevenson, a neuroscientist in his late 20s, gives a similar account: "I felt really happy to have my friends around me. I just enjoyed sitting there and spending time with them, not necessarily talking about anything, but not to the degree that I felt particularly attracted or warm to people I didn't know. I was very friendly and open to meeting people, but there wasn't anything inappropriate about the feeling."

Adam Newman, an Internet specialist in his 20s, believes his MDMA use has helped improve his social life. "It kind of catapulted me past a bunch of shyness and other mental and emotional blocks," he says. Even when he wasn't using MDMA, "I felt a lot better than I had in social interactions before." Bruce Rogers, a horticulturist in his 40s, says one thing he likes about MDMA is that "you can find something good in somebody that you dislike." He thinks "it would make the world a better place if everybody did it just once."

That's the kind of assertion, reminiscent of claims about LSD's earthshaking potential, that tends to elicit skeptical smiles. But the important point is that many MDMA users believe the drug has lasting psychological benefits, even when it's taken in a recreational context—the sort of thing you don't often hear about alcohol.

Not surprisingly, people who use MDMA in clubs and at raves emphasize its sensual and stimulant properties, the way it enhances music and dancing. But they also talk about a sense of connectedness, especially at raves. Jasmine Menendez, a public relations director in her early 20s who has used MDMA both at raves and with small groups of friends, says it provides "a great body high. I lose all sense of inhibition and my full potential is released. . . . It allows me to get closer to people and to myself."

Too Much Fun

Euphoria is a commonly reported effect of MDMA, which raises the usual concerns about the lure of artificial pleasure. "It was an incredible feeling of being tremendously happy where I was and being content in a basic way," Stevenson recalls of the first time he felt MDMA's effects. He used it several more times after that, but it never became a regular habit.

Menendez, on the other hand, found MDMA "easy to become addicted to" because "you see the full potential in yourself and others; you feel like you won the lottery." She began chasing that feeling one weekend after another, often taking several pills in one night. "Doing e as much as I did affected my relationship with my mother," she says. "I would come home cracked out from a night of partying and sleep the whole day. She couldn't invite anyone over because I was always sleeping. She said that my party habits were out of control. We fought constantly. I would also go to work high from the party, if I had to work weekends. The comedown was horrible because I wanted to sleep and instead I had to be running around doing errands."

Menendez decided to cut back on her MDMA consumption, and recently she has been using it only on special occasions. "I think I've outgrown it finally," she says. "I used e to do some serious soul-searching and to come out of my shell, learning all I could about who I really am. I'm grateful that I had the experiences that I did and wouldn't change it for the world. But now, being 23, I'm ready to embrace mental clarity fully. Ecstasy is definitely a constructive tool and if used correctly can benefit the user. It changed my life for the better, and because of what I learned about myself, I'm ready to start a new life without it."

Sustained heavy use of MDMA is rare, partly because it's impractical. MDMA works mainly by stimulating the release of the neurotransmitter serotonin. Taking it depletes the brain's supply, which may not return to normal levels for a week or more. Some users report a hangover period of melancholy and woolly-headedness that can last a few days. As frequency of use increases,

MDMA's euphoric and empathetic effects diminish and its unpleasant side effects, including jitteriness and hangovers, intensify. Like LSD, it has a self-limiting quality, which is reflected in patterns of use. In a 2000 survey, 8.2 percent of high school seniors reported trying MDMA in the previous year. Less than half of them (3.6 percent) had used it in the previous month, and virtually none reported "daily" use (defined as use on 20 or more occasions in the previous 30 days). To parents, of course, any use of MDMA is alarming, and the share of seniors who said they'd ever tried the drug nearly doubled between 1996 and 2000, when it reached 11 percent.

Parental fears have been stoked by reports of sudden fatalities among MDMA users. Given the millions of doses consumed each year, such cases are remarkably rare: The Drug Abuse Warning Network counted nine MDMA-related deaths in 1998. The most common cause of death is dehydration and overheating. MDMA impairs body temperature regulation and accelerates fluid loss, which can be especially dangerous for people dancing vigorously in crowded, poorly ventilated spaces for hours at a time. The solution to this problem, well-known to experienced ravers, is pretty straightforward: avoid clubs and parties where conditions are stifling, take frequent rests, abstain from alcohol (which compounds dehydration), and drink plenty of water. MDMA also interacts dangerously with some prescription drugs (including monoamine oxidase inhibitors, a class of antidepressants), and it raises heart rate and blood pressure, of special concern for people with cardiovascular conditions.

Another hazard is a product of the black market created by prohibition: Tablets or capsules sold as Ecstasy may in fact contain other, possibly more dangerous drugs. In tests by private U.S. laboratories, more than one-third of "Ecstasy" pills turned out to be bogus. (The samples were not necessarily representative, and the results may be on the high side, since the drugs were submitted voluntarily for testing, perhaps by buyers who had reason to be suspicious.) Most of the MDMA substitutes, which included caffeine, ephedrine, and aspirin, were relatively harmless, but one of them, the cough suppressant dextromethorphan (DXM), has disturbing psychoactive effects in high doses, impedes the metabolism of MDMA, and blocks perspiration, raising the risk of overheating. Another drug that has been passed off as MDMA is paramethoxyamphetamine (PMA), which is potentially lethal in doses over 50 milligrams, especially when combined with other drugs. In 2000 the DEA reported 10 deaths tied to PMA. Wary Ecstasy users can buy test kits or have pills analyzed by organizations such as DanceSafe, which sets up booths at raves and nightclubs.

Nervous Breakdown

Generally speaking, a careful user can avoid the short-term dangers of MDMA. Of more concern is the possibility of long-term brain damage. In animal studies, high or repeated doses of MDMA cause degeneration of serotonin nerve receptors, and some of the changes appear to be permanent. The relevance of these studies to human use of MDMA is unclear because we don't know whether the same changes occur in people or, if they do, at what doses and with what practical consequences. Studies of human users, which often have serious methodological shortcomings, so far have been inconclusive.

Still, the possibility of lasting damage to memory should not be lightly dismissed. There's enough reason for concern that MDMA should no longer be treated as casually as "a low-calorie martini." If the fears of neurotoxicity prove to be well-founded and a safe dose cannot be estimated with any confidence, a prudent person would need a good reason—probably better than a fun night out—to take the risk. On the other hand, the animal research suggests that it may be possible to avoid neural damage by preventing hyperthermia or by taking certain drugs (for example, Prozac) in conjunction with MDMA. In that case, such precautions would be a requirement of responsible use.

However the debate about MDMA's long-term effects turns out, we should be wary of claims that it (or any drug) makes people "engage in random sex acts." Like the idea that certain intoxicants make people lazy, crazy, or violent, it vastly oversimplifies a complex interaction between the drug, the user, and the context. As MDMA's versatility demonstrates, the same drug can be different things to different people. Michael Buchanan, a retired professor in his early 70s, has used MDMA several times with one or two other people. "It's just wonderful," he says, "to bring closeness, intimacy—not erotic intimacy at all, but a kind of spiritual intimacy, a loving relationship, an openness to dialogue that nothing else can quite match." When I mention MDMA use at raves, he says, "I don't understand how the kids can use it that way."

POSTSCRIPT

Should We Be Concerned About Club Drugs?

There is little argument that mind-altering drugs can cause physical and emotional havoc for the user. Users may become less inhibited and become involved in behaviors they would not typically do if they were not on drugs. However, is one's attendance at a rave party likely to increase his or her likelihood of using drugs? Perhaps individuals who go to raves are the type of people who would use drugs regardless. Nonetheless, if going to raves is more likely to result in drug use, then one can support the argument that they should be illegal.

The Office of National Drug Control Policy contends that rave parties are one place where club drugs are available. The clandestine nature of rave parties offers some degree of obscurity from law enforcement officials. On the other hand, if it can be demonstrated that making rave parties illegal has no impact on the use of Ecstasy, GHB, ketamine, or other so-called club drugs, then making raves illegal serves no purpose. By earmarking raves as places where drugs may be used, it is possible that this increases the possibility that drug use will occur. One may think that it is appropriate, perhaps expected, to engage in drug use at a rave party.

Sullum argues that history shows that bringing attention to certain drugs results in their increased use. Young people would not know to alter their consciousness with certain drugs unless they were alerted to their effects. However, if young people participate in an activity that is potentially harmful, one could argue that it is the government's responsibility to step in. At what point is too much information counterproductive? Balancing one's right to know about drugs with the publicity generated by informing the public about certain drugs is difficult.

The issue of whether or not we should be concerned about club drugs raises a number of interesting questions. For example, when is a drug a club drug? If a person calls a drug something different, then is it still a club drug? Can people just get together to enjoy music and to socialize without being looked upon suspiciously? If a club brings in a musical group that plays techno music, does the club become a front for a rave? If patrons at a club use illegal drugs, is that the responsibility of the club owner or manager?

There are a number of articles that look at the issue of making club drugs and rave parties. Two good articles are "The Ups and Downs of Ecstasy," by Erika Check, *Nature* (May 13, 2004) and "As Raves Go Uptown, Cities Take Aim at Drugs, Noise," by Donna Leinwand, *USA Today* (November 12, 2002). Other informative articles on this issue include "Research on Ecstasy Is Clouded by Errors," by Donald McNeil, *The New York Times* (December 2, 2003); "The Lure of Ecstasy," by John Cloud, *Time* (June 5, 2000); and, "Ecstasy Use Among Club Rave Attendees," by Amelia Arria and others, *Archives of Pediatrics and Adolescent Medicine* (March 2002). One group that sponsors research into the therapeutic benefits of Ecstasy and other drugs is the Multidisciplinary Association for Psychedelic Studies (MAPS). Its web site is www.maps.org.

ISSUE 5

Should Pregnant Drug Users Be Prosecuted?

YES: Paul A. Logli, from "Drugs in the Womb: The Newest Battle-field in the War on Drugs," *Criminal Justice Ethics* (Winter/Spring 1990)

NO: Carolyn S. Carter, from "Perinatal Care for Women Who Are Addicted: Implications for Empowerment," *Health and Social Work* (August 2002)

ISSUE SUMMARY

YES: Paul A. Logli, an Illinois prosecuting attorney, argues that it is the government's duty to enforce every child's right to begin life with a healthy, drug-free mind and body. Logli maintains that pregnant women who use drugs should be prosecuted because they harm the life of their unborn children. He feels that it is the state's responsibility to ensure that every baby is born as healthy as possible.

NO: Carolyn Carter, a social work professor at Howard University, argues that the stigma of drug use during pregnancy has resulted in the avoidance of treatment. Carter asserts that the prosecution of pregnant drug users is unfair because poor women are more likely to be the targets of such prosecution. To enable pregnant women who use drugs to receive perinatal care, it is necessary to define their drug use as a health problem rather than as a legal problem.

$\mathbf{T}$he effects that drugs have on a fetus can be mild and temporary or severe and permanent, depending on the extent of drug use by the mother, the type of substance used, and the stage of fetal development at the time the drug crosses the placental barrier and enters the bloodstream of the fetus. Both illegal and legal drugs, such as cocaine, crack, marijuana, alcohol, and nicotine, are increasingly found to be responsible for incidents of premature births, congenital abnormalities, fetal alcohol syndrome, mental retardation, and other serious birth defects. The exposure of the fetus to these substances and the long-term and involuntary physical, intellectual, and emotional effects are disturbing. In addition, the medical, social, and economic costs of treating and caring for babies who are exposed to or become addicted to drugs while in utero (in the uterus) warrant serious concern.

An important consideration regarding the prosecution of pregnant drug users is whether this is a legal problem or a medical problem. In recent years, attempts have been made to establish laws that would allow the incarceration of drug-using pregnant women on the basis of "fetal abuse." Some cases have been successfully prosecuted: mothers have been denied custody of their infants until they enter appropriate treatment programs, and criminal charges have been brought against mothers whose children were born with drug-related complications. The underlying presumption is that the unborn fetus should be afforded protection against the harmful actions of another person, specifically the use of harmful drugs by the mother.

Those who profess that prosecuting pregnant women who use drugs is necessary insist that the health and welfare of the unborn child is the highest priority. They contend that the possibility that these women will avoid obtaining health care for themselves or their babies because they fear punishment does not absolve the state from the responsibility of protecting the babies. They also argue that criminalizing these acts is imperative to protect fetuses and newborns who cannot protect themselves. It is the duty of the legal system to deter pregnant women from engaging in future criminal drug use and to protect the best interests of infants.

Others maintain that drug use and dependency by pregnant women is a medical problem, not a criminal one. Many pregnant women seek treatment, but they often find that rehabilitation programs are limited or unavailable. Shortages of openings in chemical dependency programs may keep a prospective client waiting for months, during which time she will most likely continue to use the drugs to which she is addicted and prolong her fetus's drug exposure. Many low-income women do not receive drug treatment and adequate prenatal care due to financial constraints. Women who fear criminal prosecution because of their drug use may simply avoid prenatal care altogether.

Some suggest that medical intervention, drug prevention, and education—not prosecution—are needed for pregnant drug users. Prosecution, they contend, drives women who need medical attention away from the very help they and their babies need. Others respond that prosecuting pregnant women who use drugs will help identify those who need attention, at which point adequate medical and social welfare services can be provided to treat and protect the mother and child.

In the following selections, Paul A. Logli, arguing for the prosecution of pregnant drug users, contends that it is the state's responsibility to protect the unborn and the newborn because they are least able to protect themselves. He charges that it is the prosecutor's responsibility to deter future criminal drug use by mothers who he feels violate the rights of their potential newborns to have an opportunity for a healthy and normal life. Carolyn Carter contends that prosecuting pregnant drug users may be counterproductive to improving the quality of infant and maternal health. To help women who use drugs during pregnancy, it would be more helpful to identify the problem as a medical problem and not as a legal problem.

Paul A. Logli

 **YES**

Drugs in the Womb: The Newest Battlefield in the War on Drugs

Introduction

The reported incidence of drug-related births has risen dramatically over the last several years. The legal system and, in particular, local prosecutors have attempted to properly respond to the suffering, death, and economic costs which result from a pregnant woman's use of drugs. The ensuing debate has raised serious constitutional and practical issues which are far from resolution.

Prosecutors have achieved mixed results in using current criminal and juvenile statutes as a basis for legal action intended to prosecute mothers and protect children. As a result, state and federal legislators have begun the difficult task of drafting appropriate laws to deal with the problem, while at the same time acknowledging the concerns of medical authorities, child protection groups, and advocates for individual rights.

The Problem

The plight of "cocaine babies," children addicted at birth to narcotic substances or otherwise affected by maternal drug use during pregnancy, has prompted prosecutors in some jurisdictions to bring criminal charges against drug-abusing mothers. Not only have these prosecutions generated heated debates both inside and outside of the nation's courtrooms, but they have also expanded the war on drugs to a controversial new battlefield—the mother's womb.

A 1988 survey of hospitals conducted by Dr. Ira Chasnoff, Associate Professor of Northwestern University Medical School and President of the National Association for Perinatal Addiction Research and Education (NAPARE) indicated that as many as 375,000 infants may be affected by maternal cocaine use during pregnancy each year. Chasnoff's survey included 36 hospitals across the country and showed incidence rates ranging from 1 percent to 27 percent. It also indicated that the problem was not restricted to urban populations or particular racial or socio-economic groups. More recently a study at Hutzel Hospital in Detroit's inner city found that 42.7 percent of its newborn babies were exposed to drugs while in their mothers' wombs.

From Paul A. Logli, "Drugs in the Womb: The Newest Battlefield in the War on Drugs," *Criminal Justice Ethics*, vol. 9, no. 1 (Winter/Spring 1990), pp. 23–29. Copyright © 1990 by *Criminal Justice Ethics*. Reprinted by permission of The Institute for Criminal Justice Ethics, 555 West 57th Street, Suite 601, New York, NY.

The effects of maternal use of cocaine and other drugs during pregnancy on the mother and her newborn child have by now been well-documented and will not be repeated here. The effects are severe and can cause numerous threats to the short-term health of the child. In a few cases it can even result in death.

Medical authorities have just begun to evaluate the long-term effects of cocaine exposure on children as they grow older. Early findings show that many of these infants show serious difficulties in relating and reacting to adults and environments, as well as in organizing creative play, and they appear similar to mildly autistic or personality-disordered children.

The human costs related to the pain, suffering, and deaths resulting from maternal cocaine use during pregnancy are simply incalculable. In economic terms, the typical intensive-care costs for treating babies exposed to drugs range from $7,500 to $31,000. In some cases medical bills go as high as $150,000.

The costs grow enormously as more and more hospitals encounter the problem of "boarder babies"—those children literally abandoned at the hospital by an addicted mother, and left to be cared for by the nursing staff. Future costs to society for simply educating a generation of drug-affected children can only be the object of speculation. It is clear, however, that besides pain, suffering, and death the economic costs to society of drug use by pregnant women is presently enormous and is certainly growing larger.

The Prosecutor's Response

It is against this backdrop and fueled by the evergrowing emphasis on an aggressively waged war on drugs that prosecutors have begun a number of actions against women who have given birth to drug-affected children. A review of at least two cases will illustrate the potential success or failure of attempts to use existing statutes.

People v. Melanie Green   On February 4, 1989, at a Rockford, Illinois hospital, two-day-old Bianca Green lost her brief struggle for life. At the time of Bianca's birth both she and her mother, twenty-four-year-old Melanie Green, tested positive for the presence of cocaine in their systems.

Pathologists in Rockford and Madison, Wisconsin, indicated that the death of the baby was the result of a prenatal injury related to cocaine used by the mother during the pregnancy. They asserted that maternal cocaine use had caused the placenta to prematurely rupture, which deprived the fetus of oxygen before and during delivery. As a result of oxygen deprivation, the child's brain began to swell and she eventually died.

After an investigation by the Rockford Police Department and the State of Illinois Department of Children and Family Services, prosecutors allowed a criminal complaint to be filed on May 9, 1989, charging Melanie Green with the offenses of Involuntary Manslaughter and Delivery of a Controlled Substance.

On May 25, 1989, testimony was presented to the Winnebago County Grand Jury by prosecutors seeking a formal indictment. The Grand Jury, however, declined to indict Green on either charge. Since Grand Jury proceedings in the State of Illinois are secret, as are the jurors' deliberations and votes, the reason for the decision of the Grand Jury in this case is determined more by conjecture than any direct knowledge. Prosecutors involved in the presentation observed that the jurors exhibited a certain amount of sympathy for the young woman who had been brought before the Grand Jury at the jurors' request. It is also likely that the jurors were uncomfortable with the use of statutes that were not intended to be used in these circumstances.

It would also be difficult to disregard the fact that, after the criminal complaints were announced on May 9th and prior to the Grand Jury deliberations of May 25th, a national debate had ensued revolving around the charges brought in Rockford, Illinois, and their implications for the ever-increasing problem of women who use drugs during pregnancy.

People v. Jennifer Clarise Johnson   On July 13, 1989, a Seminole County, Florida judge found Jennifer Johnson guilty of delivery of a controlled substance to a child. The judge found that delivery, for purposes of the statute, occurred through the umbilical cord after the birth of the child and before the cord was severed. Jeff Deen, the Assistant State's Attorney who prosecuted the case, has since pointed out that Johnson, age 23, had previously given birth to three other cocaine-affected babies, and in this case was arrested at a crack house. "We needed to make sure this woman does not give birth to another cocaine baby."

Johnson was sentenced to fifteen years of probation including strict supervision, drug treatment, random drug testing, educational and vocational training, and an intensive prenatal care program if she ever became pregnant again.

Support for the Prosecution
of Maternal Drug Abuse

Both cases reported above relied on a single important fact as a basis for the prosecution of the drug-abusing mother: that the child was born alive and exhibited the consequences of prenatal injury.

In the Melanie Green case, Illinois prosecutors relied on the "born alive" rule set out earlier in *People v. Bolar*. In *Bolar* the defendant was convicted of the offense of reckless homicide. The case involved an accident between a car driven by the defendant, who was found to be drunk, and another automobile containing a pregnant woman. As a result, the woman delivered her baby by emergency caesarean section within hours of the collision. Although the newborn child exhibited only a few heart beats and lived for approximately two minutes, the court found that the child was born alive and was therefore a person for purposes of the criminal statutes of the State of Illinois.

The Florida prosecution relied on a live birth in an entirely different fashion. The prosecutor argued in that case that the delivery of the controlled substance occurred after the live birth via the umbilical cord and prior to the cutting of the cord. Thus, it was argued, that the delivery of the controlled substance occurred not to a fetus but to a person who enjoyed the protection of the criminal code of the State of Florida.

Further support for the State's role in protecting the health of newborns even against prenatal injury is found in the statutes which provide protection for the fetus. These statutes proscribe actions by a person, usually other than the mother, which either intentionally or recklessly harm or kill a fetus. In other words, even in the absence of a live birth, most states afford protection to the unborn fetus against the harmful actions of another person. Arguably, the same protection should be afforded the infant against intentional harmful actions by a drug-abusing mother.

The state also receives support for a position in favor of the protection of the health of a newborn from a number of non-criminal cases. A line of civil cases in several states would appear to stand for the principle that a child has a right to begin life with a sound mind and body, and a person who interferes with that right may be subject to civil liability. In two cases decided within months of each other, the Supreme Court of Michigan upheld two actions for recovery of damages that were caused by the infliction of prenatal injury. In *Womack v. Buckhorn* the court upheld an action on behalf of an eight-year-old surviving child for prenatal brain injuries apparently suffered during the fourth month of the pregnancy in an automobile accident. The court adopted with approval the reasoning of a New Jersey Supreme Court decision and "recognized that a child has a legal right to begin life with a sound mind and body." Similarly, in *O'Neill v. Morse* the court found that a cause of action was allowed for prenatal injuries that caused the death of an eight-month-old viable fetus.

Illinois courts have allowed civil recovery on behalf of an infant for a negligently administered blood transfusion given to the mother prior to conception which resulted in damage to the child at birth. However, the same Illinois court would not extend a similar cause of action for prebirth injuries as between a child and its own mother. The court, however, went on to say that a right to such a cause of action could be statutorily enacted by the Legislature.

Additional support for the state's role in protecting the health of newborns is found in the principles annunciated in recent decisions of the United States Supreme Court. The often cited case of *Roe v. Wade* set out that although a woman's right of privacy is broad enough to cover the abortion decision, the right is not absolute and is subject to limitations, "and that at some point the state's interest as to protection of health, medical standards and prenatal life, becomes dominant."

More recently, in the case of *Webster v. Reproductive Health Services,* the court expanded the state's interest in protecting potential human life by setting aside viability as a rigid line that had previously allowed state regulation only after viability had been shown but prohibited it before viability. The court goes on to say that the "fundamental right" to abortion as described in *Roe* is now accorded the lesser status of a "liberty interest." Such language surely supports a prosecutor's argument that the state's compelling interest in potential human life would allow the criminalization of acts which if committed by a pregnant woman can damage not just a viable fetus but eventually a born-alive infant. It follows that, once a pregnant woman has abandoned her right to abort and has decided to carry the fetus to term, society can well impose a duty on the mother to insure that the fetus is born as healthy as possible.

A further argument in support of the state's interest in prosecuting women who engage in conduct which is damaging to the health of a new-born child is especially compelling in regard to maternal drug use during pregnancy. Simply put, there is no fundamental right or even a liberty interest in the use of psycho-active drugs. A perceived right of privacy has never formed an absolute barrier against state prosecutions of those who use or possess narcotics. Certainly no exception can be made simply because the person using drugs happens to be pregnant.

Critics of the prosecutor's role argue that any statute that would punish mothers who create a substantial risk of harm to their fetus will run afoul of constitutional requirements, including prohibitions on vagueness, guarantees of liberty and privacy, and rights of due process and equal protection. . . .

In spite of such criticism, the state's role in protecting those citizens who are least able to protect themselves, namely the newborn, mandates an aggressive posture. Much of the criticism of prosecutorial efforts is based on speculation as to the consequences of prosecution and ignores the basic tenet of criminal law that prosecutions deter the prosecuted and others from committing additional crimes. To assume that it will only drive persons further underground is to somehow argue that certain prosecutions of crime will only force perpetrators to make even more aggressive efforts to escape apprehension, thus making arrest and prosecution unadvisable. Neither could this be accepted as an argument justifying even the weakening of criminal sanctions. . . .

The concern that pregnant addicts will avoid obtaining health care for themselves or their infants because of the fear of prosecution cannot justify the absence of state action to protect the newborn. If the state were to accept such reasoning, then existing child abuse laws would have to be reconsidered since they might deter parents from obtaining medical care for physically or sexually abused children. That argument has not been accepted as a valid reason for abolishing child abuse laws or for not prosecuting child abusers. . . .

The far better policy is for the state to acknowledge its responsibility not only to provide a deterrant to criminal and destructive behavior by pregnant addicts but also to provide adequate opportunities for those who might seek help to discontinue their addiction. Prosecution has a role in its ability to deter future criminal behavior and to protect the best interests of the child. The medical and social welfare establishment must assume an even greater responsibility to encourage legislators to provide adequate funding and facilities so that no pregnant woman who is addicted to drugs will be denied the opportunity to seek appropriate prenatal care and treatment for her addiction.

One State's Response

The Legislature of the State of Illinois at the urging of local prosecutors moved quickly to amend its juvenile court act in order to provide protection to those children born drug-affected. Previously, Illinois law provided that a court could assume jurisdiction over addicted minors or a minor who is generally declared neglected or abused.

Effective January 1, 1990, the juvenile court act was amended to expand the definition of a neglected or abused minor. . . .

> those who are neglected include . . . any newborn infant whose blood or urine contains any amount of a controlled substance. . . .

The purpose of the new statute is to make it easier for the court to assert jurisdiction over a newborn infant born drug-affected. The state is not required to show either the addiction of the child or harmful effects on the child in order to remove the child from a drug-abusing mother. Used in this context, prosecutors can work with the mother in a rather coercive atmosphere to encourage her to enter into drug rehabilitation and, upon the successful completion of the program, be reunited with her child.

Additional legislation before the Illinois Legislature is House Bill 2835 sponsored by Representatives John Hallock (R-Rockford) and Edolo "Zeke" Giorgi (D-Rockford). This bill represents the first attempt to specifically address the prosecution of drug-abusing pregnant women. . . .

The statute provides for a class 4 felony disposition upon conviction. A class 4 felony is a probationable felony which can also result in a term of imprisonment from one to three years.

Subsequent paragraphs set out certain defenses available to the accused.

> It shall not be a violation of this section if a woman knowingly or intentionally uses a narcotic or dangerous drug in the first twelve weeks of pregnancy and: 1. She has no knowledge that she is pregnant; or 2. Subsequently, within the first twelve weeks of pregnancy, undergoes medical treatment for substance abuse or treatment or rehabilitation in a program or facility approved by the Illinois Department of Alcoholism and Substance Abuse, and thereafter discontinues any further use of drugs or narcotics as previously set forth.

. . . A woman, under this statute, could not be prosecuted for self-reporting her addiction in the early stages of the pregnancy. Nor could she be prosecuted under this statute if, even during the subsequent stages of the pregnancy, she discontinued her drug use to the extent that no drugs were present in her system or the baby's system at the time of birth. The statute, as drafted, is clearly intended to allow prosecutors to invoke the criminal statutes in the most serious of cases.

Conclusion

Local prosecutors have a legitimate role in responding to the increasing problem of drug-abusing pregnant women and their drug-affected children. Eliminating the pain, suffering and death resulting from drug exposure in newborns must be a prosecutor's priority. However, the use of existing statutes to address the problem may meet with limited success since they are burdened with numerous constitutional problems dealing with original intent, notice, vagueness, and due process.

The juvenile courts may offer perhaps the best initial response in working to protect the interests of a surviving child. However, in order to address more serious cases, legislative efforts may be required to provide new statutes that will specifically address the problem and hopefully deter future criminal conduct which deprives children of their important right to a healthy and normal birth.

The long-term solution does not rest with the prosecutor alone. Society, including the medical and social welfare establishment, must be more responsive in providing readily accessible prenatal care and treatment alternatives for pregnant addicts. In the short term however, prosecutors must be prepared to play a vital role in protecting children and deterring women from engaging in conduct which will harm the newborn child. If prosecutors fail to respond, then they are simply closing the doors of the criminal justice system to those persons, the newborn, who are least able to open the doors for themselves.

NO ↵

Carolyn S. Carter

Perinatal Care for Women Who Are Addicted: Implications for Empowerment

. . . Perinatal drug abuse is the use of alcohol and other drugs among women who are pregnant. The National Institute on Drug Abuse estimates that 5.5 percent of the women in the United States have used illicit drugs while pregnant, including cocaine, marijuana, heroin, and psychotherapeutic drugs that were not prescribed by a physician. More than 18 percent used alcohol during their pregnancy, and 20.4 percent smoked cigarettes.

Literature reports the increased use of drugs during pregnancy, using therapeutic communities and neighborhood context for addressing perinatal drug abuse; access barriers for low-income ethnic minority women who are addicted and pregnant; the importance of effective policy making; referrals to child protection services; and other responses to perinatal drug abuse.

Women who abuse drugs while pregnant face severe consequences, which include becoming stigmatized as immoral and deficient caregivers. A behavioral outcome of societal attitudes toward perinatal drug abuse is the degree to which the drug-taking behavior of pregnant women is criminalized. Criminalization refers to using legal approaches, such as incarceration, for medical problems of clients rather than referring them for treatment. Community response to the increasing number of women who give birth to infants addicted to crack cocaine, for example, has been to prosecute women for perinatal drug abuse. Similarly, the number of mentally ill inmates in jails and prisons is estimated as being twice that in state hospitals. Individuals in helping professions also display stigmatic attitudes toward perinatal drug abuse. Disparaging interactions with women in some perinatal care facilities, for example, include rude and judgmental comments to clients and violation of their confidentiality. Uncomfortable relationships with health care providers and fear of reprisal on the part of pregnant women who are addicted make women four times less likely to receive adequate care, thereby creating health risks for women who are addicted, their unborn fetuses, and their other children.

In this article I discuss contemporary responses to perinatal drug abuse, including ways in which the behavior of women who abuse drugs is criminalized

From *Health and Social Work*, vol. 27, issue 3, August 2002, pp. 166–174. Copyright © 2002 by National Association of Social Workers, Inc., Health & Social Work. Reprinted by permission. References omitted.

or subjected to legal interventions. Vignettes from an ethnographic study of 120 women who used heroin, crack cocaine, and methamphetamine while pregnant depict the attitudes and behaviors of health care providers, society at large, and women themselves toward maternal drug abuse. This article demonstrates how poor women and women of color encounter legal interventions—such as prosecution or reports to city or state child protective services (CPS)—more frequently for using drugs during pregnancy than their more affluent, white counterparts. Because criminalizing perinatal drug abuse presents substantial risks to the health of women and children, empowering strategies are suggested for redefining perinatal drug abuse less as a legal issue and more as a health concern. The strategies are consistent with elements of the national health plan of the U.S. Department of Health and Human Services (DHHS), such as creating access to health care and minimizing risks to maternal, infant, and child health.

Societal Attitudes Toward Perinatal Drug Abuse

Over the past 100 years, there has been an overall shift in obstetric medicine to a focus on fetal protection. In cases involving maternal drug abuse, the shift has sometimes resulted in adversarial attitudes with sentiment favoring the well-being of fetuses and against pregnant women. The following excerpts offer three perspectives toward perinatal drug abuse that have primary emphasis on unborn fetuses: The first comment reflects the attitudes of some drug dealers; the second statement is a common reaction of partners of pregnant women; and the third depicts the attitude of society at large.

> They [crack dealers] tell me that I shouldn't be doing this in the first place, but I'm gonna do it anyway. And they go, "You know it. I shouldn't even really sell you anything. I shouldn't sell you anything cause you're pregnant. I'm not gonna contribute to that."
>
> My baby came home with crack in her system, and he [baby's father who is himself a crack dealer] don't want to claim her now.
>
> I know one girl. She just smokes [crack] and doesn't give a damn. Her stomach is way out there, so she shouldn't be out there [using crack] anyway, cause people be like, "man, look, a pregnant woman!"

Negative attitudes like the ones in the vignettes above are pervasive and often based on assumed medical and developmental consequences of drugs on fetuses. The concerns are both supported and refuted by research. Studies of the effects of drug use on fetal development cite problems such as low birthweight, small head size, prematurity, and small size for gestational age. A study of 11,000 infants conducted by the Brown University School of Medicine, however, showed no increase in abnormalities at birth among children who had been exposed to cocaine in utero. Although the latter study has not followed the children into school age and is therefore inconclusive, other studies of adjustment among drug-exposed children also challenge the notion of devastating effects resulting from cocaine use during pregnancy. Coles concluded that the effects of the social environment are too often ignored in studies of perinatal drug abuse.

In addition to the pejorative attitudes toward women who abuse drugs during pregnancy based on ideas about adverse fetal development is the belief that drug use compromises the reproductive and caregiver roles of women. It is believed that women who abuse substances are unfit mothers undeserving of their children. Society sanctions women for failing to live up to preconceived gender-role expectations by using legal interventions, particularly against poor women of color who use drugs while they are pregnant.

Legal Interventions

Legal interventions for perinatal drug abuse may be increasing in the United States. Since 1985, 240 women in 35 states have been prosecuted for using alcohol or illegal drugs while pregnant. Eleven states have developed specific gestational-abuse statutes. The most comprehensive reporting system is in Minnesota and includes toxicological screening and "involuntary civil commitment" to drug rehabilitation of pregnant women who have used drugs. Before March 2001, eight states mandated that health care workers report neonates' positive drug toxicology as evidence of child abuse and neglect, thus paving the way for court proceedings and actions affecting the parental rights of mothers. On March 21, 2001, the U.S. Supreme Court ruled that it is unlawful to involuntarily test pregnant women who are suspected of drug abuse. In Ferguson v. City of Charleston, Charleston, South Carolina was a litigant in the Supreme Court case and, along with Florida, enforced the greatest number of legal interventions.

It is informative to place the legal interventions that occurred before the March 2001 judicial ruling within a sociocultural context. In doing so, it becomes clear that although illegal drug use is similar across class and racial lines, poor and ethnic minority women were more likely to be criminalized. The manner in which drug screening occurred is an example. Screenings commonly occurred during routine prenatal care, and the stated purpose was protecting fetuses. However, drug screenings were often limited to facilities that served low socioeconomic populations and populations of color, thus making screenings more detrimental for poor and pregnant women from ethnic minority groups.

Reports to CPS were disparate across cultural groups as well. A review of mandatory reporting of perinatal drug addiction in Florida showed that positive drug screening rates were almost equal among white and African American women and among women seen in clinics and private offices. Yet, reporting rates were much higher for African American women than for white women.

The procedures for prosecuting pregnant women for substance use were discretionary and reflected disparities across demographic groups. A 1987 review of court-ordered obstetrical interventions showed that 81 percent of the women were African American, Hispanic, or Asian and 24 percent did not speak English as a primary language. More recent study results indicate that pregnant African American women were nine times more likely to be prosecuted for substance use than pregnant white women.

Incarceration, like other legal approaches to perinatal drug abuse, also discriminated against poor women and women of color. Women with low incomes generally gave birth in public health settings. Delivering in these facilities increased their chances of incarceration compared with middle-and upper-income women who gave birth in private hospitals that rarely screened for illicit drugs. Public hospitals were more likely to have mandatory drug screenings and protocols that included reporting positive toxicology to CPS. Disclosing positive toxicology to CPS could result in incarceration. Disparities in the rate of incarceration extended to ethnic minority groups, with African American women facing the greatest burden of being imprisoned. Of the 41 pregnant women arrested for abusing drugs in South Carolina from 1989 to 1993, 40 were African American.

The American Medical Association (AMA) stated that drug addiction was an illness that required medical rather than legal intervention, and prosecution did not prevent harm to infants but it often resulted in harm. For example, fear of reprisal was a barrier to outreach and often deterred addicted pregnant women from receiving medical care. Avoiding medical care increased the risk of drug exposure before birth and ineffective parenting later. Also, women who abused drugs were more likely to physically abuse their children.

Legal interventions disregarded the treatment and advocacy roles of health care providers. For example, medical personnel often performed drug screenings without the informed consent of female patients, and the results were then used as evidence during criminal prosecutions. Addressing perinatal drug abuse through legal intervention was punitive. In large part, it operated on the assumption that although drug treatment programs for women were available in sufficient numbers, women had not made use of the services, and the research conclusively attested to the effectiveness of current drug programs for women with children. In fact, drug programs for women, and particularly pregnant women, were largely unavailable. Less than 1 percent of the federal antidrug budget was targeted for women, yet this minimal amount was expected to include women who were pregnant. Also, most drug interventions were designed with men in mind and overlooked the needs of women. Residential treatment programs, for example, rarely provided child care even though 80 percent of the women entering residential drug rehabilitation had children and half had their children living with them at the time they entered treatment. Consequently, mothers who were addicted to drugs, had other children for whom they provided primary care, and had no familial support, risked losing custody of their children by entering treatment.

Interventions based on legal ideology distorted client–worker relationships. Salient features of ethical client–helper relationships are establishing trust and respecting the confidentiality, dignity, and uniqueness of individuals. Women entering perinatal care could not be assured of these aspects of treatment. In the following scenarios involving two African American woman who were addicted to drugs, the clients' dignity and confidentiality were each violated while they received perinatal services:

> They [health care providers] look at you, they look at you foul and they tell me [sarcastic voice], "Oh, you're a crack user." And then they want to look at your record, and then this nurse look at it and this other nurse look at it, then this other nurse look at it, then . . . They talking all loud, everybody around.
>
> I know a lot of mothers say that they don't get prenatal care cause they feel like as soon as they walk through the door, they will be judged. "Oh you're a crack head. So why . . . did you get pregnant anyway?" So they don't get prenatal care . . . they are thinking how they gonna be looked at when they walk in the hospital door, like they are not good enough to be pregnant.

Experiences such as the ones above not only diminished the quality of services, but also restricted access by causing women to retreat before obtaining the care they sought.

The strained client–worker relationships precipitated by legal interventions also created parallel care systems that were not in the best interest of clients. Prototypes were nontraditional birthing methods. Parallel care also delayed registering the birth of children and reduced opportunities for health care providers to assist women in obtaining required immunizations and other follow-up care for their infants. In these ways, parallel systems for perinatal care placed both mothers who are addicted and infants at risk.

> I'm gonna have my baby at home and then I'm gonna register the birth at three or four months.

Health-Related Interventions

Health-related approaches to perinatal drug abuse are notably unlike legal interventions. As the Healthy People 2010 plan states, useful approaches to improving health build community partnerships and are systemic, multidisciplinary, absent of disparities across population groups, and attuned to the reciprocal relationship between individual health and community health. Reciprocal means community health is affected by the beliefs, attitudes, and behaviors of everyone in a given community and vice versa.

Components of Healthy People 2010—the national plan for improving public health in the United States—include two discrete goals, 467 objectives, and 28 focal areas. Among the focal areas of the plan are maternal, infant, and child health and substance abuse. Healthy People 2010 proposes to improve maternal, infant, and child health by decreasing maternal drug abuse. Because of the relevant focal areas and strategies of Healthy People 2010 and because the plan creates opportunities for individuals to make healthy lifestyle choices for themselves and their families, it has implications for developing empowerment strategies in perinatal care settings.

Implications for Empowerment

Of concern to social workers is that perinatal drug abuse, a health-related issue of families and children, is often criminalized. Basing perinatal approaches on empowerment strategies that target women who are addicted and health care providers promises to overcome legal interventions and address disparaging attitudes toward perinatal drug abuse.

Empowerment refers to increasing clients' personal, social, and political power so that they can change their situations and prevent reoccurrence of problems. Because empowerment theory emerged from efforts to develop more effective and responsive services for women and people of color, it is highly relevant to perinatal drug abuse.

The empowerment practice goals are helping client systems achieve a sense of personal power, become more aware of the connection between individual and community problems, develop helpful skills, and work toward social change. Studies cite the usefulness of empowerment practice in improving the contexts of human services organizations in ethnically diverse metropolitan areas and helping women of color in oppressed neighborhoods overcome unequal access to resources. Empowerment strategies include role playing as a technique for skills training, raising self-esteem, and helping women see the impact of the political environment on issues in their own lives. In empowerment practice, power is shared, clients are helped to "experience a sense of power" within helping relationships, and professionals are collaborators rather than superiors.

Perhaps the most empowering perinatal service about which social workers and their clients who are addicted can collaborate is helping women become alcohol and drug free. The specific strategies for motivating clients to seek drug rehabilitation, attain sobriety, and use relapse prevention measures are documented in the literature but are not a focus of this article. This article is concerned with empowering strategies for addressing the adverse attitudes and practices to which pregnant women who are addicted are often subjected. Examples include

- teaching pregnant women who are addicted to make formal complaints when they receive unprofessional services in perinatal care settings
- improving access by overcoming scheduling issues and advocating for adequate resources
- enhancing communication skills among women who are pregnant and addicted to drugs
- conducting culturally sensitive in-service training for health care providers
- addressing the unique issues of women of color
- promoting gender-sensitive programs
- overcoming systemic factors that create barriers to health care
- developing community partnerships with relevant groups
- recommending national policies that redefine perinatal drug abuse as a health issue.

Addressing Professional Attitudes and Practices

Social workers can help addicted women become empowered in perinatal care settings in which existing professional attitudes and practices are esteem lowering and potentially disempowering by conveying their own positive regard for the worth and dignity of individuals. This includes validating with clients that rude, judgmental, and other unethical practices are oppressive and unacceptable in health care settings. Collaborating with women about the best ways to file formal complaints against perinatal care personnel who fail to meet professional standards enhances women's personal power and is a model for social change.

Two of the most insurmountable barriers for low-income women seeking perinatal care are (1) the pejorative attitudes of providers and (2) the distrust of the health care system. Stressful interactions with health care providers can adversely affect the drug abuse recovery of women in perinatal care, further damage their self-esteem, and be intimidating as well.

The health of individuals and communities depends on access to quality health care. Case management approaches in which social workers appropriately assist in referring women who require perinatal care are potentially empowering because they facilitate access to services. Social workers can enhance their referrals by becoming knowledgeable about the practices and expectations for clients in perinatal care agencies and using the increased knowledge to improve clients' involvement in their own perinatal care regime. Examples are raising clients' general awareness of an agency's intake procedures and working collaboratively to overcome access barriers that are common in some perinatal care facilities. Access barriers include long waiting periods in facilities and scheduling problems—for example, consistently busy telephone lines and too few available appointments. Short-term strategies for overcoming barriers could involve scheduling appointments far in advance and adequately planning for such support services as extended child care, transportation, and meals when clients are scheduled for appointments. Long-term strategies should include advocating for increased resources.

By means of role playing or related techniques, addicted clients who require perinatal care can be taught more assertive, and thus personally empowering, means of communicating in health care settings. For instance, it is more useful for both clients and services professionals if a woman states, "Hello, I am [name] and I am here for my 3:00 appointment or the results of my lab work" than for her to say, "Hello, I am here for my appointment." Improved client communication may increase access and signal to providers that clients expect dignified, respectful services.

Health-related approaches to perinatal care have informed views on diversity. In-service training in which social workers help providers become more culturally sensitive to poor and ethnic minority clients is empowering because it can improve the overall environment of perinatal care settings. Our knowledge of human diversity and ethical commitment to ethnic-sensitive practice can enhance our role as trainers. Social workers understand, for instance, the usefulness of community intervention and how to use natural helping networks and extended families when working with poor families and families of color. Natural helpers, such as neighbors who can offer transportation or child care, are invaluable to perinatal drug abuse services. Lack of child care and transportation are access barriers that are personally disempowering to many wom en who require perinatal care.

It is also important to address the unique issues of women of color. For example, HIV infections are common among women who abuse intravenous drugs, but African American women are seven times more likely to die from HIV/AIDS. Patient education on preventing HIV infections and other sexually transmitted diseases and planning for loss of parents and other effects of AIDS on families are important topics of discussion during perinatal care to African American women.

Counteracting Legal Interventions

Some experts believe the current political climate produces gender-biased, racist, and classist policies. An example is contemporary policy defining perinatal drug abuse as if it were strictly a legal issue and then targeting for prosecution poor women and women of color. Because of social workers' mandate to promote social justice, it is important that we advocate on behalf of vulnerable populations, for example, pregnant women who are addicted and their unborn children.

In recommending policies that foster adequate income, health insurance, and education, we can raise the socioeconomic status of mothers and, in turn, enhance the health status of drug-exposed babies. Being poor and less educated are linked to systemic issues like restricted access to health care, living in unsafe neighborhoods, inadequate housing, and limited opportunities to engage in health promotion. Many contemporary drug policies, however, blame women and divert attention from systemic forces, such as poverty, that promote substance abuse. A study of 1,000 substance abuse cases in four large cities showed that a sizable number of the parents lost their children to custodial care because of inadequate housing and poverty rather than explicit drug abuse. Healthy People 2010 embraces the empowering strategy of focusing on systemic factors that affect the health status of addicted women and their unborn fetuses.

Although it is important that social workers advocate for health-related perinatal care policies, it is even more empowering if the resulting programs are gender sensitive. Gender-sensitive perinatal programs take into account, among other factors, protecting women's physical health, access issues, and the rate of depression among women who are addicted. Depression, for example, is strongly correlated with high levels of personal stress, inadequate housing, lack of money for basic needs, and other factors associated with poverty. Because depressive symptoms are predictable among women who abuse drugs and can deter health-seeking behaviors, assessing depression in perinatal care settings is gender sensitive. Assessing depression is also a biopsychosocial strategy that favors health promotion. By treating depression, social workers can help clients in perinatal care settings overcome feelings of helplessness and become more available to engage in social change. Therefore, examining depression in perinatal care settings is personally, politically, and socially empowering to clients.

Social workers can intensify their perinatal advocacy efforts by developing community partnerships with CPS and perinatal care programs that fulfill the programs' missions while also protecting families and children. Perinatal toxicology screenings are allegedly designed to protect children, and CPS's primary mission is protecting children. However, between 1982 and 1989, when the number of substance abuse-related CPS cases doubled, child welfare agencies began separating children from their mothers solely on the basis of positive toxicology, without attempts to apply preventive measures or family rehabilitation. It is expedient that social workers help CPS and perinatal care providers refocus their dialogue on the needs of families within social and political contexts. Partnering agencies may then stop relying heavily on legal strategies and instead advocate for financial and other resources that can improve the health status of all family members—for example, by locating medical facilities in local communities and providing culturally specific health education. Because advocating community partnerships highlights the relatedness of individuals' problems and environmental conditions, it fulfills tenets of empowerment practice and Healthy People 2010.

Community partnerships that reach out to nontraditional partners can be among the most effective tools for improving health in communities. Social workers can further strengthen their campaigns to eliminate legal interventions for perinatal drug abuse by broadening their community partnerships with CPS and perinatal care programs to incorporate women, private companies, and community-based organizations such as criminal justice agencies, legal clinics, employment agencies, and churches. By providing research data, social workers can demonstrate to partners how legal means of "protecting" families and children are, in fact, injurious to them. Incarceration, for example, complicates birth outcomes in various ways. When women are released from prison, their own as well as their children's Medicaid eligibility is compromised for at least a month or more. If women and their children have chronic illnesses such as diabetes, HIV/AIDS, or hypertension, treatment adherence is essential, but health care is inaccessible without medical coverage. Women with low incomes, already at the highest risk of poor birth outcomes, are at greater risk of incarceration.

Once community partners are better informed, they can then educate politicians and other policymakers and thereafter solicit their help in adopting national policies that redefine perinatal drug abuse as a health-related issue. One example of such a policy is greater incentives for private corporations to develop partnerships with community-based drug rehabilitation organizations that accommodate mothers who are addicted as well as their children. Another is a policy that rewards medical schools for teaching students how to identify risk factors for substance use during pregnancy. In a survey of primary care physicians, only 17 percent could diagnose illicit drug use, a mere 30 percent were prepared to diagnose misuse of prescription drugs, and only 20 percent could confidently diagnose alcoholism. On the other hand, 82 percent of the physicians could identify patients with diabetes, and

83 percent could diagnose patients with hypertension. Increasing physicians' ability to identify risk factors for drug use during pregnancy is not only a preventive measure for improving maternal, infant, and child health, but a means of reinforcing among physicians and other health care providers the health-related definition of perinatal drug abuse.

Conclusion

Health care professionals and society at large exhibit negative attitudes toward women who abuse drugs. By means of empowerment strategies, social workers can potentially help clients who are addicted and pregnant to seek and complete perinatal treatment programs, improve the environment in which perinatal care services are provided, and advocate for policies that define perinatal drug abuse more as a health problem than a legal issue. Desired outcomes of these efforts are improved health care access and quality of life for families in which perinatal drug abuse is an issue.

POSTSCRIPT

Should Pregnant Drug Users Be Prosecuted?

Babies born with health problems as a result of their mother's drug use is a tragedy that needs to be rectified. The issue is not whether this problem needs to be addressed, but what course of action is best. The need for medical intervention and specialized treatment programs serving pregnant women with drug problems has been recognized. The groundwork has been set for funding and developing such programs. The Office of Substance Abuse Prevention is funding chemical dependency programs specifically for pregnant women in several states.

It has been argued that drug use by pregnant women is a problem that requires medical, not criminal, attention. One can contend the notion that pregnant drug users and their drug-exposed infants are victims of drug abuse. Critics contend that there is an element of discrimination in the practice of prosecuting women who use drugs during pregnancy because these women are primarily low-income, single, members of minorities, and recipients of public assistance. Possible factors leading to their drug use—poverty, unemployment, poor education, and lack of vocational training—are not addressed when the solution to drug use during pregnancy is incarceration. Moreover, many pregnant women are denied access to treatment programs.

Prosecution proponents contend that medical intervention is not adequate in preventing pregnant women from using drugs and that criminal prosecution is necessary. Logli argues that "eliminating the pain, suffering and death resulting from drug exposure in newborns must be a prosecutor's priority." He maintains that the criminal justice system should protect newborns and, if legal cause does exist for prosecution, then statutes should provide protection for the fetus. However, will prosecution result in more protection or less protection for the fetus? If a mother stops using drugs for fear of prosecution, the fetus benefits. If the mother avoids prenatal care because of potential legal punishment, the fetus suffers.

If women can be prosecuted for using illegal drugs such as cocaine and narcotics during pregnancy because they harm the fetus, should women who smoke cigarettes and drink alcohol during pregnancy also be prosecuted? The evidence is clear that tobacco and alcohol place the fetus at great risk; however, most discussions of prosecuting pregnant drug users overlook women who use these drugs. Also, the adverse health effects from secondhand smoke are well documented. Should people be prosecuted if they smoke around pregnant women?

An excellent review of the effects of prenatal exposure to alcohol is "Alcohol and Pregnancy, Highlights from Three Decades of Research," by

Carrie L. Randall, *Journal of Studies on Alcohol* (vol. 62, 2001). Three articles that examine this issue thoroughly are "The Rights of Pregnant Women: The Supreme Court and Drug Testing," by Lawrence O. Gostin, *The Hastings Center Report* (September-October 2001); "Inside the Womb: Interpreting the Ferguson Case," by Samantha Weyrauch, *Duke Journal of Gender Law and Policy* (Summer 2002); and, "Who Is the Guilty Party? Rights, Motherhood, and the Problem of Prenatal Drug Exposure," by Karen Zivi, *Law and Society Review* (vol. 34, no. 1, 2000).

ISSUE 6

Should Drug Addiction Be Considered a Disease?

YES: Lisa N. LeGrand, William G. Iacono, and Matt McGue, from "Predicting Addiction," *American Scientist* (March–April 2005)

NO: Jacob Sullum, from "H: The Surprising Truth About Heroin and Addiction," *Reason* (June 2003)

ISSUE SUMMARY

YES: Psychologists Lisa LeGrand, William Iacono, and Matt McGue maintain that certain personality characteristics, such as hyperactivity, acting-out behavior, and sensation-seeking may have their bases in genetics. LeGrand, Iacono, and McGue acknowledge the role of environment, but they feel that genes play a substantial role in drug-taking behavior.

NO: Jacob Sullum, a senior editor with *Reason* magazine, contends that drug addiction should not be considered a disease, a condition over which one has no control. Numerous individuals who have used drugs extensively have been able to stop drug use. Sullum maintains that drug use is a matter of behavior, not addiction. Classifying behavior as socially unacceptable does not prove that it is a disease.

Is drug addiction caused by an illness or disease, or is it caused by inappropriate behavioral patterns? This distinction is important because it has both legal and medical implications. Should people be held accountable for behaviors that stem from an illness over which they have no control? For example, if a person cannot help being an alcoholic and hurts or kills someone as a result of being drunk, should that person be treated or incarcerated? Likewise, if an individual's addiction is due to lack of self-control, rather than due to a disease, should taxpayer money go to pay for that person's treatment?

It can be argued that the disease concept of drug addiction legitimizes or excuses behaviors. If addiction is an illness, then blame for poor behavior can be shifted to the disease and away from the individual. Moreover, if drug addiction is incurable, can people ever be held responsible for their behavior?

Lisa Legrand, William Iacono, and Matt McGue contend that addiction is caused by heredity, biochemistry, and environment influences. If drug addiction is the result of factors beyond the individual's control, then one should not be held responsible for one's behavior and that loss of control is not inevitable. Critics assert that many individuals have the ability of alcoholics to stop their abuse of drugs. For example, it has been shown that many cocaine and heroin users do not lose control while using these drugs. In their study of U.S. service personnel in Vietnam, epidemiologist Lee N. Robins and colleagues showed that most of the soldiers who used narcotics regularly during the war did not continue using them once they returned home. Many service personnel in Vietnam reportedly used drugs because they were in a situation they did not want to be in. Additionally, without the support of loved ones and society's constraints, they were freer to gravitate to behaviors that would not be tolerated by their families and friends.

Attitudes toward treating drug abuse are affected by whether it is perceived as an illness or as an act of free will. The disease concept implies that one needs help in overcoming addiction. By calling drug addiction a medical condition, the body is viewed as a machine that needs fixing; character and will become secondary. Also, by calling addiction a disease, the role of society in causing drug addiction is left unexplored. What roles do poverty, crime, unemployment, inadequate health care, and poor education have in drug addiction?

Jacob Sullum argues that the addictive qualities of drugs, especially heroin, are exaggerated. By claiming that certain drugs are highly addictive, it is easier to demonize those drugs and the people who use them. Sullum maintains that legal drugs such as alcohol and tobacco result in higher rates of addiction. Sullum also cites studies in which a number of heroin users are weekend users. This dispels the notion that heroin use always causes addiction.

According to the disease perspective, an important step for addicts to take in order to benefit from treatment is to admit that they are powerless against their addiction. They need to acknowledge that their drug addiction controls them and that drug addiction is a lifelong problem. The implication of this view is that addicts are never cured. Addicts must therefore abstain from drugs for their entire lives.

Is addiction caused by psychological or biological factors? Can drugs produce changes in the brain that result in drug addiction? How much control do drug addicts have over their use of drugs? In the following selections, Legrand, Iacono, and McGue argue that addiction is a disease while Sullum contends that the concept of drug addiction is a social construct, not based in science.

YES ⤶

Lisa N. LeGrand, William G. Iacono, and Matt McGue

Predicting Addiction

In 1994, the 45-year-old daughter of Senator and former presidential nominee George McGovern froze to death outside a bar in Madison, Wisconsin. Terry McGovern's death followed a night of heavy drinking and a lifetime of battling alcohol addiction. The Senator's middle child had been talented and charismatic, but also rebellious. She started drinking at 13, became pregnant at 15 and experimented with marijuana and LSD in high school. She was sober during much of her 30s but eventually relapsed. By the time she died, Terry had been through many treatment programs and more than 60 detoxifications.

Her story is not unique. Even with strong family support, failure to overcome an addiction is common. Success rates vary by treatment type, severity of the condition and the criteria for success. But typically, fewer than a third of alcoholics are recovered a year or two after treatment. Thus, addiction may be thought of as a chronic, relapsing illness. Like other serious psychiatric conditions, it can cause a lifetime of recurrent episodes and treatments.

Given these somber prospects, the best strategy for fighting addiction may be to prevent it in the first place. But warning young people about the dangers of addiction carries little force when many adults drink openly without apparent consequences. Would specific warnings for individuals with a strong genetic vulnerability to alcoholism be more effective? Senator McGovern became convinced that his daughter possessed such a vulnerability, as other family members also struggled with dependency. Perhaps Terry would have taken a different approach to alcohol, or avoided it altogether, if she had known that something about her biology made drinking particularly dangerous for her.

How can we identify people—at a young enough age to intervene—who have a high, inherent risk of becoming addicted? Does unusual susceptibility arise from differences at the biochemical level? And what social or environmental factors might tip the scales for kids at greatest risk? That is, what kind of parenting, or peer group, or neighborhood conditions might encourage—or inhibit—the expression of "addiction" genes? These questions are the focus of our research.

From *American Scientist*, vol. 93, March-April 2005, pp. 140–147. Copyright © 2005 by American Scientist. Reprinted by permission.

Minnesota Twins

We have been able to answer some of these questions by examining the life histories of almost 1,400 pairs of twins. Our study of addictive behavior is part of a larger project, the Minnesota Center for Twin Family Research (MCTFR), which has studied the health and development of twins from their pre-teen years through adolescence and into adulthood. Beginning at age 11 (or 17 for a second group), the participants and their parents cooperated with a barrage of questionnaires, interviews, brainwave analyses and blood tests every three years. The twin cohorts are now 23 and 29, respectively, so we have been able to observe them as children before exposure to addictive substances, as teenagers who were often experimenting and as young adults who had passed through the stage of greatest risk for addiction.

Studies of twins are particularly useful for analyzing the origins of a behavior like addiction. Our twin pairs have grown up in the same family environment but have different degrees of genetic similarity. Monozygotic or identical twins have identical genes, but dizygotic or fraternal twins share on average only half of their segregating genes. If the two types of twins are equally similar for a trait, we know that genes are unimportant for that trait. But when monozygotic twins are more similar than dizygotic twins, we conclude that genes have an effect.

This article reviews some of what we know about the development of addiction, including some recent findings from the MCTFR about early substance abuse. Several established markers can predict later addiction and, together with recent research, suggest a provocative conclusion: that addiction may be only one of many related behaviors that stem from the same genetic root. In other words, much of the heritable risk may be nonspecific. Instead, what is passed from parent to child is a tendency toward a group of behaviors, of which addiction is only one of several possible outcomes.

Markers of Risk

Personality

Psychologists can distinguish at-risk youth by their personality, family history, brainwave patterns and behavior. For example, certain personality traits do not distribute equally among addicts and nonaddicts: The addiction vulnerable tend to be more impulsive, unruly and easily bored. They're generally outgoing, sociable, expressive and rebellious, and they enjoy taking risks. They are more likely to question authority and challenge tradition.

Some addicts defy these categories, and having a certain personality type doesn't doom one to addiction. But such traits do place individuals at elevated risk. For reasons not completely understood, they accompany addiction much more frequently than the traits of being shy, cautious and conventional.

Although these characteristics do not directly cause addiction, neither are they simply the consequences of addiction. In fact, teachers' impressions of their 11-year-old students predicted alcohol problems 16 years later, according to a Swedish study led by C. Robert Cloninger (now at Washington University in St. Louis). Boys low in "harm avoidance" (ones who lacked fear and inhibition) and high in "novelty seeking" (in other words, impulsive, disorderly, easily bored and distracted) were almost 20 times more likely to have future alcohol problems than boys without these traits. Other studies of children in separate countries at different ages confirm that personality is predictive.

Family Background

Having a parent with a substance-abuse disorder is another established predictor of a child's future addiction. One recent and intriguing discovery from the MCTFR is that assessing this risk can be surprisingly straightforward, particularly for alcoholism. The father's answer to "What is the largest amount of alcohol you ever consumed in a 24-hour period?" is highly informative: The greater the amount, the greater his children's risk. More than 24 drinks in 24 hours places his children in an especially risky category.

How can one simple question be so predictive? Its answer is laden with information, including tolerance—the ability, typically developed over many drinking episodes, to consume larger quantities of alcohol before becoming intoxicated—and the loss of control that mark problematic drinking. It is also possible that a father who equivocates on other questions that can formally diagnose alcoholism—such as whether he has been unsuccessful at cutting down on his drinking or whether his drinking has affected family and work—may give a frank answer to this question. In our society, episodes of binge drinking, of being able to "hold your liquor," are sometimes a source of male pride.

Brainwaves

A third predictor comes directly from the brain itself. By using scalp electrodes to detect the electrical signals of groups of neurons, we can record characteristic patterns of brain activity generated by specific visual stimuli. In the complex squiggle of evoked brainwaves, the relative size of one peak, called P300, indicates addiction risk. Having a smaller P300 at age 17 predicts the development of an alcohol or drug problem by age 20. Prior differences in consumption don't explain this observation, as the reduced- amplitude P300 (P3-AR) is not a consequence of alcohol or drug ingestion. Rather, genes strongly influence this trait: P3-AR is often detectable in the children of fathers with substance-use disorders even before these problems emerge in the offspring. The physiological nature of P300 makes it an especially interesting marker, as it may originate from "addiction" genes more directly than any behavior.

Precocious Experimentation

Lastly, at-risk youth are distinguished by the young age at which they first try alcohol without parental permission. Although the vast majority of people try alcohol at some point during their life, it's relatively unusual to try alcohol *before* the age of 15. In the MCTFR sample of over 2,600 parents who had tried alcohol, only 12 percent of the mothers and 22 percent of the fathers did so before the age of 15. In this subset, 52 percent of the men and 25 percent of the women were alcoholics. For parents who first tried alcohol after age 19, the comparable rates were 13 percent and 2 percent, respectively. So, what distinguishes alcoholism risk is not *whether* a person tries alcohol during their teen years, but *when* they try it.

In light of these data, we cannot regard very early experimentation with alcohol as simply a normal rite of passage. Moreover, drinking at a young age often co-occurs with sex, the use of tobacco and illicit drugs, and rule-breaking behaviors. This precocious experimentation could indicate that the individual has inherited the type of freewheeling, impulsive personality that elevates the risk of addiction. But early experimentation may be a problem all by itself. It, and the behaviors that tend to co-occur with it, decrease the likelihood of sobriety-encouraging experiences and increase the chances of mixing with troubled peers and clashing with authority figures.

A General, Inherited Risk

Some of these hallmarks of risk are unsurprising. Most people know that addiction runs in families, and they may intuit that certain brain functions could differ in addiction-prone individuals. But how can people's gregariousness or their loathing of dull tasks or the age at which they first had sex show a vulnerability to addiction? The answer seems to be that although addiction risk is strongly heritable, the inheritance is fairly nonspecific. The inherited risk corresponds to a certain temperament or disposition that goes along with so-called *externalizing* tendencies. Addiction is only one of several ways this disposition may be expressed.

Externalizing behaviors include substance abuse, but also "acting out" and other indicators of behavioral under control or disinhibition. In childhood, externalizing traits include hyperactivity, "oppositionality" (negative and defiant behavior) and antisocial behavior, which breaks institutional and social rules. An antisocial child may lie, get in fights, steal, vandalize or skip school. In adulthood, externalizing tendencies may lead to a personality marked by low constraint, drug or alcohol abuse, and antisocial behaviors, including irresponsibility, dishonesty, impulsivity, lawlessness and aggression. Antisociality, like most traits, falls on a continuum. A moderately antisocial person may never intentionally hurt someone, but he might make impulsive decisions, take physical and financial risks or shirk responsibility.

It's worth reiterating that an externalizing disposition simply increases the risk of demonstrating problematic behavior. An individual with such tendencies could express them in ways that are not harmful to themselves and actually help society: Fire fighters, rescue workers, test pilots, surgeons and entrepreneurs are often gregarious, relatively uninhibited sensation-seekers—that is, moderate externalizers.

So a genetic inclination for externalizing can lead to addiction, hyperactivity, acting-out behavior, criminality, a sensation-seeking personality or *all* of these things. Although the contents of this list may seem haphazard, psychologists combine them into a single group because they all stem from the same *latent factor*. Latent factors are hypothesized constructs that help explain the observed correlations between various traits or behaviors.

For example, grades in school generally correlate with one another. People who do well in English tend to get good marks in art history, algebra and geology. Why? Because academic ability affects grades, regardless of the subject matter. In statistical lingo, academic ability is the "general, latent factor" and the course grades are the "observed indicators" of that factor. Academic ability is latent because it is not directly measured; rather, the statistician concludes that it exists and causes the grades to vary systematically between people.

Statistical analyses consistently show that externalizing is a general, latent factor—a common denominator—for a suite of behaviors that includes addiction. Furthermore, the various markers of risk support this conclusion: Childhood characteristics that indicate later problems with alcohol also point to the full spectrum of externalizing behaviors and traits. Thus, drinking alcohol before 15 doesn't just predict future alcohol and drug problems, but also future antisocial behavior. A parent with a history of excessive binge drinking is apt to have children not only with substance-use problems, but with behavioral problems as well. And a reduced-amplitude P300 not only appears in children with a familial risk for alcoholism, but in kids with a familial risk for hyperactivity, antisocial behavior or illicit drug disorders.

The associations between externalizing behaviors aren't surprising to clinicians. Comorbidity—the increased chance of having other disorders if you have one of them—is the norm, not the exception, for individuals and families. A father with a cocaine habit is more likely to find that his daughter is getting into trouble for stealing or breaking school rules. At first glance, the child's behavioral problems look like products of the stress, conflict and dysfunction that go with having an addict in the family. These are certainly aggravating factors. However, the familial and genetically informative MCTFR data have allowed us to piece together a more precise explanation.

Environment has a strong influence on a child's behavior—living with an addict is rife with challenges—but genes also play a substantial role. Estimates of the genetic effect on externalizing behaviors vary by indicator and age, but among older adolescents and adults, well over half of the differences between people's externalizing tendencies result from inheriting different genes.

Our analysis of the MCTFR data indicates that children inherit the general, latent factor of externalizing rather than specific behavioral factors. Thus, an antisocial mother does not pass on genes that code simply for antisocial behavior, but they do confer vulnerability to a range of adolescent disorders and behaviors. Instead of encounters with the law, her adolescent son may have problems with alcohol or drugs. The outcomes are different, but the same genes—expressed differently under different environmental conditions—predispose them both.

The Role of the Environment

Even traits with a strong genetic component may be influenced by environmental factors. Monozygotic twins exemplify this principle. Despite their matching DNA, their height, need for glasses, disease susceptibility or personality (just to name a few) may differ.

When one member of a monozygotic pair is alcoholic, the likelihood of alcoholism in the other is only about 50 percent. The high heritability of externalizing behaviors suggests that the second twin, if not alcoholic, may be antisocial or dependent on another substance. But sometimes the second twin is problem free. DNA is never destiny.

Behavioral geneticists have worked to quantify the role of the environment in addiction, but as a group we have done much less to specify it. Although we know that 50 percent of the variance in alcohol dependence comes from the environment, we are still in the early stages of determining what those environmental factors are. This ignorance may seem surprising, as scientists have spent decades identifying the environmental precursors to addiction and antisocial behavior. But only a small percentage of that research incorporated genetic controls.

Instead, many studies simply related environmental variation to children's eventual problems or accomplishments. A classic example of this failure to consider genetic influence is the repeated observation that children who grow up with lots of books in their home tend to do better in school. But concluding that books create an academic child assumes (falsely) that children are born randomly into families—that parent-child resemblance is purely social. Of course, parents actually contribute to their children's environment *and* their genes. Moreover, parents tend to provide environments that complement their children's genotypes: Smart parents often deliver both "smart" genes and an enriched environment. Athletic parents usually provide "athletic" genes and many opportunities to express them. And, unfortunately, parents with addiction problems tend to provide a genetic vulnerability coupled with a home in which alcohol or drugs are available and abusing them is normal.

To understand the true experiential origins of a behavior, one must first disentangle the influence of genes. By using genetically informative samples, we can subtract genetic influences and conclude with greater confidence that a particular environmental factor affects behavior. Using this approach, our data suggest that deviant peers and poor parent-child relationships exert true environmental influences that promote substance use and externalizing behaviors during early adolescence.

When considering the effect of environment on behavior, or any complex trait, it's helpful to imagine a continuum of liability. Inherited vulnerability determines where a person begins on the continuum (high versus low risk). From that point, psychosocial or environmental stressors such as peer pressure or excessive conflict with parents can push an individual along the continuum and over a disease threshold.

However, sometimes the environment actually modifies gene expression. In other words, the relative influence of genes on a behavior can vary by setting. We see this context-dependent gene expression in recent, unpublished work comparing study participants from rural areas (population less than 10,000) with those from more urban settings. Within cities of 10,000 or more, genes substantially influence which adolescents use illicit substances or show other aspects of the externalizing continuum—just as earlier research indicated. But in very rural areas, environmental (rather than genetic) factors overwhelmingly account for differences in externalizing behavior.

One way to interpret this finding is that urban environments, with their wider variety of social niches, allow for a more complete expression of genetically influenced traits. Whether a person's genes nudge her to substance use and rule-breaking, or abstinence and obedience, the city may offer more opportunities to follow those urges. At the same time, finite social prospects in the country may allow more rural parents to monitor and control their adolescents' activities and peer-group selection, thereby minimizing the impact of genes. This rural-urban difference is especially interesting because it represents a gene-by-environment interaction. The genes that are important determinants of behavior in one group of people are just not as important in another.

The Future of Addiction Research

This complex interplay of genes and environments makes progress slow. But investigators have the data and statistical tools to answer many important addiction-related questions. Moreover, the tempo of discovery will increase with advances in molecular genetics.

In the last fifteen years, geneticists have identified a handful of specific genes related to alcohol metabolism and synapse function that occur more often in alcoholics. But the task of accumulating the entire list of contributing genes is daunting. Many genes influence behavior, and the relative importance of a single gene may differ across ethnic or racial populations. As a result, alcoholism-associated genes in one population may not exert a measurable influence in a different group, even in well-controlled studies. There are also different pathways to addiction, and some people's alcoholism may be more environmental than genetic in origin. Consequently, not only is any one gene apt to have small effects on behavior, but that gene may be absent in a substantial number of addicts.

Nonetheless, some day scientists should be able to estimate risk by reading the sequence of a person's DNA. Setting aside the possibility of a futuristic dystopia, this advance will usher in a new type of psychology. Investigators will be able to observe those individuals with especially high (or low) genetic risks for externalizing as they respond, over a lifetime, to different types of environmental stressors.

This type of research is already beginning. Avshalom Caspi, now at the University of Wisconsin, and his colleagues divided a large group of males from New Zealand based on the expression level of a gene that encodes a neurotransmitter-metabolizing enzyme, monoamine oxidase A or MAOA. In combination with the life histories of these men, the investigators demonstrated that the consequences of an abusive home varied by genotype. The gene associated with high levels of MAOA was protective—those men were less likely to show antisocial behaviors after childhood maltreatment than the low-MAOA group.

Further advances in molecular genetics will bring opportunities for more studies of this type. When investigators can accurately rank experimental participants by their genetic liability to externalizing, they will gain insight into the complexities of gene-environment interplay and answer several intriguing questions: What type of family environments are most at-risk children born into? When children with different genetic risks grow up in the same family, do they create unique environments by seeking distinct friends and experiences? Do they elicit different parenting styles from the same parents? Could a low-risk sibling keep a high-risk child from trouble if they share a close friendship? Is one type of psychosocial stressor more apt to lead to substance use while another leads to antisocial behavior?

Molecular genetics will eventually deepen our understanding of the biochemistry and biosocial genesis of addiction. In the interim, quantitative geneticists such as ourselves continue to characterize the development of behavior in ways that will assist molecular geneticists in their work. For example, if there is genetic overlap between alcoholism, drug dependence and antisocial behavior—as the MCTFR data suggest—then it may help to examine extreme externalizers, rather than simply alcoholics, when searching for the genes that produce alcoholism vulnerability.

Much Left to Learn

Although the MCTFR data have resolved some addiction-related questions, many others remain, and our team has just begun to scratch the surface of possible research. Our work with teenagers indicates that externalizing is a key factor in early-onset substance-use problems, but the path to later-life addiction may be distinct. Some evidence suggests that genes play a lesser role in later-onset addiction. Moreover, the markers of risk may vary. Being prone to worry, becoming upset easily and tending toward negative moods may, with age, become more important indicators. We don't yet know. However, the MCTFR continues to gather information about its participants as they approach their 30s, and we hope to keep following this group into their 40s and beyond.

Meanwhile, the evidence suggests that for early-onset addiction, most relevant genes are not specific to alcoholism or drug dependence. Instead, the same genes predispose an overlapping set of disorders within the externalizing spectrum. This conclusion has significant implications for prevention: Some impulsive risk-takers, frequent rule-breakers and oppositional children may be just as much at risk as early users.

At the same time, many kids with a genetic risk for externalizing don't seem to require any sort of special intervention; as it is, they turn out just fine. DNA may nudge someone in a certain direction, but it doesn't force them to go there.

Bibliography

Burt, S. A., M. McGue, R. F. Krueger and W. G. Iacono. 2005. How are parent-child conflict and childhood externalizing symptoms related over time? Results from a genetically informative cross-tagged study. *Development and Psychopathology* 17:1–21.

Caspi, A., J. McClay, T. E. Moffitt, J. Mill, J. Martin, I. W. Craig, A. Taylor and R. Poulton. 2002. Role of genotype in the cycle of violence in maltreated children. *Science* 297:851–854.

Cloninger, C. R., S. Sigvardsson and M. Bohman. 1988. Childhood personality predicts alcohol abuse in young adults. *Alcoholism: Clinical and Experimental Research* 12:494–505.

Hicks, B. M., R. F. Krueger, W. G. Iacono, M. McGue and C. J. Patrick. 2004. Family transmission and heritability of externalizing disorders: A twin-family study. *Archives of General Psychiatry* 61:922.–928.

Iacono, W. G., S. M. Malone and M. McGue. 2003. Substance use disorders, externalizing psychopathology, and P300 event- related potential amplitude. *International Journal of Psychophysiology* 48:147–178.

Krueger, R. F., B. M. Hicks, C. J. Patrick, S. R. Carlson, W. G. Iacono and M. McGue. 2002. Etiologic connections among substance dependence, antisocial behavior, and personality: Modeling the externalizing spectrum. *Journal of Abnormal Psychology* 111:411–424.

Malone, S. M., W. G. Iacono and M. McGue. 2002. Drinks of the father: Father's maximum number of drinks consumed predicts externalizing disorders, substance use, and substance use disorders in preadolescent and adolescent offspring. *Alcoholism: Clinical and Experimental Research* 26:1823–1832.

McGovern, G. 1996. *Terry: My Daughter's Life-and-Death Struggle With Alcoholism.* New York: Random House.

McGue, M., W. G. Iacono, L. N. Legrand, S. Malone and I. Elkins. 2001. The origins and consequences of age at first drink. I. Associations with substance-abuse disorders, disinhibitory behavior and psychopathology, and P3 amplitude. *Alcoholism: Clinical and Experimental Research* 25:1156–1165.

Porjesz, B., and H. Begleiter. 2003. Alcoholism and human electrophysiology. *Alcohol Research & Health* 27:153–160.

Turkheimer, E., H. H. Goldsmith and I.I. Gottesman. 1995. Some conceptual deficiencies in "developmental" behavioral genetics: Comment. *Human Development* 38:142–153.

Walden, B., M. McGue, W. G. Iacono, S. A. Burt and I. Elkins. 2004. Identifying shared environmental contributions to early substance use: The respective roles of peers and parents. *Journal of Abnormal Psychology* 113:440–450.

Jacob Sullum

H: The Surprising Truth About Heroin and Addiction

In 1992, *The New York Times* carried a front-page story about a successful businessman who happened to be a regular heroin user. It began: "He is an executive in a company in New York, lives in a condo on the Upper East Side of Manhattan, drives an expensive car, plays tennis in the Hamptons and vacations with his wife in Europe and the Caribbean. But unknown to office colleagues, friends, and most of his family, the man is also a longtime heroin user. He says he finds heroin relaxing and pleasurable and has seen no reason to stop using it until the woman he recently married insisted that he do so. "The drug is an enhancement of my life," he said. "I see it as similar to a guy coming home and having a drink of alcohol. Only alcohol has never done it for me."

The Times noted that "nearly everything about the 44-year-old executive . . . seems to fly in the face of widely held perceptions about heroin users." The reporter who wrote the story and his editors seemed uncomfortable with contradicting official anti-drug propaganda, which depicts heroin use as incompatible with a satisfying, productive life. The headline read, "Executive's Secret Struggle With Heroin's Powerful Grip," which sounds more like a cautionary tale than a success story. And *The Times* hastened to add that heroin users "are flirting with disaster." It conceded that "heroin does not damage the organs as, for instance, heavy alcohol use does." But it cited the risk of arrest, overdose, AIDS, and hepatitis—without noting that all of these risks are created or exacerbated by prohibition.

The general thrust of the piece was: Here is a privileged man who is tempting fate by messing around with a very dangerous drug. He may have escaped disaster so far, but unless he quits he will probably end up dead or in prison.

That is not the way the businessman saw his situation. He said he had decided to give up heroin only because his wife did not approve of the habit. "In my heart," he said, "I really don't feel there's anything wrong with using heroin. But there doesn't seem to be any way in the world I can persuade my wife to grant me this space in our relationship. I don't want to lose her, so I'm making this effort."

From Reason, vol. 35, issue 12, June 2003, pp. 32–40. Copyright © 2003 by Reason Foundation. Reprinted by permission.

Judging from the "widely held perceptions about heroin users" mentioned by *The Times*, that effort was bound to fail. The conventional view of heroin, which powerfully shapes the popular understanding of addiction, is nicely summed up in the journalist Martin Booth's 1996 history of opium. "Addiction is the compulsive taking of drugs which have such a hold over the addict he or she cannot stop using them without suffering severe symptoms and even death," he writes. "Opiate dependence . . . is as fundamental to an addict's existence as food and water, a physio-chemical fact: an addict's body is chemically reliant upon its drug for opiates actually alter the body's chemistry so it cannot function properly without being periodically primed. A hunger for the drug forms when the quantity in the bloodstream falls below a certain level. . . . Fail to feed the body and it deteriorates and may die from drug starvation." Booth also declares that "everyone . . . is a potential addict"; that "addiction can start with the very first dose"; and that "with continued use addiction is a certainty."

Booth's description is wrong or grossly misleading in every particular. To understand why is to recognize the fallacies underlying a reductionist, drug-centered view of addiction in which chemicals force themselves on people—a view that skeptics such as the maverick psychiatrist Thomas Szasz and the psychologist Stanton Peele have long questioned. The idea that a drug can compel the person who consumes it to continue consuming it is one of the most important beliefs underlying the war on drugs, because this power makes possible all the other evils to which drug use supposedly leads.

When Martin Booth tells us that anyone can be addicted to heroin, that it may take just one dose, and that it will certainly happen to you if you're foolish enough to repeat the experiment, he is drawing on a long tradition of anti-drug propaganda. As the sociologist Harry G. Levine has shown, the original model for such warnings was not heroin or opium but alcohol. "The idea that drugs are inherently addicting," Levine wrote in 1978, "was first systematically worked out for alcohol and then extended to other substances. Long before opium was popularly accepted as addicting, alcohol was so regarded." The dry crusaders of the 19th and early 20th centuries taught that every tippler was a potential drunkard, that a glass of beer was the first step on the road to ruin, and that repeated use of distilled spirits made addiction virtually inevitable. Today, when a kitchen wrecked by a skinny model wielding a frying pan is supposed to symbolize the havoc caused by a snort of heroin, similar assumptions about opiates are even more widely held, and they likewise are based more on faith than facts.

Withdrawal Penalty

Beginning early in the 20th century, Stanton Peele notes, heroin "came to be seen in American society as the nonpareil drug of addiction—as leading inescapably from even the most casual contact to an intractable dependence, withdrawal from which was traumatic and unthinkable for the addict." According to this view, reflected in Booth's gloss and other popular portrayals, the potentially fatal agony of withdrawal is the gun that heroin holds to the addict's head. These accounts greatly exaggerate both the severity and the importance of withdrawal symptoms.

Heroin addicts who abruptly stop using the drug commonly report flu-like symptoms, which may include chills, sweating, runny nose and eyes, muscular aches, stomach cramps, nausea, diarrhea, or headaches. While certainly unpleasant, the experience is not life threatening. Indeed, addicts who have developed tolerance (needing higher doses to achieve the same effect) often voluntarily undergo withdrawal so they can begin using heroin again at a lower dose, thereby reducing the cost of their habit. Another sign that fear of withdrawal symptoms is not the essence of addiction is the fact that heroin users commonly drift in and out of their habits, going through periods of abstinence and returning to the drug long after any physical discomfort has faded away. Indeed, the observation that detoxification is not tantamount to overcoming an addiction, that addicts typically will try repeatedly before successfully kicking the habit, is a commonplace of drug treatment.

More evidence that withdrawal has been overemphasized as a motivation for using opiates comes from patients who take narcotic painkillers over extended periods of time. Like heroin addicts, they develop "physical dependence" and experience withdrawal symptoms when they stop taking the drugs. But studies conducted during the last two decades have consistently found that patients in pain who receive opioids (opiates or synthetics with similar effects) rarely become addicted.

Pain experts emphasize that physical dependence should not be confused with addiction, which requires a psychological component: a persistent desire to use the substance for its mood-altering effects. Critics have long complained that unreasonable fears about narcotic addiction discourage adequate pain treatment. In 1989, Charles Schuster, then director of the National Institute on Drug Abuse, confessed, "We have been so effective in warning the medical establishment and the public in general about the inappropriate use of opiates that we have endowed these drugs with a mysterious power to enslave that is overrated."

Although popular perceptions lag behind, the point made by pain specialists—that "physical dependence" is not the same as addiction—is now widely accepted by professionals who deal with drug problems. But under the heroin-based model that prevailed until the 1970s, tolerance and withdrawal symptoms were considered the hallmarks of addiction. By this standard, drugs such as nicotine and cocaine were not truly addictive; they were merely "habituating." That distinction proved untenable, given the difficulty that people often had in giving up substances that were not considered addictive.

Having hijacked the term addiction, which in its original sense referred to any strong habit, psychiatrists ultimately abandoned it in favor of substance dependence. "The essential feature of Substance Dependence," according to the American Psychiatric Association, "is a cluster of cognitive, behavioral, and physiological symptoms indicating that the individual continues use of the substance despite significant substance-related problems. . . . Neither tolerance nor withdrawal is necessary or sufficient for a diagnosis of Substance Dependence." Instead, the condition is defined as "a maladaptive pattern of substance use" involving at least three of seven features. In addition to tolerance and withdrawal, these include using more of the drug than intended; trying unsuccessfully to cut back; spending a lot of time getting the drug, using it, or recovering from its effects; giving up or reducing important social, occupational, or recreational activities because of drug use; and continuing use even while recognizing drug-related psychological or physical problems.

One can quibble with these criteria, especially since they are meant to be applied not by the drug user himself but by a government-licensed expert with whose judgment he may disagree. The possibility of such a conflict is all the more troubling because the evaluation may be involuntary (the result of an arrest, for example) and may have implications for the drug user's freedom. More fundamentally, classifying substance dependence as a "mental disorder" to be treated by medical doctors suggests that drug abuse is a disease, something that happens to people rather than something that people do. Yet it is clear from the description that we are talking about a pattern of behavior. Addiction is not simply a matter of introducing a chemical into someone's body, even if it is done often enough to create tolerance and withdrawal symptoms. Conversely, someone who takes a steady dose of a drug and who can stop using it without physical distress may still be addicted to it.

Simply Irresistible?

Even if addiction is not a physical compulsion, perhaps some drug experiences are so alluring that people find it impossible to resist them. Certainly that is heroin's reputation, encapsulated in the title of a 1972 book: *It's So Good, Don't Even Try It Once.*

The fact that heroin use is so rare—involving, according to the government's data, something like 0.2 percent of the U.S. population in 2001—suggests that its appeal is much more limited than we've been led to believe. If heroin really is "so good," why does it have such a tiny share of the illegal drug market? Marijuana is more than 45 times as popular. The National Household Survey on Drug Abuse indicates that about 3 million Americans have used heroin in their lifetimes; of them, 15 percent had used it in the last year, 4 percent in the last month. These numbers suggest that the vast majority of heroin users either never become addicted or, if they do, manage to give the drug up. A survey of high school seniors found that 1 percent had used heroin in the previous year, while 0.1 percent had used it on 20 or more days in the previous month. Assuming that daily use is a reasonable proxy for opiate addiction, one in 10 of the students who had taken heroin in the last year might have qualified as addicts. These are not the sort of numbers you'd expect for a drug that's irresistible.

True, these surveys exclude certain groups in which heroin use is more common and in which a larger percentage of users probably could be described as addicts. The household survey misses people living on the street, in prisons, and in residential drug treatment programs, while the high school survey leaves out truants and dropouts. But even for the entire population of heroin users, the estimated addiction rates do not come close to matching heroin's reputation. A 1976 study by the drug researchers Leon G. Hunt and Carl D. Chambers estimated there were 3 or 4 million heroin users in the United States, perhaps 10 percent of them addicts. "Of all active heroin users," Hunt and Chambers wrote, "a large majority are not addicts: they are not physically or socially dysfunctional; they are not daily users and they do not seem to require treatment." A 1994 study based on data from the National Comorbidity Survey estimated that 23 percent of heroin users never experience substance dependence.

The comparable rate for alcohol in that study was 15 percent, which seems to support the idea that heroin is more addictive: A larger percentage of the people who try it become heavy users, even though it's harder to get. At the same time, the fact that using heroin is illegal, expensive, risky, inconvenient, and almost universally condemned means that the people who nevertheless choose to do it repeatedly will tend to differ from people who choose to drink. They will be especially attracted to heroin's effects, the associated lifestyle, or both. In other words, heroin users are a self-selected group, less representative of the general population than alcohol users are, and they may be more inclined from the outset to form strong attachments to the drug.

The same study found that 32 percent of tobacco users had experienced substance dependence. Figures like that one are the basis for the claim that nicotine is "more addictive than heroin." After all, cigarette smokers typically go through a pack or so a day, so they're under the influence of nicotine every waking moment. Heroin users typically do not use their drug even once a day. Smokers offended by this comparison are quick to point out that they function fine, meeting their responsibilities at work and homey despite their habit. This, they assume, is impossible for heroin users. Examples like the businessman described by *The New York Times* indicate otherwise.

Still, it's true that nicotine's psychoactive effects are easier to reconcile with the requirements of everyday life than heroin's are. Indeed, nicotine can enhance concentration and improve performance on certain tasks. So one important reason why most cigarette smokers consume their drug throughout the day is that they can do so without running into trouble. And because they're used to smoking in so many different settings, they may find nicotine harder to give up than a drug they use only with certain people in secret. In one survey, 57 percent of drug users entering a Canadian treatment program said giving up their problem substance (not necessarily heroin) would be easier than giving up cigarettes. In another survey, 36 heroin users entering treatment were asked to compare their strongest cigarette urge to their strongest heroin urge. Most said the heroin urge was stronger, but two said the cigarette urge was, and 11 rated the two urges about the same.

In a sense, nicotine's compatibility with a wide range of tasks makes it more addictive than alcohol or heroin. But this is not the sort of thing people usually have in mind when they worry about addiction. Indeed, if it weren't for the health effects of smoking (and the complaints of bystanders exposed to the smoke), nicotine addiction probably would be seen as no big deal, just as caffeine addiction is. As alternative sources of nicotine that do not involve smoking (gum, patches, inhalers, beverages, lozenges, oral snuff) become popular not just as aids in quitting but as long-term replacements, it will be interesting to see whether they will be socially accepted. Once the health risks are dramatically reduced or eliminated, will daily consumption of nicotine still be viewed as shameful and declasse, as a disease to be treated or a problem to be overcome? Perhaps so, if addiction per se is the issue. But not if it's the medical, social, and psychological consequences of addiction that really matter.

The Needle and the Damage Done

To a large extent, regular heroin use also can be separated from the terrible consequences that have come to be associated with it. Because of prohibition, users face the risk of arrest and imprisonment, the handicap of a criminal record, and the violence associated with the black market. The artificially high price of heroin, perhaps 40 or 50 times what it would otherwise cost, may lead to heavy debts, housing problems, poor nutrition, and theft. The inflated cost also encourages users to inject the drug, a more efficient but riskier mode of administration. The legal treatment of injection equipment, including restrictions on distribution and penalties for possession, encourages needle sharing, which spreads diseases such as AIDS and hepatitis. The unreliable quality and unpredictable purity associated with the black market can lead to poisoning and accidental overdoses.

Without prohibition, then, a daily heroin habit would be far less burdensome and hazardous. Heroin itself is much less likely to kill a user than the reckless combination of heroin with other depressants, such as alcohol or barbiturates. The federal government's Drug Abuse Warning Network counted 4,820 mentions of heroin or morphine (which are indistinguishable in the blood) by medical examiners in 1999. Only 438 of these deaths (9 percent) were listed as directly caused by an overdose of the opiate. Three-quarters of the deaths were caused by heroin/morphine in combination with other drugs. Provided the user avoids such mixtures, has access to a supply of reliable purity, and follows sanitary injection procedures, the health risks of long-term opiate consumption are minimal.

The comparison between heroin and nicotine is also instructive when it comes to the role of drug treatment. Although many smokers have a hard time quitting, those who succeed generally do so on their own. Surprisingly, the same maybe true of heroin addicts. In the early 1960s, based on records kept by the Federal Bureau of Narcotics, sociologist Charles Winick concluded that narcotic addicts tend to "mature out" of the habit in their 30s. He suggested that "addiction may be a self limiting process for perhaps two-thirds of addicts." Subsequent researchers have questioned Winick's assumptions, and other studies have come up with lower estimates. But it's clear that "natural recovery" is much more common than the public has been led to believe.

In a 1974 study of Vietnam veterans, only 12 percent of those who were addicted to heroin in Vietnam took up the habit again during the three years after their return to the United States. (This was not because they couldn't find heroin; half of them used it at least once after their return, generally without becoming addicted again.) Those who had undergone treatment (half of the group) were just as likely to be re-addicted as those who had not. Since those with stronger addictions were more likely to receive treatment, this does not necessarily mean that treatment was useless, but it clearly was not a prerequisite for giving up heroin.

Despite its reputation, then, heroin is neither irresistible nor inescapable. Only a very small share of the population ever uses it, and a large majority of those who do never become addicted. Even within the minority who develop a daily habit, most manage to stop using heroin, often without professional intervention. Yet heroin is still perceived as the paradigmatic voodoo drug, ineluctably turning its users into zombies who must obey its commands.

Heroin in Moderation

The idea that drugs cause addiction was rejected in the case of alcohol because it was so clearly at odds with everyday experience, which showed that the typical drinker was not an alcoholic. But what the psychologist Bruce Alexander calls "the myth of drug-induced addiction" is still widely accepted in the case of heroin—and, by extension, the drugs compared to it—because moderate opiate users are hard to find. That does not mean they don't exist; indeed, judging from the government's survey results, they are a lot more common than addicts. It's just that people who use opiates in a controlled way are inconspicuous by definition, and keen to remain so.

In the early 1960s, however, researchers began to tentatively identify users of heroin and other opiates who were not addicts. "Surprisingly enough," a Northwestern University psychiatrist wrote in 1961, "in some cases at least, narcotic use may be confined to weekends or parties and the users may be able to continue in gainful employment for some time. Although this pattern often deteriorates and the rate of use increases, several cases have been observed in which relatively gainful and steady employment has been maintained for two to three years while the user was on what might be called a regulated or controlled habit."

A few years later, Harvard psychiatrist Norman Zinberg and David C. Lewis, then a medical resident, described five categories of narcotic users, including "people who use narcotics regularly but who develop little or no tolerance for them and do not suffer withdrawal symptoms." They explained that "such people are usually able to work regularly and productively. They value the relaxation and the 'kick' obtained from the drug, but their fear of needing more and more of the drug to get the same kick causes them to impose rigorous controls on themselves."

The example offered by Zinberg and Lewis was a 47-year-old physician with a successful practice who had been injecting morphine four times a day, except weekends, for 12 years. He experienced modest discomfort on Saturdays and Sundays, when he abstained, but he stuck to his schedule and did not raise his dose except on occasions when he was especially busy or tense. Zinberg and Lewis's account suggests that morphine's main function for him was stress relief: "Somewhat facetiously, when describing his intolerance of people making emotional demands on him, he said that he took 1 shot for his patients, 1 for his mistress, 1 for his family and 1 to sleep. He expressed no guilt about his drug taking, and made it clear that he had no intention of stopping."

Zinberg eventually interviewed 61 controlled opiate users. His criteria excluded both dabblers (the largest group of people who have used heroin) and daily users. One subject was a 41-year-old carpenter who had used heroin on weekends for a decade. Married 16 years, he lived with his wife and three children in a middle-class suburb. Another was a 27-year-old college student studying special education. He had used heroin two or three times a month for three years, then once a week for a year. The controlled users said they liked "the 'rush' (glow or warmth), the sense of distance from their problems, and the tranquilizing powers of the drug." Opiate use was generally seen as a social activity, and it was often combined with other forms of recreation. Summing up the lessons he learned from his research, Zinberg emphasized the importance of self-imposed rules dictating when, where, and with whom the drug would be used. More broadly, he concluded that "set and setting"—expectations and environment—play crucial roles in shaping a drug user's experience.

Other researchers have reported similar findings. After interviewing 12 occasional heroin users in the early 1970s, a Harvard researcher concluded that "it seems possible for young people from a number of different backgrounds, family patterns, and educational abilities to use heroin occasionally without becoming addicted." The subjects typically took heroin with one or more friends, and the most frequently reported benefit was relaxation. One subject, a 23-year-old graduate student, said it was "like taking a vacation from yourself . . . When things get to you, it's a way of getting away without getting away." These occasional users were unanimous in rejecting addiction as inconsistent with their self-images. A 1983 British study of 51 opiate users likewise found that distaste for the junkie lifestyle was an important deterrent to excessive use.

While these studies show that controlled opiate use is possible, the 1974 Vietnam veterans study gives us some idea of how common it is. "Only one-quarter of those who used heroin in the last two years used it daily at all," the researchers reported. Likewise, only a quarter said they had felt dependent, and only a quarter said heroin use had interfered with their lives. Regular heroin use (more than once a week for more than a month) was associated with a significant increase in "social adjustment problems," but occasional use was not.

Many of these occasional users had been addicted in Vietnam, so they knew what it was like. Paradoxically, a drug's attractiveness, whether experienced directly or observed secondhand, can reinforce the user's determination to remain in control. (Presumably, that is the theory behind all the propaganda warning how wonderful certain drug experiences are, except that the aim of those messages is to stop people from experimenting at all.) A neuroscientist in his late 20s who smoked heroin a couple of times told me it was "nothing dramatic, just the feeling that everything was OK for about six hours, and I wasn't really motivated to do anything." Having observed several friends who were addicted to heroin at one time or another, he understood that the experience could be seductive, but "that kind of seduction . . . kind of repulsed me. That was exactly the kind of thing that I was trying to avoid in my life."

Similarly, a horticulturist in his 40s who first snorted heroin in the mid-1980s said, "It was too nice." As he described it, "you're sort of not awake and you're not asleep, and you feel sort of like a baby in the cradle, with no worries, just floating in a comfortable cocoon. That's an interesting place to be if you don't have anything else to do. That's Sunday-afternoon-on-the-couch material." He did have other things to do, and after that first experience he used heroin only "once in a blue moon." But he managed to incorporate the regular use of another opiate, morphine pills, into a busy, productive life. For years he had been taking them once a week, as a way of unwinding and relieving the aches and pains from the hard manual labor required by his landscaping business. "We use it as a reward system," he said. "On a Friday, if we've been working really hard and we're sore and it's available, it's a reward. It's like, 'We've worked hard today. We've earned our money, we paid our bills, but we're sore, so let's do this. It's medicine.' "

Better Homes & Gardens

Evelyn Schwartz learned to use heroin in a similar way: as a complement to rest and relaxation rather than a means of suppressing unpleasant emotions. A social worker in her 50s, she injected heroin every day for years but was using it intermittently when I interviewed her a few years ago. Schwartz (a pseudonym) originally became addicted after leaving home at 14 because of conflict with her mother. "As I felt more and more alienated from my family, more and more alone, more and more depressed," she said, "I started to use [heroin] not in a recreational fashion but as a coping mechanism, to get rid of feelings, to feel OK. . . . I was very unhappy . . . and just hopeless about life, and I was just trying to survive day by day for many years."

But after Schwartz found work that she loved and started feeling good about her life, she was able to use heroin in a different way. "I try not to use as a coping mechanism," she said. "I try very hard not to use when I'm miserable, because that's what gets me into trouble. It's set and setting. It's not the drug, because I can use this drug in a very controlled way, and I can also go out of control." To stay in control, "I try to use when I'm feeling good," such as on vacation with friends, listening to music, or before a walk on a beautiful spring day. "If I need to clean the house, I do a little heroin, and I can clean the house, and it just makes me feel so good."

Many people are shocked by the idea of using heroin so casually, which helps explain the controversy surrounding a 2001 BBC documentary that explored why people use drugs. "Heroin is my drug of choice over alcohol or cocaine," said one user interviewed for the program. "I take it at weekends in small doses, and do the gardening." It may be unconventional, but using heroin to enliven housework or gardening is surely wiser than using it to alleviate grief, dissatisfaction, or loneliness. It's when drugs are used for emotional management that a destructive habit is apt to develop.

Even daily opiate use is not necessarily inconsistent with a productive life. One famous example is the pioneering surgeon William Halsted, who led a brilliant career while secretly addicted to morphine. On a more modest level,

Schwartz said that even during her years as a self-described junkie she always held a job, always paid the rent, and was able to conceal her drug use from people who would have been alarmed by it. "I was always one of the best secretaries at work, and no one ever knew, because I learned how to titrate my doses," she said. She would generally take three or four doses a day: when she got up in the morning, at lunchtime, when she came home from work, and perhaps before going to sleep. The doses she took during the day were small enough so that she could get her work done. "Aside from the fact that I was a junkie," she said, "I was raised to be a really good girl and do what I'm supposed to do, and I did."

Schwartz, a warm, smart, hard-working woman, is quite different from the heroin users portrayed by government propaganda. Even when she was taking heroin every day, her worst crime was shoplifting a raincoat for a job interview. "I never robbed," she said. "I never did anything like that. I never hurt a human being. I could never do that. . . . I'm not going to hit anybody over the head. . . .I went sick a lot as a consequence. When other junkies would commit crimes, get money, and tighten up, I would be sick. Everyone used to say: 'You're terrible at being a junkie.'"

POSTSCRIPT

Should Drug Addiction Be Considered a Disease?

There is little debate that drug addiction is a major problem. Drug addiction wreaks havoc for society and ruins the lives of numerous individuals and people who care for them. Addressing the causes of drug addiction and what to do about people who become addicted is especially relevant. Views on whether or not drug addiction is a disease diverge. Because drug abuse can be viewed as a matter of free will or as a brain disorder, there are also different views on how society should deal with drug abusers. Should drug addicts be incarcerated or treated? Does it matter whether one is responsible for one's drug addiction?

One could argue that free will and the concept of a brain disorder both apply to drug addiction. What may start out as a matter of free will may turn into an illness. Likewise, drug use may start out as an occasional behavior that may become abusive. To illustrate this point, many people may use alcohol for recreational or social purposes, but their alcohol use may develop into a chronic, abusive pattern—one that the person cannot easily overcome. Initially, one can stop using alcohol without too much discomfort. As time passes, however, and alcohol consumption becomes more frequent and the amounts increase, stopping becomes difficult for many people. By its very definition, social drinkers can stop drinking at will. Alcoholics drink out of necessity.

Many people who use addictive drugs do not become dependent on them. Perhaps there are factors beyond free will and changes in the brain that account for these people to become dependent. Is it possible that social factors come into play? Can friends and colleagues and their attitudes about drugs influence whether a drug user becomes a drug abuser? In the final analysis, drug addiction may result from the interaction of numerous factors and is not, simply, a dichotomy between psychology and biology.

Stanton Peele, an outspoken critic of the disease concept, discusses this issue in "The Surprising Truth About Addiction," *Psychology Today* (May/June 2004). In his book *Addiction Is a Choice*, Jeffrey Schaler argues against addiction as a disease. The opposite position is discussed in "Addiction Is a Brain Disease," by Alan Leshner, Issues in Science and Technology (Spring 2001). Other articles that explores whether addiction is a matter of biology is "Addiction Is a Disease," by John Halpern, *Psychiatric Times* (October 1, 2002) and "Addiction and Responsibility," by Richard J. Bonnie, *Social Research* (Fall 2001).

Do Steroids Pose a Large Risk to Athletes and Others Who Use Them?

YES: Drug Enforcement Agency, from *Steroid Abuse in Today's Society* (U.S. Department of Justice, March 2004)

NO: Charles E. Yesalis, Michael S. Bahrke, and James E. Wright, from "Societal Alternatives," in Charles E. Yesalis, ed., *Anabolic Steroids in Sport and Exercise,* 2nd ed. (Human Kinetics, 2000)

ISSUE SUMMARY

YES: Officials from the Drug Enforcement Agency warn that anabolic steroids produce numerous harmful side effects, many of which are unknown to those people using steroids. With the exception of their masculinizing effects, the long-term consequences of anabolic steroid use have not been sufficiently studied. In addition, it is estimated that more than 1 million U.S. adults and a half million 8th and 10th grade students are using steroids.

NO: Pennsylvania State University professor Charles Yesalis and his colleagues feel that anabolic steroid use would be easier to regulate if users could acknowledge taking these drugs. Also, if individuals admitted to taking steroids, they could be approached regarding the harmful side effects of these drugs. The pharmaceutical quality of steroids received by athletes and others could be assured if they were legal. In the final analysis, Yesalis and others feel that legalizing steroids would end the hypocrisy associated with their use.

Anabolic steroids are synthetic derivatives of the male hormone testosterone. Although they have legitimate medical uses, steroids are used increasingly by individuals to build up muscle quickly and to increase personal strength. Concerns over the potential negative effects of steroid use seem to be justified: an estimated 1 million Americans, including a half million adolescents, have used illegally obtained steroids. Anabolic steroids users span all ethnic

119

groups, nationalities, and socioeconomic groups. The emphasis on winning has led many athletes to take risks with steroids that are potentially destructive. Despite the widespread belief that anabolic steroids are used primarily by athletes, up to one-third of users are nonathletes who use these drugs to improve their physiques and self-images.

The emphasis society places on winning and coming out on top results in many individuals willing to make sacrifices that may compromise their health. Some people will do anything for the sake of winning. The sports headlines in many newspapers mention how various athletes have used steroids. Drug testing is a major issue every time the Olympic competition is held. Besides the adverse physical consequences of steroids, there is the ethical question regarding fair play. Do athletes who use steroids have an unfair advantage? Should they be banned even if the side effects are not harmful? Do nonsteroid users feel pressured to use these drugs to keep up with the competition?

The short-term consequences of anabolic steroids are well documented. Possible short-term effects among men include testicular atrophy, sperm count reduction, impotency, baldness, difficulty urinating, and breast enlargement. Among women, some potential effects are deepening of the voice, breast reduction, menstrual irregularities, the growth of body hair, and clitoral enlargement. Both sexes may develop acne, swelling in the feet, reduced levels of high-density lipoproteins (the type of cholesterol that is good for the body), hypertension, and liver damage. Taking steroids as an adolescent will stunt one's growth. Also related to steroid use are psychological changes, including mood swings, paranoia, and violent behavior.

The short-term effects of steroid use have been researched thoroughly; however, their long-term effects have not been substantiated. The problem with identifying the long-term effects of anabolic steroids is the lack of systematic, long-term studies. Much of the information regarding the long-term effects of steroid use comes from personal reports, not well conducted, controlled studies. However, personal stories and anecdotal evidence are often accepted as fact.

The American Medical Association opposes stricter regulation of anabolic steroids on two grounds. First, anabolic steroids have been used medically to improve growth and development, for certain types of anemia, breast cancer, endometriosis, and osteoporosis. If stricter regulations are imposed, people who may benefit medically from these drugs will have more difficulty acquiring them. Second, it is highly unlikely that illicit use of these drugs will cease if they are banned. By maintaining legal access to these drugs, more studies regarding the long-term consequences of their use can be conducted.

In the following selections, the Drug Enforcement Agency contends that people who use anabolic steroids are risking their lives as well as their athletic careers and that stricter control of these substances is essential. Charles Yesalis, Michael S. Bahrke, and James E. Wright argue that the effects of steroids are overstated. They do not advocate the use of steroids, but they argue that better regulation of these drugs can occur if they are legal. Obtaining anabolic steroids through a legitimate pharmaceutical company, they conclude, is far better than buying steroids through a questionable source.

YES ⬅

Drug Enforcement Agency

Steroid Abuse in Today's Society

Once viewed as a problem strictly associated with body builders, fitness "buffs," and professional athletes, the abuse of steroids is prevalent in today's society. This is an alarming problem because of increased abuse over the years, and the ready availability of steroids and steroid related products. The problem is widespread throughout society including school-age children, athletes, fitness "buffs," business professionals, etc. The National Institute on Drug Abuse (NIDA) estimates that more than a half million 8th and 10th grade students are now using these dangerous drugs, and increasing numbers of high school seniors don't believe steroids are risky. Another study indicated that 1,084,000 Americans, or 0.5 percent of the adult population, said that they had used anabolic steroids. These are just a couple of examples of how widespread the problem has become.

Some people are taking dietary supplements that act as steroid precursors without any knowledge of the dangers associated with their abuse. Dietary supplements are sold in health food stores, over the Internet, and through mail order. People may believe that these supplements will produce the same desired effects as steroids, but at the same time avoid the medical consequences associated with using steroids. This belief is dangerous. Supplements may also have the same medical consequences as steroids.

This guide will help you understand why steroids are being abused, and how you can educate athletes and others about the dangers of these drugs. This guide will also discuss the dangerous medical effects of illegal use of steroids on health. The short-term adverse physical effects of anabolic steroid abuse are fairly well known. However, the long-term adverse physical effects of anabolic steroid abuse have not been studied, and as such, are not known. In addition, abuse of anabolic steroids may result in harmful side-effects as well as serious injury and death. The abuser in most cases is unaware of these hidden dangers. By working together we can greatly reduce the abuse of anabolic steroids and steroid related products. It is important to recognize this problem and take preventive measures to protect athletes and other users.

From "Steroid Abuse in Today's Society", U.S. Department of Justice—Drug Enforcement Administration, March 2004.

What Are Anabolic Steroids?

Anabolic steroids are synthetically produced variants of the naturally occurring male hormone testosterone. Both males and females have testosterone produced in their bodies: males in the testes, and females in the ovaries and other tissues. The full name for this class of drugs is **androgenic** (promoting masculine characteristics) **anabolic** (tissue building) **steroids** (the class of drugs). Some of the most abused steroids include Deca-Durabolin®, Durabolin®, Equipoise®, and Winstrol®. The common street (slang) names for anabolic steroids include arnolds, gym candy, pumpers, roids, stackers, weight trainers, and juice.

The two major effects of testosterone are an androgenic effect and an anabolic effect. The term androgenic refers to the physical changes experienced by a male during puberty, in the course of development to manhood. Androgenic effects would be similarly experienced in a female. This property is responsible for the majority of the side effects of steroid use. The term anabolic refers to promoting of anabolism, the actual building of tissues, mainly muscle, accomplished by the promotion of protein synthesis.

Why Are Steroids Abused?

Anabolic steroids are primarily used by bodybuilders, athletes, and fitness "buffs" who claim steroids give them a competitive advantage and/or improve their physical performance. Also, individuals in occupations requiring enhanced physical strength (body guards, construction workers, and law enforcement officers) are known to take these drugs. Steroids are purported to increase lean body mass, strength, and aggressiveness. Steroids are also believed to reduce recovery time between workouts, which makes it possible to train harder and thereby further improve strength and endurance. Some people who are not athletes also take steroids to increase their endurance, muscle size and strength, and reduce body fat, which they believe improves personal appearance.

Where Do You Get Steroids?

Doctors may prescribe steroids to patients for legitimate medical purposes such as loss of function of testicles, breast cancer, low red blood cell count, delayed puberty, and debilitated states resulting from surgery or sickness. Veterinarians administer steroids to animals (e.g., cats, cattle, dogs, and horses) for legitimate purposes such as to promote feed efficiency, and to improve weight gain, vigor, and hair coat. They are also used in veterinary practice to treat anemia and counteract tissue breakdown during illness and trauma. For purposes of illegal use there are several sources; the most common illegal source is from smuggling steroids into the United States from other countries such as Mexico and European countries. Smuggling from these areas is easier because a prescription is not required for the purchase of steroids. Less often, steroids found in the illicit market are diverted from legitimate sources (e.g., thefts or inappropriate prescribing) or produced in clandestine laboratories.

How Are Steroids Taken?

Anabolic steroids dispensed for legitimate medical purposes are administered several ways including intramuscular or subcutaneous injection, by mouth, pellet implantation under the skin and by application to the skin (e.g., gels or patches). These same routes are used for purposes of abusing steroids, with injection and oral administration being the most common. People abusing steroids may take anywhere from 1 to upwards of a 100 times normal therapeutic doses of anabolic steroids. This often includes taking two or more steroids concurrently, a practice called "stacking." Abusers will often alternate periods (6 to 16 weeks in length) of high-dose use of steroids with periods of low-dose use or no drug at all. This practice is called "cycling." Another mode of steroid use is called "pyramiding." With this method users slowly escalate steroid use (increasing the number of drugs used at one time and/or the dose and frequency of one or more steroids), reach a peak amount at mid-cycle, and gradually taper the dose toward the end of the cycle. . . . Please see "Appendix A" for additional information on patterns of anabolic steroid abuse.

Doses of anabolic steroids used will depend on the particular objectives of the steroid user. Athletes (middle or high school, college, professional, and Olympic) usually take steroids for a limited period of time to achieve a particular goal. Others such as bodybuilders, law enforcement officers, fitness buffs, and body guards usually take steroids for extended periods of time. The length of time that steroids stay in the body varies from a couple of days to more than 12 months. . . .

Physical & Psychological Dangers

There is increasing concern regarding possible serious health problems that are associated with the abuse of steroids, including both short-term and long-term side effects (see Appendix B). The short-term adverse physical effects of anabolic steroid abuse are fairly well known. Short-term side effects may include sexual and reproductive disorders, fluid retention, and severe acne. The short-term side effects in men are reversible with discontinuation of steroid use. Masculinizing effects seen in women, such as deepening of the voice, body and facial hair growth, enlarged clitoris, and baldness are not reversible. The long-term adverse physical effects of anabolic steroid abuse in men and in women, other than masculinizing effects, have not been studied, and as such, are not known. However, it is speculated that possible long-term effects may include adverse cardiovascular effects such as heart damage and stroke.

Possible Physical Side Effects Include the Following:

- High blood cholesterol levels—high blood cholesterol levels may lead to cardiovascular problems
- Severe acne
- Thinning of hair and baldness
- Fluid retention
- High blood pressure

- Liver disorders (liver damage and jaundice)
- Steroids can affect fetal development during pregnancy
- Risk of contracting HIV and other blood-borne diseases from sharing infected needles
- Sexual & reproductive disorders:

Males	Females
• Atrophy (wasting away of tissues or organs) of the testicles	• Menstrual irregularities
• Loss of sexual drive	• Infertility
• Diminished or decreased sperm production	• Masculinizing effects such as facial hair, diminished breast size, permanently deepened voice, and enlargement of the clitoris.
• Breast and prostate enlargement	
• Decreased hormone levels	
• Sterility	

Possible Psychological Disturbances Include the Following:

- Mood swings (including manic-like symptoms leading to violence)
- Impaired judgment (stemming from feelings of invincibility)
- Depression
- Nervousness
- Extreme irritability
- Delusions
- Hostility and aggression

Laws and Penalties for Anabolic Steroid Abuse

The Anabolic Steroids Control Act of 1990 placed anabolic steroids into Schedule III of the Controlled Substances Act (CSA) as of February 27, 1991. Under this legislation, anabolic steroids are defined as any drug or hormonal substance chemically and pharmacologically related to testosterone (other than estrogens, progestins, and corticosteroids) that promotes muscle growth.

The possession or sale of anabolic steroids without a valid prescription is illegal. Simple possession of illicitly obtained anabolic steroids carries a maximum penalty of one year in prison and a minimum $1,000 fine if this is an individual's first drug offense. The maximum penalty for trafficking is five years in prison and a fine of $250,000 if this is the individual's first felony drug offense. If this is the second felony drug offense, the maximum period of imprisonment and the maximum fine both double. While the above-listed penalties are for federal offenses, individual states have also implemented fines and penalties for illegal use of anabolic steroids. State executive offices have also recognized the seriousness of steroid abuse and other drugs of abuse in schools. For example, the State of Virginia enacted a new law that will allow student drug testing as a legitimate school drug prevention program. Some other states and individual school districts are considering implementing similar measures.

The International Olympic Committee (IOC), National Collegiate Athletic Association (NCAA), and many professional sports leagues (e.g., Major League Baseball, National Basketball Association, National Football League [NFL], and National Hockey League) have banned the use of steroids by athletes, both because of their potential dangerous side effects and because they give the user an unfair advantage. The IOC, NCAA, and NFL have also banned the use of steroid precursors (e.g., androstenedione) by athletes for the same reason steroids were banned. The IOC and professional sports leagues use urine testing to detect steroid use both in and out of competition.

Common Types of Steroids Abused

The illicit anabolic steroid market includes steroids that are not commercially available in the U.S. as well as those which are available. Steroids that are commercially available in the U.S. include fluoxymesterone (Halotestin®), methyltestosterone, nandrolone (Deca-Durabolin®, Durabolin®), oxandrolone (Oxandrin®), oxymetholone (Anadrol®), testosterone, and stanozolol (Winstrol®). Veterinary steroids that are commercially available in the U.S. include boldenone (Equipoise®), mibolerone, and trenbolone (Revalor®). Other steroids found on the illicit market that are not approved for use in the U.S. include ethylestrenol, methandriol, methenolone, and methandrostenolone.

Steroid Alternatives

A variety of nonsteroid drugs are commonly found within the illicit anabolic steroid market. These substances are primarily used for one or more of the following reasons: 1) to serve as an alternative to anabolic steroids; 2) to alleviate short-term adverse effects associated with anabolic steroid use; or 3) to mask anabolic steroid use. Examples of drugs serving as alternatives to anabolic steroids include clenbuterol, human growth hormone, insulin, insulin-like growth factor, and gamma-hydroxybutyrate (GHB). Examples of drugs used to treat the short-term adverse effects of anabolic steroid abuse are erythropoietin, human chorionic gonadotropin (HCG), and tamoxifen. Also, diuretics and uricosuric agents may be used to mask steroid use. The following chart illustrates how masking is accomplished:

Drug Group	Drug or Effect	How Drug Masks Steroid Use
Uricosuric agents	Probenecid	Decreases entry of steroids into the urine
Diuretics	Spironolactone, furosemide	Dilutes steroid concentration in the urine
Epitestosterone	Decreases testosterone to epitestosterone ratio	Reduces detection of testosterone usage

Over the last few years, a number of metabolic precursors to either testosterone or nandrolone have been marketed as dietary supplements in the U.S. These dietary supplements can be purchased in health food stores without a prescription. Some of these substances include androstenedione, androstenediol, norandrostenedione, norandrostenediol, and dehydroepiandtrosterone (DHEA), which can be converted into testosterone or a similar compound in the body. Whether they promote muscle growth is not known.

Are Anabolic Steroids Addictive?

An undetermined percentage of steroid abusers may become addicted to the drug, as evidenced by their continuing to take steroids in spite of physical problems, negative effects on social relations, or nervousness and irritability. Steroid users can experience withdrawal symptoms such as mood swings, fatigue, restlessness, and depression. Untreated, some depressive symptoms associated with anabolic steroid withdrawal have been known to persist for a year or more after the abuser stops taking the drugs.

How Widespread Is the Problem?

In today's society, people are willing to take great risk to excel in sports and perform their jobs better. Also, we live in a society where image is paramount to some people. Therefore, the popularity of performance-enhancing drugs such as anabolic steroids and anabolic steroid substitute products are the choice of some people to achieve these goals. Steroid abuse is still a problem despite the illegality of the drug and the banning of steroids by various sports authorities and sports governing bodies. The following examples indicate how diverse this problem is and how widespread it is across all age groups.

General Public

The Substance Abuse and Mental Health Services Administration's National Household Survey on Drug Abuse determined 1,084,000 Americans, or 0.5 percent of the adult population, said that they had used anabolic steroids. In the 18 to 34 age group, about 1 percent had ever used steroids.

School-Age Children

The "Monitoring the Future" study conducted in 2002 determined that since 1991 there has been a significant increase of steroid use by school-age children. This annual study, supported by the NIDA and conducted by the Institute for Social Research at the University of Michigan, surveys drug use among eighth, tenth, and twelfth graders in the United States. The first year data was collected on younger students was in 1991. Since 1991 there has been a significant increase in reported steroid use by teenagers. For all three grades, the 2002 levels represent a significant increase from 1991. The following chart illustrates the increase of steroid abuse among teenagers who reported using steroids at least once in their lifetime:

Percent of Students Reporting Steroid Use 1991–2002

Year	Eighth Grade	Tenth Grade	Twelfth Grade
1991	1.9%	1.8%	2.1%
1999	2.7%	2.7%	2.9%
2002	2.5%	3.5%	4.0%

The 2002 survey also indicated additional data related to steroid abuse by school-age children:

Percent of Students Reporting Steroid Use in 2002

Student Steroid Use	Eighth Grade	Tenth Grade	Twelfth Grade
Past month use	0.8%	1.0%	1.4%
Past year use	1.5%	2.2%	2.5%
Lifetime use	2.5%	3.5%	4.0%

In addition, the 2002 survey also determined how easy it was for school-aged children to obtain steroids. The survey indicated 22% of eighth graders, 33.2% of tenth graders, and 46.1% of twelfth graders surveyed in 2002 reported that steroids were "fairly easy" or "very easy" to obtain. More than 57% of twelfth graders surveyed in 2002 reported that using steroids was a "great risk." Also, another study indicated that steroids are used predominately by males. The survey determined the annual prevalence rates were two to four times as high among males as among females.

The "Monitoring the Future" study also determined that misuse and abuse of steroids is a major concern among school-aged children. Some of their findings are alarming and indicate a need for concern:

- A survey in 1999 determined that 479,000 students nationwide, or 2.9 percent, had used steroids by their senior year of high school.
- A survey in 2001 determined the percentage of 12th graders who believed that taking these drugs causes "great risk" to health declined from 68 percent to 62 percent.

The Center for Disease Control and Prevention (CDC) conducts the Youth Risk Behavior Surveillance Study, a survey of high school students across the United States. A survey conducted in 2001 indicated that 5% of all high school students reported lifetime use of steroid tablets/injections without a doctor's prescription. The survey also indicated that 5.8% of ninth graders, 4.9% of tenth graders, 4.3% of eleventh graders, and 4.3% of twelfth graders reported lifetime illegal use of steroids.

A majority of the studies performed on steroid abuse indicate males are twice as likely to abuse steroids as females.

Professional & College Sports

The NFL suspended running back Mike Cloud of the New England Patriots, defensive back Lee Flowers of the Denver Broncos, and Keith Newman of the Atlanta Falcons for violating the league's steroid policy. All three players tested positive for steroids and received a four game suspension without pay during the regular season. Three members of the Norwick University (located in Northfield, Vermont) football team were arrested for possession of 1,000 anabolic steroid tablets. During interviews with the three football players, they advised authorities that several other students and football players were using steroids. In professional baseball it is widely believed that steroid abuse is rampant. The news media has reported countless instances where players were taking steroids or other performance-enhancing drugs. There is also continuous debate about steroid testing and other drug testing in professional baseball.

Law Enforcement

Despite the illegality of steroids without a prescription and the known dangers of steroid abuse the problem continues to grow in the law enforcement community. In Minneapolis, a police sergeant was charged for possession of steroids. He admitted to being a user of steroids. In Miami, a police officer was arrested for the purchase of human growth hormone kits (HGH) from a dealer. The dealer had also informed Federal officials that the police officer had purchased anabolic steroids from him on four other occasions. In Tampa, a police officer was sentenced to 70 months in jail for exchanging 1,000 ecstasy tablets from police custody for steroids.

How Can We Curtail Their Abuse?

The most important aspect to curtailing abuse is education concerning dangerous and harmful side effects, and symptoms of abuse. Athletes and others must understand that they can excel in sports and have a great body without steroids. They should focus on getting proper diet, rest, and good overall mental and physical health. These things are all factors in how the body is shaped and conditioned. Millions of people have excelled in sports and look great without steroids. For additional information on steroids please see our website at www.DEAdiversion.usdoj.gov

Appendix A: Facts About Steroids and Athletic Performance Enhancement[1]

Patterns of Anabolic Steroid Abuse

Cycling

- Alternating periods of anabolic steroid use (on cycle) with periods of either no use or the use of low doses of anabolic steroids (off cycle)
- Cycling periods usually last from 6 to 16 weeks

- Anecdotal reasons for cycling
  - Reduction of tolerance development
  - Reduction of adverse effects
  - Prevent detection of steroid use
  - Insure peak performance during competition

Stacking

- Never done in medical practice
- Concurrent use of two or more steroids together
- Injectables may be stacked with oral preparations
- Short-acting steroids may be stacked with longer-acting steroids

Stacking the Pyramid

- A stacking regimen wherein there is a progressive increase in the doses and types of steroids used in the initial part of the cycle and a gradual reduction in the doses and types of steroids used in the latter half of the cycle
- This regimen is believed to give the optimal, desired steroid effects while decreasing the likelihood of detection of anabolic steroid use . . .

Doses of Anabolic Steroids Abused

Steroid abusers select doses depending upon their particular objectives. For athletes, the doses selected are to some extent determined by the sporting event.

- **Endurance athletes:** At or slightly below replacement levels of 5 to 10 mg/day
- **Sprinters:** 1.5 to 2 times replacement levels
- **Weightlifters & body builders:** 10 to 100 times normal doses
- **Women:** Regardless of sport tend to use lower doses than men

Appendix B: Physical & Mental Effects of Steroid Abuse on Males and Females[1]

Short-Term Adverse Physical Effects of Anabolic Steroids in Men

- Acne
- Skin tissue damage at the site of injection
- Shrinkage of the testicles
- Decreased sperm production and motility
- Decreased semen volume
- Frequent or continuing erections
- Enlargement of the breast (gynecomastia)
- Elevated blood pressure
- Increased LDL cholesterol levels
- Decreased HDL cholesterol levels
- Fluid retention leading to swelling
- Abnormal liver function
- Prostate enlargement
- Bleeding (usually nose)

Short-Term Adverse Physical Effects of Anabolic Steroids in Prepubertal Boys

- Precocious sexual development
- Penis enlargement
- Painful, prolonged penile erections
- Increased frequency of penile erections
- Premature closure of the growth plates in long bones resulting in a decrease in the total height achieved
- Fluid retention leading to swelling

Short-Term Adverse Physical Effects of Anabolic Steroids in Women

- Acne
- Oily skin
- Tissue damage at injection site
- Deepening of the voice
- Increased body and facial hair growth
- Enlargement of the clitoris
- Male pattern baldness
- Decreased breast size
- Menstrual irregularities (missed periods or no periods)
- Fluid retention leading to swelling

Adverse Cardiovascular Effects of Anabolic Steroids in Men and Women

- Increased blood pressure → potential coronary artery disorder
- Increased LDL cholesterol → potential coronary artery disorder
- Enlargement of the heart
- Actual death of heart cells
- Heart attacks (cardiac infraction)
  - Spasms of the coronary arteries
  - Increased blood clotting
- Stroke

Possible Long-Term Consequences of Anabolic Steroid Abuse in Men and Women

- Adverse cardiovascular effects
- Liver dysfunction
- Liver tumors
- Liver cancer
- Cancer of the prostate (men only)

Other Potential Risks Faced by Anabolic Steroid Abusers in Men and Women

- Skin infections
- HIV infection (needle sharing) → AIDS

- Hepatitis infections
- Violent trauma

Psychological Effects of Anabolic Steroid Abuse in Men and Women

Psychotic and Manic Reactions (Rare Occurrence)

- Most likely seen in people with prior mental illness

Anger, Hostility, Aggression and/or Violent Behavior

- Occurs in some but not all anabolic steroid users
- Unpredictable who will respond
- Increased likelihood with higher doses
- Minor provocations evoke exaggerated responses
- Presents danger to spouse, family, and friends
- Presents danger to law enforcement

Note

1. Dr. James Tolliver (Pharmacologist), DEA, Drug and Chemical Evaluation Section (ODE)

Charles E. Yesalis, Michael S. Bahrke, and James E. Wright

NO

Societal Alternatives

When the first edition of this book [*Anabolic Steroids in Sport and Exercise*] was published in 1993, this chapter opened with a quote from Robert Voy, MD (1991), former Chief Medical Officer of the U.S. Olympic Committee:

> If we will have reached a point of no return with this win at all costs attitude, the gold medals won't shine as brightly, the flags won't wave as boldly, the torch will flicker dimly, and we will have lost one of the greatest treasures ever known.

With this second edition, it appears that Dr. Voy's predictions have already come to pass. In 1998 alone, the public was bombarded with continual reports of drug scandals (Dickey, Helmstaedt, Nordland, & Hayden, 1999; "Drug Trial, Take II," 1998; "Snowboarder Loses Medal," 1998; "Drugs and Cycling," 1998; "Track Star Blazed Trail," 1998), including the following:

1. Chinese swimmers being ejected from the World Championships in Australia after having tested positive for banned substances.
2. Former East German coaches and physicians tried for their roles in the systematic doping of East German athletes over three decades.
3. Canadian snowboarder Ross Rebagliati testing positive for marijuana after having won a gold medal at the Winter Olympics in Nagano, Japan.
4. Olympic gold medalist Michelle Smith de Bruin accused of "manipulating" her urine sample in an out-of-competition drug test.
5. Cyclists, coaches, physicians, and trainers participating in the Tour de France implicated in a widespread, systematic doping scheme.
6. Olympic champion Randy Barnes testing positive for androstenedione.
7. Home run king Mark McGwire admitting the use of androstenedione.
8. Olympic champion Florence Griffith Joyner dying at age 38. Rumors of prior performance-enhancing drug use that surrounded her victories at the Seoul Olympic Games are resurrected.

Portions of chapter reproduced and adapted, with permission, from Yesalis CE: Winning and performance-enhancing drugs-our dual addition. *Phys Sportsmed* 1990; 18(3):161–167 © 2005 The McGraw-Hill Companies. All rights reserved.

9. Uta Pippig, three-time winner of the Boston Marathon, testing positive for a high level of testosterone.
10. Australian Open champion Petr Korda testing positive for an anabolic steroid.

When discussing the problem of performance-enhancing drug use, it is important to remember that sport is a microcosm of our society and the problems in sport are not limited to drug use. During the 1980s, 57 of 106 universities in Division I-A were punished by the NCAA via sanctions, censure, or probation for rule violations (Leaderman, 1990). These offenses did not involve illicit drug use by athletes but rather the unethical behavior of coaches, athletic administrators, staff, and faculty, the very men and women who should be setting the example. More recently, collegiate athletes have been convicted of criminal offences related to sports gambling (Lassar, 1998; Saum, 1998). In addition, an NCAA survey of 2,000 Division I male football and basketball players found 72% had gambled in some form, and 25% reported gambling on collegiate sports; 4% bet on games in which they played (Saum, 1998; "Study: Gambling in NCAA Rampant," 1999). Among members of the International Olympic Committee (IOC), bribery, graft, and other corruption appear entrenched in the culture of the organization (Simson & Jennings, 1992; Swift, 1999). A common factor among all these scandals is money. In the 1990s there is no doubt sport has become a multinational industry of huge proportions. The IOC, NCAA, NFL, NBA, and MLB, among others, are all billion-dollar businesses ("A Survey of Sport," 1998; Hiestand, 1999).

A free society relies on the news media to inform the populace of the incidence and magnitude of social problems such as doping in sport. Even though the epidemic of drug use in sport has been common knowledge among insiders, the news media, especially in the United States, have not engaged in a widespread concerted effort to chronicle this issue. Unfortunately the media, in particular television news, are often influenced by conflicts of interest within their parent companies between those reporting the news and those responsible for the broadcast of major sporting events. Few would argue that an in-depth exposé of drug use, for example, in the NFL or the Olympics, would enhance the marketing of these highly lucrative sporting events.

Before any effort can be made to address the issue of doping in sport, it is critical that all of the stakeholders acknowledge that a problem exists. In this regard, we need to fully appreciate the high entertainment value placed on sport by society. Some go so far as to argue that sport is the opiate of the masses—a contention made earlier by Karl Marx regarding religion. If sport has become the opiate of the masses, then we must be prepared for the public to be indifferent to drug use in sport, at least at the elite level. Moreover, it could be argued that if substantial progress is made in the fight against epidemic doping, fans may express anger, rather than appreciation, toward those fighting drug use. Many people view competitive sports to escape from the problems of daily life and do not wish to be confronted with the moral and ethical aspects of doping. Besides, if antidoping efforts are successful, the once bigger-than-life idols could begin to appear all too human in stature and the eclipsing of records at national, Olympic, and world levels could become so rare that the fervor of fans would wane and the business of sports would suffer. Even high school sport appears to be expanding as a source of entertainment for adults, as shown by the increasing level of television coverage of high school football and basketball games. Consequently, it can be argued that the growth of the high school sport entertainment business is contributing to the increase in anabolic steroid use among adolescents during the 1990s.

Sport has also been used by governments as a tool to control the masses or as justification for their social, political, and economic systems. "Bread and circuses" (panem et circenses) were used in this fashion by the emperors of Rome (Benario, 1983). Nazi Germany, the Soviet Union, East Germany, and Communist China all used sport for political advantage (Hoberman, 1984). Consequently, such governments, arguably, would be less than enthusiastic participants in the fight against doping or, for that matter, even in publicly acknowledging the existence of widespread doping. On the contrary, there is a reasonable amount of evidence that the governments of the Soviet Union, East Germany, and Communist China all played significant roles in the systematic doping of their athletes.

With many societal problems, identifying potential solutions is easy, but agreeing on a proper course of action and successfully completing it are difficult. The following are our alternatives for dealing with the use of anabolic steroids and other performance-enhancing drugs: legalization, interdiction, education, and alteration of societal values and attitudes related to physical appearance and winning in sport.

Legalization: An End to Hypocrisy?

The legalization of illicit drugs has for some time been the subject of heated debate: comments range from "morally reprehensible" to "accepting reality." Legalization would reduce the law enforcement costs associated with illicit anabolic steroid use as well as the substantial cost of drug testing. Even some opponents of legalization must concede that such an action would lessen the level of hypocrisy in sport. It can be argued that society and sports federations have turned a blind eye or have subtly encouraged drug use in sport as long as the athletes have not been caught or spoken publicly about their use of anabolic steroids (Bamberger & Yaeger, 1997; Dubin, 1990; Lemonick, 1998; "Drugs and Cycling," 1998; "Longtime Drug Use," 1999; Voy, 1990; Yesalis & Friedl, 1988).

Legalization of anabolic steroid use in sport would involve two levels of authority. At one level, federal and state laws related to the possession, distribution, and prescription of anabolic steroids would have to be changed. If in the future anabolic steroids become an accepted means of contraception or as treatment for "andropause," it is difficult to understand how anabolic steroids could remain a Schedule III controlled substance. At the second level, bans on anabolic steroids now in place in virtually every sport would have to be rescinded. Legalization would bring cries that the traditional ideals of sport and competition were being further eroded. On the other hand, given the continued litany of drug and other sport scandals (see above) that have taken pace in full public view, it is hard to imagine in this jaundiced age that many people believe that the so-called traditional ideals in elite sports even exist.

It has long been asserted that the legalization of anabolic steroids would force athletes to further expose themselves to possible physical harm or else to compete at a disadvantage. Others have even questioned the basic premise that banning drugs in sport benefits the health of athletes and have argued that "the ban has in fact increased health risks by denying users access to medical advice and caused users to turn to high risk black market sources" (Black, 1996).

Further, legalization would allow athletes to use pharmaceutical grade steroids while being monitored by a physician. It can also be argued that the "danger" of steroid use is not, in itself, a realistic deterrent given the existing levels of tobacco, alcohol, and other illicit drug use.

In 1999 it seems that legalization of anabolic steroid use in sport is not acceptable. However, if the impotence of drug testing, now in full public view, persists for much longer, it is easy to imagine the IOC or other sport federations throwing up their hands in frustration and allowing the athlete with the best chemist to prevail.

Interdiction: A Question of Cost-Effectiveness

The U.S. federal government and all state governments currently have laws regarding the distribution, possession, or prescription of anabolic steroids (USDHHS, 1991). The Federal Food, Drug, and Cosmetic Act (FFDCA) was amended as part of the Anti-Drug Abuse Act of 1988 such that distribution of steroids or possession of steroids with intent to distribute without a valid prescription became a felony. This legislation not only increased the penalties for the illicit distribution of steroids but also facilitated prosecution under the FFDCA. In 1990 the Anabolic Steroids Control Act was signed into law by President [George H. W.] Bush and added anabolic steroids to Schedule III of the Controlled Substances Act. This law institutes a regulatory and criminal enforcement system whereby the Drug Enforcement Administration (DEA) controls the manufacture, importation, exportation, distribution, and dispensing of anabolic steroids. However, the act did not provide extra resources to the DEA to shoulder the added responsibility.

Furthermore, as the use of anabolic steroids is increasingly criminalized, drug use will likely be driven further underground, and the source of the drugs will increasingly be clandestine laboratories, the products of which are of questionable quality. It also appears that in some areas criminalization has already altered the distribution network for anabolic steroids; athletes used to sell to other athletes, but sellers of street drugs are now becoming a major source (U.S. Department of Justice, 1994).

Even though the legal apparatus to control steroid trafficking exists, enforcement agents already are struggling to handle the problems of importation, distribution, sales, and use of other illicit drugs such as cocaine and heroin (U.S. Department of Justice, 1994). Based on what we know about the physical, psychological, or social effects of steroids, it is neither realistic nor prudent that enforcement efforts for steroids take precedent over those for more harmful drugs. On the other hand, this line of reasoning should not be used as a rationale for a lack of effective action against steroids. Nevertheless, the outlook that limited resources can be stretched to cover yet another class of drugs is not optimistic (U.S. Department of Justice, 1994), especially given the increase in recreational drug use among adolescents (Office of Applied Studies, 1999). The availability of anabolic steroids in this country suggests there is some reason to believe the United States may simply not have sufficient law enforcement personnel to deal with apprehending and punishing sellers of anabolic steroids and other performance-enhancing drugs.

Nonetheless, between February 1991 and February 1995, 355 anabolic steroid investigations were initiated by the DEA (Yesalis & Cowart, 1998). There have been more than 400 arrests, and more than 200 defendants have been convicted. However, because of the way criminal penalties were developed for steroid infractions, an individual brought to court on charges of distribution or selling must be a national-level dealer to receive more than a "slap on the wrist" and perhaps a short visit to a "country club" prison. For this reason, law enforcement agents often do not bother pursuing small cases because the costs of prosecution vastly outweigh any penalties that will be assessed.

Drug testing by sport federations is yet another form of interdiction. Such testing has been partially successful when directed at performance-enhancing drugs that, to be effective, must be in the body at the time of competition, such as stimulants and narcotics. . . . [D]rug testing has been even less effective against anabolic steroids that are used during training or used to enhance an athlete's capacity to train. Testing can be circumvented by the steroid user in several ways. Generally, to avoid a positive test, athletes can determine when to discontinue use prior to a scheduled test, or, in the case of an unannounced test, they titrate their dose using transdermal patches or skin creams containing testosterone so as to remain below the maximum allowable level. Further confounding the testing are other drugs used by athletes, such as human growth hormone and erythropoietin, for which no effective tests currently exist. Moreover, testing for anabolic steroids is expensive (approx. $120 per test), and although organizations like the IOC, NFL, or NCAA may be able to institute such procedures, the cost is prohibitive for the vast majority of secondary schools. Consequently, only a handful of secondary school systems test for anabolic steroids.

In summary, although interdiction through law enforcement and drug testing has intuitive appeal, its impact on the nonmedical use of anabolic steroids and other performance-enhancing drugs is open to debate. Since the flurry of legislative activity at the state and national levels regarding the control of the manufacture, distribution, prescription, and possession of steroids in the late 1980s and the early 1990s, use among adolescents has increased significantly. As for the future of testing, it is difficult to be optimistic: over the past 30 years, drug users have consistently outplayed the drug testers. In addition, one can only speculate as to the future challenges to testing created by impending advances in genetic engineering. Will we be able to genetically enhance muscle mass, aerobic capacity, vision, and neurological response (Barton-Davis, Shoturma, Musaro, Rosenthal, & Sweeney, 1998)?

Education: Is Anybody Listening?

Since the 1980s, the U.S. Public Health Service, the U.S. Department of Education, as well as many state education departments, state and local medical societies, private foundations, and sport federations have been involved in prevention efforts related to steroid abuse. For the most part, these have centered on the development and distribution of educational materials and programs such as posters, videos, pamphlets, and workshops. For example, the Iowa High School Athletic Association has developed an educational booklet that provides information on the effects of steroid use, but also includes strength-enhancing alternatives to steroids and prevention ideas (Beste, 1991). The U.S. Department of Education and other sources have developed a variety of informational posters targeted at high school students to provide facts about steroids, their adverse effects, alternatives to their use, and their illegal status (American Academy of Orthopaedic Surgeons; U.S. Department of Health & Human Services [USDHHS], 1988). Video distributors now have a wide range of videotape programs available on steroid use prevention as well as bodybuilding techniques (William C. Brown Communications Inc., 1993). Educational consulting firms provide antisteroid training, program, and curriculum development to junior and senior high schools across the United States (Griffin & Svendsen, 1990; Harding Ringhofer, 1993). Major television networks have presented special programming targeted at adolescent audiences to relay the possible consequences of steroid use (*ABC Afterschool Special:* "Testing Dirty" and *CBS Schoolbreak Special:* "The Fourth Man"; Disney Educational Productions: "Benny and the Roids").

Health educators have made some inroads in changing several high-risk behaviors, such as high-fat diets, sedentary lifestyles, and smoking. Educators are well armed with vast quantities of scientific data regarding the deleterious nature of these activities. Furthermore, these are behaviors on which society has increasingly frowned. In sports, on the other hand, athletes who use anabolic steroids have enjoyed significant improvements in physical performance and appearance. Society is much less likely to shun these people. The adulation of fans, the media, and peers is a strong secondary reinforcement, as are financial, material, and sexual rewards.

Another fly in the education ointment is the possibility that anabolic steroids taken intermittently in low to moderate doses may have only a negligible impact on health, at least in the short term. In 1989, several experts at the National Steroid Consensus Meeting concluded that according to the existing evidence, these drugs represent more of an ethical dilemma than a public health problem (Yesalis, Wright, & Lombardo, 1989). Although there is still little available evidence regarding the long-term health effects of anabolic steroids, many current or potential anabolic steroid users unfortunately mistake absence of evidence for evidence of absence. Even more frustrating is the fact that in two national studies, a substantial minority of the anabolic steroid users surveyed expressed no intention to stop using anabolic steroids if deleterious health effects were unequivocally established (Yesalis, Herrick, Buckley, Friedl, Brannon, & Wright, 1988; Yesalis, Streit, Vicary, Friedl, Brannon, &

Buckley, 1989). Clearly, the paucity of scientific information has impeded the formulation of effective health education strategies. Far more than that, the unsubstantiated claims of dire health effects made by some in sports medicine and sensationalized by the news media have further eroded communication between athletes and doctors. However, even if long-term deleterious effects were well documented for anabolic steroids, our experience with teenagers and smoking suggests that substantial abuse would probably persist (Centers for Disease Control and Prevention, 1994; U.S. Department of Health and Human Services, 1989).

All of these problems and limitations in developing and disseminating effective prevention and intervention strategies could largely explain the significant increase in anabolic steroid use among adolescents since 1990.

Changing a behavior that has resulted in major benefits to the user, such as improved appearance and athletic performance, presents a monumental challenge. Traditional cognitive and affective education approaches to tobacco, alcohol, and drug abuse prevention have not been effective (Schaps, Bartolo, Moskowitz, Palley, & Churgin, 1981). In fact, there is evidence that providing a prevention program that uses "scare tactics" to dissuade adolescents from becoming involved with anabolic steroids may actually lead to increased usage, possibly because additional information stimulated curiosity (Goldberg, Bents, Bosworth, Trevisan, & Elliot, 1991). This observation helped lead to a prevention program (ATLAS) focused, in part, on positive educational initiatives related to nutrition and strength training. The program also focused on increasing adolescents' awareness of the types of social pressures they are likely to encounter to use anabolic steroids, and attempts to "inoculate" them against these pressures. Adolescents are taught specific skills for effectively resisting both peer and media pressures to use anabolic steroids. Periodic monitoring and reporting of actual anabolic steroid use among adolescents was conducted in an effort to dispel misinformation concerning the widespread use of anabolic steroids among peers. Using peers as program leaders is an additional component. This program has been successful in significantly affecting attitudes and behaviors related to steroid use and remained effective over several years (Goldberg et al., 1996).

Unfortunately, the generalizability of the ATLAS program is open to question. The program focused on male high school football players and was not designed specifically to address anabolic steroid use among teenage girls, whose rate of steroid use . . . has doubled since 1990. In addition, the long-term effectiveness of this school-based program is still unknown and the program has yet to be replicated in other states. Moreover, there are two important and, as yet, unanswered questions regarding the ATLAS program. First, are school boards, in an age of constrained resources, willing to commit time and money to this relatively demanding program? Efficacy aside, it would be far easier and cheaper to continue to give only "lip service" to this problem and limit efforts to an occasional talk by the coach and the use of readily available educational videos and posters.

The second question is even more threatening to school officials. In an era when some believe that the "win at all costs" philosophy is gaining the upper hand, will some schools hesitate to unilaterally "disarm"? That is, will some schools hesitate to institute a program that could significantly reduce steroid use at the cost of conferring an advantage to an opponent who chooses to maintain a "see no evil" stance on the use of performance-enhancing drugs? This question is given some legitimacy by pervasive anecdotal accounts of high school coaches encouraging the use of, and in some instances selling, so-called supplements such as creatine, DHEA, and androstenedione to their athletes.

In summary, although educating athletes about the health risks and ethical issues associated with anabolic steroid use can help reduce use, this strategy is not a panacea.

Conclusion: Our Values Must Change

Compared with legalization, interdiction, and education, the influence of our social environment on anabolic steroid use receives far less attention. Yet in many ways the social environment exerts a more fundamental influence on drug use in sport than do the more superficial strategies to reduce use described earlier.

A number of performance-enhancing drugs, including anabolic steroids, are not euphorigenic, or mood altering, immediately following administration. Instead, the appetite for these drugs was created predominantly by our societal fixation on winning and physical appearance. An infant does not innately believe that a muscular physique is desirable—our society teaches this. Likewise, children play games for fun, but society preaches the importance of winning— seemingly, at an increasingly younger age.

Ours is a culture that thrives on competition, both in business and in sport. However, we long ago realized that competition of all types must exist within some boundaries. A primary goal of competition is to win or be the very best in any endeavor. Philosophically, many in our society appear to have taken a "bottom-line" attitude and consider winning the *only* truly worthwhile goal of competition. If we accept this philosophy, then it becomes easy to justify, or be led to the belief, that one should win at any cost. At that point doping becomes a very rational behavior, with the end (winning) justifying the means (use of anabolic steroids and other drugs).

This "win at any cost/winner take all" philosophy is not new. The winners in the ancient Greek Olympics were handsomely rewarded, and episodes of athletes cheating to obtain these financial rewards are well documented (Thompson, 1986a, 1986b; Young, 1985). Smith (1988) argued persuasively that the level of cheating in college athletics at the turn of the century exceeded what we see today. Even the legendary Knute Rockne was quoted as saying, "Show me a good and gracious loser and I'll show you a failure." Vince Lombardi went a step further with his philosophy that winning isn't everything—it's the only thing. Indeed episodes of cheating, including drug use, have been commonplace at the collegiate, professional, and Olympic levels over the past four decades (Dealy, 1990; Dickey et al., 1999; Dubin, 1990; Francis, 1990; Sperber, 1990; Swift, 1999; Telander, 1989; Voy, 1990). Moreover, because of reports in the news media as well as written and oral testimonials by athletes, adolescents are aware that anabolic steroids and other performance-enhancing drugs have played a part in the success of many so-called role-model athletes (Alzado, 1991; Bamberger & Yaeger, 1997; Dickey et al., 1999).

Our fixation on appearance, especially the muscularity of males, is also long lived. An entire generation of young men aspired to the physique of Charles Atlas, followed by yet another generation who marveled at the muscles of Mr. Universe, Steve Reeves, who played Hercules in several movies in the 1950s. Today's children look with envy at the physiques of Sylvester Stallone, Jean-Claude Van Damme, Wesley Snipes, Linda Hamilton, and other actors *and actresses* whose movie roles call for a muscular athletic build. In addition, a number of professional wrestlers such as Hulk Hogan and "Stone Cold" Steve Austin as well as some elite athletes like Mark McGwire are admired in part for their bigger-than-life muscularity. Anabolic steroid use among professional wrestlers, including Hulk Hogan, was given national attention during a steroid trafficking trial in 1991 (Demak, 1991). President Bush's appointment of Arnold Schwarzenegger, an individual who attained his prominence as a bodybuilder and movie star at least in part as a result of steroid use, as chair of the President's Council on Physical Fitness and Sports was yet another inappropriate message sent to our children. Such messages of material reward and fame as a result of drug-assisted muscularity and winning grossly overshadow posters on gym walls and videos that implore "Just Say No to Steroids."

Some might argue that our attitudes and values related to sports and appearance are too deeply entrenched to change. That may be so, in particular when it comes to elite sport—there is simply too much money involved. However, if we cannot control our competitive and narcissistic natures, we then must resign ourselves to anabolic steroid use, even among our children.

Society's current strategy for dealing with the use of anabolic steroids in sport is multifaceted and primarily involves interdiction and education. However, 10 years after our society was made aware that our children were using steroids, our efforts to deal with this problem have not been very successful. Since 1989 a number of national conferences on anabolic steroid use have been held, sponsored by either the U.S. federal government or sport and educational organizations. The purpose of these meetings was to gather and or disseminate information or to achieve a consensus for action. At this point all these activities appear to have been a sincere effort to deal with the problem, but this strategy of attacking the symptoms while ignoring the social influence of drug use in sport is obviously ineffective. If we maintain our current course in the face of increased high levels of anabolic steroid use (or use of other performance-enhancing drugs), then we as sports medicine professionals, parents, teachers, and coaches are guilty of duplicity—acting for the sake of acting. We plan and attend workshops, distribute educational materials, lobby for the passage of laws, and seek the assistance of law enforcement. All these activities merely soothe our consciences in the face of our inability, or unwillingness, to deal with our addiction to sport and our fixations on winning and appearance.

References

Alzado, L. (1991, July 8). I'm sick and I'm scared. *Sports Illustrated*, 20–27.

American Academy of Orthopaedic Surgeons and the U.S. Department of Health and Human Services. *STEROIDS DON'T WORK OUT!* (a poster). Washington, DC: Center for Substance Abuse Prevention, Substance Abuse and Mental Health Services Administration.

Bamberger, M., & Yaeger, D. (1997, April 14). Over the edge. *Sports Illustrated*, 60–70.

Barton-Davis, E.R., Shoturma, D.I., Musaro, A., Rosenthal, N., & Sweeney. H.L. (1998). Viral mediated expression of insulin-like growth factor I blocks the aging-related loss of skeletal muscle function. *Proceedings of the National Academy of Sciences*, *95*, 15603–15607.

Benario, H. (1983). Sport at Rome. *The Ancient World*, *7*, 39.

Beste A. (1991). *Steroids: You make the choice*. N.p.: Iowa High School Athletic Association Printing Department.

Black, T. (1996). Does the ban on drugs in sport improve societal welfare? *International Review for Sociology of Sport*, *31*, 367–380.

Centers for Disease Control and Prevention (1994). *Preventing tobacco use among young people: A report of the Surgeon General*. Atlanta: Author.

Dealy, F (1990). *Win at any cost: The sell out of college athletics*. New York: Birch Lane Press Books.

Demak, R. (1991, July). The sham is a sham. *Sports Illustrated*, 8.

Dickey. C., Helmstaedt, K., Nordland, R., & Hayden, T. (1999, February 15). The real scandal. *Newsweek*, pp. 48–54.

Drug trial, take II. (1998, August 19). *USA Today*, p. 3C.

Drugs and cycling. (1998, September 29). *USA Today*, p. 1C.

Dubin, C. (1990). *Commission of inquiry into the use of drugs and banned practices intended to increase athletic performance* (Catalogue No. CP32-56/1990E, ISBN 0-660-13610-4). Ottawa, ON: Canadian Government Publishing Centre.

Francis, C. (1990). *Speed trap*. New York: St. Martin's Press.

Goldberg, L., Bents, R., Bosworth, E., Trevisan, L., & Elliot, D. (1991). Anabolic steroid education and adolescents: Do scare tactics work? *Pediatrics*, *87*, 283–286.

Goldberg, L., Elliot D.L., Clarke G., MacKinnon, D., Zoref, L., Moe, E., Green, C., & Wolf, S. (1996). The Adolescents Training and Learning to Avoid Steroids (ATLAS) prevention program: Background and results of a model intervention. *Archives of Pediatrics and Adolescent Medicine*, *150*, 713–721.

Griffin T., & Svendsen R. (1990). *Steroids and our students: A program development guide*. St. Paul: Health Promotion Resources and WBA Ruster Foundation.

Harding Ringhofer & Associates and Media One. (1993). *Students and steroids: The facts . . . straight up* (a steroid use prevention program for adolescents). Minnetonka, MN: Author.

Hiestand, M. (1999, January 12). The B word—billion—no longer out of bounds. *USA Today*, pp. 1–2a.

Hoberman, J. (1984). *Sport and political ideology*. Austin, TX: University of Texas Press.

Lassar, S. (1998, December 3). Four former Northwestern football players indicted on perjury charges related to sports gambling investigation (press release). U.S. Justice Department, U.S. Attorney, Northern District of Illinois.

Leaderman, D. (1990, January 3). 57 of 106 universities in NCAA's top unit punished in 1980s. *Chronicle of Higher Education*, p. A31.

Lemonick, M. (1998, August 10). Le Tour des Drugs. *Time*, p. 76.

Longtime drug use. (1999, January 28). *USA Today*, p. 3C.

Office of Applied Studies (1999). *National Household Survey on Drug Abuse: Main findings, 1997* (SMA # 99-3295). Rockville, MD: U.S. Department of Health and Human Services, Substance Abuse and Mental Health Services Administration.

Saum, B. (1998, November 10). Written testimony of Bill Saum, Director of Agent and Gambling Activities, National Collegiate Athletic Association, before the National Gambling Impact Study Commission, Las Vegas, Nevada.

Schaps, E., Bartolo, R., Moskowitz, J., Palley, C., & Churgin, S. (1981). Review of 127 drug abuse prevention program evaluations. *Journal of Drug Issues, 2,* 17–43.

Simson, V., & Jennings, A. (1992). *The lords of the rings: Power, money, and drugs in the modern Olympics.* London: Simon & Schuster.

Smith, R. (1988). *Sports and freedom: The rise of big-time college athletics.* New York: Oxford University Press.

Snowboarder loses medal after drug test. (1998, February 11). *USA Today,* p. 9E.

Sperber. M. (1990). *College sports inc.* New York: Holt.

Study: Gambling in NCAA rampant. (1999, January 12). *USA Today,* p. 3C.

A survey of sport: Not just a game. (1998). *Economist, 347,* 2–23.

Swift. E. (1999, February 1). Breaking point. *Sports Illustrated,* 34–35.

Telander, R. (1989). *The hundred yard lie.* New York: Simon & Schuster.

Thompson, J. (1986a). Historical errors about the ancient Olympic games. *Gamut, 17*(winter), 20–23.

Thompson, J. (1986b). The intrusion of corruption into athletics: An age-old problem. *Journal of General Education, 23,* 144–153.

Track star blazed trail. (1998, September 22). *USA Today,* pp. 1–2C.

U.S. Department of Health and Human Services, Department of Education. (1988). *Steroids: Playing with trouble* (a poster). Washington, DC: U.S. Government Printing Office, 1988-0-208-087.

U.S. Department of Health and Human Services. (1989, March). *Health United States: 1988* (DHHS Publication [PHS] 89-1232, U.S.). Hyattsville, MD: USDHHS, National Center for Health Statistics.

U.S. Department of Health and Human Services, Public Health Service. (1991, January). *Interagency Task Force on Anabolic Steroids.* Washington, DC: Author.

U.S. Department of Justice (1994). *Report of the International Conference on the Abuse and Trafficking of Anabolic Steroids.* Washington, DC: Drug Enforcement Administration.

Voy, R. (1990). *Drugs, sport, and politics.* Champaign, IL: Leisure Press.

Wm. C. Brown Communications. (1993). *1992–1993 Weight training fitness and conditioning catalog.* Dubuque, IA: Brown and Benchmark.

Yesalis, C., & Cowart, V. (1998). *The steroids game.* Champaign, IL: Human Kinetics.

Yesalis, C., & Friedl, K. (1988). Anabolic steroid use in amateur sports: An epidemiologic perspective. In R. Kretchmar (Ed.), *Proceedings of the US Olympic Academy XII* (pp. 83–89). Colorado Springs: U.S. Olympic Committee.

Yesalis, C.E., Herrick, R.T., Buckley, W.E., Friedl, K.E., Brannon, D., & Wright, J.E. (1988). Self-reported use of anabolic-androgenic steroids by elite power lifters. *The Physician and Sportsmedicine, 16,* 91–100.

Yesalis, C., Wright, J., & Lombardo, J. (1989, July 30–31). *Anabolic androgenic steroids: A synthesis of existing data and recommendations for future research.* Keynote research address, National Steroid Consensus Meeting, Los Angeles.

Yesalis, C., Streit, A., Vicary, J., Friedl, K., Brannon, D., & Buckley, W. (1989). Anabolic steroid use: Indications of habituation among adolescents. *Journal of Drug Education, 19,* 103–116.

Young, D. (1985). *The Olympic myth of Greek amateur athletics.* Chicago: Ares.

POSTSCRIPT

Do Steroids Pose a Large Risk to Athletes and Others Who Use Them?

There are several reasons why long-term research into the effects of anabolic steroids is lacking. First, it is unethical to give drugs that may prove harmful, even lethal, to people. Also, the amount of steroids given to subjects in a laboratory setting may not replicate what illegal steroid users actually take. Users who take steroids illegally may take substantially more than the dosage subjects are given in a clinical trial.

Second, to determine the true effects of drugs, double-blind studies need to be conducted. This means that neither the researcher nor the people receiving the drugs know whether the subjects are receiving the steroids or the placebos (inert substances). This is not practical with steroids because subjects can always tell if they received the steroids or the placebos. The effects of steroids could be determined by following up with people who are known steroid users. However, this method lacks proper controls. If physical or psychological problems appear in a subject, for example, it cannot be determined whether the problems are due to the steroids or to other drugs the person may have been taking. Also, the type of person who uses steroids may be the type of person who has emotional problems in the first place.

Even though the Drug Enforcement Administration estimates the black-market trade in anabolic steroids to be several hundred million dollars a year, one could argue that steroids are symptomatic of a much larger social problem. Society places much emphasis on appearance and performance. From the time we are children, we are bombarded with constant reminders that we must do better than the next person. If you want to make the varsity team, if you want that scholarship, if you want to be a professional athlete, then you better do whatever it takes to get there. We are also constantly reminded of the importance of appearance—to either starve ourselves or pump ourselves up (or both) in order to satisfy the cultural ideal of beauty. If we cannot achieve these cultural standards through exercising, dieting, or drug use, then we can turn to surgery. As males grow up, many are given the message that they should be "big and strong." One shortcut to achieving that look is through the use of steroids. Steroid use fits into the larger social problem of people not accepting themselves and their limitations.

The use of steroids in sports is dealt with in "Drugs and the Olympics," *The Economist* (August 7, 2004); "Risks of Doping Often Overlooked for Rewards," by Mark Emmons, *San Jose Mercury News* (November 12, 2003); Campbell Aitken's article "Lifting Your Game: Campbell Aitken Probes the Use of Steroids in

Sports," *Meanjin* (June 2002); and, "Can Drug Busters Beat New Steroids? It's Scientist Vs. Scientist as the Athens Olympics Approach," by Arline Weintraub, *Business Week* (June 14, 2004). The dangers of steroids are discussed in "Anabolic Steroids and Dependence," by Helen Keane, *Contemporary Drug Problems* (Fall 2003). The effects of tetrahydrogestrinone (THG), another performance-enhancing drug, is described in Deeanna Franklin's article "FDA Warns About Dangers of THG: Banned Steroid," *Pediatric News* (January 2004).

On the Internet . . .   DUSHKIN ONLINE

National Institute on Alcohol Abuse and Alcoholism (NIAAA)

This site provides research on the causes, consequences, treatment, and prevention of alcoholism and alcohol-related problems.

http://niaaa.nih.gov

American Medical Association (AMA)

Information regarding the development and promotion of standards in medical practice, research, and education are included on this Web site.

http://www.ama-assn.org

Columbia University College of Physicians and Surgeons Complete Home Medical Guide

This site provides information about health and medicine, including information dealing with psychotherapeutic drugs.

http://cpmcnet.columbia.edu/texts/
guide/hmg06_005.html

American Psychological Association (APA)

Research concerning different psychological disorders and the various types of treatments, including drug treatments that are available, can be accessed through this site.

http://www.apa.org

CDC's Tobacco Information and Prevention Source

This location contains current information on smoking prevention programs. Much data regarding teen smoking can be found at this site.

http://www.cdc.gov/tobacco

U.S. Food and Drug Administration, Center for Drug Evaluation and Research: Over-the-Counter (OTC) Drugs

Current information regarding over-the-counter drugs is highlighted in this site.

http://www.fda.gov/cder/otc/index.htm

National Organization for the Reform of Marijuana Laws

This site contains informaiton regarding the legalization of marijuana.

http://www.natlnorml.org

PART 2

Drugs and Social Policy

*E*xcept for the debate over whether laws prohibiting marijuana use should be relaxed, each debate in this section focuses on drugs that are already legal. Despite concerns over the effects of illegal drugs, the most frequently used drugs in society are legal drugs. Because of their prevalence and legal status, the social, psychological, and physical impact of drugs like tobacco, caffeine, alcohol, and prescription drugs are often minimized or negated. However, tobacco and alcohol cause far more death and disability than all illegal drugs combined.

   The recent trend toward medical self-help raises questions of how much control one should have over one's health. The current tendency to identify nicotine as an addictive drug and to promote the moderate use of alcohol to reduce heart disease has generated much controversy. In the last several years, the increase in consumers requesting prescription drugs for themselves and Ritalin for their children also has created much concern. Lastly, should marijuana be prescribed for people with certain illnesses for which some have suggested the drug could be beneficial?

- Are the Adverse Effects of Smoking Exaggerated?

- Should Laws Prohibiting Marijuana Use Be Relaxed?

- Are Psychotherapeutic Drugs Effective for Treating Mental Illness?

- Do the Consequences of Caffeine Consumption Outweigh Its Benefits?

- Is Ritalin an Effective Drug for Treating Attention Deficit/Hyperactivity Disorder (ADHD)?

- Do Consumers Benefit When Prescription Drugs Are Advertised?

ISSUE 8

Are the Adverse Effects of Smoking Exaggerated?

YES: Robert A. Levy and Rosalind B. Marimont, from "Lies, Damned Lies, and 400,000 Smoking-Related Deaths," *Regulation* (vol. 21, no. 4, 1998)

NO: Centers for Disease Control, from *The Health Consequences of Smoking: A Report of the Surgeon General* (Centers for Disease Control, 2004)

ISSUE SUMMARY

YES: Robert A. Levy, a senior fellow at the Cato Institute, and Rosalind B. Marimont, a mathematician and scientist who retired from the National Institute of Standards and Technology, claim that the government distorts and exaggerates the dangers associated with cigarette smoking. Levy and Marimont state that factors such as poor nutrition and obesity are overlooked as causes of death among smokers. They note that cigarette smoking is harmful, but the misapplication of statistics should be regarded as "junk science."

NO: The 2004 Surgeon General's report on smoking states that the evidence pointing to the dangers of smoking is overwhelming. The report clearly links cigarette smoking to various forms of cancer, cardiovascular diseases, respiratory diseases, reproductive problems, and a host of other medical conditions.

Most people, including those who smoke, recognize that cigarette smoking is harmful. Because of tobacco's reputation as an addictive substance that jeopardizes people's health, many activists are requesting that more stringent restrictions be placed on it. As it stands now, cigarette packages are required to carry warnings describing the dangers of tobacco products. In many countries, tobacco products cannot be advertised on television or billboards. Laws that prevent minors from purchasing tobacco products are being more vigorously enforced than they have ever been before. However, the World Health Organization feels that global leadership in curtailing the proliferation of cigarette smoking is lacking.

Defenders of the tobacco industry point to benefits associated with nicotine, the mild stimulant that is the chief active chemical in tobacco. In previous centuries, for example, tobacco was used to help people with a variety of ailments, including skin diseases, internal and external disorders, and diseases of the eyes, ears, mouth, and nose. Tobacco and its smoke were employed often by Native Americans for sacramental purposes. For users, nicotine provides a sense of euphoria, and smoking is a source of gratification that does not impair thinking or performance. One can drive a car, socialize, study for a test, and engage in a variety of activities while smoking. Nicotine can relieve anxiety and stress, and it can reduce weight by lessening one's appetite and by increasing metabolic activity. Many smokers assert that smoking cigarettes enables them to concentrate better and that abstaining from smoking impairs their concentration.

Critics paint a very different picture of tobacco products, citing some of the following statistics: Tobacco is responsible for about 30 percent of deaths among people between ages 35 and 69, making it the single most prominent cause of premature death in the developed world. The relationship between cigarette smoking and cardiovascular disease, including heart attack, stroke, sudden death, peripheral vascular disease, and aortic aneurysm, is well documented. Even as few as one to four cigarettes daily can increase the risk of fatal coronary heart disease. Cigarettes have also been shown to reduce blood flow and the level of high-density lipoprotein cholesterol, which is the beneficial type of cholesterol.

Cigarette smoking is strongly associated with cancer, accounting for over 85 percent of lung cancer cases and 30 percent of all deaths due to cancer. Cancer of the pharynx, larynx, mouth, esophagus, stomach, pancreas, uterus, cervix, kidney, and bladder has been related to smoking. Studies have shown that smokers have twice the rate of cancer than nonsmokers.

According to smokers' rights advocates, the majority of smokers are already aware of the potential harm of tobacco products; in fact, most smokers tend to overestimate the dangers of smoking. Adults should therefore be allowed to smoke if that is their wish. Many promote the idea that the Food and Drug Administration (FDA) and a number of politicians are attempting to deny smokers the right to engage in a behavior that they freely choose. On the other hand, tobacco critics maintain that due to the addictiveness of nicotine—the level of which some claim is manipulated by tobacco companies—smokers really do not have the ability to stop their behavior. That is, after a certain point, smoking cannot be considered freely chosen behavior.

In the following selections, Robert A. Levy and Rosalind B. Marimont argue that the scientific evidence demonstrating that tobacco use is harmful to smokers is disputable. Levy and Marimont state that smoking has been demonized unfairly. Cigarette smoking is not illegal and does not cause intoxication, violent behavior, or unemployment. *The Health Consequences of Smoking: A Report of the Surgeon General* identifies statistics that clearly demonstrate the high level of harm associated with cigarette smoking. Numerous bodily systems, ranging from the cardiovascular to the pulmonary to the digestive systems, are adversely affected by cigarette smoking.

Robert A. Levy and
Rosalind B. Marimont

 **YES**

Lies, Damned Lies, and 400,000 Smoking-Related Deaths

Truth was an early victim in the battle against tobacco. The big lie, repeated ad nauseam in anti-tobacco circles, is that smoking causes more than 400,000 premature deaths each year in the United States. That mantra is the principal justification for all manner of tobacco regulations and legislation, not to mention lawsuits by dozens of states for Medicaid recovery, class actions by seventy-five to eighty union health funds, similar litigation by thirty-five Blue Cross plans, twenty-four class suits by smokers who are not yet ill, sixty class actions by allegedly ill smokers, five hundred suits for damages from secondhand smoke, and health-related litigation by twelve cities and counties—an explosion of adjudication never before experienced in this country or elsewhere.

The war on smoking started with a kernel of truth—that cigarettes are a high risk factor for lung cancer—but has grown into a monster of deceit and greed, eroding the credibility of government and subverting the rule of law. Junk science has replaced honest science and propaganda parades as fact. Our legislators and judges, in need of dispassionate analysis, are instead smothered by an avalanche of statistics—tendentious, inadequately documented, and unchecked by even rudimentary notions of objectivity. Meanwhile, Americans are indoctrinated by health "professionals" bent on imposing their lifestyle choices on the rest of us and brainwashed by politicians eager to tap the deep pockets of a pariah industry.

The aim of this paper is to dissect the granddaddy of all tobacco lies—that smoking causes 400,000 deaths each year. To set the stage, let's look at two of the many exaggerations, misstatements, and outright fabrications that have dominated the tobacco debate from the outset.

Third-Rate Thinking About Secondhand Smoke

"Passive Smoking Does Cause Lung Cancer, Do Not Let Them Fool You," states the headline of a March 1998 press release from the World Health Organization. The release begins by noting that WHO had been accused of suppressing its own study because it "failed to scientifically prove that there is an association between passive smoking . . . and a number of diseases, lung cancer in particular." Not true, insisted WHO. Smokers themselves are not the only ones who suffer health problems because of their habit; secondhand smoke can be fatal as well.

The press release went on to report that WHO researchers found "an estimated 16 percent increased risk of lung cancer among nonsmoking spouses of smokers. For workplace exposure the estimated increase in risk was 17 percent." Remarkably, the very next line warned: "Due to small sample size, neither increased risk was statistically significant." Contrast that conclusion with the hype in the headline: "Passive Smoking Does Cause Lung Cancer." Spoken often enough, the lie becomes its own evidence.

The full study would not see the light of day for seven more months, until October 1998, when it was finally published in the *Journal of the National Cancer Institute.* News reports omitted any mention of statistical insignificance. Instead, they again trumpeted relative risks of 1.16 and 1.17, corresponding to 16 and 17 percent increases, as if those ratios were meaningful. Somehow lost in WHO's media blitz was the National Cancer Institute's own guideline: "Relative risks of less than 2 [that is, a 100 percent increase] are considered small. . . . Such increases may be due to chance, statistical bias, or effects of confounding factors that are sometimes not evident." To put the WHO results in their proper perspective, note that the relative risk of lung cancer for persons who drink whole milk is 2.4. That is, the increased risk of contracting lung cancer from whole milk is 140 percent—more than eight times the 17 percent increase from secondhand smoke.

What should have mattered most to government officials, the health community and concerned parents is the following pronouncement from the WHO study: After examining 650 lung cancer patients and 1,500 healthy adults in seven European countries, WHO concluded that the "results indicate no association between childhood exposure to environmental tobacco smoke and lung cancer risk."

EPA's Junk Science

Another example of anti-tobacco misinformation is the landmark 1993 report in which the Environmental Protection Agency declared that environmental tobacco smoke (ETS) is a dangerous carcinogen that kills three thousand Americans yearly. Five years later, in July 1998, federal judge William L. Osteen lambasted the EPA for "cherry picking" the data, excluding studies that "demonstrated no association between ETS and cancer," and withholding "significant portions of its findings and reasoning in striving to confirm its *a priori* hypothesis." Both "the record and EPA's explanation," concluded the court, "make it clear that using standard methodology, EPA could not produce statistically significant results." A more damning assessment is difficult to imagine, but here are the court's conclusions at greater length, in its own words.

EPA publicly committed to a conclusion before research had begun; excluded industry [input thereby] violating the [Radon Research] Act's procedural requirements; adjusted established procedure and scientific norms to validate the Agency's public conclusion, and aggressively utilized the Act's authority to disseminate findings to establish a de facto regulatory scheme intended to restrict Plaintiff's products and to influence public opinion. In conducting the ETS Risk Assessment, EPA disregarded information and made findings on selective information; did not disseminate significant epidemiologic information; deviated from its Risk Assessment Guidelines; failed to disclose important findings and reasoning; and left significant questions without answers. EPA's conduct left substantial holes in the administrative record. While so doing, EPA produced limited evidence, then claimed the weight of the Agency's research evidence demonstrated ETS causes Cancer.

—*Flue-Cured Tobacco Coop. Stabilization Corp. v. United States Environmental Protection Agency*, 4 F. Supp. 2d 435, 465–66 (M.D.N.C. 1998)

Hundreds of states, cities, and counties have banned indoor smoking—many in reaction to the EPA report. California even prohibits smoking in bars. According to Matthew L. Myers, general counsel of the Campaign for Tobacco-Free Kids, "the release of the original risk assessment gave an enormous boost to efforts to restrict smoking." Now that the study has been thoroughly debunked, one would think that many of the bans would be lifted. Don't hold your breath. When science is adulterated and debased for political ends, the culprits are unlikely to reverse course merely because they have been unmasked.

In reaction to the federal court's criticism EPA administrator Carol M. Browner said, "It's so widely accepted that secondhand smoke causes very real problems for kids and adults. Protecting people from the health hazards of secondhand smoke should be a national imperative." Like *Alice in Wonderland*, sentence first, evidence afterward. Browner reiterates: "We believe the health threats . . . from breathing secondhand smoke are very real." Never mind science; it is Browner's beliefs that control. The research can be suitably tailored.

For the EPA to alter results, disregard evidence, and adjust its procedures and standards to satisfy agency prejudices is unacceptable behavior, even to a first-year science student. Those criticisms are about honesty, carefulness, and rigor—the very essence of science.

Classifying Diseases as Smoking-Related

With that record of distortion, it should come as no surprise that anti-tobacco crusaders misrepresent the number of deaths due to smoking. Start by considering the diseases that are incorrectly classified as smoking-related. The Centers for Disease Control and Prevention (CDC) prepares and distributes information on smoking-attributable mortality, morbidity and economic costs (SAMMEC). In its *Morbidity and Mortality Weekly Report* for 27 August 1993, the CDC states that 418,690 Americans died in 1990 of various diseases that they contracted because, according to the government, they smoked.

Diseases are categorized as smoking-related if the risk of death for smokers exceeds that for nonsmokers. In the jargon of epidemiology, a relative risk that is greater than 1 indicates a connection between exposure (smoking) and effect (death). Recall, however, the National Cancer Institute's guideline: "Relative risks of less than two are considered small. . . . Such increases may be due to chance, statistical bias, or effects of confounding factors that are sometimes not evident." And the *Federal Reference Manual on Scientific Evidence* confirms that the threshold test for legal significance is a relative risk of two or higher. At any ratio below two, the results are insufficiently reliable to conclude that a particular agent (e.g., tobacco) caused a particular disease.

What would happen if the SAMMEC data were to exclude deaths from those diseases that had a relative risk of less than two for current or former smokers? Table 1 shows that 163,071 deaths reported by CDC were from diseases that should not have been included in the report. Add to that another 1,362 deaths from burn injuries—unless one believes that Philip Morris is responsible when a smoker falls asleep with a lit cigarette. That is a total of 164,433 misreported deaths out of 418,690. When the report is properly limited to diseases that have a significant relationship with smoking, the death total declines to 254,257. Thus, on this count alone, SAMMEC overstates the number of deaths by 65 percent.

Table 1

Disease Category	Relative Risk	Deaths From Smoking
Cancer of pancreas	1.1–1.8	2,931*
Cancer of cervix	1.9	647*
Cancer of bladder	1.9	2,348*
Cancer of kidney, other urinary	1.2–1.4	353
Hypertension	1.2–1.9	5,450
Ischemic heart disease (age 35–64)	1.4–1.8	15,535*
Ischemic heart disease (age 65+)	1.3–1.6	64,789
Other heart disease	1.2–1.9	35,314
Cerebrovascular disease (age 35–64)	1.4	2,681*
Cerebrovascular disease (age 65+)	1.0–1.9	14,610
Atherosclerosis	1.3	1,267*
Aortic aneurysm	1.3	448*
Other arterial disease	1.3	372*
Pneumonia and influenza	1.4–1.6	10,552*
Other respiratory diseases	1.4–1.6	1,063*
Pediatric diseases	1.5–1.8	1,711
Sub-total		160,071
Environmental tobacco smoke	1.2	3,000
Total		163,071

* Number of deaths for this category assumes population deaths distributed between current and former smokers in same proportion as in Cancer Prevention Survey CPS-II, provided by the American Cancer Society.

Calculating Excess Deaths

But there is more. Writing on "Risk Attribution and Tobacco-Related Deaths" in the 1993 *American Journal of Epidemiology,* T. D. Sterling, W. L. Rosenbaum, and J. J. Weinkam expose another overstatement—exceeding 65 percent— that flows from using the American Cancer Society's Cancer Prevention Survey (CPS) as a baseline against which excess deaths are computed. Here is how one government agency, the Office of Technology Assessment (OTA), calculates the number of deaths caused by smoking:

The OTA first determines the death rate for persons who were part of the CPS sample and never smoked. Next, that rate is applied to the total U.S. population in order to estimate the number of Americans who would have died if no one ever smoked. Finally, the hypothetical number of deaths for assumed never-smokers is subtracted from the actual number of U.S. deaths, and the difference is ascribed to smoking. That approach seems reasonable if one important condition is satisfied: The CPS sample must be roughly the same as the overall U.S. population with respect to those factors, other than smoking, that could be associated with the death rate. But as Sterling, Rosenbaum, and Weinkam point out, nothing could be further from the truth.

The American Cancer Society bases its CPS study on a million men and women volunteers, drawn from the ranks of the Society's members, friends, and acquaintances. The persons who participate are more affluent than average, overwhelmingly white, married, college graduates, who generally do not have hazardous jobs. Each of those characteristics tends to reduce the death rate of the CPS sample which, as a result, enjoys an average life expectancy that is substantially longer than the typical American enjoys.

Because OTA starts with an atypically low death rate for never-smokers in the CPS sample, then applies that rate to the whole population, its baseline for determining excess deaths is grossly underestimated. By comparing actual deaths with a baseline that is far too low, OTA creates the illusion that a large number of deaths are due to smoking.

That same illusion pervades the statistics released by the U.S. Surgeon General, who in his 1989 report estimated that 335,600 deaths were caused by smoking. When Sterling, Rosenbaum, and Weinkam recalculated the Surgeon General's numbers, replacing the distorted CPS sample with a more representative baseline from large surveys conducted by the National Center for Health Statistics, they found that the number of smoking-related deaths declined to 203,200. Thus, the Surgeon General's report overstated the number of deaths by more than 65 percent simply by choosing the wrong standard of comparison.

Sterling and his coauthors report that not only is the death rate considerably lower for the CPS sample than for the entire U.S. but, astonishingly, even smokers in the CPS sample have a lower death rate than the national average for both smokers and nonsmokers. As a result, if OTA were to have used the CPS death rate for smokers, applied that rate to the total population, then subtracted the actual number of deaths for all Americans, it would have found that smoking saves 277,621 lives each year. The authors caution, of course, that their calculation is sheer nonsense, not a medical miracle. Those "lives would be saved only if the U.S. population would die with the death rate of smokers in the affluent CPS sample."

Unhappily, the death rate for Americans is considerably higher than that for the CPS sample. Nearly as disturbing, researchers like Sterling, Rosenbaum, and Weinkam identified that statistical predicament many years ago; yet the government persists in publishing data on smoking-related deaths that are known to be greatly inflated.

Controlling for Confounding Variables

Even if actual deaths were compared against an appropriate baseline for nonsmokers, the excess deaths could not properly be attributed to smoking alone. It cannot be assumed that the only difference between smokers and nonsmokers is that the former smoke. The two groups are dissimilar in many other respects, some of which affect their propensity to contract diseases that have been identified as smoking-related. For instance, smokers have higher rates of alcoholism, exercise less on average, eat fewer green vegetables, are more likely to be exposed to workplace carcinogens, and are poorer than nonsmokers. Each of those factors can be a "cause" of death from a so-called smoking-related disease; and each must be statistically controlled for if the impact of a single factor, like smoking, is to be reliably determined.

Sterling, Rosenbaum, and Weinkam found that adjusting their calculations for just two lifestyle differences—in income and alcohol consumption—between smokers and nonsmokers had the effect of reducing the Surgeon General's smoking-related death count still further, from 203,200 to 150,000. That means the combined effect of using a proper standard of comparison coupled with controls for income and alcohol was to lower the Surgeon General's estimate 55 percent—from 335,600 to 150,000. Thus, the original estimate was a disquieting 124 percent too high, even without adjustments for important variables like occupation, exercise, and nutritional habits.

What if smokers got plenty of exercise and had healthy diets while nonsmokers were couch potatoes who consumed buckets of fast food? Naturally, there are some smokers and nonsmokers who satisfy those criteria. Dr. William E. Wecker, a consulting statistician who has testified for the tobacco industry, scanned the CPS database and found thousands of smokers with relatively low risk factors and thousands of never-smokers with high risk factors. Comparing the mortality rates of the two groups, Dr. Wecker discovered that the smokers were "healthier and die less often by a factor of three than the never-smokers." Obviously, other risk factors matter, and any study that ignores them is utterly worthless.

Yet, if a smoker who is obese; has a family history of high cholesterol, diabetes, and heart problems; and never exercises dies of a heart attack, the government attributes his death to smoking alone. That procedure, if applied to the other causal factors identified in the CPS study, would produce more than twice as many "attributed" deaths as there are actual deaths, according to Dr. Wecker.

For example, the same calculations that yield 400,000 smoking-related deaths suggest that 504,000 people die each year because they engage in little or no exercise. Employing an identical formula, bad nutritional habits can be shown to account for 649,000 excess deaths annually. That is nearly 1.6 million deaths from only three causes—without considering alcoholism, accidents, poverty, etc.—out of 2.3 million deaths in 1995 from all causes combined. And on it goes—computer-generated phantom deaths, not real deaths—constrained neither by accepted statistical methods, by common sense, nor by the number of people who die each year.

Adjusting for Age at Death

Next and last, we turn to a different sort of deceit—one pertaining not to the number of smoking-related deaths but rather to the misperception that those deaths are somehow associated with kids and young adults. For purposes of this discussion, we will work with the far-fetched statistics published by CDC—an annual average from 1990 through 1994 of 427,743 deaths attributable to tobacco. Is the problem as serious as it sounds?

At first blush, it would seem that more than 400,000 annual deaths is an extremely serious problem. But suppose that all of the people died at age ninety-nine. Surely then, the seriousness of the problem would be tempered by the fact that the decedents would have died soon from some other cause in any event. That is not far from the truth: while tobacco does not kill people at an average age of ninety-nine, it does kill people at an average age of roughly seventy-two–far closer to ninety-nine than to childhood or even young adulthood. Indeed, according to a 1991 RAND study, smoking "reduces the life expectancy of a twenty-year-old by about 4.3 years"—not a trivial concern to be sure, but not the horror that is sometimes portrayed.

Consider Table 2, which shows the number of deaths and age at death for various causes of death: The three nonsmoking categories total nearly 97,000 deaths—probably not much different than the correctly calculated number of smoking-related deaths—but the average age at death is only thirty-nine. As contrasted with a seventy-two-year life expectancy for smokers, each of those nonsmoking deaths snuffs out thirty-three years of life—our most productive years, from both an economic and child-rearing perspective.

Perhaps that is why the Carter Center's "Closing the Gap" project at Emory University examined "years of potential life lost" (YPLL) for selected diseases, to identify those causes of death that were of greatest severity and consequence. The results were reported by R.W. Amler and D.L. Eddins, "Cross-Sectional Analysis: Precursors of Premature Death in the United States," in the 1987 *American Journal of Preventive Medicine*. First, the authors determined for each disease the annual number of deaths by age group. Second, they multiplied for each age group the number of deaths times the average number of years remaining before customary retirement at age sixty-five. Then they computed YPLL by summing the products for each disease across age groups.

Table 2

Cause of Death	Number of Deaths per Year	Mean Age at Death
Smoking-attributed	427,743	72
Motor vehicle accidents	40,982	39
Suicide	30,484	45
Homicide	25,488	32

Source: Centers for Disease Control and Prevention

Table 3

Cause	Deaths	YPLL
Alcohol-related	99,247	1,795,458
Gaps in primary care*	132,593	1,771,133
Injuries (excluding alcohol-related)	64,169	1,755,720
Tobacco-related	338,022	1,497,161

* Inadequate access, screening and preventive interventions.

Thus, if smoking were deemed to have killed, say, fifty thousand people from age sixty through sixty-four, a total of 150,000 years of life were lost in that age group—i.e., fifty thousand lives times an average of three years remaining to age sixty-five. YPLL for smoking would be the accumulation of lost years for all age groups up to sixty-five.

Amler and Eddins identified nine major precursors of preventable deaths. Measured by YPLL, tobacco was about halfway down the list—ranked four out of nine in terms of years lost—not "the number one killer in America" as alarmists have exclaimed. Table 3 shows the four most destructive causes of death, based on 1980 YPLL statistics. Bear in mind that the starting point for the YPLL calculation is the number of deaths, which for tobacco is grossly magnified for all of the reasons discussed above.

According to Amler and Eddins, even if we were to look at medical treatment—measured by days of hospital care—nonalcohol-related injuries impose a 58 percent greater burden than tobacco, and nutrition-related diseases are more burdensome as well.

Another statistic that more accurately reflects the real health repercussions of smoking is the age distribution of the 427,743 deaths that CDC mistakenly traces to tobacco. No doubt most readers will be surprised to learn that—aside from burn victims and pediatric diseases—*tobacco does not kill a single person below the age of 35.*

Each year from 1990 through 1994, as shown in Table 4, only 1,910 tobacco-related deaths—less than half of 1 percent of the total—were persons below age thirty-five. Of those, 319 were burn victims and the rest were infants whose parents smoked. But the relationship between parental smoking and pediatric diseases carries a risk ratio of less than 2, and thus is statistically insignificant. Unless better evidence is produced, those deaths should not be associated with smoking.

Table 4

U.S. Smoking-Attributable Mortality by Cause and Age of Death
1990–1994 Annual Average

Age at Death	Pediatric Diseases	Burn Victims	All Other Diseases	Total
Under 1	1,591	19	0	1,610
1–34	0	300	0	300
35–49	0	221	21,773	21,994
50–69	0	286	148,936	149,222
70–74	0	96	62,154	62,250
75–84	0	133	120,537	120,670
85+	0	45	71,652	71,697
Totals	1,591	1,100	425,052	427,743

Source: Private communication from the Centers for Disease Control and Prevention

On the other hand, the National Center for Health Statistics reports that more than twenty-one thousand persons below age thirty-five died from motor vehicle accidents in 1992, more than eleven thousand died from suicide, and nearly seventeen thousand died from homicide. Over half of those deaths were connected with alcohol or drug abuse. That should put smoking-related deaths in a somewhat different light.

Most revealing of all, almost 255,000 of the smoking-related deaths—nearly 60 percent of the total—occurred at age seventy or above. More than 192,000 deaths—nearly 45 per-cent of the total—occurred at age seventy-five or higher. And roughly 72,000 deaths—almost 17 percent of the total—occurred at the age of 85 or above. Still, the public health community disingenuously refers to "premature" deaths from smoking, as if there is no upper age limit to the computation.

The vast overestimate of the dangers of smoking has had disastrous results for the health of young people. Risky behavior does not exist in a vacuum; people compare uncertainties and apportion their time, effort, and money according to the perceived severity of the risk. Each year, alcohol and drug abuse kills tens of thousands of people under the age of thirty-five. Yet according to a 1995 survey by the U.S. Department of Health and Human Services, high school seniors thought smoking a pack a day was more dangerous than daily consumption of four to five alcoholic beverages or using barbiturates. And the CDC reports that the number of pregnant women who drank frequently quadrupled between 1991 and 1995—notwithstanding that fetal alcohol syndrome is the largest cause of preventable mental retardation, occurring in one out of every one thousand births.

Can anyone doubt that the drumbeat of antismoking propaganda from the White House and the health establishment has deluded Americans into thinking that tobacco is the real danger to our children? In truth, alcohol and drug abuse poses an immensely greater risk and antismoking zealots bear a heavy burden for their duplicity.

Conclusion

The unvarnished fact is that children do not die of tobacco-related diseases, correctly determined. If they smoke heavily during their teens, they may die of lung cancer in their old age, fifty or sixty years later, assuming lung cancer is still a threat then.

Meanwhile, do not expect consistency or even common sense from public officials. Alcoholism contributes to crime, violence, spousal abuse, and child neglect. Children are dying by the thousands in accidents, suicides, and homicides. But states go to war against nicotine—which is not an intoxicant, has no causal connection with crime, and poses little danger to young adults or family members.

The campaign against cigarettes is not entirely dishonest. After all, a seasoning of truth makes the lie more digestible. Evidence does suggest that cigarettes substantially increase the risk of lung cancer, bronchitis, and emphysema. The relationship between smoking and other diseases is not nearly so clear, however; and the scare-mongering that has passed for science is appalling. Not only is tobacco far less pernicious than Americans are led to believe, but its destructive effect is amplified by all manner of statistical legerdemain—counting diseases that should not be counted, using the wrong sample as a standard of comparison, and failing to control for obvious confounding variables.

To be blunt, there is no credible evidence that 400,000 deaths per year—or any number remotely close to 400,000—are caused by tobacco. Nor has that estimate been adjusted for the positive effects of smoking—less obesity, colitis, depression, Alzheimer's disease, Parkinson's disease and, for some women, a lower incidence of breast cancer. The actual damage from smoking is neither known nor knowable with precision. Responsible statisticians agree that it is impossible to attribute causation to a single variable, like tobacco, when there are multiple causal factors that are correlated with one another. The damage from cigarettes is far less than it is made out to be.

Most important, the government should stop lying and stop pretending that smoking-related deaths are anything but a statistical artifact. The unifying bond of all science is that truth is its aim. When that goal yields to politics, tainting science in order to advance predetermined ends, we are all at risk. Sadly, that is exactly what has transpired as our public officials fabricate evidence to promote their crusade against big tobacco.

The Health Consequences of Smoking: A Report of the Surgeon General

Executive Summary

This report of the Surgeon General on the health effects of smoking returns to the topic of active smoking and disease, the focus of the first Surgeon General's report published in 1964. The first report established a model of comprehensive evidence evaluation for the 27 reports that have followed: for those on the adverse health effects of smoking, the evidence has been evaluated using guidelines for assessing causality of smoking with disease. Using this model, every report on health has found that smoking causes many diseases and other adverse effects. Repeatedly, the reports have concluded that smoking is the single greatest cause of avoidable morbidity and mortality in the United States.

Of the Surgeon General's reports published since 1964, only a few have comprehensively documented and updated the evidence on active smoking and disease. The 1979 report provided a broad array of information, and the 1990 report on smoking cessation also investigated major diseases caused by smoking. Other volumes published during the 1980s focused on specific groups of diseases caused by smoking, and the 2001 report was devoted to women and smoking. Because there has not been a recent systematic review of the full sweep of the evidence, the topic of active smoking and health was considered an appropriate focus for this latest report. Researchers have continued to identify new adverse effects of active smoking in their ongoing efforts to investigate the health effects of smoking. Lengthy follow-ups are now available for thousands of participants in long-term cohort (follow-up) studies.

This report also updates the methodology for evaluating evidence that the 1964 report initiated. Although that model has proved to be effective, this report establishes a uniformity of language concerning causality of associations so as to bring greater specificity to the findings of the report. Beginning with this report, conclusions concerning causality of association will be placed into one of four categories with regard to strength of the evidence: (1) sufficient to

From "The Health Consequences of Smoking: A Report of the Surgeon General", Centers for Disease Control, 2004. References omitted.

infer a causal relationship, (2) suggestive but not sufficient to infer a causal relationship, (3) inadequate to infer the presence or absence of a causal relationship, or (4) suggestive of no causal relationship.

This approach separates the classification of the evidence concerning causality from the implications of that determination. In particular, the magnitude of the effect in the population, the attributable risk, is considered under "implications" of the causal determination. For example, there might be sufficient evidence to classify smoking as a cause of two diseases but the number of attributable cases would depend on the frequency of the disease in the population and the effects of other causal factors.

This report covers active smoking only. Passive smoking was the focus of the 1986 Surgeon General's report and subsequent reports by other entities. The health effects of pipes and cigars, also not within the scope of this report, are covered in another report (NCI 1998).

In preparing this report, the literature review approach was necessarily selective. For conditions for which a causal conclusion had been previously reached, there was no attempt to cover all relevant literature, but rather to review the conclusions from previous Surgeon General's reports and focus on important new studies for that topic. The enormous scope of the evidence precludes such detailed reviews. For conditions for which a causal conclusion had not been previously reached, a comprehensive search strategy was developed. Search strategies included reviewing previous Surgeon General's reports on smoking, publications originating from the largest observational studies, and reference lists from important publications; consulting with content experts; and conducting focused literature searches on specific topics. For this report, studies through 2000 were reviewed.

In addition, conclusions from prior reports concerning smoking as a cause of a particular disease have been updated and are presented in this new format based on the evidence evaluated in this report (Table 1). Remarkably, this report identifies a substantial number of diseases found to be caused by smoking that were not previously causally associated with smoking: cancers of the stomach, uterine cervix, pancreas, and kidney; acute myeloid leukemia; pneumonia; abdominal aortic aneurysm; cataract; and periodontitis. The report also concludes that smoking generally diminishes the health of smokers.

Despite the many prior reports on the topic and the high level of public knowledge in the United States of the adverse effects of smoking in general, tobacco use remains the leading preventable cause of disease and death in the United States, causing approximately 440,000 deaths each year and costing approximately $157 billion in annual health-related economic losses. Nationally, smoking results in more than 5.6 million years of potential life lost each year. Although the rates of smoking continue to decline, an estimated 46.2 million adults in the United States still smoked cigarettes in 2001. In 2000, 70 percent of those who smoked wanted to quit. An increasingly disturbing picture of widespread organ damage in active smokers is emerging, likely reflecting the systemic distribution of tobacco smoke components and their high level of toxicity. Thus, active smokers are at higher risk for cataract, cancer of the cervix, pneumonia, and reduced health status generally.

Table 1

Diseases and Other Adverse Health Effects for which Smoking is Identified as a Cause in the Current Surgeon General's Report

Disease	Highest Level Conclusion from Previous Surgeon General's Reports (year)	Conclusion from the 2004 Surgeon General's Report
Cancer		
Bladder cancer	"Smoking is a cause of bladder cancer; cessation reduces risk by about 50 percent after only a few years, in comparison with continued smoking." (1990, p. 10)	"The evidence is sufficient to infer a causal relationship between smoking and . . . bladder cancer."
Cervical cancer	"Smoking has been consistently associated with an increased risk for cervical cancer." (2001, p. 224)	"The evidence is sufficient to infer a causal relationship between smoking and cervical cancer."
Esophageal cancer	"Cigarette smoking is a major cause of esophageal cancer in the United States." (1982, p. 7)	"The evidence is sufficient to infer a causal relationship between smoking and cancers of the esophagus."
Kidney cancer	"Cigarette smoking is a contributory factor in the development of kidney cancer in the United States. The term 'contributory factor' by no means excludes the possibility of a causal role for smoking in cancers of this site." (1982, p. 7)	"The evidence is sufficient to infer a causal relationship between smoking and renal cell, [and] renal pelvis . . . cancers."
Laryngeal cancer	"Cigarette smoking is causally associated with cancer of the lung, larynx, oral cavity, and esophagus in women as well as in men. . . ." (1980, p. 126)	"The evidence is sufficient to infer a causal relationship between smoking and cancer of the larynx."
Leukemia	"Leukemia has recently been implicated as a smoking-related disease. . .but this observation has not been consistent." (1990, p. 176)	"The evidence is sufficient to infer a causal relationship between smoking and acute myeloid leukemia."
Lung cancer	"Additional epidemiological, pathological, and experimental data not only confirm the conclusion of the Surgeon General's 1964 Report regarding lung cancer in men but strengthen the causal relationship of smoking to lung cancer in women." (1967, p. 36)	"The evidence is sufficient to infer a causal relationship between smoking and lung cancer."
Oral cancer	"Cigarette smoking is a major cause of cancers of the oral cavity in the United States." (1982, p. 6)	"The evidence is sufficient to infer a causal relationship between smoking and cancers of the oral cavity and pharynx."
Pancreatic cancer	"Smoking cessation reduces the risk of pancreatic cancer, compared with continued smoking, although this reduction in risk may only be measurable after 10 years of abstinence." (1990, p. 10)	"The evidence is sufficient to infer a causal relationship between smoking and pancreatic cancer."
Stomach cancer	"Data on smoking and cancer of the stomach . . . are unclear." (2001, p. 231)	"The evidence is sufficient to infer a causal relationship between smoking and gastric cancers."

Table 1 (Continued)

Disease	Highest Level Conclusion from Previous Surgeon General's Reports (year)	Conclusion from the 2004 Surgeon General's Report
Cardiovascular diseases		
Abdominal aortic aneurysm	"Death from rupture of an atherosclerotic abdominal aneurysm is more common in cigarette smokers than in nonsmokers." (1983, p. 195)	"The evidence is sufficient to infer a causal relationship between smoking and abdominal aortic aneurysm."
Atherosclerosis	"Cigarette smoking is the most powerful risk factor predisposing to atherosclerotic peripheral vascular disease." (1983, p. 8)	"The evidence is sufficient to infer a causal relationship between smoking and subclinical atherosclerosis."
Cerebrovascular disease	"Cigarette smoking is a major cause of cerebrovascular disease (stroke), the third leading cause of death in the United States." (1989, p. 12)	"The evidence is sufficient to infer a causal relationship between smoking and stroke."
Coronary heart disease	"In summary, for the purposes of preventive medicine, it can be concluded that smoking is causally related to coronary heart disease for both men and women in the United States." (1979, p. 1–15)	"The evidence is sufficient to infer a causal relationship between smoking and coronary heart disease."
Respiratory diseases		
Chronic obstructive pulmonary disease	"Cigarette smoking is the most important of the causes of chronic bronchitis in the United States, and increases the risk of dying from chronic bronchitis." (1964, p. 302)	"The evidence is sufficient to infer a causal relationship between active smoking and chronic obstructive pulmonary disease morbidity and mortality."
Pneumonia	"Smoking cessation reduces rates of respiratory symptoms such as cough, sputum production, and wheezing, and respiratory infections such as bronchitis and pneumonia, compared with continued smoking." (1990, p. 11)	"The evidence is sufficient to infer a causal relationship between smoking and acute respiratory illnesses, including pneumonia, in persons without underlying smoking-related chronic obstructive lung disease."
Respiratory effects in utero	"In utero exposure to maternal smoking is associated with reduced lung function among infants. . . ." (2001, p. 14)	"The evidence is sufficient to infer a causal relationship between maternal smoking during pregnancy and a reduction of lung function in infants."
Respiratory effects in childhood and adolescence	"Cigarette smoking during childhood and adolescence produces significant health problems among young people, including cough and phlegm production, an increased number and severity of respiratory illnesses, decreased physical fitness, an unfavorable lipid profile, and potential retardation in the rate of lung growth and the level of maximum lung function." (1994, p. 41)	"The evidence is sufficient to infer a causal relationship between active smoking and impaired lung growth during childhood and adolescence." "The evidence is sufficient to infer a causal relationship between active smoking and the early onset of lung function decline during late adolescence and early adulthood."

(continues)

Table 1 (Continued)

Disease	Highest Level Conclusion from Previous Surgeon General's Reports (year)	Conclusion from the 2004 Surgeon General's Report
		"The evidence is sufficient to infer a causal relationship between active smoking and respiratory symptoms in children and adolescents, including coughing, phlegm, wheezing, and dyspnea."
		"The evidence is sufficient to infer a causal relationship between active smoking and asthma-related symptoms (i.e., wheezing) in childhood and adolescence."
Respiratory effects in adulthood	"Cigarette smoking accelerates the age-related decline in lung function that occurs among never smokers. With sustained abstinence from smoking, the rate of decline in pulmonary function among former smokers returns to that of never smokers." (1990, p. 11)	"The evidence is sufficient to infer a causal relationship between active smoking in adulthood and a premature onset of and an accelerated age-related decline in lung function."
		"The evidence is sufficient to infer a causal relationship between sustained cessation from smoking and a return of the rate of decline in pulmonary function to that of persons who had never smoked."
Other respiratory effects	"Smoking cessation reduces rates of respiratory symptoms such as cough, sputum production, and wheezing, and respiratory infections such as bronchitis and pneumonia, compared with continued smoking." (1990, p. 11)	"The evidence is sufficient to infer a causal relationship between active smoking and all major respiratory symptoms among adults, including coughing, phlegm, wheezing, and dyspnea."
		"The evidence is sufficient to infer a causal relationship between active smoking and poor asthma control."
Reproductive effects		
Fetal death and stillbirths	"The risk for perinatal mortality—both stillbirth and neonatal deaths—and the risk for sudden infant death syndrome (SIDS) are increased among the offspring of women who smoke during pregnancy." (2001, p. 307)	"The evidence is sufficient to infer a causal relationship between sudden infant death syndrome and maternal smoking during and after pregnancy."
Fertility	"Women who smoke have increased risks for conception delay and for both primary and secondary infertility." (2001, p. 307)	"The evidence is sufficient to infer a causal relationship between smoking and reduced fertility in women."
Low birth weight	"Infants born to women who smoke during pregnancy have a lower average birth weight . . . than . . . infants born to women who do not smoke." (2001, p. 307)	"The evidence is sufficient to infer a causal relationship between maternal active smoking and fetal growth restriction and low birth weight."

Table 1 (Continued)

Disease	Highest Level Conclusion from Previous Surgeon General's Reports (year)	Conclusion from the 2004 Surgeon General's Report
Pregnancy complications	"Smoking during pregnancy is associated with increased risks for preterm premature rupture of membranes, abruptio placentae, and placenta previa, and with a modest increase in risk for preterm delivery." (2001, p. 307)	"The evidence is sufficient to infer a casual relationship between maternal active smoking and premature rupture of the membranes, placenta previa, and placental abruption." "The evidence is sufficient to infer a causal relationship between maternal active smoking and preterm delivery and shortened gestation."
Other effects		
Cataract	"Women who smoke have an increased risk for cataract." (2001, p. 331)	"The evidence is sufficient to infer a causal relationship between smoking and nuclear cataract."
Diminished health status/morbidity	"Relationships between smoking and cough or phlegm are strong and consistent; they have been amply documented and are judged to be causal . . . ." (1984, p. 47) "Consideration of evidence from many different studies has led to the conclusion that cigarette smoking is the overwhelmingly most important cause of cough, sputum, chronic bronchitis, and mucus hypersecretion." (1984, p. 48)	"The evidence is sufficient to infer a causal relationship between smoking and diminished health status that may be manifest as increased absenteeism from work and increased use of medical care services." "The evidence is sufficient to infer a causal relationship between smoking and increased risks for adverse surgical outcomes related to wound healing and respiratory complications."
Hip fractures	"Women who currently smoke have an increased risk for hip fracture compared with women who do not smoke." (2001, p. 321)	"The evidence is sufficient to infer a causal relationship between smoking and hip fractures."
Low bone density	"Postmenopausal women who currently smoke have lower bone density than do women who do not smoke." (2001, p. 321)	"In postmenopausal women, the evidence is sufficient to infer a causal relationship between smoking and low bone density."
Peptic ulcer disease	"The relationship between cigarette smoking and death rates from peptic ulcer, especially gastric ulcer, is confirmed. In addition, morbidity data suggest a similar relationship exists with the prevalence of reported disease from this cause." (1967, p. 40)	"The evidence is sufficient to infer a causal relationship between smoking and peptic ulcer disease in persons who are *Helicobacter pylori* positive."

Sources: U.S. Department of Health, Education, and Welfare 1964, 1967, 1979; U.S. Department of Health and Human Services 1980, 1982, 1983, 1984, 1989, 1990, 1994, 2001.

This new information should be an impetus for even more vigorous programs to reduce and prevent smoking. Smokers need to be aware that smoking carries far greater risks than the most widely known hazards. Health care providers should also use the new evidence to counsel their patients. For example, ophthalmologists may want to warn patients about the increased risk of cataract in smokers, and geriatricians should counsel their patients who smoke, even the oldest, to quit. This report shows that smokers who quit can lower their risk for smoking-caused diseases and improve their health status generally. Those who never start can avoid the predictable burden of disease and lost life expectancy that results from a lifetime of smoking. . . .

Major Conclusions

Forty years after the first Surgeon General's report in 1964, the list of diseases and other adverse effects caused by smoking continues to expand. Epidemiologic studies are providing a comprehensive assessment of the risks faced by smokers who continue to smoke across their life spans. Laboratory research now reveals how smoking causes disease at the molecular and cellular levels. Fortunately for former smokers, studies show that the substantial risks of smoking can be reduced by successfully quitting at any age. The evidence reviewed in this and prior reports of the Surgeon General leads to the following major conclusions:

1. Smoking harms nearly every organ of the body, causing many diseases and reducing the health of smokers in general.
2. Quitting smoking has immediate as well as longterm benefits, reducing risks for diseases caused by smoking and improving health in general.
3. Smoking cigarettes with lower machine-measured yields of tar and nicotine provides no clear benefit to health.
4. The list of diseases caused by smoking has been expanded to include abdominal aortic aneurysm, acute myeloid leukemia, cataract, cervical cancer, kidney cancer, pancreatic cancer, pneumonia, periodontitis, and stomach cancer.

POSTSCRIPT

Are the Adverse Effects of Smoking Exaggerated?

Much data indicate that smoking cigarettes is injurious to human health. For example, more than 400,000 people die from tobacco-related illnesses each year in the United States, costing the United States health care system billions of dollars annually. Not only does the smoker bear the cost of tobacco-related illness, so do millions of taxpayers.

Thousands more people develop debilitating conditions such as chronic bronchitis and emphysema. Levy and Marimont, however, question the accuracy of the data. How the data are presented and interpreted may affect how one feels about the issue of placing more restrictions on tobacco products. If cigarette smoking is demonized, as Levy and Marimont suggest, it is not difficult to influence people's positions on regulating tobacco. There is currently a great deal of antismoking sentiment in society because of how the statistics are presented. Levy and Marimont do not recommend that people use tobacco products; however, they state only that the consequences linked to it are exaggerated. If the health effects of cigarette smoking were not deemed as hazardous as they are, would people feel differently about smoking?

Despite the reported hazards of tobacco smoking, numerous proponents of smokers' rights assert that cigarette smoking is a matter of choice. However, many people could argue that smoking is not a matter of choice because smokers become addicted to nicotine. Others contend that the decision to start smoking is a matter of choice, but once tobacco dependency occurs, most smokers are in effect deprived of the choice to stop smoking. Yet, it has been shown that millions of smokers have been able to quit smoking. Contributing to the tobacco dilemma is the expansion of tobacco manufacturers into many developing countries and the proliferation of advertising despite its ban from television and radio. Print advertisements and billboards are popular tools for advertsing tobacco products.

Nevertheless, tobacco proponents maintain that people make all types of choices, and if the choices that people make are ultimately harmful, then that is their responsibility. A basic question is, "do people have the right to engage in self-destructive behavior?" If people are looked down upon because they smoke cigarettes, then should people be looked down upon if they eat too much or exercise too little? Does one have the right to eat a half-dozen double cheeseburgers, to be a couch potato, to drink until one passes out? At what point does one lose the right to engage in deleterious behaviors—assuming that the rights of others are not adversely affected?

There are many articles that address the impact of tobacco on society. One article that focuses on reasons that teenagers smoke is "Too Many Kids

Smoke," by Dianna Gordon, *State Legislatures* (March 2004). Kendall Morgan looks at the addictiveness of nicotine in "More Than a Kick," *Science News* (March 22, 2003). Several times a year the SmokeFree Educational Services publishes *SmokeFree Air*, a newsletter describing actions that have been taken to limit smoking in public locations. Mike Mitka's article "Surgeon General's Newest Report on Tobacco," *Journal of the American Medical Association* (September 20, 2000), describes current smoking-related statistics and efforts to stem cigarette smoking.

ISSUE 9

Should Laws Prohibiting Marijuana Use Be Relaxed?

YES: Ethan A. Nadelmann, from "An End to Marijuana Prohibition," *National Review* (July 12, 2004)

NO: Office of National Drug Control Policy, from *Marijuana Myths and Facts: The Truth Behind 10 Popular Misconceptions* (2004)

ISSUE SUMMARY

YES: Ethan Nadelmann, founder and executive director of the Drug Policy Foundation, argues that law enforcement officials are over-zealous in prosecuting individuals for marijuana possession. Eighty-seven percent of marijuana arrests are for possession of small amounts of the drug. The cost of marijuana enforcement to U.S. tax-payers ranges from $10 to $15 billion. In addition, punishments are unjust because they vary greatly.

NO: The Office of National Drug Control Policy (ONDCP) contends that marijuana is not a harmless drug. Besides causing physical prob-lems, marijuana affects academic performance and emotional adjustment. Moreover, dealers who grow and sell marijuana may become violent to protect their commodity.

Despite marijuana being the most commonly used illegal drug in the United States, the federal government maintains that it is a potentially dan-gerous substance. Also, its use represents a danger, not just to the user, but to others. The government claims that marijuana can be addictive and that more young people are in treatment for marijuana than for other illegal drugs.

The federal government argues that relaxing laws against marijuana use, even for medical purposes, is unwarranted. However, since the mid-1990s, voters in California, Arizona, Oregon, Colorado, and other states have passed referenda to legalize marijuana for medical purposes. Despite the position of these voters, however, the federal government does not support the medical use of marijuana, and federal laws take precedence over state laws. A major concern of opponents of these referenda is that legalization of marijuana for medicinal purposes will lead to its use for recreational purposes.

The use of marijuana dates back at least 5000 years ago. It was utilized medically as far back as 2737 B.C., when Chinese emperor Shen Nung recommended marijuana, or cannabis, for medical use. By the 1890s, some medical reports had stated that cannabis was useful as a pain reliever. Despite its historical significance, the use of marijuana for medical treatment is still a widely debated and controversial topic. The easing of marijuana laws, despite the drug's possible medical benefits, is viewed as a slippery slope.

Marijuana has been tested in the treatment of glaucoma, asthma, convulsions, epilepsy, and migraine headaches, and in the reduction of nausea, vomiting, and loss of appetite associated with chemotherapy treatments. Many medical professionals and patients believe that marijuana shows promise in the treatment of these disorders and others, including spasticity in amputees and multiple sclerosis.

Another consideration of relaxing marijuana laws, even for medical purposes, is what constitutes a legitimate medical use. For example, many people would agree that the medicinal use of marijuana for someone who has glaucoma or is receiving chemotherapy would be a valid use of marijuana. Would smoking marijuana to get rid of a headache or because one has muscle soreness be reasonable medical uses for marijuana?

Advocates for relaxing marijuana laws feel that the drug is unfairly labeled as a dangerous drug. For example, many more people throughout the world die from tobacco smoking and alcohol than from marijuana use. Yet, adults using those products do not go to jail and are not deprived of rights that other citizens enjoy. There are as many people in jail today for marijuana offenses as from cocaine, heroin, methamphetamine, Ecstasy, and all other illegal drugs combined, claims Nadelmann.

Another point raised by those people in favor of relaxing marijuana laws is that it would be easier to educate young people about marijuana's effects if it was legal. By simply keeping the drug illegal, the message is DON'T USE MARIJUANA, rather than how to reduce harms associated with it. Proponents such as Nadelmann and others do not advocate the unregulated use of marijuana. They favor a more reasoned, controlled approach.

Marijuana opponents argue that the evidence in support of marijuana as being medically useful suffers from far too many deficiencies. The DEA, for example, believes that studies supporting the medical value of marijuana are scientifically limited, based on biased testimonies of ill individuals who have used marijuana and their families and friends, and grounded in the unscientific opinions of certain physicians, nurses, and other hospital personnel.

In the following selections, Ethan A. Nadelmann asserts that the federal government is overzealous in its enforcement of marijuana laws. Besides having approximately 700,000 people in jail for marijuana offenses, the government has set up needless political roadblocks to prevent the use of marijuana for medicinal purposes. The Office of National Drug Control Policy (ONDCP) argues that marijuana is far more dangerous than many young people realize and tries to dispel many of the myths associated with its use. The ONDCP maintains that marijuana should not be used for legal medical purposes because the current research on marijuana's medicinal benefits is inconclusive.

YES ↰

Ethan A. Nadelmann

An End to Marijuana Prohibition

Never before have so many Americans supported decriminalizing and even legalizing marijuana. Seventy-two percent say that for simple marijuana possession, people should not be incarcerated but fined: the generally accepted definition of "decriminalization."[1] Even more Americans support making marijuana legal for medical purposes. Support for broader legalization ranges between 25 and 42 percent, depending on how one asks the question.[2] Two of every five Americans—according to a 2003 Zogby poll—say "the government should treat marijuana more or less the same way it treats alcohol: It should regulate it, control it, tax it, and only make it illegal for children."[3]

Close to 100 million Americans—including more than half of those between the ages of 18 and 50—have tried marijuana at least once.[4] Military and police recruiters often have no choice but to ignore past marijuana use by job seekers.[5] The public apparently feels the same way about presidential and other political candidates. Al Gore,[6] Bill Bradley,[7] and John Kerry[8] all say they smoked pot in days past. So did Bill Clinton, with his notorious caveat.[9] George W. Bush won't deny he did.[10] And ever more political, business, religious, intellectual, and other leaders plead guilty as well.[11]

The debate over ending marijuana prohibition simmers just below the surface of mainstream politics, crossing ideological and partisan boundaries. Marijuana is no longer the symbol of Sixties rebellion and Seventies permissiveness, and it's not just liberals and libertarians who say it should be legal, as William F. Buckley Jr. has demonstrated better than anyone. As director of the country's leading drug policy reform organization, I've had countless conversations with police and prosecutors, judges and politicians, and hundreds of others who quietly agree that the criminalization of marijuana is costly, foolish, and destructive. What's most needed now is principled conservative leadership. Buckley has led the way, and New Mexico's former governor, Gary Johnson, spoke out courageously while in office. How about others?

A Systemic Overreaction

Marijuana prohibition is unique among American criminal laws. No other law is both enforced so widely and harshly and yet deemed unnecessary by such a substantial portion of the populace.

Police make about 700,000 arrests per year for marijuana offenses.[12] That's almost the same number as are arrested each year for cocaine, heroin, methamphetamine, Ecstasy, and all other illicit drugs combined.[13] Roughly 600,000, or 87 percent, of marijuana arrests are for nothing more than possession of small amounts.[14] Millions of Americans have never been arrested or convicted of any criminal offense except this.[15] Enforcing marijuana laws costs an estimated $10–15 billion in direct costs alone.[16]

Punishments range widely across the country, from modest fines to a few days in jail to many years in prison. Prosecutors often contend that no one goes to prison for simple possession—but tens, perhaps hundreds, of thousands of people on probation and parole are locked up each year because their urine tested positive for marijuana or because they were picked up in possession of a joint. Alabama currently locks up people convicted three times of marijuana *possession* for 15 years to life.[17] There are probably—no firm estimates exist—100,000 Americans behind bars tonight for one marijuana offense or another.[18] And even for those who don't lose their freedom, simply being arrested can be traumatic and costly. A parent's marijuana use can be the basis for taking away her children and putting them in foster care.[19] Foreign-born residents of the U.S. can be deported for a marijuana offense no matter how long they have lived in this country, no matter if their children are U.S. citizens, and no matter how long they have been legally employed.[20] More than half the states revoke or suspend driver's licenses of people arrested for marijuana possession even though they were not driving at the time of arrest.[21] The federal Higher Education Act prohibits student loans to young people convicted of any drug offense;[22] all other criminal offenders remain eligible.[23]

This is clearly an overreaction on the part of government. No drug is perfectly safe, and every psychoactive drug can be used in ways that are problematic. The federal government has spent billions of dollars on advertisements and anti-drug programs that preach the dangers of marijuana—that it's a gateway drug, and addictive in its own right, and dramatically more potent than it used to be, and responsible for all sorts of physical and social diseases as well as international terrorism.[24,25] But the government has yet to repudiate the 1988 finding of the Drug Enforcement Administration's own administrative law judge, Francis Young, who concluded after extensive testimony that "marijuana in its natural form is one of the safest therapeutically active substances known to man."[26]

Is marijuana a gateway drug? Yes, insofar as most Americans try marijuana before they try other illicit drugs. But no, insofar as the vast majority of Americans who have tried marijuana have never gone on to try other illegal drugs, much less get in trouble with them, and most have never even gone on to become regular or problem marijuana users.[27] Trying to reduce heroin addiction by preventing marijuana use, it's been said, is like trying to reduce motorcycle fatalities by cracking down on bicycle riding.[28] If marijuana did not exist, there's little reason to believe that there would be less drug abuse in the U.S.; indeed, its role would most likely be filled by a more dangerous substance.

Is marijuana dramatically more potent today? There's certainly a greater variety of high-quality marijuana available today than 30 years ago. But anyone who smoked marijuana in the 1970s and 1980s can recall smoking pot that was just as strong as anything available today.[29] What's more, one needs to take only a few puffs of higher-potency pot to get the desired effect, so there's less wear and tear on the lungs.[30]

Is marijuana addictive? Yes, it can be, in that some people use it to excess, in ways that are problematic for themselves and those around them, and find it hard to stop. But marijuana may well be the least addictive and least damaging of all commonly used psychoactive drugs, including many that are now legal.[31] Most people who smoke marijuana never become dependent.[32] Withdrawal symptoms pale compared with those from other drugs. No one has ever died from a marijuana overdose, which cannot be said of most other drugs.[33] Marijuana is not associated with violent behavior and only minimally with reckless sexual behavior.[34] And even heavy marijuana smokers smoke only a fraction of what cigarette addicts smoke. Lung cancers involving only marijuana are rare.[35]

The government's most recent claim is that marijuana abuse accounts for more people entering treatment than any other illegal drug. That shouldn't be surprising, given that tens of millions of Americans smoke marijuana while only a few million use all other illicit drugs.[36] But the claim is spurious nonetheless. Few Americans who enter "treatment" for marijuana are addicted. Fewer than one in five people entering drug treatment for marijuana do so voluntarily.[37] More than half were referred by the criminal justice system.[38] They go because they got caught with a joint or failed a drug test at school or work (typically for having smoked marijuana days ago, not for being impaired), or because they were caught by a law-enforcement officer—and attending a marijuana "treatment" program is what's required to avoid expulsion, dismissal, or incarceration.[39] Many traditional drug treatment programs shamelessly participate in this charade to preserve a profitable and captive client stream.[40]

Even those who recoil at the "nanny state" telling adults what they can or cannot sell to one another often make an exception when it comes to marijuana—to "protect the kids." This is a bad joke, as any teenager will attest. The criminalization of marijuana for adults has not prevented young people from having better access to marijuana than anyone else. Even as marijuana's popularity has waxed and waned since the 1970s, one statistic has remained constant: More than 80 percent of high school students report it's easy to get.[41] Meanwhile, the government's exaggerations and outright dishonesty easily backfire. For every teen who refrains from trying marijuana because it's illegal (for adults), another is tempted by its status as "forbidden fruit."[42] Many respond to the lies about marijuana by disbelieving warnings about more dangerous drugs. So much for protecting the kids by criminalizing the adults.

The Medical Dimension

The debate over medical marijuana obviously colors the broader debate over marijuana prohibition. Marijuana's medical efficacy is no longer in serious dispute. Its use as a medicine dates back thousands of years.[43] Pharmaceutical products containing marijuana's central ingredient, THC, are legally sold in the U.S., and more are emerging.[44,45,46] Some people find the pill form satisfactory, and others consume it in teas or baked products. Most find smoking the easiest and most effective way to consume this unusual medicine,[47] but non-smoking consumption methods, notably vaporizers, are emerging.[48]

Federal law still prohibits medical marijuana.[49] But every state ballot initiative to legalize medical marijuana has been approved, often by wide margins— in California, Washington, Oregon, Alaska, Colorado, Nevada, Maine, and Washington, D.C.[50] State legislatures in Vermont,[51] Hawaii,[52] and Maryland[53] have followed suit, and many others are now considering their own medical marijuana bills—including New York,[54] Connecticut,[55] Rhode Island,[56] and Illinois.[57] Support is often bipartisan, with Republican governors like Gary Johnson and Maryland's Bob Ehrlich taking the lead.[58,59] In New York's 2002 gubernatorial campaign, the conservative candidate of the Independence party, Tom Golisano, surprised everyone by campaigning heavily on this issue.[60] The medical marijuana bill now before the New York legislature is backed not just by leading Republicans but even by some Conservative party leaders.[61]

The political battleground increasingly pits the White House—first under Clinton and now Bush—against everyone else. Majorities in virtually every state in the country would vote, if given the chance, to legalize medical marijuana.[62] Even Congress is beginning to turn; last summer about two-thirds of House Democrats and a dozen Republicans voted in favor of an amendment co-sponsored by Republican Dana Rohrabacher to prohibit federal funding of any Justice Department crackdowns on medical marijuana in the states that had legalized it.[63,64] (Many more Republicans privately expressed support, but were directed to vote against.) And federal courts have imposed limits on federal aggression: first in *Conant* v. *Walters*,[65] which now protects the First Amendment rights of doctors and patients to discuss medical marijuana, and more recently in *Raich* v. *Ashcroft*[66] and *Santa Cruz* v. *Ashcroft*,[67] which determined that the federal government's power to regulate interstate commerce does not provide a basis for prohibiting medical marijuana operations that are entirely local and non-commercial. (The Supreme Court let the *Conant* decision stand,[68] but has yet to consider the others.)

State and local governments are increasingly involved in trying to regulate medical marijuana, notwithstanding the federal prohibition. California, Oregon, Hawaii, Alaska, Colorado, and Nevada have created confidential medical marijuana patient registries, which protect bona fide patients and caregivers from arrest or prosecution.[69] Some municipal governments are now trying to figure out how to regulate production and distribution.[70] In California, where dozens of medical marijuana programs now operate openly, with tacit approval by local authorities, some program directors are asking to be licensed and regulated.[71,72] Many state and local authorities, including law enforcement, favor this but are intimidated by federal threats to arrest and prosecute them for violating federal law.[73]

The drug czar and DEA spokespersons recite the mantra that "there is no such thing as medical marijuana," but the claim is so specious on its face that it clearly undermines federal credibility.[74] The federal government currently provides marijuana—from its own production site in Mississippi—to a few patients who years ago were recognized by the courts as bona fide patients.[75] No one wants to debate those who have used marijuana for medical purposes, be it

Santa Cruz medical-marijuana hospice founder Valerie Corral or NATIONAL REVIEW's Richard Brookhiser.[76] Even many federal officials quietly regret the assault on medical marijuana. When the DEA raided Corral's hospice in September 2002, one agent was heard to say, "Maybe I'm going to think about getting another job sometime soon."

The Broader Movement

The bigger battle, of course, concerns whether marijuana prohibition will ultimately go the way of alcohol Prohibition, replaced by a variety of state and local tax and regulatory policies with modest federal involvement.[77] Dedicated prohibitionists see medical marijuana as the first step down a slippery slope to full legalization.[78] The voters who approved the medical-marijuana ballot initiatives (as well as the wealthy men who helped fund the campaigns[79]) were roughly divided between those who support broader legalization and those who don't, but united in seeing the criminalization and persecution of medical marijuana patients as the most distasteful aspect of the war on marijuana. (This was a point that Buckley made forcefully in his columns about the plight of Peter McWilliams, who likely died because federal authorities effectively forbade him to use marijuana as medicine.[80])

The medical marijuana effort has probably aided the broader anti-prohibitionist campaign in three ways. It helped transform the face of marijuana in the media, from the stereotypical rebel with long hair and tie-dyed shirt to an ordinary middle-aged American struggling with MS or cancer or AIDS.[81] By winning first Proposition 215, the 1996 medical-marijuana ballot initiative in California, and then a string of similar victories in other states, the nascent drug policy reform movement demonstrated that it could win in the big leagues of American politics.[82] And the emergence of successful models of medical marijuana control is likely to boost public confidence in the possibilities and virtue of regulating nonmedical use as well.

In this regard, the history of Dutch policy on cannabis (i.e., marijuana and hashish) is instructive. The "coffee shop" model in the Netherlands, where retail (but not wholesale) sale of cannabis is de facto legal, was not legislated into existence. It evolved in fits and starts following the decriminalization of cannabis by Parliament in 1976, as consumers, growers, and entrepreneurs negotiated and collaborated with local police, prosecutors, and other authorities to find an acceptable middle-ground policy.[83] "Coffee shops" now operate throughout the country, subject to local regulations.[84] Troublesome shops are shut down, and most are well integrated into local city cultures. Cannabis is no more popular than in the U.S. and other Western countries, notwithstanding the effective absence of criminal sanctions and controls.[85] Parallel developments are now underway in other countries.

Like the Dutch decriminalization law in 1976, California's Prop 215 in 1996 initiated a dialogue over how best to implement the new law.[86] The variety of outlets that have emerged—ranging from pharmacy-like stores to medical "coffee shops" to hospices, all of which provide marijuana only to people with a patient ID card or doctor's recommendation—play a key role as the most public symbol and manifestation of this dialogue. More such outlets will likely pop up around the country as other states legalize marijuana for medical purposes and then seek ways to regulate distribution and access. And the question will inevitably arise: If the emerging system is successful in controlling production and distribution of marijuana for those with a medical need, can it not also expand to provide for those without medical need?

Millions of Americans use marijuana not just "for fun" but because they find it useful for many of the same reasons that people drink alcohol or take pharmaceutical drugs. It's akin to the beer, glass of wine, or cocktail at the end of the workday, or the prescribed drug to alleviate depression or anxiety, or the sleeping pill, or the aid to sexual function and pleasure.[87] More and more Americans are apt to describe some or all of their marijuana use as "medical" as the definition of that term evolves and broadens. Their anecdotal experiences are increasingly backed by new scientific research into marijuana's essential ingredients, the cannabinoids.[88] Last year, a subsidiary of *The Lancet,* Britain's leading medical journal, speculated whether marijuana might soon emerge as the "aspirin of the 21st century," providing a wide array of medical benefits at low cost to diverse populations.[89]

Perhaps the expansion of the medical-control model provides the best answer—at least in the U.S.—to the question of how best to reduce the substantial costs and harms of marijuana prohibition without inviting significant increases in real drug abuse. It's analogous to the evolution of many pharmaceutical drugs from prescription to over-the-counter, but with stricter controls still in place. It's also an incrementalist approach to reform that can provide both the control and the reassurance that cautious politicians and voters desire.

In 1931, with public support for alcohol Prohibition rapidly waning, President Hoover released the report of the Wickersham Commission.[90] The report included a devastating critique of Prohibition's failures and costly consequences, but the commissioners, apparently fearful of getting out too far ahead of public opinion, opposed repeal.[91] Franklin P. Adams of the *New York World* neatly summed up their findings:

> Prohibition is an awful flop.
> We like it.
> It can't stop what it's meant to stop.
> We like it.
> It's left a trail of graft and slime
> It don't prohibit worth a dime
> It's filled our land with vice and crime,
> Nevertheless, we're for it.[92]

Two years later, federal alcohol Prohibition was history.

What support there is for marijuana prohibition would likely end quickly absent the billions of dollars spent annually by federal and other governments to prop it up. All those anti-marijuana ads pretend to be about reducing drug abuse, but in fact their basic purpose is sustaining popular support for the war on marijuana. What's needed now are conservative politicians willing to say enough is enough: Tens of billions of taxpayer dollars down the drain each year. People losing their jobs, their property, and their freedom for nothing more than possessing a joint or growing a few marijuana plants. And all for what? To send a message? To keep pretending that we're protecting our children? Alcohol Prohibition made a lot more sense than marijuana prohibition does today—and it, too, was a disaster.

Notes

1. Joel Stein, "The New Politics of Pot," *Time,* 4 November 2002. Available online at http://www.time.com/time/covers/1101021104/story.html. For more polling information, see http://www.drugpolicy.org/library/publico-pinio/.

2. Ibid.; "Poll Finds Increasing Support For Legalizing Marijuana," *Alcoholism and Drug Abuse Weekly,* 15, No. 27 (2003): 8; Zogby International, "National Views on Drug Policy," (Utica, New York: Zogby, April 2003). The Poll was conducted during April 2003. Forty-one percent of respondents stated that marijuana should be treated in similar manner as alcohol.

3. Ibid.

4. Substance Abuse and Mental Health Services Administration, Department of Health and Human Services, *National Survey on Drug Use and Health, 2002* (Maryland: U.S. Department of Health and Humans Services, 2003): Table 1.31A.

5. Jesse Katz, "Past Drug Use, Future Cops," *Los Angeles Times*, 18 June 2000; "Alcohol and drug disqualification," Military.com, Military Advantage, 2004, <http://www.military.com/Recruiting/Content/0,13898,rec_step07_DQ_alcohol_drug,,00.html>(17 June 2004).

6. Yvonne Abraham, "Campaign 2000/McCain: Crime and Drugs the Topic in South Carolina," *The Boston Globe,* 9 February 2000.

7. Greg Freeman, "Blagojevich's Pot Use Is Raising Eyebrows, But It Isn't Big News," *St. Louis Post-Dispatch*, 19 September 2002.

8. Bob Dart, "Democrat Hopefuls Pin Hearts on Sleeves; Political 'Oprahization' Means That Confession Is Good for the Poll," *The Austin American Statesman,* 8 December 2003.

9. John Stossel and Sam Donaldson, "Give Me a Break: Politicians Don't Always Do What They Say Or What They Do," *20/20 Friday,* ABC News, 25 August 2000.

10. Ibid.

11. See http://www.norml.org/index.cfm?Group_ID=3461.

12. Federal Bureau of Investigation, Division of Uniform Crime Reports, *Crime in the United States: 2002* (Washington, D.C.: U.S. Government Printing Office, 2003): 234. Available online at http://www.fbi.gov/ucr/02cius.htm.

13. 840,000 arrests were made for all other drugs combined. Ibid.

14. Ibid.

15. There have been more than 11 million marijuana arrests made in the U.S. since 1970. See Federal Bureau of Investigation, *Uniform Crime Reports,* Washington, D.C.: Department of Justice, 1966–2002.

16. See http://www.norml.org/index.cfm?Group_ID=4444&wtm_format=print#prohibcost. See also Marijuana Policy Project, "Marijuana Prohibition Facts 2004," 2004, <http://mpp.org/pdf/prohfact.pdf> (18 June 2004); Mitch Earleywine, *Understanding Marijuana: A New Look at the Scientific Evidence* (New York: Oxford University Press, 2002): 235.

17. The Alabama Sentencing Commission, *Recommendations for Reform of Alabama's Criminal Justice System 2003 Report* (Alabama: Alabama Sentencing Comission, March 2003): 22, 23.

18. Estimated by Marijuana Policy Project, based on Bureau of Justice Statistics, *Prisoners in 2001,* U.S. Department of Justice (Washington, D.C.: U.S. Government Printing Office, 2002); Bureau of Justice Statistics, U.S. Department of Justice, *Prison and Jail Inmates at Midyear 2001* (Washington, D.C.: U.S. Government Printing Office, 2002); Bureau of Justice Statistics, U.S. Department of Justice, *Profile of Jail Inmates, 1996* (Washington, D.C.: U.S. Government Printing Office, 1998); Bureau of Justice Statistics, U.S. Department of Justice, *Substance Abuse and Treatment, State and Federal Prisoners 1997* (Washington, D.C.: U.S. Government Printing Office, 1999). All reports available online at http://www.ojp.usdoj.gov/bjs/pubalp2.htm.

19. Judy Appel and Robin Levi, *Collateral Consequences: Denial of Basic Social Services Based on Drug Use* (California: Drug Policy Alliance, June 2003). Available online at http://www.drugpolicy.org/docUploads/Postincarceration_abuses_memo.pdf.

20. Carl Hiassen, "New Rules Trap Immigrants with Old Secrets," *The Miami Herald,* 30 May 2004.

21. Paul Samuels and Debbie Mukamal, *After Prison: Roadblocks to Reentry: A Report on State Legal Barriers Facing People With Criminal Records* (New York: Legal Action Center, 2004). Available online at http://www.lac.org/lac/upload/lacreport/LAC_PrintReport.pdf.

22. *Higher Education Act of 1998, U.S. Code,* Title 20, Sec. 1091.

23. According to data from the Department of Education analyzed by Students for Sensible Drug Policy, over 150,000 students have lost aid thus far due to the provision. See Greg Winter, "A Student Aid Ban for Past Drug Use is Creating a Furor," *The New York Times,* 13 March 2004; Alexandra Marks, "No Education Funds for Drug Offenders," *Christian Science Monitor,* 24 April 2001; John Kelly, "Students Seeking Aid Not Answering Drug Questions," *The Associated Press,* 21 March 2000.

24. See http://www.mediacampaign.org/mg/index.html.

25. Theresa Howard, "U.S. Crafts Anti-Drug Message," *USA Today,* 15 March 2004.

26. Drug Enforcement Administration, *In the Matter of Marijuana Rescheduling Petition* [Docket#86-22] (Washington, D.C.: U.S. Department of Justice, 6 September 1988): 57.

27. Based on data from *National Household Survey on Drug Abuse: Population Estimates 1994* (Rockville, MD: U.S. Department of Health and Human Services, 1995); *National Household Survey on Drug Abuse: Main Findings 1994* (Rockville, MD: U.S. Department of Health and Human Services, 1996). See also D.B. Kandel and M. Davies, "Progression to Regular Marijuana Involvement: Phenomenology and Risk Factors for Near-Daily Use," *Vulnerability to Drug Abuse,* Eds. M. Glantz and R. Pickens (Washington, D.C.: American Psychological Association, 1992): 211–253.

28. Lynn Zimmer and John P. Morgan, *Marijuana Myths, Marijuana Facts: A Review of the Scientific Evidence* (New York: Drug Policy Alliance, 1997): 37–38.

29. Ibid., 134–141.

30. Mitch Earleywine, *Understanding Marijuana: A New Look at the Scientific Evidence* (New York, Oxford University Press, 2002): 130.

31. Janet E. Joy, Stanley J. Watson Jr., and John A. Benson Jr., Eds., *Marijuana and Medicine: Assessing the Science Base* (Washington, D.C.: National Academy of Sciences Institute of Medicine, 1999): 89–91. Available online at http://books.nap.edu/html/marimed/.

32. See the findings of the Canadian Committee on Illegal Drugs, available at `http://www.parl.gc.ca/37/1/parlbus/commbus/senate/come/ille-e/` `rep-e/summary-e.pdf`. Pierre Claude Nolin, Chair, Senate Special Committee on Illegal Drugs, *Cannabis: Our Position for a Canadian Public Policy: Summary Report* (Ontario: Senate of Canada, 2002).

33. I Geenberg, "Psychiatric and Behavioral Observations of Casual and Heavy Marijuana Users," *Annals of the New York Academy of Sciences*, 282 (1976): 72–84; N. Solowij et al., "Biophysical Changes Associated with Cessation of Cannabis Use: A Single Case Study of Acute and Chronic Effects, Withdrawal and Treatment," *Life Sciences* 56 (1995): 2127–2135; A.D. Bensusan, "Marihuana Withdrawal Symptoms," *British Journal of Medicine*, 3 (1971):112.

34. Numerous government commissions investigating the relationship between marijuana and violence have concluded that marijuana does not cause crime. See National Commission on Marihuana and Drug Abuse, *Marihuana: A Signal of Understanding* (Washington, D.C.: U.S. Government Printing Office, 1972): 77; Pierre Claude Nolin Chair, Senate Special Committee on Illegal Drugs, *Cannabis: Our Position for a Canadian Public Policy: Summary Report* (Ontario: Senate of Canada, 2002). See also Lynn Zimmer and John P. Morgan, *Marijuana Myths, Marijuana Facts: A Review of the Scientific Evidence* (New York: Drug Policy Alliance, 1997): 7, 88–91.

35. S. Sidney, C.P. Quesenberry, G.D. Friedman, and I.S. Tekawa, "Marijuana Use and Cancer Incidence," *Cancer Cause and Control* 8 (1997); 722–728; Lynn Zimmer and John P. Morgan, *Marijuana Myths, Marijuana Facts: A Review of the Scientific Evidence* (New York: Drug Policy Alliance, 1997): 7, 112–116; Mitch Earleywine, *Understanding Marijuana: A New Look at the Scientific Evidence* (New York, Oxford University Press, 2002): 155–158.

36. Substance Abuse and Mental Health Services Administration, Department of Health and Human Services, *National Survey on Drug Use and Health, 2002* (Maryland: U.S. Department of Health and Humans Services, 2003): 4, 5.

37. Substance Abuse and Mental Health Services Administration, *2003 Treatment Episode Data Set: 1992–2001,* National Admissions to Substance Abuse Treatment Services, DASIS Series: S-20 (Maryland: U.S. Department of Health and Human Services, 2003): 122.

38. Ibid.

39. Ibid.

40. Substance Abuse and Mental Health Services Administration, Department of Health and Human Services, "Coerced Treatment Among Youths: 1993 to 1998," *The DASIS Report,* 21 September 2001.

41. L.D. Johnston, P.M. O'Malley, and J.G. Bachman, *Monitoring the Future: National Results on Adolescent Drug Use: Overview of Key Findings, 2003* (Bethesda, Maryland: National Institute on Drug Abuse, 2004); Ann L. Pastore and Kathleen Maguire, Eds., U.S. Department of Justice, Bureau of Justice Statistics, *Sourcebook of Criminal Justice Statistics 2001* (Washington, D.C.: U.S. Government Printing Office, 2002): 173.

42. Svetlana Kolchik, "More Americans Used Illegal Drugs in 2001, U.S. Study Says," *USA Today,* 6 September 2002; Corky Newton, *Generation Risk: How to Protect Your Teenager from Smoking and Other Dangerous Behaviors* (New York: M. Evans and Company, 2001).

43. Ernest Abel, *Marijuana: The First Twelve Thousand Years* (New York: McGraw Hill, 1982); Martin Booth, *Cannabis: A History* (London: Doubleday, 2003); Janet E. Joy, Stanley J. Watson Jr., and John A. Benson Jr., Eds., *Marijuana and Medicine: Assessing the Science Base* (Washington, D.C.: National Academy of Sciences Institute of Medicine, 1999): 19. Available online at `http://books.nap.edu/html/marimed/`.

44. Janet E. Joy, Stanley J. Watson Jr., and John A. Benson Jr., Eds., *Marijuana and Medicine: Assessing the Science Base* (Washington, D.C.: National Academy of Sciences Institute of Medicine, 1999): 16. Available online at http://books.nap.edu/html/marimed/.

45. "Marijuana-Based Drug Developed to Treat MS," *Calgary Sun,* 12 May 2004.

46. Heather Stewart, "Late Again: GW's Cannabis-Based Painkiller," *The Guardian,* 1 May 2004.

47. See Janet E. Joy, Stanley J. Watson Jr., and John, A. Benson Jr., Eds., *Marijuana and Medicine: Assessing the Science Base* (Washington, D.C.: National Academy of Sciences Institute of Medicine, 1999); 27–29; and Mitch Earleywine, *Understanding Marijuana: A New Look at the Scientific Evidence* (New York, Oxford University Press, 2002): 171.

48. Dale Gieringer, Joseph St. Laurent, and Scott Goodrich, "Cannabis Vaporizer Combines Efficient Delivery of THC with Effective Suppression of Pyrolytic Compounds," *Journal of Cannabis Therapeutics* 4(2004): 7–27. A British pharmaceutical company, GW Pharmaceuticals, has developed an oral spray to dispense cannabis to medical-marijuana patients. See http://gwpharm.co.uk/ for more information.

49. *Schedules of Controlled Substances, U.S. Code,* Title 21, Sec. 812.

50. Bill Piper et al., *State of the States: Drug Policy Reforms: 1996–2002* (New York: Drug Policy Alliance, 2003): 42. Available online at http://states.drugpolicy.org.

51. David Gram, "Vermont's Medical Marijuana Bill to Be Law," *Associated Press,* 20 May 2004.

52. Associated Press, "Hawaii Becomes First State to Approve Medical Marijuana Bill," *The New York Times,* 15 June 2000.

53. Craig Whitlock and Lori Montgomery, "Ehrlich Signs Marijuana Bill; Maryland Governor Weighs Independence, GOP Loyalty," *The Washington Post,* 23 May 2003; Angela Potter, "Maryland Governor Signs Medical Marijuana Bill Into Law," *Associated Press,* 22 May 2003.

54. Ellis Henican, "High Hopes for Pot," *Newsday,* 16 June 2004.

55. Ken Dixon, "State Urged to Legalize Medical Marijuana Use," *Connecticut Post,* 2 April 2004.

56. "Medical Marijuana in Rhode Island," *The Providence Journal,* 19 May 2004.

57. "Medical Marijuana Debate on Hold," *The State Journal-Register,* 3 March 2004.

58. Matthew Miller, "He Just Said No to the Drug War," *The New York Times Magazine,* 20 August 2000.

59. Richard Willing, "Attitudes Ease Toward Medical Marijuana," *USA Today,* 22 May 2003.

60. Seanne Adcox, "Golisano Proposes Medical Use of Marijuana," *New York Newsday,* 17 October 2002.

61. John H. Wilson, "Medical Marijuana Helps Serious Ill," *Albany Times Union,* 24 March 2004.

62. See Janet E. Joy, Stanley J. Watson Jr., and John A. Benson Jr., Eds., *Marijuana and Medicine: Assessing the Science Base* (Washington, D.C.: National Academy of Sciences Institutes of Medicine, 1999): 18; and Richard Schmitz and Chuck Thomas, *State-By-State Medical Marijuana Laws: How to Remove the Threat of Arrest* (Washington, D.C.: Marijuana Policy Project, 2001): Appendix D. Available at http://www.mpp.org/statelaw/app_d.html. For a list of polls results, see http://www.drugpolicy.org/library/publicopinio/.

63. Edward Epstein, "Bill to Protect Medicinal Pot Users Falls Short in House," *San Francisco Chronicle,* 24 July 2003.

64. In July 2004, a similar amendment was voted on and once again fell short of passage. See `http://www.drugpolicy.org/news/07_08_04hincheyvote.cfm`.

65. See `http://www.drugpolicy.org/marijuana/medical/challenges/cases/conant/index.cfm`.

66. The U.S. Supreme Court will hear *Raich v. Ashcroft* this fall. See `http://www.drugpolicy.org/library/legalmateria/wamm_raich_facts.cfm`; Eric Bailey, "State Set for Legal Showdown Over Pot," *Los Angeles Times,* 19 May 2004.

67. "Leave Medical Marijuana Group Alone, Judge Tells Government," *The New York Times,* 22 April 2004. See also `http://www.drugpolicy.org/law/marijuana/santacruz/`.

68. Linda Greenhouse, "Supreme Court Roundup; Justices Say Doctors May Not Be Punished for Recommending Medical Marijuana," *The New York Times,* 15 October 2003.

69. National Organization for the Reform of Marijuana Laws, "Summary of active State Medical Marijuana Programs," July 2002, <`http://www.norml.org/index.cfm?Group_ID=3391`> (June 2004).

70. Laura Counts, "Oakland to Limit Marijuana Outlets," *Tri-Valley Herald,* 18 April 2004. Also see information on San Franciscos" Proposition S, available at `http://www.drugpolicy.org/news/11_06_02props.cfm`.

71. Amy Hilvers, "'Pot Club' Thrives in Oildale," *The Bakersfield Californian,* 26 May 2004.

72. Laura Counts, "Medical Marijuana Merchant Defies Oakland Order to Close," *The Oakland Tribune,* 2 June 2004.

73. Doug Bandow, "Where's the Compassion?," *National Review Online,* 19 December 2003. Available at `http://www.mapinc.org/drugnews/v03/n1964/a06.html`. See also Michael Gougis, "Medical Marijuana Tug of War: Lenient Sentences Underscore Conflicting State and Federal Pot Laws," *Daily News of Los Angeles,* 12 December 2003; Clarence Page, "Drug Warriors Trampling Rights of Medical Marijuana Proponents," *Salt Lake Tribune,* 12 February 2003.

74. Andrea Barthwell, "Haze of Myths Clouds Value of Medical 'Pot,'" *The Republican,* 27 July 2003; Alan W. Bock, "UNSPIN/Marijuana, Medicine, and Ed Rosenthal: The Issue: Medical Marijuana and Federal Law," *Orange County Register,* 9 February 2003; Ian Ith and Carol M. Ostrom, "Feds Pose Challenge to Use of Medical Marijuana," *The Seattle Times,* 16 September 2002; and Josh Richman, "Drug Czar Coolly Received in Bay Area; Federal Stance on Medical Marijuana Won't be Relaxed, Walters Says," *The Daily Review,* 18 November 2003.

75. David Brown, "NIH Panel Cautiously Favors Medical Study of Marijuana," *The Washington Post,* 21 February 1997; Ray Delgado, "Many Patients Call Government Marijuana Weak; Medicinal Cigarettes Loaded With Stems, Seeds, Researchers Say," *San Francisco Chronicle,* 16 May 2002; Lester Grinspoon and James B. Bakalar, *Marihuana: The Forbidden Medicine* (Connecticut: Yale University Press, 1997): 45–66.

76. Richard Brookhiser, "Drug Warriors Are Repeating Earlier Errors; Considering His Past Abuse, Bush Should Be Sympathetic to Reforms," *Chicago Sun-Times,* 25 May 2001; Richard Brookhiser, "In Dull Election, My Vote Is Going To Marijuana Man," *New York Observer,* 4 November 2002; Richard Brookhiser, "Madness of Pot Prohibition Claims Yet Another Victim," *New York Observer,* 24 July 2000; Richard Brookhiser, "The Sick Shouldn't Be Victims of the Drug War," *Buffalo News,* 20 July 2003; Richard Brookhiser, "Why I Support Medical Marijuana," Congressional Testimony, House Judiciary committee, Subcommittee on Crime, 6 March 1996. Available online at `http://www.norml.org/index.cfm?Group_ID=4451`.

77.   Raymond B. Fosdick, *Toward Liquor Control* (New York: Harper, 1993): David E. Kyvig, *Repealing national Prohibition*, 2nd Edition (Ohio: Kent State University Press, 2000).

78.   John L. Mica, "Should the Federal Government Study the Effects of Medical Marijuana? Do Not Waste Taxpayers' Dollars," *Roll Call*, 21 June 1999.

79.   George Soros, "The Drug War 'Cannot Be Won:' It's Time to Just Say No To Self-Destructive Prohibition," *The Washington Post*, 2 February 1997.

80.   William F. Buckley Jr., "The Legal Jam," *National Review Online*, 15 May 2001; William F. Buckley, Jr., "Peter McWilliams, R.I.P.," *National Review*, 17 July 2000; William F. Buckley, Jr., "Reefer Madness," *National Review*, 14 July 2003.

81.   Compare the photographs that accompany the following two articles: Tom Morganthau et al., "Should Drugs Be Legal?," *Newsweek*, 30 May 1988; Geoffrey Cowley et al., "Can Marijuana Be Medicine?," *Newsweek*, 3 February 1997.

82.   Bill Piper et al., *State of the States: Drug Policy Reforms: 1996–2002* (New York: Drug Policy Alliance, 2003). Available online at http://states.drugpolicy.org.

83.   Robert J. MacCoun and Peter Reuter, *Drug War Heresies: Learning from Other Vices, Times, and Places* (New York: Cambridge University Press, 2001): 238–264.

84.   A.C.M. Jansen, "The Development of a 'Legal' Consumers' Market for Cannabis—the 'Coffee Shop' Phenomenon," *Between Prohibition and Legalization: The Dutch Experiment in Drug Policy*, E. Leuw and I. Haen Marshall, Eds., (New York: Kugler Publications, 1996).

85.   Craig Reinarman, Peter D.A. Cohen, and Hendrien L. Kaal, "The Limited Relevance of Drug Policy: Cannabis in Amsterdam and in San Francisco," *American Journal of Public Health* 94 (2004): 836–842.

86.   Michael Pollan, "Living With Medical Marijuana," *New York Times Magazine*, 20 July 1997.

87.   See Pierre Claude Nolin, Chair, Senate Special Committee on Illegal Drugs, *Cannabis: Our Position for a Canadian Public Policy: Summary Report* (Ontario: Senate of Canada, 2002): Mitch Earleywine, *Understanding Marijuana: A New Look at the Scientific Evidence* (New York, Oxford University Press, 2002).

88.   J. M. McPartland and E. B. Russo, "Cannabis and Cannabis Extracts: Greater Than the Sum of Their Parts?," *Journal of Cannabis Therapeutics* 1 (2001): 103–132; R. Mechoulam, L. A. Parker, and R. Gallily, "Cannabidiol: An Overview of Some Pharmacological Aspects," *Journal of Clinical Pharmacology*, 42 (2002): 11S–19S; R. G. Pertwee, "The Pharmacology and Therapeutic Potential of Cannabidiol," *Cannabinoids*, Ed. V. DiMarzo (The Netherlands: Kluwer Academic Publishers, 2004).

89.   David Baker, Alan Thompson et al., "The Therapeutic Potential of Cannabis," *The Lancet Neurology*, 2 (2003): 294.

90.   See http://www.drugtext.org/library/reports/wick/Default.htm for the complete text of the Commission's report.

91.   David E. Kyvig, *Repealing National Prohibition*, 2nd Edition (Ohio: Kent State University Press, 2000): 111–115.

92.   As cited in David E. Kyvig, *Repealing National Prohibition*, 2nd Edition (Ohio: Kent State University Press, 2000): 114.

Marijuana & The Truth Behind 10 Popular Misperceptions

Introduction

Marijuana is the most widely used illicit drug in the United States. According to the National Survey on Drug Use and Health (formerly called the National Household Survey on Drug Abuse), 95 million Americans age 12 and older have tried "pot" at least once, and three out of every four illicit-drug users reported using marijuana within the previous 30 days.

Use of marijuana has adverse health, safety, social, academic, economic, and behavioral consequences. And yet, astonishingly, many people view the drug as "harmless." The widespread perception of marijuana as a benign natural herb seriously detracts from the most basic message our society needs to deliver: It is not OK for anyone—especially young people—to use this or any other illicit drug.

Marijuana became popular among the general youth population in the 1960s. Back then, many people who would become the parents and grandparents of teenage kids today smoked marijuana without significant adverse effects, so now they may see no harm in its use. But most of the marijuana available today is considerably more potent than the "weed" of the Woodstock era, and its users tend to be younger than those of past generations. Since the late 1960s, the average age of marijuana users has dropped from around 19 to just over 17. People are also lighting up at an earlier age. Fewer than half of those using marijuana for the first time in the late 1960s were under 18. By 2001, however, the proportion of under-18 initiates had increased to about two-thirds (67 percent).

Today's young people live in a world vastly different from that of their parents and grandparents. Kids these days, for instance, are bombarded constantly with pro-drug messages in print, on screen, and on CD. They also have easy access to the Internet, which abounds with sites promoting the wonders of marijuana, offering kits for beating drug tests, and, in some cases, advertising pot for sale. Meanwhile, the prevalence of higher potency marijuana, measured by levels of the chemical delta-9-tetrahydrocannabinol (THC), is increasing. Average THC levels rose from less than 1 percent in the mid-1970s to more than 6 percent in 2002. Sinsemilla potency increased in the past two decades from

From "Are Psychotherapeutic Drugs Effective for Treating Mental Illness", Office of National Drug Control Policy, 2004. References omitted.

6 percent to more than 13 percent, with some samples containing THC levels of up to 33 percent. . . .

Myth 1: Marijuana Is Harmless

Marijuana harms in many ways, and kids are the most vulnerable to its damaging effects. Use of the drug can lead to significant health, safety, social, and learning or behavioral problems, especially for young users. . . .

Short-term effects of marijuana use include memory loss, distorted perception, trouble with thinking and problem-solving, and anxiety. Students who use marijuana may find it hard to learn, thus jeopardizing their ability to achieve their full potential.

Cognitive Impairment

That marijuana can cause problems with concentration and thinking has been shown in research funded by the National Institute on Drug Abuse (NIDA), the federal agency that brings the power of science to bear on drug abuse and addiction. A NIDA-funded study at McLean Hospital in Belmont, Massachusetts, is part of the growing body of research documenting cognitive impairment among heavy marijuana users. The study found that college students who used marijuana regularly had impaired skills related to attention, memory, and learning 24 hours after they last used the drug.

Another study, conducted at the University of Iowa College of Medicine, found that people who used marijuana frequently (7 or more times weekly for an extended period) showed deficits in mathematical skills and verbal expression, as well as selective impairments in memory-retrieval processes. These findings clearly have significant implications for young people, since reductions in cognitive function can lead to poor performance in school. . . .

Mental Health Problems

Smoking marijuana leads to changes in the brain similar to those caused by cocaine, heroin, and alcohol. All of these drugs disrupt the flow of chemical neurotransmitters, and all have specific receptor sites in the brain that have been linked to feelings of pleasure and, over time, addiction. Cannabinoid receptors are affected by THC, the active ingredient in marijuana, and many of these sites are found in the parts of the brain that influence pleasure, memory, thought, concentration, sensory and time perception, and coordinated movement.

Particularly for young people, marijuana use can lead to increased anxiety, panic attacks, depression, and other mental health problems. One study linked social withdrawal, anxiety, depression, attention problems, and thoughts of suicide in adolescents with past-year marijuana use. Other research shows that kids age 12 to 17 who smoke marijuana weekly are three times more likely than non-users to have thoughts about committing suicide. A recently published longitudinal study showed that use of cannabis increased the risk of major depression fourfold, and researchers in Sweden found a link between marijuana use and an increased risk of developing schizophrenia.

According to the American Society of Addiction Medicine, addiction and psychiatric disorders often occur together. The latest National Survey on Drug Use and Health reported that adults who use illicit drugs were more than twice as likely to have serious mental illness as adults who did not use an illicit drug.

Researchers conducting a longitudinal study of psychiatric disorders and substance use (including alcohol, marijuana, and other illicit drugs) have suggested several possible links between the two: (1) people may use drugs to feel better and alleviate symptoms of a mental disorder; (2) the use of the drug and the disorder share certain biological, social, or other risk factors; or (3) use of the drug can lead to anxiety, depression, or other disorders. . . .

Long-Term Consequences

The consequences of marijuana use can last long after the drug's effects have worn off. Studies show that early use of marijuana is strongly associated with later use of other illicit drugs and with a greater risk of illicit drug dependence or abuse. In fact, an analysis of data from the National Household Survey on Drug Abuse showed that the age of initiation for marijuana use was the most important predictor of later need for drug treatment.

Regular marijuana use has been shown to be associated with other long-term problems, including poor academic performance, poor job performance and increased absences from work, cognitive deficits, and lung damage. Marijuana use is also associated with a number of risky sexual behaviors, including having multiple sex partners, initiating sex at an early age, and failing to use condoms consistently.

Myth 2: Marijuana Is Not Addictive

. . . According to the 2002 National Survey on Drug Use and Health, 4.3 million Americans were classified with dependence on or abuse of marijuana. That figure represents 1.8 percent of the total U.S. population and 60.3 percent of those classified as individuals who abuse or are dependent on illicit drugs.

The desire for marijuana exerts a powerful pull on those who use it, and this desire, coupled with withdrawal symptoms, can make it hard for long-term smokers to stop using the drug. Users trying to quit often report irritability, anxiety, and difficulty sleeping. On psychological tests they also display increased aggression, which peaks approximately one week after they last used the drug.

Many people use marijuana compulsively even though it interferes with family, school, work, and recreational activities. What makes this all the more disturbing is that marijuana use has been shown to be three times more likely to lead to dependence among adolescents than among adults. Research indicates that the earlier kids start using marijuana, the more likely they are to become dependent on this or other illicit drugs later in life. . . .

Myth 3: Marijuana Is Not as Harmful to Your Health as Tobacco

Although some people think of marijuana as a benign natural herb, the drug actually contains many of the same cancer-causing chemicals found in tobacco. Puff for puff, the amount of tar inhaled and the level of carbon monoxide absorbed by those who smoke marijuana, regardless of THC content, are three to five times greater than among tobacco smokers.

Consequently, people who use marijuana on a regular basis often have the same breathing problems as tobacco users, such as chronic coughing and wheezing, more frequent acute chest illnesses, and a tendency toward obstructed airways. And because respiratory problems can affect athletic performance, smoking marijuana may be particularly harmful to kids involved in sports.

Researchers at the University of California, Los Angeles, have determined that marijuana smoking can cause potentially serious damage to the respiratory system at a relatively early age. Moreover, in a review of research on the health effects of marijuana use, the researchers cited findings that show "the daily smoking of relatively small amounts of marijuana (3 to 4 joints) has at least a comparable, if not greater effect" on the respiratory system than the smoking of more than 20 tobacco cigarettes.

Recently, scientists in England produced further evidence linking marijuana use to respiratory problems in young people. A research team at the University of Birmingham found that regular use of marijuana, even for less than six years, causes a marked deterioration in lung function. . . .

Myth 4: Marijuana Makes You Mellow

. . . Research shows that kids who use marijuana weekly are nearly four times more likely than non-users to report they engage in violent behavior. One study found that young people who had used marijuana in the past year were more likely than non-users to report aggressive behavior. According to that study, incidences of physically attacking people, stealing, and destroying property increased in proportion to the number of days marijuana was smoked in the past year. Users were also twice as likely as non-users to report they disobey at school and destroy their own things.

In another study, researchers looking into the relationship between ten illicit drugs and eight criminal offenses found that a greater frequency of marijuana use was associated with a greater likelihood to commit weapons offenses; except for alcohol, none of the other drugs showed such a connection. . . .

Myth 5: Marijuana Is Used to Treat Cancer and Other Diseases

Under the Comprehensive Drug Abuse Prevention and Control Act of 1970, marijuana was established as a Schedule I controlled substance. In other words, it is a dangerous drug that has no recognized medical value.

Whether marijuana can provide relief for people with certain medical conditions, including cancer, is a subject of intense national debate. It is true that THC, the primary active chemical in marijuana, can be useful for treating some medical problems. Synthetic THC is the main ingredient in Marinol®, an FDA-approved medication used to control nausea in cancer chemotherapy patients and to stimulate appetite in people with AIDS. Marinol, a legal and safe version of medical marijuana, has been available by prescription since 1985.

However, marijuana as a smoked product has never proven to be medically beneficial and, in fact, is much more likely to harm one's health; marijuana smoke is a crude THC delivery system that also sends many harmful substances into the body. In 1999, the Institute of Medicine (IOM) published a review of the available scientific evidence in an effort to assess the potential health benefits of marijuana and its constituent cannabinoids. The review concluded that smoking marijuana is not recommended for any long-term medical use, and a subsequent IOM report declared, "marijuana is not a modern medicine." . . .

Myth 6: Marijuana Is Not as Popular as MDMA (Ecstasy) or Other Drugs among Teens Today

Recent survey data show that about 15 million people—6.2 percent of the U.S. population—are current marijuana users, and that nearly a third of them (4.8 million people) used the drug on 20 or more days in the past month. Among kids age 12 to 17, more than two million (8.2 percent) reported past-month marijuana use. By contrast, fewer than 250,000 young people (1 percent) reported past-month use of hallucinogens, and of that number, only half (124,000) had used MDMA.

The 2003 Monitoring the Future Study showed that marijuana is not only popular today, it has been the most widely used illicit drug among high school seniors for the entire 29 years of the study. Meanwhile, Ecstasy use among American teens appears to be declining after record increases. Between 2001 and 2003, past-month use of MDMA among students in the three grades surveyed dropped by more than half, from 1.8 percent to 0.7 percent (8th grade), 2.6 percent to 1.1 percent (10th grade), and 2.8 percent to 1.3 percent (12th grade). . . .

Myth 7: If I Buy Marijuana, I'm Not Hurting Anyone Else

Violence at Home

. . . The trade in domestically grown marijuana often turns violent when dealers have conflicts or when growers feel their crops are threatened. But drug criminals are not the only ones threatened by the violence of the marijuana trade.

Much of the marijuana produced in America is grown on public lands, including our national forests and parks—areas set aside to preserve wildlife habitats, provide playgrounds for our children, and serve as natural refuges for recreation. Traffickers grow their crops in these areas because the land is free and accessible, crop ownership is hard to document, and because growers are immune to asset forfeiture laws. Law enforcement officials report that many marijuana growers, seeking to protect their crops from busybodies and rival "pot pirates," surround their plots with crude booby traps, including fishhooks dangling at eye level, bear traps, punji sticks, and rat traps rigged with shotgun shells.

Most of the marijuana on America's public lands is grown in the vast national forests of California, where more than 540,000 plants were seized or eradicated on land managed by the U.S. Forest Service in 2003 alone. This figure does not include the 309,000 marijuana plants taken from Forest Service land in other states, nor does it take into account the hundreds of thousands of plants removed from land managed by other government agencies. For example, in 2003 more than 134,000 marijuana plants were seized or eradicated from areas in California administered by the U.S. Department of the Interior's Bureau of Land Management.

According to officers with the Forest Service and other agencies, many of California's illegal marijuana fields are controlled not by peace-loving flower children but by employees of Mexican drug-trafficking organizations carrying high-powered assault weapons. During the growing season, the officers say, the cartels smuggle hundreds of undocumented Mexican nationals into the U.S. to work the fields, bringing with them pesticides, equipment, and guns. Hunters, campers, and others have been threatened at gunpoint or fired upon after stumbling into these illegal gardens. . . .

Myth 8: My Kids Won't Be Exposed to Marijuana

. . . More than half (55 percent) of youths age 12 to 17 responding to the National Survey on Drug Use and Health in 2002 reported that marijuana would be easy to obtain. The survey indicated that most marijuana users got the drug from a friend, and that almost nine percent of youths who bought marijuana did so inside a school building. Moreover, nearly 17 percent of the young people surveyed said they had been approached by someone selling drugs in the past month. In the 2000 survey, more than a quarter of 12- to 17-year-olds (26.6 percent) reported that drug-selling occurs frequently in their neighborhoods.

Kids are also exposed to a relentless barrage of marijuana messages in the popular culture—in the music they listen to, the movies they watch, and the magazines they read. And then there's the Internet, a crowded landscape of pro-marijuana and drug legalization Web sites. More often than not, the culture glamorizes or trivializes marijuana use and fails to show the serious harm it can cause. . . .

Not Just an Inner-City Problem

Some people have the impression that kids in the inner city are those most likely to get involved with drugs. Research shows, however, that marijuana use among youth in cities, rural areas, and the suburbs is roughly the same, and that use rates are similar regardless of population density. For example, annual prevalence rates of marijuana use among 10th graders are 28 percent in non-urban areas, 29 percent in large metropolitan statistical areas, and 32 percent in other metropolitan areas.

Myth 9: There's Not Much Parents Can Do to Stop Their Kids from Experimenting with Marijuana

Many people are surprised to learn that parents are the most powerful influence on their children when it comes to drugs. By staying involved, knowing what their kids are doing, and setting limits with clear rules and consequences, parents can increase the chances their kids will stay drug free. Research shows that appropriate parental monitoring can reduce future drug use even among adolescents who may be prone to marijuana use, such as those who are rebellious, cannot control their emotions, and experience internal distress. . . .

Parental Involvement

Kids who learn about the risks of drugs from their parents or caregivers are less likely to use drugs than kids who do not. Parents can create situations that help them connect with their children and stay involved in their lives. Experts suggest that parents try to be home with their kids after school, if possible, because evidence indicates that the riskiest time for kids with regard to drug involvement is between the hours of 3 p.m. and 6 p.m. Parents who can't be home with their children should consider enrolling them in after-school programs, sports, or other activities, or arrange for a trusted adult to oversee them.

It's also important for families to participate in activities such as eating meals together; holding meetings in which each person gets a chance to talk; and establishing regular routines of doing something special (like taking a walk) that allow parents to talk to their kids. Opening channels of communication between parents and children, as well as between families and the greater community, gives young people greater confidence and helps them make healthy choices.

Myth 10: The Government Sends Otherwise Innocent People to Prison for Casual Marijuana Use

On the contrary, it is extremely rare for anyone, particularly first-time offenders, to get sent to prison just for possessing a small amount of marijuana. In most states, possession of an ounce or less of pot is a misdemeanor offense, and some states have gone so far as to downgrade simple possession of marijuana to a civil offense akin to a traffic violation.

. . . In 1997, according to the U.S. Department of Justice's Bureau of Justice Statistics (BJS), only 1.6 percent of the state inmate population had been convicted of a marijuana-only crime, including trafficking. An even smaller percentage of state inmates were imprisoned with marijuana *possession* as the only charge (0.7 percent). And only 0.3 percent of those imprisoned just for marijuana possession were first-time offenders.

More recent estimates from the BJS show that at midyear 2002, approximately 8,400 state prisoners were serving time for possessing marijuana in any amount. Fewer than half of that group, or about 3,600 inmates, were incarcerated on a first offense. In other words, of the more than 1.2 million people doing time in state prisons across America, only a small fraction were first-time offenders sentenced just for marijuana possession. And again, this figure includes possession of *any* amount.

On the federal level, prosecutors focus largely on traffickers, kingpins, and other major drug criminals, so federal marijuana cases often involve hundreds of pounds of the drug. Cases involving smaller amounts are typically handled on the state level. This is part of the reason why hardly anyone ends up in federal prison for simple possession of marijuana. The fact is, of all drug defendants sentenced in federal court for marijuana offenses in 2001, the vast majority were convicted of trafficking. Only 2.3 percent—186 people—were sentenced for simple possession, and of the 174 for whom sentencing information is known, just 63 actually served time behind bars. . . .

Conclusion

The clutter of messages about marijuana in the popular culture creates an atmosphere of confusion and sends kids mixed signals about the drug. But what should be clear is that no responsible person thinks young people should use marijuana. Kids can learn the truth about marijuana at www.freevibe.com.

Parents can help keep their children away from marijuana by letting them know its dangers, and by monitoring their activities and staying involved in their lives. For more information and useful tips about talking to kids about marijuana, visit www.theantidrug.com. Both of these Web sites are supported by the Office of National Drug Control Policy.

Schools and communities can also play an important role by providing activities that keep kids interested and involved in healthy, drug-free programs.

If you want to help dispel misperceptions and spread the truth about marijuana to help kids grow up drug-free, you can:

- Educate yourself about the dangers of marijuana and keep up with scientific research into its harmful effects. For a wealth of good information, visit the Web site for the National Institute on Drug Abuse at http://www.nida.nih.gov
- Help kids in trouble with marijuana get into drug treatment programs
- Be an advocate for better, more informed drugged-driving laws

- Support after-school programs and get involved in local anti-drug coalitions
- Stay informed about the marijuana laws in your state, and take a stand against changes in legislation that would increase the drug's availability in your community
- Support efforts to launch a student drug-testing program in your local schools
- See "What You Need to Know About Drug Testing in Schools," available by calling 800-666-3332 and online at `http://www.whitehouse-drugpolicy.gov/pdf/drug_testing.pdf`
- To learn more about drug and alcohol abuse, visit the Substance Abuse & Mental Health Services Administration's National Clearinghouse for Alcohol and Drug Information at `http://www.health.org/` or call its 24-hour hotline: 1-800-729-6686 or 1-800-788-2800

POSTSCRIPT

Should Laws Prohibiting Marijuana Use Be Relaxed?

The restrictive laws against marijuana, according to Nadelmann, have resulted in a burgeoning number of people in prison for marijuana offenses. Nadelmann does not contend that marijuana is a safe drug, but that legalizing it would enable officials to have better control over its use. In addition, he feels that the federal government prevents people from receiving medication that is both therapeutic and benign. The government's objection to marijuana, says Nadelmann, is based more on politics than on scientific evidence.

From perspective of the federal government, promoting marijuana as a medicinal agent would be a mistake because it has not been proven medically useful or safe. Moreover, it feels that the availability of marijuana should not be predicated on personal accounts of its benefits or whether the public supports its use. Also, the federal government asserts that studies showing that marijuana may have medical value have been based on bad scientific methodology and other deficiencies. The results of previous research, according to the federal government, do not lend strong credence to marijuana's medicinal value.

Some people have expressed concern about what will happen if marijuana is approved for medicinal use. Would it then become more acceptable for non-medical, recreational use? There is also a possibility that some people would misinterpret the government's message and think that marijuana cures cancer when, in fact, it would only be used to treat the side effects of the chemotherapy.

Despite its popularity, the federal government notes that parents should and can assert more influence on their children's desire to use marijuana. The government claims that marijuana is not the harmless drug that many proponents believe. Marijuana can have adverse effects on mental health, physical well-being, and academic performance. In addition, thousands of young people enter substance abuse treatment for their addiction to marijuana. It is important, states the Office of National Drug Control Policy, to counteract how culture trivializes the dangers of marijuana use.

Many marijuana proponents contend that the effort to prevent the legalization of marijuana for both medical and nonmedical use is purely a political battle. Detractors maintain that the issue is purely scientific—that the data supporting marijuana's medical usefulness are inconclusive and scientifically unsubstantiated. And although the chief administrative law judge of the Drug Enforcement Administration (DEA) made a recommendation to change the status of marijuana from Schedule I to Schedule II, the DEA and other federal agencies are not compelled to do so and have resisted any change in the law.

A number of articles debate the merits of relaxing laws against marijuana use. David Wahlberg, in "Stronger Pot, Bigger Worries" (*The Sacramento Bee*,

May 5, 2004), argues that one danger with marijuana today it that its potency has gotten increasingly stronger. In "Tokin' Politics: Making Marijuana Law Reform An Election Issue" (*Heads,* May 2004), Paul Armentano writes that politicians have refused to relax marijuana laws because that decision would be politically unpopular. The on-going dispute between the United States and Canada regarding marijuana laws is discussed by Donna Leinwand in "U.S., Canada Clash on Pot Laws" (*USA Today,* May 8, 2003). Articles that discuss whether or not marijuana should be legalized as a medication include "The Growing Debate on Medical Marijuana: Federal Power Vs. States Rights," by Alreen Hussein, *California Western Law Review* (Vol. 37, No. 2, 2001); and "Cannabis Control: Costs Outweigh the Benefits," by Alex Wodak and others, *British Medical Journal* (January 12, 2002). Lester Grinspoon's and James Bakalar's book *Marihuana, the Forbidden Medicine* (Yale University Press, 1997) provides a thorough history and overview of marijuana's medical benefits.

ISSUE 10

Are Psychotherapeutic Drugs Effective for Treating Mental Illness?

YES: Bruce M. Cohen, from "Mind and Medicine: Drug Treatments for Psychiatric Illnesses," *Social Research* (Fall 2001)

NO: Charles L. Whitfield, from *The Truth About Depression: Choices for Healing* (Health Communications, 2003)

ISSUE SUMMARY

YES: Medical doctor Bruce M. Cohen maintains that psychiatric medicines are very beneficial in enabling individuals with a variety of illnesses to return to normal aspects of consciousness. Cohen points out that people with conditions such as anxiety, depression, and psychosis respond very well to medications. These types of drugs have been utilized successfully for hundreds of years.

NO: Medical doctor Charles Whitfield questions the effectiveness of psychiatric drugs, especially antidepressant drugs. Whitfield maintains that the increase in the use of psychotherapeutic drugs results from their promotion by the pharmaceutical industry. The Food and Drug Administration (FDA), the government agency charged with protecting the public from harmful drugs, has an advisory committee consisting of members who are paid by drug companies.

One of the most common emotional problems in America is mental illness, especially depression. It is estimated that approximately 10 percent of Americans experience some type of depression during their lives. Although some of the newer antidepressant drugs such as Prozac, Paxil, and Zoloft have not been available that long, they account for billions of dollars in sales. Does this mean that more people are becoming mentally ill or are people more likely to be diagnosed with mental illness today?

Although antidepressant drugs were originally developed to treat depression—for which they are believed to be about 60 percent effective—these drugs are now prescribed for an array of other conditions. Some of these conditions include eating disorders like bulimia and obesity, obsessive-compulsive disorders, panic attacks, and anxiety. An important question about these drugs is currently under debate: Are they prescribed too casually? Some experts feel that physicians are giving antidepressant drugs to patients who do not need chemical treatment to overcome their afflictions. Yale University professor Sherwin Nuland has argued that drugs like Prozac are relatively safe for approved applications but that they are inappropriate for less severe problems.

As with most other drugs, antidepressants produce a number of adverse side effects. These effects include hypotension (low blood pressure), weight gain, and irregular heart rhythms. Other side effects that may be experienced are headaches, fatigue, profuse sweating, anxiety, reduced appetite, jitteriness, dizziness, stomach discomfort, nausea, sexual dysfunction, and insomnia. Because these drugs are relatively new, long-term side effects have yet to be determined.

Soon after Prozac was introduced, several lawsuits were filed against Eli Lilly and Company, the drug's manufacturer, due to Prozac's side effects. The drug was linked to violent and suicidal behavior. Some individuals charged with violent crimes have used the defense that Prozac made them act violently and that they should not be held accountable for their actions while on the drug. Prozac also has been implicated in a number of suicides although it is unclear whether Prozac caused these individuals to commit suicide or whether they would have committed suicide anyway. Paxil and Zoloft, which were introduced after Prozac, reportedly have fewer side effects.

Psychiatrist Peter R. Breggin, who feels that antidepressant drugs are prescribed too frequently, has argued that they are used to replace traditional psychotherapy. Breggin claims that psychiatry has given in to the pharmaceutical companies. In contrast to psychiatry, antidepressant drugs are less expensive and more convenient. However, do these drugs get at the root of the problems that many people have? The United States Public Health Service recommends drug therapy for severe cases of depression but psychotherapy for mild or moderate cases of depression.

One may accept the use of drug therapy when one's medical condition is caused by a chemical imbalance. However, should drugs be employed to alter one's personality—to help one become more confident and less introverted? One could argue that if drugs help people with these personal qualities, then that is a healthy use of these drugs. Are using these drugs any different than people using cigarettes to relax or using alcohol to overcome one's shyness?

In the following selections, Bruce M. Cohen argues that antidepressant drugs are invaluable drugs because they effectively treat anxiety, depression, and psychosis. The benefits of these drugs, claims Cohen, far outweigh their potential side effects. Charles Whitfield is concerned that antidepressant drugs are prescribed too quickly and that physicians are too aggressive in prescribing these drugs. Moreover, Whitfield questions the effectiveness of these drugs. He claims that antidepressant drugs are no more effective than placebos.

Bruce M. Cohen

 **YES**

Mind and Medicine: Drug Treatments for Psychiatric Illnesses

Psychiatric Disorders as Medical Illnesses

Psychiatric illnesses are conditions of the brain that lead to alternations in thinking, mood, and behavior. These illnesses are observed in cultures throughout the world and are probably at least as old as human beings. Recognizable features of psychiatric disorders are described in the texts of many early societies, including those of ancient Egypt, Israel, Greece, India, and China. Also ancient are attempts to treat people with disorders of cognition and emotion by what today would be called psychosocial therapies (including counseling, asylum, and exploration of thought) and psychopharmacologic therapies (that is, plant products or other drugs).

The most common symptoms experienced by those with psychiatric disorders fall into a few categories. Mood may be abnormally high or low. Irritability and anxiety are often felt. Thinking, and its expression in speech and other behaviors, may be illogical. Delusions, which are patently false beliefs not shared by others, can be present. Obsessions and compulsions may continuously haunt the sufferers. Prominent perceptual abnormalities may occur, the most common being hallucinations, which are false sensory percepts, usually the hearing of voices within one's own head. Finally, psychiatric disorders often are associated with changes of physiologic rhythms and the basic drives of life, with disrupted sleep, appetite, and energy.

Some symptoms of psychiatric disorders, notably depression or anxiety, seem to be extremes of normal states, just as hypertension is an extreme of blood pressure. Others, such as hallucinations, appear more distinct from normal experience, although most of us have occasionally thought we heard a voice when we were alone or saw a person when no one was there. These normal experiences are fleeting, while the symptoms of psychiatric disorders last from months to a lifetime.

Symptoms rarely occur alone. Rather, they tend to occur in recognizable clusters, called syndromes. Common syndromes in internal medicine include the pneumonias or congestive heart failure. The most common psychiatric syndromes include the depressive disorders, the anxiety disorders, and the psychotic disorders, such as bipolar disorders and schizophrenia. It is the latter that are most frequently associated with hallucinations and delusions.

Psychiatric disorders are medical illnesses. Like other medical disorders, they are due to the interaction of inherited and environmental factors that, together, lead to the development of illness. While the specific genes that predispose to psychiatric disorders have not yet been identified, the presence of these genes is thoroughly and convincingly documented from family, twin, and adoption studies. Similarly, subtle but repeatedly observed differences in the brain between those with and without psychiatric disorders are now documented by post mortem studies and observation of the brain during life using technologies such as magnetic resonance imaging (MRI), positron emission tomography (PET), and single photon emission computerized tomography (SPECT).

The explicit causes of most current cases of psychiatric disorder are not yet known, but numerous medical conditions that can cause psychiatric disorders are well documented. Over a century ago, many of the patients in psychiatric hospitals had infectious, nutritional, toxic, and hormonal conditions, such as syphilis, pellagra, lead poisoning, and hyper- and hypothyroidism which affected their thinking and mood. Today these medical disorders have responded well to preventive measures, based on diet and environmental advances, or to treatment with medications.

Psychiatric illnesses of unknown cause also tend to respond well to treatment, with success rates as high as those seen in other branches of medicine. Psychotherapeutic medication can restore to normal aspects of consciousness, including feeling, perception, and cognition. For this reason medication is at the core of treatment for most psychiatric disorders.

Drugs and the Brain

Taking drugs with the intent to change aspects of consciousness is very old and quite common. Alcohol, cocaine, opiates, and peyote have been used for thousands of years. These drugs appear to act on systems built into the brain to modulate behaviors associated with eating, sleeping, sexual activity, or other drives and rewards. Co-opting receptors and processes developed to respond to internal chemical messages, these external agents alter arousal, attention, emotional state, and thinking.

Foods can have effects on mood and cognition as well. Deficiencies of some nutrients, as noted, can lead to psychiatric illness, and the oldest recreational drugs are in essence food products or derivatives. Based on this history, numerous nutritional substances are currently being examined as possible treatments for psychiatric disorders.

Hormones, including thyroid, adrenal, and sex hormones, can have profound effects on brain function, drive, cognition, and feelings, and hormonal abnormalities, as was noted, can cause psychiatric symptoms. Hormone replacement—using hormones as drugs—can restore or, occasionally, disrupt mental function.

Further links between physiology, pharmacology, and psychology are evident from the effects of drugs given for purposes unrelated to brain function, but with unwanted actions there. For example, older antihistamines for allergies, which reached receptors throughout the body (including the brain), affected alertness, concentration, and memory. Newer agents were designed that were not absorbed into brain and, therefore, have few mental side effects.

These examples provide compelling evidence that drugs can change all the aspects of consciousness. This knowledge has been used for religious, recreational, and medicinal purposes for generations. With the revolution in organic chemistry, biochemistry, and molecular biology over the past hundred years, the development of new drugs targeted to specific illnesses, such as psychiatric disorders, has become more sophisticated and more successful.

Medication for Psychiatric Disorders

Medicinal treatments for psychiatric disorders are used throughout the world and have their origins in many ancient societies. The oldest documented of these medicinal preparations, made from the plant *Rauwolfia serpentina,* appears in Ayurmedic texts of India over 2,000 years ago. It was recommended for several medical illnesses including those whose description sounds much like the psychotic disorders: the schizophrenias and bipolar disorders. The active ingredient of this preparation was likely reserpine, which was isolated in the 1930s and used briefly but effectively to treat psychotic disorders in the 1950s. It was superseded by easier to use agents, the neuroleptic antipsychotic drugs (which will be described later), in the same decade.

Another "modern" treatment for psychiatric disorders, lithium, prescribed to patients with bipolar disorders, may also have been used in ancient times. Lithium is an element related to sodium and potassium. Like these elements, it most frequently occurs in nature as a salt, often appearing in spring waters. Between A.D. 100 and 300, during the Roman Empire, Arataeus, a physician from Cappadocia, and Soranus of Ephesus recommended waters from particular alkaline springs, which probably contained lithium, for the treatment of mania. While dose could not have been carefully controlled, their advice accords with the use of lithium today.

Eastern Hemisphere plant preparations containing opium have been used to alleviate pain for centuries, and in the late nineteenth and early twentieth centuries, opiate compounds isolated from these plants were used with limited efficacy for the treatment of psychotic disorders and severe depression. Similarly, coca leaves from the Western Hemisphere, chewed by generations for their energizing effects, yielded cocaine, used by Freud and others around 1900 for its stimulating and short-lived antidepressant effects.

None of these older medicinal preparations had strong and reliable enough therapeutic effects or tolerable toxicity for the routine treatment of patients with psychiatric disorders. Breakthroughs leading to the discovery of drugs currently in use, which have good safety and efficacy, occurred in the 1950s, with the introduction of the so-called tricyclic antidepressants, such as Tofranil (imipramine); neuroleptic antipsychotic drugs, such as Thorazine (chlorpromazine); and benzodiazepine anti-anxiety agents, such as Librium (chlordiazepoxide). These drugs revolutionized the care of people with psychiatric disorders, leading to the release of many patients from institutions and the return of others to productive lives.

These first modern medications were followed by many copies and by newer generations of psychotherapeutic drugs in the 1980s and 1990s. Examples include the serotonin specific re-uptake inhibitors, such as Prozac (fluoxetine), for depression; the atypical antipsychotic agents, such as Zyprex (olanzapine), for psychotic disorders; and the mood-stabilizing anticonvulsants, such as Depakote (valproate), for bipolar disorder.

The efficacy of these medications has been proved in numerous studies, including a large number of double-blind, placebo-controlled trials in which the drug being tested is compared to inactive substances, as well as compounds that have effects on the brain, such as sedation, that are not believed to address the key symptoms of psychiatric disorders. Neither the clinical investigator nor the patient knows which drug the patient is receiving. Few drugs in medicine have ever been as thoroughly tested and proven effective.

The proper use of these drugs leads to the successful treatment of most people with depressive disorders, anxiety disorders, schizophrenias and bipolar disorders, restoring them to their proper state of mind. As with all medications, there are side effects as well as therapeutic effects, but with careful use, beneficial effects far outweigh side effects for most people. The physical mechanisms underlying these drug effects and the return to normal consciousness are beginning to be understood, providing important information on the nature of psychiatric disorders and the relationship between brain and psyche.

Medications for Anxiety

In a lifetime, nearly one in six of us will experience a disorder in which anxiety is a prominent symptom. Current anti-anxiety medications, or anxiolytics, grew out of a recognition that alcohol, prized for the comfort and disinhibition it brought, could ease feelings of anxiety. Alcohol relieves distress or discomfort whether or not these feelings are pathological, as indicated by its common social use to relax couples on an evening out or large groups at a party.

Alcohol can provide some relief for those with disorders whose cardinal symptoms include anxiety. In these illnesses, feelings of anxiety may be nearly constant or may occur in attacks of panic. In either case the degree of anxiety is out of proportion to and may even bear no relationship to life events. Unfortunately, the relief is limited by the fast metabolism of alcohol and the tendency of the body to become tolerant to its effects. In fact, as the immediate action of alcohol fades, and as tolerance develops, those who drink for recreation or to medicate themselves for anxiety can find that a physiologic rebound opposite to the effects of alcohol occurs, and they become even more anxious.

From about 1900 on, recognizing the beneficial and toxic effects of alcohol, repeated attempts have been made to find chemical agents that share the calming or sedative effects of alcohol but lack its addictive qualities and the rebound that follows its use. These efforts have been only partially successful.

Early attempts to find safer and more effective compounds than alcohol for anxiety disorders and sedation led to discovery of the barbiturates. They were successful in producing anxiolytic effects, but toxic doses have tended to be close to therapeutic doses and tolerance and addiction are common. Barbiturates are still used for epilepsy and for sedation, but rarely in psychiatry for anxiety disorders.

In the 1950s, derivatives of mephenesin, chemically related to barbiturates, were developed and marketed under the names Miltown (meprobamate) and Equanil (tybamate). All these medications were superseded by compounds called benzodiazepine anxiolytics, which were developed in the late 1950s. The earliest of these, Librium (chlordiazepoxide) and Valium (diazepam), became exceedingly popular drugs, felt to have low risk of poisoning and to be associated only rarely with tolerance and addiction.

Today, a large number of long- and short-acting benzodiazepines are on the market as anxiolytics and sedatives. They are good and effective drugs that are neither as dangerous as alcohol or barbiturates nor as safe as early hopes and claims suggested. Tolerance is common and addiction not rare.

Like alcohol, benzodiazepines reduce anxiety whether or not an individual has an anxiety disorder. Used continuously, their anxiolytic effect tends to fade. While they often blunt the attacks or nagging presence of pathological anxiety, they rarely eliminate these symptoms entirely when used alone. Nevertheless, their powerful and consistent ability to reduce anxiety soon after they are ingested or injected suggests they may work by altering the very brain mechanisms that mediate anxiety.

Following years of fruitful study, the likely site through which the benzodiazepine anxiolytics have their clinical effects is known. Nerve cells (called neurons in the brain) process signals by both electrical and chemical means. Each cell receives chemical messages from other cells, sends electrical messages down its length, and secretes its own chemical compound or compounds, called neurotransmitters, on the cells it contacts. Neurotransmitters produce their effects by binding to specific proteins, called neurotransmitter receptors, which induce a cascade of chemical reactions in the cell to stimulate or reduce electrical activity each time a chemical signal is received.

Eighty to ninety percent of the neuron to neuron contacts in the brain involve one of two neurotransmitters: gama amino butyric acid (GABA) or glutamate. Glutamate is an excitatory neurotransmitter; its message makes a neuron more likely to fire an electrical signal. GABA is an inhibitory neurotransmitter; it quiets cells, making them less likely to fire a signal.

Benzodiazepines attach to some of the same receptors that bind the neurotransmitter GABA and change their characteristics, making them more sensitive to GABA. In this way, benzodiazepines amplify the GABA signal, shifting the overall balance between excitation and inhibition in the brain toward inhibition. At low doses, benzodiazepines may produce their calming antianxiety effect through this shift to inhibition. At high doses, inhibition becomes great enough to induce sleep, or at doses higher still, to cause coma.

GABA is used as a neurotransmitter throughout the brain, and benzodi-azepines enhance its inhibitory effects globally in the brain. It is not known if such a widespread effect is needed for relief of anxiety in humans, or if a local effect in specific regions would suffice. Medical technology is not yet ready routinely to deliver drugs solely to where they are needed. This is a common problem in using drugs in patients. Brain cells can deliver chemicals precisely, but medications go throughout the body, both to where they are needed and where they are not.

Medication for Depression

Like anxiety disorders, depressive disorders are quite common, affecting over one in eight of the population, worldwide, in a lifetime. Symptoms of depression and anxiety often occur together, and for many people, so-called antidepressant drugs are a better long-term treatment of anxiety than are the anxiolytic drugs. In chemical structure and mechanism of action, however, the two classes of drugs are unrelated.

One might think that antidepressant drugs would be derived from stim-ulants, such as the amphetamines. Stimulants can raise mood in almost any-one and can be helpful in some cases of depression. Unfortunately, they are more often not helpful and even when they improve mood, only do so tran-siently. Like anxiolytics, their short-lived effects can lead to tolerance, craving, and addiction.

The earliest current antidepressants were discovered serendipitously in patients with tuberculosis who were treated with an antibiotic called iproniaz-ide. Some of the patients not only had TB, but were severely depressed, until they received iproniazide. Tests in patients without TB, who suffered from depression, indicated that iproniazide was an effective therapeutic agent in relieving depression and restoring abnormalities of appetite, energy, and sleep that usually accompany this illness.

Pharmacologic studies determined that iproniazide was an inhibitor of an enzyme called monoamine oxidase, which metabolizes, and thereby inac-tivates, a group of chemical messengers that include norepinephrine (also called noradrenaline), serotonin, and dopamine. Like GABA, these compounds, which chemically are called monoamines, are used in the brain as neurotrans-mitters. Unlike GABA, the effects of which are rapid, appearing nearly instanta-neously and ending as quickly, the effects of the monoamine neurotransmitters are slow by the standards of the brain, lasting seconds or longer once they are released. For this reason, it has been hypothesized that the monoamines set the "tone" of activity by region in the brain.

Inhibiting the breakdown of monoamines leads to a higher concentration of these neurotransmitters in the brain, which might be the means by which iproniazide relieved depression. Evidence supportive of this speculation arises from the mechanisms by which stimulants act to more transiently elevate mood. Specifically, stimulants cause the release of monoamine neurotransmit-ters in the brain; block the re-uptake of these neurotransmitters back into the cell that released them; or mimic the effects of the monoamine neurotransmitters at the receptor proteins that recognize their presence. Based on the success of iproniazide, more monoamine oxidase inhibitor drugs (all called by the acronym MAOI) like iproniazid were developed, tested, and proved to be effective antidepressants.

Soon after the introduction of MAOIs, a new and different class of antidepressants was independently discovered. These compounds were observed in a search for agents to treat psychotic disorders, such as schizophrenia. In the early 1950s, the first modern drugs for psychosis became available. They had a structure containing three rings of carbon and occasional nitrogen, sulfur, and oxygen atoms. Many such compounds were designed, synthesized, and tested, and a clever observer noted that one compound in particular, while it lacked effects to treat psychosis, seemed to brighten mood substantially in depressed patients. The compound, imipramine, proved to be a greatly successful antidepressant, still on the market over 40 years later. Other compounds structurally similar, with three rings and, therefore, called tricyclic antidepressants, or TCAs, were developed to treat depression. Like the MAOIs, they relieve all the symptoms of depression, not just the dysphoric mood of patients.

Also like MAOIs, TCAs appear to produce their effects through actions on monoamine neurotransmitters. Specifically, they inhibit the uptake of norepinephrine back into the cells that released it. This increases the amount of norepinephrine interacting with neurons and prolongs the time over which norepinephrine acts. They have a similar, but weaker, effect on the re-uptake of serotonin. They have little effect on dopamine, which is the reverse of stimulants, which have their greatest effects on dopamine release and re-uptake.

In the late 1980s, based on the success of the TCAs but searching for a new class of antidepressants, pharmaceutical companies designed drugs that preferentially blocked the re-uptake of serotonin, rather than norepinephrine. The first of these so-called serotonin-specific re-uptake inhibitors, or SSRIs, was Prozac (fluoxetine). It and other SSRIs developed later have been extraordinarily successful, in part because they have different side effects than the TCAs, being safer and seeming to be more comfortable for most people to take. This comfort has led to an increase in the prescription of antidepressants by primary care practitioners as well as psychiatrists, with many newly treated individuals feeling relief from depression and anxiety.

Antidepressants, whether MAOIs, TCAs, or SSRIs, do not seem to benefit those who do not have symptoms of a depressive disorder. The broad use and success of the SSRIs has suggested to some that they have mood-elevating effects in people whether or not the people treated are ill. This is unlikely, as most healthy people only suffer side effects from antidepressants. Rather, as depression is a common illness, like colds in children or high blood pressure in the elderly, and physicians more readily prescribe SSRIs than previous antidepressants, more people with depressive disorders, including milder disorders, are being treated and benefiting from treatment.

Looking to why the brain responds to antidepressants, the available evidence points strongly to drug effects mediated through the monoamine neurotransmitters norepinephrine and serotonin. Two classes of drugs, the MAOIs and the TCAs, discovered independently and serendipitously, have potent actions affecting these chemical signals. A third class of agents, the SSRIs, was developed on the theory that increased serotonin messages would relieve depression. Their success helps confirm the theory. Due to crosstalk, changes in either the serotonin or norepinephrine neurotransmitter system lead to changes in the other system. Furthermore, a role for both norepinephrine and serotonin is suggested by the fact that individual antidepressant drugs whose potency is specific to one or the other monoamine appear equally efficacious in the majority of people.

It is important to note that, while drug effects on serotonin and norepinephrine can relieve depression, this outcome is not direct and immediate. Unlike benzodiazepines for anxiety, or aspirin for headache, the therapeutic effects of antidepressants do not occur in minutes or hours. They require weeks of continued use. Somehow, the brain changes its state in response to the continued presence of drug and the consequent higher levels of monoamine neurotransmitters. Brain-imaging studies suggest that depression fades as regional brain activity changes in response to altered levels of monoamine neurotransmitters induced by antidepressant drugs.

Medications for Psychosis

Psychotic disorders are among the most disabling of illnesses, disturbing thinking, perception, mood, and their interconnections, and diminishing normal human interactions. Fortunately, modern antipsychotic medications are among the more efficacious treatments in medicine today, reversing all or most symptoms in the majority of people with psychotic disorders. The effect is so dramatic that some have called antipsychotic medications the penicillin of psychiatry.

The two most common psychotic illnesses, the schizophrenias and bipolar disorders, affect over one in one hundred people. They often strike the young and can prevent a normal life or reduce successful people to homelessness. Even milder forms or episodes of psychotic illnesses can disrupt relationships among spouses, relatives, and friends. Despite obvious symptoms, including delusions, hallucinations, disrupted speech and thinking, and disorganized behavior, those in the midst of psychosis often do not realize they are ill. This peculiar lack of insight, even in those who have had multiple episodes of illness and been well in between, is another aspect of the unusual state of mind and awareness accompanying these psychotic disorders.

Many patients understand their illnesses and understand the benefits and risks of treatment. In others, lack of insight leads to considerable discussion and debate between the patient and clinicians. When there is an immediate risk of harm to the patient or others due to the symptoms of illness, medication may be started even if the patient does not accept the need for treatment. This is not common. Occasionally, patients who know medications will ameliorate their symptoms choose not to be treated. This, too, is not common, as the symptoms of psychosis are extremely uncomfortable for most people.

Others observe the symptoms of illness, of course, and for many years physicians have tried to help those with psychotic disorders. Reserpine, given in *Rauwolfia serpentina* or as the isolated chemical, had beneficial effects, but at the risk of dangerously low blood pressure and strong sedation. Opiates were used to calm patients, but had minimal effects on the key symptoms of psychosis.

It was not until the early 1950s that the first specific, well-tolerated and effective medication for psychosis, Thorazine (chlorpromazine), was introduced. This medication, and others modeled after it, were so effective that the number of patients with psychotic disorders in hospitals began to drop substantially. With the development of even newer agents that had similar therapeutic effects but fewer side effects, decreases in hospitalization continue, despite a growing population.

The antipsychotic medications were discovered by design, partly from modifying known sedatives, but mostly by looking for agents related to anesthetics, which produced a profound calming effect but not loss of consciousness. The antipsychotic drugs, however, are not all sedatives and are not, as they were once called, major tranquilizers. Some are sedative and some not. Some reduce anxiety, and some can increase it. All work similarly in reducing the symptoms of psychosis, including disrupted thinking, mood, perception, and behavior. Only one, Clozaril (clozapine), may be on average modestly more efficacious than other antipsychotic drugs.

Those without psychotic disorders gain nothing but side effects from these drugs. The drugs have little effect on people with odd or idiosyncratic ideas and behaviors, unless they have the symptoms of schizophrenia or bipolar disorder.

Given that antipsychotic medications all tend to produce a similar therapeutic outcome and were designed to be pharmacologically similar to chlorpromazine, the original antipsychotic drug, it is not surprising that they share common mechanisms of action at a molecular level. Specifically, all antipsychotic drugs block signals at some but not all receptors for the chemical messengers dopamine, norepinephrine, and serotonin.

By blocking signals at these receptors, the antipsychotic drugs produce affects in several key areas of the brain. They change activity in the nucleus accumbens, which is involved, in part, in mediating a sense of reward; the amygdala, which is involved in determining a sense of threat, disquiet, or safety; the thalamus, which appears to be involved in coordinating aspects of thought, perception, and emotion; and the prefrontal cortex, which is the most developed of all areas of the human brain and is involved in attention, decision making, and keeping thoughts in consciousness.

Like the antidepressants, therapeutic effects of antipsychotic drugs can take weeks to develop. How the immediate effects of the antipsychotic drugs become longer term effects is not known. However, there is growing evidence that modulation of signals through the monoamine receptors affected by antipsychotic drugs leads to changes in the activity of GABAergic and glutaminergic cells, which mediate much of the function of the brain.

It is not surprising that even though the antipsychotic drugs have effects on only a few specific receptors in the brain, their use would change activity at many sites. Neurons that employ dopamine, norepinephrine, and serotonin as their chemical messengers are few, but they contact vast numbers of cells throughout the brain. In addition, because cells in the brain are interconnected in a dense network, a limited direct effect can translate into a broad distributed effect.

Most well-described functions of the brain, such as the processing of visual information or the control of movement, are handled by cells distributed across many different, but sometimes overlapping, areas of the brain. It is possible, and even likely, that emotions and thoughts are also a consequence of changes in the activity of specific groups of cells linked to one another but representing different aspects of feeling or cognition and existing in different locations within the brain. The wide distribution of neurons responding to antipsychotic drugs, and mediating their effects, illustrates this point.

Psychiatric Disorders, Psychotherapeutic Medication, and Consciousness

Medications are a key component of the treatment of most psychiatric disorders. They are not, of course, the sole treatment. Proper care requires attention to the psychological and social aspects of illness. These may represent environmental stressors that, unaddressed, can trigger illness in those predisposed. Also, psychological and social problems are frequently consequences of the disruption of mood, thought, and behavior caused by illness. Patients need support in reconstituting their lives and sense of self once their symptoms fade.

It is remarkable, however, just how powerful medications are in relieving the symptoms of psychiatric disorders. Along with genetic, structural, and functional evidence, the effects of drugs are compelling findings suggesting that psychiatric illnesses arise from abnormal activity of the brain; that is, they are medical disorders of the brain.

Arguments can be made for and against the recreational use of drugs. Society accepts some, such as alcohol, and not others, such as marijuana. By comparison, there is little basis for argument about the treatment of psychiatric disorders with medication. For most people, the benefits clearly outweigh the risks.

The effects of psychotherapeutic medications also speak to questions beyond that of the origin and nature of psychiatric disorders. They speak to the nature of consciousness.

Drugs can disturb all aspects of consciousness and drugs can restore aspects of consciousness. As drugs act on the structure, chemistry, and electrical activity of the brain, it is logical to conclude that all aspects of consciousness depend on physical states of the brain.

Evidence is growing as to the precise molecular sites at which drugs act, as well as on the specific changes that occur in cellular metabolism and the state of neural circuits during drug treatment. Pharmacologic studies point to particular regions of the brain or particular distributed groups of nerve cells as being involved in mediating mood, awareness, cognition, or the integration of experience. Studies of the consequences of lesions associated with epilepsy, tumors, strokes, and trauma also suggest that particular parts of the brain are necessary, if not sufficient, to determine aspects of consciousness. Results from pharmacology and pathology agree strongly on which areas are associated with which aspects of consciousness.

No simple connections are likely to exist between a molecule and a thought or a nerve cell and a mood. However, it is reasonable to expect that the state of networks of nerve cells in the brain may be closely related to conscious states of thinking or feeling. Drugs and medications can change the patterns of firing in neural circuits and the tone of neural activity in the brain. By doing so, they can alter those aspects of consciousness that make us most human. The study of drug effects will remain an important tool for designing and testing models of how mind may arise from brain. Equally or more important, the use of currently available drugs and the arrival of new drugs under development will continue to provide good treatments, and some day cures, for the devastating illnesses classified as psychiatric disorders.

NO ↲

Charles L. Whitfield

The Truth about Depression: Choices for Healing

Do Antidepressant Drugs Work?

Yes, they do appear to work, but at best by only a few percentage points (e.g., 2 to 10 percent) better than placebo. More likely, for most people they work only about as well as placebo. But, with their high expense and fairly high incidence of toxic side effects, are they worth it? Here are some considerations.

Saying that antidepressant drugs (ADPs) may not work flies in the face of seemingly firm medical opinion and could put more demands on clinicians and threaten to damage the large incomes and profits of the drug industry. Antidepressant drugs may have selected uses, and in some cases could even be life-saving. But could we have bought into using these sometime helpful drugs too enthusiastically and often prematurely? For example, the long-term usefulness of benzodiazepine sedative drugs (e.g., the Valium, Ativan, Xanax family) proved to be largely unture but only after we learned painful lessons over a four-decade span of clinical and personal experience about their limited efficacy, bothersome and sometimes dangerous side effects, and high addiction rates.

We have also had the same four decades of experience with modern antidepressants. These drugs include four kinds, starting with 1) the monoamine oxidase inhibitor ADPs (MAOIs), and then 2) the tricyclic ADPs, and over the past twenty years 3) the highly marketed selective serotonin reuptake inhibitors (SSRIs) and finally 4) the atypical ADPs. In spite of these categorical differences and the drug companies' heavy promotion of their individual drugs, numerous therapeutic trials have shown that none of these different categories or kinds of antidepressants is any better than another, nor is any individual brand name any better.

Drug Promotions

Drug companies that make psychiatric drugs are big business. While over time they have produced some effective drugs, such as antibiotics and diuretics, drug companies are not generally run by clinicians, they do not take a Hippocratic oath, and they do not appear to always act in the best interest of sick

From THE TRUTH ABOUT DEPRESSION: CHOICES FOR HEALING, March 2003, pp. 121–125, 128–145. Copyright © by Health Communications, Inc. Reprinted by permission.

people. They function in most ways like any other big business. Their only regulation, often with minimal success, is by limited agencies of the federal government. Most of the psychiatric drug types they have produced were discovered by accident. Most of these drugs are nonspecific in their action. That is, they tend to have broad-spectrum effects, both positive and negative, beneficial and toxic. Most of the drug company clinical trials are limited to only a few weeks' duration, yet they and their representatives regularly recommend that patients take their drugs long-term, often without full knowledge of toxic and detrimental consequences that come only later (remember thalidomide).

Behind the Scenes

Behind the scenes, many psychiatrists on the faculty of medical schools and testing companies, and others who give lectures and workshops about psychiatric drugs, are paid by drug companies to do much of their research and help promote their drugs. A recent survey of one hundred authors of published *clinical practice guidelines,* which offer "state-of-the-art" diagnostic and treatment advice to physicians, nurses and allied clinicians, revealed that 87 percent of the authors had been paid by drug companies and/or were their prior employees or consultants. Might this represent what lawyers would call a conflict of interest? Thirty years ago, medical ethics probably would not have allowed this kind of behavior. While this information is minimally disclosed to most of the speakers' continuing education audiences, it is not published in the medical journal articles in which they write about these drugs and is not usually known to the general public. As this book goes to press, apparently instigated by critics, some medical journals have just begun to require such disclosure of the authors of its published articles. Another study found that *over half* of the U.S. Food and Drug Administration's (FDA) *advisory committee* members are paid by drug companies that have an interest in FDA decision. These kinds of deceptions can have important implications and cautions for all of medicine and psychiatry.

Regarding the clinical trials of each drug, there is no requirement by the government or any other authority that the drug company report any negative results to clinicians or the public. Instead, they tend to report only positive results. Similar to the tobacco companies, many drug companies have tended to deny or minimize the toxic effects of their drugs. . . . They downplay these toxic effects in various ways, including calling them "side effects," when they actually often indicate drug *toxicity.* One of the more bothersome effects of most of the ADPs, some antipsychotics, and all of the benzodiazepine drugs is a *painful* and often *confusing, prolonged* and *disabling withdrawal syndrome.* Drug companies have tended to deny the existence of such withdrawal, claiming instead that the symptoms are simply a "reemergence" of the original complaints. After being pressured for years to disclose this information as a warning to clinicians and pharmacists, they finally began to list cursory warnings. . . .

Drug companies tend to assign drugs their names not by their chemical properties, but for marketing purposes only. They make up both the generic and trade or brand names, which usually have nothing to do with the drug's chemical structure. More deception: They may also disguise the names of some drugs to make more money from them, including when their patent for a drug has expired. For example, Serafem for the treatment of severe premenstrual problems (premenstrual dysphoric disorder) is actually only Prozac (fluoxetine), and Zyban for helping people stop smoking is simply Welbutrin (bupropion).

Even though many antidepressant drugs have been shown to differ only very little in effectiveness from placebo (sugar pills), drug companies have frequently exaggerated this small and often insignificant difference in their advertisements to physicians and other clinicians in medical journals. And seventeen years later, when the patent runs out for a particular drug, they may change their original promotional claims. For example, in 1984 Eli Lilly launched Prozac (fluoxetine) as one of the first "effective" SSRI antidepressant drugs. Over the next seventeen years, associated with heavy marketing and promotion, it made billions of dollars from its sales to health consumers who took their clinicians' word that it was effective for lessening their symptoms of depression. In late 2001, when its patent ran out on exclusive rights to making and selling fluoxetine as Prozac, they appear to have changed their tune. At this point, Lilly representatives published evidence that Prozac was *no better than a placebo* (sugar pill) to treat depression. Why? Because not only had their patent run out on Prozac, but now they had a new antidepressant (generic name duloxetine) to market and sell to clinicians and the public that was "more effective." How might the public interpret this kind to behavior? Could the company have known it all along? How did this knowledge pass the academics who conducted the clinical trials for Lilly? And how and why did it pass the government agency that originally approved the licensing of Prozac?

My Clinical Experience

My own clinical experience includes: 1) hearing more than four hundred (a conservative estimate) of my patients recount their experiences of having "depression" for which they had been prescribed by others one or many ADPs—and often a string of them—mostly unsuccessfully, and 2) prescribing these drugs myself for more than over two hundred of my own patients (also a conservative estimate). (My approach has always been to look first for the cause of the symptoms of depression that the patient could address, with or without my or others' assistance, to help lessen their pain.)

Unpredictable

From that experience, I observed that about a third of my patients reported experiencing an acceptable relief of their symptoms of depression *for a time*; another third had some, though not ideal relief for a time; and the final third reported no relief. I say "for a time" because they usually reported that most of their relief lasted for only a few weeks or months, and then their symptoms returned—although a small number said they were helped for a year or more. Many reported only a *partial* relief of their symptoms, and their overall quality of life had not significantly improved. Many of them went on to try a different ADP, which had about the same one-third/one-third/one-third effect described above. Their histories often included having tried a string of several to as many as eight or ten different ADPs, mostly tricyclics and SSRIs, and since 1990 mostly the latter. Of course, many of them stopped taking one or more ADPs because of their bothersome or even intolerable side effects.

ADPs are unpredictable in their actions, results and toxic effects. Different people may react in totally opposite ways to the same drug. For example, I have seen one person become quite sedated on paroxetine (Paxil), and another feel overstimulated on the same drug and dose. I have seen similar results from other ADP drugs. And more often than not, when they do work, people tend to benefit from these drugs only somewhat, if at all. The following is a summary of a patient I assisted in her recovery.

> **Case History 10.1:** Margaret was a forty-six-year-old divorced woman who grew up in a troubled family wherein she experienced repeated physical, mental and emotional abuse. She presented with a long history of recurring episodes of major depression, with a strong component of anxiety. Over the years she had seen several different clinicians and had been diagnosed with depression. She was treated over time with eight different antidepressant drugs, most of which had little or no lasting effect on her depressive symptoms. On further evaluation I found her to fulfill the *DSM-IV* diagnostic criteria for PTSD. When she voluntarily withdrew from taking her current antidepressant drug she became more aware of her childhood trauma history and the effects that it caused, including her anxiety and depression. She slowly began to express these painful experiences to safe people, and over the next few months her mood began to lift. She is currently still working a recovery program in group and individual therapy.

Margaret's story represents a common experience that I have observed among childhood trauma survivors. After the trauma, they develop one or more painful conditions or disorders, such as depression, an anxiety disorder, PTSD, an addiction or the like, and often seek aid from physical medicine or mental health clinicians in the community. These clinicians focus on the presenting complaints and make a limited diagnosis based on *DSM* or other diagnostic criteria. Influenced by health insurance companies, they then prescribe or recommended a limited form of treatment, such as drugs or, less often, brief psychotherapy. They tend not to connect the person's current problems with their past traumas, and thereby may miss a major opportunity to make an effective therapeutic intervention. . . .

Having realized some of the above dynamics, psychiatrists J. Douglas Bremner describes his experience. He said:

> *I asked some of my more experienced psychiatric colleagues at Yale whether or not they felt that childhood abuse was an important topic for research study for a psychiatrist. They gave me their opinions that childhood abuse was not very common, and in any case was not an important topic. . . . I then asked the other psychiatrists and social workers in the psychiatric clinic at the VA [Veterans Administration Hospital] if they would be willing to screen their patients for a history of childhood abuse, in order to participate in my studies using brain imaging to examine the effects of abuse on the brain. They felt that they couldn't ask their patients about anything in their childhoods, because if their patients had been*

abused, that subject would make them much more upset, and then the psychiatrists and social workers would have trouble dealing with them. I offered to screen everyone coming into the clinic for abuse myself, and to take on as my personal patients anyone who became extremely upset as a result of this screening. Fascinatingly, the results of the screening procedure were the opposite of my colleagues' fears. The patients who did have abuse histories were extremely appreciative that at last their psychiatrists were finally figuring out how to properly assess them as patients.

At times a trial of antidepressant drugs may be indicated and helpful for some childhood trauma survivors, but that should not be the primary treatment aid. Here, the primary focus should be on the gradual cognitive and experiential connecting of the person's current pain and issues with their past trauma, which is often best accomplished by using recovery aids. . . . In this context, when they are effective, ADP drugs may take the edge off of otherwise distracting and disabling pain, so that the person can work more constructively on healing from the long-term trauma effects.

For the minority of people with depression who grew up in a healthy family, ADP drugs or individual psychotherapy—or a combination of both—may be effective in lessening their symptoms. I have assisted some such people as well. However, knowing how common childhood trauma is and that full trauma memories may be slow to emerge, even for them I keep an open ear for that possibility. Our mistake may have been to assume that there is no connection between past trauma and subsequent mental illness.

When I read the independent London researcher Charles Medawar's comprehensive review of the state of our understanding of ADPs, I noticed that his summary, and others', supported what I had observed in my clinical experience: that ADP drugs are not as effective as we would like them to be and/or as the drug companies would like us to believe. For example, regarding ADPs, he wrote, ". . . patients generally respond (some very well, others less so) in about 50–70% of cases." Research psychiatrist John Greden said, ". . . up to 70 percent of patients being treated for depression are not finding satisfactory relief of their depressive symptoms." . . . I will summarize some of Medawar's and others' most salient findings. I recommend that anyone interested in this topic read their original articles, some of which are available on the Internet.

Recent History of Antidepressant Drugs

During the past forty years, the politics of marketing and prescribing these and other drugs developed and escalated hand-in-hand with ". . . the biological approach to psychiatry—treating mental illness as a genetically influenced disorder of brain chemistry—[which] has been [either] a smashing success" or a subtle failure.

In the 1950s, monoamine oxidase inhibitors (MAOIs) were discovered and developed from the finding that some patients with tuberculosis who took the antibiotic drug *iproniazid* experienced a lifted mood (Table 10.1). This finding led to drug companies and some academics looking for more profits by theorizing a possible biochemical basis for depression and developing drugs to try to treat it, in that they speculated that depression might be due to a lack

Table 10.1

Risk-Benefit Ratio Analysis of Common Psychiatric Drugs
The Ideal Ratio Is as Close to Zero as Possible

(ratios estimated by author 2002)

Drug	Estimated R/B Ratio	Risk	Benefit
SSRI Antidepressant*	Medium	• 25–80% bothersome adverse effects, including akathesia & suicide/ homicide; • 33–86% have a withdrawal syndrome	On average, most are only 2–10% better than placebo in reducing symptoms of depression by 50%
Benzodiazepine Sedative**	Medium to high	• High addiction rate • Block healthy feelings & grieving • High withdrawal rate & potential long disability	Excellent for acute severe fear (anxiety) The longer taken, the less effective (drug tolerance) in reducing fear
Buspirone (Anti-fear/anxiety)***	Low	Low risk	About 80% helped
Major Tranquilizers****	Medium to High	• Tardive dyskinesia • Withdrawal syndrome	Helps some psychotics function Helps family & staff
Placebo†	Zero	Lowest risk	33–70% helped in depression

Comments:

*Of 2/3 of people who are helped some, 1/3 are helped partially & 1/3 are helped more. Often help lasts for only a few months. The last 1/3 of people are not helped at all.

**If used, do so for only a few days to avoid risk effects. For serious ongoing fear (anxiety): buspirone plus psycho-social-spiritual aids (see Table 12.1) may help.

***Takes edge off fear (anxiety); helps many with PTSD & panic. Expensive (as for most drugs)

****See *The Truth about Mental Illness* for further comments

† Show how poorly many drugs work

of brain noradrenaline (also called norepinephrine), and later thought caused by a lack of another neurotransmitter, serotonin (5-hydroxytryptamine). Unknown to many clinicians and others, both of these theories were eventually disproved.

Until the 1980s, up to 80 percent of cases of depression were thought to be self-limiting. This observation may have been related to the fact that in the 1960s some drug companies began a slow marketing campaign to find "depressed" patients—who should naturally be prescribed their patented ADP drugs.

Psychiatrist and author Frank Ayd said, "To a certain extent, it was necessary for Merck [a drug company in the 1960s and beyond] to educate the physicians in order to market the illness [depression] so they would know what to prescribe for that illness, which was Merck's drug [amytriptyline/ Elavil]."

⌑⟐⌑

This process continues even today. Drug companies develop psychoactive drugs and then teach physicians how to use them. With pressure from the "managed care" arms of insurance companies, other professions commonly buy into this process. As an example, currently psychologists are lobbying government agencies to allow them to prescribe psychiatric drugs. As psychiatrist Ashley Wazana of McGill University said, "The tail seems to be wagging the dog." Today drug companies are further violating ethical guidelines by marketing their drugs to the public through often misleading TV commercials.

Like all good business people, to keep them financially well afloat, the drug companies looked for more and better drugs. When they found more kinds of tricyclic antidepressant drugs in the 1960s and 1970s and the SSRIs in the 1980s, they escalated their marketing campaign to try to convince clinicians and the public that depression was common and, of course, that those afflicted needed their drugs.

Over time, drug companies have presented a storyline of the medical necessity to treat the world's now large "depressed" population, which they had themselves assumed and promoted, with any one or a combination of their own ADPs or benzodiazepine sedative drugs long-term. With minimal evidence, they appear to have planned, believed and marketed that depression was a genetically transmitted biochemical brain disorder. After more than forty years of clinical and research experience, we now know that much of that storyline has been embellished to some extent by the drug companies in concert with some academics, and others in government agencies and the helping professions. Most of what they have promoted appears to be untrue. . . .

Drug Versus Placebo: Biases and Problems

From numerous clinical trials, the therapeutic differences between the efficacy of ADP drugs when compared to placebo have been neither great nor impressive. Even so, with the growing belief in and promotion of the "biologic basis" of depression and the discounting of placebo factors at work in these trials, intense marketing and subtle politics seem to have overtaken the data, such that prescribing ADPs has, since at least the early 1980s, become routine. Clinical and research psychiatrist David Healy said, "Almost anyone who was unhappy for any reason could now be diagnosed as depressed. It was at this point, I believe, that psychiatrists unwittingly handed the agenda over to the pharmaceutical industry."

But problems, often carefully hidden or overlooked, developed. Unfortunately, many companies' original drug *trials*, for example, have tended to have several important *biases*.

1. Many of their test patients also *took other psychoactive drugs* at the *same time* that they were being "tried" on an ADP. In several studies, 25 percent of these "trial" patients were also taking benzodiazepine drugs at the same time. Medawar notes that the *one* study that did not permit the use of other drugs was the *only one* of four trial studies to find *no* satistically *significant difference* between treatment results for fluoxetine (Prozac) and placebo. This means that in each of the other three (i.e., 75 percent of these fluoxetine [Prozac] trials), *other drugs were*

allowed to contaminate the results—and that these were therefore not appropriately conducted or "clean" trials.

2. A second flaw was that among all four of the pivotal trials on fluoxetine (Prozac), the investigators used what is called a *placebo washout* period to *exclude the early responders to placebo.* In this manipulative procedure, *all of the test subjects* received placebo for the first week, and every one of them whose Hamilton Depression Scale rating dropped below 80 percent of their original value was [inappropriately] excluded. The investigators may argue that "half" of the eliminated subjects would have been given the fluoxetine anyway. But we don't know that for a fact, since many drug companies often vary their drug/placebo ratios (I have seen ratios of 4/1), so why tamper with proven experimental procedure and introduce such a potentially major bias into the credibility of any important drug trial?[1]

3. A third potential flaw is that trials on SSRIs before 1990 typically *lasted* for only about *six weeks,* and more recently for only *eight weeks.* This is hardly enough time for drug companies to provide clinicians with crucial data to make informed decisions about whether to prescribe an ADP for a several-month period or longer—which drug companies and their spokespeople recommend (some suggest that depressed people take their drugs for a year to life).

4. A fourth flaw is that the *double-blind procedure* (where neither researcher nor subject knows whether drug or placebo was taken) is *often blocked or invalidated* when the person experiences one or more *side effects* from the drug, thus potentially *telling* both researcher and subject that they have in fact *taken the active drug.*

5. A fifth potential problem involves the inherent *motivation bias* of the drug company that develops the drug. A drug company has to spend several million dollars to develop a new drug, as it jumps through the numerous hoops that are required for licensure. The enormous cost of every new drug project that does not result in a licensed and successful drug can be a financial drain on their coffers, and so there is naturally great pressure to produce "positive" results from their trials. Could it be that the researchers that they pay, within and outside the company, sometimes find positive results because their salaries and grants depend on it? Another variation on this influence may involve Heisenberg's classic *Uncertainty Principle,* which says that the experimenter inherently influences the results of the experiment, and that by the simple act of *observing,* this influence unknowingly occurs.

6. A sixth potential bias is that investigators and reporters can *misreport* or *misinterpret* a subject's HAM-D Scale (Hamilton Depression Scale, used almost universally in ADP drug trials). As clinical and research psychiatrist Bruce Greyson said, "The 'gold standard' scale for measuring depression in drug studies is the Hamilton Depression Scale [HAM-D], and most drug studies use as a criterion for improvement a 50 percent decrease in a patient's score. On the HAM-D, generally 7 points is considered depressed, and 15 is severely depressed; so if a patient enters a drug study with a HAM-D score of 32, and after 4 weeks of Prozac has a score of 16, that's counted as a successful treatment because the patient's score fell by 50 percent, even though they still score in the 'severely depressed' range!"

This potential bias may be associated with how the drug companies, researchers and now probably most psychiatrists and other helping professionals define "improvement." Greyson added, "With the advent of the *DSM-III* and then *DSM-IV*, psychiatrists got away from identifying depression in terms of how the patient feels, and started defining it with their 'Chinese-menu' symptom lists. So now to be depressed you need to have at least five symptoms, only one of which is feeling sad; the others are diminished interest in activities, weight change, sleep change, psychomotor change, feelings of worthlessness, diminished concentration, and recurrent thoughts of death. . . . What that means is that if antidepressants correct your insomnia and restore your appetite and give you more energy, they can by definition make you no longer depressed, even though you still feel like death warmed over. And there are lots of data to show that antidepressants do just that: They help correct what are called the 'vegetative signs of depression'—the decreased sleep, appetite, energy, libido, etc.—but don't necessarily help you feel any better."

David Healy said that when drug companies test their antidepressants, they generally measure not only depression (by scales like the HAM-D) but also the reported quality of life. But although they are quick to publish the improved depression scores, they almost never make public the quality-of-life data, because antidepressants don't, in fact, improve quality of life, and in some cases, they worsen it.

When combined with these six serious potential and often real drug trial biases, the information summarized in this book shows that ADPs are, as a whole, at best only a few percentage points better than placebo. More realistically they are *about equal* to placebo in their effectiveness in helping ameliorate depression. Plus, their downside is that they are *expensive,* . . . they have *bothersome side effects,* . . . and rarely, especially if involved in drug interactions and overdoses, they can be fatal.

Analysis of Drug Versus Placebo Trials

Perhaps even stronger evidence comes from recent independent analyses of the numerous clinical drug trials that were previously conducted or sponsored by the drug companies themselves. For example, research psychiatrist Arif Khan and colleagues evaluated the treatment trials for nine FDA-approved *antidepressant* drugs between 1985 and 2000 on 10,030 depressed patients who participated in fifty-two trials evaluating ninety-three treatment arms of a new or prior drug. They also looked at thirteen FDA-approved *antianxiety* drugs trials on 8,340 anxious patients between 1985 and 2000 who participated in forty trials evaluating seventy-five treatment arms of a new or prior drug. Their remarkable finding was that *fewer than half* (48 percent, 45/93) of the *antidepressant drug* treatment trial arms showed superiority to placebo. Among *antianxiety* drugs, the same percentage of 48 percent (36/75) showed superiority over placebo. These data show that conventional drug treatments for depression and anxiety are superior to placebo *less than half the time*. Thus, in over half of the trials (52 percent), the response to antidepressants and anxiolytics was *indistinguishable* from that of *placebo*. These results replicate previous reports by independent researchers on the small difference between antidepressant drugs and placebo. They also call into serious question the proposal that placebo controls can be done away with in clinical trials. Based on these data, if new antidepressants and anxiolytics were tested against "standard" treatment rather than placebo, about half of the trials would yield invalid results.

Prozac (fluoxetine) took seven trials to find two that showed superiority over placebo, and Paxil (paroxtine) and Zoloft (sertraline) required even more. These few analyzed drug trial studies are thus the most positive results that the drug companies could complete in order to submit their most new-drug favorable findings to the FDA for approval. Thus, Khan et al's study was not able to look at the five negative studies that showed that Prozac was no better than placebo because its drug company had apparently not submitted them to the FDA.

The same applies to other drug makers. In fact, drug companies have among the most minimal of requirements that the Food and Drug Administration has ruled as being adequate to show the "effectiveness" of any new ADP drug. Their only requirement is to produce two placebo-controlled, randomized, double-blind studies that show a 50 percent improvement on the Hamilton Depression Scale over five to eight weeks of taking the drug that significantly exceeds the antidepressant effectiveness of placebo, which often is by only a few percentage points. For example, two study results in the neighborhood of 55 percent success for drug receivers compared to 45 percent of placebo receivers would possibly warrant FDA approval, even if the same studies had failed to show any drug advantage six times previously.

For most people who take them, antidepressant drugs don't work well. An ideal ADP drug would specifically lessen the symptoms of depression without causing bothersome of toxic side effects. But there is no such ideal drug today. In spite of drug company claims to the contrary, these drugs tend to have broad and nonspecific effects, many or which prompt people to stop taking them, such as oversedation, overstimulation, weight gain and anorgasmia—to name some of the more common ones. In the field of medicine we call these "shotgun" effects, as opposed to a single-bullet kind of effect. Clinical and research psychiatrist Thomas Moore said, "Antidepressant drugs are a kind of bull in a China shop." Harvard psychiatrist and author Joseph Glenmullen said, "Normal functioning of the brain is impaired by antidepressant drugs." When they do work, for some people they may be just as effective at lower than recommended doses (especially in elderly people), which we have learned over time with many of the ADP drugs. In this book, I am not saying that we should not use them at all. I believe that for some people they may help to some degree, even though for a majority who use them they do not work as well as we would like.

Risks and Benefits

Another way to look at this problem is to compare the relative risk for taking a drug to its potential benefit. For at least thirty years, physicians and other health professionals have been aware of the importance of weighing these two key realities. While they have spoken of risk-benefit ratios and more recently risk-benefit analysis, I have not found a clear description and discussion of them for commonly used psychiatric drugs.

Based on my thirty-year experience in the fields of addiction medicine and trauma psychology, I have estimated the risk-benefit ratios of commonly and some uncommonly used psychiatric drugs. I also base this information on my knowledge of the literature. Given this overview, readers may make their own inquiries and decisions regarding their and others' personal situations wherein any of these drugs may be involved.

In my clinical work, I have seen many patients who wasted money and time trying antidepressant drugs, who went through painful withdrawal periods, and of course, many others who have suffered toxic effects of antidepressants, many of whom received little or no relief from their depressive symptoms as well. I have also seen countless patients who became addicted to stimulants and benzodiazepines, frequently prescribed for depressed and anxious people, who went through painful withdrawals and drug-seeking behaviors. By contrast, I have never seen a patient addicted to barbiturates, the antianxiety drug buspirone or to major tranquilizers, although I know that especially the latter are often toxic.

Based on his vast clinical and research career on depression and ADP drugs, David Healy said, "With the increasing use of these drugs, there has been a huge upsurge in the numbers of people who are depressed. This is not what is supposed to happen when treatments work. . . . Their capacity to sell to us far outstrips their capacity to help us. This is the point at which the antidepressants become part of the problem of depression rather than part of the solution." Psychiatrist Joseph Glenmullen said, "I don't think there is an epidemic of depression, but there is an epidemic of prescribing antidepressant drugs."

Perhaps their biggest detriment has to do with the way that antidepressant drugs have been used for their more than forty years of existence. This use has too often allowed the helping professions that recommend and prescribe them often to *overlook* what appears to be the most common cause of or association with depression: a history of trauma, most commonly *repeated childhood trauma*. These traumatic experiences appear to be woven into a web of other subtle and overt factors that may predate depression or aggravate it. These factors may include: 1) the presence of other "co-morbid" disorders; 2) a poor to marginal diet or nutrition; 3) a lack of regular exercise; 4) an overexposure to a television, movie and print media that commonly portrays a negative distortion of our human potential and reality; 5) an out-of-date and often ineffective educational system; 6) a religious system that is often not nourishing to our spirits; and 7) ongoing traumas and significant stressors in the person's adult life. . . .

Even though ADP drugs have became a mainstay of treatment of depressive symptoms today, there are at least twelve other treatment aids. . . .

Note

1. Originally, early in the forty-year sequence of properly conducted ADP drugs trials, Smith and colleagues found that the median placebo improvement response rate was 46 percent (versus 61 percent) for active drugs. But later,

these often hidden placebo washouts reduced the actual placebo response rate by about 13 percent (a potentially significant figure) from 46 percent down to 33 percent. Some thirty years later, in 1998, Kirsch and Sapirstein calculated the mean effect sizes (i.e., effectiveness) for changes in depression among 2,318 patients who had been randomly assigned to either antidepressant medication or placebo in nineteen double-blind clinical trials. They found that the effect size for active medications that are *not regarded to be antidepressants* was as large as that for those classified as antidepressants, and in both cases, these "inactive placebos" produced improvement that was at least 75 percent of the effect of the active drug. A more careful examination of pre- and post-effect sizes, i.e., the differences among depressed individuals assigned to no-treatment or wait-list control groups, suggested that about one-quarter of the drug response is caused by the administration of an active medication, *one half is a placebo effect,* and the remaining *quarter* is caused by other nonspecific factors. Research psychologist Irving Kirsch (1998) said, "What is the proportion of the response to antidepressant medication that is duplicated by placebo administration? Sapirstein and I calculated this figure to be about 75 percent (Kirsch & Sapirstein, 1998). Joffe and colleagues' (1996) data indicate the figure to be 65 percent. Pharmaceutical company statistics yield an estimate of 71 percent (Kirsch 1998). These data, all of which are from published sources, indicate that, at best, the pharmacological effect of antidepressant medication is somewhere between 25 and 35 percent of the total drug response."

POSTSCRIPT

Are Psychotherapeutic Drugs Effective for Treating Mental Illness?

Many mental health practitioners maintain that antidepressant drugs can be effective in treating the majority of people with less severe forms of depression. However, there is a sharp disagreement as to whether these drugs are prescribed too readily and whether they are taking the place of traditional talk therapy. Of course, this debate does not focus on which type of treatment is best. Many people receive both drug therapy and psychotherapy. In addition, it has been shown that drug therapy and psychotherapy work best when used in combination.

The debate regarding antidepressant drugs has spurned other concerns. Should they be prescribed for common problems that people encounter on a daily basis, such as stress, feelings of anxiety, phobias, shyness, and obsessive-compulsive behavior? Many people experience these problems. A certain degree of anxiety, shyness, and compulsivity is not unusual. Should people rid themselves of these conditions even if they may incur adverse side effects?

The pursuit of happiness seems to be of paramount importance in our society. Yet, can one find happiness in a pill? Should one turn to pills to find happiness? Do these drugs represent a quick and easy fix? Is it ethical to chemically alter an individual's mood and personality in order to make that person happy? Will psychopharmacology replace traditional psychotherapy? Is the rapid growth of antidepressant drugs a well-conceived promotion on the part of pharmaceutical companies? In a society that values solving problems quickly and easily, these drugs seem to effectively fulfill a need. However, do their advantages outweigh their disadvantages?

A popular slogan many years ago referred to "better living through chemistry." If a drug is available that will make people happier, more confident, and more socially adept, shouldn't that drug be available for people who would derive some degree of benefit from it? One concern is that some individuals may rely on drugs to remedy many of their problems rather than to work through those issues that caused the problems in the first place. It is much easier to drop a pill than to engage in self-exploration and self-reflection. One could make some analogy between antidepressant drugs and other drugs. Many people now use alcohol, tobacco, over-the-counter medicines, and illegal drugs to cope with life's problems. Drugs, whether they are legal or illegal, are used increasingly for dealing with our daily problems.

Consumer Report magazine (October 2004) assessed the advantages of drug therapy versus talk therapy and found that both work best when used in combination. Gordon Marino argues against psychotherapeutic drugs in "Altered States: Pills Alone Won't Cure the Blues" (*Commonweal*, May 21, 2004). The negative publicity regarding psychotherapeutic drug may prevent young people from deriving their benefits, according to Nancy Shute in "Teens, Drugs, and Sadness" (*U.S. News and World Report*, August 30, 2004). In his article "Is It Really Our Chemicals That Need Balancing?" *Journal of American College Health* (July 2002), Christopher Bailey argues that society is falling into the trap of making minor problems into mental illnesses. The article "Generation Rx: The Risk of Raising Our Kids on Pharmaceuticals" by Rob Waters, *Psychotherapy Networker* (March/April 2000), maintains that children are being put on drugs like stimulants and antidepressants at too early an age. Carl Elliott writes in "Pursued by Happiness and Beaten Senseless: Prozac and the American," *Hastings Center Report* (March/April 2000), that too many people are using antidepressant drugs simply because they feel alienated.

ISSUE 11

Do the Consequences of Caffeine Consumption Outweigh Its Benefits?

YES: Men's Health, from "Start Me Up," *Men's Health* (October 2004)

NO: Harvard Women's Health Watch, from "Coffee: For Most It's Safe," *Harvard Women's Health Watch* (September 2004)

ISSUE SUMMARY

YES: The writers from *Men's Health* describe caffeine as an addictive substance whose use results in withdrawal symptoms. The stimulating effects of caffeine are muted by tolerance that develops to the drug. In large amounts, caffeine consumption can cause anxiety and panic.

NO: The writers from the *Harvard Women's Health Watch* discuss the benefits of coffee. Although caffeine may have addictive qualities, its dangers are overstated. Caffeine's effects on the cardiovascular system are modest. Benefits of caffeine include reducing the risk of developing type 2 diabetes, gallstones, liver disease, and Parkinson's disease. In addition, caffeine improves cognitive functioning and physical performance.

$\mathbf{C}$affeine is one of the most widely consumed legal drugs in the world. In the United States, more than 9 out of every 10 people drink some type of caffeinated beverage, mostly for its stimulating effects. Caffeine elevates mood, reduces fatigue, increases work capacity, and stimulates respiration. Caffeine often provides the lift that people need to start the day. Although many people associate caffeine primarily with coffee, caffeine also is found in numerous soft drinks, over-the-counter medications, chocolate, and tea. Because caffeinated drinks are common in society and there are very few legal controls regarding the use of caffeine, its physical and psychological effects frequently are overlooked, ignored, or minimized.

In recent years, coffee consumption has declined; however, the amount of caffeine being consumed has not declined appreciably because of the increase in caffeinated soft drink consumption. To reduce their levels of caffeine intake, many people have switched to decaffeinated drinks and coffee. Although this results in less caffeine intake, decaffeinated coffee still contains small amounts of caffeine.

Research studies evaluating the effects of caffeine consumption on personal health date back to the 1960s. In particular, the medical community has conducted numerous studies to determine whether or not there is a relationship between caffeine consumption and cardiovascular disease, because heart disease is the leading cause of death in many countries, including the United States. In spite of the many studies on this subject, a clear relationship between heart disease and caffeine is not yet apparent. Studies have yielded conflicting results. Rather than clarifying the debate regarding the consequences of caffeine use, the research only adds to the confusion. As a result, studies suggesting that there is a connection between caffeine consumption and adverse physical and psychological effects have come under scrutiny by both the general public and health professions.

One serious limitation of previous research indicating that caffeine does have deleterious effects is that the research focused primarily on coffee use. Coffee may contain other ingredients besides caffeine that produce harmful effects. Moreover, an increasing percentage of the caffeine being consumed comes from other sources, such as soft drinks, tea, chocolate, antihistamines, and diet pills. Therefore, caffeine studies involving only coffee are not truly representative of the amount of caffeine that people ingest.

Another important criticism of caffeine research, especially studies linking caffeine use and heart disease, is gender bias. Until recently, research has focused primarily on the caffeine consumption of men. The bias in medical research is not limited to caffeine studies; men have traditionally been the primary group studied for research in many facets of health. This situation is changing. There is increasing research into the potential consequences of caffeine use on the fetus and nursing mother.

People who believe that drinking caffeine in moderation does not pose a significant health threat are critical of previous and current studies. This is particularly true of those studies that demonstrate a relationship between caffeine and heart disease. Critics contend that it is difficult to establish a definitive relationship between caffeine and heart disease due to a myriad of confounding variables. For example, cardiovascular disease has been linked to family history, a sedentary lifestyle, cigarette smoking, obesity, fat intake, and stress. Many individuals who consume large amounts of coffee also smoke cigarettes, drink alcohol, and are hard-driven. Several factors also affect caffeine's excretion from the body. Cigarette smoking increases caffeine metabolization, while the use of oral contraceptives and pregnancy slow down metabolization. Therefore, determining the extent to which caffeine use causes heart disease while adjusting for the influence of these other factors is difficult.

In the following selections, the writers of *Men's Health* caution readers about the use of caffeine, even in moderate amounts. They claim that small amounts can cause panic and anxiety. In contrast, the writers from *Harvard Women's Health Watch* cast doubt on the negative effects associated with caffeine intake and state that the effects of caffeine may not be as harmful as many people speculate.

Start Me Up

Caffeine. It's America's buzz word. And with spiked sodas and goosed gums, it's easier than ever to ingest. But is there a price for living a wired life? I'm an unnervous wreck. Stuporously groggy on this, the first full day of "Caffeine Cold Turkey," my head feels like it's been crushed in a vice. It's nearly impossible to think.

I slap myself three times, happy for the jolts of fleeting alertness each cheek sting provides. Alas, this exercise quickly proves too exhausting to continue. It's now 10:40 a.m., and I've been up since 8:45, nearly 2 full hours. Surely I've earned the right to take my first nap. But no: I shan't succumb to sleep's siren call so swiftly. I will struggle to stay awake till, at the very least, noonish. Given the headache, lethargy, and sundry other unpleasant symptoms involved so far in my withdrawal, you may be wondering about my reason for this exercise in abstention. Excellent question. Let's start with the basic truth that, God help me, I've become a slave to the bean. Our family's commercial-grade coffeemaker brews up to 10 cups at a time. When I first purchased this gizmo in the mid-'90s, I typically limited myself to 2 or 3 cups each morning. Over time, however, my usage incrementally escalated—3 cups gave way to 4, then 5, then 6, then . . . Honestly, I'm at a loss to explain how things got so out of whack. But for the past few years, my habit upon awakening has been to pack the basket with pro-digious quantities of Colombian Supremo, hit the strongest brew button, then drink the resulting 10 cups of black coffee over the next hour. If the synapses of my brain can be compared to an obstinate mule team, then caffeine has become the lash that drives them. By lunch, I'm usually ready to follow up my morning dosage with one or two 12-ounce cans of Coke, nothing too serious. But by 5 o'clock, the workday done, I'm ready to resume heavy usage again—not to hone cognitive performance, but rather to boost physical endurance. As a mas-ters swimmer averaging 17,000 yards a week, I've gotten in the habit of stopping off at a local convenience store en route to evening practice. Here I purchase and quickly down a 24-ounce cappuccino to goad my efforts in the pool. Unfortu-nately, I've become so habituated to my favorite drug that it no longer works terri-bly well for me. That's the main reason I decided to decaffeinate my body: I have a key swim meet coming up, and I've been concerned about my chances for some time. So concerned that I sought advice from Lawrence Armstrong, Ph.D., a

From *Men's Health*, vol. 19, issue 8, October 2004, pp. 172. Copyright © 2004 by Roland Press. Reprinted by permission.

professor of exercise at the University of Connecticut's human-performance lab and a longtime researcher into caffeine's sports-enhancing effects. "If you've developed a tolerance to caffeine" he told me, "you should try withdrawal until you become caffeine naive again, then come back to it for your meet, when it's likely you'll get a greater response per dose." That's the plan, anyway. Right now, I feel like a java junkie, even though, technically, I'm not one. Caffeine isn't a drug like amphetamines or cocaine, in that it doesn't act on the areas of the brain related to reward, motivation, and addiction. So I can't be "hooked" in the heroin sense of the word. On this, my first day of withdrawal, I absolutely crave caffeine, but I don't absolutely need it. It's now 11:18 a.m. What I do absolutely need is a nap. Though my personal usage is undeniably extreme, my affection for caffeine is hardly unique. According to Harriet de Wit, Ph.D., an associate professor of psychiatry at the University of Chicago, caffeine is by far the most widely used psychoactive drug in the world, easily surpassing both alcohol and nicotine. A study of java-drinking trends by the National Coffee Association (NCA) showed that, as of 2000, a record 79 percent of U.S. adults consumed coffee. As a nation, we down 350 million cups of coffee a day, with men swallowing significantly more than women. Of course, since many of us also imbibe tea, Big Gulps, and "energy" drinks such as Red Bull, these stats don't begin to measure the extent of America's buzz. Caffeine is ubiquitous. It's in everything from chocolate bars to over-the-counter analgesics, many cold remedies, and weight loss pills. There's even a new caffeinated gum on the market: Jolt Caffeine Energy Gum—available in Spearmint and Icymint. Two Chiclet-size pieces are capable of leaching, in about 5 minutes, 70 milligrams (mg)—or about a coffee cup's worth—of caffeine into the blood vessels under the tongue. (Coffee, by comparison, takes at least 45 minutes to produce peak caffeine levels in the bloodstream.)

Obviously, mankind has come a long way since Sufi priests made the first caffeinated drink out of coffee-bean husks, then used the liquid to fuel all-night religious ceremonies. Early Europeans witnessing these maniacal events dubbed the participants "whirling dervishes"—and the truth is, there's no shortage of us would-be dervishes around today.

So what exactly has made caffeine the Official Drug of the Human Race? The story of this plant-derived compound clearly begins with its action in the brain. Inside each human noggin, a slew of neurotransmitters and related compounds carry on cascading interactions that somehow result in everything from sleep to wakefulness, thoughts to emotions. Some of these molecules have a generally stimulating effect, while others work to dampen down nervous activity. Until about 20 years ago, scientists thought caffeine fell squarely into the brain-jazzing category. Then, in 1982, researchers discovered an evolutionary fluke: Caffeine's molecular structure is very similar to that of adenosine, an inhibitory brain substance found in many animals, including humans. "Animal studies have suggested that adenosine could be the 'somnolent,' or sleep-inducing, factor," explains Tom McLellan, Ph.D., a scientist at Defence R&D Canada in Toronto who studies caffeine for the Canadian military. "when people need sleep, their adenosine levels are high, which seems to trigger the brain into wanting to shut down." The longer you're awake, the more adenosine gradually accumulates in your brain. The growing surfeit, in turn, binds to specialized adenosine receptors, depressing nervous-system activity and making you groggy.

In ways that are not yet understood, getting enough sleep clears the chemical from your system, allowing you to begin the next day fully restored, your sleep debt paid in full. There is, however, an alternative to clearing adenosine: You can block it before it has a chance to make you sleepy. Caffeine does this by binding to adenosine receptors before the adenosine gets there. It's like jamming a toothpick into a keyhole so the key can't fit. To the holistic, health-food-store crowd, such molecular monkey-wrenching probably smacks of fooling Mother Nature in a way similar to pumping heifers full of bovine growth hormone. Surely we caffeine fiends can't keep doing this to ourselves day after day without having to pay some kind of penalty. Right?

The Health Impact

For decades, studies have attempted to find links between caffeine intake and a host of heavy-duty ailments, from heart disease to cancer. But no luck. The famed Framingham Heart Study, for example, concluded that caffeine consumption showed no influence on the rate of heart disease or stroke. Another investigation of 45,000 men published in *The New England Journal of Medicine* reached a similar conclusion. As for the cancer connection, a Norwegian study of 15,000 people found no significant correlation between coffee use and cancer, or any other disease, for that matter. The International Agency for the Research of Cancer reaffirmed this finding. "Caffeine, however, has been condemned by 'clean living' advocates because it has no nutritional value, is not needed for any physiologic function, and is commonly abused by the tired and stressed," concludes nutrition expert Nancy Clark, R.D., in a review paper published in *The Physician and Sportsmedicine*. "As a result, many coffee drinkers worry that their early-morning mugful will contribute to health problems. The truth is, coffee and other caffeinated beverages in moderation are not health demons." In fact, some health conditions may actually be helped by those judicious jolts of java. Harvard researchers recently connected caffeine intake to a reduced risk of type-2 diabetes, and just last year, scientists in Italy discovered that coffee may decrease a person's chances of developing oral or esophageal cancer.

The Emotional Effects

Even caffeine's greatest boosters have long acknowledged that in a certain subset of users, the drug can trigger unpleasant side effects, including anxiety and even panic attacks. Several years ago, University of Chicago researcher de Wit attended a lecture by German geneticist Jurgen Deckert, who reported his finding that a genetic variation in a type of adenosine receptor was strongly linked to panic disorder. "Since I knew that caffeine works on adenosine receptors," recalls de Wit, "I knew it would be easy to see whether this same gene variation is related to people's different responses to caffeine" In a study published in the journal *Neuropsychopharmacology,* de Wit and her colleagues gave 94 randomly selected volunteers 150 mg caffeine (the equivalent of 2 cups of coffee) or a placebo, then measured their responses in terms of mood, alertness, heart rate, and blood pressure. The researchers also genotyped each individual. On nearly all measures, from increased vigilance to relief from fatigue, caffeine proved to affect the test subjects identically. The only difference was that those with the specific genetic variation—about 30 percent of the total—reported anxiety, whereas the other 70 percent didn't. "What our data suggest," says de Wit, "is that if you have an unusual response to caffeine, there's probably a biological basis for why it's happening to you" Bottom line: If moderate doses of the bean give you the heebie-jeebies, it's best to cut it out entirely.

The Brain Benefits

Of all caffeine's purported effects, the one most touted by users themselves is its ability to provide a temporary mental edge. Unfortunately, for those who are hoping to ace a critical exam through a short-lived boost in IQ, the current evidence indicates that caffeine doesn't make you smarter. "What's been shown with caffeine is that it does have a dramatic effect on alertness," says McLellan, "but as you move to higher-order cognitive functioning, such as decision making, it doesn't really have an impact." Still, alertness is essential for most jobs, especially those in the military. In a new U.S. Air Force-funded study, researchers had 16 healthy men alternate 28 hours of consciousness with 14 hours of sleep for 1 month—an eccentric schedule designed to mimic shift work or jet lag. Every hour that the men were awake, they received tablets containing either a placebo substance or roughly 20 mg caffeine, the amount in 1/4 cup of coffee. The results proved unequivocal, with caffeine users consistently outperforming the placebo group on a host of computerized tests. The findings also showed something else—that it doesn't make sense to wake up and smell the coffee. "Caffeine had a very strong effect when delivered in small, incremental doses over time," says study author James Wyatt, Ph.D. "I hate to say it, but most of us have been using caffeine the wrong way." Wyatt bases his hypothesis on the fact that soporific adenosine levels are lowest when we first awake, precisely the time most of us reach for our Folgers. By the time adenosine starts to build, the morning caffeine spike is already waning. For those wedded to their caffeine fix, Wyatt recommends waiting till after lunch, when adenosine levels are starting to rise significantly. Thereafter, you'll get a more effective and consistent hit with small, regular doses, such as 1/4 cup per hour. It's important not to overdo it and end up compromising your ability to sleep at night. For most people, this probably means avoiding caffeine within 4 hours of bedtime. "Remember the big picture here," says Wyatt. "If everyone simply got 8.3 to 8.4 hours of quality sleep on a regular nightly basis, we wouldn't need caffeine in the first place."

The Endurance Angle

Studies have long shown that caffeine has ergogenic (i.e., sports-enhancing) effects in a multitude of activities, from swimming to tennis. The main effect seems to be improving endurance. In a 2002 study published in the *Journal of*

Applied Physiology, McLellan and his colleagues found that the time it took for cyclists to exercise to exhaustion was significantly longer in those receiving caffeine than in those given a placebo. Moreover, this benefit was greatest in those who didn't use caffeine regularly. "More and more," says McLellan, "it's looking like caffeine works on motivation within the brain itself. It affects your perception of effort and makes you feel you're not working as hard as you might otherwise feel." It doesn't take whopping doses to get this effect. In McClellan's recent study of 9 men, the equivalent of 2 cups of coffee was sufficient to provide a longer exercise duration to exhaustion, with the consumption of more caffeine providing no additional benefit. If you're planning to try out the caffeine edge the next time you challenge a buddy, say, to five sets of tennis, keep in mind that coffee can sometimes trigger gastrointestinal distress, possibly because of acids and other components in the brew. In his studies for the Canadian military, McLellan found what he believes is an optimum delivery system: caffeinated gum. "I found it great, myself," he says. "It's really quick—the concentration peaks in 5 to 10 minutes. And it doesn't give me any stomach symptoms."

It's exactly 3 weeks since my last cup of coffee, and my system is presumably as caffeine-free now as the day I was born. The headaches and urge to hibernate that plagued me during the first 5 days of abstinence have faded, restoring a baseline normalcy—no less nor, alas, more energetic than I was during the long days of my high-octane dependency.

I stifle a yawn. In yesterday's mail, my secret weapon for my swim meet finally arrived: a dozen packs of Jolt Caffeine Energy Gum (available at convenience stores and `joltgum.com`). In exactly 1/2 hour, I'll mount the starting blocks for the 500-yard freestyle at the Pennsylvania State Games. In preparation for this, I finally break my fast, popping a single piece of gum into my mouth. It takes a mere 10 minutes for the wad under my tongue to utterly obliterate any further urge to yawn.

Five minutes before the race, I chew a second piece, providing my system with the total caffeine equivalent of a single cup of coffee. The effect is nothing short of exhilarating. I explode off the blocks and find myself swimming with a remarkable degree of verve and indefatigability. When the splashing stops, I've placed first in the event—by 27 seconds—in the process swimming the second-fastest 500 of my life. Suspecting a possible fluke, I repeat the same two-hit caffeine-gum protocol for each race over the next 2 days. I easily win them all—the 100 backstroke, plus the 50, 100, and 200 freestyles—achieving close to lifetime bests in each race. True, this success hasn't come cheap. During the nights following both days of competition, I found it nearly impossible to sleep and, in fact, averaged no more than 3 fitful hours. And a day after getting home from the swim meet, I came down with the worst cold I've had in years. I'm sure the caffeine did not directly cause this. But could my immune system have been compromised by sleeplessness and by extraordinary effort made to seem effortless? In any event, this whole experience has given me a new appreciation—and respect—for a drink I'd come to think of as little more than hot brown water. Gone forever is my old gallon-a-day approach. From now on, I plan to keep my coffee drinking and gum chewing below moderate, saving occasional indulgences only for those times when this dervish truly needs to whirl.

← **NO**

Coffee: For Most, It's Safe

Despite 20 years of reassuring research, many people still avoid coffee[*] because they worry about its health effects. Their concerns are understandable. Older studies had linked coffee to a range of health problems, including pancreatic cancer and heart disease. But this early research didn't take into account the real culprit: cigarette smoking, which was once a common habit of many coffee drinkers. We now know that in moderation—that is, a few cups per day—coffee is a safe beverage. New research suggests it even offers some health benefits.

Coffee isn't totally innocuous. Its main active ingredient, caffeine, is a mildly addictive stimulant. Getting too much may give you the jitters, keep you awake, and make you irritable. If you're a regular coffee drinker and miss your morning dose, you may get a splitting headache. Some people develop indigestion, stomach problems, or other intestinal distress when they drink coffee. And inconclusive research suggests that high doses of coffee can contribute to bone loss. But for most people, coffee in moderation is harmless.

If you don't enjoy coffee or it bothers you, don't drink it. But if you consider it one of life's pleasures, a rundown of some of the latest findings on coffee's health effects may assuage your concerns.

Cardiovascular Effects Are Modest

Coffee has several cardiovascular effects.

Constricted arteries   The caffeine in a cup of coffee can constrict arteries that lie in areas away from the heart and lungs, such as the brain. This is one reason drinking a cup of coffee sometimes relieves a throbbing headache caused by dilated blood vessels in the brain. It's also why caffeine is added to several over-the-counter analgesics.

Increased heart rate   In some people, coffee can slightly speed the heart rate.

---

[*] Unless otherwise indicated, "coffee" refers to coffee containing caffeine, not to decaffeinated coffee.

Increased blood pressure   A cup of coffee temporarily boosts blood pressure, in much the same way as an activity such as climbing stairs does. But a coffee habit doesn't cause chronic high blood pressure. And several studies have found that blood pressure changes tend to occur only in people who don't usually drink coffee.

Irregular heartbeat   The American Heart Association says that caffeine (which is also found in tea, some soft drinks, and chocolate) may cause an occasional irregular heartbeat. If you think coffee affects you this way, slowly cut back on the amount you drink each day, and talk to your clinician.

Increased cholesterol levels   The coffee oils kahweol and cafestol can increase levels of total and LDL (bad) cholesterol. Paper filters trap these compounds, so they're not found in most cups of coffee in America, and are a problem only for those who drink espresso, pressed, boiled, or other unfiltered coffee.

Homocysteine   Several studies have linked coffee consumption to increased levels of homocysteine, a substance in the blood that may increase the risk for heart disease. A Dutch study found that while caffeine alone (the amount in 4 cups of strong coffee) raised homocysteine levels by 5%, getting that amount in coffee more than doubled the effect. This suggests that compounds other than caffeine are involved. But high homocysteine levels are also associated with some nutritional deficiencies (such as low folate). In one study, coffee had no effect on homocysteine levels in people who ate a healthy diet.

Heart disease   The American Heart Association has concluded that moderate coffee use (which it defines as 1–2 cups per day) is not harmful. And large, long-term studies (including Harvard's Nurses' Health Study) have found that drinking even as many as 5–6 cups of coffee a day doesn't increase the risk for heart disease.

For Women Only

Many women, particularly those of childbearing age, wonder whether coffee and other caffeine-containing foods and drinks are safe for them. Fortunately, there's plenty of scientific evidence about the effects of coffee and caffeinated beverages on women's health.

Fertility   There's no credible evidence that caffeine lowers a woman's fertility.

Pregnancy   Although the evidence is somewhat mixed, low caffeine consumption (1–2 cups per day) appears to be safe during pregnancy. Most of the studies that have linked caffeine to miscarriage, birth defects, or low birth weight have either not taken into account other factors, or involved higher levels of caffeine or coffee consumption (more than 300 mg of caffeine, or more than 3 cups of coffee, per day). Last year, a Danish study published in the *British Medical Journal* found that pregnant women who drank 4 or more cups of coffee per day were at increased risk of stillbirth. Most authorities, including the FDA, the March of Dimes, and the American College of Obstetricians and Gynecologists, agree that pregnant women should limit their consumption of caffeine to the equivalent of no more than 1–2 cups of coffee (about 100–200 mg of caffeine) per day.

Breast health   Some women believe that abstaining from coffee and caffeinated beverages alleviates the symptoms of fibrocystic breast disease (a condition of benign lumps in the breast). The available research does not support this association.

Cancer   Over the years, some flawed studies have linked caffeine and coffee to several cancers, including cancers of the breast and ovaries as well as the pancreas and bladder. More thorough investigations carried out in the past 10–15 years have found no connection between coffee and cancer. The American Cancer Society has concluded that caffeine is not a risk factor for cancer.

Osteoporosis   Although caffeine can increase urinary excretion of calcium, the jury is still out on whether it's a factor in osteoporosis. Some studies, including Harvard's Nurses' Health Study, suggest that drinking 4 cups or more per day can contribute to bone loss and hip fracture. On the other hand, one study of lifetime coffee drinking (amounting to 2 cups per day) found no evidence of bone loss in women who also drank at least 1 cup of milk per day. Until we know more, it's best to avoid heavy coffee consumption. Women who regularly drink coffee and caffeinated beverages should also be sure they get adequate calcium (1,000–1,200 mg per day) from food and supplements.

Caffeine Content of Some Foods and Beverages

Product	Range (mg)	Typical (mg)
Coffee, 8 oz, drip-brewed	80–240	100
Coffee, decaffeinated, 8 oz	2–4	3
Espresso, 2 oz	60–100	80
Tea, 8 oz, brewed, domestic	20–90	40
Tea, 8 oz, imported	25–110	60
Caffeinated soft drinks, 12 oz	22–55	36
Chocolate milk, 8 oz	2–7	5
Semisweet chocolate, 1 oz	5–35	20

Sources: Various. The amount of caffeine in foods and beverages varies widely.

A potentially fatal oral dose of caffeine is estimated to be 10–14 grams (10 grams = 10,000 mg).
Sources: Institute of Medicine (2001), *Caffeine for the Sustainment of Mental Task Performance.*

Possible Benefits

Most studies investigating the health effects of coffee or caffeine consumption have focused on possible harms. But some large investigations have identified several potential benefits from coffee drinking.

Diabetes The risk for type 2 diabetes is lower among regular coffee drinkers than among those who don't drink coffee. In two studies, Harvard researchers found that women who drank 6 cups or more per day reduced their risk for type 2 diabetes by 30% (*Annals of Internal Medicine*, Jan. 6, 2004). This result is particularly significant because the studies tracked a total of 125,000 men and women for a dozen years or more. Similarly, Finnish scientists following nearly 15,000 men and women, ages 35–64, found that women who drank 3–4 cups per day had a 29% lower risk for diabetes, and drinking 10 or more cups per day lowered the risk even further (*Journal of the American Medical Association,* March 10, 2004). But no one is recommending that women drink 10 cups a day, or even more than 3 or 4 cups. Not enough is known about its other effects at high doses. We know that it may be harmful in some circumstances, including pregnancy.

Gallstones A Harvard study found that women who drink 4 cups of coffee per day have a reduced risk of developing gallstones. Coffee may alter the metabolism of bile acids, which trigger the formation of the cholesterol crystals that become gallstones. Coffee also stimulates gallbladder contractions, which may curb stone formation.

Colon cancer Several studies have found a reduced risk of colon cancer in people who drink 4 or more cups of coffee per day, compared with those who rarely or never drink coffee. German researchers reported last year that they identified an antioxidant in coffee called methylpyridinium, which boosts the activity of enzymes that may discourage the development of colon cancer. The compound is found in both regular (caffeine-containing) and decaffeinated coffee.

Cognitive function Research involving older men and women participating in the Rancho Bernardo Study found that lifetime coffee intake is associated with better performance by women (but not men) on several cognitive tests. No relationship was found between cognitive function and decaffeinated coffee consumption.

Performance Caffeine has been shown to improve endurance performance in long-duration physical activities such as running, cross-country skiing, and cycling. Studies suggest this effect occurs at doses of 2–9 mg of caffeine per 2.2 pounds of body weight. This is about the amount of caffeine found in 2–5 cups of coffee.

Liver disease Researchers at the National Institute of Diabetes and Digestive and Kidney Diseases have found a strong association between coffee drinking and a reduced risk for liver damage in people at high risk for liver disease. This includes heavy drinkers of alcohol, people with hepatitis B or C, and those with iron overload disorders, such as hemochromatosis. The highest consumption, more than 2 cups of coffee per day, was correlated with the greatest benefit.

Parkinson's disease Several large studies have shown a reduced risk for Parkinson's disease in coffee drinkers. Although most of the data come from research in men, a 2001 Harvard School of Public Health study found that women who consumed 1–3 cups of coffee per day had a 50% reduction in risk for Parkinson's disease, with no increased benefit at higher levels of intake.

The Upshot

Those who view their morning coffee as a guilty pleasure can banish their misgivings. The latest research discounts the notion that moderate coffee consumption—which we interpret to be about 2–4 cups per day—causes significant or lasting harm. Indeed, some studies suggest that coffee and caffeine may offer some real health benefits.

POSTSCRIPT

Do the Consequences of Caffeine Consumption Outweigh Its Benefits?

Although caffeine is commonly consumed by millions of people without much regard to its physical and psychological effects, many studies have questioned its safety. However, other studies have reported very few hazards. The basic question is whether people who drink several cups of coffee or other caffeinated beverages daily should be more concerned than they are. Are the claims of caffeine's benefits or hazards exaggerated?

Determining if certain foods or beverages promote disease or have health benefits can be trying because the research is unclear. Many people become frustrated because quite a few of the things that we eat or drink are suspected of being unhealthy. For example, various reports indicate that the fat in beef can lead to various forms of cancer and heart disease, that we should consume less salt and sugar, that processed foods should be avoided, and that whole milk, butter, and margarine should be reduced or eliminated from our diets. If people paid attention to every report about the harmful effects of the foods and beverages they consumed, they would not be able to eat much at all. What is the average consumer supposed to do?

A legitimate question is whether or not food studies are worth pursuing because so many of the products that are reportedly bad are enjoyed by millions of people. Caffeine is simply one more example of a commonly used product that has come under scrutiny. In addition, although the research is vast, it is inconclusive and contradictory. One study, for instance, linked caffeine to pancreatic cancer, only to find later that the culprit was not caffeine but cigarette smoking. Research on caffeine's effects on cancers of the bladder, urinary tract, and kidney has also proven to be inconsistent and inconclusive. Because caffeinated products are consumed by millions of people, it is important to know if its dangers are exaggerated. However, if professional researchers cannot agree as to whether a product is safe or harmful, how can the average person know what to believe?

The writers from *Men's Health* claim that caffeine may cause dependence because it shares some of the same characteristics of cocaine, alcohol, and nicotine. They state that too much caffeine causes tolerance as well as withdrawal symptoms. The writers from *Harvard Women's Health Watch* counter that caffeine's adverse effects are overstated. Furthermore, they indicate that caffeine may have possible benefits.

Other articles that examine caffeine's psychological and physical effects are "Communicating the Message: Clarifying the Controversies About

Caffeine," by Edith H. Hogan, Betsy A. Hornick, and Ann Bouchoux, *Nutrition Today* (January-February 2002); Brian Rowley's "The Buzz on Caffeine: The Latest Research on What's Brewing on This Popular Bodybuilding Pick-Me-Up, and How to Use It Wisely," *Muscle and Fitness* (March 2002); Eric Metcalf's "Coffee to Go: Research Shows That Caffeine, in the Right Amount, Can Boost Performance Without Harming Your Health," *Runner's World* (January 2002); and, Jeff Novick's "Waking Up to the Effects of Caffeine: How Important Is That Morning Cup of Coffee?" *Health Science* (Spring 2002).

ISSUE 12

Is Ritalin an Effective Drug for Treating Attention Deficit/ Hyperactivity Disorder (ADHD)?

YES: Michael Fumento, from "Trick Question," *The New Republic* (February 3, 2003)

NO: Farhang Khosh and Deena Beneda, from "Attention Deficit/Hyperactivity Disorder," *Townsend Letter for Doctors and Patients* (January 2003)

ISSUE SUMMARY

YES: Writer Michael Fumento disputes the idea that Ritalin is over-prescribed. He notes that there are many myths associated with Ritalin. Its use does not lead to abuse and addiction. Fumento argues that Ritalin is an excellent medication for ADHD. It is possible that the drug is underutilized.

NO: Writers Farhang Khosh and Deena Beneda contend that Ritalin addresses the symptoms, but not the causes, of attention deficit/hyperactivity. Moreover, Ritalin has short- and long-term side effects such as appetite suppression, weight loss, and stunted growth. Khosh and Beneda state that Ritalin may cause paranoid symptoms in individuals who take it in large amounts. In addition, they say that Ritalin inhibits emotions. Khosh and Beneda recommend exploring alternative treatments like nutritional therapies, herbs, and homeopathy.

The number one childhood psychiatric disorder in the United States is attention deficit/hyperactivity disorder, which affects approximately 6 million American school children. ADHD is characterized by inattentiveness, hyperactivity, and impulsivity. Many children are diagnosed as having only attention deficit disorder (ADD), which is ADHD without the hyperactivity. The most commonly prescribed drug for ADHD is the stimulant Ritalin (generic name methylphenidate). American children consume 90 percent of all Ritalin produced worldwide. Only a very small percentage of European children are diagnosed with ADHD. Ritalin is therefore much less likely to be prescribed in Europe.

The use of stimulants to treat such behavioral disorders dates back to 1937. The practice of prescribing stimulants for behavioral problems increased dramatically beginning in 1970, when it was estimated that 150,000 American children were taking stimulant medications. It seems paradoxical for physicians to be prescribing a stimulant such as Ritalin for a behavioral disorder that already involves hyperactivity. However, Ritalin appears to be effective for many children, as well as many adults, who suffer from this condition. Looking at this issue from a broader perspective, one needs to ask whether behavioral problems should be treated as a disease. Also, does Ritalin really address the problem? Or could it be covering up other maladies that should be treated?

Ritalin enhances the functioning of the brain's reticular activating system, which helps one to focus attention and to filter out extraneous stimuli. The drug has been shown to improve short-term learning. Ritalin also produces adverse effects such as insomnia, headaches, irritability, nausea, dizziness, weight loss, and growth retardation. Psychological dependence may develop, but physical dependence is unlikely. The effects of long-term Ritalin use are unknown.

Since 1990 the number of children receiving Ritalin has increased 500 percent. This large increase in the number of children diagnosed with ADHD may be attributed to a broader application of the criteria for diagnosing ADHD, heightened public awareness, and changes in American educational policy regarding schools' identifying children with the disorder. Some people feel that the increase in prescriptions for Ritalin reflects an increased effort to satisfy the needs of parents whose children exhibit behavioral problems. Ritalin has been referred to as "mother's little helper." Regardless of the reasons for the increase, many people question whether Ritalin is overprescribed and children are overmedicated or whether Ritalin is a miracle drug.

One problem with the increased prevalence of Ritalin prescriptions is that illegal use of the drug has also risen. There are accounts of some parents getting prescriptions for their children and then selling the drugs illegally. On a number of college campuses, there are reports of students using Ritalin to get high or to stay awake in order to study. Historically, illegal use of Ritalin has been minimal, although officials of the Drug Enforcement Administration (DEA) are now concerned that its illegal use is proliferating. Problems with its use are unlikely to rival those of cocaine because Ritalin's effects are more moderate than those of cocaine or amphetamines.

The fact is that children now receive prescriptions for Ritalin rather readily. Frequently, parents will pressure their pediatricians into writing the prescriptions. One survey found that almost one-half of all pediatricians spent less than an hour assessing children before prescribing Ritalin. On the other hand, if there is a medication available that would remedy a problem, shouldn't it be prescribed? If a child's academic performance can improve through the use of Ritalin, should that child be denied the drug?

In the following selections, Michael Fumento maintains that ADHD is underdiagnosed in many instances. He asserts that Ritalin's bad reputation arises from many misconceptions regarding the drug. Farhang Khosh and Deena Beneda question the long-term safety of Ritalin and contend that alternative procedures should be used instead of Ritalin.

YES ⬅

Michael Fumento

Trick Question

It's both right-wing and vast, but it's not a conspiracy. Actually, it's more of an anti-conspiracy. The subject is Attention Deficit Disorder (ADD) and Attention Deficit Hyperactivity Disorder (ADHD), closely related ailments (henceforth referred to in this article simply as ADHD). Rush Limbaugh declares it "may all be a hoax." Francis Fukuyama devotes much of one chapter in his latest book, *Our Posthuman Future*, to attacking Ritalin, the top-selling drug used to treat ADHD. Columnist Thomas Sowell writes, "The motto used to be: 'Boys will be boys.' Today, the motto seems to be: 'Boys will be medicated.'" And Phyllis Schlafly explains, "The old excuse of 'my dog ate my homework' has been replaced by 'I got an ADHD diagnosis.'" A March 2002 article in *The Weekly Standard* summed up the conservative line on ADHD with this rhetorical question: "Are we really prepared to redefine childhood as an ailment, and medicate it until it goes away?"

Many conservative writers, myself included, have criticized the growing tendency to pathologize every undesirable behavior—especially where children are concerned. But, when it comes to ADHD, this skepticism is misplaced. As even a cursory examination of the existing literature or, for that matter, simply talking to the parents and teachers of children with ADHD reveals, the condition is real, and it is treatable. And, if you don't believe me, you can ask conservatives who've come face to face with it themselves.

Myth: ADHD Isn't a Real Disorder

The most common argument against ADHD on the right is also the simplest: It doesn't exist. Conservative columnist Jonah Goldberg thus reduces ADHD to "ants in the pants." Sowell equates it with "being bored and restless." Fukuyama protests, "No one has been able to identify a cause of ADD/ADHD. It is a pathology recognized only by its symptoms." And a conservative columnist approvingly quotes Thomas Armstrong, Ritalin opponent and author, when he declares, "ADD is a disorder that cannot be authoritatively identified in the same way as polio, heart disease or other legitimate illnesses."

The Armstrong and Fukuyama observations are as correct as they are worthless. "Half of all medical disorders are diagnosed without benefit of a lab procedure," notes Dr. Russell Barkley, professor of psychology at the College of Health Professionals at the Medical University of South Carolina. "Where are the lab tests for headaches and multiple sclerosis and Alzheimer's?" he asks. "Such a standard would virtually eliminate all mental disorders."

Often the best diagnostic test for an ailment is how it responds to treatment. And, by that standard, it doesn't get much more real than ADHD. The beneficial effects of administering stimulants to treat the disorder were first reported in 1937. And today medication for the disorder is reported to be 75 to 90 percent successful. "In our trials it was close to ninety percent," says Dr. Judith Rapoport, director of the National Institute of Mental Health's Child Psychiatry Branch, who has published about 100 papers on ADHD. "This means there was a significant difference in the children's ability to function in the classroom or at home."

Additionally, epidemiological evidence indicates that ADHD has a powerful genetic component. University of Colorado researchers have found that a child whose identical twin has the disorder is between eleven and 18 times more likely to also have it than is a non-twin sibling. For these reasons, the American Psychiatric Association (APA), American Medical Association, American Academy of Pediatrics, American Academy of Child Adolescent Psychiatry, the surgeon general's office, and other major medical bodies all acknowledge ADHD as both real and treatable.

Myth: ADHD Is Part of a Feminist Conspiracy to Make Little Boys More Like Little Girls

Many conservatives observe that boys receive ADHD diagnoses in much higher numbers than girls and find in this evidence of a feminist conspiracy. (This, despite the fact that genetic diseases are often heavily weighted more toward one gender or the other.) Sowell refers to "a growing tendency to treat boyhood as a pathological condition that requires a new three R's— repression, re-education and Ritalin." Fukuyama claims Prozac is being used to give women "more of the alpha-male feeling," while Ritalin is making boys act more like girls. "Together, the two sexes are gently nudged toward that androgynous median personality . . . that is the current politically correct outcome in American society." George Will, while acknowledging that Ritalin can be helpful, nonetheless writes of the "androgyny agenda" of "drugging children because they are behaving like children, especially boy children." Anti-Ritalin conservatives frequently invoke Christina Hoff Sommers's best-selling 2000 book, *The War Against Boys*. You'd never know that the drug isn't mentioned in her book—or why.

"Originally I was going to have a chapter on it," Sommers tells me. "It seemed to fit the thesis." What stopped her was both her survey of the medical literature and her own empirical findings. Of one child she personally came to know she says, "He was utterly miserable, as was everybody around him. The drugs saved his life."

Myth: ADHD Is Part of the Public School System's Efforts to Warehouse Kids Rather Than to Discipline and Teach Them

"No doubt life is easier for teachers when everyone sits around quietly," writes Sowell. Use of ADHD drugs is "in the school's interest to deal with behavioral and discipline problems [because] it's so easy to use Ritalin to make kids compliant: to get them to sit down, shut up, and do what they're told," declares Schlafly. The word "zombies" to describe children under the effects of Ritalin is tossed around more than in a B-grade voodoo movie.

Kerri Houston, national field director for the American Conservative Union and the mother of two ADHD children on medication, agrees with much of the criticism of public schools. "But don't blame ADHD on crummy curricula and lazy teachers," she says. "If you've worked with these children, you know they have a serious neurological problem." In any case, Ritalin, when taken as prescribed, hardly stupefies children. To the extent the medicine works, it simply turns ADHD children into normal children. "ADHD is like having thirty televisions on at one time, and the medicine turns off twenty-nine so you can concentrate on the one," Houston describes. "This zombie stuff drives me nuts! My kids are both as lively and as fun as can be."

Myth: Parents Who Give Their Kids Anti-ADHD Drugs Are Merely Doping Up Problem Children

Limbaugh calls ADHD "the perfect way to explain the inattention, incompetence, and inability of adults to control their kids." Addressing parents directly, he lectures, "It helped you mask your own failings by doping up your children to calm them down."

Such charges blast the parents of ADHD kids into high orbit. That includes my Hudson Institute colleague (and fellow conservative) Mona Charen, the mother of an eleven-year-old with the disorder. "I have two non-ADHD children, so it's not a matter of parenting technique," says Charen. "People without such children have no idea what it's like. I can tell the difference between boyish high spirits and pathological hyperactivity. . . . These kids bounce off the walls. Their lives are chaos; their rooms are chaos. And nothing replaces the drugs."

Barkley and Rapoport say research backs her up. Randomized, controlled studies in both the United States and Sweden have tried combining medication with behavioral interventions and then dropped either one or the other. For those trying to go on without medicine, "the behavioral interventions maintained nothing," Barkley says. Rapoport concurs: "Unfortunately, behavior modification doesn't seem to help with ADHD." (Both doctors are quick to add that ADHD is often accompanied by other disorders that are treatable through behavior modification in tandem with medicine.)

Myth: Ritalin Is "Kiddie Cocaine"

One of the paradoxes of conservative attacks on Ritalin is that the drug is alternately accused of turning children into brain-dead zombies and of making them Mach-speed cocaine junkies. Indeed, Ritalin is widely disparaged as "kiddie cocaine." Writers who have sought to lump the two drugs together include Schlafly, talk-show host and columnist Armstrong Williams, and others whom I hesitate to name because of my long-standing personal relationships with them.

Mary Eberstadt wrote the "authoritative" Ritalin-cocaine piece for the April 1999 issue of *Policy Review*, then owned by the Heritage Foundation. The article, "Why Ritalin Rules," employs the word "cocaine" no fewer than twelve times. Eberstadt quotes from a 1995 Drug Enforcement Agency (DEA) background paper declaring methylphenidate, the active ingredient in Ritalin, "a central nervous system (CNS) stimulant [that] shares many of the pharmacological effects of amphetamine, methamphetamine, and cocaine." Further, it "produces behavioral, psychological, subjective, and reinforcing effects similar to those of d-amphetamine including increases in rating of euphoria, drug liking and activity, and decreases in sedation." Add to this the fact that the Controlled Substances Act lists it as a Schedule II drug, imposing on it the same tight prescription controls as morphine, and Ritalin starts to sound spooky indeed.

What Eberstadt fails to tell readers is that the DEA description concerns methylphenidate *abuse*. It's tautological to say abuse is harmful. According to the DEA, the drugs in question are comparable when "administered the same way at comparable doses." But ADHD stimulants, when taken as prescribed, are neither administered in the same way as cocaine nor at comparable doses. "What really counts," says Barkley, "is the speed with which the drugs enter and clear the brain. With cocaine, because it's snorted, this happens tremendously quickly, giving users the characteristic addictive high." (Ever seen anyone pop a cocaine tablet?) Further, he says, "There's no evidence anywhere in literature of [Ritalin's] addictiveness when taken as prescribed." As to the Schedule II listing, again this is because of the potential for it to fall into the hands of abusers, not because of its effects on persons for whom it is prescribed. Ritalin and the other anti-ADHD drugs, says Barkley, "are the safest drugs in all of psychiatry." (And they may be getting even safer: A new medicine just released called Strattera represents the first true non-stimulant ADHD treatment.)

Indeed, a study just released in the journal *Pediatrics* found that children who take Ritalin or other stimulants to control ADHD cut their risk of future substance abuse by 50 percent compared with untreated ADHD children. The lead author speculated that "by treating ADHD you're reducing the demoralization that accompanies this disorder, and you're improving the academic functioning and well-being of adolescents and young adults during the critical times when substance abuse starts."

Myth: Ritalin Is Overprescribed Across the Country

Some call it "the Ritalin craze." In *The Weekly Standard*, Melana Zyla Vickers informs us that "Ritalin use has exploded," while Eberstadt writes that "Ritalin use more than doubled in the first half of the decade alone, [and] the number of schoolchildren taking the drug may now, by some estimates, be approaching the *4 million mark.*"

A report in the January 2003 issue of *Archives of Pediatrics and Adolescent Medicine* did find a large increase in the use of ADHD medicines from 1987 to 1996, an increase that doesn't appear to be slowing. Yet nobody thinks it's a problem that routine screening for high blood pressure has produced a big increase in the use of hypertension medicine. "Today, children suffering from ADHD are simply less likely to slip through the cracks," says Dr. Sally Satel, a psychiatrist, AEI fellow, and author of *PC, M.D.: How Political Correctness Is Corrupting Medicine.*

Satel agrees that some community studies, by the standards laid down in the APA's *Diagnostic and Statistical Manual of Mental Disorders (DSM)*, indicate that ADHD may often be over-diagnosed. On the other hand, she says, additional evidence shows that in some communities ADHD is *under*-diagnosed and *under*-treated. "I'm quite concerned with children who need the medication and aren't getting it," she says.

There *are* tremendous disparities in the percentage of children taking ADHD drugs when comparing small geographical areas. Psychologist Gretchen LeFever, for example, has compared the number of prescriptions in mostly white Virginia Beach, Virginia, with other, more heavily African American areas in the southeastern part of the state. Conservatives have latched onto her higher numbers—20 percent of white fifth-grade boys in Virginia Beach are being treated for ADHD—as evidence that something is horribly wrong. But others, such as Barkley, worry about the lower numbers. According to LeFever's study, black children are only half as likely to get medication as white children. "Black people don't get the care of white people; children of well-off parents get far better care than those of poorer parents," says Barkley.

Myth: States Should Pass Laws That Restrict Schools From Recommending Ritalin

Conservative writers have expressed delight that several states, led by Connecticut, have passed or are considering laws ostensibly protecting students from schools that allegedly pass out Ritalin like candy. Representative Lenny Winkler, lead sponsor of the Connecticut measure, told *Reuters Health*, "If the diagnosis is made, and it's an appropriate diagnosis that Ritalin be used, that's fine. But I have also heard of many families approached by the school system [who are told] that their child cannot attend school if they're not put on Ritalin."

Two attorneys I interviewed who specialize in child-disability issues, including one from the liberal Bazelon Center for Mental Health Law in Washington, D.C., acknowledge that school personnel have in some cases stepped over the line. But legislation can go too far in the other direction by declaring, as Connecticut's law does, that "any school personnel [shall be prohibited] from recommending the use of psychotropic drugs for any child." The law appears to offer an exemption by declaring, "The provisions of this section shall not prohibit *school medical staff* from recommending that a child be evaluated by an appropriate medical practitioner, or prohibit school personnel from consulting with such practitioner, with the consent of the parent or guardian of such child." [Emphasis added.] But of course many, if not most, schools have perhaps one nurse on regular "staff." That nurse will have limited contact with children in the classroom situations where ADHD is likely to be most evident. And, given the wording of the statute, a teacher who believed a student was suffering from ADHD would arguably be prohibited from referring that student to the nurse. Such ambiguity is sure to have a chilling effect on any form of intervention or recommendation by school personnel. Moreover, 20-year special-education veteran Sandra Rief said in an interview with the National Education Association that "recommending medical intervention for a student's behavior could lead to personal liability issues." Teachers, in other words, could be forced to choose between what they think is best for the health of their students and the possible risk of losing not only their jobs but their personal assets as well.

"Certainly it's not within the purview of a school to say kids can't attend if they don't take drugs," says Houston. "On the other hand, certainly teachers should be able to advise parents as to problems and potential solutions. . . . [T]hey may see things parents don't. My own son is an angel at home but was a demon at school."

If the real worry is "take the medicine or take a hike" ultimatums, legislation can be narrowly tailored to prevent them; broad-based gag orders, such as Connecticut's, are a solution that's worse than the problem.

The Conservative Case for ADHD Drugs

There are kernels of truth to every conservative suspicion about ADHD. Who among us has not had lapses of attention? And isn't hyperactivity a normal condition of childhood when compared with deskbound adults? Certainly there are lazy teachers, warehousing schools, androgyny-pushing feminists, and far too many parents unwilling or unable to expend the time and effort to raise their children properly, even by their own standards. Where conservatives go wrong is in making ADHD a scapegoat for frustration over what we perceive as a breakdown in the order of society and family. In a column in *The Boston Herald*, Boston University Chancellor John Silber rails that Ritalin is "a classic example of a cheap fix: low-cost, simple and purely superficial."

Exactly. Like most headaches, ADHD is a neurological problem that can usually be successfully treated with a chemical. Those who recommend or prescribe ADHD medicines do not, as *The Weekly Standard* put it, see them as "discipline in pill-form." They see them as pills.

In fact, it can be argued that the use of those pills, far from being liable for or symptomatic of the Decline of the West, reflects and reinforces conservative values. For one thing, they increase personal responsibility by removing an excuse that children (and their parents) can fall back on to explain misbehavior and poor performance. "Too many psychologists and psychiatrists focus on allowing patients to justify to themselves their troubling behavior," says Satel. "But something like Ritalin actually encourages greater autonomy because you're treating a compulsion to behave in a certain way. Also, by treating ADHD, you remove an opportunity to explain away bad behavior."

Moreover, unlike liberals, who tend to downplay differences between the sexes, conservatives are inclined to believe that there are substantial physiological differences—differences such as boys' greater tendency to suffer ADHD. "Conservatives celebrate the physiological differences between boys and girls and eschew the radical-feminist notion that gender differences are created by societal pressures," says Houston regarding the fuss over the boy-girl disparity among ADHD diagnoses. "ADHD is no exception."

But, however compatible conservatism may be with taking ADHD seriously, the truth is that most conservatives remain skeptics. "I'm sure I would have been one of those smug conservatives saying it's a made-up disease," admits Charen, "if I hadn't found out the hard way." Here's hoping other conservatives find an easier route to accepting the truth.

Farhang Khosh
and Deena Beneda

 **NO**

Attention Deficit/
Hyperactivity Disorder

. . . Attention Deficient Hyperactive Disorder, better known as ADHD, is becoming more common in children throughout the United States. It is reaching epidemic portions and yet few advancements have been done to effectively treat, manage or eliminate ADHD. Current treatment relies on pharmaceutical drugs, which not only do not eliminate the condition but have both short and long-term side effects. Alternative therapies focus on nutrition, vitamins and minerals, amino acids, herbs, homeopathy, food and environmental allergies, and proanthocyanidins. In addition, hypothyroidism and adrenal glands have also been mentioned in the literature in relation to ADHD. An integrative alternative approach should be considered in the treatment and management of ADHD.

The term ADHD was originally derived from the term ADD (attention deficit disorder). ADD was further subcategorized as ADD with hyperactivity or ADD without hyperactivity. However, in the 1994 DSM-IV the official term was stated as ADHD.[1]

A child with ADHD has a wide range of symptoms including hyperactivity, short attention span, distractibility, and difficulty with organizational skills and not paying attention to details. These children are restless, forgetful and react impulsively.[2] They may have mood swings, temper tantrums and are unable to cope with stress.[1] Boys seem to be two to three times more likely to be diagnosed with ADHD.[2] Some of the current research examines the possibility that ADHD is inherited. Twin and adoption studies suggest that ADHD has a relatively high degree of hereditability. However, to date there is insufficient data linking ADHD to an inherited trait.[1]

In order to diagnose a child with ADHD the behaviors must appear before age seven and be present at a minimum of six months. ADHD occurs in 3% to 5% of children in the United States, and approximately half of those children continue to have ADHD symptoms as adults.[2] Those that continue to have symptoms into adulthood may develop antisocial behavior, substance abuse, suffer from poor self-esteem and social skill deficits.[3] In 1993, more than two million children were diagnosed with ADHD; this was an increase from 902,000 in 1990. It is estimated that as many as four million children currently have been diagnosed with ADHD.[1]

Currently, conventional medical interventions include pharmaceutical drugs. Psychostimulants are the first line of defense used in ADHD. Methylphenidate or Ritalin is the most common drug prescribed to treat ADHD. In 1993, more than 2.5 million prescriptions were written for Ritalin.[1] Other stimulants that can be used are dextroamphetamine (Dexedrine), a mixture of four salts of dextroamphetamine (Adderall), methamphetamine (Desoxyn) or pemoline (Cylert). Ritalin and Ritalin-SR are preparations of methyl-alpha-pheny1-2-piperidineacetate hydrochloride. Ritalin acts on the central nervous system with a dopamine-agonistic effect that works slower but is mechanically almost identical to cocaine and amphetamines.[1,4] Most all of the mood altering drugs (alcohol, cigarettes, caffeine, heroin, cocaine, and the stimulant medications for hyperactive children) affect dopamine.[5]

Research has found that ADHD children have a deficiency in dopamine, a chemical in the brain necessary for several vital brain functions. The dopamine system is involved in the reward-seek behavior, sexual behavior, control of movements, regulation of the pituitary-hormone secretion and memory functions. Dopamine has been shown in young animals to exert a protective influence against hyperactivity.[6] It is thought ADHD children have too many molecules that use up the dopamine before it can be used for its vital functions. Ritalin binds to these molecules allowing the dopamine levels to increase in the brain and be used for the normal vital functions.[4]

Even though Ritalin is the drug of choice for children with ADHD, it has many side effects and presents many risks for the children who use it. A child who is treated with Ritalin is moved from a hyperactive state to the opposite state. Children develop appetite suppression, weight loss, retarded growth, emotional blunting and detachment, and many parents complain that the child acts like a "zombie."[6] Children on higher doses and chronic use may develop paranoid symptoms—withdrawal, anger, restlessness, and suspicious behavior. It has been shown that adults who abuse amphetamines regularly develop psychotic states with paranoid features.[6] Other serious side effects of methylphenidate are auditory and visual hallucinations, drug abuse-rebound depression, psychic dependence, increased euphoria and cocaine-like activity, insomnia and tachycardia. Also, researchers reported that Ritalin caused liver cancer in mice. No drug that affects the dopamine system is free of long-term toxicity to the motor system. Ritalin may produce disruption of movement control and facial and head tics may appear.[6] Amphetamines are commonly referred to as "speed" or "uppers" and are one of the most dangerous medications ever discovered. They are chemically similar to dopamine and are the synthetic replacement in the dopamine receptor sites of the brain. Amphetamines have the potential to cause injury to healthy tissue, interfere with growth and development, sleep problems, or aggressive and depressed moods in children.[7]

How can we increase dopamine levels in children with ADHD naturally without using Ritalin or other amphetamines? Dopamine is made from the amino acids tyrosine, or phenylalanine. These amino acids are converted by enzymes into L-dopa. Folic acid, niacin and iron are required for the enzyme to make L-dopa from tyrosine. Finally, another enzyme converts L-dopa to dopamine as long as vitamin B6 is available. By supplementing nutrients and amino acids the body can make dopamine naturally, increasing its levels in the brain.[7] In addition, one study examined the plasma amino acids in 28 patients diagnosed with ADD and 20 control subjects. Compared to the controls, the ADD subjects had significantly lower levels of phenylalanine, tyrosine, tryptophan, histidine, and isoleucine. This suggests there may be a general deficiency in amino acid transport, absorption or both in ADD.[8]

Rhodiola rosea (Rose root) has been used in traditional European medicine for over 3,000 years and it is a way to increase dopamine in the brain. Current research shows that it increases the body's resistance to any type of stress by regulation of the hormonal response in the body. It has a protective effect upon neurotransmitters such as serotonin and dopamine in the brain. It improves neurotransmitter activity by inhibiting their enzymatic destruction and preventing their decline caused by excessive stress hormone release.[9]

Much has been said in the literature relating diet to ADHD. Dietary influences such as food and environmental allergies and nutritional deficiencies have been linked to hyperactivity. By focusing on nutrition, proanthocyanidins, essential fatty acids, supplementing with vitamins/minerals, and eliminating allergens have been very effective in treating ADHD.

Food allergies and food chemistry are important in causing learning and behavior problems in children. When children are sick or influenced by food and/or airborne chemicals, it can compromise brain function. Their learning is impaired and behavior may be disturbed.[6] Feingold research found that up to 50% of all hyperactive children were sensitive to food additives (artificial food colors, flavorings and preservatives) plus salicylates occurring naturally in some foods, making the connection between food allergies and hyperactivity.[1] Since then research has made the connection with foods and ADHD. Seventy-eight children with hyperactive behavior were placed on an elimination diet. Fifty-nine (76%) of the children improved in behavior. These 59 children who responded were then challenged with various foods and some food additives. It was found the additive containing foods were the worst offenders (70% reacted). Then the list was as follows: chocolate (64%), cow's milk (64%), orange (57%), cow's cheese (45%), wheat (45%), other fruits (35%), tomato (22%) and egg (18%).[10] Another study with 26 children who met the criteria for ADHD were put on a multiple item elimination diet and showed 19 children responding favorably and with an open challenge all 19 children reacted to many foods, dyes and/or preservatives. This study shows the benefit of eliminating reactive foods and artificial colors in the diets of children with ADHD.[11] Finally; a study involving 40 children who were given a diet free of artificial food dyes and other additives for five days; 20 of the children were classified as hyperactive and the other 20 were controls without a hyperactive classification. On oral challenges with food dyes the performance of the hyperactive children was impaired relative to their performance after receiving the placebo. The performance of the nonhyperactive group was not affected by the challenge of the food dyes.[12] The United States consumes an enormous amount of food additives. Per capita daily consumption of food additives is 13–15 grams, and the population's total annual consumption of food colors alone is approximately 100 million pounds. There are some 5,000 additives currently in widespread use. Other countries have significantly restricted artificial food additives. The removal of artificial food colorings and preservatives from the diet of a child with ADHD is vital and a realistic clinical intervention.[1]

Environmental illness can play an important role in ADHD. Environmental toxins include everything from molds, dust, and pollens to toxic chemicals (pesticides, herbicides, solvents, etc.). All of these toxins have been linked to changes in behavior, perception, cognition or motor ability. Children who have been exposed to lead, arsenic, aluminum, mercury or cadmium can have permanent neurological damage including attention deficits, emotional and behavioral problems.[1]

Nutritional deficiencies have been shown throughout the literature to make a significant impact on the learning and behavior of children. For example, in one study reading skills and IQ tests improved significantly after children started taking multivitamins.[13] Another study showed that learning-disabled children who were placed on vitamin/mineral supplements improved in reading comprehension, their grades improved and those in special education classes were able to become mainstreamed. Those that discontinued the treatment saw their skills drop off, and those who remained on the therapy continued to improve.[14] Research continues to show that poor nutritional habits in children lead to low concentrations of water-soluble vitamins in the blood, impair brain function and subsequently cause violence and other serious antisocial behavior. After correcting the nutrient intake, either by a well-balanced diet or low-dose vitamin/mineral supplementation, this corrected the low concentrations of vitamins in the blood, improved brain function and subsequently lowered institutional violence and antisocial behavior by almost half.[15] The brain and the rest of the body need nutrients for normal vital functioning. Therefore, brain function can be affected by any nutrient deficiency or imbalance. ADHD children often have nutrition deficiencies or imbalances that if corrected can make a significant impact on their behavior.[1]

Zinc deficiency has been noted in children with ADHD. Hyperactive children had significantly lower zinc levels in hair, blood, fingernail and urine compared to the age and sex-matched controls. The yellow food dye tartrazine may bind to zinc in the blood as a chelating agent and reduce levels of zinc in the blood.[16] Another study found that ADHD children with zinc deficiency had a poorer response to amphetamine treatment.[17]

Magnesium was linked with ADHD in a study involving ADHD children with a recognized magnesium deficiency in the blood. In a period of six months, those examined regularly took magnesium preparations in a dose of approximately 200 mg/day. After a period of six months, there was an increase in magnesium content in hair and a significant decrease of hyperactivity compared to their clinical state before the supplementation and the control group, which was not treated with magnesium.[18]

Vitamin B6 (pyridoxine) is an essential component in a majority of the metabolic pathways of amino acids, including decarboxylation pathways for dopamine, adrenaline and serotonin.[1] One study reported that B vitamins improved the behavior of some children with ADHD in comparison to methylphenidate. In addition, it was further investigated giving children who were responsive to methylphenidate, supplementation of B6. In a double blind, multiple crossover trial, each child received placebo, low and high doses of methylphenidate, and low and high doses of B6 in a 21-week period. Results showed that serotonin blood levels increased dramatically on B6, and teacher ratings showed a 90% level of statistical trend in favor of B6 being slightly more effective than methylphenidate.[19]

There is an abundance of information correlating the connection of ADHD and essential fatty acids (EFA). There are two main classes of fatty acids— omega-3 and omega-6. Fatty acids function as pro-homeostatic parts of cell membranes and as precursors to smaller molecules (eicosanoids) that transduce information inward to the cell interior, and outward from each cell to influence other cells. One consistent symptom of EFA deficiency in both animals and humans is excessive thirst (polydypsia) without the matching frequent urination (polyuria). C22:6 omega-3 (docosahexaenoic acid, DHA) and C20:4 omega-6 (arachidonic acid) are in human breast milk.[11] Unfortunately, the average DHA content of breast milk in the U.S. is the lowest in the world; probably due to the fact Americans eat comparatively little fish. DHA is the building block of human brain tissue and is abundant in the gray matter of the brain and in the retina. Low levels of DHA have been associated with depression, memory loss, dementia, and visual problems. Low DHA levels have been linked to low brain serotonin levels, which can be connected to depression, suicide and violence.[20] Researchers at Purdue University found that subclinical deficiency in DHA is responsible for the abnormal behavior of children with ADHD. They pointed out the supplementation with a long-chain omega-6 fatty acid (evening primrose oil) was unsuccessful in ameliorating ADHD and this is believed to be due to ADHD children needing more omega-3 fatty acids than omega-6 acids. The researchers also found that children with ADHD were less often breastfed as infants than were children without ADHD. Breast milk is an excellent source of DHA.[21] Another research study at the School of Medicine at the University of Auckland in Auckland, New Zealand found that upon blood analyses, hyperactive children had significantly depressed levels of docosahexaenoic, dihomogammalinolenic and arachidonic acids. The researchers pointed out that male animals require three times as much EFA as do females in order to achieve normal neonatal and infant development; this is consistent with the finding that hyperactivity is more common among boys than among girls.[22]

Proanthocyanidins may prove effective in treating ADHD. It was reported in a pediatric practice that children were treated with nutritional supplements similar to pycnogenol (pine bark extract). The biologically active compounds found in pycnogenol are oligomeric proanthocyanidins (OPCs). The results showed that patients in areas relating to sustained attention and distractibility, rather than hyperactivity and impulsivity, found the most significant improvement. A few side effects were noted in some children becoming irritable and having decreased energy. OPCs are a class of flavonoids. Flavonoids are a group of polyphenolic substances, which are present in most plants. OPCs have been extracted from many plants including apples, berries, grapes, raspberries and may also be present in many red wines.[23]

When treating ADHD, homeopathy should be considered as a treatment option. In a study comparing the effectiveness of homeopathy vs. methylphenidate, it was found that in cases where treatment of the hyperactive child was not immediate, homeopathy is a valuable alternative to methylphenidate. The reported results of the homeopathic treatment appear to be similar to the effects of methylphenidate. Only children who did not achieve the high level of sensory integration for school had to be changed to methylphenidate. In preschoolers, homeopathy appears to be particularly useful in the treatment of ADHD.[24]

Chinese herbal therapies have been used in numerous studies with children who had ADHD and proved to be very effective. From a traditional Chinese medical viewpoint, ADD is caused by a "kidney essence deficiency" that affects brain development. Furthermore, the yin aspect of the kidney is mainly deficient, which leads to excessive statement of yang. This excessive yang can manifest as hyperactivity and wandering of the mind. Therefore ADD should be treated by nourishing the kidney yin, opening the heart orifices (which are the passages that affect the brain function), and settling the agitated yang. The main herbs that can be used for nourishing the kidney in ADD children are rehmannia, tortoise shell, deer antler gelatin, lycium, and cornus. In clearing the heart orifices and enhancing the mental function, the main herbs used are acorus, polygala, curcuma, and alpinia. To settle an agitated yang energy (manifesting as hyperactivity and insomnia) the alleged "heavy sedating agents" are used. The traditional idea is that these mineral-rich substances bear down on the rising and disordered yang. The main substances given for ADD by Chinese doctors are dragon bone or dragon teeth, oyster shell or mother of pearl, succinum, and cinnabar.

One study showing the effectiveness of Chinese herbals on ADHD children used a sugar paste. Two formulas were made in this form—Zhili Tangjiang, composed mainly of acorus and polygala, and Kangyi Tangjiang, which contained acorus, polygala, plus tortoise shell, hoelen, dragon bone, alpinia, dioscorea, and lotus seeds. The dose of these pastes was 10–15 ml each time, two to three times per day. Of 170 cases (two studies), 132 (77%) were improved. Treatment time was approximately one month.[25] Another study showed 30 children with ADD were treated with a syrup and powder for two to four months, with the result that 22 (73%) showed improvements. The syrup was made with alpinia, hoshou-wu, lycium, dragon bone, oyster shell, acorus, curcuma, and salvia, boiled down to a thick liquid and preserved with benzoic acid. Three times per day, the children would take 25 ml of the liquid and 2 grams of deer antler powder. A similar method was used in a study of 50 children with ADD who consumed a decoction of acorus polygala, dragon bone, and oyster shell, modified by adding three to six herbs according to symptoms, and who also consumed a powder of succinum. The duration of the therapy was not specified but 38 of the children (76%) showed improvements.[25]

Another study showed interesting results using an Ayurvedic formulation—Mentat. In this study, 40 hyperactive children were enrolled in a double-blind placebo-controlled study to receive either an active drug Mentat or a placebo. One group of 20 received Mentat syrup and another a placebo. The drugs were given for 3 to 7 months in both groups. Evaluation was done on Yale's Behavior Inventory before and after the twelve weeks of treatment. It was observed that there was remarkable improvement in behavioral pattern along with an increase in concentration. There was significant reduction in hyperactivity, temper tantrums and improvement in language usage. Social behavior improved in those who received Mentat treatment as opposed to those on placebo. Mentat is an Ayurvedic formulation (Himalayan) that has been reported to be effective in disorders involving memory and attention.[26]

Thyroid should be examined in children with ADHD. One study was done examining the relationship between thyroid hormone and attention in 85 seven-year old children with congenital hypothyroidism. It was found that children with higher circulating levels of thyroxine (T4) had significantly more distractibility on an index of cognitive attention.[27] Another study showed that ADHD was strongly associated with generalized resistance to thyroid hormone.[28]

A study of ADHD children suggests that the lack of ability to control impulsive thoughts and actions may be caused by an underactive rather than an overactive adrenal hormone response. The ability to control behavior is thought to be related to the body's release of stress hormones such as cortisol. Researchers compared cortisol secretion in two groups of children: those who had ADHD symptoms for over a year, and those whose symptoms had declined. Salivary cortisol assays performed on both groups showed that children with persistent ADHD had a significantly lower adrenal response. In addition, after performing a series of academic and psychological tests, these children exhibited cortisol responses that were two to three times lower than those children who no longer were experiencing ADHD symptoms. It was concluded that a blunted cortisol response to stress might indicate a more developmentally persistent form of ADHD.[29]

This paper discusses some of the alternative options for treating attention deficit hyperactivity disorder in children. This has become a serious condition that is affecting many children today. Ritalin, the most popular pharmaceutical choice in treating ADHD, has many short- and long-term side effects. Alternative therapies should be considered as viable options to Ritalin. There are many effective alternative treatments that can be used to treat and manage ADHD.

References

1. Kidd P. Attention Deficit/Hyperactivity Disorder (ADHD) in Children: Rationale for its Integrative Management. Altern Med Rev 2000 Oct; 5(5): 402–28.

2. www.parentsofallergicchildren.org

3. Mannuzza S., Klein RG. Long-term Prognosis in Attention-Deficit/Hyperactivity Disorder. Child Adolesc Psychiatr Clin N Am 2000 Jul; 9(3):711–26.

4. Volkow N., Wang G., Fowler J., Logan J., Gerasimov M., Maynard L., Ding Y., Gatley S., Gifford A., Franceschi D. Therapeutic Doses of Oral Methylphenidate Significantly Increase Extracellular Dopamine in the Human Brain The Journal of Neuroscience, 2001, 21:RC121:1–5.

5. Teresa Gallagher. Born to explore the other side of the ADD. http://borntoexplore.org/whatisadd.htm

6. Stephen J. Gislason, MD; Alpha Nutrition Health Education Series: Special Children, Hyperactivity/ADHD.www.nutramed.com

7. Charles E. Gant, MD, PhD, It's Your Chemistry. 1995–1998, Great Connections[R] http://www.oneaddplace.com/articles/itsyour.htm

8. Bernstein RA, Baker GB, Carroll A, King G, Wong JT, Douglass AB. Plasma Amino Acids in Attention Deficit Disorder. Psychiatry Res 1090 Sep; 33(3): 301–306.

9. Solgar Vitamins. Solgar New Product Information. Rhediola Vegicaps. Solgar Vitamins, Tring, Herts. 1998.

10. Carter CM, Urbanowicz M, Hemsley R, Mantilla L, Strobel S, Graham PJ, Taylor E. Effects of a Few Food Diet in Attention Deficit Disorder. Arch Dis Child 1993 Nov; 69(5):564–8.

11. Boris M, Mandel FS. Foods and Additives are Common Causes of the Attention Deficit Hyperactive Disorder in Children. Ann Allergy 1994 May; 72(5):462–8.

12. Swanson JM, Kinsbourne M. Food Dyes Impair Performance of Hyperactive Children on a Laboratory Learning Test. Science 1980 Mar 28; 207(4438): 1485–7.

13. Colgan M, Colgan L. Nutr Health 1984; 3(1.2):69.77.

14. Carlton, et al.; Altern Ther Health Med 2000 May; 6(3):85–91.

15. Schoenthaler SJ, Bier ID; J Altern Complement Med 2000 Feb; 6(1):7–17.

16. Shaw W. Importance of Zinc to the Immune System. www.parentsofallergicchildren.org/importance_of_zinc.htm

17. Arnold LE, Votolato NA, Kleykamp D, Baker GB, Bornstein RA. Does Hair Zinc Predict Amphetamine Improvement of ADD/Hyperactivity? Int J Neurosci 1990 Jan; 50(1–2):103–107.

18. Starobrat-Hermelin B, Kozielec T. The Effects of Magnesium Physiological Supplementation on Hyperactivity in Children with Attention Deficit Hyperactivity Disorder (ADHD). Positive Response to Magnesium Oral Loading Test. Magnes Res 1997 Jun; 10(2):149–56.

19. Coleman M, Steinberg G, Tippett J, et al. A Preliminary Study of the Effect of Pyridoxine. Biol Psychiaty 1979; 14:741–751.

20. Levine, Barbara S. Most Frequently Asked Questions About DHA. Nutrition Today 1997 November/December, vol. 32, pp. 248–49.

21. Burgess JR, Stevens L, Zhang W, Peck L. Long-Chain Polyunsaturated Fatty Acids in Children with Attention-Deficit Hyperactivity Disorder. Am J Clin Nutr 2000 Jan; 71(1 Suppl): 327S.30S.

22. Mitchell, E.A., et al. Clinical Characteristics and Serum Essential Fatty Acid Levels in Hyperactive Children. Clinical Pediatrics, Vol. 26, August 1987, pp. 406–11.

23. Greenblatt James, M.D.. Nutritional Supplements In ADHD. J.Am.Acad. Child Adolesc. Psychiatry 38:10, October 1999, pp. 1209–1210.

24. Frei H, Thurneysen A. Treatment for Hyperactive Children: Homeopathy and Methylphenidate Compared in a Family Setting. Br Homeopath J 2001 Oct; 90(4): 1838.

25.   Chinese Herbal Treatment for Attention Deficit Disorder. By Subhuti Dharmananda, Ph.D., Director, Institute for Traditional Medicine, Portland Oregon. Note: The clinical trials mentioned in this paper were described in Chinese language literature. Heiner Fruehauf, Ph.D., L.Ac., at the Institute for Traditional Medicine, prepared rough translations of the information.

26.   Experience with Mentat in Hyperkinetic Children. Mrs. Renu B. Patel, M.D., D.C.H., Professor and Head of the Dept. of Pediatrics, Institute of Child Health, Grant Medical College and J.J. Group of Hospitals, Bombay And Mrs. Leela Pereira Medical and Psychiatric Social Worker

27.   Revert J, Alvarez M. Thyroid Hormone and Attention in School-Age Children with Congenital Hypothyroidism. J Child Psychol Psychiatry 1996 Jul; 37(5):579–85.

28.   Hauser P, Zametkin AJ, Martinez P, Vitiello B, Matochik JA, Mixson AJ, Weintraub BD. Attention Deficit-Hyperactivity Disorder in People with Generalized Resistance to Thyroid Hormone. N Engl J Med 1993 April 8; 328(14):997–1001.

29.   King J., Borkley R., Barrett S. Attention-Deficit Hyperactivity Disorder and the Stress Response. Journal of Biological Psychiatry 1998; 44:73–74

POSTSCRIPT

Is Ritalin an Effective Drug for Treating Attention Deficit/ Hyperactivity Disorder (ADHD)?

To satisfy their own emotional needs, many parents push their physicians into diagnosing their children with ADHD. These parents believe that their children will benefit if they are labeled ADHD. The pressure for children to do well academically in order to get into the right college and graduate school is intense. Some parents feel that if their children are diagnosed with ADHD, then they may be provided special circumstances or allowances such as additional time when taking college entrance examinations. Some parents also realize that if their children are identified as having ADHD, their children will be eligible for extra services in school. In some instances, the only way to receive such extra help is to be labeled with a disorder. Also, some teachers favor the use of Ritalin to control students' behavior. During the last few years, there has been increasing emphasis on controlling school budgets. The result is larger class sizes and higher student-to-teacher ratios. Thus, it should not be surprising that many teachers welcome the calming effect of Ritalin on students whose hyperactivity is disruptive to the class.

Whether or not drug therapy should be applied to behaviors raises another concern. What is the message that children are receiving about the role of drugs in society? Perhaps children will generalize the benefits of using legal drugs like Ritalin to remedy life's problems to using illegal drugs to deal with other problems that they may be experiencing. Children may find that it is easier to ingest a pill rather than to put the time and effort into resolving personal problems. For many adults, drugs seem to represent a shortcut to correcting life's difficulties. Through its reliance on drugs, is American society creating a wrong impression for its children, an illusion of believing that there is a pill for every ill?

When to prescribe Ritalin for children also places physicians in a quandary. They may see the benefit of helping students function more effectively in school. However, are physicians who readily prescribe Ritalin unintentionally promoting an antihumanistic, competitive environment in which performance matters regardless of cost? On the other hand, is it the place of physicians to dictate to parents what is best for their children? In the final analysis, will the increase in prescriptions for Ritalin result in benefits for the child, for the parents, and for society?

An article that question the validity of Attention Deficit/Hyperactivity Disorder is Jonathon Leo's "Broken Brains or Flawed Studies? A Critical Review of ADHD Neuroimaging Research," in *The Journal of Mind and Behavior* (Winter 2003).

How Ritalin functions is reviewed in "Methylphenidate: Mechanism of Action and Clinical Update" by Lawrence Scahill, Deirdre Carroll, and Kathleen Burke (*Journal of Child and Adolescent Psychiatric Nursing,* April-June, 2004). Jeff Evans reports on the role of stimulants in school performance in "ADHD Medications Affect School Attendance and Substance Abuse: Retrospective Studies" (*Family Practice News,* April 1, 2004). Another review of Ritalin's effects is discussed in "Ritalin Update for Counselors, Teachers, and Parents" by Hazel L. White (*Education,* Winter 2003).

ISSUE 13

Do Consumers Benefit When Prescription Drugs Are Advertised?

YES: Merrill Matthews, Jr., from "Advertising Drugs Is Good for Patients," *Consumers' Research Magazine* (August 2001)

NO: Katharine Greider, from *The Big Fix: How the Pharmaceutical Industry Rips Off American Consumers* (Public Affairs, 2003)

ISSUE SUMMARY

YES: Merrill Matthews, Jr., a health policy advisor with the American Legislative Exchange Council, feels that the advertising of prescription drugs directly to consumers will result in better-informed consumers. Concerns that the cost of prescription drugs will rise due to the cost of advertising drugs are unfounded. Instead, advertising drugs creates competition among manufacturers, resulting in lower costs. Additionally, communication between doctors and patients may improve because patients are more knowledgeable about drugs.

NO: Writer Katharine Greider notes that drug advertising has increased the number of visits by patients to their physicians as well as the number of prescriptions written at the request of consumers. Also, many consumers may not have the clinical or pharmacological background to comprehend information in drug advertisements.

The prescription drug business is one of the most lucrative businesses in the world today. Billions of dollars are spent every year for prescription drugs in the United States alone. But, the *only* way for consumers to obtain a prescribed drug is through a physician. In the early 1980s, U.S. drug companies began to advertise directly to the consumer. It is logical for drug companies to advertise to physicians because they are responsible for writing prescriptions. However, is it logical for pharmaceutical manufacturers to advertise their drugs directly to consumers? Are consumers capable of making informed, rational decisions regarding their pharmaceutical needs? Do consumers derive any benefits when prescription drugs are advertised?

An increasing number of individuals are assuming more responsibility for their own health care. In the United States, over one-third of all prescriptions are written at the request of patients. Also, many patients do not take their doctors' prescriptions to pharmacies to be filled. Both of these scenarios raise the question of whether consumers are adequately educated to make decisions pertaining to their pharmaceutical needs or to assess risks associated with prescription drugs. Evidence suggests that many are not. Prescription drugs, for example, cause more worksite accidents than do illegal drugs.

Some commentators argue that there are several advantages to directly advertising drugs to consumers. One advantage is that direct advertisements make consumers better informed about the benefits and risks of certain drugs. For example, it is not unusual for a person to experience side effects from a drug without knowing that the drug was responsible for the side effects. Advertisements can provide this information. Another advantage for consumers is that they may learn about medications that they might not have known existed. Furthermore, advertising lowers the cost of prescription drugs because consumers are able to ask their physicians to prescribe less-expensive drugs than the physician might be inclined to recommend. Finally, prescription drug advertising allows consumers to become more involved in choosing the medications that they need or want.

Critics argue that there are a number of risks associated with the direct advertising of prescription drugs. One concern is with the content of drug advertisements. Consumers may not pay enough attention to information detailing a drug's adverse effects. Also, sometimes a drug's benefits are exaggerated. Another problem is that there are many instances in which drugs that have been approved by the Food and Drug Administration (FDA) for one purpose have been promoted for other purposes. Is the average consumer capable of understanding the purposes of the drugs that are being advertised?

Opponents of direct-to-consumer drug advertisements express concern with the way in which the information in the advertisements is presented. Promotions for drugs that appear as objective reports are often actually slick publicity material. In such promotions, medical experts are shown providing testimony regarding a particular drug. Many consumers may not be aware that these physicians have financial ties to the pharmaceutical companies. Celebrities—in whom the public often places its trust despite their lack of medical expertise—are also used to promote drugs. Finally, the cost of the drugs advertised, a major concern to most consumers, is seldom mentioned in the advertisements.

In the following selections, Merrill Matthews argues that the marketing of prescription drugs helps consumers because it lowers the cost of drugs and effectively informs consumers about the benefits of new drugs. Katharine Greider does not believe that consumers gain from prescription drug advertising because many people lack clinical and pharmacological expertise. Some patients spend more money because they schedule more visits with their physicians.

YES

Merrill Matthews, Jr.

Advertising Drugs Is Good for Patients

Many health policy experts believe that direct-to-consumer (DTC) advertising by pharmaceutical companies misinforms gullible consumers, encourages drug overconsumption, increases health care costs, strains doctor-patient relationships and undermines the quality of patient care. For example:

- The American College of Physicians and the American Society of Internal Medicine, in a joint policy statement, wrote: "We are concerned that advertising will result in increased consumption of these highly advertised drugs; though their use may be neither appropriate nor necessary." The organizations also wrote: "Many times, physicians will give in to the demand and when they don't, often patients will 'doctor shop' until they find a physician who will prescribe the medication."
- Sen. Tim Johnson (D-S.D.) also questioned the growth of DTC. "Is the information value worth the yearly increases in drug costs that advertising inevitably causes? Are patients getting the best individual choices of medicines or just the best advertised ones? Are generic drugs, often an excellent cost-effective alternative, getting equal consideration?"
- Finally, members of the Committee on Bioethical Issues of the Medical Society of the State of New York wrote: "Direct drug advertising provides no real benefit to patients, is potentially harmful, and is costly. We therefore urge the U.S. Food and Drug Administration to review and strengthen its policies concerning this practice."

Are these criticisms accurate? In some cases, yes. For example, DTC advertising does encourage more drug consumption—which can lower some health care costs when drug therapy precludes the need for other, more expensive therapies.

However, the above-mentioned concerns largely are misdirected. They focus on the evolving pharmaceutical marketplace when in fact the whole health care system is in transition. And direct-to-consumer pharmaceutical ads are a response to the transitional process, not the cause of it.

The U.S. health care system has reached a cross-roads, and the direction the country takes will determine the type, availability and quality of care for years to come. Pharmaceutical advertising pre-supposes that health care consumers can

From Merrill Matthews, Jr., "Advertising Drugs Is Good for Patients," *Consumers Research Magazine,* vol. 84, no. 8 (August 2001). Copyright © 2001 by The Institute for Policy Innovation. Reprinted by permission.

make choices for themselves—and that's the type of health care system people want. Those who have no choice in health care have no need of advertising.

A health care system in transition   America is in the forefront of the information economy. One of the hallmarks of this new economy is access to much more information by many more people. Patients have much greater access to health care information, especially through the Internet and through advertising. Indeed, the most important change occurring in the health care system is this access to information. According to health care consultant Lyn Siegel:

- About 25% of on-line information is related to health;
- More than 50% of adults who go on the Web use it for health care information; and
- More than 26% of people who go to disease-oriented Web sites ask their doctors for a specific brand of medication. Thus information is driving the transition to a patient-directed health care system.

A generation ago physicians were the possessors of all medical information. Patients went to physicians and accepted evaluations and diagnoses almost without question. Patients who want second opinions and physicians who gracefully accede to their wishes are relatively new phenomena.

In a physician-directed health care system:

- Physicians have all the extant medical knowledge and skills;
- Physicians perform all patient examinations;
- Patients accept their physicians' diagnoses and insurers pay for the care;
- Hospitals admit patients based on physicians' orders and pharmacists fill the prescriptions; and,
- Drug and medical device companies market to the physicians who control all access to patients.

In this model, no one reaches patients without a physician's consent. The physician-directed system worked well for several decades. The vast majority of working Americans had good health insurance benefits that protected them, their families and their assets from catastrophic losses due to a major accident or illness. Third-party payers were generous in their reimbursement policies while doctors and hospitals could do only so much. Whatever doctors recommended, insurers covered.

Once the amazing medical advances of the 1970s and 1980s began to appear, health care costs began to soar. Insured workers and seniors on Medicare were insulated from the cost of care, and so had little incentive to control health care spending. Employers and the government, who paid most health care bills, desperately sought cost-control mechanisms. That's when managed care came in. Its proponents claimed that managed care could lower the cost of comprehensive health care coverage, in part by controlling utilization. While the arguments continue over how well managed care controlled costs and whether it sacrificed quality to achieve savings, the growth in health care spending did slow during the 1990s. Recently, though, the rate of growth has escalated and engendered fears of more double-digit increases in health care spending.

Meanwhile, the expansion of managed care helped to undermine the physician-directed health care system. Insurers and employers gained the power to question and even override doctors' decisions, which put doctors in an uncomfortable and unsatisfactory position.

Patients also reacted negatively. Many believed their doctors were willing or able to give them only the level of care their insurers would cover. This distrust undermined the doctor-patient relationship and spurred patients to seek health care information directly, rather than from their doctor or insurer. Thus health care consumers began to exploit the information economy.

Increasingly, patients are entering the health care system armed with information—and sometimes misinformation. They may not know how to practice medicine, but many know something about their medical condition and the options available to them. And they raise questions if the doctor follows a different path from the one they expect.

As Dr. Thomas R. Reardon, past president of the American Medical Association, has insightfully noted: "Patients themselves are also creating a strong impetus for change. Disillusioned by restrictions on coverage and care, they are increasingly demanding choice of physician, hospital, and even type of health plan. More than ever, patients see physicians as the essential point of trust in a changing system, and demand choice and stability in their vital relationships with their doctors. . . . At the same time, patients themselves are becoming better educated, not only about insurance options but also about medical treatments. Today, thanks to the Internet, trends in product advertising, and the massive proliferation of medical information, patients are better equipped to take part in their care than ever before. Rather than simplifying the physician's job, however, this increased patient knowledge base is creating new challenges."

We are transitioning toward a patient-directed health care system—if the federal and state governments don't intervene—in which all of the components cater to the patient, rather than the physician. It is impossible to overstate the magnitude of the change. We aren't there yet, but the system is moving—or being pulled—in that direction.

In the new system, insurers and employers, doctors and other health care providers, researchers and pharmaceutical companies will view the patient rather than the provider as the primary consumer. And in the new system:

- Insurers will have to create products that consumers rather than their employers want;
- Doctors will have to please their patients rather than insurers, reinvigorating the weakened doctor-patient relationship; and
- Pharmaceutical and medical device companies increasingly will market directly to the consumers who use their products.

Because health care consumers are becoming better informed, they will, on balance, make better decisions. And they will want even more information. But how do companies and providers reach individuals with the information the latter want and need? One way is through advertising.

Every Sunday newspaper is filled with advertising flyers for department stores, office products, computers, cars, food and clothing. Yet people don't complain they can't afford food because all the grocery stores advertise. And does anyone really think they would be able to get a computer for less money if none of the computer manufacturers and retail outlets advertised?

In virtually every sector of the economy, those with products or services to sell must get information to those who will buy. Advertising is the vehicle for getting information to the intended customers. It tells prospective customers about product availability, quality and cost—the information those prospects need in order to make comparisons. While some people may consider it annoying if they are not looking for a particular product, those in the market for the advertised item often will pay close attention to ads and other marketing techniques such as direct mail and communication from sales representatives.

The general assumption is that advertising raises the costs of products. This assumption recently has entered the debate over the impact of drug companies' advertisements aimed at consumers. But advertising can—and should—lower costs. For example, according to economist John Calfee of the American Enterprise Institute:

> A pioneering study compared the prices of eye-glasses in states that either permitted or restricted advertising for eyeglass services. Prices were about 25% higher where advertising was restricted or banned (and prices were highest for the least educated consumers). A later study by the Federal Trade Commission (FTC) staff showed that product quality in the states without advertising was not higher despite the higher prices. Studies also found higher prices in the absence of advertising for such diverse products as gasoline, prescription drugs and legal services.

How is it that advertising can actually lower prices? Most products have certain fixed costs, plus some variable costs. While variable costs are imputed to each item produced, fixed costs are divided by the number of products sold. The goal of advertising is to expand consumer awareness and increase sales. The more items sold, the greater the economies of scale and the lower the fixed costs per consumer.

Holman Jenkins of the Wall Street Journal explains the rationale: "The media also complain about advertising as if this were an extra cost borne by drug users. Drug companies spend on advertising because it's profitable—it pays for itself by generating additional sales, allowing development costs to be spread over a larger number of users. The average price to each user is lower."

In the absence of competition, advertising might raise prices. But in the absence of competition, vendors would likely raise prices whether they advertised or not. Competition keeps manufacturers from charging as much as they would like, except in cases where there is an unusually high demand for a particular product (as when everyone decides they want a Cabbage Patch doll, a Tickle Me Elmo or a Furby for Christmas). Thus, even when advertising doesn't increase sales, vendors cannot add the cost on top of the product if there are other competitively priced alternatives on the market.

DTC ads and the health care system   Putting information in the hands of consumers who didn't have that information before is a revolutionary business—and revolutions engender change. Critics know this and raise concerns that DTC advertising will increase health care spending, strain doctor-patient relationships and confuse consumers and patients. Worst of all, they believe going directly to the consumer is only a drug company technique to increase prices and therefore profits. Are any of these concerns valid?

Will DTC advertising increase health care spending?   Probably, but that is not necessarily bad. Increased health care spending is bad only when it is wasteful and inefficient. For example, if doctors were to prescribe medicines for patients who had no medical need, that would be wasteful—and unethical. However, very few doctors would prescribe medicines their patients do not need. In fact, a new *Prevention* magazine survey found that about half of those who talk to a doctor as a result of a DTC ad receive no drug therapy.

A greater concern is that patients, having seen an expensive brand-name drug advertised, will want it rather than a generic equivalent. When patients or their doctors choose brand names over generics, their choices may increase total health care spending. But, again, that may not be bad. The brand name may be higher in quality or slightly different in composition. And it may have fewer side effects. Thus it may offer additional benefits, in which case the additional cost may be justified.

If an expansion of DTC advertising means that we are treating more people who otherwise might have just suffered in pain or endured a debilitating condition, then increased medical spending is positive. Some have argued that increased drug spending may lower total health care costs if less expensive drug therapy replaces more expensive surgery or other procedures. This may be true for individual patients, but it cannot be aggregated to apply to the whole health care system. Total spending will continue to rise because the American health care system will continue to do more and more for patients.

Will DTC advertising strain the doctor-patient relationship?   Historically, doctors informed and patients performed. That is, doctors diagnosed and issued instructions that patients followed—or at least were supposed to. With more information at the patients' fingertips, that relationship is changing. Patients are asking questions, and doctors are beginning to see the questions as opportunities to enhance patients' understanding and sense of responsibility about their own health. (The author himself has asked a physician about an advertised prescription drug, and neither he nor the doctor saw anything unusual or unethical about the exchange.)

Doctors may have to take more time to discuss with their patients why Drug A, which the patient saw advertised on TV, would not in the doctor's opinion be as good a choice as Drug B. Cost, efficacy and suitability all may play a role in that discussion. Some irascible patients may refuse to accept the doctor's advice. But this occurs even without DTC advertising. Indeed, current DTC advertising is very subtle. No announcer tells the audience to demand Drug A from a doctor because it has been clinically proven to be better than

Drug B. DTC ads tend to convey too little information rather than too much. This may change, but the medical community already is learning to deal with people who come to the doctor not just as patients but as consumers.

Will DTC ads confuse patients? Economist John Calfee contends that three decades of research on advertising has led to two basic understandings:

> First, advertising has an unsuspected power to improve consumer welfare. As a market-perfecting mechanism, advertising arises spontaneously to attack serious defects in the marketplace. Advertising is an efficient and sometimes irreplaceable mechanism for bringing consumers information that would otherwise languish on the sidelines. Advertising's promise of more and better information also generates ripple effects in the market. These include enhanced incentives to create new information and develop better products. Theoretical and empirical research has demonstrated what generations of astute observers had known intuitively, that markets with advertising are far superior to markets without advertising.
>
> The second finding is that competitive advertising is fundamentally a self-correcting process. Some people may find this surprising. Well informed observers once thought that unregulated advertising would bring massive distortion of consumer information and decisions. Careful research, however, has shown these fears to be groundless. Self-correcting competitive forces in advertising generate markets in which information is richer and more fundamentally balanced than can be achieved through detailed controls over advertising and information.

Is DTC just a way to increase drug prices? Drug companies advertise for the same reason every other company and industry advertises: to increase sales with a view to increasing profits. The consumer benefit is that, as competition grows, prices usually fall. By contrast, in the absence of marketing, prices would not go down, but up. Just consider under which scenario a manufacturer is more likely to charge high prices for low quality: where there is no advertising and consumers have no way to comparison-shop without taking their own time to go from store to store to compare price and quality, or where advertising takes that information directly to the consumer? It is not advertising that increases the price of products, it's the lack of it. High prices thrive in an atmosphere of ignorance. If critics want to see the price of prescription drugs fall, they should encourage even more advertising and competition.

The missing ingredient: value As long as patients are insulated from the cost of medical care and doctors stand between patients and their prescriptions, the health care marketplace cannot work exactly like a normal market in which consumers demand from vendors quality, service and reasonable prices—that is, value.

But the U.S. health care system can take on some of the dynamics of a market, and in fact is already doing so. There is some competition; there is some DTC advertising; and prices at least for some health care products and services are relatively low.

As we continue to move into a patient-directed system, market forces may become more apparent. For example, if most people chose to combine a Medical Savings Account (MSA) for small expenses with a catastrophic health insurance policy for large expenses, patients would pay for their prescription drugs out of the MSA and thus be more cost-conscious.

In addition, the realization is growing in Washington that the current tax subsidy for health insurance causes problems. As a result, Congress may pass a tax credit that will help the uninsured purchase a policy. This in turn may lead to a fundamental shift in the type of health insurance policy people purchase—and facilitate the move to a patient-directed system.

The Big Fix: How the Pharmaceutical Industry Rips Off American Consumer's

Drugmakers' efforts to influence doctors' behavior are ultimately aimed at influencing ours. And more than ever before, these companies are bringing their pitch straight into Americans' everyday lives, advertising on radio, in popular magazines, and especially on TV. Here the message eschews the dry language of clinical research, its end points and data sets, for the powerful emotional image: a flower opening, an old person frolicking like a colt, people of all colors linking arms. Or to strike a different mood, an apparently healthy middle-aged woman suddenly dropping from the frame.

Although magazine ads weren't uncommon in the 1980s, direct-to-consumer (DTC) drug advertising is largely a phenomenon that arose in the 1990s. A 1997 FDA rule making it more practical to advertise on television—companies could now substitute a toll-free number or web address for the "small print" details about drug side effects and contraindications—was undoubtedly an important catalyst. Then a few bold and enormously successful campaigns convinced other big players that they couldn't afford to stay on the sidelines. Spending on consumer ads surged from a scant $266 million in 1994 to $2.6 billion in 2001. Controversial in the United States, the practice of pushing prescription medicine much the same way as soda pop is virtually unheard of elsewhere in the developed world. As Boston University's Sager says, "They're laughing at us again."

Traditionally, prescription drugmakers have emphasized as a defining feature of their industry that they did not advertise to the consumer, but only to the learned physician. Among other things, this approach facilitated the industry's close association with scientific authority. The recent promotional focus on patients reflects a sea change in medicine and in culture itself. As Mickey Smith, Ph.D., an expert in pharmaceutical marketing at the University of Mississippi, puts it, "People are much better educated—not smarter necessarily, but better educated. The ads you see right now, if they'd run in the Fifties, would have fallen on deaf ears because people wouldn't have had a clue what you were talking about." Now that you, Consumer, are trawling the

Internet for health information, now that you're motivated to take care of yourself and empowered to make decisions about your own medical care, the drug industry would like a moment of your time.

The ads seem to be getting the job done, reaching the great majority of Americans, winning their trust, and, in more than a few cases, prompting people to ask for a drug by name. Nine out of ten consumers surveyed in 2000 by *Prevention Magazine* said they'd seen or heard a drug ad. When queried by the Henry J. Kaiser Family Foundation in 2001, 30 percent of consumers reported having talked with their doctor about a drug they'd seen advertised. Nearly half of those who asked for an advertised drug—13 percent of all consumers—came away with a script. In another Kaiser study, co-sponsored by *The News-Hour with Jim Lehrer,* nearly half of American consumers said they trust advertisements to provide them with accurate information. But perhaps most telling are these results of a recent NIHCM study: Between 1999 and 2000, prescriptions for the fifty most heavily advertised drugs rose at six times the rate of all other drugs. Sales of those fifty intensively promoted drugs were responsible for a almost half the increase in Americans' overall drug spending that year. Makers of the new arthritis drug Vioxx spent $160 million pushing it to consumers in 2000, more advertising dollars than were dropped on Pepsi Cola, Budweiser beer, Nike shoes, or Campbell's soups. Vioxx sales shot up 360 percent.

The way industry spokespeople tell it, Americans should count themselves lucky—drug ads are educational, informing us about health conditions so we can seek appropriate treatment. "The bottom line is that direct-to-consumer advertising is good for patients and good for public health," says a PhRMA spokesman. Sometimes public-health goals do overlap with marketing goals: More people recognizing the signs of clinical depression might boost antidepressant sales and bring relief to many. But skeptics of the drug industry's ads-equal-education equation point out that plenty of important public-health messages go begging for want of profit potential. For example, several pharmaceutical companies have introduced discount programs for low-income seniors. "Have you seen one ad promoting those discount cards?" asks Wennar, of United Health Alliance in Vermont. "Do they do anything on TV to tell people about them?"

What we're getting from DTC drug advertising is lots of exposure to a relatively small number of drugs—generally speaking, new medicines with huge markets and plenty of patent life left. The Kaiser Family Foundation reports that with thousands of drugs on the market, 60 percent of DTC spending in 2000 went to plug just twenty products. This intensive exposure creates what ad people call "brand awareness." A recent survey by market research firm Insight-Express found that, for example, 74 percent of respondents knew Claritin by name. More than half recognized Paxil, 45 percent knew the cholesterol-lowering Zocor, and nearly 80 percent were aware of the pharmaceutical phenomenon Viagra. All have been among the most heavily advertised drug products.

As for what else people take away from the ads, opinions are mixed, and consumer research is limited. One AARP survey found that one-third of the DTC audience failed to notice fine-print information on indications, side effects, and other issues included in magazine ads. Of those who did notice the information, two-thirds said they weren't in the habit of reading it. TV ads have to direct consumers to a phone number, web side, or other ad where they can get more information. But in a Kaiser Family Foundation study, nine out of ten respondents shown three televised drug ads couldn't remember where to get this additional information. Respondents who were shown the drug ads (which included mention of major side effects) judged the side effects to be more serious than those who hadn't seen the ads, but just after viewing the ad, only about half could identify the side effects.

As in all advertising, the main event isn't the discursive information the ads deliver directly, but the suggestive fantasies buried in their music and pictures. "The Nexium ads are so phenomenal that I'd like to take the drug and I don't even have the problem," says Gerstein. "They show a variety of people, very diverse, all standing on jagged stone promontories, and they all start moving together . . . If Disney had done it, you'd say 'Wonderful!'" An ad for an oral contraceptive shows a couple grinning and nuzzling, with the tag line, "Isn't it great when you finally find the right one?" The sound track is a tune whose words—not heard in the ad—are, "This will be an everlasting love."

Other drug ads trade on the cachet of various famous people—baseball legend Cal Ripken Jr., pitching a blood-pressure drug, figure skater Dorothy Hamill praising arthritis medicine, journalist Joan Lunden flogging an allergy med. *Med Ad News* recently reported on a team-up between pharmaceutical-marketing firm Catalyst Communications and a sports-marketing company founded by a former New York Yankees VP. Catalyst's chief stated, "We chose Perello & Company because it understands the divergent worlds of pharmaceuticals and sports." So much for the square in the white coat. Indeed, the use of celebrities has facilitated the industry's bringing together any number of divergent worlds. Is it journalism or is it advertising? Is it fantasy or real life?

Naturally reporters' and editors' in-boxes are stuffed with company press releases and ready-made copy—perhaps a feature on a golf pro's arthritis and how he overcame it with Drug X. That's par for the course. What's surprising and not a little disturbing is that some big stars have been getting air on major news outlets to chat about their conditions and urge others to seek treatment—without anyone mentioning they were being paid by a drug company. Newspeople were chagrined by a *New York Times* exposé in the summer of 2002 that depicted a veritable three-ring circus: Kathleen Turner raving to *Good Morning America*'s Diane Sawyer about "extraordinarily effective" new medications to treat her rheumatoid arthritis (thank you, Wyeth); Lauren Bacall spooking the daylights out of *Today* viewers over an eye disease that can cause blindness (thank you, Novartis); actor Noah Wyle being interviewed as if he were an expert in post-traumatic stress disorder, even as his fictional character on *ER* endured the aftermath of a violent attach (thanks, Pfizer). A week after the *Times* report, CNN did a story telling viewers that some celebrities interviewed on it own network had been paid by drug companies. It announced a new policy of asking famous people scheduled to talk about medical issues whether they have financial ties to related companies and to reveal any such ties on the air.

As long as they don't mention a drug by name, celebs stirring up interest in a particular disease don't have to adhere to the FDA's "fair balance" rule, which requires that any claim linking a specific drug to a specific action be accompanied by mention of the drug's limitations and side effects. Ads can accomplish this, too. "Reminder" ads feature the name of a drug without saying what it's for; they may have the stylized vagueness of ads for hip perfumes. Other drug ads come off as public-service announcements: Bob Dole wants to talk to you about erectile dysfunction. These "help-seeking" ads mention a condition and may flash the company name, but won't name the drug (Viagra) you'll get when you follow the ad's exhortation to see your doctor.

Indeed, to browse the archives of FDA notices of violation to drug companies for misleading ads is to get a sense of how utterly at a loss the agency is to address the various ways expert image makers get across their "claims." Here's what the FDA had to say about an ad for the sleep aid Ambien: "The reminder advertisement presents graphics of the sun and the earth going from night to day, a flower closing and opening, and the Ambien tablet falling on a sheet or pillow, together with the verbal statement 'the rhythm of life.' Thus, the advertisement in total, with the graphics and verbal statement, makes a representation about the product." "Reminder" ads—which don't have to name side effects—aren't supposed to make claims either. But *every* ad makes a representation about a product. What else is an ad for?

Another FDA notice complained that the "totality of the images, the music, and the audio statements" in a sixty-second TV spot for arthritis med Celebrex overstated the drug's efficacy. The ad showed silver-haired arthritis sufferers rowing boats and riding scooters to the joyous sound track, "Celebrate, celebrate, do what you like to do!" (Celebrex hasn't been shown to reduce pain any more effectively than, for example, the generic ibuprofen that sells for a fraction of the cost.) The Celebrex spots have changed—most ads cited by the FDA are either modified or pulled without further regulatory action—but they communicate the same basic idea, with an attractive, well-dressed older couple dancing energetically to happy music. You could argue that the ads associate Celebrex not only with pain relief (whether exaggerated or not is subjective) but also with energy, wealth, youth, beauty, and a happy marriage. That's how the medium works. As one professor of pharmacy puts it, "They're making it look chic to take certain drugs. You don't focus on the product or the disease, you focus on the lifestyle that the drug allows or creates. They're selling lifestyles, not drugs."

Still another FDA missive ordered the discontinuation of a consumer mailer that touted brand-name tamoxifen (Nolvadex) for prevention of breast cancer in women at high risk for the disease. The agency said the mailer overstated the drug's efficacy in this role, minimized side effects, and failed to make clear that women who score 1.7 on a breast-cancer risk assessment, though they may be considered "high risk," have only a 1.7 percent chance of getting breast cancer. But FDA enforcers didn't mention—and in fact are not empowered to address—how the brochure, titled "Are You a Helpless Female?" capitalized on women's terror, with models who stare fixedly at the reader and the tag line: "Now *predict* your chances of getting *breast cancer*. And *act* on it."

Even a drug's trade name is an advertisement, enlisting the deep and not always conscious associations of language to tout the drug's wonderful qualities wherever and whenever it's mentioned. Hardly indifferent to this fact, drugmakers put a good deal of effort into inventing brand names, sometimes hiring outside consultants to conduct market research and screen the name for unfortunate connotations in an array of languages. Sildenafil is one thing—but Viagra, with its suggestion of vitality, virility, and the mighty flow of the Niagara, is quite another. According to one report, Lilly's new impotence drug Cialis was derived from the French word for sky, *ciel,* to give users the impression that "the sky's the limit." The alchemy of naming turns the rather awkward atorvastatin into Lipitor, which combines the word for blood fats, "lipid," with a hint of the avenging action hero. And Baycol (a cholesterol reducer withdrawn from the market for safety reasons)—can it be a coincidence that the name invokes a certain tasty (if fatty) breakfast meat?

The fact is, it's not the job of advertising (or "branding," as marketers call it) to educate, to put it all in context. In the Kaiser study, respondents who'd seen an ad for Nexium were more likely to know that heartburn and acid reflux can lead to more serious stomach problems—but did they understand that more often than not, this doesn't happen? And did the ad give them insight into whether this problem affects them personally? It's extremely rate for an ad to give information about a drug's mechanism of action, success rate, or length of treatment, much less about alternative treatments or cost. "Let's pretend that a drug ad is completely accurate," says Bodenheimer. "It doesn't mention that there's an alternative drug that costs ten times less and is just as good."

Defenders of prescription-drug advertising suggest it's all about promoting conversations between patients and their doctors, the only people empowered to write prescriptions. But often patients simply ask for a drug, and doctors see their way clear to giving it. "Believe me there's definitely pressure," says Steinman. "Some patients will be quite insistent. Also there's just a question of time. You're always running late. It's a lot easier to say, 'Sure I'm going to give you that prescription' than to go into a lengthy explanation of why you're not going to give it." One in five consumers surveyed by AARP reported having asked their doctor about a drug the doctor didn't even know about. Few physicians would send a patient off with a script that's potentially dangerous or clearly inappropriate (one doc recalls declining to prescribe a drug for male-pattern baldness to a woman). But most often the decision falls into a "gray area," says Steinman. There might be something cheaper out there, the patient might not need *this* drug—but it's not going to hurt the patient and it'll probably help. Like the availability of free drug samples, consumer ads lower the threshold for prescribing whatever the drug companies happen to be promoting this year.

And like its approach to the doctor, the industry's engagement of consumers is becoming ever more creative, at times straining the limits of good taste, In 2000, Pfizer's adorable "Zithromax zebra," the mascot for an antibiotic used to treat the ubiquitous childhood ear infection, dangled from the stethoscopes of pediatricians and "sponsored" episodes of *Sesame Street*. This drew the fire of media watchdog group Fairness and Accuracy in Reporting, upset over the commercialization of kids' public television. It also irritated some public-health experts, since the ink was hardly dry on a recommendation by the Centers for Disease Control to use a cheaper antibiotic for ear infections. Officials of the U.S. Drug Enforcement Agency (DEA) were taken aback when in 2001, the makers of stimulants to treat kids with attention deficit hyperactivity disorder (ADHD) decided to pitch their new long-acting versions straight to moms via women's magazines and cable TV; this broke with a thirty-year-old voluntary international agreement to abstain from promoting controlled substances—drugs with addictive or abuse potential—to consumers. One DEA policy official told *USA Today* that the campaign, picturing happy kids and smiling mothers, evinced "the mentality of 'mother's little helpers' from the '60s." Likewise, breastfeeding advocates were disturbed to find the logo of a major producer of baby formula on the cover of the American Academy of Pediatrics' *New Mother's Guide to Breastfeeding*. Still others expressed doubts about the appropriateness of a new drug-ad vehicle called the Patient Channel, which would wrap the ads around educational segments about particular conditions and send them into hospital rooms, where patients lay convalescing. File this one under "Really gross, presumably rare": Warner-Lambert (now part of Pfizer) is accused in a whistle-blower lawsuit of promoting an epilepsy drug by, among other things, paying doctors to work as consultants, to participate in clinical trials—and to let drug reps watch while they examined patients, sometimes allowing the reps to make recommendations for treatment, Pfizer has denied many of the changes, which date from before it acquired Warner-Lambert. . . .

POSTSCRIPT

Do Consumers Benefit When Prescription Drugs Are Advertised?

Opponents of prescription drug advertising contend that drug companies' promotions are frequently inaccurate or deceptive. Furthermore, they maintain that drug companies are more interested in increasing their profits, not in truly providing additional medical benefit to the average consumer. Drug companies do not deny that they seek to make profits from their drugs, but they argue that they are offering an important public service by educating consumers about new drugs through their advertisements.

An important issue is whether or not the average consumer is capable of discerning information distributed by pharmaceutical companies. Are people without a background in medicine, medical terminology, or research methods sufficiently knowledgeable to understand literature disseminated by drug companies? With the help of the Internet and other media, prescription drug advertising proponents maintain that the average consumer is capable of understanding information about various drugs. On the other hand, will most people take the time to follow up on drugs they see advertised?

Some critics argue that restricting drug advertisements is a moot point because consumers cannot obtain prescriptions without the approval of their physicians. Yet, in numerous instances, physicians acquiesce to the wishes of their patients and write prescriptions upon their request. If patients receive prescriptions that are not appropriate for their needs, who is responsible: the patient, the physician, or the drug manufacturer and advertiser?

When drug manufacturers introduce a new drug, they get a patent on the drug to protect their investment. Drug companies, therefore, receive financial rewards for introducing new drugs. Of course, drug companies also take financial risks when developing new drugs. However, some critics maintain that many of these new drugs are merely "me-too" drugs that are similar to existing drugs and that they do not provide any additional benefit. Are consumers being fooled into requesting more expensive drugs that are no better than drugs already on the market?

Two excellent articles that explore the benefits of prescription drug advertising are "Americans Find Prescription Drug Advertising Helpful, Survey Says," in *Biotech Business Week* (March 1, 2004) and "Media and Message Effects on DTC Prescription Drug Print Advertising Awareness," by Martin S. Roth in *Journal of Advertising Research* (June 2003). Other articles that address this issue are "Promotion of Prescription Drugs to Consumers," by Meredith Rosenthal and associates, *The New England Journal of Medicine* (February 14, 2002), "What You Should Know about Direct-to-Consumer Advertising of Prescription Drugs," by David E. Dukes, James F. Rogers and Eric A Paine, *Defense*

Counsel Journal (January 2001), and "The Direct-to-Consumer Advertising Dilemma" by Anne B. Brown in *Patient Care* (March 30, 2001). Finally, whether or not Great Britain will allow direct-to-consumer advertising is discussed in "Consumer Choice or Chaos?" in *Chemist and Druggist* (June 10, 2000).

National Clearinghouse for Alcohol and Drug Information (NCADI)

Information regarding a variety of drugs as well as research published by the federal government are available through this site. Up-to-date developments in drug use are available through NCADI.

http://www.health.org

Narcotics Anonymous

This site provides information on Narcotics Anonymous groups, which are structured similar to the 12-step model of Alcoholics Anonymous.

http://www.na.org

The Weiner Nusim Foundation

This private foundation located in Connecticut publishes information regarding drug education. The information is free.

http://www.weinernusim.com

DrugHelp

This site, a service of the American Council for Drug Education (an affiliate of Phoenix House Foundation), provides information, counsel, and referral to treatment centers.

http://www.drughelp.org

Partnership for a Drug-Free America

Extensive information on the effects of drugs and the extent of drug use by young people is available at this Web site.

http://www.drugfreeamerica.org

American Lung Association

The American Lung Association Web site contains includes numerous statistics on teen smoking.

http://www.lungUSA.org

National Council on Alcoholism and Drug Dependence

This site contains objective information and referral for individuals, families, and others seeking intervention and treatment.

http://www.ncadd.org

PART 3

Drug Prevention and Treatment

*I*n spite of their legal consequences and the government's interdiction efforts, drugs are widely available and used. Two common ways of dealing with drug abuse is to incarcerate drug users and to intercept drugs before they enter the country. However, many drug experts believe that more energy should be put into preventing and treating drug abuse. An important step toward prevention and treatment is to find out what contributes to drug abuse and how to nullify these factors.

By educating young people about the potential hazards of drugs and by developing an awareness of social influences that contribute to drug use, many drug-related problems may be averted. The debates in this section focus on different prevention and treatment issues such as the effect that tobacco advertisements have on smoking behavior, whether schools should drug-test students, and the effectiveness of drug abuse treatment.

- Does Secondhand Smoke Endanger the Health of Nonsmokers?

- Is Alcoholism Hereditary?

- Should Moderate Alcohol Consumption Be Encouraged?

- Should Schools Drug-Test Students?

- Does Drug Abuse Treatment Work?

- Do Tobacco Advertisements Influence People to Smoke?

ISSUE 14

Does Secondhand Smoke Endanger the Health of Nonsmokers?

YES: Georgina Lovell, from "Secondhand Smoke—Firsthand Pollution: Tiny Smokestacks Poison a Room," *You Are the Target. Big Tobacco: Lies, Scams—Now The Truth* (Chryan Communications, 2002)

NO: J.B. Copas and J.Q. Shi, from "Reanalysis of Epidemiological Evidence on Lung Cancer and Passive Smoking," *British Medical Journal* (February 12, 2000)

ISSUE SUMMARY

YES: Author Georgina Lovell argues that secondhand smoke is the third-leading cause of preventable disease, disability, and death in the United States. Secondhand smoke, according to Lovell, is never totally removed from any indoor room. Moreover, secondhand smoke has greater levels of poisons than the smoke inhaled by smokers through a filtered tip of a cigarette.

NO: Statisticians J. B. Copas and J.Q. Shi argue that research demonstrating that secondhand smoke is harmful is biased. They contend that many journals are more likely to publish articles if secondhand smoke is shown to be deleterious and that the findings of many studies exaggerate the adverse effects of secondhand smoke.

T he movement to restrict secondhand smoke—the smoke that a person breathes in from another person's cigarette, cigar, or pipe—is growing. Smoking is banned on all commercial airplane flights within the continental United States. Canada, Australia, and many other countries have enacted similar bans. Smoking is prohibited or restricted in all federal public areas and workplaces. The right to smoke in public places is quickly being eliminated. Is this fair, considering tobacco's addictive hold over smokers? Former surgeon general C. Everett Koop and many researchers point out that smoking is an addiction that is as difficult to overcome as an addiction to cocaine or heroin. Should smokers be penalized—prevented from smoking or isolated from nonsmokers—for having a nicotine addiction?

Articles describing passive smoking or secondhand smoking can be confusing because several terms frequently are used to describe it. *Passive smoking* has been referred to as involuntary smoking, and the smoke itself has been identified as both *secondhand smoke* and *environmental tobacco smoke*, or *ETS*. Secondhand smoke can be further broken down into *mainstream smoke* and *sidestream smoke*. Mainstream smoke is the smoke that the smoker exhales. Sidestream smoke is the smoke comes off the end of the tobacco product as it burns. Sidestream smoke has higher concentrations of carbon monoxide and other gases than mainstream smoke. Scientists also believe that sidestream smoke contains more carcinogens than mainstream smoke.

The issue of passive smoking is extremely divisive. On one side of the debate are the nonsmokers, who strongly believe that their rights to clean air are compromised by smokers. Their objections are based on more than aesthetics; it is not simply a matter of smoke being unsightly, noxious, or inconvenient. Nonsmokers are becoming more concerned about the toxic effects of secondhand smoke. Groups of nonsmokers and numerous health professionals have initiated a massive campaign to educate the public on the array of health-related problems that have been associated with secondhand smoke.

On the other side are smokers, who believe that they should have the right to smoke whenever and wherever they wish. This group is backed by the tobacco industry, which has allocated vast sums of money and resources to conduct research studies on the effects of secondhand smoke. Based on the results of these studies, smoking rights groups claim that the health concerns related to secondhand smoke are based on emotion, not on scientific evidence. They argue that there are too many variables involved to determine the exact impact of secondhand smoke. For example, to what extent does a polluted environment or a poorly ventilated house contribute to the health problems attributed to secondhand smoke? These groups maintain any studies concluding that secondhand smoke is harmful are questionable.

Many smokers who acknowledge that smoking may have adverse effects on health argue that their freedoms should not be limited. They feel that they should have the right to engage in behaviors that affect only themselves, even if those behaviors are unhealthy. Some smokers reason that if smoking behavior is regulated, perhaps other personal behaviors also will become regulated. They fight against the regulation of smoking because they believe that behavior regulation is a potentially harmful trend.

If smoking is restricted, many people employed in the tobacco industry may lose their livelihoods. What may be a health benefit for some people may be detrimental to the economic health of others. Are the people who want to restrict smoking willing to help those individuals who would be economically affected by such a restriction?

In the following sections, Georgina Lovell stresses that the dangers associated with secondhand smoke are clear. Secondhand smoke, says Lovell, causes medical conditions ranging from sudden infant death syndrome to asthma to lung cancer. J. B. Copas and J. Q. Shi maintain that much of the information about the health hazards of secondhand smoke has been distorted and accepted as fact without adequate critical questioning.

Georgina Lovell  **YES**

Second Hand Smoke—Firsthand Pollution: Tiny Smokestacks Poison a Room, You Are the Target, Big Tobacco: Lies, Scams—Now the Truth

Tobacco industry commentary prefers to label secondhand smoke as *environmental tobacco smoke* (ETS), trivializing what it is: a substance known to cause cancer in humans. Use of the word "environmental" implies indigenous and natural conditions. There is nothing natural or acceptable about the toxic waste produced as the by-product of combustion from a lighted cigarette, pipe or cigar.

Nine out of ten pediatricians said cigarette smoke is the greatest environmental contributor to the number and/or severity of diseases and conditions among their patients.

Secondhand smoke is the third leading cause of preventable disease, disability and death in the U.S.; the second is alcohol use; the first is active smoking.

Because the organic material in tobacco doesn't burn completely, cigarette smoke contains more than 4,700 chemical compounds, including carbon monoxide, ammonia, formaldehyde, benzene and arsenic. Of these, 43 are known to cause cancer.

Tobacco smoke poses two serious problems in an enclosed indoor space. Firstly, ventilation can only limit peak concentration and cannot be increased beyond what is cost effective. Based on random samples taken during a research project in Washington, D.C. metropolitan areas, 19 micro environments (bingo halls, bowling alleys, etc.) were studied where smokers smoked. Two-thirds of these locations were out of compliance with ventilation rates much less than local codes.

As a conservative average, at least one cigarette will be constantly burning for every three smokers in a room. A condensed and very basic explanation of Einstein's *gedanken* experiment illustrates why toxic tobacco smoke can never be completely removed from any indoor room. Steady generation of tobacco smoke in a room of smokers can be compared to a bathtub filled to capacity, drain open, and a steady flow of water into the tub to maintain the equilibrium. Water drains from the bathtub at the same rate as it is being filled, and the water level in the bathtub remains constant. Slowly add a big bottle of India ink to the water in the bathtub, causing the water to darken. During this ongoing process, the color of the water will become lighter, but will never clear completely.

Substitute a room of air for the water in the bathtub of water, and substitute tobacco smoke for the India ink in this analogy, and you have a simplified illustration of the mechanics of ventilation systems. Limited control can be achieved in raising and lowering concentration of tobacco smoke in the room, depending on how much ventilation is installed—and utilized—but the tobacco smoke will never be completely eliminated.

Solutions embracing increases in ventilation, the argument typically presented by the tobacco cartel, use an unrealistic hypothetical situation where inhabitants of a room remain stationery, do not increase in number, and limit their smoking to only one cigarette burning at any given time for every three smokers.

A ventilation engineer designs the system to comply with standards in ventilation codes specifying so many cubic feet per minute, per occupant. Except in the State of California, no requirement exists in the U.S. to ensure ongoing operation of the installed system according to specifications. Canadian requirements vary and remain difficult if not impossible to monitor. Complicated and expensive research becomes necessary to determine whether ventilation systems are being utilized according to code. The moment the scientist completes such research studies, no guarantees exist such a system will continue to be used in compliance with standards. Secondly, tobacco smoke conforms to the scientific definition of a toxic and carcinogenic chemical, and appears on the national list of carcinogens posted by the U.S. National Toxicology Program, on the same list as asbestos, arsenic and mustard gas for which no safe level of exposure exists.

Hands up, how many smokers would like to volunteer to go into a room where mustard gas, arsenic and asbestos are in use, or have recently been used? Tobacco smoke is no different in its toxicity. It also leaves a residue of toxic waste containing gases and particles on the ceiling, walls, floor and in the ventilation system. It is toxic waste. Smokers "choose" to inhale Class A carcinogens directly into their lungs on average of ten times with each cigarette smoked. The majority of the population whose preference is to remain smoke-free become unwillingly exposed to these poisons unless smoke-free ordinances protect them.

Until recent years, tobacco smoke exposure had been the norm. Many boomers' grew up with one or more smoking parents and remained ignorant of the information known by the tobacco industry about the toxic effects of secondhand smoke on nonsmokers—information the tobacco industry carefully and deliberately kept secret from the general public for many decades, until a court order forced them to disclose their research documents. Tobacco reacted by producing lists of additional dangerous commonplace substances in a transparent attempt to normalize involuntary exposure to tobacco smoke. Their soundbytes proclaiming the dangers of exhaust fumes, barbeques and perfume in elevators do nothing to alter the inherent danger of tobacco smoke. When challenged, tobacco spokespeople solemnly ruminate over global disasters such as earthquakes, floods and nuclear accidents, suggesting the smoke-free who want protection from secondhand smoke concentrate, instead, on more pressing issues. People typically discount risks with which they are familiar, and disproportionately fear risks with which they are unfamiliar.

Tobacco vindicators' tunnel vision believes only one social issue can be addressed at a time and for them, predictably, tobacco has the lowest priority. Drunk driving, drug use by teens and domestic violence—which, combined, do not claim as many lives each year as tobacco—absorb tobacco supporters' total focus, leaving no time or energy to address the health outcome of tobacco use and involuntary exposure to secondhand smoke. In comical contradiction, a prominent concern always mentioned in defense of unrestricted smoking is the "real pollution" caused by vehicle exhaust, barbeques and campfires. Their list of what-about's grows ever long, while the health consequences of passive smoking remain as serious as they've ever been.

Meanwhile, tobacco's only agenda continues to be normalization of the bizarre behavior of placing a tube of dried leaves in the mouth, and setting it on fire for the sole purpose of sucking smoke directly into the lungs on average of 200 times each day for the pack a day smoker.

> *"Children can leave the room if they are bothered by smoke.* Reminded that infants cannot leave, he responded, *"When they are older, they can crawl away.*
>
> —Mike Harper, the former CEO of R. J. Reynolds Tobacco, answered a shareholder's question in 1996 about smoking around children. (Minnesota Smoke-Free Coalition, *In Their Own Words*)

James Repace, M.Sc. and Science Policy Analyst and Staff Scientist at the U.S. Environmental Protection Agency from 1979–1998, has set out in an international campaign to monitor exposure to tobacco smoke effectively. This doesn't mean going into restaurants, bars and workplaces to measure smoke levels, but to measure levels of the nicotine, metabolite, cotinine, in bodily fluids. Results of his research confirm the exposure of the general public to tobacco smoke exceeds general opinion. The level of air pollution can be back calculated from cotinine levels and his Hong Kong study confirmed that with only one exception, every single restaurant waiter in that study violated the U.S. Environmental Protection Agency standards of air quality, both for the annual and the twenty-four hour standards. Tobacco apologists argue cotinine levels can be affected by nicotine content in some vegetables. To detect the equivalent cotinine concentrations present in children from households where two or more family members smoke, 90 kilograms (198 lbs.) of raw tomatoes would have to be eaten *every day*.

Tobacco smoke is a regulated air pollutant in terms of its impact on the lungs on fine particle concentrations in the air, and it violates all EPA standards.

Clean air never exists in any room where people are smoking. Second-hand smoke contains higher concentrations of poisons than those inhaled by smokers through a filter tip. Secondhand smoke means firsthand pollution.

Secondhand Smoke Exposure Is a Type of Child Abuse

James Gabarino, Director of Cornell University's Family Life Development Centre, says "More young children are killed by parental smoking than by all unintentional injuries combined. Let's call it what it is: Parental smoking is child abuse."

Pregnant women who smoke and nonsmoking pregnant women exposed daily to tobacco smoke are more likely to have low birth weight babies at risk for death and disease in infancy and early childhood.

Nursing mothers who smoke can pass along harmful chemicals from cigarettes to their babies in breast milk.

More than one-third (35 percent) of all deaths from Sudden Infant Death Syndrome (SIDS) are due to maternal tobacco use. U.S. Children are three times more likely to die from SIDS caused by maternal smoking than die from homicide or child abuse.

Children of parents who smoke have a higher prevalence of symptoms of respiratory irritation such as cough, phlegm, and wheeze.

Exposure to secondhand smoke substantially increases the risk of lower respiratory tract infections, and is responsible for an estimated 350,000 cases of bronchitis and 152,000 cases of pneumonia annually or 16 percent of all lung infections in U.S. children under the age of five.

Involuntary exposure to tobacco smoke is responsible for an estimated 1.2 million ear infections each year in the United States, or approximately 7 percent of the total.

Children exposed to household smoking are at greater risk of requiring surgery for recurrent ear infections or tonsillitis; an estimated 86,000 tube insertions (14 percent of the total) and 18,000 tonsillectomies/adenoidectomies (removal of the tonsils or adenoids—20 percent of the total) each year in the United States are attributable to secondhand smoke.

Secondhand smoke exposure is associated with higher risk of developing asthma and more frequent and severe asthma attacks in children who already have the disease. Each year in the United States, an estimated 11 percent of all asthma cases and more than half a million physician visits for asthma are due to smoking in the home.

Exposure to the smoking of one or both parents has also been shown to be a highly important predictor of smoking among adolescents.

It takes more than three hours to remove 95 percent of the smoke from one cigarette from the room once smoking has ended.

Secondhand Smoke and Custody Decisions

In divorce agreements, the corollary to a smoking parent who remains deluded about the harm caused by exposure to secondhand smoke is court ordered visitation restriction and in extreme cases, denial of parental rights.

In an alarming number of cases, parents place the gratification of their addiction to nicotine above not only the welfare of their child, but also jeopardize their custody rights. Court orders have been required before some smoking parents stop exposing their children to secondhand smoke. Some custody decisions influenced by parental exposure to secondhand smoke:

1988, Roofeh v. Roofeh, (NY Family Ct., Nassau County, Mineola) Mr. Jahanshah Roofeh's attorney, Stephen W. Schlissel of Mineola, NY's Ruskin, Schlissel, Moscou, Evans & Faltischek, P.C.; Ms. Elizabeth Roofeh represented by Joel R. Brandes of Garden City, NY. Nassau County Judge Ralph Diamond in Mineola issued order forbidding Elizabeth to smoke in front of her husband and three children. Ms. Roofeh was also directed to confine her cigarette smoking to a small television room in the couple's Kings Point mansion.

1988, Reeves v. Reeves, Pricilla Bullock (married name Reeves) complained about a judge's order restricting her from smoking in confined areas around her four-year-old son. Fourth Circuit Court Judge Bill Swann made the ruling and said his decision was based on the child's welfare Swann granted a request by the ex-husband's lawyer to prohibit her from smoking around the child in a confined environment, such as the home or in an automobile. {Knoxville News-Sentinel, 6/4/88}

1989, Badeau v. Badeau, (LA). In LaPlace, LA, an appeals court upheld a lower court decision reducing a father's visitation rights because his smoking aggravated his child's bronchial problem.

> "I was overwhelmed about the amount of information there was that the rest of us didn't know . . . The documents I reviewed had 'secret' stamped all over them."
>
> —Dr. Richard Hurt, Director of the Mayo Clinic's Nicotine
> Dependence Center

1989, in Denton, MD, a judge placed a three-year-old girl with severe asthma in a foster home because her parents ignored medical advice to protect the child from their tobacco smoke. {WSJ, 10/18/90}

1990, De Beni Souza v. Kallweit (Sacramento, CA, August) Judge David Stirling ordered a woman (Anna Maria de Beni Souza) not to smoke in front of her five-year-old son; judge issued the ruling at the request of the boy's father, Manfred Kallweit, who had complained of health risks associated with inhaling secondhand smoke.

1991, Robert Strathmann v. Linda Foster Judge Stephanie Domitrovich ordered that there will be no smoking in the natural father's home for at least 48 hours before children are to visit. The natural father shall provide a smoke-free environment for all of the children while he is exercising his partial custody with them. Natural mother shall also provide a smokefree environment.

1991, Mitchell v. Mitchell In this divorce case, the court refused to return custody of an asthmatic child to the mother although the mother had joined a smoking cessation program. The father had been awarded custody because the child suffered from asthma, and despite the pediatrician's advice, the mother and grandmother had not stopped smoking. The trial judge had found that the failure of the mother and grandmother to stop smoking was strong evidence of lack of proper concern for the welfare of the child.

1991, Brett Lee Bryant/Department of Social Services v. Wakely, et al. The Michigan Court of Appeals upheld the decision of a Civil Court that placement with a grandmother who smoked would not be in a child's best interest. The child had serious respiratory problems and it was highly recommended that he live in close proximity to a hospital in Traverse City (where his grandparents were unable to relocate) and that he should live in a smokefree environment.

1991, Lamacchia v. Lamacchia Temporary order that neither parent will smoke in front of their three-year-old son who suffers from lung ailments.

1992, Sulva v. Isaacson (IL) Judge William Ward signed an order barring Isaacson from smoking when he visited his son. It was the first time in Illinois history that such an order has been signed. Alex, the son, suffers from bronchitis and it was alleged that his father's smoking might aggravate his condition. The order meant that to have a smoke this father by court order, will either have to abstain or leave his apartment every other weekend from about 9:30 a.m. Saturday to 6:30 p.m. Sunday, as well as for about a month during the summer when he has his son for visitation. One smoke in front of his son could lead to a contempt of court finding and a jail sentence of up to 6 months.

1993, Masone v. Tanner A county judge granted a nonsmoking father's request to remove an 8-year-old girl from the custody of her mother, his ex-wife. The child had only 43 percent of her breathing capacity because the mother continued to violate an earlier court order, obtained five years ago, that she not smoke around or near the child. The smoking continued until the child had an asthma attack and a doctor stated that she would end-up in an emergency room if her exposure to tobacco smoke continued. The child was placed in the custody of her grandmother.

1993, Montufar v. Navot Judge Orlando granted post-judgment relief to a nonsmoking father whose child, aged ten, was exposed to tobacco smoke by his mother and maternal relatives and suffered adverse effects. The order stated that the custodial mother shall provide the child a complete smokefree environment in the home in which he resides. There must be no smoking by other residents or by visitors. All smoking must be carried on outdoors. The custodial mother is also under obligation to take all reasonable steps in assuring that the child is not unduly exposed to secondhand smoke. The custodial mother must remove the child from any situation or location where he is exposed to passive smoke. As far as the grandparents are concerned (they live close to the mother) the order compels the mother to remove the child from the grandparents' presence if they are smoking. There is to be no smoking in any vehicle in which the child is a passenger.

National Toxicology Program Classification of Tobacco Smoke and Secondhand Smoke

In May 2000, the U.S. National Toxicology included Environmental Tobacco Smoke, Smoking and Smokeless Tobacco on its list in its biennial *Report on Carcinogens* ("RoC"). This report outlines individual substances, mixtures of chemicals, or exposure circumstances which are known to be human carcinogens or which may reasonably be anticipated to be human carcinogens; it also contains information received from other federal agencies relating to estimated exposures and exposure standards or guidelines.

The National Toxicology Program Report on Carcinogens (*RoC*) classified secondhand smoke, smoking and smokeless tobacco in the same category as benzene, mustard gas, asbestos and arsenic.

Environmental tobacco smoke—Environmental tobacco smoke, generated from sidestream and exhaled mainstream smoke of cigarettes, pipes, and cigars is listed as a known human carcinogen. The *RoC* indicates this listing is based on the observed causal relationship between passive exposure to tobacco smoke and human lung cancer. The listing states that there are conclusive published studies that indicate increased risk of lung cancer in nonsmoking women living with smoking husbands or working with smoking co-workers.

Tobacco smoking—Tobacco smoking (i.e. directly inhaled tobacco smoke) is listed as a known human carcinogen. Cigarette smoking has been known to cause cancer in humans for many years, and is now considered to be the leading preventable cause of cancer in developed countries. Separate chemicals identified in tobacco smoke were already listed as carcinogens in the *RoC*. The new listing of tobacco smoking is the result of the 1996 revision in the review process that allows for the review and listing of exposure circumstances in the *RoC*.

Predictably, tobacco front groups claim secondhand smoke, smoking and smokeless tobacco also appear on the same list as "sunshine", once again illustrating their lack of understanding between "sunshine" and carcinogenic solar UV radiation and exposure to sunlamps and sunbeds. If only a parallel to sunblock cream existed to block out the harmful effects of secondhand smoke!

> "What the smoker does to himself may be his business, but what the smoker does to the non-smoker is quite a different matter. . . . six out of ten believe that smoking is hazardous to the nonsmoker's health, up sharply over the last four years. . . This we see as the most dangerous development yet to the viability of the tobacco industry that has yet occurred. . . The issue, as we see it, is no longer what the smoker does to himself, but what he does to others." "[Philip Morris' world-wide strategy is to] coordinate and pay so many scientists on an international basis to keep the environmental tobacco smoke controversy alive."
>
> —(Roper Organization. A Study of Public Attitudes toward Cigarette Smoking and the Tobacco Industry in 1978. Vol. 1. Roper Organization, 1978)

Smoke-free Workplace Safety

Riddle: How many employers insist their staff must involuntarily be exposed to dangerous limits of heavy metals, Class A Carcinogens and poisons not allowed to be dumped in sanitary landfill sites?

Answer: All those employers who receive funding from the tobacco industry to resist clean indoor air ordinances.

In addition to the toxicity of individual chemicals contained in tobacco smoke, the chemicals contained in tobacco smoke interact with each other, enhancing and increasing toxicity and carcinogenicity. Many of the poisons contained in secondhand smoke do not need to be inhaled to cause harm. They are absorbed through the skin, and include the following:

Chemicals in Secondhand Smoke (Absorbed Through Skin Contact) Carcinogenic to Humans:

4-Aminobiphenyl has been called one of the most potent known bladder carcinogens and absorption occurs through the skin.

Benzene is known to cause leukemia in humans, produce chromosomal aberrations and can take 2–50 years to manifest following exposure. Benzene exposure occurs in absorption through the skin.

2-Aminonaphthalene causes cancer in humans and is absorbed both by inhalation and through the skin.

Vinyl Chloride causes lung and liver cancer in humans. It is readily absorbed through the skin.

Cadmium, Nickel and Polonium-210 (Radon) are also present in secondhand smoke. Exposure to these chemicals through inhalation causes cancer in humans.

Chemicals in Secondhand Smoke (Absorbed Through the Skin) Possibly and Probably Carcinogenic to Humans

1-Aminonaphthalene used industrially for dyes and weed control has been shown to cause lung, liver and leukemia cancers in animals. Absorption through the skin can occur without any irritation or other warning.

Acetaldehyde Animal studies in which pregnant rats were exposed found that acetaldehyde gave birth to offspring with growth retardation, malformation, delayed bone growth and stillbirth. Small amounts of acetaldehyde irritates the eyes, skin and respiratory tract of humans and animals.

Acetone is a irritant to eyes, nose and throat and causes liver damage. Absorption occurs through inhalation and skin contact.

Acrylonitrile is suspected to cause cancer in humans, and is similar to cyanide in toxicity. Acrylonitrile is also known as vinyl cyanide. Pregnant animals exposed to acrylonitrile showed significant maternal toxicity and increase in deformed fetuses and offspring. It is absorbed from the respiratory and gastrointestinal tract and through skin contact.

Benzo[a]pyrene has been found to cause cancer in animals and fish in every study to date. Absorption occurs through inhalation and through skin contact. When combined with catechol (also in tobacco smoke), the result is co-carcinogenic.

Cresol promotes tumors in mice, and long term human exposure results in headaches, nausea, vomiting and impaired kidney function, it is absorbed through the skin.

Lead is known to cause cancer in animals, and is soluble in body fluids when inhaled. Lead poisoning effects on the brain may not be reversible, and long term exposure may lead to kidney disease.

Phenol damages the lungs and central nervous system, irritates the skin, mucous membranes and eyes of humans. It is absorbed by inhalation and through the skin.

Quinoline causes genetic mutations and prolonged exposure causes liver damage and nosebleeds. Absorption occurs by inhalation and through the skin.

"Carcinogens are found in practically every class of compounds in smoke . . . flavor substances and carcinogenic substances come from the same classes, in many instances."

—Confidential Philip Morris report *Tobacco and Health Research & Development Approach page seventeen November 15, 1961 Bates number 2024947191*

NO ↵

J. B. Copas and J. Q. Shi

Reanalysis of Epidemiological Evidence on Lung Cancer and Passive Smoking

Objective   To assess the epidemiological evidence for an increase in the risk of lung cancer resulting from exposure to environmental tobacco smoke.

Design   Reanalysis of 37 published epidemiological studies previously included in a meta-analysis allowing for the possibility of publication bias.

Main outcome measure   Relative risk of lung cancer among female lifelong non-smokers, according to whether her partner was a current smoker or a lifelong non-smoker.

Results   If it is assumed that all studies that have ever been carried out are included, or that those selected for review are truly representative of all such studies, then the estimated excess risk of lung cancer is 24%, as previously reported (95% confidence interval 13% to 36%, P < 0.001). However, a significant correlation between study outcome and study size suggests the presence of publication bias. Adjustment for such bias implies that the risk has been overestimated. For example, if only 60% of studies have been included, the estimate of excess risk falls from 24% to 15%.

Conclusion   A modest degree of publication bias leads to a substantial reduction in the relative risk and to a weaker level of significance, suggesting that the published estimate of the increased risk of lung cancer associated with environmental tobacco smoke needs to be interpreted with caution.

Introduction

Exposure to environmental tobacco smoke (passive smoking) is widely accepted to increase the risk of lung cancer, but different epidemiological studies have produced varying estimates of the size of the relative risk. Hackshaw et al. reviewed the results of 37 such studies that estimated the relative risk of lung cancer among female lifelong non-smokers, comparing those whose spouses (or

From J. B. Copas and J. Q. Shi, "Reanalysis of Epidemiological Evidence on Lung Cancer and Passive Smoking," *British Medical Journal,* vol. 320 (February 12, 2000). Copyright © 2000 by The BMJ Publishing Group. Reprinted by permission. Notes omitted.

partners) were current smokers with those whose spouses had never smoked.[1] Of the 37 studies, 31 reported an increase in risk, and the increase was significant in seven studies. The remaining six studies reported negative results, but none of these was significant. Pooling these results using a method which allows for statistical heterogeneity between studies, Hackshaw et al concluded that there is an overall excess risk of 24% (95% confidence interval 13% to 36%).[1] This is strong epidemiological evidence for an association between lung cancer and passive smoking (P < 0.001).

The approach used by Hackshaw et al does not allow for the possibility of publication bias—that is, the possibility that published studies, particularly smaller ones, will be biased in favour of more positive results. We reanalysed the results and looked for evidence of publication bias.

Methods and Results

. . . [T]he relative risks from the 37 epidemiological studies analysed by Hackshaw et al[1] [were] plotted against a measure of the uncertainty in that relative risk. This uncertainty (s) decreases as the size of the study increases so that large studies are on the left of the plot and small studies on the right. The plot shows a trend for smaller studies to give more positive results than the larger studies (correlation = 0.35, P < 0.05, or P = 0.012 by Egger's test[2]). This graph is similar to the funnel plot used in the meta-analysis of clinical trials, when a trend such as this is interpreted as a sign of publication bias.[3] This bias arises when a study is more likely to be written up and submitted to a journal and more likely to be accepted for publication if it reports positive results than if its results are inconclusive or negative. Since it is reasonable to assume that publication is more likely for larger (small s) than smaller (large s) studies, the problem of publication bias will be most evident among the smaller studies, as suggested by the figure. By "publication" we mean the whole process of selecting a study for review.

We reanalysed the results of the 37 epidemiological studies to allow for the trend evident in the figure. Our method describes the apparent relation between relative risk and study size by a curve. This gives a good fit to the observed points. The basic idea of the method is that there is no real relation between study outcome and study size, the relation that we observe is simply an artefact of the process of selecting these studies.

Our method has been published,[4] and further details are available from us on request. The estimated average relative risk depends on a statistical parameter that can be interpreted as the probability that a paper with a certain value of s is published (publication probability). If the publication probability is 1, all papers are published and so there is no possibility of publication bias; the relative risk is then estimated as 1.24 (24% risk excess), agreeing as expected with Hackshaw et al's result.[1] But smaller values of publication probability give smaller estimates of relative risk. We do not know how many unpublished studies have been carried out. Therefore there is no way of estimating the publication probability from any data: all we know is that there is a significant correlation in the funnel plot, so that some degree of publication bias is needed to explain this trend.

Table 1

Estimated Relative Risk and Number of Unpublished Smaller and Larger Studies for Various Values of Publication Probability

Publication probability	Relative risk (95% CI)	P value	No of unpublished studies (*)	
			Small	Large
0.6	1.11 (0.97 to 1.27)	0.110	36	24
0.7	1.13 (1.00 to 1.27)	0.052	23	15
0.8	1.15 (1.03 to 1.28)	0.014	14	9
0.9	1.18 (1.07 to 1.31)	0.002	7	4
n	1.24 (1.13 to 1.36)	<0.001	0	0

(*) Smaller studies s > 0.4; larger studies s [is less than or equal to] 0.4.

Table 1 gives the estimated relative risk for values of publication probability between 0.6 and 1, together with 95% confidence intervals and P values. The P value is less than 5% only when the publication probability is more than about 0.7. The indirect estimate of 19% excess risk derived from studies on biochemical markers (table 5 of Hackshaw et al's paper[1]) agrees with the epidemiological analysis when the publication probability is about 0.9.

For any given value of publication probability it is possible to estimate the number of studies which have been undertaken but not published. This is shown in the final two columns of Table 1. If the publication probability is 0.8 then there are a total of 23 unpublished studies so that the 37 selected ones represent a sample of 37/60 = 62% of all such studies that have been undertaken. If this is the case, then the excess risk is likely to be closer to 15% than 24%. . . .

Conclusions

Although the trend . . . seems clear, Bero et al suggest that the number of unpublished studies is unlikely to be large,[5] and so the problem of publication bias may be less severe here than in systematic reviews of other aspects of medicine. However, the possibility of publication bias cannot be ruled out altogether, and at least some publication bias is needed to explain the trend we found. Our results show that the publication probability does not have to fall much below 1.0 before there is quite a substantial reduction in the estimated risk.

References

1. Hackshaw AK, Law MR, Wald NJ. The accumulated evidence on lung cancer and environmental tobacco smoke. BMJ 1997;315:980–988.
2. Egger M, Smith GD, Schneider M, Minder C. Bias in meta-analysis detected by a simple graphical test. BMJ 1997;315:629–634.

3.   Egger M, Smith GD. Misleading meta-analysis. BMJ 1995;310:752–754.

4.   Copas JB. What works; selectivity models and meta analysis. J R Stat Soc Am 1999; 162:95–109.

5.   Bero LA, Glantz SA, Rennie D. Publication bias and public health policy on environmental tobacco smoke. JAMA 1994;272:133–136.

POSTSCRIPT

Does Secondhand Smoke Endanger the Health of Nonsmokers?

In today's health-conscious society, many people seem to be more aware of what they eat, whether or not they get enough exercise, if they get an adequate amount of sleep, and how much stress they experience. Thus, it is only logical that people also are concerned about possible environmental threats to their health, such as secondhand smoke.

Whether or not secondhand smoke is injurious to nonsmokers is relevant because many businesses have adopted policies and many cities and states have passed laws based on the premise that secondhand smoke is a significant health risk. A number of states restrict smoking in the workplace; most shopping malls prohibit smoking; the military has banned or restricted smoking in many of its facilities; and numerous restaurants forbid smoking in their establishments. New York City and other cities have even banned smoking in bars. Many colleges prohibit smoking in residence halls.

The issue of smoking also has become a point of contention in child custody cases. It has been argued that parents who smoke around their children are unfit parents. Is smoking around children a form of child abuse? Should parental smoking be a consideration in children custody cases? If one thinks that smoking around children is abusive, then would overfeeding children or using television as a babysitter also be considered child abuse?

Increasingly, smokers are being isolated in society; they are almost pictured as social outcasts. There appears to be a growing contempt and disdain shown toward smokers. The emotionality of this issue often puts smokers on the defensive. This confrontational stance is not conducive to addressing the issue of smokers' rights in a constructive way.

A report released by the Environmental Protection Agency (EPA) links environmental tobacco smoke (ETS) to lung cancer and heart disease in nonsmokers and to respiratory infections in children. The report states that passive smoking is responsible for an estimated 3,000 lung cancer deaths annually in adults, as many as 300,000 childhood cases of bronchitis and pneumonia, and between 8,000 and 26,000 new cases of asthma in children. Although groups in support of restricting environmental tobacco smoke cite the EPA's report as evidence for their position, the report has been criticized for exaggerating and distorting the harmful effects of passive smoke.

The effects of secondhand smoke are studied in "Adverse Health Effects of Prenatal and Postnatal Tobacco Smoke Exposure on Children" by W. Hofhuis, J. C. de Jongste, and P. J. Merkus (*Archives of Disease in Childhood*, December 2003). F. D. Galliland and associates examined the role of secondhand smoke on schoolchildren in "Environmental Tobacco Smoke and Absenteeism Related to Respiratory Illness in Schoolchildren," (*American Journal of Epidemiology*, May 15, 2003). "Second Hand Smoke and Risk Assessment: What Was in It for the Tobacco Industry?" by Norbert Hirschhorn and Stella A. Bialous in *Tobacco Control* (December 2001) addresses how the tobacco industry tries to refute the claims regarding the harms related to secondhand smoke. An overview of the government's position and that of the tobacco industry on the issue of passive smoking is discussed in Elisa Ong and Stanton Glantz's article "Tobacco Industry Efforts Subverting International Agency for Research on Cancer's Second-Hand Smoke Study," *The Lancet* (April 8, 2000).

ISSUE 15

Is Alcoholism Hereditary?

YES: National Institute on Alcohol Abuse and Alcoholism,
from "The Genetics of Alcoholism," *Alcohol Alert* (July 2003)

NO: Grazyna Zajdow, from "Alcoholism's Unnatural History:
Alcoholism Is Not a 'Health' Issue, But One of Personal and Existential
Pain. Recognising This Would Force Us to Acknowledge One of the
Most Successful Methods of Dealing With Alcohol Addiction," *Arena
Magazine* (April–May 2004)

ISSUE SUMMARY

YES: The National Institute on Alcohol Abuse and Alcoholism
(NIAAA) contends that heredity plays a large role in the development of alcoholism. Family environment may play a role in whether
one becomes an alcoholic, but individuals inherit characteristics that
increase the possibility of developing alcoholism. The NIAAA notes
that identical twins are twice as likely to become alcoholic as fraternal twins.

NO: Grazyna Zajdow, a lecturer in sociology at Deakin University,
maintains that the concept of alcoholism results from a social construct of what it means to be alcoholic. Because alcoholism is a social
stigma, it is viewed as a disease rather than as a condition caused by
personal and existential pain. Environmental conditions, especially
consumerism, says Zajdow, are the root cause of alcoholism.

Alcoholism is a serious health problem throughout the world. The number
of people with an addiction to alcohol surpasses the number of addicts of any
other drug. Estimates from the National Institute on Alcohol Abuse and Alcoholism indicate that there are approximately 10 million to 20 million alcoholics
in the United States and millions more who are problem drinkers. Yet, it is not
fully understood what determines a person's disposition to alcoholism. For
years, scientists have been reporting that there is a genetic tendency toward
alcoholism. Research shows that specific biochemical and behavioral differences may exist in the way sons and daughters of alcoholics respond to alcohol.
These factors may be a key as to why these children are more prone to becoming addicted to or abusive of the drug.

Children of alcoholics have been consistently shown to have higher rates of alcoholism than children of nonalcoholics. Children of alcoholics are two to four times more likely to become alcoholic than children of nonalcoholic parents, according to the National Council on Alcoholism. Thus, alcoholism has been called a "family disease" because it tends to run in families.

The degree to which hereditary and biological risk factors make some individuals more likely candidates for addiction once they begin drinking is unknown. Psychological forces and environmental influences may also play a major role in predisposing one to alcoholism. Certainly, there is agreement among experts that a combination and interplay of all three of these factors—biological, psychological, and environmental—are responsible for alcoholic behaviors.

In one of the largest studies ever conducted on females and alcoholism, the *Journal of the American Medical Association* reports that heredity plays a major role in determining whether a woman becomes an alcoholic. Researchers found that genes do not automatically cause alcoholism, but they do account for 50 to 61 percent of a woman's risk of becoming an alcoholic. The report mirrors the results for men. Another research group found that college-aged sons of alcoholics tend to have a lower hormonal response to alcohol and feel less drunk when they drink too much when compared to young men whose parents are not alcoholic. And, many adoption and twin studies indicate a genetic predisposition to alcoholism among children of alcoholic parents.

Although many scientists and psychologists believe that there is a genetic component of alcoholism for many people, genetic theories remain inconclusive. Researchers have not identified a single gene that carries a predisposition to alcohol abuse. Some argue that risk factors for alcoholism cannot be translated directly into genetic and biological terms and that factors such as personality traits, values, individual needs, attitudes, family upbringing, peers, and other sociocultural influences in a person's life affect one's use or abuse of alcohol.

Studies of family members show (1) common causal factors that are shared among relatives and (2) risk factors that are unique to an individual family member's life experiences and environment. In addition to sharing genes, many family members share similar environments, customs, culture, diet, and patterns of behavior. The interaction of these factors may be the foundation for a pattern of alcoholism in the family or individual family member. Thus, the conclusion that the sole cause of alcoholism is genetic is viewed skeptically because there are too many other psychological and environmental factors that play a key role in the onset of alcoholism.

The National Institute on Alcohol Abuse and Alcoholism (NIAAA) argues that alcoholism has a genetic component and is not the result of family environment. The NIAAA maintains that there are differences in the brains of alcoholics that may account for their alcoholism. Grazyna Zajdow contends that alcoholism is not based on genetics but on society's view of what constitutes alcoholism. Zajdow argues addictive drinking results from a variety of environmental and psychological factors and personal choice.

The Genetics of Alcoholism

Research has shown conclusively that familial transmission of alcoholism risk is at least in part genetic and not just the result of family environment.[1] The task of current science is to identify what a person inherits that increases vulnerability to alcoholism and how inherited factors interact with the environment to cause disease. This information will provide the basis for identifying people at risk and for developing behavioral and pharmacologic approaches to prevent and treat alcohol problems. The advances being made now are built on the discovery 50 years ago of the role in inheritance of DNA, the genetic material in cells that serves as a blueprint for the proteins that direct life processes. Alcoholism research, like other fields, is capitalizing on the scientific spinoffs of this milestone, among them the Human Genome Project and related efforts to sequence the genomes, the complete DNA sequences, of selected animals.

A Complex Genetic Disease

Studies in recent years have confirmed that identical twins, who share the same genes, are about twice as likely as fraternal twins, who share on average 50 percent of their genes, to resemble each other in terms of the presence of alcoholism. Recent research also reports that 50 to 60 percent of the risk for alcoholism is genetically determined, for both men and women.[2–5] Genes alone do not preordain that someone will be alcoholic; features in the environment along with gene–environment interactions account for the remainder of the risk.

Research suggests that many genes play a role in shaping alcoholism risk. Like diabetes and heart disease, alcoholism is considered genetically complex, distinguishing it from genetic diseases, such as cystic fibrosis, that result primarily from the action of one or two copies of a single gene and in which the environment plays a much smaller role, if any. The methods used to search for genes in complex diseases have to account for the fact that the effects of any one gene may be subtle and a different array of genes underlies risk in different people.

Scientists have bred lines of mice and rats that manifest specific and separate alcohol-related traits or phenotypes, such as sensitivity to alcohol's

From "Alcohol Alert:, the National Institute on Alcohol Abuse and Alcoholism", no. 60, July 2003.

intoxicating and sedative effects, the development of tolerance, the susceptibility to withdrawal symptoms, and alcohol-related organ damage.[6,7] Risk for
alcoholism in humans reflects the mix and magnitude of these and other
phenotypes, shaped by underlying genes, in interaction with an environment
in which alcohol is available. Genetic research on alcoholism seeks to tease
apart the genetic underpinnings of these phenotypes and how they contribute
to risk.

One well characterized relationship between genes and alcoholism is the
result of variation in the liver enzymes that metabolize (break down) alcohol.
By speeding up the metabolism of alcohol to a toxic intermediate, acetaldehyde, or slowing down the conversion of acetaldehyde to acetate, genetic variants in the enzymes alcohol dehydrogenase (ADH) or aldehyde dehydrogenase
(ALDH) raise the level of acetaldehyde after drinking, causing symptoms that
include flushing, nausea, and rapid heartbeat. The genes for these enzymes and
the alleles, or gene variants, that alter alcohol metabolism have been identified.
Genes associated with flushing are more common among Asian populations
than other ethnic groups, and the rates of drinking and alcoholism are correspondingly lower among Asian populations.[8,9]

Genes, Behavior, and the Brain

Addiction is based in the brain. It involves memory, motivation, and emotional state. The processes involved in these aspects of brain function have thus
been logical targets for the search for genes that underlie risk for alcoholism.
Much of the information on potential alcohol-related genes has come from
research on animals. Research has demonstrated a similarity in the mechanisms of many brain functions across species as well as an overlap between the
genomes of animals—even invertebrates—and humans.

One approach to identifying alcohol-related genes is to start with an
aspect of brain chemistry on which alcohol is thought to have an impact, and
work forward, identifying and manipulating the underlying genes and ultimately determining whether the presence or absence of different forms, or
alleles, of a gene influence alcoholism risk. For example, genetic technology
now permits scientists to delete or inactivate specific genes, or alternatively, to
increase the expression of specific genes, and watch the effects in living animals. Because genes act in the context of many other genes, interpretation of
these studies can be difficult. If one gene is disabled, for example, others may
compensate for the loss of function. Alternatively, the loss of a single gene
throughout development may be harmful or lethal. Nonetheless, these techniques can provide important clues to function. These approaches have been
used to study how altering the expression of genes encoding the receptors (or
their subunits) for neurotransmitters and intracellular messenger molecules
alters the response to alcohol.[10]

Scientists also have an increasing array of methods for locating alcohol-
related genes and gene locations and only then determining how the genes
function, an approach known as reverse genetics. Quantitative trait loci
(QTL) analysis seeks to identify stretches of DNA along chromosomes that

influence traits, like alcohol sensitivity, that vary along a spectrum (height is another quantitative trait). QTLs have been identified for alcohol sensitivity, alcohol preference, and withdrawal severity.[11] Ultimately, the goal is to identify and determine which candidate genes within the QTLs are responsible for the observed trait. Among the candidate genes already known to lie near alcohol-related QTLs are several that encode neurotransmitter receptors and neurotransmitters themselves. One of these, neuropeptide Y (NPY), lies within a QTL for alcohol preference in rats. NPY is a small protein molecule that is abundant in the brain and has been shown to influence the response to alcohol.[12]

Scientists also can scan the genome to identify genes whose activity differs among animals that respond differently to alcohol. The methods used are designed to measure the amount of messenger RNA which, as the first intermediary in the process by which DNA is translated into protein, is a reflection of gene expression. The advantage of this approach is its power to survey the activities of thousands of genes, some of which might not otherwise have been identified as candidates for involvement in alcohol-related behavior. Recent work in rats identified a gene that is differentially expressed in brain regions of alcohol-preferring rats and nonpreferring rats. The gene is within an already identified QTL for alcohol preference and codes for alpha-synuclein, a protein that has been shown to regulate dopamine transmission.[13]

Genetic Studies in Humans

Knowledge gained from animal studies has assisted scientists in identifying the genes underlying brain chemistry in humans. Much research suggests that genes affecting the activity of the neurotransmitters serotonin and GABA (gamma-aminobutyric acid) are likely candidates for involvement in alcoholism risk. A recent preliminary study looked at five genes related to these two neurotransmitters in a group of men who had been followed over a 15-year period.[14] The men who had particular variants of genes for a serotonin transporter and for one type of GABA receptor showed lower response to alcohol at age 20 and were more likely to have met the criteria for alcoholism. Another study found that college students with a particular variant of the serotonin transporter gene consumed more alcohol per occasion, more often drank expressly to become inebriated, and engaged more frequently in binge drinking than students with another variant of the gene.[15] The relationships between neurotransmitter genes and alcoholism are complex, however; not all studies have shown a connection between alcoholism risk and these genes.

Individual variation in response to stressors such as pain is genetically influenced and helps shape susceptibility to psychiatric diseases, including alcoholism. Scientists recently found that a common genetic variation in an enzyme (catechol-0-methyltransferase) that metabolizes the neurotransmitters dopamine and norepinephrine results in a less efficient form of the enzyme and increased pain susceptibility.[16] Scientists in another study found that the same genetic variant influences anxiety in women. In this study, women who had the enzyme variant scored higher on measures of anxiety and exhibited an electroencephalogram (EEG) pattern associated with anxiety disorders and alcoholism.[17]

The drug naltrexone has been shown to help some, but not all, alcohol-dependent patients reduce their drinking. Preliminary results from a recent study showed that alcoholic patients with different variations in the gene for a receptor on which naltrexone is known to act (the mu-opioid receptor) responded differently to treatment with the drug.[18] This work demonstrates how genetic typing may in the future be helpful in tailoring treatment for alcoholism to each individual.

NIAAA's Collaborative Study on the Genetics of Alcoholism (COGA) is searching for alcohol-related genes through studies of families with multiple generations of alcoholism. Using existing markers—known variations in the DNA sequence that serve as signposts along the length of a chromosome—and observing to what extent specific markers are inherited along with alcoholism risk, they have found "hotspots" for alcoholism risk on five chromosomes and a protective area on one chromosome near the location of genes for alcohol dehydrogenase.[19] They have also examined patterns of brain waves measured by electroencephalogram. EEGs measure differences in electrical potential across the brain caused by synchronized firing of many neurons. Brain wave patterns are characteristic to individuals and are shaped genetically—they are quantitative genetic traits, varying along a spectrum among individuals. COGA researchers have found that reduced amplitude of one wave that characteristically occurs after a stimulus correlates with alcohol dependence, and they have identified chromosomal regions that appear to affect this P300 wave amplitude.[20] Recently, COGA researchers found that the shape of a characteristic brain wave measured in the frequency stretch between 13 and 25 cycles per second (the "beta" wave) reflected gene variations at a specific chromosomal site containing genes for one type of GABA receptor.[21] They suggest that this site is in or near a previously identified QTL for alcoholism risk. Thus, brain wave patterns reflect underlying genetic variation in a receptor for a neurotransmitter known to be involved in the brain's response to alcohol. Findings of this type promise to help researchers identify markers of alcoholism risk and ultimately, suggest ways to reduce the risk or to treat the disease pharmacologically.

Genetics Research—A Commentary by NIAAA Director, Ting-Kai Li, M.D.

Even from the first drink, individuals differ substantially in their response to alcohol. Genetics research is helping us understand how genes shape the metabolic and behavioral response to alcohol and what makes one person more vulnerable to addiction than another. An understanding of the genetic underpinnings of alcoholism can help us identify those at risk and, in the long term, provide the foundation for tailoring prevention and treatment according to the particular physiology of each individual.

References

1. **National Institute on Alcohol Abuse and Alcoholism (NIAAA).** The Genetics of Alcoholism. *Alcohol Alert* No. 18. Rockville, MD: NIAAA, 1992.

2. **Heath, A.C.;** Bucholz, K.K.; Madden, P.A.F.; et al. Genetic and environmental contributions to alcohol dependence risk in a national twin sample: Consistency of findings in women and men. *Psychological Medicine* 27:1381–1396, 1997.

3. **Heath, A.C.,** and Martin, N.G. Genetic influences on alcohol consumption patterns and problem drinking: Results from the Australian NH&MRC twin panel follow-up survey. *Annals of the New York Academy of Sciences* 708:72–85, 1994.

4. **Kendler, K.S.;** Neale, M.C.; Heath, A.C.; et al. A twin-family study of alcoholism in women. *American Journal of Psychiatry* 151:707–715, 1994.

5. **Prescott, C.A.,** and Kendler, K.S. Genetic and environmental contributions to alcohol abuse and dependence in a population-based sample of male twins. *American Journal of Psychiatry* 156: 34–40, 1999.

6. **Crabbe, J.C.** Alcohol and genetics: New models. *American Journal of Medical Genetics (Neuropsychiatric Genetics)* 114:969–974, 2002.

7. **Tabakoff, B.,** and Hoffman, P.L. Animal models in alcohol research. *Alcohol Research & Health* 24(2):77–84, 2000.

8. **Li, T.K.** Pharmacogenetics of responses to alcohol and genes that influence alcohol drinking. *Journal of Studies on Alcohol* 61:5–12, 2000.

9. **Makimoto, K.** Drinking patterns and drinking problems among Asian-Americans and Pacific Islanders. *Alcohol Health & Research World* 22(4):270–275, 1998.

10. **Bowers, B.J.** Applications of transgenic and knockout mice in alcohol research. *Alcohol Research & Health* 24(3):175–184, 2000.

11. **Crabbe, J.C.;** Phillips, T.J.; Buck, K.J.; et al. Identifying genes for alcohol and drug sensitivity: Recent progress and future directions. *Trends in Neurosciences* 22(4):173–179, 1999.

12. **Pandey, S.C.;** Carr, L.G.; Heilig, M.; et al. Neuropeptide Y and alcoholism: Genetic, molecular, and pharmacological evidence. *Alcoholism: Clinical and Experimental Research* 27:149–154, 2003.

13. **Liang, T.;** Spence, J.; Liu, L.; et al. -Synuclein maps to a quantitative trait locus for alcohol preference and is differentially expressed in alcohol-preferring and nonpreferring rats. *Proceedings of the National Academy of Sciences of the U.S.A.* 100(8): 4690–4695, 2003.

14. **Schuckit, M.A.;** Mazzanti, C.; Smith, T.L.; et al. Selective genotyping for the role of 5-HT_{2A}, 5-HT_{2C}, and $GABA_{\alpha 6}$, receptors and the serotonin transporter in the level of response to alcohol: A pilot study. *Biological Psychiatry* 45:647–651, 1999.

15. **Herman, A.I.;** Philbeck, J.W.; Vasilopoulos, N.L.; and Depetrillo, P.B. Serotonin transporter promoter polymorphism and differences in alcohol consumption behaviour in a college student population. *Alcohol and Alcoholism* 38: 446–449, 2003.

16. **Zubieta, J.-K.;** Heitzeg, M.M.; Smith, Y.R.; et al. COMT val[158]met genotype affects μ-opioid neurotransmitter responses to a pain stressor. *Science* 299: 1240–1243, 2003.

17. **Enoch, M.A.;** Xu, K.; Ferro, E.; et al. Genetic origins of anxiety in women: A role for a functional catechol-O-methyltransferase polymorphism. *Psychiatric Genetics* 13(1):33–41, 2003.

18.   **Oslin, D.W.;** Berrettini, W.; Kranzler, H.R.; et al. A functional polymorphism of the μ-opioid receptor gene is associated with naltrexone response in alcohol-dependent patients. *Neuropsychopharmacology* 28:1546–1552, 2003.

19.   **Edenberg, H.J.** The collaborative study on the genetics of alcoholism: An update. *Alcohol Research & Health* 26(3):214–217, 2002.

20.   **Begleiter, H.;** Porjesz, B.; Reich, T.; et al. Quantitative trait loci analysis of human event-related brain potentials: P3 voltage. *Electroencephalography and Clinical Neurophysiology* 103(3):244–250, 1998.

21.   **Porjesz, B.;** Almasy, L.; Edenberg, H.J.; et al. Linkage disequilibrium between the beta frequency of the human EEG and a $GABA_A$ receptor gene locus. *Proceedings of the National Academy of Sciences of the U.S.A.* 99:3729–3733, 2002.

NO ↰

Grazyna Zajdow

Alcoholism's Unnatural History: Alcoholism Is Not a "Health" Issue, But One of Personal and Existential Pain. Recognising This Would Force Us to Acknowledge One of Most Successful Methods of Dealing With Alcohol Addiction

Watching former Tasmanian premier Jim Bacon on TV, resigning himself to continuing a course of palliative care for lung cancer and urging young Australians not to be "idiots" and smoke, reminds one that there is such a thing as addiction. Bacon prefers to say he was stupid rather than addicted. And this is to a substance that is not mind-altering!

This example gives us an interesting view of how we deal with addictive substances on a social and personal level. Addiction is a problem for the late modern world because it questions the very basis of consumption and choice. In a wider social world, choice is everything; for the addict, choice can be death. Yet the Australian response to addiction is marked by ambivalence, particularly in the case of addiction to alcohol. Despite the widespread acknowledgement of the serious nature of this social problem, the attitude to one of the most successful ways of dealing with alcoholism—through Alcoholics Anonymous—is often one of downright antagonism. As a sociologist who reads the literature on addictions and problematic drug use, I often wonder why—and here I will try to unravel the mystery.

The most prominent narrative of addiction in the last few years in Australia and other places is the narrative of social construction. This narrative presents drug use as an integral part of the social world and cuts it loose from biology and physiology. Addiction only exists if there is a stigmatised role of "addict." Without this deviant category there would not be a notion of addiction. Thomas de Quincey wrote about his seventeen-year addiction to opium and even lengthier time with laudanum. He could write so openly because there was

From *Arena Magazine*, issue 70, April–May 2004, pp. 41–43. Copyright © 2004 by Arena Magazine.

no notion of addiction as a stigmatised social category at the time, but what he described was addiction nonetheless.

There is also the postmodern, discursive view of addiction as an extension of social constructionism. Discourses of addiction, in this view, are part of the Foucauldian notion of disciplinary power and knowledge. The addict is part of the "web of power" that plugs him/her into a network that constrains and limits the individual. This is a particularly abstract notion of addiction that rarely admits to material reality of the individual body, or even the social body. This narrative comes not from the sociological study of the experience of addiction, but cultural studies research on written texts such as the book *What's Wrong with Addiction* by Helen Keane.

These narratives of addiction often merge and become entangled in academic discussions. Combine these with the antagonism-towards-the-disease model of addiction that is sometimes—erroneously in my view—linked to Temperance and Prohibition and we might get an idea of why AA and its models have had such bad press, particularly on the social welfare Left. Take a typical example from a major textbook called *Drug Use in Australia,* in which one chapter refers to the AA model of addiction as the grand narrative of the "alcoholic as sinner." The evidence the authors present is one person's reported statements in an AA meeting from another academic text! Another chapter presents it as a disease model of addiction—but nowhere in the text is any of the large-scale and in-depth studies of AA referred to.

I would argue that the fundamental fact about alcoholism must be that this problem lies in the individual body as much as the social body and it is experienced as a highly individual pain. This pain is materially real and cannot be explained away as a form of discourse, amenable to the linguistic contortions of postmodernity or dismissed as simply a social construction. Alcoholics are different from non-alcoholics. The difference is not easy to distinguish—it only really becomes apparent in its most extreme manifestations—but it is there. I cannot say that my first drink of alcohol changed my life—I cannot even remember it—but I know plenty of alcoholics who say just that. They remember their first drink and how it made them feel. For some who always believed they were different or outsiders, their first drink made them feel part of humanity. For others, their natural shyness disappeared and they became loquacious and humorous. Again others just drank themselves into a stupor from the first moment because they hated the world so much and never seemed to leave this state, at least not until the pain became too great and they permanently left this world.

The sociologist Norman Denzin, in his opus *The Alcoholic Society*, wrote that every alcoholic he talked to drank "to escape an inner emptiness of self." Of course, many of us experience an inner emptiness at many times of our lives, but what Denzin talks about is an emptiness which is a constant. For Denzin, the "alcoholic self" is constantly in search of fulfilment through alcohol, but alcohol just pushes the alcoholic further away from him/herself and all others. No drug or cognitive therapy produces permanent fulfilment—only sobriety through the experience of likeminded others. One could suggest that the divided self produced by alcoholism precedes the first drink, and an existential pain must exist which is married to some physiological and bio-chemical response to alcohol. There is some genetic component, but what it is and how it works is not understood, and it is unlikely that any pharmaceutical therapy can ever offer a solution—though medical experts, along with phar-maceutical companies are always hinting at the possibility. For Denzin, the answer to the individual alcoholic's pain is the community of others, specifi-cally the community of alcoholics. He is talking, of course, about Alcoholics Anonymous.

A Parallel World

Many years ago, I worked as a youth worker in what was known as the Com-munity Youth Support Scheme. We worked out of an old house, but there was one room that we did not use and which was generally locked. One day I had to go in to do something and I felt that I had stumbled on the meeting room of a secret order, like the Masons. What struck me at first was the terri-ble odour of tobacco (this was in the days when we could smoke absolutely anywhere) and then I noticed the banners on the wall. They were full of strange language which included the terms God, higher power and surren-der. It looked to me as if I had fallen through a hole in the floor and found myself in a parallel world. My stoned friends and I lived off jokes about it for years.

Thus, as a sociologist and a materialist, feminist and atheist, my first AA meeting—which I attended as a non-alcoholic—came as a shock to me. I imagined it had to be a cult, that it produced automatons who were close to born-again Christians. For me, the answer to alcohol and drug problems was to sweep away poverty and inequality; the social and personal body were indistinguishable—what was good for one was equally good for the other. After listening to the unmediated stories of pain, anguish and redemption, I came to believe that I was wrong. Not that poverty and inequality should not be swept away, but that alcoholism would be swept away with them. How-ever, I did meet many stalwarts of the Left in those AA meetings and stalwarts they stayed. I know academics, unionists, politicians, writers, folk singers, musos from the 1970s who regularly maintain their sober conditions through AA. To get to this position and stay in AA, these people had to cross a line that would have been unimaginable, and the only explanation can be the intense, existential pain they experienced when they drank.

Many, whatever the drug of choice had originally been, ended up drink-ing themselves into oblivion. It may only have been because alcohol was the cheapest and most freely available. There are many paths into addiction and many different categories of addicts. In the end, I never truly understood what they were doing or what they were feeling. I could not understand, ever. I am not like them. I do not feel their pain, I could never cause pain to people the way they did, and nothing I do could ease their suffering. I suspect this is one of the reasons there is such a distrust of AA and its notion of alcoholism—that alcoholism produces a different category of individual, one not amenable to the niceties of living in the world as nonaddicts might do.

But I do know people who are like them. They come together in rooms (no longer smoke-ridden) and recite a prayer at the end of their meetings. Most of them have found some kind of religious understanding; many are still atheists; but all have some form of spiritual fulfilment. Those meetings are more egalitarian than almost any other community they may belong to, although sexism and racism still exist to some extent.

Here people seek to change the way they live in the world and it is a change in morality, as much as in alcohol consumption. We may find the way that television has taken up this public confession distasteful, but the AA meeting is not an episode of Oprah—it is not a mediated televisual experience. To the same extent as any conversation, it is unmediated. It also demands an ethical understanding of individual experience. Obviously some people are better at it than others. An old AA saying is that a sober horse-thief is still a horse-thief.

There are many well-known people who admit to membership of AA. Even in death, however, many people's friends and relatives often refuse to acknowledge the importance of AA in their lives. It is as if acknowledging AA is a recognition that some things (like sobriety) are more important than motherhood or friendship or other social roles.

Why are we so reluctant to recognise this state of addiction that some people find themselves in? There are strong cultural and economic forces that make alcoholism almost impossible to speak about. To recognise it would mean having to do something about it. In Australia at the moment, it would mean having to deal with the availability of help to overcome the problems of drunkenness, and it would mean facing up to the key issue of whether it should be portrayed to any degree as a "health" issue. While it has health consequences, it is not a health issue; it is an issue of personal and existential pain. Even after his public humiliation, Democrats leader Andrew Bartlett would not admit to an alcohol problem. He called it instead a "health" problem. More people are now willing to admit to problems with depression but few mention that they have been compulsively drinking a depressant for most of their adult lives. They are happy to admit to Prozac but not the sobriety (or lack of).

It is more than likely that it is a cultural distrust of AA, its religiosity and its American influence, that keeps many antagonistic to it. Ultimately, one of the most powerful arguments in AA's favour is that it works. A sixty-year follow-up by the writer George Vaillant—carried out fifteen years after the release of his *The Natural History of Alcoholism,* which looked at American men with clear alcohol problems in the 1940s—found that those who were still alive were most likely to be abstinent.

Beyond that, most alcohol-related problems in Australia are not connected to alcoholism or addiction, but to drunkenness and its consequences. Indeed, alcoholics or chronic heavy drinkers make up between 5 and 15 percent of the drinking population. Mixed with aggressive forms of masculinity, drunkenness contributes to all forms of violent crime, from the minor altercation in the pub between drunken bulls, to domestic assault and then to deaths of all sorts. It does not matter whether it is used as a form of excuse or "time-out"—without the intoxicating effects of alcohol, violent crime would be much reduced.

Large and small epidemiological studies show quite clearly that the cheaper and more readily available the alcohol is, and the greater the number of alcohol outlets, the greater the problems that exist. Some cultural factors may ameliorate or enhance its worst effects, but the reality is that humans, especially those in societies which are based on endless consumerism, will endlessly consume alcohol and other intoxicating substances. Attempting to minimise its most harmful effects without dealing with supply is to park an ambulance at the bottom of the cliff. I am not saying we should not provide the ambulance, but we cannot pretend that it is anything more than that. It is here that the abstract nature of academic discussions combines with libertarian constructions of personal choice. Resistance, then, to the restriction of the supply of alcohol means that we are really unable to effectively deal with the worst aspects of alcohol consumption.

POSTSCRIPT

Is Alcoholism Hereditary?

Is there a significant, substantiated relationship between heredity and alcoholism? The National Institute on Alcohol Abuse and Alcoholism (NIAAA) notes that numerous studies demonstrate a high probability of biological vulnerability to alcohol addiction. The NIAAA claims that there are differences in the brains of alcoholics and the brains of nonalcoholics. Critics agree that alcoholism runs in families, but they argue that there are critical environmental and psychological risk factors for alcoholism that cannot be overlooked. In the final analysis, this issue comes down to which research findings one chooses to accept.

Some experts have expressed concern for certain people who feel that alcoholism is a family legacy. An individual who believes that he or she is destined to become an alcoholic because his or her mother, father, aunt, uncle, or grandparent has suffered from alcoholism may become alcoholic to satisfy a self-fulfilling prophecy. Some psychologists believe this may have lamentable consequences for such individuals who feel that alcoholism is their destiny.

Whether or not alcoholism is genetic or environmental has serious implications. For example, if a genetic predisposition to alcoholism was conclusively proven, then medical therapies could be designed to help those who had the hereditary risk. Second, if individuals were diagnosed as having a genetic predisposition, they could adopt behaviors that would help them avoid problem drinking. That is, they would become aware of the hereditary factor and adjust their attitudes and actions accordingly. If alcoholism is environmental, then one's environment could be altered to influence drinking behavior.

Because of the lack of conclusive evidence identifying heredity as the primary cause for alcoholism, it may be wise to err on the side of caution with regard to consigning children of alcoholics to a fate of alcoholism. On the other hand, research that consistently finds higher rates of alcoholism and alcohol abuse among children of alcoholics cannot be dismissed. This link alone provides ample support for additional funding of research studies that may delineate the exact nature of and risk factors for alcoholism. Still, efforts against the perils of alcoholism via progressive alcohol prevention and education programs to meet the needs of children of alcoholics as well as the general public need to be strengthened.

Two interesting publications that provide a different look at the genetic basis of alcoholism are "Recent Progress in the Genetics of Alcoholism," in *10th Special Report to the U.S. Congress on Alcohol and Health* and *Alcohol: The World's Favorite Drug* by Griffith Edwards (St. Martin's Press, 2001). In "Finding the Future Alcoholic," (*The Futurist*, May/June 2002), Steven Stocker describes attempts to identify children who may become alcoholic. In "Research Finds Alcohol Tolerance Gene," (*The San Francisco Chronicle*, December 12, 2003), Carl Hall examines why some people can tolerate alcohol's effects better than others.

ISSUE 16

Should Moderate Alcohol Consumption Be Encouraged?

YES: Kenneth J. Mukamal, et al., from "Roles of Drinking Pattern and Type of Alcohol Consumed in Coronary Heart Disease in Men," *The New England Journal of Medicine* (January 9, 2003)

NO: National Institute on Alcohol Abuse and Alcoholism, from *State of the Science Report on the Effects of Moderate Drinking* (National Institutes of Health, December 19, 2003)

ISSUE SUMMARY

YES: Kenneth J. Mukamal, a physician at the Beth Israel Deaconess Medical Center in Boston, and associates report that men who consume alcohol at least three to four times a week have less risk of coronary heart disease, regardless of the type of alcohol consumed. Binge drinking, not moderate use, increases the risk of coronary heart disease.

NO: The report from the National Institute on Alcohol Abuse and Alcoholism (NIAAA) cautions against the moderate use of alcohol because individuals vary in their response to alcohol. In addition, the benefits of moderate alcohol consumption may be overstated because people who drink alcohol moderately may engage in healthier practices such as eating more nutritiously and exercising more regularly.

Heart disease is the leading cause of death in the United States; therefore, it is reasonable to assume that people are interested in reducing the risks that lead to heart disease. Magazines are replete with articles describing ways to control factors that are linked to heart disease, such as minimizing the amount of saturated fats we consume, managing stress in our lives, controlling blood pressure, and exercising to counter the effects of a sedentary lifestyle. Is it possible to diminish the likelihood of heart disease through the moderate consumption of alcohol? This issue focuses on the relationship between alcohol and heart disease and whether or not physicians should recommend moderate alcohol consumption.

Discussions regarding the effects of alcohol usually center on the consequences associated with its excessive use. Alcoholism is a devastating problem. Individuals and families have been ruined by the unhealthy use of alcohol. Businesses lose billions of dollars due to higher health insurance costs, worker absenteeism, and lower productivity. Despite a decline in the number of fatalities linked to driving while intoxicated during the previous decade, almost 20,000 people are killed annually by drivers under the influence of alcohol. Alcoholism is often described as a national epidemic that poses a threat to every member of society. Thus, is it a wise idea for physicians to promote moderate use of alcohol, even though such behavior may reduce the risk of heart disease?

An important aspect of this debate is what constitutes moderate use. The concept of moderation varies from one individual to another. To a social drinker, moderation may involve one, two, or three drinks per week. To an alcoholic, moderation is probably much more. To college students, binge drinking may be viewed as moderate if it is limited to weekends and special occasions. Also, how much alcohol does one need to drink to reduce heart disease? Due to individual and cultural differences, many experts feel that no one definition of moderation is adequate. Some critics question the value of promoting moderate alcohol consumption in individuals who maintain a lifetime of sobriety. Yet, research indicates that moderate alcohol use is beneficial to those people who drink.

Some experts maintain that the evidence demonstrating the benefits of moderate alcohol use is misleading because these studies are based on self-reports. Others concur that excessive alcohol use entails potential harm, but that it is reasonable to advocate moderate alcohol consumption. Moreover, educators and public health officials are preoccupied with discussing the negative effects of alcohol and researchers downplay the positive effects of alcohol because they fear that people would drink more than a moderate amount if they were told of alcohol's benefits. Another argument against advancing the notion that moderate alcohol use is beneficial is that some people are genetically predisposed to becoming an alcoholic and moderate consumption may turn into excessive, unhealthy use.

One major concern with regard to promoting moderate alcohol consumption to lessen the likelihood of heart disease is that some people may misconstrue the information. Heavy drinkers, for example, may rationalize their behavior and claim that their drinking is for health purposes. If moderate alcohol use acts as a protective behavior against heart disease, some people may disregard other risk factors that are clearly harmful, such as smoking, hypertension, stress, inadequate exercise, and poor nutrition.

The following selections discuss whether moderate alcohol consumption should be encouraged. K.J. Mukamal and associates argue that the evidence is clear—moderate alcohol use reduces against the risk of heart disease. The National Institute on Alcohol Abuse and Alcoholism contends that the benefits of moderate alcohol use should not be encouraged because people may not engage in other healthy behaviors.

YES ⤵   Kenneth J. Mukamal, et al.

Roles of Drinking Pattern and Type of Alcohol Consumed in Coronary Heart Disease in Men

Important questions remain about the effect of alcohol consumption on coronary heart disease. Among these are the roles that the type of beverage consumed, the pattern of drinking, and the consumption of alcohol with meals have in modifying the apparent benefits of moderate alcohol consumption. Furthermore, most studies have used single measurements of alcohol use and hence have not assessed the importance of updating alcohol intake or the effect of changes in consumption over time.

Although the consumption of wine in particular has been hypothesized to be associated with a lower risk of cardiovascular disease, systematic reviews differ about the specific effects of beer, wine, and liquor. Likewise, an episodic pattern of drinking, with alcohol consumption concentrated over a few days, confers a higher risk of myocardial infarction, but few studies have sought to clarify the relative roles of the quantity and frequency of alcohol consumption or consumption with meals.

To address these questions, we extended our analysis of data from the Health Professionals Follow-up Study to 12 years, having previously reported on alcohol use and coronary heart disease after 2 years.

Methods

The Health Professionals Follow-up Study includes 51,529 U.S. male dentists, veterinarians, optometrists, osteopathic physicians, and podiatrists 40 to 75 years of age who returned a mailed questionnaire regarding diet and medical history in 1986. Participants return follow-up questionnaires every two years to update information on exposures and current illnesses. At base line, we excluded 5528 men who reported a history of myocardial infarction, angina, stroke, transient ischemic attack, claudication, or cancer (other than nonmelanoma skin cancer); 1703 men whose data on alcohol consumption were missing; 202 men whose questionnaires had other technical problems; and 6019

From *New England Journal of Medicine*, 348:2, January 9, 2003, pp. 109–118. Copyright © 2003 by Massachusetts Medical Society. Reprinted by permission. References omitted.

men who currently consumed no alcohol but reported having consumed alcohol in the preceding 10 years. A total of 38,077 men were therefore included in this analysis.

We assessed average alcohol consumption with a semiquantitative food-frequency questionnaire, which included separate questions about beer, white wine, red wine, and liquor. We standardized portions as a 12-oz (355-ml) bottle or can of beer, a 4-oz (118-ml) glass of wine, and a shot of liquor. For each beverage, participants reported their usual average consumption in the preceding year, with nine response categories. We determined alcohol intake by multiplying the consumption of each beverage by its ethanol content (12.8 g for beer, 11.0 g for wine, and 14.0 g for liquor) and summing all beverages. This process was repeated in 1990 and 1994, and a similar question about light beer (containing 11.3 g of ethanol) was added in 1994. We categorized daily ethanol intake in grams into seven categories: none, 0.1 to 4.9, 5.0 to 9.9, 10.0 to 14.9, 15.0 to 29.9, 30.0 to 49.9, and 50.0 g or more.

We assessed the validity of self-reported alcohol consumption by comparing estimates from the food-frequency questionnaire with two seven-day dietary records among 127 participants who returned questionnaires in 1986 and 1987. The Spearman correlation coefficients between alcohol use assessed on the basis of the first and second questionnaires and dietary records were 0.83 and 0.86, respectively.

In 1986, men reported the number of days per week that they typically drank any alcohol, with five response categories. The correlation coefficient between drinking frequency with the use of this measure and dietary records was 0.79. To determine the usual quantity of alcohol consumed per drinking day, we divided average weekly alcohol consumption (from the food-frequency questionnaire) by the number of drinking days per week. In 1994, men reported the proportion of their alcohol that was consumed with meals in four response categories.

We confirmed a reported myocardial infarction if it met World Health Organization criteria, including the presence of symptoms and either typical electrocardiographic changes or elevated cardiac enzyme levels. We included probable myocardial infarctions when we could not obtain medical records but the participant required hospitalization and supplementary correspondence corroborated the diagnosis.

We confirmed deaths when reported by families, postal officials, or the National Death Index, with a combined follow-up rate exceeding 98 percent. Fatal coronary heart disease included fatal myocardial infarction that was confirmed by hospital records or, if coronary heart disease was listed as the cause of death on the death certificate, was the most plausible cause and if evidence of previous coronary heart disease was available. We included sudden death from cardiac causes, defined as death within one hour after the onset of symptoms in a man with no previous serious illness and no other plausible cause. Physicians reviewing medical records were unaware of participants' reported alcohol intake.

We calculated person-years from the date of return of the 1986 questionnaire to the date of the first coronary heart disease event, death, or January 31,

1998. We estimated relative risks with cumulative incidence ratios, adjusted for age in five-year categories and smoking in six categories. In multivariate analyses, we used pooled logistic regression to control for age; smoking status; quintiles of body-mass index (the weight in kilograms divided by the square of the height in meters); use or nonuse of aspirin; physical exertion (in five categories); presence or absence of hypertension, diabetes, and a parental history of premature myocardial infarction; energy intake (in quintiles); and energy-adjusted intakes of vitamin E, folate, saturated fat, trans fatty acids, and dietary fiber (in quintiles). Dietary variables were updated every four years, and other covariates every two years. We assigned missing variables their values from the previous questionnaire.

For base-line alcohol consumption, we assessed the risk of subsequent myocardial infarction according to a single estimate of alcohol consumption. In updated analyses, we prospectively assessed the risk of myocardial infarction in four-year increments, based on alcohol consumption in the preceding questionnaire. We assessed the risk associated with individual types of beverages using updated intake, controlling for standard covariates and the intake of the other beverages. To assess changes in alcohol use, we determined whether the change from 1986 to 1990 predicted the risk of myocardial infarction from 1990 to 1994 and whether the change from 1990 to 1994 predicted the risk from 1994 to 1998. . . .

Pattern of Alcohol Consumption

The frequency of alcohol consumption was strongly inversely associated with the risk of myocardial infarction (Table 1). To assess the relative effects of the quantity and frequency of alcohol consumption, we subdivided the categories of frequency according to the amount of alcohol consumed per drinking day. We found consistently similar risks within categories of frequency, regardless of the amount of alcohol consumed per drinking day.

We next compared a frequency of alcohol use of less than three times per week with a weekly frequency of three or more times within narrow categories of average alcohol consumption. Among men who consumed 0.1 to 4.9, 5.0 to 9.9, 10.0 to 14.9, 15.0 to 29.9, or 30.0 to 49.9 g of alcohol per day on average, more frequent use consistently predicted a reduced risk, with adjusted relative risks of 0.66 (95 percent confidence interval, 0.37 to 1.18), 0.77 (95 percent confidence interval, 0.57 to 1.03), 0.72 (95 percent confidence interval, 0.52 to 1.01), 0.74 (95 percent confidence interval, 0.44 to 1.23), and 0.76 (95 percent confidence interval, 0.18 to 3.21), respectively. The inclusion of both the frequency and average quantity of consumption (in seven categories) in a single model did not change the relative risks associated with the frequency of use, but it markedly attenuated the estimated effect of the quantity of consumption, with relative risks for myocardial infarction ranging from 1.06 to 1.20.

The inverse association between the frequency of alcohol consumption and the risk of myocardial infarction was similar among men in 10-year age groups from 40 to 49 years to 70 to 79 years (data not shown), including men 40 to 49 years of age who reported no change in their alcohol consumption in

Table 1

Relative Risks of Myocardial Infarction among 38,077 U.S. Male Health Professionals According to the Base-Line Frequency of Alcohol Consumption and the Quantity of Ethanol Consumed per Drinking Day.

Variable*	<1 Drinking Day/Wk	1–2 Drinking Days/Wk	3–4 Drinking Days/Wk	5–7 Drinking Days/Wk	P Value†
Cases of myocardial Infarction	411	428	188	388	
Person-yr	97,913	118,794	65,689	112,114	
Relative risk‡ 95% CI	1.00 —	0.84 0.73–0.96	0.63 0.53–0.75	0.63 0.55–0.73	<0.001
Multivariate relative risk‡ 95% CI	1.00 —	0.88 0.77–1.01	0.68 0.55–0.84	0.63 0.54–0.74	<0.001
Multivariate relative risk§ 95% CI	1.00 —	0.83 0.70–0.99	0.66 0.50–0.85	0.62 0.48–0.78	0.001

		1–2 Drinking Days/Wk			3–4 Drinking Days/Wk			5–7 Drinking Days/Wk		
	<1 Drinking Day/Wk	<10.0 g/ drinking day	10.0–29.9 g/drinking day	≥30.0 g/ drinking day	<10.0 g/ drinking day	10.0–29.9 g/drinking day	≥30.0 g/ drinking day	<10.0 g/ drinking day	10.0–29.9 g/ drinking day	≥30.0 g/ drinking day
No. of cases	411	82	195	151	10	118	60	8	185	195
Person-yr	97,913	19,658	54,096	45,039	2,818	41,749	21,122	2,193	56,940	52,982
Relative risk‡ 95% CI	1.00 —	0.84 0.66–1.06	0.86 0.73–1.02	0.79 0.65–0.95	0.65 0.34–1.22	0.61 0.50–0.75	0.65 0.50–0.86	0.57 0.28–1.15	0.61 0.51–0.73	0.65 0.55–0.78
Multivariate relative risk‡ 95% CI	1.00 —	0.85 0.67–1.08	0.93 0.78–1.10	0.84 0.70–1.02	0.63 0.33–1.19	0.67 0.55–0.83	0.71 0.54–0.93	0.68 0.33–1.37	0.68 0.57–0.82	0.63 0.52–0.76

* CI denotes confidence interval.
† P values were derived from tests of linear trend across increasing categories of frequency of alcohol use by treating the midpoint of frequency in each category as a continuous variable.
‡ Relative risks and multivariate relative risks were adjusted for the covariates listed in Table 2.
§ Multivariate relative risks were adjusted for the covariates listed in Table 2 as well as for the estimated quantity of alcohol consumed in 1986, with use of the seven categories of alcohol consumption given in Tables 1 and 2.

the 10 years before enrollment. The use or nonuse of aspirin and the body-mass index also did not modify the association of the frequency of alcohol use with the risk of myocardial infarction.

Type of Beverage

We found inverse relations between the risk of myocardial infarction and consumption of the four types of beverage, with similar relative risks at levels of consumption of at least 15.0 g of alcohol daily (Table 2). The associations were strongest for beer and liquor, intermediate for white wine, and weakest for red wine. Multivariate adjustment weakened the association of myocardial infarction with wine consumption but strengthened the associations with beer and liquor consumption.

Timing of Alcohol Intake with Respect to Meals

Of the 20,986 eligible men who reported their alcohol intake with respect to meals in 1994, 43 percent consumed less than 25 percent of their overall intake with meals, 22 percent consumed 25 to 74 percent with meals, 24 percent

Table 2

Relative Risks of Myocardial Infarction (MI) among 38,077 U.S. Male Health Professionals, According to the Type of Alcoholic Beverage Consumed.

Variable*	0 g/day	0.1–9.9 g/day	10.0–14.9 g/day	≥15.0 g/day		P Value†
Red wine						
No. of cases of MI	814	560	36	8		
person-yr	211,361	171,979	8,952	4,681		
Relative risk	1.00	0.94	1.14	0.48		0.14
95% CI	—	0.84–1.05	0.81–1.59	0.24–0.97		
Multivariate relative risk	1.00	1.06	1.48	0.64		0.34
95% CI	—	0.95–1.19	1.05–2.09	0.32–1.29		
White wine						
No. of cases of MI	671	709	26	12		
person-yr	168,438	214,784	8,346	5,404		
Relative risk	1.00	0.93	0.82	0.62		0.06
95% CI	—	0.83–1.03	0.55–1.21	0.35–1.10		
Multivariate relative risk	1.00	1.04	0.98	0.74		0.87
95% CI	—	0.93–1.17	0.65–1.46	0.41–1.32		

	0 g/day	0.1–9.9 g/day	10.0–14.9 g/day	15.0–49.9 g/day	≥50.0 g/day	
Beer						
No. of cases of MI	747	574	72	21	4	
person-yr	184,927	173,592	26,914	9,657	1883	
Relative risk	1.00	0.91	0.74	0.58	0.45	<0.001
95% CI	—	0.81–1.01	0.58–0.94	0.38–0.90	0.17–1.22	
Multivariate relative risk	1.00	0.93	0.78	0.57	0.34	<0.001
95% CI	—	0.83–1.04	0.61–1.01	0.37–0.89	0.12–0.92	
Liquor						
No. of cases of MI	646	515	156	87	14	
person-yr	186,506	142,782	41,587	22,390	3706	
Relative risk	1.00	1.02	0.80	0.73	0.67	<0.001
95% CI	—	0.91–1.15	0.67–0.96	0.58–0.92	0.39–1.14	
Multivariate relative risk	1.00	1.03	0.79	0.67	0.54	<0.001
95% CI	—	0.91–1.16	0.66–0.95	0.53–0.84	0.31–0.92	

*Relative risks were directly adjusted for age and smoking status. Multivariate relative risks were adjusted for all other types of beverage and the covariates listed in Table 2. CI denotes confidence interval.

† P values were derived from tests of linear trend across increasing categories of alcohol consumption by treating the midpoint of consumption in each category as a continuous variable.

consumed 75 to 100 percent with meals, and 11 percent did not drink. Among men who consumed 5.0 to 29.9 g of alcohol daily, drinking 25 to 74 percent of the total with meals and drinking at least 75 percent of the total with meals were associated with relative risks of 0.66 (95 percent confidence interval, 0.40 to 1.09) and 1.21 (95 percent confidence interval, 0.81 to 1.82), respectively, as compared with drinking less than 25 percent of the total with meals (P for trend, 0.51). The relative effect of alcohol was similar among men with different patterns of consumption with meals (Table 3).

Change in Consumption Over Time

Among men who were free of cardiovascular disease or cancer in 1994, mean daily alcohol consumption declined from 13.1 g in 1986 to 12.0 g in 1994. . . . Men who substantially decreased their consumption had a higher prevalence of diabetes and symptoms triggering a visit to a physician, and men who substantially increased consumption had a lower prevalence of hypercholesterolemia (Table 4).

As compared with consumption that remained constant or increased by less than 5.0 g, an increase of 5.0 to 9.9 g was not associated with a decreased risk of myocardial infarction . . . , but an increase of at least 10.0 g was. Among men whose consumption remained stable or increased, a 12.5-g increase in

Table 3

Multivariate Relative Risk of Myocardial Infarction (MI) among 20,986 U.S. Male Health Professionals, According to Alcohol Consumption and the Proportion of Alcohol Consumed with Meals in 1994.*

Variable	0.1–4.9 g/day	5.0–29.9 g/day	≥30.0 g/day	P value†
<25% of total alcohol intake consumed with meals				
No. of cases of MI	45	70	22	
Relative risk	1.00	0.67	0.57	0.05
95% CI	—	0.45–0.99	0.32–1.03	
25–74% of total alcohol intake consumed with meals				
No. of cases of MI	6	21	8	
Relative risk	1.00	0.78	0.51	0.28
95% CI	—	0.29–2.07	0.15–1.77	
≥75% of total alcohol intake consumed with meals				
No. of cases of MI	20	41	3	
Relative risk	1.00	0.92	0.33	0.16
95% CI	—	0.52–1.63	0.09–1.27	

* The analysis includes cases of myocardial infarction that occurred from 1994 to 1998. Multivariate relative risks were adjusted for the same variables listed in Table 2. Only subjects with information on the consumption of alcohol with meals are included.

† P values were derived from tests of linear trend across increasing categories of alcohol consumption by treating the midpoint of consumption in each category as a continuous variable.

daily alcohol consumption (as a linear variable) was associated with a relative risk of myocardial infarction of 0.78. . . . Conversely, among men whose consumption was stable or decreased during follow-up, a 12.5-g decrease in daily alcohol intake was associated with a nonsignificant trend toward a higher risk of infarction . . . , with similar risks among men whose consumption decreased by 5.0 to 9.9 g per day and those with a decrease of 10.0 g or more per day.

Discussion

Among these 38,077 men, alcohol consumption was consistently associated with a lower risk of coronary heart disease, regardless of the type of beverage, the proportion consumed with meals, or the type of coronary outcome. The drinking pattern had an important effect, with the lowest relative risks among men who consumed alcohol three or more days per week, even if the amount consumed per drinking day was small to moderate.

Episodic consumption of large amounts of alcohol has been associated with a high risk of coronary heart disease in several studies. For example, in the Australian World Health Organization MONICA (Monitoring of Trends and Determinants in Cardiovascular Disease) project, men who consumed nine or more drinks per drinking day, as compared with those who did not drink at all, had odds ratios for acute myocardial infarction of approximately 2 even if they drank only one to two days per week, whereas men who consumed one to two drinks on five to six drinking days per week had an odds

Table 4

Characteristics of 25,692 U.S. Male Health Professionals, According to Average Alcohol Consumption in 1986 and 1994.*

Characteristic†	Alcohol Consumption in 1986 and 1994‡								
	Light in 1986 and 1994 (N = 8534)	Light in 1986 and Moderate in 1994 (N = 1812)	Light in 1986 and Heavy in 1994 (N = 53)	Moderate in 1986 and Light in 1994 (N = 2626)	Moderate in 1986 and 1994 (N = 8229)	Moderate in 1986 and Heavy in 1994 (N = 1130)	Heavy in 1986 and Light in 1994 (N = 248)	Heavy in 1986 and Moderate in 1994 (N = 1143)	Heavy in 1986 and 1994 (N = 1917)
Mean age at base line (yr)	52.3	50.9	53.4	53.2	52.4	52.9	53.4	54.4	54.2
Mean alcohol intake in 1986 (g/day)	1.5	2.9	2.3	10.1	13.5	18.0	47.5	42.2	47.9
Mean alcohol intake in 1994 (g/day)	1.1	9.9	42.0	2.1	13.9	41.1	0.7	18.5	48.7
Full-time or part-time work status in 1994 (%)	78	78	74	78	78	75	75	77	73
No physical examination within 2 yr preceding 1994 (%)	23	19	31	20	20	23	24	23	26
Physical examination for symptoms within 2 yr preceding 1994 (%)	16	14	12	16	14	12	21	15	13
Current smoker in 1994 (%)	4	4	18	7	5	11	15	10	16
Hypertension in 1994 (%)	19	20	27	22	20	25	31	25	26
Diabetes in 1994 (%)	4.2	2.1	4.7	3.7	2.0	2.0	7.1	3.2	2.6
Hypercholesterolemia in 1994 (%)	23	26	16	24	25	27	29	30	26
Aspirin use in 1994 (%)	29	36	32	31	36	42	34	37	38

* This subgroup of men in the Health Professionals Follow-up Study comprised men who reported their alcohol consumption in both 1986 and 1994 and who were free of cardiovascular disease and cancer at both time points.

† Except for age, all variables have been adjusted by direct standardization to the age distribution of the entire study population.

‡ Light, moderate, and heavy refer to an average daily consumption of less than 5.0, 5.0 to 29.9, and 30.0 or more g of alcohol, respectively.

ratio of 0.36. In contrast, our results emphasize the frequency of alcohol consumption as the primary determinant of its inverse association with the risk of myocardial infarction. Our results concur with the findings of one meta-analysis of alcohol consumption and nonfatal myocardial infarction: an average consumption of more than a single drink every two days offered only a small incremental benefit. The inverse association between recent alcohol exposure and the risk of myocardial infarction, though debated, also offers evidence in support of a benefit of frequent consumption.

Studies differ on whether the drinking pattern modifies high-density lipoprotein cholesterol levels. The drinking pattern does not clearly influence fibrinogen levels, but it may have an important effect on blood pressure. The Intersalt study found that a highly variable pattern of alcohol consumption predicted a high mean blood-pressure level among heavy drinkers, regardless of the amount of alcohol consumed in the 24 hours before measurement. Likewise, platelet aggregability appears to be lower among moderate drinkers than among those who did not drink but higher during withdrawal among heavy users of alcohol.

When we used two methods of assessing alcohol consumption—at base line and updated every four years during follow-up—we found a stronger association with myocardial infarction for the updated reports. Because alcohol use changes over time, updating this information should improve the accuracy of assessment during the follow-up period, an important feature for exposures with short-term effects on risk.

We found the strongest associations between alcohol consumption and the risk of myocardial infarction for beer and liquor, the predominant types of alcoholic beverages consumed by this population. Our findings support the hypothesis that the beverage most widely consumed by a given population is the one most likely to be inversely associated with the risk of myocardial infarction in that population. This may occur because heavily consumed beverages are more likely to be consumed frequently, as confirmed by their closer correlation with the frequency of drinking in our analyses. The fact that multivariate adjustment strengthened the inverse associations of myocardial infarction with beer and liquor but weakened the associations with red wine and white wine suggests that uncontrolled confounding may explain the greater benefits attributed to red wine in some studies.

Few studies have assessed increases in alcohol consumption and the risk of myocardial infarction. In three studies, increased consumption over time was associated with a decrease in the risk of subsequent cardiovascular events of a magnitude similar to that in our study, although one study found no significant difference in the rate of death from coronary or cardiovascular causes. Since advising patients at high risk for myocardial infarction to drink moderately is controversial, the finding that a moderate increase in consumption over time appears beneficial may inform this debate.

Recent reviews suggest that alcohol consumption is mainly associated with a decreased risk of myocardial infarction among men over 45 years of age and women over 55 years of age. We found that frequent drinking was associated with a decreased risk even among men 40 to 49 years of age who had previously had stable levels of consumption, implying that this association is not limited to adults over a specific age. However, the absolute benefits of moderate drinking will be most apparent among older adults at increased risk for myocardial infarction, whereas many of the risks of alcohol consumption, such as trauma, are of paramount concern for younger persons. For example, among the middle-aged healthy men in our study, the incidence of myocardial infarction among those who abstained was 420 cases per 100,000 person-years, yielding a difference in risk associated with frequent alcohol use of approximately 145 cases per 100,000 person-years. In younger populations at decreased risk for myocardial infarction, the difference in risk associated with frequent alcohol use would be smaller.

Although differences among participants in factors other than alcohol consumption could influence our findings, we found little additional confounding by diet, exercise, body-mass index, family history, aspirin use or nonuse, or the presence or absence of hypertension and diabetes after we controlled for age and smoking status, and our population was homogeneous, by design, with respect to occupational class and sex. In order to have produced these results, any uncontrolled confounder would need to be associated with both exposure and the outcome and unrelated to the covariates included. Our exclusion of former drinkers, the elimination of myocardial infarctions that occurred early in the follow-up period, and the similarity in risk among those who abstained and those who were very light drinkers argue against the "sick quitter" hypothesis as an explanation for our findings.

Our ability to separate the associations of the quantity and the frequency of alcohol consumption with the risk of myocardial infarction was limited, because the two were correlated. Also, only 3.5 percent of study participants reported consumption of 50 g or more of alcohol daily, a fact that limited our ability to study the detrimental effects of heavy drinking.

National guidelines recommend caution when applying the results of epidemiologic studies of alcohol consumption to individual patients, since clinical care requires consideration of the myriad health effects of alcohol and of individual susceptibility to those effects. We encourage adults to discuss alcohol use with their physicians and together make individualized decisions about appropriate consumption.

National Institute on Alcohol
Abuse and Alcoholism

 **NO**

State of the Science Report on the Effects of Moderate Drinking

I. Background Information

. . . About 35% of the adult U.S. population abstains from alcohol use, about 60% are occasional to moderate drinkers, and about 5 to 7 % are diagnosable with alcohol abuse or dependence. Of the some 16 million Americans who meet the diagnostic criteria for abuse or dependence, only about 1.5 million seek and receive treatment.

Alcohol consumption causes some 100,000 deaths annually in the U.S., including more than 16,000 alcohol related traffic fatalities. Compared with abstainers, drinkers—particularly heavy or excessive drinkers—have higher death rates from injuries, violence, suicide, poisoning, cirrhosis, certain cancers, and possibly hemorrhagic strokes.

However, because of alcohol's apparent protective effect against coronary heart disease (CHD) and other atherosclerotic diseases, which are the most common causes of death in the U.S., the consequences of alcohol use must be evaluated in conjunction with its potential benefits. For example, at least one estimate predicts that if all current consumers of alcohol abstained from drinking, another approximately 80,000 CHD deaths would occur each year.

Over the past 50 years, numerous studies have investigated the relationship of alcohol consumption and the development of many medical conditions including cancers, cardiovascular disease, diabetes and dementia. Studies have also investigated the relationship of maternal alcohol consumption during pregnancy and breast feeding to the health and development of infants and children. Many of these studies have evaluated dose response relationships and therefore may provide comparative information about zero, low, moderate and heavy levels of ethanol consumption and the various outcomes of interest. Both epidemiologic and basic science studies have addressed the relationship of moderate alcohol consumption and medical consequences and both must be considered in evaluating the relationship of moderate drinking and health. However, certain complications are inherent in interpreting this

From "State of the Science Report on the Effects of Moderate Drinking", National Institute on Alcohol Abuse and Alcoholism, December 19, 2003. References omitted.

literature. "Moderate" drinking is the only level of drinking that has been shown to have potential health benefits, and the levels of drinking that are classified as "moderate" and "heavy" have not been defined consistently across studies. Further, they are not always consistent with the definition of moderate drinking in the USDA/DHHS Dietary Guidelines (i.e., no more than one drink per day for women and no more than two drinks per day for men). Furthermore, the amount considered moderate in some situations may be excessive under other circumstances (e.g., pregnancy; intent to drive). Also, it is important to note that many "moderate drinkers" have occasions of high-risk drinking, including heavy episodic drinking and acute intoxication leading to injuries and violence.

The difficulty in defining moderate drinking is to some extent a result of individual differences. The amount a person can drink without intoxication may vary according to drinking experience and tolerance. Individual metabolic differences can lead to a wide range of blood alcohol content (BAC) levels for the same consumption. Also important is the time over which the alcohol is consumed: 3 drinks in one hour will produce a much higher BAC than 3 drinks over the course of 3 hours, and therefore different effects. Thus, definitions solely based on the number of drinks are not the best approach.

Another complicating factor in the interpretation of this complex literature is the interaction of genetic vulnerability to a particular medical condition with the effects of alcohol consumption: risk and protection from alcohol's effects may vary considerably across groups or individuals in the population. Confounding and modification by lifestyle variables also could be a factor in the observed health differences between drinkers and non-drinkers. Various studies have found that nondrinkers are less likely to exercise regularly and have a higher body mass index than their drinking counterparts; they also report lower vegetable intakes and higher fat consumption. Moderate drinkers are found to monitor their health (e.g., blood pressure and preventive dental care) more often than abstainers and heavy drinkers, and female drinkers over age 50 report significantly higher mammography rates than nondrinkers. Studies suggest that life-long abstainers tend to be older, poorer, religious, disabled or in poor health, less physically and socially active, and to have more symptoms of depression; while some of these traits (e.g., health status) may stem from their abstention, others obviously do not.

Research on basic mechanisms of alcohol effects may explain observed epidemiological phenomena associated with moderate drinking. In this report, we summarize both the epidemiological and selected basic research studies that may contribute to the understanding of the consequences and benefits of moderate drinking. However, it is important to note that there is a difference between epidemiological data (e.g., population-based averages) and experimental/clinical data (e.g., looking at specific individuals in specific confounding or co-occurring environmental, physiological, and genetic contexts). Moreover, the interpretation of and conclusions drawn from all of these studies must be tempered by the following considerations. . . .

Definition of "Moderate"

Moderate drinking can mean drinking in moderation, where the term "moderation" is defined by Webster's Dictionary as "within limits; reasonable; of average or medium quantity or extent"—that is, drinking such that there is no ensuing harm. Alternatively, the term "moderate drinking" can be used as a descriptor of quantity/frequency of intake, particularly in comparison to the "extremes" of total abstinence and heavy drinking. Both of these definitions share the problem of not accounting for the pattern of intake over time, which can be a major determinant of whether drinking is harmful or beneficial. Other conceptions of moderate include nonintoxicating; noninjurious; or statistically "normal," definitions which can vary by individual or by socio-cultural context. Studies cited throughout this report use a wide range of consumption levels to represent moderate drinking: some consider it to be 1 drink per week or less while others use as many as 4 drinks per day, making comparisons and generalizations across studies and across areas of harm difficult.

Drinking Patterns

Drinking patterns are as important as total consumption, not only in terms of alcohol's benefits, but also its harmful consequences. Risks for alcohol abuse and/or dependence jump dramatically for men who exceed 4 drinks per occasion and for women who exceed 3 drinks per occasion. Some of the studies addressed in this report have specifically looked at the differences between low per-occasion consumption occurring regularly (e.g., 1 or 2 drink per day, 4 days per week) and the same total weekly consumption occurring all at once. However, the pattern of drinking was not assessed by many of the studies, and so the consumption level of "an average of 1 drink per day" could reflect either a true "daily" drinker; a 3-times-per-week, 2-drinks-per-occasion pattern; or a weekend heavy drinker, making comparison across studies and the determination of clear conclusions difficult.

Drink Size

Because some researchers present results in terms of number of drinks and others in terms of "grams of alcohol" (which differs across alcoholic beverage types and according to portion sizes), this report will use the approximation of 1 drink = 15 grams of alcohol in presenting all data in order to facilitate evaluations. However, drink sizes vary by country, alcohol content varies by type of beverage, and recall/reporting by the study participants may be inaccurate (intentionally or not). Thus, while this report "standardizes" drink size for ease of readability, a true comparison of actual alcohol ingestion level across studies is unreliable.

In summary, discrepancies in findings across studies can arise from pattern of alcohol consumption and differences in modes of administration, differences in definition of drink size or in the number of drinks that constitutes "moderate" use, differences between in vivo and in vitro reactivity, and the use of different animal models and the validity of their extrapolation to humans. In human studies, gene-environment interactions, co-morbidity, medications, age, self-reporting and alcohol use assessment, gender and lifestyle effects further complicate interpretation.

II. Areas of Specific Focus

A. Cardiovascular Disease

Cardiovascular disease, in particular coronary heart disease (CHD) and associated myocardial infarction (MI), is the leading cause of death among adults in the United States. Cardiovascular causes account for about 45% of all deaths among men over 35 years old and 37% of all deaths among women over 35. In numerous studies—cross-sectional, longitudinal, cohort, case-control, individual, meta-analysis—differing considerably in their adjustments for confounding risk factors, the data on CHD-related death are remarkably consistent: the relationship between alcohol consumption and mortality follows a J-shaped or U-shaped curve, with one to four drinks daily significantly reducing risk and five or more drinks daily significantly increasing risk. This inverse association between light-to-moderate alcohol consumption and CHD morbidity and mortality had been demonstrated independent of age, sex, smoking habits, and body mass index.

Most recent studies have found that the trend for beneficial CHD effects first appears when daily drinking exceeds 1 and 1.5 drinks per day for women and men, respectively. The relative risk of MI is reduced by 25% in men consuming up to 2 drinks per day and by 50% in those consuming more than 2 drinks. The association holds even for men with a prior history of MI. Lower levels of consumption were not significantly associated with CHD. However, recently Mukamal et al. found that the protective effect was more a function of frequency of consumption than of volume; small amounts consumed several times a week reduced risk to a greater extent than the same amount consumed over fewer occasions. In pre-menopausal women, for whom overall CHD risk is lower, the effects of alcohol are less likely to reach significance, although there have been studies showing significant HDL cholesterol-increasing and LDL cholesterol-decreasing effects. However, in one of the few studies large enough to offset the rarity of CHD in younger women (age 34–59 at start), a 20–40% lower CHD risk was found for moderate drinkers as compared with nondrinkers. In post-menopausal women, for whom CHD risk is higher than for their younger counterparts, similar lipid profile effects, as well as reduced CHD risk, have been found to correspond with moderate (1–2 drinks/day) alcohol consumption. However, for both men and women, any report of heavy episodic drinking was associated with a significantly increased risk of CHD, at 2.26 for men and 1.10 for women.

There are also cardiovascular risks associated with alcohol consumption, at least at heavier drinking levels. Consistent heavy consumption of alcohol often leads to impairment of left ventricular function, which can result in cardiomyopathy. Although most likely pluri-causal with at least some genetic component, alcoholic cardiomyopathy is often a complication of longstanding alcohol abuse, related to a person's lifetime dose of ethanol; it can eventually lead to congestive heart failure. Alcoholism is one of the most important factors in dilative cardiomyopathy, associated with up to 30% of the cases and typically occurring in men between age 30 and 55 who have regularly consumed more than 5 drinks per day for more than 10 years. Total abstinence has been the standard treatment for alcoholic cardiomyopathy, based on the assumption that any further alcohol consumption is deleterious. However, an evaluation of the effect of reduced drinking in patients with cardiomyopathy found that cardiac contractility improved in all patients who reduced their daily intake to 1–4 drinks/day (n = 15). Drinking at a level of 4–5 drinks/day had mixed results, and functional deterioration continued in most of those who continued to exceed 5 drinks/day. An exception within the last (i.e., > 5 drinks) group were those who, although exceeding 5 drinks/day, nonetheless decreased their previous intake by 50% or more; these 4 patients actually demonstrated a functional improvement. . . .

Summary—CHD

The J-shaped curve has accumulated considerable evidence in cohorts of individuals 40 and over, and it persists after the empirical testing of major alternative explanations such as lifestyle and dietary factors, or composition of abstainer group. The largest potential benefits of alcohol use in terms of CHD mortality and morbidity apply to older individuals and those otherwise at risk for heart disease; insufficient research has been done on the lifetime accumulation of CHD benefits—or risks—that may accompany moderate drinking begun in young adulthood.

B. Breast Cancer

The effect of alcohol on the risk for breast cancer remains controversial. Methodological problems are common, including the lack of reporting information about other breast cancer risk factors such as family history and estrogen replacement therapy (ERT). Even in well done case control and cohort studies, researchers use a variety of somewhat arbitrary cutoffs in assessing levels, doses, or amounts of alcohol consumed (Ginsburg, 1999). Thus, when comparing the outcomes of various studies, results for pre- and post-menopausal women are inconclusive; there is no clear evidence of a dose-response relationship; there is a large range of threshold values (between <1/2 and 4 or 5 drinks per day); and, as the strength of the association seems to decrease with an increase in follow-up time, results from 5 year versus 15 year follow-ups are often in conflict.

Although some studies have found a positive correlation between alcohol and breast cancer, others have not; there have even been a few findings of lowered relative risk among light-to-moderate drinkers as compared with abstainers. A substantial number of the "positive" findings have failed to reach standard levels of statistical significance; the researchers generally attribute this to their study's sample size and subsequent limited power to detect associations of the low magnitude observed for alcohol and breast cancer. Other studies report a "significant trend for increasing risk with increasing consumption," although none of the individual levels of consumption actually demonstrate a statistically significant risk. Even when results are statistically significant, in some studies the magnitude of the change in risk for an individual woman is quite small, making the clinical importance of such findings debatable; however, the public health implications, when the change in risk level is applied across 150 million U.S. women, may be substantial.

In a large collaborative re-analysis of 53 studies, one of the larger analyses with statistically significant findings, compared with women who reported drinking no alcohol, the relative risk of breast cancer was increased by a third for an intake of 2 ½ to 3 drinks per day and by nearly half for more than 3 drinks per day. Specifically, the relative risk of breast cancer increased by 7% for each additional two-thirds drink per day. This means that the cumulative incidence of breast cancer by 80 years is estimated to increase from 8.8 per 100 women in non-drinkers to 9.4, 10.1, 10.8, 11.6, 12.4, and 13.3 per 100 women consuming an average of 1, 2, 3, 4, 5, and 6 drinks per day. The risk at higher doses (e.g., 7–8 drinks per day) is difficult to determine, because in most studies the vast majority of participants report less than 4 drinks per day.

One group that does seem to be at substantially increased risk even at low doses is women with a family history of breast cancer. Vachon et al. found a risk ratio of 2.45 in daily drinkers who were first-degree relatives of breast cancer probands, as compared with never-drinkers. The risk for second degree relatives was not significant, and there was no association for women who had married into the families (i.e., were not biologically related).

A number of pooled studies and meta-analyses have been undertaken to provide the level of statistical power needed to resolve the issue of nonsignificant findings. One pooled analysis of 6 cohort studies found a significant dose response effect with 1 or more drinks per day increasing breast cancer risk by 9%, and 2–5 drinks per day increasing it by 41%. A meta-analysis of 38 studies indicates a steady but modest increase in risk of breast cancer with increasing daily alcohol consumption. However, the association is a relatively weak one, and researchers have suggested that, not only can associations of this magnitude be due to bias or measurement error, but that investigation of other factors that may differ by alcohol use (e.g., age, obesity, smoking, reproductive factors, etc.) is necessary before any conclusions can be drawn. There is some evidence of a monotonic increase in the relative risk of breast cancer with alcohol consumption; however, the magnitude of the risk was modest—in comparison with non-drinkers, there is a 10% increase in risk for women averaging 1 drink/day.

The picture for older women is slightly different. Although there is no consensus on the comparative risks for premenopausal versus postmenopausal women overall, findings for a subset of postmenopausal women have been consistent. Epidemiological evidence indicates that estrogen replacement therapy (ERT) after menopause increases breast cancer risk, and there are data suggesting that ERT combined with alcohol use magnifies that risk. In particular, a significant risk is associated with intake of more than 2 drinks/day over a period of years. However, in some studies, even lower levels of alcohol consumption add risk. The Iowa Women's Health Study found that women who consumed an average of one-half drink per day or more manifested increased risk of breast cancer with estrogen administration; lesser consumption or none at all showed no increased risk. A prospective cohort of 44,187 postmenopausal women found that, while there was no significant increase in risk for women who drank at least 1 ½ drinks per day but did not use ERT, the women consuming that amount of alcohol and also using ERT for 5 or more years had a relative risk twice that of non-drinking, non ERT users (i.e., a woman whose lifetime risk for breast cancer is 4% would increase her risk to 8% with 5 or more years of current ERT use and the consumption of >1 ½ drinks daily). . . .

Summary—Breast Cancer

In summary, overall evidence from epidemiologic data seems to indicate that alcohol may be associated with an increase in the risk of breast cancer in the population overall, but that the relative effect of moderate consumption is small at the individual level but can be substantial at the population level; the increase in risk is most clearly evident for women with a family history of breast cancer, and for those using ERT. A degree of uncertainty remains about the effect of a given amount of alcohol on the risk of developing breast cancer in the absence of confounding risk factors, as well as whether there may be a threshold dose below which alcohol has no effect. Although not well-investigated other than via consideration as confounds, individual genetic variations in metabolism and their interaction with carcinogens and dietary factors may play a role. Individual women, with the help of their physicians, must weigh their potential increased risk for breast cancer against their potential reduced risk for CHD in determining whether alcohol consumption should be reduced.

C. Obesity

Obesity results from an imbalance between energy intake and energy expenditure over a prolonged period of time. Given the energy content of alcohol (7.1 kcal/g, as compared to 4.5 kcal/g for protein, 5 kcal/g for carbohydrate and 9 kcal/g for fat), weight gain attributable to drinking could arise if corresponding food intake was not adjusted sufficiently to maintain energy balance. DeCastro and Orozco found that alcohol supplements rather than displaces food-supplied calories. However, a recent animal model study designed to evaluate the effects of chronic moderate alcohol intake (5% ethanol in drinking water) on energy balance using male rats that are maintained on either a low-fat or a high-fat diet suggests that rats fully compensate for the excess calories associated with alcohol and maintain energy balance regardless of the fat content of the diet. Looking at actual changes in weight or body mass index (BMI) rather than calorie-source replacement, a prospective study by Wannamethee and Shaper found that, over a five year follow-up period, mean body mass index and the prevalence of men with a BMI of 28 or greater (i.e., top quintile of the BMI distribution) increased significantly from the light-moderate to the very heavy alcohol (defined in this study as 2 or more drinks per day) intake group even after adjustment for potential confounding factors. However, a prospective study with a ten year follow-up found that changes in levels of alcohol consumption were not associated with changes in waist circumference. Over a shorter timeframe, Cordain et al. found that the addition of two glasses of red wine to the evening meals for 6 weeks did not adversely affect body weight. Thus far, the evidence on the relationship between moderate alcohol consumption and obesity remains inconclusive. . . .

Diabetes
The relationship between alcohol intake and the relative risk of developing Type II diabetes is U- or J-shaped. Several studies have demonstrated that moderate drinking is associated with a reduced incidence of Type 2 diabetes in both men and women. The risk is lower by about 1/3 in moderate drinkers as compared to abstainers, and the association is even stronger for those who drink at levels somewhat beyond the limits of moderation, with the risk decreasing progressively up to 6 drinks/day in some populations. In a ten year follow-up study, Wannamethee et al. found a progressively decreasing risk for those consuming ½ (20% reduction) through 2 drinks (nearly 60% reduction) per day, but 3 or more drinks per day conferred the same level of risk as total abstention. Looking at Native American Indian populations, Lu et al. found a similar pattern, but at lower consumption levels: light (3 drinks/week) and moderate (4–12 drinks/week) drinkers had a lower relative risk of developing Type 2 diabetes while heavier drinkers had an increased risk.

The diabetes-related benefits seem to derive from alcohol's effects on insulin secretion, resistance and sensitivity. Regular moderate alcohol consumption (4.5 to 11.5 drinks/week) is associated with decreased insulin resistance. Alcohol consumption of 1–2 drinks per day by both men and women was associated with enhanced insulin-mediated glucose uptake, lower plasma glucose and insulin concentrations in response to oral glucose. The exact mechanism underlying the insulin sensitizing action of alcohol remains unresolved.

Summary—Obesity & Related Conditions
The relationship between moderate alcohol consumption and weight gain, BMI, or obesity remains inconclusive. However, there appears to be some protective effect of moderate consumption on two of the major sequelae of obesity, i.e., metabolic syndrome and diabetes.

D. Birth Defects

Research over three decades in both human epidemiological studies and animal models has clearly established that alcohol at high consumption levels can cause both physical and neurobehavioral birth defects. These findings have led to the issuance of a Health Advisory from the Surgeon General of the United States. A specific dysmorphic syndrome, named "fetal alcohol syndrome" (FAS) was identified and confirmed through research. As research has clearly identified three domains of deficits in FAS—in growth, physical malformations, and neurological/cognitive effects—it is principally in these domains that potential effects of moderate alcohol exposure could be looked for. However, to date few studies have been undertaken on the effects of low-or-moderate alcohol exposure levels and therefore findings are more limited.

Effects on Growth

A longitudinal study of alcohol exposure in pregnancy reported a 4 pound decrease in weight at ages 10 and 14 resulting from first trimester exposure to an average daily volume of one drink compared with zero exposure. Among women who drank one or more drinks per day during the third trimester, Day et al. observed continuing smaller size of offspring, including a 1.6 pound decrease in weight at age 3, compared to the offspring of abstainers. In a longitudinal study, Sampson et al. found that effects on size were observable at birth and at 8 months, but not thereafter. A recent case-control study by Yang et al. provided no evidence of an independent association between moderate maternal alcohol consumption (<14 drinks per week) and risk for intrauterine growth retardation (IUGR). However, unlike the previous studies cited, Yang et al. collected the maternal alcohol data retrospectively rather than during pregnancy, an approach that appears to be less effective in detecting subtle alcohol effects. Additionally, the outcome measure used was a major growth deficit rather than continuous measures of growth, another difficulty in determining subtle effects. Therefore, studies on the risks of moderate prenatal alcohol exposure associated with effects on growth have not yet been definitive. . . .

Impact on Stillbirths

With respect to risk for the adverse outcome of stillbirth, Kesmodel et al. found a nearly 3-fold increase in risk of stillbirth among women who reported consuming five or more drinks weekly. The mechanism of action was unclear, as the increased risk could not be attributed to low birth weight, preterm delivery, or malformation, and there was no association between fetal alcohol exposure and risk of first-year death for live-born infants. . . .

Summary—Birth Defects

There is no question about the effects of excessive consumption: heavy drinking during pregnancy can produce a range of behavioral and psychosocial problems, malformations, and mental retardation in the offspring. The question of whether there is a safe level of drinking during pregnancy still remains to be established, with studies indicating that low-to-moderate drinking during pregnancy does not appear to be associated with an increased risk of fetal physical malformations, but may have behavioral or neurocognitive consequences. There is some evidence for a dose-response association, but so far there is not an established threshold level below which consumption is not teratogenic. In the absence of definitive information on low- or moderate-level drinking, in 1981 the Surgeon General recommended that women maintain abstinence during pregnancy.

Summary—Breastfeeding

Because the level of alcohol in breast milk mirrors the mother's blood alcohol content (i.e., it decreases as time-since-consumption lengthens), nursing mothers can limit their infants' exposure to alcohol by timing their drinking so it does not coincide with feeding schedules. However, while folklore has perpetuated the belief that alcohol is an aid to lactation, and new mothers have often been encouraged to use low or moderate consumption as a way to increase milk production, the research indicates that alcohol ingestion does not enhance lactational performance, and may actually decrease it, at least in the several hours immediately following the consumption period. . . .

Hepatic Effects

Alcohol abuse is the leading cause of liver-related mortality in the U.S., accounting for at least 40%, and perhaps as many as 90%, of cirrhosis deaths. The level of alcohol consumption associated with increased risk for liver disease is uncertain; some studies have suggested levels as low as 14 drinks per week for men and 7 for women while others have observed considerably higher thresholds. However, the largest body of evidence suggests that intake of at least 5 drinks/day over a period of at least 5 years is necessary for the development of cirrhosis, while the odds ratio for hepatocellular carcinoma shows a linear increase after more than 4 drinks/day, and becomes statistically significant when consumption levels exceed 5 ½ drinks/day. . . .

Cancer—General

Considering all cancers combined, an American Cancer Society study of middle-aged men found that mortality from cancer was significantly lower among those consuming up to one drink daily, as compared to abstainers. However, it seems that any cancer-related benefits conferred occur only at the lower end of the "moderate drinking" range.

Injuries/Accidents

Studies on the role of alcohol in injury from falls and violence/abuse frequently do not distinguish between moderate and excessive drinking. However, many "moderate drinkers" have episodes of high-risk drinking, including heavy episodic drinking and acute intoxication leading to injuries and violence. Additionally, studies of the acute effects of alcohol show that even moderate-dose consumption compromises brain performance in terms of error detection, processing speed, and response time, impairments that may be particularly important in terms of driving-related risk. Several reports have indicated that low levels of drinking (e.g., 1 or fewer per day) and BACs below the legal limit of 0.08% (e.g., 0.05%) increase risk of driving-related accidents.

Total (All-Cause) Mortality

A meta-analysis on all cause-mortality using approximately 50 studies demonstrated an inverse association between light to moderate drinking and total mortality under all scenarios, although the extent of the effect (i.e., nadir of risk curve; magnitude of effect) may differ according to demographics (e.g., women versus men; older populations versus younger). The resulting J-shaped curve, with the lowest mortality risk occurring at the level of 1–2 drinks per day, is likely due primarily to the protective effects of alcohol consumption on CHD and ischemic stroke, which comprise the leading cause of death in the U.S.

IV. Conclusions

Government dietary guidelines commonly indicate a minimum daily requirement necessary for good health. Health care consumers are familiar with this approach and may easily confuse low-risk guidelines for alcohol use with recommended levels of intake for good health. Thus, "moderate alcohol use" should not be construed as "healthy alcohol use."

Furthermore, as described in the "Background" section of this report, the relationship between moderate alcohol consumption and disease outcome is confounded and modified by numerous individual differences—age, gender, genetic susceptibility, metabolic rate, co-morbid conditions, lifestyle factors, and patterns of consumption, just to name a few. Protective and detrimental levels of alcohol consumption cannot be generalized across the population, but instead should be determined by an individual in consultation with her or his physician.

Finally, most of the research refers to the risk of disease occurrence. Some of these illnesses may detract from quality of life without increasing mortality; most differ in prognosis, either via the natural history of the disease or due to currently available treatment options. The potential for moderate alcohol consumption to increase risk for one disease may be offset or outweighed by its potential to decrease risk for another disease, depending on the individual's family history, medical history, genetic makeup, and lifestyle.

POSTSCRIPT

Should Moderate Alcohol Consumption Be Encouraged?

Approximately 10 percent of adults in the United States are alcoholics. Public health programs emphasize the risks associated with excessive alcohol consumption. Heavy drinking leads to increased health care costs, accidents, premature death, family disruption, and reduced productivity in the workplace. The social and economic burdens placed on society are immense. In view of the myriad of problems caused by excessive alcohol use, is it prudent for public health officials to promote moderate alcohol consumption? Will the promotion of moderate alcohol consumption result in alcohol-related problems rather than reduced heart disease?

Experts agree that heavy drinking is a problem in society; however, heart disease is a grave concern also. Heart disease is the leading cause of death in the United States. Numerous public health education programs strive to reduce the risk factors associated with heart disease. If it can be shown that moderate alcohol use lessens that risk, would it not make sense to advocate moderate consumption?

An important point to consider is the effect of a program that promotes moderate alcohol use. Would such a program result in heavy drinkers reducing their alcohol consumption? Or would nondrinkers initiate drinking, and would people predisposed to alcoholism become alcoholic? Advocates for moderate drinking believe that these concerns are unwarranted. Heavy drinkers will continue to drink heavily and most people will not consume more alcohol even if they are told to do so. Moreover, promoting moderate use, especially among young people, will help them develop a healthy attitude toward alcohol.

The National Institute for Alcohol Abuse and Alcoholism (NIAAA) questions whether or not nondrinkers will have lower rates of heart disease if they starting drinking moderately. There are other potential problems that may arise from advocating moderate alcohol consumption. One may get the wrong message about alcohol. Also, moderate drinking may be defined differently so that some people may end up drinking too much. Advocating a message of moderate alcohol use may send the wrong message.

There are numerous papers and studies that examine the issue of heart disease and moderate alcohol use. In a paper entitled "Frequency of Light-to-Moderate Drinking Reduces Heart Disease in Men," the National Institutes of Health argues that men who drank alcohol three or more days per week had a reduced risk of heart attacks compared to men who drank less frequently. In "Analysis: Moderate Alcohol Consumption and Stroke Risk," (*American Family Physician*, June 1, 2003), Caroline Wellbery writes that moderate alcohol use reduces the risk of strokes. Janet Raloff discusses the benefits of moderate alcohol use in "When Drinking Helps," (*Science News*, March 3, 2003).

ISSUE 17

Should Schools Drug-Test Students?

YES: Office of National Drug Control Policy, from *What You Need to Know About Drug Testing in Schools* (2002)

NO: Fatema Gunja, Alexandra Cox, Marsha Rosenbaum, and Judith Appel, from *Making Sense of Student Drug Testing: Why Educators Are Saying No* (American Civil Liberties Union and the Drug Policy Alliance, January 2004)

ISSUE SUMMARY

YES: The Office of National Drug Control Policy (ONDCP), an agency of the federal government, maintains that it is important to test students for illicit drugs because academic achievement is impaired by drug use. Use of drugs such as marijuana impedes memory and learning, and Ecstasy use may result in long-term brain damage.

NO: Fatema Gunja and associates maintain that drug testing is ineffective and that the threat of drug testing may dissuade students from participating in extracurricular activities. In addition, drug testing is costly, it may make schools susceptible to litigation, and it undermines relationships of trust between students and teachers. Drug testing, according to Gunja and others, does not effectively identify students who may have serious drug problems.

Attempting to reduce drug use by students is a desirable goal. Whether or not drug-testing students is a means to achieve this goal is the subject of this debate. If it can be shown that drug testing results in less student drug use, then it is worthwhile. However, people on both sides of this issue do not agree on whether drug use is curtailed by drug testing.

According to the Office of National Drug Control Policy (ONDCP), drug testing acts as a deterrent to drug use. The threat of drug testing, states the ONDCP, has been shown to be extremely effective in reducing drug use by students who participate in extracurricular activities as well as by individuals in the workplace. On the other hand, Fatema Gunja and associates believe that drug testing does not have an impact on drug use. They indicate that drug testing is counterproductive in that the threat of drug testing will cause many students to avoid extracurricular activities. Moreover, drug testing may lead to false positives in which students may be erroneously accused of using drugs.

Should the expense of drug testing be a factor in whether schools test students? Very few students are detected as having used illegal drugs. When school districts are strapped for funds, is drug testing a good use of funds? Critics maintain that a more effective strategy for reducing drug use would be better drug education programs that are geared to having students understand the hazards associated with drugs. Drug testing is geared to preventing drug use, not to reducing the harms that come from drug use.

An important question evolves around the legality of drug testing. Does drug testing unfairly discriminate against student athletes? In June 2002, the Supreme Court, in a 5 to 4 decision, ruled that random drug testing for all middle and high school students participating in extracurricular activities is allowable. Prior to 2002, only student athletes could be tested. Should students who participate in school government, band, plays, or other school-related activities undergo drug testing?

One reason the federal government supports drug testing is that students who use drugs do not perform as well academically as those students who do not use drugs. The point of drug testing, states the federal government, is to help students, not to punish them. One criticism of drug testing is that it focuses on illegal drugs. Teenagers are far more likely to use tobacco and alcohol than illegal drugs. Drug testing does not address the problem of tobacco and alcohol use. Tobacco and alcohol cause far more harm than illegal drugs. Drug testing proponents agree that tobacco and alcohol are not adequately addressed, but that does not mean that students should not be tested for illegal drugs.

In the following selections, the Office of National Drug Control Policy (ONDCP) advocates drug testing as a means of reducing illegal drug use by students. The ONDCP claims that the threat of drug testing is sufficient for stopping drug use or preventing drug use from occurring in the first place. Fatema Gunja and her associates question the effectiveness of drug testing. They maintain that drug testing has the opposite effect in that many students will choose not to participate in extracurricular activities for fear of testing positive for illegal drugs.

What You Need to Know About Drug Testing in Schools

"[W]e find that testing students who participate in extracurricular activities is a reasonably effective means of addressing the School District's legitimate concerns in preventing, deterring, and detecting drug use."

—Justice Clarence Thomas U.S. Supreme Court (June 27, 2002)

Introduction

Should Schools Test Children for Illegal Drugs?

It is an important question, and ultimately one best left to parents, teachers, and school administrators. There is no single right or wrong answer, no "one size fits all" solution. A decision in June 2002 by the U.S. Supreme Court expands the authority of public schools to test students for drugs. Still, it is up to individual communities and schools to decide if drugs are a significant threat, and if testing is an appropriate response.

The question of whether to test students for drugs or alcohol should never be taken lightly. It involves myriad complex issues that must be fully understood and carefully weighed before testing begins. The Office of National Drug Control Policy has put together *What You Need To Know About Drug Testing in Schools* to shed light and offer perspective on this multifaceted and sometimes controversial topic. Our aim is to provide anyone who is considering a drug-testing program in his or her community with a broad understanding of the issue and solid, up-to-date information on which to base a decision.

Included in this booklet are answers to questions that students, parents, school officials, and other concerned individuals might have about the process. It explains, generally, what drug testing is all about, who pays for it, who does the testing, what it tells you about an individual's drug use, and, equally important, what it does *not* tell you. The booklet describes what services should be in place for communities to deal effectively with students who test positive for drugs, and it also offers case histories showing how several schools used testing

From "What You Need to Know About Drug Testing in Schools", Office of National Drug Control Policy, 2002.

to address their drug problems. Their experiences may help others determine whether testing is right for their communities.

Drug Testing: An Overview

What Did the Court Rule?

In the case of the Board of Education of Independent School District No. 92 of Pottawatomie County et al. *v.* Earls et al., the U.S. Supreme Court upheld a drug-testing program for students involved in competitive extracurricular activities. Although the ruling allows schools to test greater numbers of students for drugs, it is not a blanket endorsement of drug testing for all students. Before implementing a drug-testing program, schools should engage legal counsel familiar with the law regarding student drug testing.

Why Drug-Test Students?

Thanks to advances in medical technology, researchers are now able to capture pictures of the human brain under the influence of drugs. As these images clearly show, the pleasurable sensations produced by some drugs are due to actual physical changes in the brain. Many of these changes are long-lasting, and some are irreversible. Scientists have recently discovered that the brain is not fully developed in early childhood, as was once believed, but is in fact still growing even in adolescence. Introducing chemical changes in the brain through the use of illegal drugs can therefore have far more serious adverse effects on adolescents than on adults.

Even so-called soft drugs can take a heavy toll. Marijuana's effects, for example, are not confined to the "high"; the drug can also cause serious problems with memory and learning, as well as difficulty in thinking and problem solving. Use of methamphetamine or Ecstasy (MDMA) may cause long-lasting damage to brain areas that are critical for thought and memory. In animal studies, researchers found that four days of exposure to Ecstasy caused damage that persisted for as long as six or seven years. Kids on drugs cannot perform as well in school as their drug-free peers of equal ability. So if testing reduces students' use of illicit drugs, it will remove a significant barrier to academic achievement.

CASE HISTORY: A REWARD FOR STAYING CLEAN

Autauga County School System

In rural Autauga County, Alabama, students have a special incentive to stay off drugs. As part of a voluntary drug-testing program, participating students who test negative for drugs in random screenings receive discounts and other perks from scores of area businesses.

Community leaders and school officials, prompted by a growing concern about the use of drugs, alcohol, and cigarettes among students, launched the program in 2000 with the help of a local drug-free coalition called Peers Are Staying Straight (PASS). "Our community was awakening to the fact that we needed to do something," says PASS Executive Director Martha Ellis.

The Independent Decision program began with just the 7th grade but will expand each year to include all grade levels. In the 2001–2002 school year, more than half of all 7th and 8th graders at public and private schools participated.

To enter the program, kids take a urine test for nicotine, cocaine, amphetamines, opiates, PCP, and marijuana. Those who test negative get a picture ID that entitles them to special deals at more than 55 participating restaurants and stores. Students keep the ID as long as they test negative in twice-yearly random drug tests.

Those who test positive (there have been only three) must relinquish their cards and any special privileges. The school counselor notifies the parents and, if appropriate, offers advice about where to find help. At that point, the matter is strictly in the parents' hands. If the child tests negative in a subsequent random test, his or her card is returned. "Our whole purpose," says Ellis, "is to reward kids who stay clean and help them see the benefits of a drug-free lifestyle."

Surveys taken by PRIDE (the National Parents' Resource Institute for Drug Education) before the program began and again in 2002 showed significant reductions in drug use among Autauga County's 8th graders: from 35.9 percent to 24.4 percent for nicotine, 39.9 percent to 30 percent for alcohol, and 18.5 percent to 11.8 percent for marijuana.

Substance abuse should be recognized for what it is—a major health issue—and dealt with accordingly. Like vision and hearing tests, drug testing can alert parents to potential problems that continued drug use might cause, such as liver or lung damage, memory impairment, addiction, overdose, even death. Once the drug problem has been identified, intervention and then treatment, if appropriate, can begin.

Testing can also be an effective way to prevent drug use. The expectation that they may be randomly tested is enough to make some students stop using drugs—or never start in the first place.

That kind of deterrence has been demonstrated many times over in the American workplace. Employees in many national security and safety-sensitive positions—airline pilots, commercial truck drivers, school bus drivers, to name a few—are subject to pre-employment and random drug tests to ensure public safety. Employers who have followed the Federal model have seen a 67-percent drop in positive drug tests. Along with significant declines in absenteeism, accidents, and healthcare costs, they've also experienced dramatic increases in worker productivity.

While some students resist the idea of drug testing, many endorse it. For one thing, it gives them a good excuse to say "no" to drugs. Peer pressure among young people can be a powerful and persuasive force. Knowing they may have to submit to a drug test can help kids overcome the pressure to take drugs by giving them a convenient "out." This could serve them well in years to come: Students represent the workforce of tomorrow, and eventually many will need to pass a drug test to get a job.

It is important to understand that the goal of school-based drug testing is not to punish students who use drugs. Although consequences for illegal drug use should be part of any testing program—suspension from an athletic activity or revoked parking privileges, for example—the primary purpose is to deter use and guide those who test positive into counseling or treatment. In addition, drug testing in schools should never be undertaken as a stand-alone response to the drug problem. Rather, it should be one component of a broader program designed to reduce students' use of illegal drugs.

What Are the Benefits of Drug Testing?

Drug use can quickly turn to dependence and addiction, trapping users in a vicious cycle that destroys families and ruins lives. Students who use drugs or alcohol are statistically more likely to drop out of school than their peers who don't. Dropouts, in turn, are more likely to be unemployed, to depend on the welfare system, and to commit crimes. If drug testing deters drug use, everyone benefits—students, their families, their schools, and their communities.

Drug and alcohol abuse not only interferes with a student's ability to learn, it also disrupts the orderly environment necessary for all students to succeed. Studies have shown that students who use drugs are more likely to bring guns and knives to school, and that the more marijuana a student smokes, the greater the chances he or she will be involved in physical attacks, property destruction, stealing, and cutting classes. Just as parents and students can expect schools to offer protection from violence, racism, and other forms of abuse, so do they have the right to expect a learning environment free from the influence of illegal drugs.

What Are the Risks?

Schools should proceed with caution before testing students for drugs. Screenings are not 100 percent accurate, so every positive screen should be followed by a laboratory-based confirming test. Before going ahead with tests, schools should also have a good idea of precisely what drugs their students are using. Testing for just one set of illegal drugs when others pose an equal or greater threat would do little to address a school's drug problem.

Confidentiality is a major concern with students and their parents. Schools have a responsibility to respect students' privacy, so it is vital that only the people who need to know the test results see them—parents and school administrators, for example. The results should not be shared with anyone else, not even teachers. . . .

What Kinds of Tests Are Available?

Urinalysis, the most common drug testing method, has been studied exhaustively and used extensively, has undergone rigorous challenge in the courts, and has proved to be accurate and reliable. As a result, urinalysis currently is the only technique approved for drug testing in the Federal workforce. Some employers, however, have already begun using other types of drug tests—on hair, sweat, and oral fluids. Each of these new tests has benefits as well as drawbacks.

What Does Each Test Measure?

Drug tests are used to determine whether a person has used alcohol or illegal drugs. Some tests show recent use only, while others indicate use over a longer period. Each type of test has different applications and is used to detect a specific drug or group of drugs. The Federal Drug-Free Workplace program, which serves as a model for accuracy and quality assurance in drug testing, relies on a urine test designed to detect the use of marijuana, opiates, cocaine, amphetamines, and phencyclidine (PCP). Urine tests can also be used to detect alcohol, LSD, and cotenine, the major metabolite of nicotine.

Following are summaries of the most commonly used tests:

Urine
Results of a urine test show the presence or absence of specific drugs or drug metabolites in the urine. Metabolites are drug residues that remain in the system for some time after the effects of the drug have worn off. A positive urine test does not necessarily mean the subject was under the influence of drugs at the time of the test. Rather, it detects and measures use of a particular drug within the previous few days.

Hair
Analysis of hair may provide a much longer "testing window" for the presence of drugs and drug metabolites, giving a more complete drug-use history that goes back as far as 90 days. Like urine testing, hair testing does not provide evidence of current impairment, only past use of a specific drug. Hair testing cannot be used to detect alcohol.

Sweat Patch
Another type of drug test consists of a skin patch that measures drugs and drug metabolites in perspiration. The patch, which looks like a large adhesive bandage, is applied to the skin and worn for some length of time. A gas-permeable membrane on the patch protects the tested area from dirt and other contaminants. The sweat patch is sometimes used in the criminal justice system to monitor drug use by parolees and probationers, but so far it has not been widely used in workplaces or schools.

Oral Fluids
Traces of drugs, drug metabolites, and alcohol can be detected in oral fluids, the generic term for saliva and other material collected from the mouth. Oral fluids are easy to collect—a swab of the inner cheek is the most common way. They are harder to adulterate or substitute, and collection is less invasive than with urine or hair testing. Because drugs and drug metabolites do not remain in oral

fluids as long as they do in urine, this method shows more promise in determining current use and impairment.

Breath Alcohol
Unlike urine tests, breath-alcohol tests do detect and measure current alcohol levels. The subject blows into a breath-alcohol test device, and the results are given as a number, known as the Blood Alcohol Concentration, which shows the level of alcohol in the blood at the time the test was taken. In the U.S. Department of Transportation regulations, an alcohol level of 0.04 is high enough to stop someone from performing a safety-sensitive task for that day.

What Do Drug Tests NOT Measure?

The five-drug urine test used in the Federal Drug-Free Workplace Program does not detect all drugs used by young people. For example, it does not detect so-called "club" drugs such as gamma hydroxybutyrate (GHB) and Ecstasy, for example, although other urine tests can determine use of these drugs, and hair tests can easily detect Ecstasy use. No standard test, however, can detect inhalant abuse, a problem that can have serious, even fatal, consequences. (Inhalant abuse refers to the deliberate inhalation or sniffing of common household products—gasoline, correction fluid, felt-tip markers, spray paint, air freshener, and cooking spray, to name a few—with the purpose of "getting high.") . . .

CASE HISTORY: TESTING MADE THE DIFFERENCE

Hunterdon Central Regional High School

Teachers and administrators at Hunterdon Central Regional High School in Flemington, New Jersey, were alarmed. A survey taken during the 1996–1997 school year revealed that 45 percent of the school's 2,500 students had smoked marijuana, 70 percent were drinking alcohol, and 13 percent of all seniors had used cocaine. More than 10 percent of the student population had used hallucinogens, and 38 percent of seniors reported that heroin was readily available to them.

"Our drug problem was probably no worse than that of other high schools," says Principal Lisa Brady. "But for us, this was just unacceptable."

In September 1997, Hunterdon began a random drug-testing program for all student athletes. Urine was tested for marijuana, cocaine, heroin/codeine, amphetamine/methamphetamine, PCP, steroids, and alcohol. If a student tested positive, the school notified the parents and set up a meeting with the student, his or her parents, and a school counselor to discuss treatment options. The student attended a mandatory 4-week drug education course and was suspended from athletic activity until a subsequent test showed the drug use had stopped.

"We had one of the best random testing implementations in the country," says Brady. "It was working well." Indeed, a survey in 1999 showed that drug use at Hunterdon had declined in 20 of 28 key categories. For example, cocaine use among seniors had dropped from 13 percent to 4 percent, according to the survey. In another encouraging finding, the number of 10th graders reporting little or no use of drugs or alcohol increased from 41.8 percent to 47.3 percent.

Brady credits drug testing for the decline. "It was the only variable in the equation," she says. "Nothing else had changed." Hunterdon expanded its testing program in February 2000 to include students participating in any extracurricular activity. Even kids who wanted to act in school plays or obtain a parking permit could be called in to take a drug test. Eventually, problems with adulterated urine samples prompted school officials to give up urine testing and start testing oral fluids.

In September 2000, however, the school suspended all random testing when the American Civil Liberties Union filed a lawsuit in New Jersey state court on behalf of students who claimed their Fourth Amendment rights were violated. (The suit is still pending.) Since the school halted testing, Brady has seen what she believes to be clear evidence that drug use at Hunterdon has begun to rise. "There's no question it's gotten worse," she says.

Before drug testing began at Hunterdon, many people in the community resisted the idea, explains Brady. "Now parents are demanding that we test their kids."

What Happens If the Test Is Positive?

Results of a positive drug test should not be used merely to punish a student. Drug and alcohol use can lead to addiction, and punishment alone may not necessarily halt this progression. However, the road to addiction *can* be blocked by timely intervention and appropriate treatment.

When a positive test result has been reviewed and confirmed for illegal drug use, the school's crucial next step is to contact the parents and help them stop their child's drug use. Parents play a key role in drug-abuse prevention, so they need lots of guidance and support. They also need to know that anger, accusations, and harsh punishment could make the situation worse. The best approach for parents is usually to stay firm and to treat their child with respect as they work together as a family to change his or her behavior.

After involving the parents, school officials may refer the student to a trained substance-abuse counselor, who can perform a drug assessment and determine whether the child needs treatment or other specialized help. For young people who use drugs occasionally, a few words from the counselor or parents—coupled with the prospect of future drug tests—may be enough to put an end to the drug use. For frequent users or those in danger of becoming drug dependent, treatment will likely be necessary.

Many schools require drug-positive students to enroll in a drug education course or activity. Some also offer Student Assistance Programs, whose trained counselors are linked to resources in the greater community and can help students cope with a variety of problems, including substance abuse. In any case, the school will want to perform follow-up drug tests on students with positive results to make sure they stay drug free.

Can Students "Beat" the Tests?

Many drug-using students are aware of techniques that supposedly detoxify their systems or mask their drug use. Some drink large amounts of water just before the test to dilute their urine; others add salt, bleach, or vinegar to their sample. In some cases, users call on their drug-free friends to leave bottles of clean urine in the bathroom stalls.

Popular magazines and Internet sites give advice on how to dilute urine samples, and there are even companies that sell clean urine or products designed to distort test results. A number of techniques and products are focused on urine tests for marijuana, but masking products increasingly are becoming available for tests of hair, oral fluids, and multiple drugs.

Most of these masking products do not work, cost a lot of money, and are almost always easily identified in the testing process. But even if the specific drug is successfully masked, the product itself can be detected, in which case the student using it would become an obvious candidate for additional screening and attention. . . .

How Much Do Drug Tests Cost?

The price of drug testing varies according to the type of test and the drugs involved, but generally the cost is between $10 and $30 per test, with hair testing somewhat higher. The price for onsite alcohol tests usually ranges from $1 to $10 per test.

Some schools have paid for drug tests through Federal grants from SAMHSA or the U.S. Department of Education's Safe and Drug-Free Schools Program. Others get money for testing from private foundations. When school-based programs begin to expand, testing providers will likely start offering volume price incentives.

Fatema Gunja, et al.

Making Sense of Student Drug Testing: Why Educators Are Saying No

Executive Summary

Comprehensive, rigorous, and respected research shows that there are many reasons why random student drug testing is not good policy:

- Drug testing is not effective in deterring drug use among young people;
- Drug testing is expensive, taking away scarce dollars from other, more effective programs that keep young people out of trouble with drugs;
- Drug testing can be legally risky, exposing schools to potentially costly litigation;
- Drug testing may drive students away from extracurricular activities, which are a proven means of helping students stay out of trouble with drugs;
- Drug testing can undermine relationships of trust between students and teachers and between parents and their children;
- Drug testing can result in false positives, leading to the punishment of innocent students;
- Drug testing does not effectively identify students who have serious problems with drugs; and
- Drug testing may lead to unintended consequences, such as students using drugs that are more dangerous but less detectable by a drug test, and learning the wrong lessons about their constitutional rights.

There *are* alternatives to drug testing which emphasize education, discussion, counseling, extracurricular activities, and build trust between students and adults.

Random Drug Testing Does Not Deter Drug Use

Largest National Study Shows Drug Testing Fails

The first large-scale national study on student drug testing found no difference in rates of drug use between schools that have drug testing programs and those that do not. Based on data collected between 1998 and 2001 from 76,000 students nationwide in 8th, 10th, and 12th grades, the study found that drug testing did not have an impact on illicit drug use among students, including athletes. Dr. Lloyd D. Johnston, an author of the study, directs *Monitoring the Future*, the leading survey by the federal government of trends in student drug use and attitudes about drugs. According to Dr. Johnston, "[The study] suggests that there really isn't an impact from drug testing as practiced . . . I don't think it brings about any constructive changes in their attitudes about drugs or their belief in the dangers associated with using them."[2] Published in the April 2003 *Journal of School Health*, the study was conducted by researchers at the University of Michigan and funded in part by the National Institute on Drug Abuse.

The strongest predictor of student drug use, the study's authors note, is students' attitudes toward drug use and their perceptions of peer use. The authors recommend policies that address "these key values, attitudes, and perceptions" as effective alternatives to drug testing. The results of the national study are supported by numerous surveys and studies that examine the effectiveness of different options for the prevention of student drug misuse.

Set against the evidence from this national study and expert opinion, a handful of schools claim anecdotally that drug testing has reduced drug use. The only formal study to claim a reduction in drug use was based on a snapshot of six schools and was suspended by the federal government for lack of sound methodology.

Who Says No to Random Drug Testing?

There has been a groundswell of opposition to random drug testing among school officials, experts, parents, and state legislatures.

SCHOOL OFFICIALS AND PARENTS SAY NO TO DRUG TESTING

We stopped testing because "we didn't think it was the deterrent that we thought it would be . . . we didn't think it was as effective with the money we spent on it."

—*Scott Dahl, Vice President of School Board in Guymon, Oklahoma*

We decided not to drug test because "it's really a parental responsibility . . . it is not our job to actually test [students]."

—Harry M. Ward, Superintendent in Matthews County, Virginia

"The concerns of parents [in opposing a student drug testing proposal] have ranged from the budgetary issues to losing our focus on education to creating a threatening environment."

—Laura Rowe, President of Band Aids, parent association of the HS band program in Oconomowoc, Wisconsin

"We object to the urine-testing policy as an unwarranted invasion of privacy. We want schools to teach our children to think critically, not to police them."

—Hans York, Parent and Deputy Sheriff in Wahkiakum, Washington

"I would have liked to see healthy community participation that stimulates thoughtful interaction among us. Instead, this [drug testing] policy was steamrolled into place, powered by mob thinking."

—Jackie Puccetti, Parent in El Paso, Texas

Educators and School Officials

The majority of school officials—including administrators, teachers, coaches, school counselors, and school board members—have chosen not to implement drug testing programs. They object to drug testing for a variety of reasons, including the cost of testing, the invasion of privacy, and even the unfair burden that student drug testing places on schools, with their concerns rooted in knowledge and experience about students. For many educators and school officials, drug testing simply fails to reflect the reality of what works to establish safe school environments.

Experts

"Social workers, concerned with a child's well-being, question whether [drug testing] will do more harm than good . . . What is most effective in keeping kids away from drugs and alcohol are substance abuse prevention programs based on scientific research."

—Elizabeth J. Clark, PhD, ACSW, MPH
Executive Director of the National Association of Social Workers

In regards to drug testing, "what was once a tool to help physicians diagnose and treat substance abuse has been extended for non-medical uses . . . This testing, however has been frequently mistaken as the method, rather than as an aide, for detecting substance abuse."

—Policy Statement of the American Academy
of Child & Adolescent Psychiatry

The Oklahoma policy "falls short doubly if deterrence is its aim: It invades the privacy of students who need deterrence least, and risks steering students at greater risk for substance abuse away from extracurricular involvement that potentially may palliate drug problems."

—Supreme Court Justice Ruth Bader Ginsburg's
Dissenting Opinion in the Earls *Decision*

Physicians, social workers, substance abuse treatment providers, and child advocates agree that student drug testing cannot replace pragmatic drug prevention measures, such as after school activities. Many prominent national organizations representing these groups have come forward and opposed drug testing programs in court. These groups include the American Academy of Pediatrics, the National Education Association, the American Public Health Association, the National Association of Social Workers, and the National Council on Alcoholism and Drug Dependence. These experts stated: "Our experience—and a broad body of relevant research—convinces us that a policy of [random student drug testing] *cannot* work in the way it is hoped to and will, for many adolescents, interfere with more sound prevention and treatment processes."

Parents

Many parents oppose drug testing for the same reasons as school personnel and administrators. In addition, some parents believe that schools are misappropriating their roles when they initiate drug testing programs. They believe that it is the role of parents, not schools, to make decisions about their children's health.

State Governments

In 2003, several state legislatures opposed student drug testing after hearing community and experts' concerns about privacy, confidentiality, potential liability, and overall effectiveness. For example, the Hawaii legislature tabled a bill that would establish a drug testing pilot program at several public high schools. In Louisiana, a bill that would have mandated drug testing state scholarship recipients was defeated.

MOST SCHOOLS SAY NO TO DRUG TESTING

A national survey of schools conducted six years after the U.S. Supreme Court upheld drug testing for school athletes found that:

- 95% of schools do not randomly drug test student athletes.
- No public school district randomly drug tests all of its students.
- None of the ten largest U.S. school systems randomly drug test their students.

Drug Testing Has a Negative Impact on the Classroom

Drug testing can undermine student-teacher relationships by pitting students against the teachers and coaches who test them, eroding trust, and leaving students feeling ashamed and resentful.

As educators know, student-teacher trust helps create an atmosphere in which students can address their fears and concerns, both about drug use itself and the issues in their lives that can lead to drug use, including depression, anxiety, peer pressure, and unstable family lives. Trust is jeopardized if teachers act as confidants in some circumstances but as police in others.

Drug Testing Is Expensive and a Waste of School Resources

. . . Drug testing costs schools an average of $42 per student tested, which amounts to $21,000 for a high school testing 500 students. This figure is for the initial test alone and does not include the costs of other routine components of drug testing, such as additional tests throughout the year or follow-up testing for positive results.

The cost of drug testing sometimes exceeds the total a school district spends on existing drug education, prevention, and counseling programs. In fact, drug testing may actually take scarce resources away from the health and treatment services necessary for students who are misusing drugs—seriously undermining the original purpose of the drug test.

The process for dealing with a positive test is usually long and involved; not only must a second test be done to rule out a false-positive result, but treatment referral and follow-up systems must be in place. In one school district, the cost of detecting only 11 students who tested positive amounted to $35,000. . . .

Beyond the initial costs, there are long-term operational and administrative costs associated with student drug testing, including:

- Monitoring students' urination to collect accurate samples;
- Documentation, bookkeeping, and compliance with confidentiality requirements; and
- Tort or other insurance to safeguard against potential lawsuits.

Not All Drug Testing Is Protected Under the Law

In 2002, by a margin of 5 to 4, the U.S. Supreme Court permitted public school districts to drug test students participating in competitive, extracurricular activities in the case *Pottawatomie v. Earls*. In its ruling, however, the Court only interpreted *federal* law. Schools are also subject to *state* laws—which may provide greater protections for students' privacy rights. These laws vary greatly from state to state, and in many states, the law may not yet be well defined by the courts. For instance, random drug testing programs in Iowa are prohibited because the State Constitution forbids suspicionless searches of any kind. An Iowa school district's drug testing program, then, could still be challenged under state law.

In many states, including Arkansas, Indiana, Maryland, Michigan, Ohio, Oklahoma, Oregon, Texas, and Washington, lawsuits have been filed against school districts for their drug testing policies. Many of these school districts spend years and thousands of taxpayer dollars battling these lawsuits with no guarantee of success.

In late 2003, the Supreme Court of Pennsylvania struck down the random, suspicionless drug testing of student participants in extracurricular activities and those with parking passes, finding that this program violated the heightened privacy protections provided by the Pennsylvania constitution.

U.S. SUPREME COURT *DID NOT* SAY . . .

- The Court DID NOT say that schools are required to test students involved in competitive extracurricular activities.
- The Court DID NOT say drug testing of all students or specific groups of students outside of those participating in competitive, extracurricular activities (i.e., student drivers) is constitutional.
- The Court DID NOT say it is constitutional to drug test elementary school children.
- The Court DID NOT say that it is constitutional to test by means other than urinalysis.
- The Court DID NOT say that schools are protected from lawsuits under their respective state laws.

Random Drug Testing Is a Barrier to Joining Extracurricular Activities

Random drug testing is typically directed at students who want to participate in extracurricular activities, including athletics. However, drug testing policies may prevent some students from engaging in these activities. Research shows the vastly disproportionate incidence of adolescent drug use and other dangerous behavior occurs during the unsupervised hours between the end of classes and parents' return home in the evening.

Research also shows that students who participate in extracurricular activities are:

- Less likely to develop substance abuse problems;
- Less likely to engage in other dangerous behavior such as violent crime; and
- More likely to stay in school, earn higher grades, and set—and achieve—more ambitious educational goals.

In addition, after school programs provide students who are experimenting with or misusing drugs with productive activities and contact with a teacher, coach, or even a peer who can help them identify and address problematic drug use.

One of many school districts facing lawsuits regarding privacy concerns and confidentiality, the Tulia Independent School District has seen a dramatic reduction in student participation in extracurricular activities since implementing drug testing. One female student explains:

> "I know lots of kids who don't want to get into sports and stuff because they don't want to get drug tested. That's one of the reasons I'm not into any [activity]. Cause . . . I'm on medication, so I would always test positive, and then they would have to ask me about my medication, and I would be embarrassed. And what if I'm on my period? I would be too embarrassed."

Drug Testing Results in False Positives that Punish Innocent Students

A positive drug test can be a devastating accusation for an innocent student. The most widely used drug screening method—urinalysis—will falsely identify some students as illicit drug users when they are not actually using illicit drugs at all, because drug testing does not necessarily distinguish between drug metabolites that have closely similar structures. For example:

- Over-the-counter decongestants may produce positive results for amphetamine.
- Codeine can produce a positive result for heroin.
- The consumption of food products with poppy seeds can produce a positive result for opiates.

Violating Confidentiality

When Tecumseh High School in Oklahoma enacted its random drug testing program, the school failed to ensure the protection of private information concerning prescription drug use submitted under the testing policy. The Choir teacher, for instance, looked at students' prescription drug lists and left them where other students could see them. The results of a positive test, too, were disseminated to as many as 13 faculty members at a time. Other students figured out the results when a student suddenly was suspended from his/her activity shortly after the administration of a drug test. This not only violates students' privacy rights, but can also lead to costly litigation.

In a desire to eliminate the possibility for false positives, schools often ask students to identify their prescription medications before taking a drug test. This both compromises students' privacy rights and creates an added burden for schools to ensure that students' private information is safely guarded.

WHAT NATIONAL EXPERTS SAID TO THE U.S. SUPREME COURT

A mandatory drug testing policy "injects the school and its personnel, unnecessarily, into a realm where parental and medical judgment should be preeminent."

—*American Academy of Pediatrics, et al.*

School drug testing policies often operate "in disregard for prevention and treatment principles that doctors and substance abuse experts view as fundamental . . ."

—*American Public Health Association, et al.*

"There is growing recognition that extracurricular involvement plays a role in protecting students from substance abuse and other dangerous health behaviors."

—*National Education Association, et al.*

The risk that testing students for illicit drugs "will be understood to signal that alcohol and tobacco are of less danger is not an idle concern."

—*National Council on Alcoholism and Drug Dependence, et al.*

Drug Testing Is Not the Best Way to Identify Students With a Drug Problem

Drug testing says very little about who is misusing or abusing drugs. Hundreds or even thousands of students might be tested in order to detect a tiny fraction of students who may have used the drugs covered by the test. Additionally, students misusing other harmful substances not detected by drug tests will not be identified. If schools rely on drug testing, they may undervalue better ways of detecting young people who are having problems with drugs. Most often, problematic drug use is discovered by learning to recognize its common symptoms. Teachers, coaches, and other school officials can identify students with a drug problem by paying attention to such signs as student absences, erratic behavior, changes in grades, and withdrawal from peers.

Drug Testing Has Unintended Consequences

Students May Turn to More Dangerous Drugs or Binge Drinking

Because marijuana is the most detectable drug, students may switch to drugs they think the test will not detect, like Ecstasy (MDMA) or inhalants. Knowing alcohol is less detectable, they may also engage in binge drinking, creating greater health and safety risks for students and the community as a whole.

Students Can Outsmart the Drug Test

Students who fear being caught by a drug test may find ways to cheat the test, often by purchasing products on the internet. A quick search on the Internet for "passing a drug test" yields over 8,000 hits, linking students to web sites selling drug-free replacement urine, herbal detoxifiers, hair follicle shampoo, and other products designed to beat the drug test. In addition, a new subculture of students might emerge that makes a mockery of the drug testing program. For example, in one school district in Louisiana, students who were facing a hair test shaved their heads and body hair.

Students Learn that They Are Guilty Until Proven Innocent

Students are taught that under the U.S. Constitution, people are presumed innocent until proven guilty and that they have a reasonable expectation of privacy. Random drug testing undermines both lessons; students are assumed guilty until they can produce a clean urine sample, with little regard given to students' privacy rights.

FIRST, ASK THESE HARD QUESTIONS

- Has the drug test been proven to identify students likely to have future problems and to clear those who will not?
- Have schools been proven to be more cost-effective places to perform these tests than a doctor's office?
- Are resources in place to assist students who "fail" the test, regardless of health insurance status or parental income?
- Is the financial interest of a drug testing company behind the test's promotion?
- Is school staff using precious time to elicit parental permission, explain the test, make the referrals, and assure follow-up?

Adapted from the American Association of School Administrators web site

Alternatives to Student Drug Testing

The current push to increase drug testing comes from the drug testing industry, but also from well-intentioned educators and parents frustrated by the lack of success of drug prevention programs such as Drug Abuse Resistance Education

(DARE). However, there are more effective ways to keep teens out of trouble with drugs.

Engage Students in After School Programs

Schools and local communities should help engage students in extracurricular activities and athletics since these are among the best deterrents for drug misuse.

Incorporate Reality-Based Drug Education Into the School Curriculum

Drugs of all sorts abound in our society. We are constantly confronted with a wide variety of substances that have recreational and medicinal uses and that can be purchased over the counter, by prescription, and illegally. Since decisions to use drugs of all kinds is ongoing, quality drug education should be incorporated into a broad range of science classes, including physiology, chemistry, and biology, as well as psychology, history, and sociology. Drug education should avoid dishonest scare tactics, and it should also recognize the wide spectrum of drug use and misuse, and the reasons why young people might choose to use (or not use) drugs.

Provide Counseling

Schools should provide counseling for students who are using drugs in a way that is causing harm to themselves or others. An emerging model, which stresses relationships between students and counselors, is that of a comprehensive Student Assistance Program (SAP). Both prevention education and intervention can occur in such a program. Counselors who teach about drugs can remain an important resource for students after the formal session ends. Trained student counselors can engage students who may feel more comfortable talking about their problems with their peers.

Allow Students to be Assessed and Treated by Health Care Professionals

Schools can refer students to health care professionals who can play a role in screening, intervening, and referring adolescents to treatment. Several screening tools, other than urinalysis, such as questionnaires, are available to health care professionals in diagnosing drug abuse among adolescents.

Encourage Parents to Become Better Informed

Informed parents play a key role in preventing and detecting drug misuse, so they should learn as much as they can. Schools can encourage parents to open a dialogue when adolescents are actually confronted with alcohol and other intoxicating drugs, usually in middle school. At this point, "drug talks" should be two-way conversations. It is important for parents to teach as well as learn from their children.

Cultivate Trust and Respect Among Students and Adults

Trust and respect are perhaps the most important elements of a relationship with teens. Young people who have the confidence of their parents and teachers, and are expected to assume responsibility for their actions, are the most likely, in turn, to act responsibly. They need to practice responsibility while still in high school where they have a parental and school "safety net."

The combination of these methods will help ensure that students:

1. Receive comprehensive, science-based information;
2. Receive help when they need it; and
3. Stay busy and involved in productive activities when the school day ends.

Resources

Studies on Students, Drug Testing, and/or After School Activities

Ryoko Yamaguchi, Lloyd D. Johnston, Patrick M. O'Malley, "Relationship Between Student Illicit Drug use and School Drug Testing Policies," *Journal of School Health* 73–4 (2003): 159–64. Available at: http://www.monitoringthefuture.org/pubs/text/ryldjpom03.pdf

Robert Taylor, "Compensating Behavior and the Drug Testing of High School Athletes," *The Cato Journal* 16–3 (1997). Available at: http://www.cato.org/pubs/journal/cj16n3-5.html

William J. Bailey, M.P.H., C.P.P, "Suspicionless Drug Testing in Schools," *Current Issues in Drug Abuse Prevention* (1998). Available at: http://www.drugs.indiana.edu/issues/suspicionless.html

U.S. Department of Justice, "Safe and Smart: Making After-School Hours Work for Kids" (1998). Available at: http://www.ed.gov/pubs/SafeandSmart

U.S. Department of Health and Human Services, "Adolescent Time Use, Risky Behaviors and Outcomes" (1995). Available at: http://aspe.hhs.gov/hsp/cyp/xstimuse.htm

Recommended Reading and Viewing

Andrew Weil, M.D. and Winifred Rosen, *From Chocolate to Morphine: Everything You Need to Know About Mind-Altering Drugs*, (Boston: Houghton Mifflin, 1998).

Marsha Rosenbaum, *Safety First: A Reality-Based Approach to Teens, Drugs and Drug Education*, (San Francisco: Drug Policy Alliance, 2002). This 17-page booklet provides parents and educators with pragmatic ways to address teenage drug use. It is available in hard copy or at http://www.safety1st.org in English, Spanish, Russian, and Hebrew.

Friend-of-the-Court brief of the American Academy of Pediatrics, et al. in Support of Lindsay Earls, for *Earls*, 536 U.S. 822 (2002). Available at: http://www.drugtestingfails.org/pdf/amicus_brief.pdf

"Larry v. Lockney," writers and directors Mark Birnbaum and Jim Schermbeck, Public Broadcasting System, 1 July 2003. This is a documentary about a parent's fight against a student drug testing program in his son's school, and the web site

includes lesson plans and other related resources. Available at: http://
www.pbs.org/pov/pov2003/larryvlockney/index.html
"Teaching about Drug Testing in Schools," American Bar Association, adapted from
Street Law, Inc (1999). This is a lesson plan that educates students about drug
testing in schools and allows them to consider and discuss the consequences of a
student drug testing policy. Available at: http://www.abanet.org/publiced/
lawday/schools/lessons/hs_drugs.html

Recommended Web Sites

"Drug Testing Fails" provides resources for parents, educators, coaches, and other
interested and concerned adults who believe that safe and trusting learning environments are critical to our young people's health and safety, and that student
drug testing programs get in the way of creating that kind of environment.
Available at: http://www.drugtestingfails.org
"A Test You Can't Study For" is a special ACLU web feature on student drug testing
that includes a guide for students, fact sheets, reports, and other materials. Available at: http://www.aclu.org/DrugPolicy

POSTSCRIPT

Should Schools Drug-Test Students?

Advocates for random drug testing and people opposed to drug testing do not agree on whether such programs reduce illegal drug use. Regardless of whether drug testing curtails the use of drugs, some critics are concerned that drug testing programs undermine relationships of trust between students and teachers. Teachers are often put in the position of enforcers.

An important question evolves around the role of parents regarding their children. Is it the responsibility of schools to test students for drug use? Should parents be responsible for their children's behavior? In addition, if students test positive for drugs, is it the schools' or the parents' responsibility to deal with this problem?

Another concern regarding drug testing is that some schools may be susceptible to litigation. What is the school's role if a student is falsely identified as having used drugs? The federal government recognizes this risk and strongly supports that school districts that randomly drug-test students have safeguards for students who test positive. Moreover, what actions should schools take if students test positive for drugs? Is the purpose to punish or help students who test positive? Lastly, which school personnel should have access to the results of drug tests? Generally, it is recommended that only school administrators and parents have access to this confidential information.

Some school administrators oppose drug testing on the grounds that such programs create a threatening environment. In addition, some administrators feel that drug testing represents an unwarranted invasion of privacy. Others maintain that student drug use is the responsibility of parents, not schools. Proponents of drug testing point out that many parents abdicate their parental responsibilities. They claim that schools are the logical place to implement drug testing.

One concern is that students will try to outsmart the drug test. Whether or not one can fool a drug test is not the point. The point is that students may engage in unhealthy practices to avoid detection. One only has to surf the Internet to find hundreds of advertisements for products that can beat drug tests. One can purchase herbal detoxifiers, hair follicle shampoo, or drug-free replacement urine.

According to Supreme Court Justice Ruth Bader Ginsburg, drug testing ". . . risks steering students at greater for substance abuse away from extracurricular involvement that potentially may palliate drug problems." At the present time, the vast majority of schools do not randomly drug-test student athletes. Also, no public school randomly drug-tests all of its students.

The Office of National Drug Control Policy (ONDCP) does not support that all schools drug test students. Its position is that a school should drug-test if it or the community feels that there is a drug problem among its students. Without community support, drug testing is not advocated. Because the ONDCP recognizes that some students may test falsely positive, it recommends that reputable drug testing laboratories be used.

Two articles that point to the effectiveness of drug testing programs to reduce drug use are "High School Drug Testing Program Dramatically Reduces Drug Use," in *Medical Letter on the CDC and FDA* (February 2, 2003) and Norm Brodsky's article "Street Smarts," in *INC Magazine* (November 2004). In the article "Relationship Between Student Illicit Drug Use and School-testing Policies," (*Journal of School Health*, April 2003), Ryoko Yamaguchi, Lloyd D. Johnston, and Patrick O'Malley argue that drug testing had no impact on whether high school students used illegal drugs.

ISSUE 18

Does Drug Abuse Treatment Work?

YES: Office of Applied Studies, from *Services Research Outcomes Study (SROS)* (U.S. Department of Health and Human Services, January 28, 2004)

NO: United Nations, from *Investing in Drug Abuse Treatment* (United Nations Office on Drugs and Crime, 2003)

ISSUE SUMMARY

YES: The Office of Applied Studies, a research branch of the U.S. Department of Health and Human Services, contends that individuals in drug treatment are less likely to use drugs following treatment and are less likely to engage in criminal behavior. Moreover, the longer a person stays in treatment, the more effective it is.

NO: The report from the United Nations Office on Drugs and Crime argues that drug abuse treatment does not cure drug abuse. Most people who go through drug treatment relapse. Drug abuse treatment does not get at the root causes of drug abuse: crime, family disruption, loss of economic productivity, and social decay. At best, treatment may minimize drug abuse.

Numerous drug experts feel that more funding should go toward preventing drug use from starting or escalating and toward treating individuals who are dependent on drugs. Today, when budget battles loom and taxpayers dispute how their tax monies are spent, the question of whether government funds should be used to treat people who abuse drugs is especially relevant. Questions surrounding this debate include: Does drug abuse treatment reduce criminal activity associated with drugs? Will drug addicts stop their abusive behavior if they enter treatment? Will more drug addicts seek treatment if services are expanded? Will the availability and demand for illegal drugs decline?

The research on the effectiveness of drug treatment is mixed. In *The Effectiveness of Treatment for Drug Abusers Under Criminal Justice Supervision* (National Institute of Justice, 1995), Douglas S. Lipton states that drug abuse treatment not only reduces the rate of arrests but also reduces crime and lowers the cost to taxpayers over the long run. Also, it has been shown that illicit drug use is curtailed by drug abuse treatment. Perhaps most important, drug treatment may prove beneficial in curbing the escalation of HIV (human immunodeficiency virus), the virus that causes AIDS. The logic here is that when drug users (a high-risk population for HIV) enter treatment, they can be advised about the behaviors that lead to HIV transmission.

Some experts contend that reports regarding the effectiveness of drug treatment are not always accurate and that research on drug abuse has not been subjected to rigorous standards. Some question how effectiveness should be determined. If a person relapses after one year, should the treatment be considered ineffective? Would a reduction in an individual's illegal drug use indicate that the treatment was effective, or would an addict have to maintain complete abstinence? Also, if illegal drug use and criminal activity decline after treatment, it is possible that these results would have occurred anyway, regardless of whether the individual had been treated?

There are a variety of drug treatment programs. One type of treatment program developed in the 1960s is *therapeutic communities*. Therapeutic communities are usually residential facilities staffed by former drug addicts. Although there is no standard definition of what constitutes a therapeutic community, the program generally involves task assignments for residents (the addicts undergoing treatment), group intervention techniques, vocational and educational counseling, and personal skill development. Inpatient treatment facilities, such as the Betty Ford Center, are the most expensive type of treatment and are often based on a hospital model. These programs are very structured and include highly regimented schedules, demanding rules of conduct, and individual and group counseling.

Outpatient treatment, the most common type of drug treatment, is less expensive, less stigmatizing, and less disruptive to the abuser's family than other forms of treatment. Vocational, educational, and social counseling are provided. One type of treatment that has proliferated in recent years is the self-help group. Members of self-help groups are bound by a common denominator, whether it is alcohol, cocaine, or narcotics. Due to the anonymous and confidential nature of self-help groups, however, it is difficult to conduct follow-up research to determine their effectiveness.

Individuals addicted to narcotics are often referred to methadone maintenance programs. Methadone is a synthetic narcotic that prevents narcotic addicts from getting high and eliminates withdrawal symptoms. Because methadone's effects last about 24 hours, addicts need to receive treatment frequently. Unfortunately, the relapse rate is high once addicts stop treatment. Because there is much demand for methadone maintenance in some areas, there are lengthy waiting lists. A newer, more effective drug for treating narcotic addiction is buprenorphine.

In the following selections, the Office of Applied Statistics maintains that drug abuse treatment is beneficial if addicts stay in treatment for an extended period of time. In addition, addicts who undergo treatment are less likely to engage in criminal activity. The United Nations International Drug Control Program argues that drug abuse treatment is ineffective because treatment programs do not get at the root cause of addiction.

Services Research Outcomes Study (SROS)

Changes in Client Behavior and Circumstances in the Five Years Before and After Treatment

. . . The SROS interview led respondents through a series of explicit comparisons between the five-year period preceding the index treatment episode and the five years after the treatment episode, using identically worded items to compare the clients' drug and alcohol use, criminal behavior, housing characteristics, physical and mental health, and employment and other sources of income across these two periods. This section presents an analysis of changes on these measures, weighted to reflect the 967,000 clients represented by SROS as a whole as well as subgroups divided on a variety of dimensions. The findings generally reflect appreciable changes across these periods, particularly in the drug and alcohol use and criminal activity measures, and these changes correlate in important ways with factors such as the length of stay in treatment. The observation that statistically significant changes occurred from the period before treatment to the period after treatment does not necessarily mean that treatment was a sole cause (nor, strictly speaking, does it prove that treatment caused *any*) of these changes, but it does mean that real changes occurred, that something caused these changes, that treatment is associated with these changes, and that further analysis is warranted to isolate and assess the contributions of the potential causes.

Changes in Drug and Alcohol Use Among Clients as a Whole

There were substantial decreases in the percentage of respondents who reported using *any* illicit drugs after treatment, compared with the period before treatment. Those using any illicit drug decreased from 75 percent before treatment to 59 percent after treatment, which is a statistically significant difference of minus 16 points, and a percentage difference . . . of 21 percent. This decrease was also found for almost every individual drug, from the most prevalent (marijuana and cocaine, down 28 and 45 percent) to those rarely used,

From "Services Research Outcome Study", Office of Applied Studies—U.S. Department of Health and Human Services, January 28, 2004.

such as PCP. The only listed drug for which the decrease in use was not statistically significant was illegal methadone. . . .

. . . [Clients] who used marijuana before treatment used it an average (mean) of 15 days per month; after treatment, the same group used marijuana half as often, or fewer than seven days per month. The use of cocaine by pretreatment cocaine users fell by 63 percent, from 12 days to five days per month, and the use of crack by pretreatment crack users fell by 49 percent, from 16 days to eight days per month. . . .

[The number of days alcohol], marijuana, cocaine, and crack [are] used per month decreased by 15, 28, 21, and 11 percent, respectively. [In contrast, clients who used illegal methadone both before and after treatment increased their rate of use from around six days to eight days per month on average. Although this finding was statistically significant, the number of cases in the sample was small, and additional analyses in later research will be needed to interpret this finding correctly.]

To summarize, among the client population as a whole, the percentage of clients using all drugs and any specific drug was lower after treatment than before; users of specific drugs before treatment used them less after treatment; and even clients who continued to use the most prevalent drugs after treatment used them less frequently than before. In the following discussion of changes in drug use by sociodemographic and treatment subgroups, attention is focused on only the first of these measures (i.e., the percentage of clients using drugs before versus after treatment).

Changes in Drug Use by Sociodemographic and Treatment Subgroups

There were distinct differences in the level of change in drug use depending on sex, age, and racial/ethnic group. Both male and female clients were less likely to use drugs after treatment than before. However, for any illicit drug overall and for each of the most frequently used illicit drugs (marijuana, cocaine, crack, and heroin), the decrease was greater among female clients than male. Adults and adolescents differed as well. No statistically significant decreases were detected for adolescents in overall use of any illicit drug during the five years after treatment or in the specific use of marijuana, cocaine, and heroin. However, adolescents significantly increased their use of crack after treatment, albeit from a low pretreatment base of 5 percent, because the age of first use of crack is typically more than 20 years. Among adults, there were gradients in the extent of change by age, with older age groups generally reducing their drug use to a greater degree (percentage change) after treatment than younger age groups did. Finally, among black, white, and Hispanic clients, there were similar decreases in the overall measure of any illicit drug use. However, only the black clients reduced their crack and heroin use to a statistically significant extent (23- and 18-percent declines); in both instances, black clients had been more likely to use these drugs before treatment than the other two racial/ethnic groups.

. . . [There are] changes in drug use rates by the type of treatment that the client received. Clients in methadone treatment facilities composed the only group showing a significant decrease in heroin use (27-percent decline); methadone treatment had lesser effects on cocaine and crack use, but this finding corresponds well to the predominance of heroin use in the methadone treatment group's pretreatment profile. By far the largest decrease in crack use was among residential clients (32-percent decline). Cocaine use also decreased most among residential clients (55-percent decline), although the contrast with other treatment types was less pronounced in this case. . . .

Length of Stay and Change in Drug Use after Treatment

In addition to the type of treatment, the length of stay in treatment was consistently associated with the extent of change in drug use. Although the pattern does not appear strictly linear, this is a consequence of grouping clients in types of treatment with shorter (generally the 24-hour facilities) and longer (outpatient) planned terms. By and large, the "less than one week" and "less than six month" groups are more heavily weighted with clients with suboptimal lengths of stay. The multivariate regression results reported below make it more clear that, after controlling for type of treatment (and therefore planned length of stay), length of stay is associated with the extent of decrease in drug use. Clients who completed their treatment plan were more likely to reduce their pretreatment drug use than noncompleters for every principal drug except crack. . . .

Changes in Criminal Behavior

Just as clients reported overall reductions in drug use in the five years after treatment, they reported overall reductions in criminal activities. . . . Virtually all of the measures of individual types of income-producing crimes (such as breaking and entering, larceny, prostitution, and drug sales), as well as more violent and disorderly offenses (such as driving under the influence and weapons use), declined by roughly one-third (the range is 23 to 38 percent; a few of the rarer offenses in the client population, such as auto theft, rape, and murder, are outside this range). However, self-reported arrests declined by a smaller proportion (17 percent) than crimes, incarceration actually increased by 17 percent, and violations of probation or parole conditions rose by 26 percent. These findings seem paradoxical. It is possible that the same circumstances that led clients to seek treatment also placed them under more stringent supervision in the form of probation, parole, and incarceration, and this increase in supervision reduced the commission of primary offenses. Another possibility is that treatment had the effect of making clients both less prone to committing offenses and more visible or easily collared when they did. The evidence in SROS cannot further discriminate among these or other possible explanations. . . .

Changes in Criminal Behavior by Sociodemographic and Treatment Subgroups

. . . Percentage changes in specific criminal activities before and after treatment differed somewhat by sex and race/ethnicity but with no unifying pattern of consistent differences. In contrast, changes by age group showed a strong positive association between age and the extent of change: Older age groups were much more inclined to reduce criminal activities after treatment than younger ones. This is particularly dramatic with respect to driving under the influence or while intoxicated, selling drugs, and committing acquisitive crimes, some of which increased in the five years after treatment among the youngest age group. Increase in criminal activity from the early teenage years into young adulthood is an extremely common observation in cohort studies, and in order to isolate more precisely the intervention effects, investigative efforts must adopt the assumption of a steeply rising growth curve. Although the consistent finding of greater reductions in post-treatment criminal activity with increasing age is striking, this relationship continued to hold only for drug selling in the multivariate analyses discussed in the next section.

Changes in Criminal Behavior by Length of Stay

There were no consistent patterns of before/after change in criminal activity across type of treatment, but lengths of stay greater than six months and completion of the treatment plan were clearly associated with greater reductions in crime than were shorter lengths of stay and noncompletion of the treatment plan. The decreases in crime were about one-half larger for completers and clients who had at least a six-month stay; these results were consistent with the findings for drug use. In addition, for most of the crimes listed, the decline in criminal activity after treatment for those discharged from their first treatment experience was larger, and in some cases twice as large, as the decline for those who had one or more treatment experiences. For example, rates of theft/larceny and breaking and entering declined by 52 and 62 percent, respectively, among clients receiving their first lifetime treatment, but declined by only about 30 percent for those receiving a second or greater treatment. . . .

Changes in Lifestyle Characteristics

. . . After treatment there was a shift toward retaining and regaining child custody, having more reliable housing, [Homelessness was fairly common; more than one out of every five clients (22 percent) had been homeless for at least two nights prior to treatment. One-half of these of these people (10 percent of the total population) spent that time on the streets, while the other one-half spent time both on the streets and in shelters. However, after treatment, the percentage who spent at least two nights homeless had decreased by 34 percent. The percentage who spent this time on the streets decreased by 40 percent.] avoiding physical abuse, and not attempting suicide, which dropped from 15 percent to 9 percent—despite a continuation of the earlier prevalence of sadness in the clients.

No change was found in the overall rate of full-time employment: About three-quarters of clients had been employed full time for some period before and after treatment. However, this stability masked significant negative trends: Clients were less likely to be employed in a full-time job after treatment than before if they were Hispanic (12-percent reduction), were black (17-percent), were 30 to 39 or 40 years or older (10- and 24-percent), had 9 or fewer years of education (10-percent), were in methadone facilities (25-percent), or reported heroin as their main drug (25-percent).

National Estimates: Converting Percentage Change to Net Differences

This section develops estimates based on the *net differences* for the entire discharged client population—that is, changes in the behavior of treatment clients when the differences in the *before/after* behavior are statistically significant. Estimates of how many individuals changed their behavior after treatment were developed by multiplying the raw differences in before/after behavior by the size of the relevant population. For example, the number of individuals who both had used any illicit drug in the five years before the 1989–1990 treatment episode and did not use any illicit drug in the five years after the episode would be computed by multiplying the 967,012 population by the 16.1-percent raw difference (i.e., 967,012 × –0.161 = 155,689). As a result, there were 155,689 fewer individuals (which will be rounded to the nearest 1,000; i.e., 156,000) using any illicit drug in the five years after the SROS episode than in the five years before the treatment episode. Additional computations lead to the following national estimates for drug use and crime:

Drug Use

- 156,000 fewer users of any illicit drug in the five years after treatment than before;
- 152,000 fewer marijuana users in the five years after treatment than before;
- 187,000 fewer cocaine users in the five years after treatment than before;
- 46,000 fewer crack users in the five years after treatment than before;
- 18,000 fewer heroin users in the five years after treatment than before;
- 22,000 fewer inhalant users in the five years after treatment than before;
- 26,000 fewer PCP users in the five years after treatment than before;
- 71,000 fewer hallucinogen users in the five years after treatment than before;
- 26,000 fewer narcotics users in the five years after treatment than before; and
- 126,000 fewer alcohol users in the five years after treatment than before.

Crime (using the naive assumption that each individual only commits these crimes once in five years [In "Does Crime Pay?" James Q. Wilson and Allan Abhahamse (Justice Quarterly, 9(3):359–376, 1992) write that "mid–rate" burglars/thieves commit crimes at the following rates: theft/larceny, 11.1 per year; fraud/forgery, 0.6 per year; drug selling, 98.6 per year; and vehicle theft, 0.9 per year.]:

- 48,000 fewer vehicle thefts in the five years after treatment than before;
- 165,000 fewer driving-while-intoxicated cases in the five years after treatment than before;
- 131,000 fewer driving-under-the-influence cases in the five years after treatment than before;

- 82,000 fewer cases of public disorder in the five years after treatment than before;
- 101,000 fewer drug sales in the five years after treatment than before;
- 31,000 fewer cases of prostitution/procurement in the five years after treatment than before;
- 34,000 fewer cases of fraud/forgery in the five years after treatment than before;
- 96,000 fewer cases of theft/larceny in the five years after treatment than before;
- 50,000 fewer cases of breaking and entering in the five years after treatment than before; and
- 28,000 fewer cases of threat/attack in the five years after treatment than before.

These estimates represent the pool of behavior change within which, if treatment had any success in meeting its goals, the extent of that success is to be found. As discussed previously, the association in time between an episode of treatment and a variety of changes in behavior is not conclusive, but it encourages a search for greater precision and certainty. . . .

 **NO**

Investing in Drug Abuse Treatment

Summary

Drug addiction produces serious, pervasive and expensive social problems. Regardless of whether substance abuse is a sin, a crime, a bad habit or an illness, society has a right to expect that an effective public policy or approach to the "drug abuse problem" will reduce drug-related crime, unemployment, family dysfunction and disproportionate use of medical care.

Science has made great progress over the past several years, but it is still not possible to account fully for the physiological and psychological processes that transform controlled, voluntary "use" of alcohol and/or other drugs into uncontrolled, involuntary "dependence" on those substances, and there is still no cure. What can be done is to treat use "effectively" and to provide an attractive return on societal investment in treatment. . . .

Importantly, the research shows that while motivation for treatment plays an important role in maintaining treatment participation, most substance-abusing patients enter treatment with combinations of internal motivation and family, employment or legal pressure. Those pressures can be combined with treatment interventions for the benefit of the patient and society.

The evidence is compelling that, at the present state of knowledge, addiction is best considered a chronic relapsing condition. It is true that not all cases of addiction are chronic and some who meet diagnostic criteria for substance dependence recover completely without treatment. However, many of those who develop addiction disorders suffer multiple relapses following treatments and are thought to retain a continuing vulnerability to relapse for years or perhaps a lifetime. Like so many other illnesses, it is impossible to predict whether or when an acute care strategy is likely to achieve complete remission. For example, while change in diet, exercise and lifestyle can reduce high blood pressure in some patients without medication or continuing treatment, many others require sustained management with medications as well as regular monitoring of diet, stress and exercise. In considering addiction a chronic

From "Investing in Drug Abuse Treatment", United Nations International Drug Control Programme, 2003.

condition, it is no longer surprising that incarcerations or brief stabilizations are not effective.

The available research is quite clear on these points:

- Education does not correct drug dependence: it is not simply a problem of lack of knowledge.
- Consequences of drug use (e.g. hangovers, loss of job, arrest, etc.) appear to be important stimuli leading to entry into drug abuse treatment.
- Very few addicted individuals are able to profit from a corrections-oriented approach by itself. Relapse rates are over 70 per cent from all forms of criminal justice interventions.
- Addiction is not simply a matter of becoming stabilized and getting the drugs out of one's system. Relapse rates following detoxifications are approximately the same as those following incarceration. . . .

Introduction

Problems of substance dependence produce dramatic costs to all societies in terms of lost productivity, transmission of infectious diseases, family and social disorder, crime and, of course, excessive utilization of health care. These alcohol- and drug-related problems not only reduce the safety and quality of daily life, they are also a source of substantial expense. For example, it has been estimated that, in the United States of America, the total cost of alcohol abuse in 1990 was 99 billion United States dollars and drug abuse cost approximately US$ 67 billion, while the total cost of illicit drug abuse in Australia was estimated to be 1,684 million Australian dollars (or US$ 1,237 million) in 1992. In Canada, the total cost of alcohol abuse in 1992 was estimated to be 7,522 million Canadian dollars (US$ 6,223 million) and the total cost of illicit drug abuse Can$ 1,371 million (US$ 1,134).

Understandably, such problems also produce heated debates regarding what a family, a school, an employer, a Government and/or a society should do to reduce the costs and the threats of substance abuse to the public health and safety of citizens.

There are few countries—regardless of their economic development—with a well developed public treatment system designed to address different substances of abuse and different levels or manifestations of the addiction spectrum. Why have treatment options not been more favourably considered and better developed and disseminated to address the problems of substance dependence? Perhaps the first reason for this is the relative prominence of the social problems caused by drug and alcohol abuse. Crime, family disruption, loss of economic productivity and social decay are the most observable, potentially dangerous and expensive effects of drugs on the social systems of most countries. This is a powerful factor in shaping the general view that the "drug issue" is primarily a criminal problem requiring a social-judicial remedy rather than a health problem requiring prevention and treatment.

A second reason for a diminished role of treatment in most public policies regarding drug abuse is that most societies are sceptical about the effectiveness of substance abuse treatments and most Governments question whether treatment is "worth it." Moreover, recent surveys show that even a majority of general practice physicians and nurses feel that the currently available medical or health-care interventions are not appropriate or effective in treating addiction.

A third reason why treatment options may not have received more attention in public policies regarding drug abuse is the pervasive view that a treatment approach to substance abuse conveys an implicit message that the addiction—and the addiction-related problems—are not the fault of the addicted person; that they "can't help themselves" and that they have no responsibility for the actions that led to—or resulted from—the addiction. In that regard, the view exists that treatments are designed exclusively to help the drug user but not society. Why should a society expend resources to help an individual who may have produced social harms? These are messages that many people find offensive and unfair.

Thus, treatment interventions that admittedly cannot cure addiction and that may be seen as focused only on helping socially stigmatized addicted individuals are not popular in many segments of society. Are those perceptions correct? Is there a role for addiction treatment in public policy aimed at reducing drug-related problems? In the text that follows the issue is considered from several perspectives. The first part of the paper considers the perspective of a Government or public agency questioning the value of any intervention aimed at "drug problems": What would an "effective" intervention do, regardless of whether the intervention were a punitive, criminal justice intervention, an educational intervention, a new social policy or a treatment intervention? Here the paper examines the characteristics of patients who enter addiction treatments—asking where they have come from, who or what agency has referred them to treatment and what goals are expected by those agencies and organizations. This examination is used to develop a set of outcome expectations that would make treatment "worth it" to a society that might be asked to support such an intervention or policy. . . .

Why Are Addiction Treatments Not as Effective as Treatments for Other Illnesses?

Implications for the Delivery and Evaluation of Addiction Treatment

The previous sections of this paper have examined the addiction treatment field from the perspective of its value to society. It would seem that this review would provide a relatively simple answer to what appears to be a direct question of cost and value. Yet it is not a direct question at all. This paper has tried to show that the reasonable expectations of a society regarding any form of intervention designed to "take care of the drug problem" must address many different issues, all typically related to the "addiction-related" problems that are so frightening and costly to society. Multiple perspectives on outcome are not typical in evaluations of medical illnesses. In the treatment of most chronic illnesses "effective" treatments are expected to reduce symptoms, increase function and prevent relapse, especially costly relapse. Thus, as a final perspective on the issue of the effectiveness and worth of addiction treatments, this section now considers an evaluation of the effectiveness of addiction treatments using the criteria typical for evaluations of other chronic illnesses.

Compliance, Symptom Remission and Relapse in Addiction Treatment

It is important to note that addiction does not need to be considered chronic. Many who meet diagnostic criteria for substance dependence recover completely even without treatment. Others have long remissions following treatment. However, many of those who develop addiction disorders suffer multiple relapses following treatments and are thought to retain a continuing vulnerability to relapse for years or perhaps a lifetime. It is possible to argue that as yet there is no reliable "cure" for drug dependence. For the reasons outlined above, those dependent upon alcohol and/or other drugs who attempt to continue but reduce their use are likely to have problems in maintaining "controlled use." Among those who become addicted, patients who comply with the recommended regimen of education, counselling and medication have favourable outcomes during and for at least 6–12 months following treatment. However, most of those who start any type of treatment drop out prior to completion or they ignore their physician's advice to remain on medication and to continue participation in aftercare or self-help groups. It is also well known that problems of low socio-economic status, co-morbid psychiatric conditions and lack of family or social supports are among the most important variables associated with lack of compliance in addiction treatment and with relapse following treatment. Because of multiple co-morbid medical and social conditions and because of poor compliance with the medical and behavioural components of the treatment regimen, one-year follow-up studies have typically shown that only about 40–60 per cent of treated patients are abstinent, although an additional 15–30 per cent have not resumed dependent use during that period.

It is quite discouraging to many in the addiction treatment field that so many drug- and alcohol-dependent patients fail to comply with the recommended course of treatment and that so many subsequently resume substance use. As indicated above, there are now several medications that have demonstrated effectiveness in the treatment of alcohol and opiate dependence. However, for those medications to be effective, they must be taken on a regular basis and lack of patient compliance has severely limited their impact. Ongoing clinical research in this area is focused upon the development of longer-acting or "depot" forms of these medications, as well as behavioural strategies to increase patient compliance.

Compliance, Symptom Remission and Relapse in the Treatment of Chronic Illnesses

Hypertension, diabetes and asthma are well-studied, chronic disorders, requiring continuing care for most if not all of a patient's life. At the same time, these disorders are not necessarily unremitting or unalterably lethal, as long as the treatment regimen of medication, diet and behavioural change are followed. This last point requires elaboration. Treatments for these medical disorders are heavily dependent upon behavioural change and medication compliance to achieve their potential effectiveness. In a recently published review of treatment outcome studies of these disorders, patient compliance with the recommended medical regimen was the most significant determinant of treatment outcome. However, studies have shown that less than 60 per cent of type-1, insulin-dependent, adult diabetics fully comply with their medication schedule and less than 40 per cent of hypertensive or asthmatic patients comply fully with their medication regimens. The problem is even worse for the behavioural and diet changes that are so important for the maintenance of short-term gains in these chronic illnesses. Again, a review of recent studies in the fields of adult-onset diabetes, hypertension and asthma indicates that less than 30 per cent of patients in treatment for these disorders comply with prescribed diet and/or behavioural changes that are designed to increase functional status and to reduce risk factors for reoccurrence of the disorders. Across all three of these chronic medical illnesses, compliance, and ultimately outcome, is poorest among patients with low socio-economic status, low family and social supports or significant psychiatric co-morbidity, as summarized in table 1.

This review of medication and behavioural compliance in the treatment of other chronic medical illnesses suggests important parallels with the treatment of drug dependence. In all these disorders, lack of patient compliance with the treatment regimen is a major contributor to the reoccurrence of symptoms; and in all these disorders compliance is poorest among those with co-morbid medical, psychiatric, family and social problems. Perhaps because of these similarities in treatment compliance there is also similarity in relapse or reoccurrence rates across all these disorders. In fact, outcome studies indicate that 30–50 per cent of insulin-dependent adult diabetic patients and approximately 50–70 per cent of adult hypertensive and asthmatic patients suffer reoccurrences of their symptoms each year to the point that they require, at least, re-stabilization of their medication and/or additional medical care to re-establish symptom remission. Many of these reoccurrences result in serious health complications. For example, limb amputations and blindness are common results of treatment non-compliance among diabetics. Stroke and cardiac disease are common problems associated with exacerbation of hypertension.

Table 1

Factors Associated with Relapse in Hypertension, Diabetes and Asthma

- Lack of adherence to prescribed medication, diet or behavioural change regimens
- Low socio-economic status
- Low family supports
- Psychiatric co-morbidity

A Chronic Illness Perspective on Treatment and Evaluation Designs

This section focuses on the question of whether the assumptions underlying interventions for acute conditions or those for chronic conditions are more appropriate for the treatment of addiction.

There are no definitive "cures" for any of the chronic medical illnesses reviewed here. Yet it is interesting that despite rather comparable rates of compliance and relapse across all of the disorders examined, there is no serious argument as to whether the treatments for diabetes, hypertension or asthma are "effective" or whether they should be supported by contemporary health insurance. However, this issue is very much in question with regard to treatments for drug dependence. In this regard, it is interesting that the relatively high relapse rates among diabetic, hypertensive and asthmatic patients following cessation of their medications have been considered evidence of the effectiveness of those medications and of the need for compliance enhancement strategies. In contrast, relapses to drug and alcohol use following cessation of addiction treatments has often been considered evidence of treatment failure.

Drug dependence treatments are not provided and especially are not evaluated under the same assumptions that pertain to other chronic illnesses. Particularly important in this regard is that drug dependence treatments are rarely delivered under a continuing care model that would be appropriate for a chronic illness. Indeed, with the exception of methadone maintenance and self-help groups most contemporary treatments for drug dependence are acute-care episodes. For example, it is common for a drug-dependent individual to be admitted to an outpatient rehabilitation programme lasting 30–90 days, rarely accompanied by medical monitoring or medication. This period of treatment is typically followed by discharge with referral to "community sources." While addiction treatment might be conceptualized as ongoing by those in the treatment field, from an operational perspective addiction treatments are delivered in much the same way as one might treat a surgical patient following a joint replacement. Outcome evaluations are typically conducted 6–12 months following treatment discharge, because addiction treatments have been expected to produce lasting reduction in symptoms following termination of treatment. Unlike the treatments for other chronic conditions, the reduction of symptoms during treatment has not been considered adequate to the expectations underlying addiction treatment.

This argument has nothing to do with whether addiction is fundamentally a disease, a bad habit, a social problem or all of the above. Moreover, it does not matter whether the essence of the intervention is the correction of some biological abnormality, the resolution of a psychological process, the teaching of some new behaviour or the development of some improved social support system. The expectations have been that some finite combination of medications, counselling and therapy, social services and/or social support systems should effect essential change in the root causes of addiction, remove those causal factors and result in lasting benefits.

A more realistic expectation is that the interventions currently available will not permanently correct the essence of the problem, only reduce the number and severity of the symptoms and improve personal function, as long as the patient participates in the intervention. This is precisely the same expectation that currently prevails in the treatment of chronic illnesses. Further, an "acute-care" expectation placed upon those types of treatment produces some perverse and even absurd results. For example, consider contemporary goals and the prevailing evaluation strategy for addiction treatments—applied to a hypertension treatment regimen. Patients who meet diagnostic criteria for hypertension would be admitted to an outpatient "hypertension rehabilitation" programme lasting 30–90 days in which they might receive medication, behavioural change therapy, dietary education and an exercise regimen. At the end of that period, the medication would be tapered during the last days of the treatment and the patients would be referred to community sources. The evaluation team would recontact the patient six months later and determine whether the patient had been continuously normotensive throughout that post-treatment period. Only those patients who met that criterion would be considered "successfully treated." Obviously, this hypothetical treatment management strategy and its associated evaluation approach are absurd for any chronic illness, including drug dependence.

POSTSCRIPT

Does Drug Abuse Treatment Work?

Much of the research on drug abuse treatment effectiveness is inconclusive; furthermore, researchers do not agree on the best way is to measure effectiveness. Determining the effectiveness of drug abuse treatment is extremely important because the federal government and a number of state governments debate the amount of funding allocated to drug treatment. Many experts in the drug field agree that much of the money allocated to problems related to drugs has not been spent wisely. To prevent further waste of taxpayer funds, it is essential to find out if drug abuse treatment works before funding for it is increased.

Another concern related to this issue is that addicts who wish to receive treatment often face many barriers. One of the most serious barriers is a lack of available treatment facilities. Compounding the problem is the fact that many communities resist the idea of having a drug treatment center in their neighborhoods, even though there is little research on the effects of treatment facilities on property values and neighborhood crime rates. Another barrier to treatment is cost, which, with the exception of self-help groups, is expensive. Furthermore, some addicts avoid organized treatment altogether for fear that if they go for treatment, they will be identified as drug abusers by law enforcement agencies. Likewise, many female drug addicts avoid drug treatment because they fear they will lose custody of their children.

Many addicts in treatment are there because they are given a choice of entering either prison or treatment. Are people who are required to enter treatment more or less likely to succeed than people who enter treatment voluntarily? Early studies show that treatment was more effective for voluntary clients. However, a study conducted by the U.S. federal government of 12,000 clients enrolled in 41 publicly funded treatment centers found that clients referred by the criminal justice system fared as well as, if not better than, voluntary clients in terms of reduced criminal activity and drug use. People who enter treatment voluntarily have an easier time walking away from treatment. One emerging trend is to provide drug treatment to people in prison. Drug abuse treatment to prison inmates has been shown to reduce recidivism.

Two articles that discuss the benefits of drug abuse treatment are "Drug Treatment: The Willard Option," in *Corrections Today* (April 2004) and "Coming Clean; Drug Treatment," in *The Economist* (October 16, 2004). Donna Lyons examines whether drug addicts should be sent to prison or to treatment in "Conviction for Addiction: States Are Considering No-nonsense Drug Policy Should Mean Prison or Treatment," in *State Legislatures* (June 2002). The benefits of providing drug abuse treatment to addicts in prison are discussed in Peter Anderson's article, "Treatment With Teeth: A Judge Explains Why Drug

Courts That Mandate and Supervise Treatment Are an Effective Middle Ground to Help Addicts Stay Clean and Reduce Crime," in *The American Prospect* (December 2003). In "Is Drug Abuse Treatment Effective?" (*The American Enterprise*, March/April 1994), Robert Apsler questions the value of drug abuse treatment.

ISSUE 19

Do Tobacco Advertisements Influence People to Smoke?

YES: Georgina Lovell, from "Women and Children First: Tobacco Targets the Vulnerable," *You Are the Target. Big Tobacco: Lies, Scams—Now The Truth* (Chryan Communications, 2002)

NO: Alyse R. Lancaster and Kent M. Lancaster, from "Teenage Exposure to Cigarette Advertising in Popular Consumer Magazines," *Journal of Advertising* (Fall 2003)

ISSUE SUMMARY

YES: Author Georgina Lovell maintains that the tobacco industry purposely targets women and children with advertisements. Cigarette advertisements appeal to women by emphasizing the independence that comes from smoking and by showing that smoking helps to keep one slim. To illustrate the effectiveness of cigarette advertisements, smoking by high school girls increased dramatically throughout the 1990s. One of the most successful advertising campaigns was the use of Joe Camel to get adolescents to smoke.

NO: Alyse R. Lancaster and Kent M. Lancaster, communication professors at the Universities of Florida and Michigan, respectively, argue that the vast majority of teens are exposed to cigarette advertisements, yet only a small percentage actually take up smoking.

This debate is not about whether tobacco is hazardous, but whether advertising influences young people to smoke. Several questions need to be considered: Do tobacco advertisements encourage smoking, especially among adolescents? Will a ban on tobacco advertisements reduce smoking behavior? Should tobacco companies have the right to promote their products as they wish and are they protected by freedom of speech?

If tobacco advertisements are prohibited because tobacco products are harmful, should advertisements for other potentially unhealthy products such as high-fat foods, tanning beds, and guns be prohibited also? Are tobacco companies being unfairly targeted? Does the prohibition of tobacco advertisements violate the democratic rights of tobacco companies? How much responsibility do consumers, including adolescents, have for their behavior?

In 1970, the Public Health Cigarette Smoking Act was passed, which banned cigarette advertisements from television and radio. Since the 1970 ban, cigarette advertisements have become much more prevalent in the print media and on roadside billboards. Although cigarettes are not directly advertised on television, their presence on television is unmistakable. Tobacco companies sponsor many televised sporting activities, especially automobile racing. Signs at various stadiums, which are frequently seen on camera, prominently display tobacco products. Critics contend that many of these advertisements are geared toward target populations, notably adolescents and minorities. One of the most successful advertising campaigns is R.J. Reynolds Tobacco Company's Joe Camel. Over half of 6-year-olds were able to match the Joe Camel cartoon character with the cigarette it was promoting. Sales of Camel cigarettes escalated from $6 million to $476 million after the Joe Camel advertisements were introduced.

Many critics contend that stricter controls need to be put in place to eliminate the manipulative effects that tobacco advertising campaigns have on target audiences as well as on the general public. There is much concern that tobacco is a "gateway drug" that paves the way for the use of other, illegal types of drugs, such as marijuana, cocaine, heroin, and Ecstasy. The longer young people wait before they smoke cigarettes, if they even do choose to smoke, the less likely they will be to use other drugs. Many critics argue that marketing tobacco products to young people is unconscionable because of the potential long-term effects.

Supporters of the tobacco industry and advertising executives claim that there is no compelling evidence of a causal link between advertising and smoking initiation and behavior. Moreover, advertisers contend that they do not market their tobacco products to young people. Advertising, they claim, is used to enhance brand loyalty. They also argue that banning advertising violates their rights to free speech. It is their contention that advertisers have a constitutional right to disseminate their advertisements and that consumers have the right to view tobacco advertisements. How much responsibility for adolescent smoking lies with young people?

Curiosity and experimentation are very common among many adolescents. If a young person experiments with cigarettes out of curiosity, can advertising be blamed? Cultural attitudes toward smoking are another factor. There is a growing negative attitude in society in regard to smoking. However, not everyone looks at smoking in an adverse way. What is the effect of their attitudes on the smoking behavior of people around them? Advertisers become easy scapegoats if people choose to use tobacco or engage in other unhealthy activities.

In the following selections, Georgina Lovell argues that cigarette advertising successfully targets youths and women. Lovell points to particular advertising campaigns and the subsequent increase in cigarette use as evidence. Restricting tobacco advertising is an important first step in decreasing smoking rates, particulary among young people and women, says Lovell. Alyse Lancaster and Kent Lancaster maintain the majority of young people do not smoke, despite the fact that they are exposed to large amounts of cigarette advertising. The Lancasters argue that limiting tobacco advertisements would have little impact on whether young people choose to smoke.

YES

Georgina Lovell

You Are the Target: Big Tobacco: Lies, Scams—Now the Truth

I. Women and Children First: Tobacco Targets the Vulnerable

Women—"Project Magic"

. . . Towards the end of the 19th century, the tobacco industry understood the importance of peddling nicotine to women via traditional images of sweet children, fortified with an appeal to the newly emerging suffragette. Even the most coddled of women welcomed the novel opportunity to make their own choices independently of male influence. Inveterate cigarette advertising directed to the untapped female market carried images of a barefoot little girl cuddling a cat, and apple-cheeked babies in prams who declared in cute captions that "PET cigarettes are the best!" Bold new advertising, reflecting newly-found female independence, showed naughty-but-nice young ladies flashing forbidden ankles as they bent over to take a closer look at a package of cigarettes on the ground, the double-entendre caption declaring: "Worth Picking Up!"

Until the years following World War I, only women of loose morals would dare to be seen smoking in public. Tobacco capitalized on the excitement of the forbidden-fruit connection with smoking pitted against traditionally accepted ladylike behavior. This appealing dichotomy has been the foundation for a century to market nicotine to women, particularly young women, with the false claim that only the free-thinking and independent dare to smoke, while thumbing their metaphorical noses at anyone who objects. From the dainty Victorian matron lighting a "Little Darling" cigarette in the privacy of her own parlor, to the party animal 1920's flapper; from WWII Rosie the Riveter, to the 1950's June Cleaver clones; from the bra-burning women's liberationists of the 1960's to the pierced punk rockers of the 1990's—the underlying theme of enticing women to smoke has embraced the fundamental feminine requisites all women share: to make their own decisions—and above all else, do whatever they are convinced is necessary to stay slim.

The counter-image of the smoke-free woman as a puritanical prude whose rejection of nicotine addiction means, as the tobacco ads have said for a hundred years, she loses out in the dating game, doesn't know how to enjoy herself, and secretly resents her bolder, free-thinking (and, of course, smoking) sisters. This image of the female smoker continues to be promoted today.

The roaring twenties of post WWI reflected the metamorphosed woman who had grown weary of artificially laced-up wasp waists and bustles, elaborate coiffures, ankles tangled in cumbersome yards of voluminous skirts, crinolines and petticoats. Known as The New Generation Woman, the flapper defiantly doffed her corsets, bleached, permed and bobbed her hair, raised her hemlines scandalously high to the knees (which any self-respecting flapper curiously rouged and powdered). Fearless flappers outrageously plucked their eyebrows, painted their faces and earned themselves the proud label of "rebel" by the more gentle generation of their Gibson Girl mothers. A 1922 magazine article describes three stages of flapperdom: the semi-flapper, the flapper and the super-flapper. The author of one article as it appeared on December 6, 1922 does not take her identity lightly. She tells her parents, "Attainment of flapperhood is a big and serious undertaking!"

Venturing into previously male-only arenas included cocktails, cars, crew races—and smoking. Cigarette holders became as mandatory a fashion accessory for the fashionable flapper as fingerless fishnet gloves, feather boas and waist-length ropes of pearls. The truly chic cigarette holders collapsed into small pendants worn on a chain around the neck–concealed from the stern eye of strict parents, and available for use a needed. Later model cigarette holders mirrored the long, slim image of the flapper and extended up to 24", often fashioned from mother of pearl or silver filigree to match compacts and lipstick holders. From closet parlor smokers to wild good-time-party-girls in less than a decade, the woman of the 20's caught the attention of the tobacco industry who never fail to recognize a market ripe for the picking.

Underlying this newly found freedom of thought and action remained one of the more pervasive self-imposed conditions of women through the ages: a slender figure. 1927 Lucky Strikes advertised themselves with the slogan "Reach for a Lucky Instead of a Sweet" with the clear implication that smoking keeps a woman slim and therefore attractive to men. Packaged and sold in small satin bags, cigarettes for the female clientele in the early years of the 20th century were unfiltered and wrapped in gold leaf paper, carefully marketed as small and dainty, and sometimes perfumed. Brand names appealed to the feminine, sophisticated image tobacco still likes to promote: Little Darlings, Debs Rose Tips, Chic, Duchess, Lady Hamilton, Fems. These alluring brand names bear little association with the reality of stained teeth, yellowed fingers, halitosis and smart new hairdos reeking of stale smoke. Salome brand appealed to the saucy sisters who believed tobacco propaganda reassuring them that the only requirement for instant and irresistible sex appeal could be all theirs—via a tube of dried tobacco leaves, wrapped in gold metallic paper, set on fire, and placed dangling from the mouth, while exhaling smoke from the nostrils.

"Some women would prefer having smaller babies." Joseph Cullman, CEO, Philip Morris, when asked to comment on the results of a U.K. research project concluding that babies of smoking mothers are smaller and smoking mothers have more stillbirths and infant death with 28 days of birth.

CBS *Face the Nation* January 3, 1971 Bates 1005081714/1732

WWII saw the emergence of an even more independent women than her 1920's counterpart. With able-bodied men in uniform and away for many lonely years, women of the 1940's had to assume traditional "man's work" and proved they could tackle anything—without compromising their traditional roles of wives and mothers. Tobacco advertising adapts to current events, except when sales are adversely affected. The patriotic green "Lucky Strike Has Gone To War" military-style WWII packaging changed to white following protests from the ladies who complained the camouflage-green pack clashed with their dresses. Within six months following the package change from green to white, Lucky Strike sales increased by 38%. By 1949, 33% of women smoked, a 500% increase since WWI.

Through the baby-booming 1950's, housewives maintained a status slightly below sainthood. September, 1940 *Good Housekeeping* magazine published guidelines for Emily Post's "Smoking Etiquette" and these continued into the 1950's, as more women became addicted to nicotine. All conscientious housewives provided cut glass ashtrays for their husbands and visiting guests, and the smartest homes sported decorator coffee-table cigarette boxes made of cut crystal (with matching table lighters), regularly replenished with a fresh guest supply of cigarettes. Gracious hospitality included the offer of cigarettes as much as the offer of food and beverage.

Ever conscious of image, women responded to tobacco industry's guidelines for "Smoking Do's and Don'ts." Correct and incorrect etiquette accompanying the acceptance of a light, nostril exhales and ladylike extinguishing of a cigarette butt were taken very seriously by the 1950's woman. Emily Post remained adamant about acceptable and unacceptable behavior for smokers: it was considered the height of boorishness to light up a cigar or cigarette at a dinner table before the host or hostess did; brides may smoke, but must abstain while wearing their bridal veil (that seems only practical, if not for preservation of healthy lungs, at least for fire prevention). Always, the persistent message relentlessly reminded women they could accept a guarantee that as long as they smoked they would remain forever slim and sophisticated, while their smoke-free sisters (according to the tobacco ads) missed out on all the fun. . . .

The Virginia Slims advertising hoax of the 1960's and 1970's compared repressed turn of the century women with contemporary images of liberated ladies who enjoyed hard-earned independence and equality with men—which, of course, included nicotine addiction. In 1974, six years after the Virginia Slims 'You've come a long way, baby' campaign, the smoking initiation of twelve-year old girls in the United States had increased by 110%.

From 1991–1999, smoking among high school girls increased from 27% to 34.9%l. For twenty-five years following the 1960's publication of *The Feminine*

Mystique and *Sex and the Single Girl,* the focus of advertising to women increased dramatically to access what tobacco call "market share" of disposable income women had now acquired.

In the early 1990's, as the rate of female smokers continued to increase, the *It's a Woman Thing* campaign arrived on the heels of the *You've Come A Long Way* Virginia Slims scam. Women's independence and self-sufficiency had become established and accepted. The new marketing exploited the in-your-face attitude three generations beyond the giddy good-time-girl flapper who flaunted tradition for fun. The badge of rebellion for the great-grandmothers of modern women had been shortened skirts and bobbed hair—and, according to tobacco advertisements, smoking. The badge of rebellion for modern women became tattoos and body piercings—and, according to tobacco advertisements, smoking.

Women of the 90's took orders from nobody, with one exception: they still reacted to tobacco's false imagery of slim, chic living made possible only by smoking. Smoke-free sisters were still portrayed as spinsterish, narrow-in-the-nose nannies with no sense of fun. Smoking causes premature wrinkles and aging of the skin, due to years of collagen breakdown resulting in lack of elasticity. However, hundreds of thousands of women bought tobacco's deceptive promise of eternal youth and sophistication, made possible only by nicotine addiction. Correspondingly, women continue to die at record rates of lung cancer.

. . . Virginia Slims launched an additional *Find Your Voice* campaign, which perpetuated the myth that only nicotine addicted women have the ability to think for themselves. The *Find Your Voice* campaign launched in the late 1990's, met its nemesis—a brave lady who had once been a tobacco model and "Lucky Strike Lady" and "Chesterfield Girl" in the 1950's. Janet Sackman, a smoker and promoter of cigarette smoking for many years, lost her voice box to throat cancer in 1983. In 1990, she was diagnosed with lung cancer and lost one-third of one lung. Following speech therapy and practice in using a mechanical larynx, Janet Sackman addressed the National Press Club on May 24, 2000 to speak out, with the help of an artificial voice box, about the devastating health consequences of smoking which had not caused her to "find her voice," but to lose it.

The National Coalition FOR Women AGAINST Tobacco launched their own campaign against the marketing of tobacco to women via free giveaway cigarettes and a bought-and-paid-for female soap opera starlet. They named their counterattack *Loud and Clear,* and their coalition co-chair, Joanne Koldare, said, "The use of tobacco products continues to pose one of the greatest health threats to women. There are an estimated 23 million women smokers in this country, and we will not let the tobacco industry entice, fool, or seduce more young women with this newest attempt at recruitment."

According to the National Women's Health Information Center, since 1987, lung cancer has been the top cancer killer among American women, with an estimated 66,000 deaths in 1999. Over the past ten years, the mortality rate from lung cancer has declined in men but has continued to rise in women.

These alarming trends are under-recognized by women and are due almost exclusively to increased rates of cigarette smoking. . . .

> "A massive potential market still exists among women and young adults, cigarette industry leaders agreed, acknowledging that recruitment of these millions of prospective smokers comprises the major objective for the immediate future and on a long term basis as well."
>
> United States Tobacco Journal, 1950,
> *Cigarette Executives Expect Added Volume*

Tobacco billboard advertising has become severely restricted in North America and illegal in many places. Increased purchasing power of women becomes the target for tobacco's image of glamor, independence and free-thinking in billboard advertisements elsewhere, such as those seen in Johannesburg, South Africa for Winston Lights. The billboard-high photograph of a well-endowed naked woman about to step out of the shower clearly reveals enticing and glistening wet portions of her body. With a suggestive smile, she enticingly looks into the camera as her hand is teasingly poised to sweep the shower curtain aside. The caption, appearing directly above the cigarette logo for Winston Lights, reads: "Do I look shy?" In another, a petulant sexy blonde sitting on a park bench with a lighted cigarette in her hand looks into the camera and asks "Do I look like I'd cook you breakfast?" The desired bad-girl-in-your-face image perpetuates with another billboard-high image of a black-leather clad biker chick astride a motorcycle asking "Do I look easy to handle?"

The intended tobacco message directed at women for the last century has been clear: smoking cigarettes instantly transforms the plainest and most ordinary women into an irresistible, glamorous, mysterious and sexy rebel.

Just don't mention the tar-coated lungs.

> "Many women are angry by the suggestion of those around them that they should not smoke. For these women, smoking represents an independent and defiant stance. As women are reacting increasingly to restraints put upon them, more women are smoking (of all smokers, 53% are women, 43% are men). However, because of women's nurturing role in society, they are naturally more involved with low tar cigarettes than men (70% of low tar smokers are female)."
>
> June, 1985 Philip Morris "Project Magic" Bates Number 2501008130

Cigarettes carrying a "light" or "mild" or "low tar" label typically appeal to the feminine perspective of daintiness. Referring to cigarettes as either "light" or "mild" or "low tar" has been stopped in Canada, following confirmation of the inaccuracy of this claim. The tobacco industry manipulated test results to give false readings of low tar and nicotine content in some brands. Consumers of reduced nicotine brands of cigarettes require a deeper puff for the same nicotine delivery, and consequently develop tumors more deeply situated in the lungs than seen in smokers of "regular" brands.

Women smokers provide fertile pastures for tobacco propaganda. Appealing to their sense of responsibility to their families to take care of their health, while simultaneously promoting the "personal choice" to smoke at all, they were offered the compromise of an allegedly less dangerous "low tar" cigarette. "It is the first cigarette to offer a person the *freedom* [sic] to choose what strength it shall be."

According to the World Health Organization, 15% of women smoke in industrialized countries, compared with only 8% of women in developing countries. In addition, women in India and Asian countries use chewing tobacco with greater frequency than women in western countries. Current efforts in Vietnam, Korea and India raise the tobacco cartel's hopes of more female nicotine addiction, beginning with addressing the desires of young girls paradoxically concerned about thinking for themselves while conforming to peer pressure—and above all else, staying slim. . . .

> "Long after the adolescent preoccupation with self-image has subsided, the cigarette will pre-empt even food in time of scarcity on the smokers' priority list." *Smoker Psychology Research* by Helmut Wakeham, Presented to the PM Board of Directors November 26, 1969.
>
> Minnesota Trial Exhibit 10299 Bates #1000273741

Tobacco Targets Our Kids

The tobacco cartel have an irrefutable history of lies, fraud, conspiracy and profits über alles. The most despicable aspect of business "ethics" has been their deliberate victimization of children.

The teenage years are the years in which most smokers become addicted to nicotine, when brand selection and loyalty initiates and when conformity to peer pressure is the greatest. According to tobacco's painstaking market research, only 5% of smokers begin smoking after the age of 24. Tobacco must recruit 3,000 new smokers *every day* to replace those who quit or die (they are the ones who have quit permanently). It is not surprising to know in a secret 1983 memo summarizing the public-relations initiatives of the Tobacco Institute, Brown & Williamson Tobacco clearly stated they "will not support a youth smoking program which discourages young people from smoking."

Tobacco missed no opportunity to convey their false message that smoking is an enjoyable pastime, reserved only for adults—but children can pretend to be grown-up until they come of age. In 1946, a letter from Brown & Williamson Tobacco to a candy manufacturer gave permission for their brand labels to be copied on packages of candy cigarettes, accompanied by the comment "We have never raised any objection to the use of our labels, feeling (for your more or less private information) that it is not too bad an advertisement."

Spit tobacco (euphemistically labelled "smokeless tobacco," "chew," "dip" and "snuff" by the tobacco industry) involves placing a wad of tobacco between the gums and the cheek and sucking on it. This results in increased saliva production, and spittoons became necessary in public places to discourage disposal of brown spit on public sidewalks and pub floors. Spit tobacco is both highly addictive and a Class A Carcinogen: known to cause cancer in humans.

Skoal Long Cut Cherry spit tobacco looks and tastes like candy. Manufactured in the U.S. by the U.S. Tobacco Company it is meticulously designed to attract a youth market. The cherry flavor is strong and sweet, and lasts two–three minutes, long enough for a child to adjust to the bitter bite of raw tobacco. A former U.S. Tobacco Sales Representative refers to it as "Cherry Skoal is for somebody who likes the taste of candy, if you know what I mean."

The pH level has been exactingly adjusted to slow nicotine absorption for maximum impact on a smaller body while aiding and abetting dependency on this product, aimed for the "pre-smoker" market. Although candy flavored snuff accounts for only 2% of U.S. Tobacco sales, 47% of its total budget is spent promoting this product to young teenagers to prime them for higher impact nicotine delivery devices more commonly known as "cigarettes." . . .

> "We did not look at the underage market even though I am holding a document in my hand that says we did."
>
> (Ex-Phillip Morris President & CEO James Morgan in videotaped testimony in Minnesota St. Paul Pioneer Press, March 3, 1998)

Joe Camel

While publicly denying any direct marketing to underage children, R.J. Reynolds introduced a cartoon character representing its flagship brand whose sales were on its dromedarian knees. Joe Camel epitomized teenage cool, with wraparound sunglasses, leather jackets, white suits a la John "Stayin' Alive" Travolta, racing cars and sailboats—often with at least one beautiful woman in attendance. Entire collections of accessories were spawned, including wristwatches, clocks, t-shirts, flip-flops, baseball hats and even fishing lures. Following the arrival of this camp cartoon character, Camel cigarette sales catapulted from $6 million in 1988 to $476 million in 1991. The tobacco industry reported the brilliant invention of Joe Camel had been directly responsible for this astonishing reversal of fortune.

Joe Camel acquired cult status, especially admired by young teens who aspired to cool-ness via their favourite cartoon character. Camel cigarettes were featured by way of product placement in *Honey, I Shrunk the Kids* and *Who Framed Roger Rabbit?*

California Department of Health Services conducted a survey of 24,000 adults and 5,000 teenagers in 1990 to determine the most recognized brand of cigarettes. Camel and Marlboro were named as the two most heavily advertised brands. When the survey results were analyzed more closely by age groups, less than 10% of those respondents over the age of 45 identified Camels as first on the list of most advertised cigarettes. This percentage more than doubled to 22.7% for the 16 to 17 year olds interviewed. This figure jumped to 34% of the 12–13 year olds, who hit the R.J. Reynolds Tobacco bullseye when they identified Camel cigarettes as the most popular brand.

A second study interviewed 5,000 children. Three to six year olds had become as familiar with Joe Camel as they were with Mickey Mouse.

Joe Camel's obituary appeared in 1997 when R.J. Reynolds lost a lawsuit and agreed to not only to remove Joe Camel from their advertising but to pay $10 million for antismoking campaigns in California. Nobody mourned Joe Camel's passing except R.J. Reynolds Tobacco who would have to find a replacement for the increase of $470 million in sales resulting from a jolly cartoon they said was "not directed to children."

R.J. Reynolds would have to think of some other way to maintain the 66% increase in young teenage smokers their old pal Joe had managed to hook.

One of the most positive aspects of tobacco litigation has been the emergence of previously confidential and top secret company documents illustrating for all to see the duplicity upon which the tobacco industry depends to make billions in profit every year. Public statements bear no resemblance to the reality of the business.

One strategy proven to work effectively to educate youth about smoking has been explaining to pre teens and teenagers how they have been singled out by the tobacco cartel as dupes and profit fodder. Teenage rebellion is more effectively directed against the tobacco cartel, instead of deciding to use their products.

> And there's more . . . in the words of those swell tobacco guys who "don't target kids"
>
> "A cigarette for the beginner is a symbolic act. I am no longer my mother's child, I'm tough, I am an adventurer, I'm not square . . . As the force from the psychological symbolism subsides, the pharmacological effect takes over to sustain the habit."
>
> "The lower age limit for the profile of young smokers is to remain at 14."
>
> "From a Corporate standpoint, Philip Morris posted a 4 point gain among 14–17 year old smoker."
>
> "Respondents aged 14 to 20 are to used for the cigarette profile report."
>
> "Probability sample of 452 teen-agers ages 12–17" finds that 13 percent smoke an average of 10.6 cigarettes per day and how the data from the study are consonant [sic] with the findings of other such studies, both at Philip Morris and without."
>
> "We were trying very hard to influence kids who were 14 to start smoking." . . .

Project S.C.U.M.

Tobacco research confirms that the nicotine addicted segment of the population will assign the priority of obtaining tobacco products above life necessities such as food and shelter. In the early to mid 1990's, R.J. Reynolds Tobacco decided to increase their sales volume by observing and then closing in for the kill (literally) on distinct minorities in San Francisco. They named this campaign Project S.C.U.M., (sub culture urban marketing), and directed it towards the homeless and gay population who statistically contained a higher than average incidence of smokers. They labelled the target of their attention "rebellious" (there's that word again), "Generation X"-ers, people of "international influence" and "street people." The strategy's goal was to peddle Camel cigarettes from less than traditional retail outlets, or "head shops," and extend a tobacco friendly hand towards the wallets of an already victimized and disadvantaged segment of the population. The San Francisco areas of "Castro" and "Tenderloin" were identified as neighborhoods of particular interest, in handwritten notes in the margin of one of the documents.

Summary

In 1991, Philip Morris conducted a close-up study on women's smoking preferences to monitor the continued success of their sales and promotion of nicotine addiction to the female market.

Tobacco have targeted women for a century, appealing to women's latent sense of rebellion against a world imposing often unattainable expectations of beauty. Tobacco presents itself as the vehicle for transforming Eliza Doolittles into much-admired fair ladies with the flick of a cigarette lighter. Tobacco advertising encouraged women to think for themselves—through smoking, of course—in their Find Your Voice Campaign. This scam backfired horribly when, following surgical removal of her cancerous larynx, a former smoker and cigarette model spoke publicly through her mechanical voice box about the health consequences of tobacco use. Concerted efforts to attract women to nicotine has resulted in a higher incidence of women smokers than ever before. The unique action of female hormones places women at increased vulnerability for smoking related disease. Lung cancer now kills more women than breast cancer.

Hollywood actors disregard their responsibility to their young fans when they accept payment for smoking on camera, clearly displaying cigarette brand logos.

The tobacco industry claim they have never pursued the underage market, a claim proven false with their own research material about candy-flavored tobacco and a smoking cartoon character. Since 1982, the tobacco industry have known that spit tobacco causes oral cancer.

Disguising the bitter, foul taste of tobacco with sugary fruit flavors attracts children with the false and misleading implication that "smokeless tobacco" means "safe tobacco." Spit tobacco introduces children to the experience of a nicotine hit with each mouthful, preparing them for smoking, presented as an enticing adult activity.

The time has arrived to pay the tobacco piper. The tobacco-friendly Bush administration has waived previous restrictions preventing tobacco from advertising their products within 1,000 feet of schools and playgrounds.

Higher taxes on tobacco products have a record of reducing consumption, especially among youth. In Canada during the years 1978–1991, increases in the taxes resulted in the price of cigarettes increasing by 270%. During this same time, teenage consumption dropped from 44% to 20%.

Three out of four individuals in the western world do not smoke.

Smoking restrictions work to reduce tobacco consumption. They de-normalize smoking and reduce its social acceptance. Ensuing reductions in lung cancer rates follow. In the year 2000, California Dept. of Health Services reported a 14.4% decline in lung cancer rates since the implementation of their restrictive smoking ordinances—compare this with the national reduction of 4% for the same period of time.

Youth smoking cannot be affected without first educating adults to set the best smoke-free examples and not the do-as-I-say-not-as-I-do hypocrisy of too many nicotine addicted adults—who, if they smoke around their children are guilty of child abuse each time they do so.

> "A cigarette as a 'drug' administration system for public use has very very significant advantages. . . All we would want then is a larger bag to carry the money to the bank."
>
> BAT Marketing Strategy Document Bates Number 40045998/9956

NO

Alyse R. Lancaster and
Kent M. Lancaster

Teenage Exposure to Cigarette Advertising in Popular Consumer Magazines

One of the most prominent issues surrounding tobacco advertising is whether tobacco advertisers target teenagers with their advertising and whether this, in turn, causes teens to smoke. Certainly, this is an issue that warrants concern. In 1999, approximately 14.9% of youths 12 to 17 years of age smoked cigarettes. In 2000, 14.6% of eighth graders, 23.9% of tenth graders, and 31.4% of twelfth graders reported past-month cigarette usage. These numbers are consistent with those released in May 2002 by the Centers for Disease Control and Prevention (CDC). The CDC reported that 28.5% of high-school students currently smoke cigarettes and that lifetime cigarette usage among high-school students dropped from 70.4% in 1999 to 63.9% in 2001. Although these numbers have been declining steadily since 1996, the number of teens who smoke is still high.

Influence of Cigarette Advertising in Magazines

Following the 1971 broadcast ban on tobacco advertising, magazines have become an important medium for tobacco advertisers in the United States. In 1999, major tobacco advertisers spent approximately $442.7 million on magazine advertising. Research suggests that because magazines are targeted specifically to particular demographic groups, it is easier for advertisers, particularly tobacco advertisers, to reach various segments of the population, including women and children.

Historically, as tobacco advertising campaigns became more targeted, smoking rates among targeted groups tended to increase. For example, tobacco companies began targeting women in the mid 1920s as more women began smoking during that period. This trend strengthened in the 1960s, when tobacco companies developed marketing campaigns designed specifically

From *Journal of Advertising*, vol. 32, no. 3, Fall 2003, pp. 69–76. Copyright © 2003 by M.E. Sharpe, Inc. Reprinted by permission. References omitted.

for women. Many researchers argue that the same logic can be applied to targeting youth. Young people who report being aware of tobacco promotions are likely to be more susceptible to using tobacco products, and are encouraged to begin smoking. In addition, images in cigarette ads rely on adventure, risk, and recreation rather than on the unhealthy side effects of smoking, and these images potentially diminish perceived risks of smoking. In a longitudinal study of the association between receptivity to tobacco advertising and promotion and the initiation of smoking, Pierce et al. concluded that there is a positive relationship between the two variables and that exposure to cigarette advertising can influence non-smokers to begin smoking and become addicted to cigarettes.

One of the biggest questions surrounding teen smoking is whether cigarette usage among teens stems from exposure to cigarette advertising. Magazines are a popular medium for advertising tobacco products, and several studies have suggested that tobacco advertisers use magazines that reach children and young adults. Other studies further argue that there is indeed a relationship between exposure to tobacco advertising and smoking among teens. For example, Pollay et al. found a positive relationship between cigarette brand selection and exposure to brand advertising among teenagers. Pierce et al. found that teens who are receptive to cigarette advertising are more likely to smoke than those who are not receptive to the advertising.

Joe Camel advertisements have been controversial for many years. Several studies have suggested that children are likely to recognize the Joe Camel character and associate it with cigarettes. Some of the most heavily cited studies are those that suggest six-year-olds are more likely to recognize Joe Camel than Mickey Mouse, and that recognition of a trade character is positively associated with age. A 1995 study, however, suggested that although 25% of three-year-old children and 72% of six-year-old children correctly associated Joe Camel with cigarettes, Joe Camel was not significantly more recognized than the Disney Channel/Mickey Mouse icon. Mizerski also found that the liking for cigarettes decreased with the age of the respondent, and that with Joe Camel in particular, "liking cigarettes and recognizing Joe Camel was significantly and negatively related."

In response to studies claiming that tobacco advertisers use magazine advertising to target teens, tobacco companies such as Philip Morris have developed youth smoking-prevention programs. As part of the Master Settlement Agreement, Philip Morris stated they would not place cigarette advertising in publications directed primarily to youth under the age of 21, including college media, and that youth would not be targeted with any of their advertising. In addition, Philip Morris, along with Brown and Williamson, promised voluntarily not to place cigarette advertising in any magazine in which readership of those under the age of 18 constitutes more than 15% of the magazine's total readership or in magazines with more than 2 million readers under the age of 18.

As a result of the MSA, tobacco companies have been monitored closely in terms of their advertising. In June 2002, R.J. Reynolds was fined $20 million for violating the MSA by running magazine ads deemed to be aimed at teenagers. Reynolds was ordered to take "reasonable measures" to avoid exposing teens to its cigarette advertisements.

Measuring Exposure to Cigarette Advertising

Several studies have concluded that cigarette advertising in magazines reaches teenagers. Albright et al. found that the number of magazines with youth readership that accept cigarette advertising increased from 1971 (following the broadcast ban) until 1985. King et al. reported that cigarette brands popular among adolescents are more likely to be advertised in magazines than adult brands. Pierce et al. concluded that promotional tobacco activities, including magazine advertising, are causally related to the onset of smoking among adolescents.

A recent study by King and Siegel examined trends in advertising expenditures for 15 cigarette brands and exposure of young people to cigarette advertising in 38 youth-oriented magazines between 1995 and 2000. Youth-oriented magazines were assumed to have more than 15% of their readership comprised of teen readers, or at least 2 million readers who were between 12 and 17 years old. They found that the proportion of young people who were potentially exposed to cigarette advertising in magazines ranged from 81.9 to 88.4% for youth-brand cigarettes and from 55.5 to 80.1% for adult brands. They further found that the proportion of young people who were potentially exposed three or more times in a given year ranged from 61.3 to 87.9%. The average frequency of potential magazine advertising ranged from 10.2 to 32.8 magazine exposures per year. Throughout their study, the authors are careful to state that their analysis refers only to *potential* exposure to the cigarette advertisements contained within the magazines studied; they did not attempt to estimate exposure to cigarette advertisements themselves.

In an analysis similar to that performed by King and Siegel, Krugman and King also examined teens' exposure to consumer magazines that contained cigarette advertising. Their analysis examined 14 consumer magazines that contain cigarette advertising and have a youth readership of at least 15%. Assuming one insertion in each of the 14 magazines, they found that approximately 66.1% of teens would be reached by the magazines an average of 2.1 times. By gender, they found that these magazines reached approximately 78% of male readers and 52.9% of female readers between 12 and 17 years old. However, these figures refer to magazine reach, not message reach, which is also the case in the King and Siegel study. In other words, they refer to exposure to a magazine carrying cigarette advertisements, and not to the cigarette advertisements themselves.

A key issue in these analyses is what is meant by reach. Both the King and Siegel and the Krugman and King studies define reach as one or more exposures to a magazine containing a typical cigarette advertisement. From a public policy and media-planning perspective, however, the important issue is whether teens are being exposed not to the magazines themselves, but rather, to the cigarette ads contained within them. Not all people who read a magazine will read all of the ads contained within it. Hence, vehicle (magazine) reach is not the equivalent of message (advertisement) reach.

In addition to determining message reach, researchers must also consider the *number* of advertising exposures to estimate advertising effectiveness. Substantial academic and industry research has suggested that multiple exposures to a message are needed to communicate key message content. In fact, in its 1997 July/August issue, the *Journal of Advertising Research* devoted an entire issue to topics of effective frequency in media planning. Taking these factors into account, the current study extends the Krugman and King analysis, as they have suggested should be done. The present study examines both magazine and cigarette advertising reach and frequency using the same set of consumer magazines that were analyzed in the Krugman and King study.

Method

Krugman and King provide the percent coverage of teens (ages 12–17) for 14 magazines analyzed in their study, which they obtained from the 1998 Mediamark Research, Inc. (MRI) Teenmark Study. MRI obtains teen magazine readership using a stratified random sample that includes teens who complete self-administered surveys at home, noting frequency of reading the past four issues of various magazines. Those data are presented in Table 1.

Table 1

Teen Reach of Typical Issue of 14 Magazines

Publication	Teen Percent Reach
Vibe	10.4
Sport	8.8
Spin	5.2
Hunting	4.0
The Sporting News	4.6
Hot Rod	9.1
Rolling Stone	9.7
Popular Science	9.6
Car Craft	3.1
Vogue	9.0
Sports illustrated	22.3
Mademoiselle	4.9
Motor Trend	5.0
Jet	7.2
Total GRPs	110.2

Notes: Teens (ages 12–17) base = 22,783,000. GRP = gross rating points.

Krugman and King were not able to analyze the reach and frequency of the MRI magazine data shown in Table 1. However, Simmons Market Research Bureau, Inc. (SMRB) did provide them with a reach estimate of 66.1 and an average frequency of 2.1. These estimates were based on SMRB readership data that were not provided. Our efforts to obtain the SMRB teen readership data were precluded by the approximately $20,000 subscriber cost.

Neither the MRI nor the SMRB data reported by Krugman and King are complete, but taken together they are sufficient to duplicate Krugman and King's reach and frequency results and extend them to estimate additional measures of vehicle and message reach and frequency. SMRB and MRI use different methods for estimating publication audiences, with SMRB estimates now typically higher than MRI estimates. There has been considerable, well-publicized controversy over the years concerning the methods used by SMRB and MRI to estimate publication audiences, hut discussion of these issues is beyond the scope of this study. (A recent and detailed overview can be found in *Magazine Dimensions 2003,* for example.) Nevertheless, there is a high correlation between the two services for comparable publication audiences. For example, the correlation coefficient is .997 for the adult audiences of 168 publications for spring 1998, the time frame of the Krugman and King study, including all 14 publications in this study. Therefore, we have simulated SMRB ratings by increasing the available MRI ratings by 26% based on the ratio of SMRB to MRI GRPs (gross rating points). The well-known formula, GRPs = reach × frequency, indicates that the SMRB ratings must sum to 138.8, that is $138.8 = 66.1 \times 2.1$, which is approximately 26% higher than the MRI GRPs reported in Table 1 for these 14 publications, that is, $.26 = (138.8-110.2)/110.2$.

Given SMRB reach, average frequency, GRPs, and simulated magazine ratings, we were able to duplicate the results reported by Krugman and King for teens (ages 12–17) and extend them by estimating a complete frequency distribution. This was done using Telmar's (www.telmar.com) InterMix^{TM} multimedia, reach-frequency package and deriving the average pair-wise magazine audience duplication to be 50% greater than chance. This percentage was also used to simulate MRI pair-wise magazine audience duplication.

To extend both SMRB and MRI analyses to likely message coverage, magazine advertising recognition and readership data were obtained from *2000 STARCH Adnorms,* published by Roper Starch Worldwide, Inc. The Starch data covers the 1998–1999 time frame, which approximately matches the time period that is included in the magazine readership data used by Krugman and King and in this study. Although other magazine advertisement evaluation services exist, such as those provided by Gallup and Robinson and Readex, for example, Starch data are used in this study because they are readily available to researchers and they include a large sample of publications, product categories, and advertisements.

The STARCH Readership Service has been measuring advertising readership for more than 75 years. Advertisement readership is measured using personal interviews with a minimum sample of 100 readers per publication issue. Measures include percentage of issues for readers who saw an advertisement (*noted*); (2) associated the advertisement with a particular advertiser (*associated*); (3) read some of the advertisement (*read some*); and (4) read most of an advertisement over 50 words in length (*read most*). Noted scores were used in this study because they are the broadest recognition measure, indicating the percentage of people interviewed who remember having seen the advertisement in the issue being studied. The use of *noted* scores represents an upper bound for likely advertisement exposure. *Associated, read some,* and *read most* Starch scores would lead to *lower* estimates of advertisement readership than those reported here.

The *2000 STARCH Adnorms* study reports average noted scores for adult men, women, or readers for 14,177 full-page, four-color advertisements across 44 consumer publications sampled over a two-year period. The weighted average noted score for these data is 48.1%. Two of these 44 publications are also listed in Table 1, including *Sports Illustrated,* with an average noted score of 50% for men across 872 advertisements, and *Vogue,* with an average noted score of 52% for women across 199 advertisements.

The 14,177 full-page, four-color advertisements include a broad range of product categories, ranging from automobiles to vitamins, including cigarettes. There are readership data for approximately 139 cigarette advertisements, with a weighted average Starch noted score of 41.3%. The average noted score is 42% for 38 full-page, four-color cigarette advertisements that appeared in *Sports Illustrated,* which is the only publication of the 14 listed in Table 1 for which cigarette advertisement readership data are available. Based on this information, full-page, four-color cigarette advertisements are approximately 14.1% less likely to be noticed than the typical full-page, four-color advertisement for all measured product categories combined, that is. $141 = (48.1 - 41.3)/48.1$.

Telmar's InterMix^{TM} reach-frequency system allows message effectiveness weighting of individual publications using data such as Starch noted scores. We have done so using the specific averages reported for *Sports Illustrated* and *Vogue,* as well as the averages for all publications combined. To establish an upper bound, the analysis has been conducted using average Starch noted scores across all product categories combined, as well as those pertaining only to cigarettes.

The extent to which Starch sampling includes teens is not known. That proportion is probably small, particularly since the 44 publications used here for average readership norms range from *Architectural Digest to Woman's Day,* and include publications such as *Better Homes and Gardens, Business Week, Money, Parents Magazine, Sunset, and Traditional Home.* On the other hand, publications appealing to younger audiences are also included, such as *Car and Driver, Glamour, Parade, Reader's Digest Family Plus, Road and Track, Sports Illustrated, TV Guide,* and *Vogue.* Consequently, the results concerning the extent to which teens are likely to notice full-page, four-color cigarette advertisements should be interpreted as general tendencies rather than conclusive.

Results

Table 2 shows the results of three levels of analysis based on both SMRB and MRI magazine audience estimates, including results for the publications themselves, for full-page, four-color advertisements for all products combined

Table 2

Coverage of Teens in 14 Publications

Media Evaluation Factor	Full-page, four-color ads		
	14 Publications	All Brands	Cigarettes
Estimates based on SMRB data			
Percentage reach one or more times	66.1	46.1	41.4
Percentage reach three or more times	20.5	4.1	2.7
Average frequency	2.1	1.5	1.4
GRPs	138.8	67.7	57.5
Estimates based on MRI data			
Percentage reach one or more times	59.5	39.2	34.9
Percentage reach three or more times	13.0	2.3	1.5
Average frequency	1.9	1.4	1.3
GRPs	110.2	53.8	45.7

Notes: Teens (ages 12–17) base = 22,783,000. SMRB = Simmons Market Research Bureau, Inc.; GRP = gross rating points; MRI = Mediamark Research, Inc.

as an upper bound, and for cigarette advertisements in particular. As with the Krugman and King study, the analysis assumes one use of each of the 14 magazines. For purposes of estimating advertisement coverage, the analysis is assumed to encompass one typical brand or cigarette advertiser using one full-page, four-color advertisement in each of the 14 magazines over a one-month time frame.

Looking at Table 2 results based on SMRB data, although 66.1% of teens are likely to be exposed to 1 or more of the 14 publication issues, only 46.1% are likely to be exposed to one or more full-page, four-color advertisement for a typical brand if the readership norm for all product categories combined is used. If the cigarette readership norm is used, it is estimated that only 41.4% of teens are likely to be exposed to one or more full-page, four-color advertisement for a typical cigarette brand within the 14 publications.

Advertising scholars and practitioners have long recognized the role of frequency in achieving advertising communication effects. Table 2 provides some estimates that assume that three or more message exposures are required to be effective. Other frequency levels could certainly be analyzed as well, but three is used here as an example since it is one of the thresholds that is most typically used and studied.

Table 2 shows that only 20.5% of teens are likely to look into or read 3 or more of the 14 publications listed in Table 1. This percentage is estimated to drop substantially to 4.1% when three or more exposures to full-page, four-color advertisements for a typical consumer brand are used as the threshold. If the focus is on cigarette advertisements for a typical brand, then it is estimated that only 2.7% of teens are likely to notice three or more of the brand's advertisements, assuming one insertion in each of the 14 publications listed in Table 1.

Although the pattern of results among coverage estimates in Table 2 based on MRI data is similar to the pattern among measures based on SMRB data, each MRI estimate is substantially lower, reflecting the lower ratings and GRPs in the MRI data. For example, using MRI data it is estimated that 59.5% of teens are likely to be exposed to 1 or more of the 14 magazines, 39.2% are likely to be exposed to 1 or more of a typical brand's advertisements, and 34.9% are likely to be exposed to 1 or more of a typical cigarette brand's advertisements. Approximately 13.0% of teens are estimated to look into or read 3 or more of the 14 magazines, whereas only 2.3 % are likely to see 3 or more of a typical brand's advertisements, and only 1.5% are likely to see 3 or more of a typical cigarette brand's advertisements.

Discussion

Although other studies have applied media-planning procedures to public policy issues, this appears to be the first to apply them to the controversial issue of teen readership of tobacco advertising. Tobacco advertising often is cited as a primary reason why teens smoke. This reasoning would assume that teens not only are exposed to a particular brand's cigarette advertisements, but are exposed to them enough times for the advertisements to have a behavioral impact. The results of this study suggest that if traditional media-planning methods are applied specifically to teen reading of tobacco advertising in consumer magazines, potential message impact may be minimal, even when substantially larger annual schedules are analyzed. Although approximately 59.5–66.1% of teens are likely to be exposed to 1 or more of the 14 magazines in this study, depending on whether MRI or SMRB data are used, only approximately 13.0–20.5% of teens are likely to be exposed to 3 or more magazines. More important to note is that approximately 34.9–41.4% of teens are likely to be exposed to one or more full-page, four-color cigarette advertisement(s) for a typical brand within these magazines. Only 1.5–2.7% of teens are likely to be exposed to three or more of a typical cigarette brand's advertisements in the 14 magazines.

Perhaps the study of the media effects of cigarette advertising and of antismoking efforts on teens should not be limited to consumer magazines, as other media appear to have an influence on smoking behaviors as well. Pechmann and Shih found that positive images of smokers in movies might drive teens to begin smoking. Siegel and Biener concluded that the addition of a television component to an anti-smoking campaign aimed at adolescents may reduce the initiation of smoking, particularly among younger teens.

The 1999 National Youth Tobacco Survey questioned middle- and high-school students about exposure to media and advertising regarding tobacco. Their results were presented in four categories: (1) saw antismoking commercials on television or heard them on the radio, (2) saw actors smoking on television or in the movies, (3) saw athletes smoking on television, and (4) saw ads for tobacco products on the Internet. It is interesting to note that the survey did not appear to question respondents about exposure to magazine advertising. On average, approximately 87.3% of students saw actors smoking, and 75.3 % saw antismoking commercials. These findings suggest that perhaps traditional cigarette advertisements such as those placed in consumer magazines do not contribute to youth smoking as much as other factors do and that more effective antismoking efforts may be in order.

The 75.3% of youth that reported seeing antismoking commercials in broadcast media is higher than the magazine reach figures reported in the Krugman and King study, and in addition, they refer to actual messages, not vehicles. If it is assumed that exposure to cigarette advertising leads to an increase in smoking, then using the same logic, it can likely be assumed that exposure to equally well-designed antismoking advertisements will lead to a decrease in smoking.

This is consistent with the results of several econometric studies that look at the effects of tobacco advertising on tobacco consumption. A number of studies have concluded that over time, tobacco advertising has a limited impact on increasing the incidence of smoking and that bans on tobacco advertising are not effective in significantly reducing cigarette smoking.

In fact, several of these studies conclude that antismoking messages and health scares seem to be more effective at reducing smoking rates than bans on tobacco advertising. This suggests that if greater effort were placed on developing antismoking messages specifically targeted to youth smokers instead of banning or limiting tobacco advertising, the role of mass media in the decline of youth smoking might be strengthened.

This phenomenon already appears to have taken effect. For example, a recent antismoking campaign in Florida, the "Truth" campaign, has been coupled with a reduction in smoking among Florida teens. In fact, the *Journal of the American Medical Association* reported that in the first two years of the campaign, smoking among students in Florida declined by 40% among middle-school students and by 18% among high-school students.

In the state of Oregon, the Oregon Health Division (OHD) created the Tobacco Prevention and Education Program (TPEP) in 1997. Data suggest that, among schools funded by this program, 30-day smoking prevalence, defined as whether a cigarette was smoked in the previous month, declined among eighth graders (U.S. Department of Health and Human Services 2000). Rundall and Bruvold also found that school-based smoking interventions led to a reduction in smoking.

The most recent National Household Survey on Drug Abuse concluded that smoking among teens generally has been declining since 1996. Perhaps one reason for this decline is better school-based tobacco education programs, such as those in Oregon, and better public service campaigns targeted to teens, such as the "Truth" campaign in Florida. At the very least, these campaigns may work in conjunction with other factors to reduce smoking among teens.

It is important to note that a teen's decision not to smoke or to discontinue smoking usually is driven by variables other than media messages.

Although antismoking campaigns may contribute to a reduction in the number of teens who smoke, other factors have been shown to be highly influential as well. Peer pressure, family influence, gender, and ethnicity all may have an impact on the onset of smoking among youth. While each of these factors plays a role in a teen's decisions to smoke or abstain from smoking, perhaps the most important one is the price of cigarettes. Because most teens have low disposable incomes, the increasing cost of cigarettes and rising taxes on them often serve as a deterrent to the onset of smoking, more so than other influences. Given that price is such an important factor in a teen's decision to smoke or abstain from smoking, perhaps antismoking efforts aimed at teens should begin to focus on the high monetary cost of smoking relative to other activities of interest to teens.

Public service campaigns have often been successful in changing unhealthy behaviors, particularly those against smoking. Over time, these efforts can lead to greater awareness of the negative effects of smoking, thus leading to attitude change, and even behavior change. Therefore, stronger effort should go into the design and dissemination of well-targeted antismoking campaigns to further facilitate the decline in smoking among youth. Campaigns emphasizing peer pressure, family influences, and the high (monetary) price of smoking might prove to be relevant and meaningful to potential teen smokers. If emphasis is placed on limiting cigarette advertising in consumer magazines at the expense of developing effective antismoking programs, for example, this study suggests that a reduction in magazine advertising of cigarettes will have little effect on the decline of teen smoking.

Limitations and Future Research

The analysis presented in this study is based on several assumptions that should be noted. First, it assumes that Starch data are applicable to teens even though the extent to which Starch samples teen readers is unknown. Although most of the publications used in this study are targeted to adults, several have high teen readership as well (e.g., *Vogue, Sports Illustrated*). Therefore, it is possible that the estimates presented here might differ if Starch norms specifically for teen readers were known.

Second, the SMRB readership estimates presented in this study are simulated rather than actual due to the high cost of purchasing the SMRB teen data (approximately $20,000). Although it is likely that the estimated SMRB teen readership estimates would be approximately 26% higher, on average, than those published by MRI, the accuracy of these estimates remains unknown. This simulation would affect only those estimates of the percentage reached three or more times (Table 2), however, since reach and frequency estimates were provided by SMRB. Overall, the most "conservative" estimates were used throughout this analysis so as not to understate the likely teen readership of cigarette advertisements.

This study offers several opportunities for further research. First, the number of magazines could be extended well beyond the 14 publications used in both this and the Krugman and King studies. In addition, analyses could be performed by magazine type (e.g., general interest versus special interest magazines), by gender, and by Starch readership measures (e.g., associated, read some, read most). Magazine advertisement evaluation services provided by other organizations such as Readex and Gallup and Robinson could also be used to estimate advertisement exposure and communication effects. And finally, teenage exposure to cigarette advertisements in other media (e.g., outdoor, special promotions) could be examined for potential message reach and frequency as well.

Although teen smoking still remains a problem, the number of teenagers who smoke has continued to decline, at least in small part because of state-created programs designed to encourage youth not to smoke. Although cigarette advertising in consumer magazines is often cited as a primary influence on teen smoking, the results of this study indicate that these advertisements may not have the strong impact that previous research has suggested. If teen smoking is to continue its decline, emphasis on defining its cause should not be placed solely on cigarette advertising, but should also attempt to evaluate the impact of antismoking campaigns, peer influence, and parental influence on young people's decision to smoke.

POSTSCRIPT

Do Tobacco Advertisements Influence People to Smoke?

A study in the *Journal of the American Medical Association* reported that over half of children between ages 3 and 6 were able to identify Old Joe, the mascot for Camel cigarettes. By age 6, as many children were able to recognize Old Joe as readily as they did Mickey Mouse. Significantly, within four years after the Old Joe campaign was initiated, Camel's share of the youth market escalated from 0.5 percent to 32.8 percent. Tobacco advertisers assert that they do not market to children, but their advertising does affect what children know.

Smoking and tobacco advertising are highly charged political issues. Are the rights of tobacco companies compromised when restrictions are placed on their ability to advertise their products? If free speech is not protected for tobacco companies, are other companies subject to the same limitations if it is decided that their products are harmful? Should fastfood restaurants, tanning salons, and alcohol companies be prevented from advertising? The tobacco industry feels that government does not have the authority to regulate its freedom of speech. If government can regulate tobacco advertising, then it can regulate any activity it deems unhealthy. Also, the revenue generated by the tobacco industry goes toward state and national treasuries and thousands of people are employed by tobacco companies. The livelihood of many farmers comes from growing tobacco crops. Should these people be deprived of their livelihoods?

By exporting tobacco products, the national trade deficit may be reduced. A fundamental question is whether the role of government is to dictate what people, even teenagers, can see and do or to inform young people so that they can make informed decisions. The tobacco industry does not force anyone to smoke cigarettes, although many argue that tobacco advertisements entice children and young adults into smoking. If, at a later date, these same individuals want to give up smoking but are unable due to tobacco dependency, is the tobacco industry responsible?

Some critics argue that factors other than advertising affect people's decisions to smoke. For example, it is known that parents who smoke are more likely to have children who smoke. In addition, smoking by older siblings influences younger siblings' smoking behavior. Tobacco advertisements become an easy scapegoat. On the other hand, smoking is one of society's most harmful activities and any action, such as limiting tobacco advertisements, is viewed as positive.

In "Too Many Kids Smoke" (*State Legislatures*, March 2004), Dianna Gordon argues that teen smoking results from three factors: stress, boredom, and too much spending money. According to K.E. Warner, P.D. Jacobson, and N.J. Kaufman's article entitled "Innovative Approaches to Youth Tobacco

Control: Introduction and Overview," the biggest deterrent to youth smoking is an increase in cost (*Tobacco Control*, June 2003). Several articles discuss the impact of movies on smoking behavior of young people. These articles include Karl Miller's "Adolescent Exposure to Smoking Depicted in Movies" (*American Family Physician* (February 1, 2004); "Effect of Viewing Smoking in Movies on Adolescent Smoking Initiation: A Cohort" (*The Lancet*, July 26, 2003), by Madeline A. Dalton and others; and, Suzanne Batchelor's article "Movie Smoking Hooks Teens, Experts Say," in *National Catholic Reporter* (February 6, 2004).

Contributors to This Volume

EDITOR

RAYMOND GOLDBERG is a professor of health education at the State University of New York College at Cortland. Since 1977 he has served as coordinator for graduate programs in the School of Professional Studies. He received a B.S. in health and physical education from the University of North Carolina at Pembroke in 1969, an M.Ed. in health education from the University of South Carolina in 1971, and a Ph.D. in health education from the University of Toledo in 1981. He is the author of *Drugs Across the Spectrum,* 3rd ed. (Morton, 2000) and the author or coauthor of many articles on health-related issues, and he has made many presentations on the topic of drug education. He has received over $750,000 in grants for his research in health and drug education.

STAFF

Larry Loeppke	Managing Editor
Jill Peter	Senior Developmental Editor
Nichole Altman	Developmental Editor
Beth Kundert	Production Manager
Jane Mohr	Project Manager
Tara McDermott	Design Coordinator
Bonnie Coakley	Editorial Assistant
Lori Church	Permissions

AUTHORS

MICHAEL S. BAHRKE is an acquisitions editor in the Scientific, Technical, and Medical Division of Human Kinetics in Champaign, Illinois. He has also been an assistant professor at the University of Kansas, director of research for the U.S. Army Physical Fitness School, and fitness area coordinator at the University of Wisconsin. A fellow of the American College of Sports Medicine, he is coauthor, with Charles E. Yesalis, of *Performance-Enhancing Substances in Sport and Exercise* (Human Kinetics, 2002). He holds a master's degree in exercise physiology and a doctorate in sport psychology from the University of Wisconsin–Madison.

DEENA BENEDA received her undergraduate degree from the University of Kansas in organismal biology. She went on to receive her doctorate degree in naturopathic medicine from Bastyr University in Seattle. After graduating, she completed her residency in Norman, Oklahoma, where she worked in a complementary and alternative medical health care practice. Due to the success of the alternative health care clinic, the practice opened a satellite clinic in Tulsa, Oklahoma, which Dr. Beneda-Khosh also managed. In addition to working at the natural medical care clinic, Dr. Beneda-Khosh also works at the University of Kansas Medical Center in the Program of Integrative Medicine.

CAROLYN S. CARTER is a social work professor at Howard University.

THE CENTERS FOR DISEASE CONTROL AND PREVENTION (CDC) is one of the 13 major operating components of the Department of Health and Human Services (HHS), which is the principal agency in the U.S. government for protecting the health and safety of all Americans and for providing essential human services, especially for those people who are least able to help themselves.

BRUCE M. COHEN is a clinical instructor of psychiatry and behavioral sciences at the University of Arkansas for Medical Sciences. He is director of the Child Study Center Clinic and Community Outreach Program in the Division of Pediatric Psychiatry as well as clinical director of Arkansas CARES. His clinical work has focused on children and adolescents with ADHD, learning problems, and depression, and he has extensive experience in school consultation. He earned his B.S. in psychology and his M.S. in clinical psychology (child clinical specialty) from Memphis State University.

J. B. COPAS is a professor in the Department of Statistics at the University of Warwick in Coventry, United Kingdom. His research interests include enhancements in regression modeling and risk scoring, and he is currently researching methods of performing statistical sensitivity analysis.

THOMAS S. DEE is an assistant professor in the Department of Economics at Swarthmore College and a faculty research fellow of the National Bureau of Economic Research in Cambridge, Massachusetts. A member of the American Economic Association and the American Educational Research Association, he has also taught in the School of Economics at the Georgia Institute of Technology. His research interests include public finance, health, education, and applied econometrics. He earned his M.A. in economics and his Ph.D. in economics from the University of Maryland in 1994 and 1997, respectively.

DRUG ENFORCEMENT ADMINISTRATION (DEA) has a mission to enforce the controlled substances laws and regulations of the United States and bring to the criminal and civil justice systems of the United States, or any other competent jurisdiction, those organizations and principal members of organizations, involved in the growing, manufacture, or distribution of controlled substances appearing in or destined for illicit traffic in the United States; and to recommend and support nonenforcement programs aimed at reducing the availability of illicit controlled substances on the domestic and international markets.

MICHAEL FUMENTO is an author, journalist, and attorney specializing in science and health issues. He is a science columnist for Scripps-Howard and a senior fellow of the Hudson Institute in Washington, D.C. He has also been a legal writer for the *Washington Times* and an editorial writer for the *Rocky Mountain News* in Denver, and he was the first "National Issues" reporter for *Investor's Business Daily*. Fumento has lectured on science and health issues throughout the world, including Great Britain, France, the Czech Republic, Greece, Austria, China, and South America. His publications include *BioEvolution: How Biotechnology Is Changing Our World* (Encounter Books, 2003).

GENERAL ACCOUNTING OFFICE (GAO) is the investigative arm of the U.S. Congress. The GAO examines the use of public funds, evaluates federal programs and activities, and provides analyses, options, recommendations, and other assistance to help Congress make effective oversight, policy, and funding decisions.

KATHERINE GREIDER is the author of *The Big Fix: How the Pharmaceutical Industry Rips Off American Consumers* (Public Affairs, 2003). Greider's focus is on drug advertising in relation to the increase in the number of patients who make visits to their physicians for written prescriptions.

FATEMA GUNJA attended Cornell University. After graduating, she worked on drug policy issues, first as a communications coordinator at the American Civil Liberties Union and then as the first director of the Drug Policy Forum of Massachusetts. During her drug policy days, she became a passionate spokesperson and writer on racial justice and students' rights in the context of the War on Drugs.

ASA HUTCHINSON is former administrator with the Drug Enforcement Agency and is currently an administrator with the Department of Homeland Security (DHS). At DHS, Hutchinson is leading an effort to reform border inspections through the use of biometric technology and continues to oversee the reorganization of border agencies into a unified inspection force.

WILLIAM G. IACONO is a Distinguished McNight University Professor. He also is the director of the Clinical Science and Psychopathology Research Training Program in the Psychology Department and an adjunct professor for the Institute of Child Development.

CATHY INOUYE lives in Guatemala City and volunteers for the human rights NGO SEDEM (Seguridad en Democracia). SEDEM monitors the continuing role of the military, police, and intelligence forces in Guatemala.

FARHANG KHOSH received his Doctorate of Naturopathic Medicine from Bastyr University, a nationally accredited naturopathic medical school in Seattle. He graduated from the University of Kansas, where he earned his bachelor's degree in biochemistry and did advanced work in molecular biology. Khosh, along with his brother, formerly worked at the Kansas Clinic of Traditional Medicine and Via Christi Integrative Center in Wichita, Kansas. They developed several herbal and nutritional products that are available to health care professionals throughout the world, and both contribute articles to health-related magazines. Both brothers have published numerous papers on naturopathic approaches to diseases.

KENT M. LANCASTER is president of Media Research Institute, Inc., which provides a variety of media research and planning services and software for the advertising industry. He also is an adjunct professor of advertising at the University of Miami. Kent's research focuses on advertising media and on the economics of advertising.

ALYSE R. LANCASTER received her Ph.D. in mass communication from the University of Florida. Her research focuses on three areas: (1) health communication, concentrating on how the mass media can be used effectively to promote healthy behaviors and to discourage unhealthy behaviors such as drunk driving, illicit drug use, and unsafe sex among college students; (2) the economics and effectiveness of tobacco advertising, as well as the impact of anti-smoking campaigns; and (3) issues in advertising media planning, particularly on how various media are used to reach specified target audiences and how different research methods are used to forecast advertising effects.

LISA N. LEGRAND received her Ph.D. in behavioral genetics and clinical psychology from the University of Minnesota in 2003 and is currently a research associate at the Minnesota Center for Twin and Family Research (MCTFR).

ROBERT A. LEVY, a senior fellow in constitutional studies, joined Cato in 1997 after 25 years in business. He is a director of the Institute for Justice and a member of the board of visitors of the Federalist Society. Levy received his Ph.D. in business from the American University in 1966.

PAUL A. LOGLI is state's attorney for Winnebago County, Illinois, and a lecturer at the National College of District Attorneys. A member of the Illinois State Bar since 1974, he is a nationally recognized advocate for prosecutorial involvement in the issue of substance-abused infants. He earned his J.D. from the University of Illinois.

GEORGINA LOVELL is the B.C. Coordinator for the Tar Wars Program, a tobacco-free education program and poster contest supported by the American Academy of Family Physicians, which reaches approximately 400,000 fourth- and fifth-grade students annually in the United States and Canada. Georgina was awarded a scholarship to attend the Tar Wars annual conference in Washington, D.C. in July 2002.

ROSALIND B. MARIMONT is a retired mathematician and scientist, having done research and development for the National Institute of Standards and Technology (formerly the Bureau of Standards) for 18 years and for the

National Institute of Health (NIH) for another 19. She started in electronics defense work during World War II, then went into the logical design of the early digital computers during the 1950s. At the NIH she studied and published papers on human vision, speech, and other biomathematical subjects. Since her retirement she has been active in health policy issues, particularly the war on smoking.

ROSALIND B. MARIMONT, a retired mathematician and scientist, has done research and development for the National Institute of Standards and Technology (NIST) (or, formerly, the Bureau of Standards [NBS] for 18 years, until 1960, and NIH for another 19, until her retirement in 1979. She started in electronics defense work during World War II at NBS, then went on to the logical design of the early digital computers during the fifties. In 1960, she moved to NIH, where she studied and published papers on human vision, speech, and other biomathematical subjects. Since her retirement she has been active in health policy issues—first, the treatment of chronic pain by integrated mind/body methods, and second, the dishonest war on smoking, which has corrupted scientific research and gravely distorted the nation's health priorities.

MERRILL MATTHEWS, JR., is a public policy analyst specializing in health care, Social Security, welfare, and Internet issues, and the author of numerous studies in health policy, as well as other public policy issues. Currently a visiting scholar with the Institute for Policy Innovation, he is former president of the Health Economics Roundtable for the National Association for Business Economics and former health policy adviser for the American Legislative Exchange Council. Matthews also serves as the medical ethicist for the University of Texas Southwestern Medical Center's Institutional Review Board for Human Experimentation. He earned his Ph.D. in philosophy and humanities from the University of Texas at Dallas.

MATT McGUE is a professor of psychology at the University of Minnesota and a past president of the Behavior Genetics Association. He has co-directed the Minnesota Center for Twin and Family Research for the last dozen years.

K. J. MUKAMAL is a physician at the Beth Israel Deaconess Medical Center in Boston and assistant professor of medicine at Harvard Medical School.

ETHAN NADELMANN founded The Lindesmith Center in 1994 with the philanthropic support of George Soros. He now serves as executive director of The Lindesmith Center–Drug Policy Foundation. The two organizations merged in July 2000.

THE NATIONAL INSTITUTE ON ALCOHOL ABUSE AND ALCOHOLISM (NIAAA) provides leadership in the national effort to reduce alcohol-related problems by conducting and supporting research in a wide range of scientific areas including genetics, neuroscience, epidemiology, health risks and benefits of alcohol consumption, prevention, and treatment. The NIAAA coordinates and collaborates with other research institutes and federal programs on alcohol-related issues. It also collaborates with international, national, state, and local institutions, organizations, agencies, and programs engaged in alcohol-related work. The NIAAA translates and disseminates research findings to health care providers, researchers, policy-makers, and the public.

THE OFFICE OF APPLIED STUDIES (OAS) provides the latest national data on (1) alcohol, tobacco, marijuana, and other drug abuse, (2) drug-related emergency department episodes and medical examiner cases, and (3) the nation's substance abuse treatment system.

THE OFFICE OF NATIONAL DRUG CONTROL POLICY establishes policies, priorities, and objectives for the nation's drug control program. The goals of the program are to reduce illicit drug use, manufacturing, and trafficking; drug-related crime and violence; and drug-related health consequences.

J. Q. SHI is a research associate for the Mining and Environmental Research Group in the T. H. Huxley School of Environment, Earth Sciences and Engineering at the Imperial College of Science, Technology and Medicine in London, United Kingdom. In addition to publishing a number of research papers, he is coauthor, with B. C. Wei and G. P. Lu, of *Introduction of Statistical Diagnostics* (Southeast University Press, 1991). He earned his Ph.D. from the University of Southampton.

JACOB SULLUM is a senior editor at *Reason*, a monthly magazine that covers politics and culture from a libertarian perspective.

SANHO TREE is a fellow and director of the Drug Policy Project at the Institute for Policy Studies in Washington, D.C. The project works to end the domestic and international "War on Drugs" and replace it with policies that promote public health and safety as well as economic alternatives to the prohibition drug economy.

CHARLES L. WHITFIELD is a physician and psychotherapist, specializing in working with people with addictions and adults who have been traumatized as children. He has a private practice in Atlanta, Georgia. He is a consultant at the CDC and was a faculty member at the Rutgers University Summer program for 23 years.

JAMES E. WRIGHT, a military officer and research scientist, is the senior science editor for *Flex* and the editor of *Muscle & Fitness.* An authority on exercise program design, specific exercise techniques, and diets and nutrition for optimal physical and mental performance, he has spent most of his professional life studying ways to improve body composition, physical capacities, and performance. He has written hundreds of articles for popular health and fitness magazines, and he is coauthor, with Virginia S. Cowart, of *Altered States: The Use and Abuse of Anabolic Steroids* (Masters Press, 1994).

CHARLES E. YESALIS is a professor of health policy and administration and of exercise and sport science at Pennsylvania State University. His research focuses on the nonmedical use of anabolic-androgenic steroids and other performance-enhancing drugs. His other research interests include chemical dependency, drug use, and hormones. He holds a master's of public health from the University of Michigan and a doctoral degree from the Johns Hopkins University School of Hygiene and Public Health. He is coauthor, with Virginia S. Cowart, of *The Steroids Game* (Human Kinetics, 1998) and coeditor, with Michael S. Bahrke, of *Performance-Enhancing Substances in Sport and Exercise* (Human Kinetics, 2002).

GRAZYNA ZAJDOW is a senior lecturer at Deakin University in the school of social and international studies, primarily in the area of drugs. Zajdow's expertise is the sociology of alcohol and drug use and women's experiences in alcoholic families.

Index

Note: *Italic* page numbers indicate figures and tables.